P9-DHR-817

Enterprise Application Development in SharePoint 2010

Creating an End-to-End Application without Code

Ira Fuchs

ihf
PUBLISHING

"Enterprise Application Development in SharePoint 2010 –
Creating an End-to-End Application without Code"

Published by
IHF Publishing
Forest Hills, NY 11375

Copyright © 2010 by IHF Publishing, Forest Hills, New York

ISBN 978-1-4507-5417-0

All rights reserved. No part of the contents of this book may be reproduced or transmitted in any form or by any means without the written permission of the publisher.

Microsoft, Access, Excel, InfoPath, Office Web Applications, PerformancePoint, SharePoint, SharePoint Designer, SQL Server, Windows 7, Windows Server and Visio are either registered trademarks or trademarks of Microsoft Corporation in the United States or in other countries. Other product names mentioned in this book may be the trademarks of their respective owners.

The information in this book is provided without any express, statutory or implied warrantees. Neither the author nor the publisher will be held liable for any damages caused or alleged to be caused either directly or indirectly from the use of the information in this book.

Book design and layout by Mark Hogan
markhogandesign.com

Acknowledgements:

The author would like to acknowledge and thank the following people at Microsoft for their assistance and support in bringing this book to completion:
Rob Howard, Anson Hidajat, Nick Dallett, Cosmin Barsan, Sarah Minahan, Prakash Naravanan, Ellene Hao Klaka, JD Klaka and Scott Heim. The author greatly appreciates the time and attention that these people made available to him.

To my family — Jean Citarella, Chloe and Adam Fuchs; thank you for being the best test user accounts I could possibly hope for, and for being my favorite people in the world.

To my buddy David Adler — Thanks for working me out on the tennis courts. The exercise helped focus my mind.

The completed components, as well as the entire Employee Absence Tracking application created in this book are available for download from the book's page at **www.sharepointenterprisedevelopment.com**. The following are the components and files that can be found there:

- *SQL Server* backup file for the *Absence Tracking* database
- *InfoPath Absence Request* form
- *InfoPath EmplInfoWebPart* form
- *SharePoint Solution Package* (WSP) for the *SharePoint Designer* application workflow
- *Business Data Connectivity Service Profile* for the *Employee Information External Content Type*
- *SharePoint Solution Package* (WSP) for the entire *Employee Absence Tracking* application

Contents

Introduction

Writing a book on developing enterprise applications in *SharePoint* became possible because *SharePoint* as a development platform, which includes *SharePoint Designer 2010* and *InfoPath 2010*, has become sufficiently mature to actualize both the premise and promise of a declarative, rule-based development methodology.

A declarative development platform and methodology provides the tools that can implement the functionality of an application by allowing a developer to use rule logic, information sets, and attribute settings to describe *what* the desired functionality is. The declarative developer does not have to be concerned with creating the underlying lower-level mechanisms that control *how* the rule logic or attribute settings work.

As a declarative development platform *SharePoint* empowers programmers and non-programmers alike with accessible, efficient tools that are capable of implementing sophisticated application functionality. What can be accomplished declaratively in *SharePoint* today without writing code has grown significantly as a result of the maturity of the 2010 version. Creating custom *SharePoint* list or library actions in the previous 2007 version required writing procedural code; today this can be accomplished using the declarative development capabilities of *SharePoint Designer.*

These declarative capabilities are understandable and accessible to practically anyone. As such this book is appropriate to anyone who has an interest and stake in *SharePoint* application development. Anyone can understand the methodology and procedures described in this book; and everyone who does so will most certainly derive substantial immediate and long-term value when they put this knowledge to work for the simple reason that this methodology harnesses and exploits the most powerful inherent capabilities of SharePoint.

The significant development efficiencies and lifecycle management benefits of a declarative methodology will become apparent as we go through the process of creating a functionally complex reference application, Employee Absence Tracking, without using any code.

This book has several objectives. The first of which is to demonstrate the techniques and methodology for developing an enterprise class application in *SharePoint 2010*. We will accomplish this by creating a fully functional *Employee Absence Tracking* application that incorporates many of the characteristics of enterprise class applications. By "enterprise class" we mean applications that address the demanding use case requirements that are prevalent in large organizations. Two salient characteristics of enterprise class applications are complex functionality and user context driven behavior, attributes that we will examine in detail at various times and places in this book.

Another objective of this book is to get developers who are primarily comfortable writing code to become comfortable with the level of efficiency, power and control that *SharePoint* provides as a declarative development platform. The functional sophistication of the *Employee Absence Tracking* application that we create in this book was deliberately considered in order to demonstrate what the art of the possible is with the *SharePoint* development toolset.

The last and most important objective is to identify the best practices for developing declarative applications on the *SharePoint* platform. As with any set of development tools capable of creating sophisticated deliverables there are multiple ways to go about building an application. Some are better than others. A best practices approach is distinguished by:

A)   The coherency of the design and organization of the application artifacts and components

B)   The flexibility of modifying, interchanging and reusing the artifacts and components

C)   The exposed and self-describing functionality of the artifacts and components

D)   The ability to optimally maintain the application

Throughout the book we will point out various best practice approaches to *SharePoint* development and describe the rationale behind them and their benefits.

It is the author's hope that this book succeeds at meeting all of these objectives. *SharePoint 2010's* application development capabilities will be largely responsible for this success as it is truly an enabling development platform that is accessible to people with a wide range of development skills. Because it is a declarative development platform people who are not conventional programmers should be very comfortable working with the *SharePoint* development tools. It is also the expectation that developers who primarily work in code will become comfortable with the level of efficiency, power and control that the SharePoint platform provides.

Developer Workstation Requirements to Create and Test this Application

In order to go through the exercise of building the *Employee Absence Tracking* application you will need a *SharePoint* developer workstation with the following applications installed:

- *Windows Server 2008 R2* or *Windows 7*
- *SharePoint Server 2010 Enterprise Edition*
- *SQL Server 2008 Developer Edition*
- *SharePoint Designer 2010*
- *InfoPath 2010*
- *Visio 2010 Premium Edition* (optional for generating a run-time visualization of the workflow process)

Important Note – The *Employee Absence Tracking* application uses *SharePoint Enterprise Edition* features, specifically *InfoPath Form Services*; as such the enterprise version of *SharePoint 2010* is a pre-requisite to build and run this application. *InfoPath Form Services* are not a feature of *SharePoint 2010 Foundation Server*.

In addition, the workflow component of the application generates email notifications and in order to test this function you will need to install and configure the *SMTP Server Role* on *Windows Server 2008* or have access to an instance of *Exchange Server* for testing purposes. *SMTP Server* is only available on *Windows Server 2008*; however other SMTP applications are available for *Windows 7*.

The minimum computer requirement is a 64 bit CPU with 4 GB of RAM. The following are the workstation configuration options available:

- Use a native installation of *Windows Server 2008 R2* x64 or *Windows 7 x64* to install *SharePoint Server 2010 Enterprise Edition, SharePoint Designer 2010* and *InfoPath 2010*. *SharePoint Server 2010* will run on *Windows 7 x 64* machines as a stand-alone developer installation.

- Use *Microsoft Hyper-V* on *Windows Server 2008 R2* x64 to create a guest *Windows Server 2008 R2* x64 operating system and install *SharePoint Server Enterprise Edition, SharePoint Designer* and *InfoPath*.

For definitive information on this topic see "Setting Up the Development Environment for SharePoint 2010 on Windows Vista, Windows 7, and Windows Server 2008" at http://msdn.microsoft.com/en-us/library/ee554869(office.14).aspx.

Typographical Conventions Used In This Book

There is a lot of detailed information and procedures described in this book. In order to keep the procedural narrative from getting confusing and the text from being difficult to understand an attempt has been made to use typographical conventions to identify and differentiate certain items. The following are the typographical conventions used:

Bold text identifies an object upon which an action is taken, typically a button, a tab, or a link. The following is an example of this:

Click **OK**. Select the **View 1 (default)** View. Click the **Properties button**.

Text within "quotation marks" identifies a literal string that should be entered somewhere. The following is an example of this:

Change the View Name to "Main View"

Bold and italicized text in the body of a paragraph is used to emphasize something to indicate that it is important. The following is an example of this:

The second rule will be implemented ***later*** because

Italicized text in the *Ariel Narrow* typeface identifies the proper name for something, typically a field name which is very often two words joined by an underscore. An example of this is:

Expand the *Employee_Information* group from the *Main* data source

In addition, when something of significance is being identified the following "Note" conventions are used:

> **Development Note** – Points out a conceptual consideration or an important capability of a tool that impacts the efficiency or elegance of the development process.

> **Pattern Note** – Points out application functionality that is commonly used in many Enterprise applications.

> **Best Practice Note** – Points out a particularly advantageous way of doing something and discussing the benefits of doing so.

> **Important Note** – Points out a general piece of information that is important to keep in mind.

Application Components Available for Download from the Book Site

The completed components, as well as the entire *Employee Absence Tracking* application created in this book are available for download from the book's page at www.sharepointenterprisedevelopment.com. The following are the components and files that can be found there:

- *SQL Server* backup file for the *Absence Tracking* database
- *InfoPath Absence Request* form
- *InfoPath EmplInfoWebPart* form
- *SharePoint Solution Package* (WSP) for the *SharePoint Designer* application workflow
- *Business Data Connectivity Service Profile* for the *Employee Information External Content Type*
- *SharePoint Solution Package* (WSP) for the entire *Employee Absence Tracking* application

Characteristics and Description of an Enterprise Application – Employee Absence Tracking

In this book we use the designation "enterprise application" to describe a class of applications that are deployed in an organization that have the following characteristics:

> A) Are functionally complex with numerous procedural contingencies
>
> B) Are driven by user context
>
> C) Must integrate with and access *multiple* information sources
>
> D) Are accessed by a large population of users

An employee absence tracking application, when implemented robustly to incorporate the complex use case functionality required in large organizations is emblematic of an enterprise application. As such the exercise of designing and creating a reference implementation of this commonly used application will be an object lesson in identifying the numerous enterprise requirements relevant to an employee absence tracking application and demonstrating how the *SharePoint* platform can accommodate them effectively and efficiently.

As part of their overall compensation and benefits package organizations provide employees with vacation, sick and personal leave time, and some organizations allow carry-forward balances from year to year as well. Employees typically draw down these allocations through an absence request process. Employee absence tracking applications manage the process, policies and contingencies of employees using their allocated leave time.

In large organizations leave time allocation and record keeping is a function of a centralized Human Resource or Payroll system, but the actual transactional process of requesting and approving leave time is executed in a separate application and very often in multiple instances of such applications.

The reason for this is that the policies and contingencies governing the consumption of leave time are typically set and managed differently within the multiple operational and regional units of an enterprise. Attempting to accommodate all of the unit and regional contingencies for absence management in a single application instance is unwieldy and impractical.

Consequently the architecture of this *Employee Absence Tracking* reference implementation decentralizes the rule logic for absence request contingencies, yet centralizes the time recording and accounting information – the time away allocations, the cumulative usage and the balance of time available; as this information is typically also used by or is relevant to other HR applications such as payroll.

Multiple instances of this *Employee Absence Tracking* application can be instantiated and configured individually to implement only those rule sets that are applicable to any given operating entity; but each instance will access a common organization-wide data store that maintains the categorical absence time available and used by each employee.

We use an SQL Server 2008 database to represent this information store and we will use *SharePoint Designer* and *Business Data Connectivity Services* (BCS) to create *External Connections*, *External Content Types*, and *External Content Type Lists* to make this information available to *SharePoint* and *InfoPath*, and enable bi-directional read/write access to the database.

The functional logic of the application is implemented in an *InfoPath* form and a *SharePoint Designer* workflow and is "loosely-coupled" from the data store. It is easy to create and deploy multiple instances of the application that can be customized as required, all of which will use a BCS *External Content Type* to interact with the same database.

In a well-designed absence tracking application, when an employee starts an absence request they are presented with their entitlements and the time used and still available in each leave category. Often it will show carry forward days from a previous year and any forfeiture of accumulated leave time if not used based on the organization's policy. In this reference implementation *InfoPath* is used to create the *Absence Request* form which will be rendered in a browser using *InfoPath Form Services* as shown in **Illustration 1** at right.

Form rule logic executes automatically upon the creation of the form to auto-populate the organizational and leave time information about the user. This is accomplished by using the *userName* function of *InfoPath* to determine the identity of the user creating the form and passing the user identity as a query parameter to an *Employee Information* database created in *SQL Server* and exposed through *Business Data Connectivity Services*.

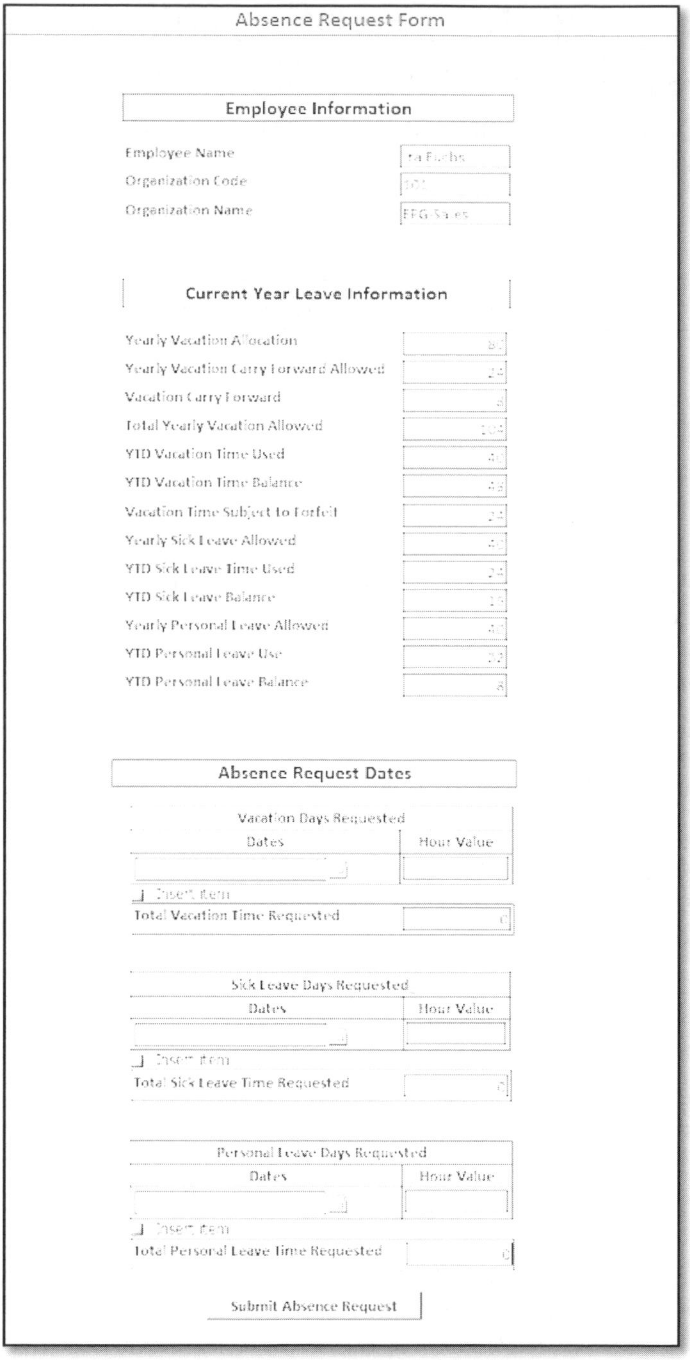

Illustration 1 - Absence Request Form rendered in a browser

The *Form Load* rule logic that auto-populates the form is shown in **Illustration 2** below.

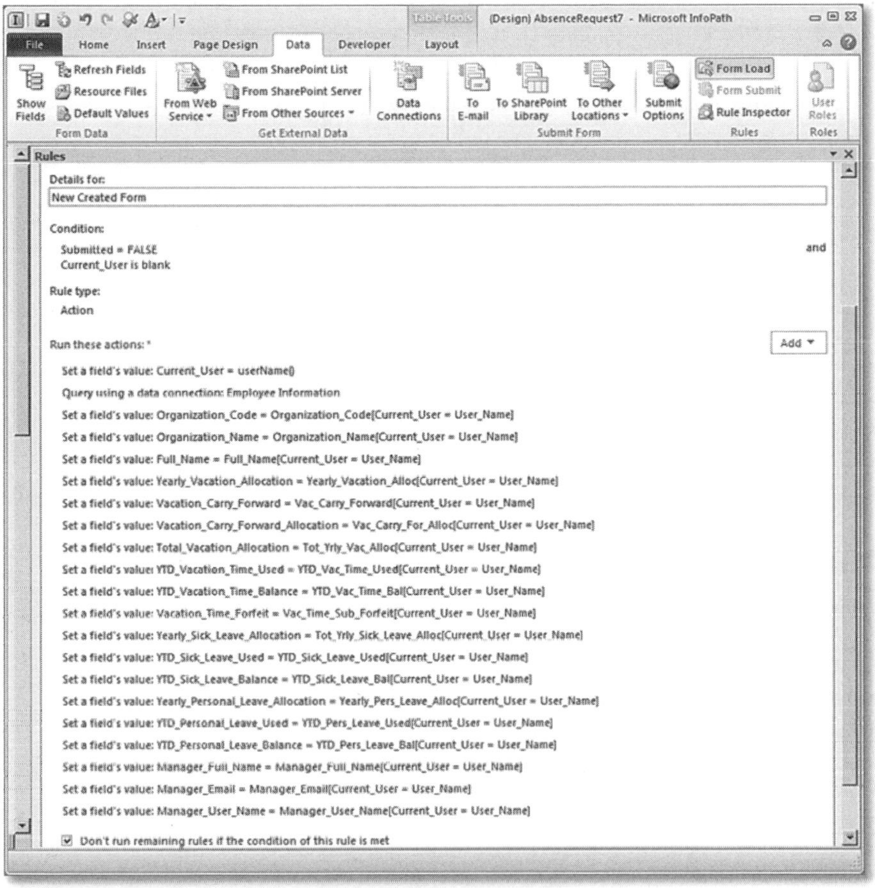

Illustration 2 - InfoPath Form Load rule set used to auto-populate the form

The *Absence Request* form presents the user with date picker controls to pick the dates that they want to take off within each leave time category. Rule logic is implemented that constrains the dates that the employee can choose as well as the behavior of the form based on the leave policies and contingencies of the organization. The leave policies and restrictions implemented as rules in the *Absence Request* form are:

- The policy that vacation time away cannot be requested for past dates. The *Absence Request* form contains rule logic that prevents picking dates prior to the current date for vacation and personal leave days; however past dates can be picked for sick leave days. Organizations want to manage time away as best as possible; allowing people to take vacation days before they request them would diminish the ability of an absence tracking system from working effectively. This policy is not applied to sick days which are typically not planned for.

- Designating restricted and reserved days that cannot be picked for vacation or personal leave time. In any operational group of an organization there are typically periods where an intense effort is required. In finance and sales the week before the end of a fiscal quarter, and certainly before the end of the year are crush times and taking time off during those periods is discouraged if not actually prohibited. Special events are also typically scheduled in advance so that people will plan around them. The *Absence Request* form contains rule logic that will check requested vacation dates against a *SharePoint* list of restricted and reserved dates by organizational code in real-time and prevent the conflicting choice to be made.

Illustration 3 below shows the *Restricted and Reserved Dates* list used for this purpose.

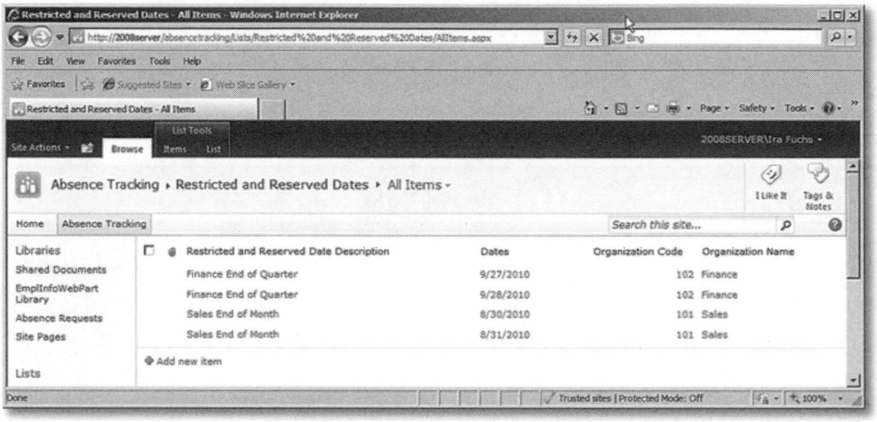

Illustration 3 - Restricted and Reserved Dates list

- Leave time requested in any allocation category cannot exceed the available balance. The *Absence Request* form will compare the total amount of time requested in each leave category with the available balance and prevent the user from requesting more time than is available. Furthermore, leave time in any category cannot be requested if the balance of available time has been depleted. The *Absence Request* form will hide the date request sections for each leave category once the balance of leave time has been exhausted.

- The requirement for management approval when the aggregate leave time requested is above a threshold in conjunction with a consideration of the employee's tenure. The *Absence Request* form uses submit rule logic to trigger an approval process if the total leave time requested exceeds a threshold for a defined tenure period.

Illustration 4 below shows the rule conditions that evaluate whether an absence request requires management approval based on the employees tenure and the amount of leave time requested.

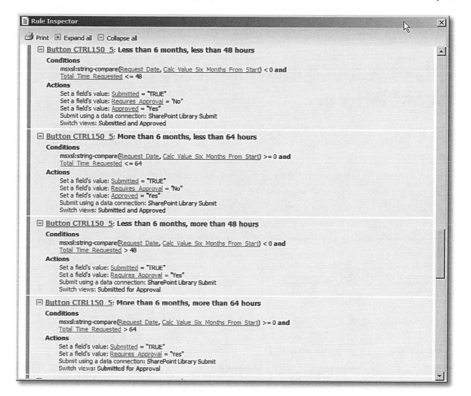

Illustration 4 - InfoPath rule set for request approval criteria

After the user selects valid leave dates for each leave category they submit the request to a *SharePoint* form library. The application generates new values for the year-to-date leave time used, and the year-to-date leave time balance in each absence request category. It does this by adding the existing year-to-date values from the *Employee Information* database with the total leave time in each category requested in the form. These new year-to-date values are written to the form library columns when the form is submitted. This serves as the interim record of the transaction prior to updating the permanent employee record in the *Employee Information* database. The workflow component of the *Employee Absence Tracking* application will update the *Employee Information* database with the new values as well as execute the rule logic for the approval contingencies.

The *Absence Request* form also contains rules to address the different behavior required when a submitted form is opened by one of three possible individuals: the original initiator of the request, the manager responsible for approving the request, or a person who is neither the initiator nor the designated approval manager. If the original initiator opens the submitted form it will open in a view that is read only. If the designated approver opens the form it will open in an editable version displaying the approval section. If a person who is neither the initiator nor the designated approver attempts to open the form they will be presented with a view that simply presents the message that "they are not authorized to view this form".

The pervasive use of user context attributes is a distinguishing characteristic of an enterprise class application. The form is designed to use the identity of the user from the outset to provide all the relevant information to the user as well as drive the form behavior in numerous ways. Without the use of contextual drivers the application would be significantly less useful in an enterprise or the required functionality would need to be implemented downstream in a far less integrated and elegant way. These contextual drivers are what define the complex use case requirements of many enterprise applications.

The Benefits of Working in a Rule Based Declarative Development Platform

One of the truly compelling reasons to build applications on the *SharePoint* platform, and specifically using *InfoPath* forms and *SharePoint Designer* workflows is that almost all of the application's functional logic is defined and executed as rules. Operational processes are driven by rules but in traditional application development the rules are first defined as conditional statements but are then re-written as procedural code that is compiled into run-time assemblies. The greater majority of lifecycle modifications to process applications are rule centric but because the rules in conventional applications are embodied in programming code and are no longer exposed as conditional statements they cannot be accessed and modified easily, and without risk of affecting the behavior of the application in unintentional ways. This significantly impacts the ability of organizations to make changes in their processes on a timely and efficient manner.

With *InfoPath* rules and *SharePoint Designer* workflows the conditional logic exists and is maintained in an accessible form that is self-documenting, transparent, and loosely-coupled from other functional aspects of the application. A rule set incorporated within *InfoPath* can be viewed and modified with confidence that the changes will not affect other functions of the application, or if there are inter-dependencies they are explicitly manifested. Any of the rules in the *Absence Request* form can be easily and readily modified to accommodate the specific leave policies and business requirements of any organization. Additional rules can be added just as easily without affecting the integrity of the overall application. The declarative workflows that can be created in *SharePoint Designer* share these same characteristics.

What will also become apparent through the exercise of creating this application is that the learning curve of mastering even the most sophisticated and leveraged capabilities of the *SharePoint* development platform is substantially lower than working in a procedural development environment, which in turn significantly impacts development efficiencies.

Artifacts, Components and Resources that Comprise the Employee Absence Tracking Application

In this book we use the term "artifact" to mean the functional building blocks provided by *SharePoint*: pages, lists, libraries, forms, web parts and workflows. "Components" are created when these artifacts are combined, configured and integrated together along with external functional resources. The following are the artifacts, components and resources that will be created for this application:

- An *SQL Server* database that stores employee HR information and employee absence records. As stated earlier, the design of this application assumes the existence of an HR or Payroll systems from which this information would be obtained using *Business Data Connectivity Services*. As such this component serves as a proxy for the system of record for this information. As described in the

Development Note below, a version of this *Employee Absence Tracking* application can be deployed without this component by using a standard *SharePoint* list to host the HR information and employee absence records instead of the *External List* generated from the BCS *External Content Type*.

- A *Business Data Connectivity Services* (BCS) data connection to the SQL database information above and a BCS *External Content Type* (ECT) that represents both the information set and operations required for this application. The ECT will be exposed as an *External List* in *SharePoint* and made accessible to *InfoPath* and to the *SharePoint Designer* workflow in that form. *Business Data Connectivity Services* will be used to access and write-back to the HR database.

- An *InfoPath* based *Absence Request* form. This component represents the majority of the work in creating this application and it is where most of the context driven techniques and rule logic is implemented.

- An *InfoPath* form used on the application's home page in an *InfoPath Form Web Part* to display an employee's categorical leave time allocations as well as time used and balances in those categories.

- A *SharePoint* list containing restricted and reserved leave dates. These are the dates that an organizational unit identifies as being important for personnel to be at work and as such cannot be used for leave days.

- A *SharePoint* library where the *Absence Request* form is published and submitted instances of the form are stored. When a form is submitted to the library information generated in the form populates the columns of the library and this information is accessed by the workflow component of the application.

- A *SharePoint Designer* workflow that is bound to the form library that completes the absence request and approval process. The workflow provides the mechanism for bringing the process to a deterministic ending in a finite period of time. Absence requests are expected to be processed in a reasonably short period of time so as not to inconvenience people. The workflow guarantees that a request is either approved or rejected within a specific duration.

- An application home page that displays the following:

    - A Web Part for the *Absence Request* form library
    - An *InfoPath Form Web Part* that displays the categorical leave time allocated, used and available balances
    - A Web Part for the *Restricted and Reserved Dates* list
    - A *Content Control* Web Part for identifying text
    - An *Announcements* Web Part for instructions and policies

Because *SharePoint* is inherently user context driven the Web Parts on the home page can be easily configured to filter and display only the information that is specific or relevant to the user.

Development Note – The working premise of this reference implementation is that it will be sufficiently robust to be suitable for actual deployment in an enterprise. As such an SQL database is used as a proxy for an enterprise HR system because in a real-world deployment it must be capable of integrating with such a legacy HR application; and the tools and methodology to accomplish this integration are available from the *SharePoint* application development platform. However, the integration with a legacy HR system or the requirement for a centralized employee information repository may not be a requirement in many small to midsize organizations. To modify this application to eliminate the inclusion of the SQL database is straightforward. Simply create a *SharePoint list* that is identical to the *External List* generated by *SharePoint Designer* from the *Business Data Connectivity Services External Content Type* and use that as the data source in the form and the workflow.

Pattern Note –User context is a defining characteristic of enterprise application development. However, this implies the ability to access identity information and its contextual attributes in order to create context driven functionality. In many cases this information is distributed among different data sources such as *Windows Profile Services*, *Active Directory Services*, *SharePoint User Profile Services* and HR systems, and consequently different methods may be required in any given situation to obtain the necessary user context information.

In this reference implementation we wanted to demonstrate the methodology for obtaining and utilizing user context information in a real-world scenario but we could not make the design assumption that certain necessary information needed for this application, specifically the identity and email address of an employee's manager responsible for approving an absence request, might reside in *Active Directory* or *SharePoint User Profile Services*. The reason we could not make this assumption is that these services might not be implemented or accessible to the reader and if we designed the application to use these facilities the reader would have an incomplete learning experience.

Consequently, we designed the application so that the SQL database representing the proxy HR system contains this information. However, since many *SharePoint* deployments will take advantage of *SharePoint User Profile Services*, we review how to use the Web Services interface to this facility to obtain user context information in the section **Accessing the SharePoint User Profile Web Service from InfoPath** on page 375.

About the SharePoint 2010 Development Platform

While you could implement enterprise functionality using the 2007 versions of *SharePoint, InfoPath,* and *SharePoint Designer,* these tools were not sufficiently mature and integrated to do so in an efficient and elegant way. Working in the 2007 version of *SharePoint* required developers to construct compensatory workarounds and write custom procedural code to implement the enterprise application functions that *SharePoint 2010* can implement intrinsically and easily today. The developer experience in *SharePoint 2007* was adequate but far from optimal. This has changed dramatically in *SharePoint 2010*. The tighter integration between *SharePoint, InfoPath* and *SharePoint Designer* provides a more coherent developer experience and the most significant development limitations that prevented *SharePoint 2007* from being a first class development platform have been addressed in *SharePoint 2010*.

SharePoint 2010 is actually a multi-functional environment that incorporates a number of valuable product offerings that have been combined and integrated together. The *SharePoint 2010 Enterprise Edition* is comprised of the following platform services:

- **Portal Collaboration Services**
- **Web Content Publishing Services**
- **Enterprise Content Management Services**
- **PerformancePoint Services**
- **Search Services**
- **InfoPath Form Services**
- **Excel Services**
- **Access Services**
- **Visio Services**
- **Business Data Connectivity Services**
- **Managed Metadata Services**
- **Content Type Publishing**
- **Workflow Services**
- **Profile Services**
- **Office Web Applications**

This veritable cornucopia of enterprise functional value easily makes *SharePoint 2010* one of the most useful and leveraged products that any organization can deploy. It provides the broad capabilities to address almost any collaborative scenarios and operational requirements that an organization will encounter. In addition to these intrinsic services, the 2010 versions of *SharePoint Designer* and *InfoPath* complement and complete *SharePoint* as a development platform. *SharePoint Designer* is available as a free download and *InfoPath* is part of the *Office 2010 Professional Plus* suite. *InfoPath Form Services* provides the ability to render form templates created in the *InfoPath* design-time tool in a browser window and in Web Parts.

The *SharePoint 2010* tools and features that we will be primarily working with are *InfoPath, Business Data Connectivity Services* through *SharePoint Designer,* and *SharePoint Designer* workflows. The following is a description of these tools and their functions.

InfoPath and Forms Server

InfoPath is a tool for creating form applications that generate structured XML information. *InfoPath 2010* actualizes its enterprise deployment potential as a result of enhancements to the capabilities of *InfoPath Form Server* and by being more tightly integrated with *SharePoint 2010*. InfoPath has many capabilities that complement and enhance *SharePoint,* but there are three distinguishing attributes of *InfoPath* that stand out:

One, *InfoPath* is a model for rules based development exemplifying one of the best implementations of the declarative development paradigm. In *InfoPath* application logic is expressed as field operations and conditional statements which in turn drive validation, formatting and action events. Both information in the form and the behavior of the form itself can be manipulated using rules. As will be seen shortly, *InfoPath* rule sets are an elegant and efficient way to implement complex application logic.

Illustration 5 below shows the *InfoPath Rule Inspector*, used to view all the rule logic in a form. The fields used in rule operations and events are hyperlinked, providing a comprehensive view of all the rules that a field participates in.

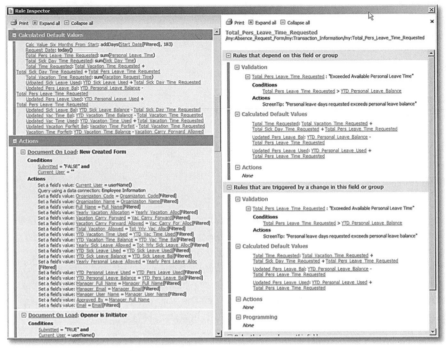

Illustration 5 - InfoPath Rule Inspector

Two, *InfoPath* forms can access an arbitrary number of data sources simultaneously and dynamically. The data sources can be Line of Business (LOB) applications, databases, Web Services and *SharePoint* lists and libraries. The information accessed from these data sources can interact with each other in the form and be manipulated in almost any way. For example, an *InfoPath* form can contain controls that consume financial market data feeds that are published as web services. Rule based logic applied to the information captured by one form control generates the analytical output values that are used to query other data sources. In this manner the *InfoPath* form functions as an interactive analytical engine with sophisticated data gathering and presentation capabilities as shown in **Illustration 6** below.

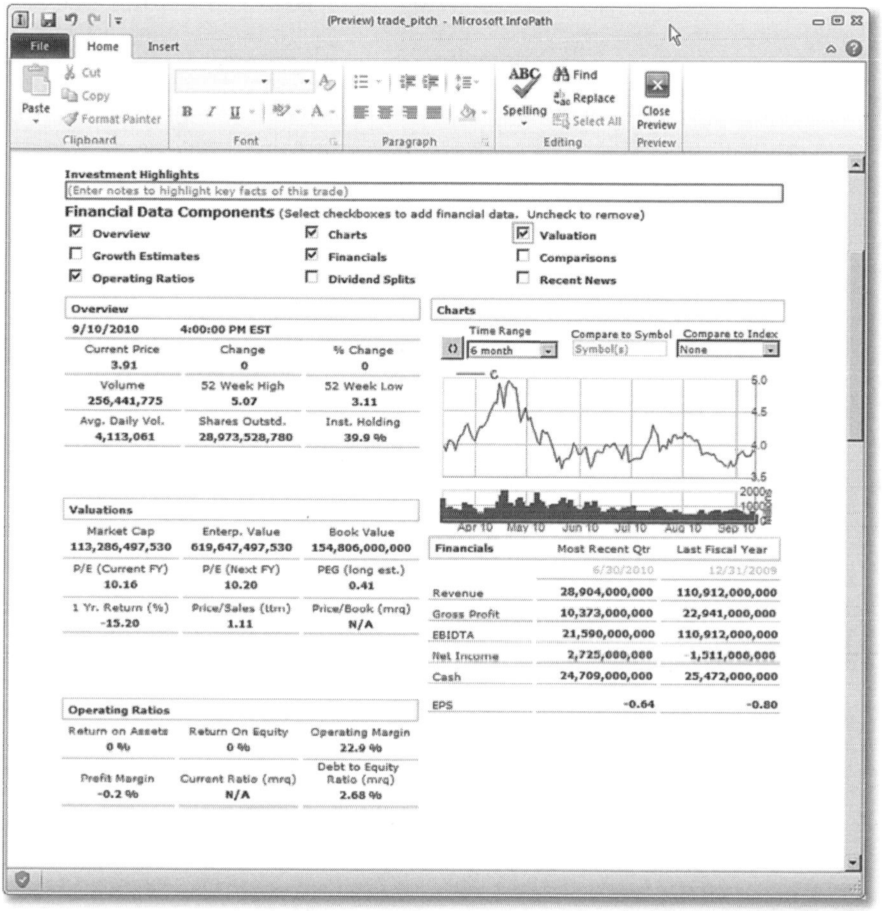

Illustration 6 - InfoPath form used for financial data gathering and presentation

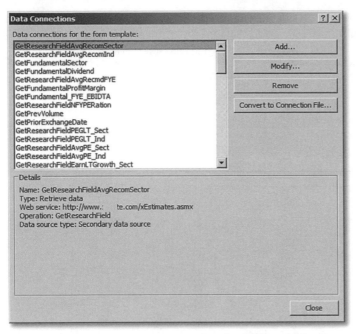

Illustration 7 at left shows the dozens of web service based data sources that this form accesses depending upon the criteria specified by the user or generated from rule logic.

Three, *InfoPath* uses *XML Schema* to represent the form's information set, and the controls used in the form to capture information are bound to the schema field nodes. The form generates an XML instance document of the captured information that is based on the organization and structure of the XML schema.

Illustration 8 below shows a section of the XML schema form fields on the right, and the corresponding form section and controls bound to the fields on the left.

Illustration 7 - Web Services Data Connections for the financial data form

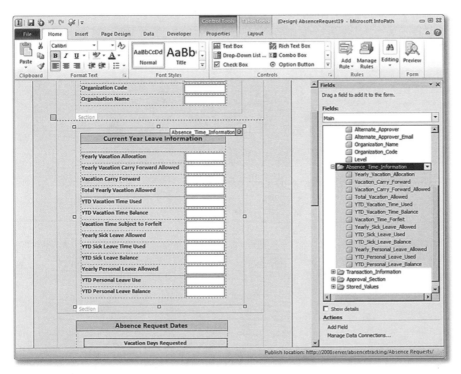

Illustration 8 - InfoPath schema segment bound to a form section

The value of creating XML documents that conform to a schema is that the meaning, function and use of the information in the document is comprehensible to and operable by any XML enabled application that can access the underlying schema for the document. Today, every industry specific initiative to develop a common vocabulary and set of procedures for the exchange and processing of information is based on *XML Schema*, as are the *Web Services* Protocols themselves. Using *InfoPath's Submit* function it is easy to send XML data from the form to any number of receiving applications.

These three capabilities allow *InfoPath* browser forms to function as smart "client" applications capable of integrating, processing, and exchanging information with diverse and distributed data sources. This smart client aspect of *InfoPath* is what makes it a uniquely versatile and leveraged tool for building sophisticated enterprise applications.

As a form development tool *InfoPath* provides a built-in library of form controls such as drop-down lists, scrollable list boxes, calendar controls, check boxes, radio buttons, repeating tables, buttons, and numerous other controls, all of which can be customized through property attributes. *InfoPath* also supports repeating sections, optional sections, and dynamic conditional formatting, all of which facilitate a very high level of design and functional flexibility. Declarative rule sets can be bound to XML nodes in the schema or to controls and sections in the form that governs the form's behavior. This behavior is manifested in the following ways:

- Displaying multiple form views
- Constraining and validating the information that can be entered in form controls
- Auto-populating the form
- Displaying and populating controls and sections based on contingencies and dependencies
- Generating automatic, derived and computed values
- Invoking events, prompts, and instructions
- Multi-conditional cascading filters
- Accessing multiple data sources
- Submitting the form
- Opening and closing form behavior

The *Employee Absence Tracking* application that we will create will take full advantage of and demonstrate all of these capabilities and features.

InfoPath Forms Server is a *SharePoint Enterprise Edition* feature that allows *InfoPath* form templates (the form application that is created with *InfoPath*) to reside and run on a *SharePoint* server and renders *InfoPath* forms in a browser. *Forms Server* delivers two benefits that make *InfoPath* a viable platform for enterprise applications: one, the *InfoPath* program does not have to be installed on an end user's computer, and two, because the application logic runs server-side rather than on the client, the lifecycle management of an InfoPath form template is simplified. Prior to the arrival of *Forms Server* in *SharePoint 2007* the only way that *InfoPath* could be used widely in an organization was to distribute copies of the program and disseminate the form templates to users. If the form template was modified, it had to be re-distributed again. This was a deal breaker and accounted to a great degree for the general lack of *InfoPath* deployment in large organizations.

InfoPath Forms Server 2007 was typical of an initial version 1.0 product; not all of the *InfoPath* client functionality was supported in browser forms. Some of the missing capabilities were the very ones required to implement the sophisticated use case requirements of Enterprise applications. While it was possible to devise workarounds around these deficiencies, it created additional work for developers and necessitated using awkward methods. These feature gaps have been eliminated with *Forms Server 2010* and it is now possible to implement the same complex form behavior in a browser form that was previously available only in the *InfoPath* client.

Furthermore, *InfoPath* now provides a valuable service to *SharePoint* that is highly complementary and enabling: the default ASP forms that SharePoint generates for lists and workflows can now be replaced with *InfoPath* forms that take advantage of all the sophisticated form behavior capabilities itemized above. *SharePoint* automatically generates Active Server Pages (ASP) for adding, editing and deleting items in lists. Additional columns can be added to a list or library with the ability to assign a datatype (single line of text, number, date) or function (a look-up from another list or library, or calculation based on other columns in the form) to the column that in turn generates an ASP.NET control on the form page. However, there are no facilities for implementing complex field and form behavior, such as validation and auto-population in *SharePoint* ASP forms without writing code. This can now be accomplished using *InfoPath*'s declarative methods.

Illustration 9 below shows the design view of an *InfoPath* form for a *SharePoint* list used for issue tracking. The rich functionality that *InfoPath* brings to *SharePoint* lists provides capabilities for manipulating, processing and displaying list information that would have previously required a substantial amount of procedural coding to accomplish.

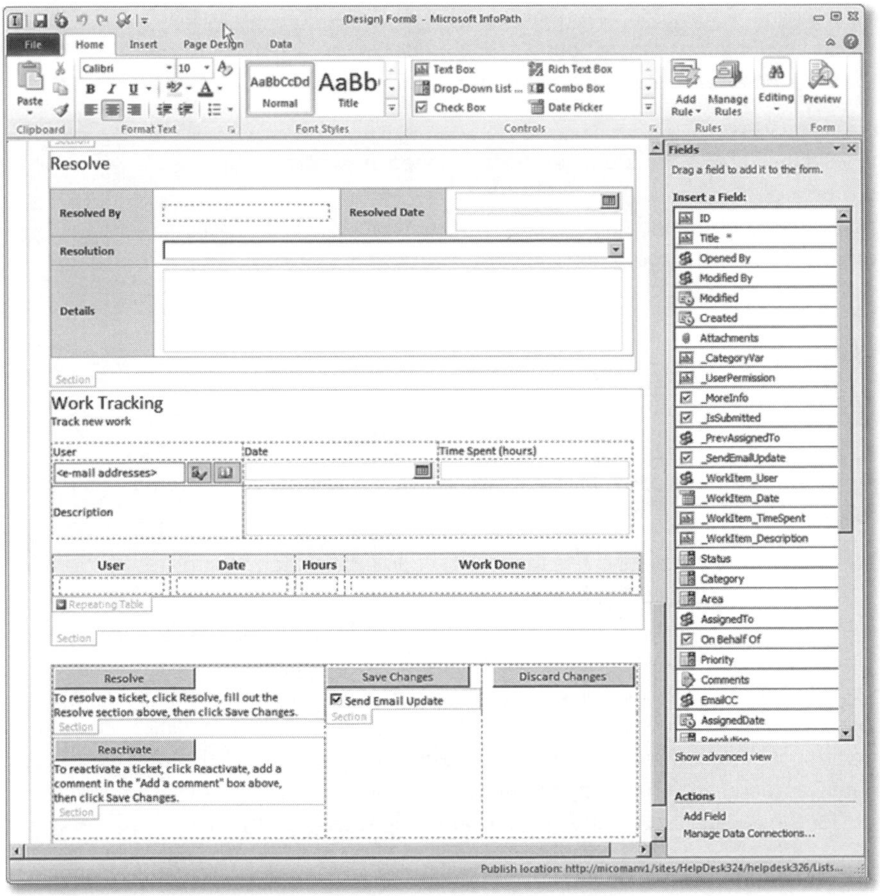

Illustration 9 - Design view of an InfoPath form for a SharePoint list

In addition, *SharePoint 2010* now has an *InfoPath Form Web Part*. You can simply insert one or more browser enabled *InfoPath* forms on any *SharePoint* page as Web Parts and interactively connect them together. This capability provides numerous options for accessing and displaying complex information sets on any *SharePoint* Web Part page. **Illustration 10** below shows an *InfoPath Form Web Part* used to display leave entitlement and usage information from an *SQL Server* database exposed through *Business Data Connectivity Services*.

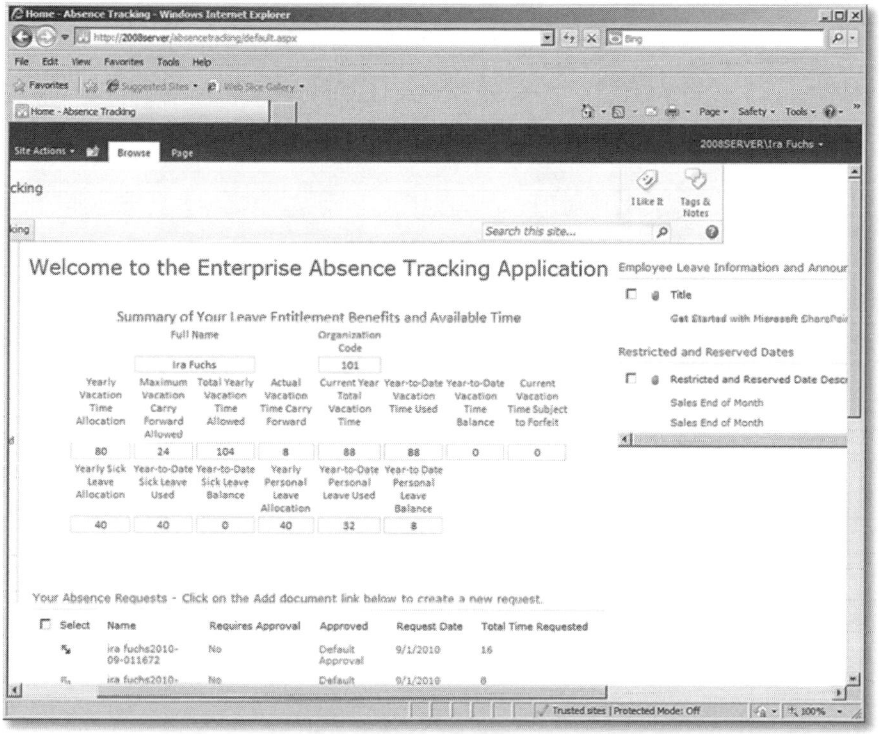

Illustration 10 - InfoPath Form Web Part accessing Line of Business information

Business Data Connectivity Services

Business Data Connectivity Services (BCS) is the new version of the *Business Data Catalog* that was originally introduced in *Microsoft Office SharePoint Server 2007*. It is now a feature of *Microsoft SharePoint Foundation 2010* with extended capabilities exposed in the *SharePoint 2010 Enterprise Edition*. BCS, through the *SharePoint Designer External Content Type* wizard, enables information from external Line of Business applications to be accessed by *SharePoint* and the *Microsoft Office* applications.

Business Data Connectivity Services uses two primary object definitions: *External Data Sources* and *External Content Types* (ECTs). *External Data Sources* are the Web Services, databases and other applications that BCS can connect to. *External Content Types* are the information sets accessed in the data sources as well as the operations that can be executed on those information sets, such as Create, Read, Update and Delete (CRUD) methods.

External Content Types are physically represented and displayed in *SharePoint 2010* as an "external list". An external list functions just like any other *SharePoint* list with all the attendant views and settings that *SharePoint* provides. The individual columns in an ECT list can also be incorporated in other *SharePoint* lists or libraries. In addition *External Content Types* can be defined so that the information set in an external source is directly accessible to *Microsoft Outlook, Word* and *Access* by mapping the ECT fields to *Microsoft Office* metadata objects.

SharePoint 2007 did not include tools for creating *Business Data Catalog* data source and ECT definitions. In *SharePoint 2010* both *SharePoint Designer* and *Visual Studio* include capabilities for creating and publishing BCS *Application Model* definitions. **Illustration 11** below shows the *SharePoint Designer* summary page for an *External Content Type*.

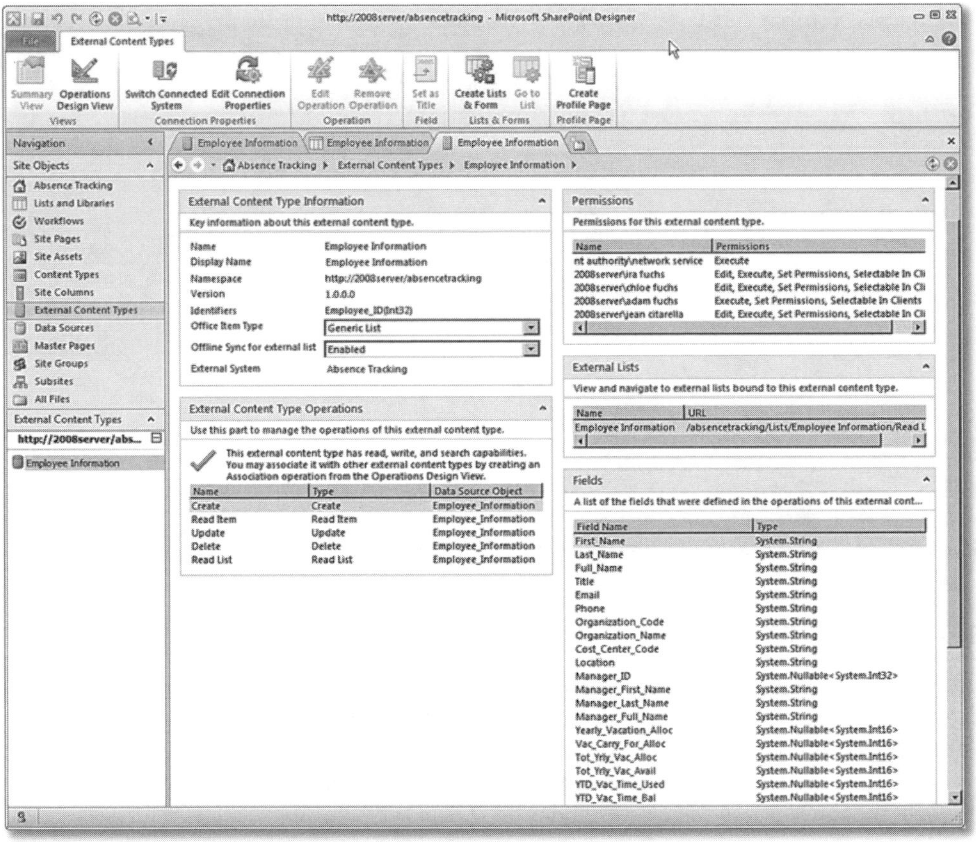

Illustration 11 - SharePoint Designer summary page for an External Content Type

Because of the substantial improvements in tools and functionality, *Business Data Connectivity Services* and *SharePoint Designer* now play a key role in the design and development of SharePoint enterprise applications. As we will demonstrate later in creating the *Employee Absence Tracking* application, *SharePoint Designer* not only provides significant efficiencies for connecting to and exposing the information and functions of external applications, but also provides capabilities for utilizing that information and functions in numerous ways.

SharePoint Designer

SharePoint Designer 2010 is a radical departure from its predecessor, *SharePoint Designer 2007*. For all intents and purposes *SharePoint Designer 2010* a completely new application with significantly enhanced capabilities to create, extend and manage *SharePoint* artifacts, as well as develop composite applications declaratively. It is the tool that ties everything together in the *SharePoint* platform, providing a development experience that is integrated, cohesive and conforms to development lifecycle best practices. There is an embarrassment of riches in *SharePoint Designer 2010* that makes it an indispensible tool for creating Enterprise applications in *SharePoint*. The user interface of *SharePoint Designer 2010* has been completely redesigned. Its governing design principle is to organize all *SharePoint* artifacts, as well as the tools to create, manipulate and integrate those artifacts, so that their relationships to each other are clearly presented and made accessible as efficiently as possible.

Every *SharePoint* artifact (site, list, library, workflow, content type, ECT) has a summary page that provides an aggregated view of all the subcomponents used by or related to that artifact, and allows the user to navigate to any summary pages for those objects. The summary page for a list will display the settings, views, forms, content type, custom actions, and workflows for that list. The summary page for a content type will reveal the forms and workflows for that content type. Any of the *SharePoint* operations and settings that can be applied to an artifact are contextually activated and made available on the summary page *Ribbon*, providing a highly efficient and flexible way of creating and managing SharePoint objects. *SharePoint Designer 2010* provides full artifact creation and editing capabilities; any function that can be executed using the SharePoint user interface can also be accomplished in *SharePoint Designer* without having to navigate between pages when using the *SharePoint* user interface. **Illustration 12** below shows how *SharePoint Designer* displays all of the lists and libraries in a site.

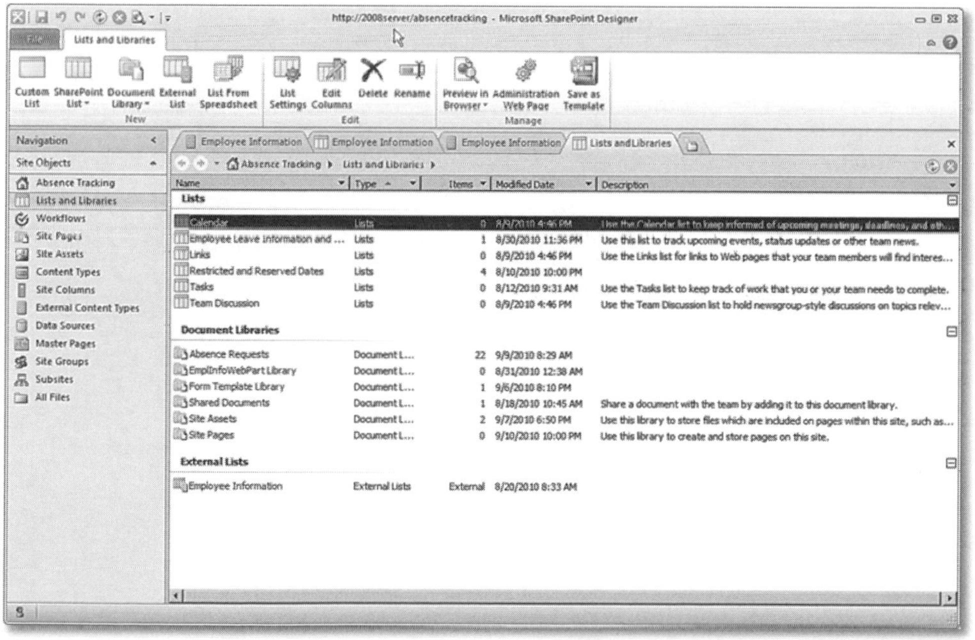

Illustration 12 – How SharePoint Designer displays all the lists and libraries in a Site

The *SharePoint Designer Navigation* pane organizes and presents the artifact categories for a *SharePoint* site collection or site. Clicking on an artifact category on the *Navigation* pane displays all the respective artifacts for that category. Clicking on a specific artifact will display its summary page. **Illustration 13** below shows the *SharePoint Designer* summary page for a form library.

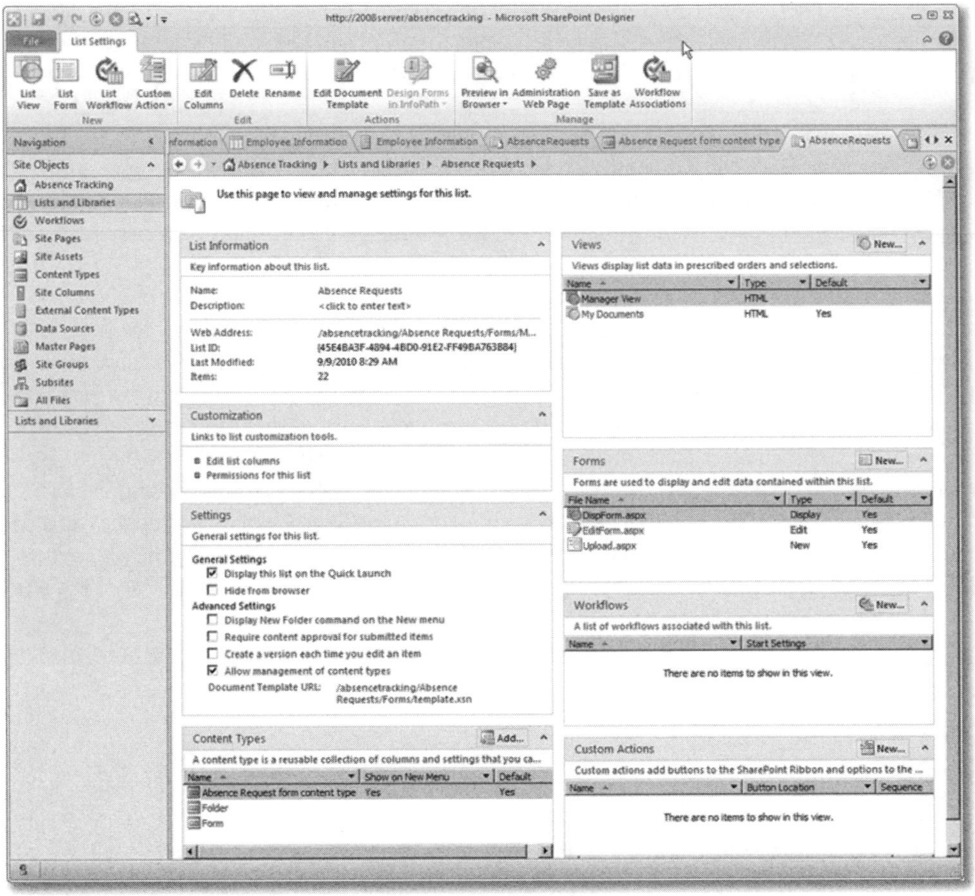

Illustration 13 - SharePoint Designer summary page for a library

SharePoint Designer now has full contextual *Ribbon* support. The *Ribbon* will display and activate the operational functions available at any given time based on the task being executed. The *Ribbon* significantly reduces the complexity of working with the numerous and rich capabilities of *SharePoint Designer*. **Illustration 14** below shows how the *Ribbon* menu in *SharePoint Designer* surfaces list and library functions when *Lists and Libraries* are selected on the *Navigation* pane.

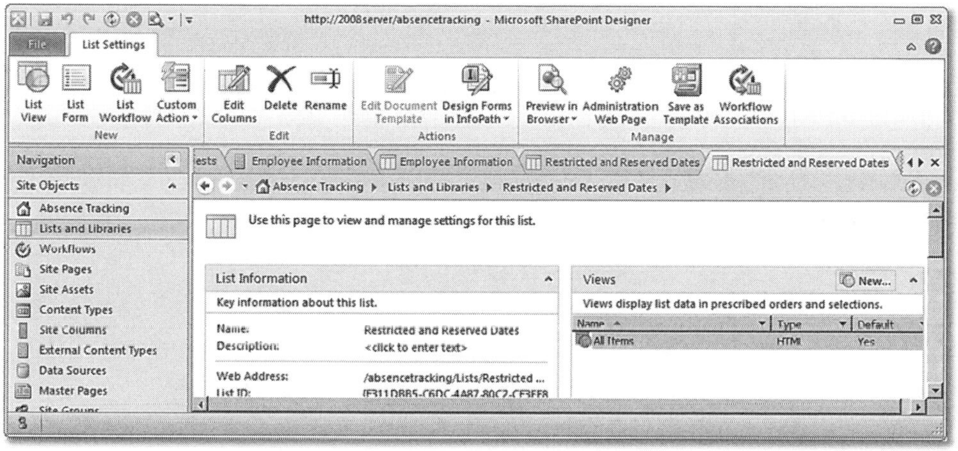

Illustration 14 – The Ribbon menu displaying the functions available for working with lists

As stated in the *InfoPath* overview earlier, the New, Display and Edit forms for list items, as well as any custom forms for a list, can now be created and modified in *InfoPath*. This can be accomplished directly from *SharePoint Designer 2010* from a list's summary page. The *Ribbon* on the summary page will activate a *Design Forms in InfoPath Ribbon* button.

By centralizing and integrating the declarative programming and configuration capabilities of *SharePoint* and *InfoPath* within *SharePoint Designer*, it now becomes a comprehensive and cohesive development console for creating *SharePoint* artifacts and applications. To further this design objective, *SharePoint Designer* has been enhanced with the following additional declarative development capabilities:

- Custom actions for list and libraries can now be created in *SharePoint Designer*. By simply clicking on the *New Custom Action* button on the Custom Actions section of the list or library's summary page a custom action can be defined to invoke opening of a form, initiate a workflow, or navigate to URL that can invoke any URL enabled function. These custom actions are represented as menu items on the *Ribbon* for the list or library or respective Web Part for the list or library. Custom actions make *SharePoint* applications easier to use by explicitly exposing the appropriate actions that can be executed for a list or library in the right context.

- *SharePoint Designer* now also includes the authoring capabilities for creating BCS artifacts, providing the facilities to connect to external data sources create external content types and publish them to the BCS instance running on a *SharePoint* server, as well as auto-generate the external list representation of the external content types and associated forms.

In addition to being able to create and modify list forms using *InfoPath*, *List Views* in *SharePoint 2010* have been reengineered as *Data Views*, which are essentially XSLT List View Web Parts or XLVs for short. XLVs provide numerous features for interacting with list information, such as paging, filtering and sorting on column headers, and inline editing. And because standard *List Views* are now *Data Views* they can be completely customized with *SharePoint Designer*, using all of the *Data View* features for working with external data sources, conditional formatting, custom styles, and related item views that display parent-child relationships between multiple lists. What's more, after customizing an XLV in *SharePoint Designer*, you can still modify that view using all of the options in the browser, such as adding or removing columns. An XLV is fully customizable both in *SharePoint Designer* and in the browser.

Illustration 15 below shows a form library in *Edit* mode from the *SharePoint* user interface with a *Current User Filter Web Part* inserted on the page. This Web Part is used to create a *Managers View* of the library items that will display only those items where the logged-in user is the manager identified in the *Manager User Name* column. Because *List Views* are now *Data View* Web Parts there is unlimited possibilities for the way in which list or library information can be manipulated, presented or made to interact with any other information in a site.

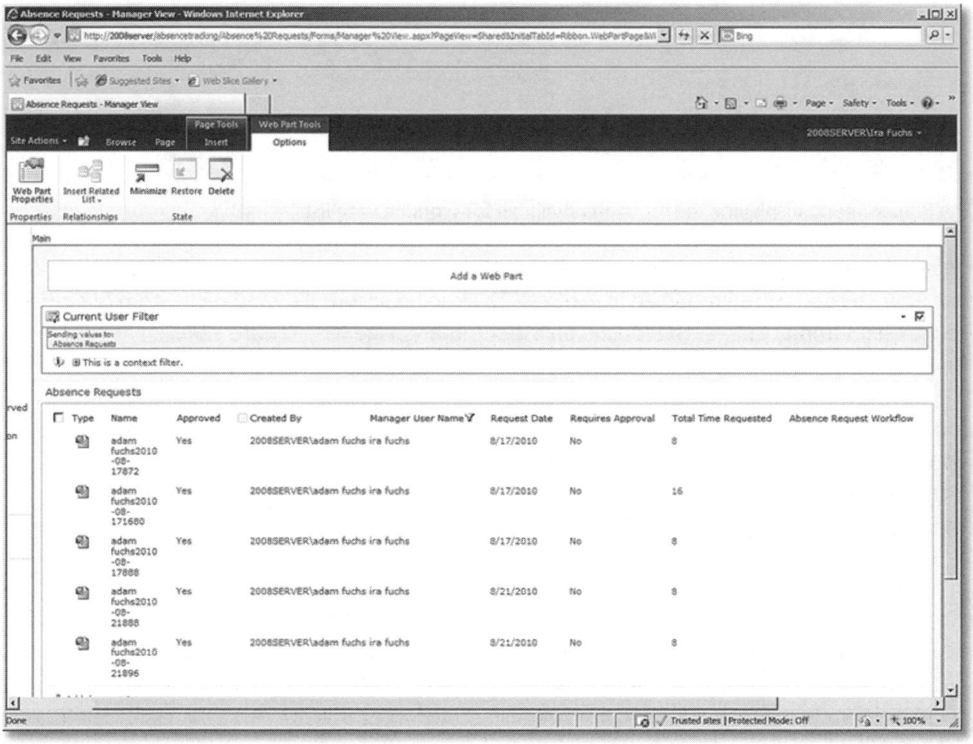

Illustration 15 - Form Library page in Edit mode showing a Current User Filter Web used to filter items for the current logged-In user

SharePoint Designer 2010 still has page editing capabilities but its primary emphasis is on creating and configuring *SharePoint* artifacts such as lists, libraries, workflows and ECTs. The experience of editing *SharePoint* Web Part pages now reflects this emphasis. Any of these artifacts can be placed and linked together inside the *main content placeholder* of a Web Part page, which is the only part of the Web Part page that is unlocked and editable in the default editing mode of *SharePoint Designer 2010*, making it significantly easier and straightforward to work with.

Illustration 16 below shows the same form library in Illustration 15 above, being edited in *SharePoint Designer*. Both the object and code view of the page are available for editing. With *SharePoint Designer* you can further customize the presentation or functional attributes of any *SharePoint* artifact.

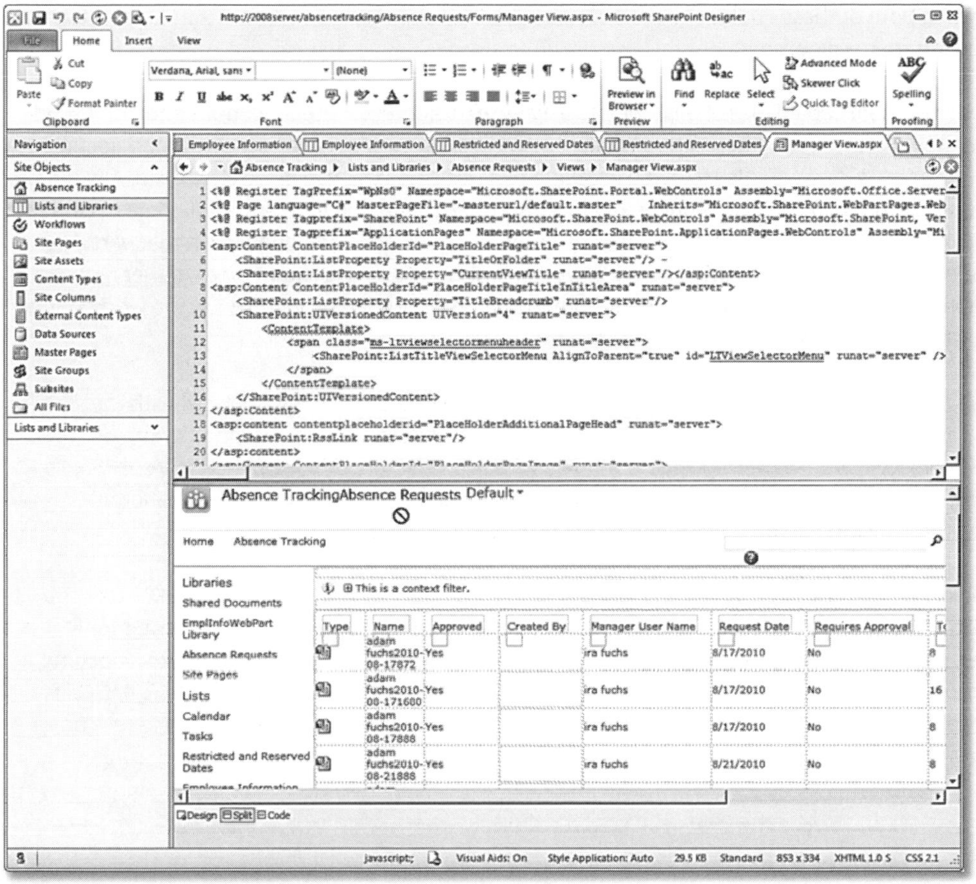

Illustration 16 - Form library page being edited in SharePoint Designer

SharePoint Workflows

Workflows are the mechanisms for executing formal processes. There are two general categories of workflow: human and document. Human workflow is the operational management of required responses by people to events in a process. Document workflow is the routing and processing of information in a process, and many organizational processes incorporate both.

SharePoint 2007 introduced an embedded workflow runtime engine, based on the *Windows Workflow Foundation* as well as several out-of-the-box common workflows (Approval, Collect Feedback, and Collect Signatures) which could be used with any list, library or content type. However these workflows could be not customized and had to be used as is, including their accompanying workflow forms. For more complex workflow requirements *SharePoint Designer* provided a workflow editor capable of creating workflows with multiple steps, with each step containing multiple conditions, actions and variables.

While the workflows that could be created in *SharePoint Designer 2007* were sophisticated enough to address a variety of use cases they were limited by being entirely bound to a specific list or library and not could not be reused. A *SharePoint Designer* workflow could not be saved and reapplied to another list, library or content type. This limitation was compounded by the fact that *SharePoint Designer* workflows could not be bound to content types either. Both of these limitations precluded flexible component reuse which is a fundamental tenet of enterprise application development.

The workflow development capabilities of *SharePoint Designer 2010* address these limitations and also include additional functional improvements that make it capable of addressing a wider range of human and document centric workflow scenarios. Any workflow created in *SharePoint Designer 2010* can be easily reused. A workflow created in the top-level site of a site collection is globally reusable; it can be bound to any list, library, or content type in the site collection. A workflow created in any site of the site collection can be reused in that particular site or a sub-site below it. *SharePoint Designer* workflows can now be bound to content types, either at the site collection level where any content types that inherit from the parent content type will include the workflow, or to just specific instances of a content type.

SharePoint Designer 2010 also introduces the ability to create a site workflow that is associated with the site itself not with a list, library or content type. In addition, a reusable *SharePoint Designer* workflow can be saved and exported as a *SharePoint Solution Package* (WSP). The workflow WSP file can be opened in *Visual Studio 2010* where it can be edited. A workflow WSP file can also be uploaded to a site collection on a different *SharePoint* farm where it can then be opened and modified by *SharePoint Designer*.

The workflow editor of *SharePoint Designer 2010* has also been improved with additional capabilities for sub steps, parallel actions, and a much broader set of workflow conditions and actions. The workflow editor is also context sensitive, displaying actions specific to a workflow association. If the workflow is bound to a document library the editor will activate a set of document library centric actions. Another feature of *SharePoint Designer* workflows is the ability to apply a workflow to a set of documents, so that a workflow action will iterate on all items in the document set.

Illustration 17 below shows the *SharePoint Designer* workflow editor user interface.

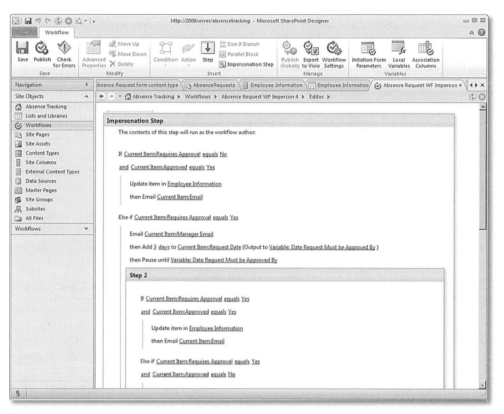

Illustration 17 - SharePoint Designer workflow editor user interface

Review of the Enterprise Employee Absence Tracking Application Scenario

- An employee who wishes to take time off goes to the *Employee Absence Tracking* site. Because *SharePoint* is user context driven the application home page displays Web Parts that shows the individual's leave time allocations and previous absence requests. In addition a list Web Part displays the restricted and reserved dates specified by the organization that the user belongs to that cannot be taken off for vacation or personal days off. An announcement Web Part displays any announcements regarding leave time as well as links to instructions for using the application and the leave policies of the organization the user belongs to.

- The user clicks on a link that opens a new *Absence Request* form. The form automatically displays the user's leave entitlements and the balance of time available to them in each entitlement category, as well as carry forward days from a previous year and any forfeiture of accumulated time off if not used based on company policy. The form obtains this information from a *SharePoint External Content Type List* that exposes HR information in an SQL database.

- The user selects the dates that they want to take off within each leave entitlement category. The date picker controls are repeating items so the user can pick as many dates as necessary. The form generates an equivalent hour value for each date for record keeping purposes. As described above rules are implemented that prevent the user from picking vacation and personal leave dates that are earlier than the current date, as well as restricted and reserved dates. Nor can the user select more leave time than the balance of time available.

- When the user submits the *Absence Request* the form calculates the total amount of time requested in all leave categories and uses a rule set that determines whether manager approval of the request is required based on the total leave time requested and the employee's tenure at the organization. A form view informs the user of this determination. The form also calculates new values for the year-to-date leave time used, and the year-to-date leave time balance in each absence request category. It does this by adding the existing year-to-date values from the *Employee Information* database with the total leave time in each category requested in the form.

- The submitted form is saved in the *Absence Request* form library. The total hour equivalent value of leave time requested in each category as well as the new year-to-date values is written to the form library columns when the form is submitted. This serves as the interim record of the transaction prior to updating the permanent employee record in the *Employee Information* database.

- A workflow is triggered upon submission of the request form to the form library. The following is a description of the workflow process:

  1. If the submitted request does not need approval (status of *Requires_Approval* equals No) then the new year-to-date values are updated in the Employee Information database and the request initiator is sent a confirmation email of this.

  2. If the submitted request requires approval (status of *Requires_Approval* equals Yes) then an email is sent to the approval manager informing them of a pending approval. The workflow calculates a duration of two days from the workflow start date during which one of the following events are anticipated:

     a. If the value of *Approved* in the form library column for the request instance is changed to "Yes", indicating that the manager has approved the request, then the new year-to-date values are updated in *the Employee Information* database and the request initiator is sent a confirmation email of this.

     b. If the value of *Approved* in the form library column for the request instance is changed to "No", indicating that the manager has rejected the request, then an email is sent to the request initiator informing them of the request rejection.

     c. If the value of *Approved* in the form library column remains empty, indicating that no action has been taken by the manager, the workflow sends a follow-up email to the manager and an additional three hours are added to the approval period time during which one of the following events will take place:

i.   The value of *Approved* in the form library column for the request instance is changed to "Yes", indicating that the manager has approved the request, then the new year-to-date values are updated in *the Employee Information* database and the request initiator is sent a confirmation email of this.

ii. The value of *Approved* in the form library column for the request instance is changed to "No", indicating that the manager has rejected the request, then an email is sent to the request initiator informing them of the request rejection.

iii. If the value of *Approved* in the form library column remains empty, indicating that no action has been taken by the manager, then the *Approved* status is set to *Yes by Default*, the new year-to-date values are updated in the *Employee Information* database and the request initiator is sent a confirmation email of this.

The execution of this workflow completes the application process. The *InfoPath Form Web Part* on the application home page displaying leave time allocated, used and available balance will display the new updated values.

Creating the Windows User Accounts and SharePoint User Profiles for the Application

Because the *Employee Absence Tracking* application is driven by user-context we will need to create several *Windows* user accounts to work with in the creation and testing of the application components. In addition, we will also create *SharePoint* user profiles for these accounts. This application utilizes the *User Profile Service* to provide the account name used in the *Current User Filter* for the *Absence Request* library and *Restricted and Reserved Dates* list. In addition, many other *SharePoint* applications will require user-context information that resides in the *User Profile Service* store.

Creating the Windows User Accounts

In *Windows Server 2008* select **Administrative Tools**, then **Computer Management** from the *Start* menu. The *Computer Management* console will open as shown in **Illustration 18** below.

Illustration 18 - Windows Server 2008 Computer Management console

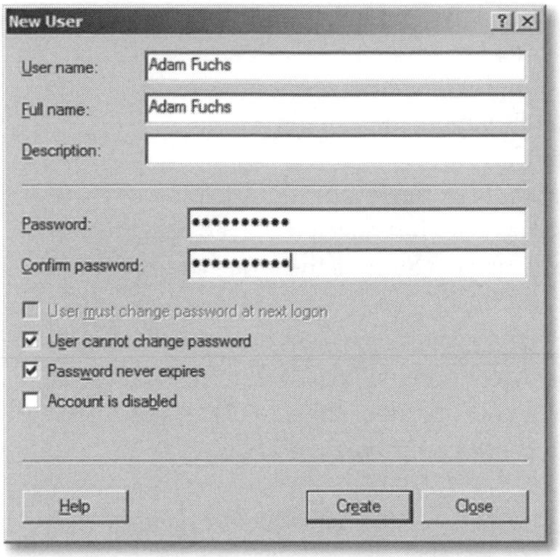

Select the *Local User and Groups* folder and then the *Users* folder. Right click and choose **New User**. The *New User* dialogue screen will appear as shown in **Illustration 19** at left. De-select the **User must change password at next logon** checkbox and select **User cannot change password** and **Password never expires** check boxes. Create at least two user accounts.

Click **Create**. When you are done you can close the *Computer Management* application.

Illustration 19 - New User dialogue box

Creating the SharePoint User Profiles

From the *Start* menu select and click on the SharePoint *Central Administration* application which will look like **Illustration 20** below when opened. Click on **Manage service applications** from the *Application Management* group.

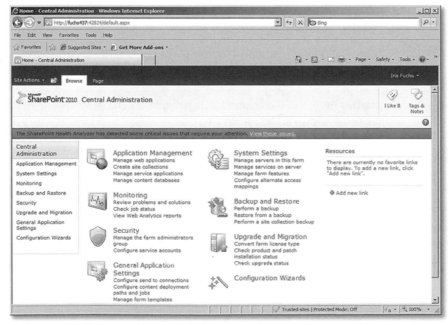

Illustration 20 - SharePoint Central Administration main page

The SharePoint *Service Applications* page will display as shown in **Illustration 21** below. Scroll down to the **User Profile Service Application** and click on it.

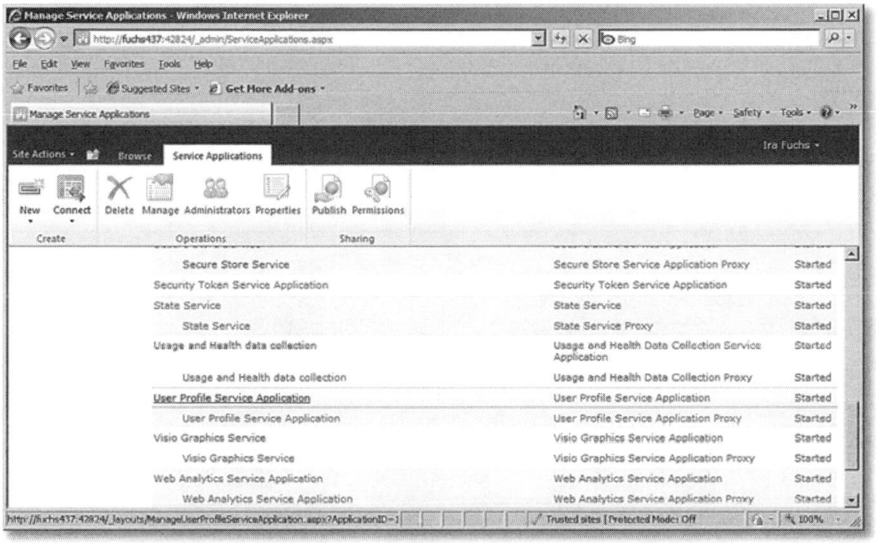

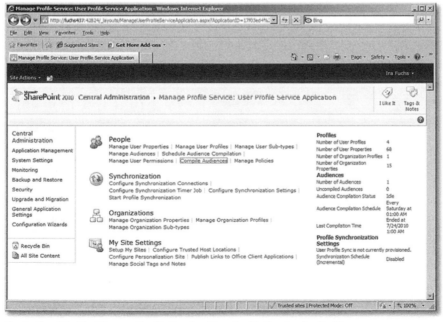

Illustration 21 - SharePoint Central Administration Service Applications page

The *Manage Profile Service: User Profile Service Application* page will display as shown in **Illustration 22** below.

Illustration 22 - The Manage Profile Service: User Profile Service Application page

Click on **Manage User Profiles**. The *Manage User Profiles* page will display as shown in **Illustration 23** below.

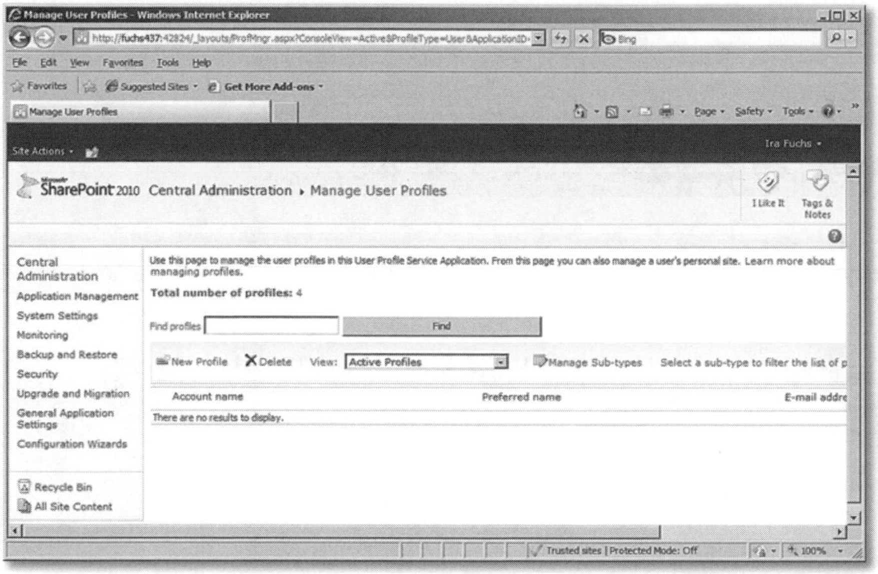

Illustration 23 - The Manage User Profiles page

Click **New Profile**. The *User Profile* data entry page will display as shown in **Illustration 24** on the next page. *User Profiles* can be created only for people who have Active Directory or Windows user accounts; or exist in some other directory service that *User Profile Services* synchronizes with. Enter the *Windows* user account name that you just created in the *Account name* field and click on the **People Picker** control icon to the right to resolve the full domain account name for the person. You can also do a directory look-up by clicking on the directory look-up control icon.

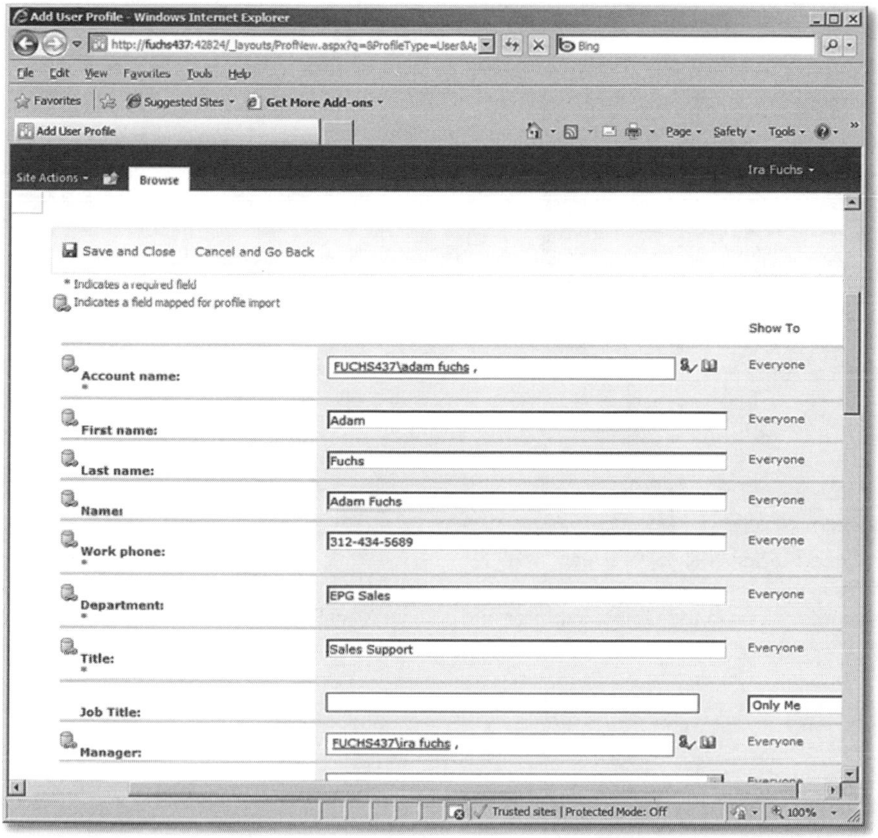

Illustration 24 - The User Profile data entry page

Enter the *First name, Last name, Name* (First and Last combined) at a minimum.

Creating the Supporting SQL Database and Employee Information Table

We will now create the *SQL Server* database and table that serves as the proxy for an actual HR or Payroll application that would contain the employee leave time allocations and other relevant employee information. The information in this database will be exposed in SharePoint through *Business Data Connectivity Services* as the *Employee Information External Content Type*.

> **Note** - The backup file for this SQL 2008 database is available from the book's web site. Instructions for installing the application and database can be found there.

Open *SQL Server Management Studio* and connect to an instance of the Database Engine as shown in **Illustration 25** below.

Illustration 25 - SQL Server Connect to Server dialogue screen

Right click on the **Databases** folder icon in the **Object Explorer** and choose **New Database** as shown in **Illustration 26** below.

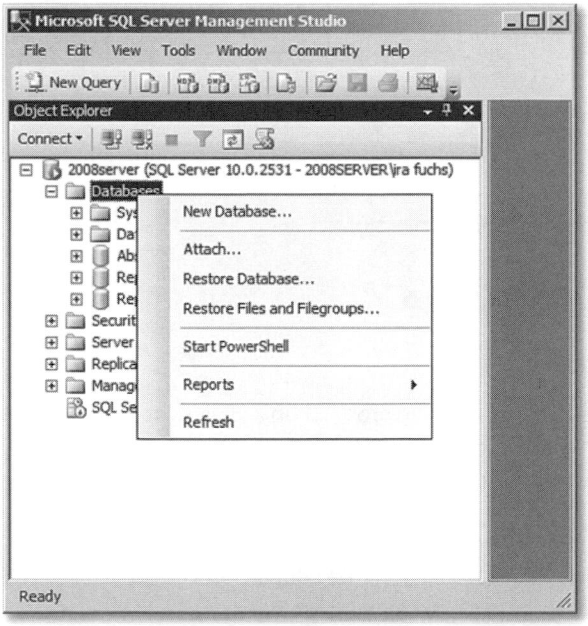

Illustration 26 - SQL Server New Database dialogue screen

Name the Database "Absence Tracking" as shown in **Illustration 27** below.

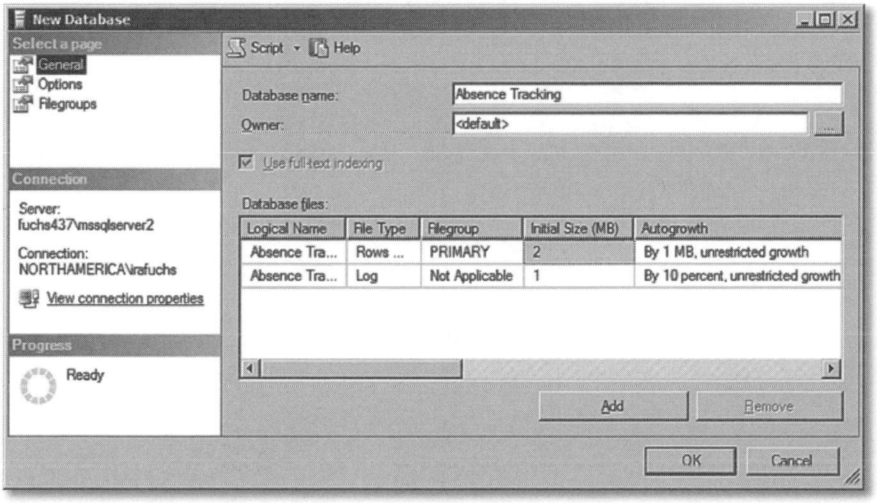

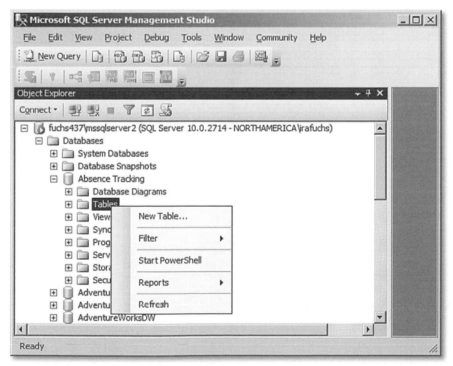

Illustration 27 - SQL Server New Database creation page

In the *Object Explorer* you will now see the *Absence Tracking* Database under *Databases.* Expand the *Absence Tracking* Database icon where you will see the related folders containing the various database objects. Right click on the **Tables** folder icon and pick **New Table** as shown in **Illustration 28** below.

Illustration 28 - SQL Server New Table dialogue screen

The *Table Design* palette will display allowing you to create the database columns and define their attributes. **Illustration 29** below shows the completed *Employee_Information* table. Create each of these table column items with their respective Data Types and Null values.

Column Name	Data Type	Allow Nulls
Employee_ID	int	☐
First_Name	nvarchar(50)	☐
Last_Name	nvarchar(50)	☐
Full_Name	nvarchar(50)	☑
Title	nvarchar(50)	☑
Email	nvarchar(50)	☐
Phone	nvarchar(50)	☐
Organization_Code	nvarchar(50)	☐
Organization_Name	nvarchar(50)	☐
Cost_Center_Code	nvarchar(50)	☑
Location	nvarchar(50)	☑
Manager_ID	int	☑
Manager_First_Name	nvarchar(50)	☑
Manager_Last_Name	nvarchar(50)	☑
Manager_Full_Name	nvarchar(50)	☑
Yearly_Vacation_Alloc	smallint	☑
Vac_Carry_For_Alloc	smallint	☑
Tot_Yrly_Vac_Alloc	smallint	☑
Tot_Yrly_Vac_Avail	smallint	☑
YTD_Vac_Time_Used	smallint	☑
YTD_Vac_Time_Bal	smallint	☑
Vac_Time_Sub_Forfeit	smallint	☑
Tot_Yrly_Sick_Leave_...	smallint	☑
YTD_Sick_Leave_Used	smallint	☑
YTD_Sick_Leave_Bal	smallint	☑
Yearly_Pers_Leave_Al...	smallint	☑
YTD_Pers_Leave_Used	smallint	☑
YTD_Pers_Leave_Bal	smallint	☑
Start_Date	date	☑
[Level]	smallint	☑
User_Name	nvarchar(50)	☑
Manager_User_Name	nvarchar(50)	☑
Manager_Email	nvarchar(50)	☑
Vac_Carry_Forward	smallint	☑

Illustration 29 - SQL Server Table Design palette

Note - The *User_Name, Manager_User_Name, Manager_Email* and *Vac_Carry_Forward* fields appear to be out of sequence in Illustration 29 above. This is because they were added later and cannot be "inserted" into the table, just added. Their placement in the table has no effect on their functional utility.

For this application we want the *Employee_ID* column to auto-generate a sequential numeric data type and be the primary key. Select the **Empolyee_ID row** and scroll down in the *Column Properties* tab to display the *Identity Specification* property. Right click on the drop-down property selection button and choose **Yes** as shown in **Illustration 30** below.

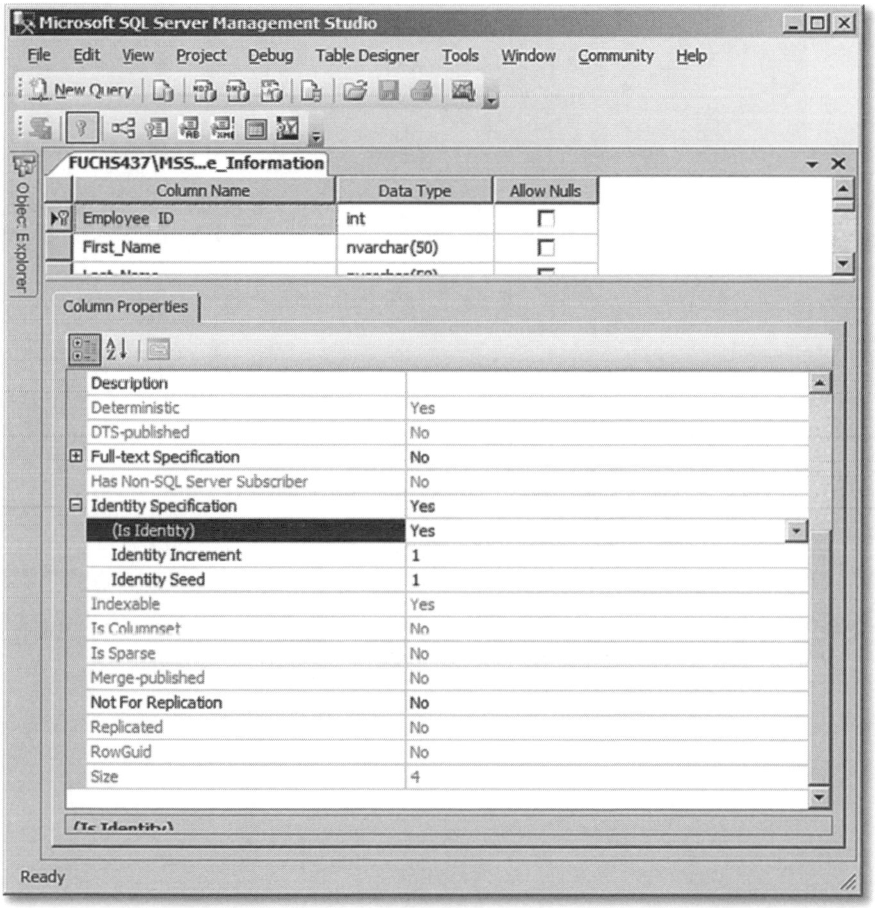

Illustration 30 - SQL Server Column Property palette

While the *Employ_ID* row is still selected right click on it and select **Set Primary Key**. From the *File* menu save the *Employee_Information* table.

To populate the table with information click on the **dbo.Employee_Information** table in *Object Explorer* and select **Edit Top 200 Rows**. From here you will be able to create the records in the table as shown in **Illustration 31** below. Add at least one record to the table.

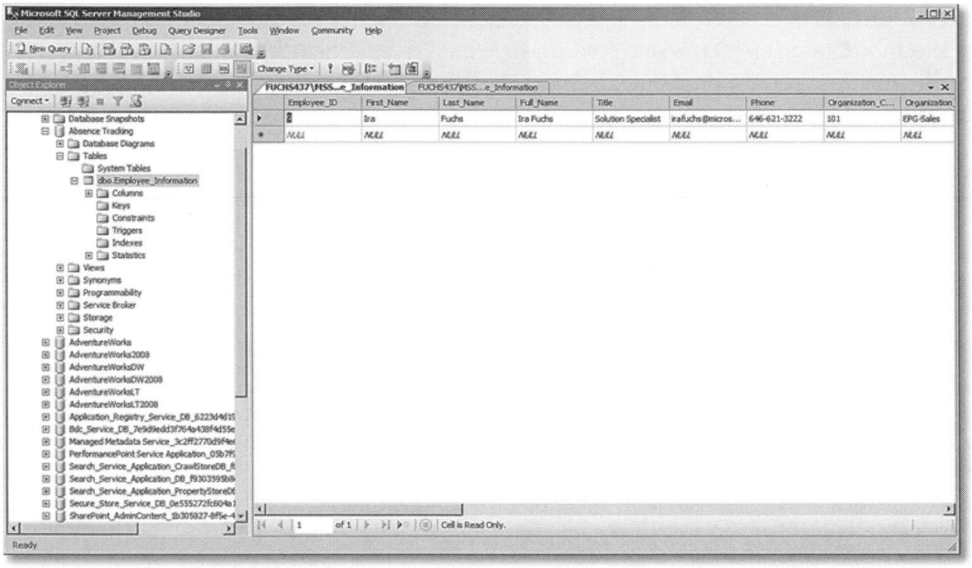

Illustration 31 - SQL Server table record creation screen

The last thing that we need to do in *SQL Server Management Studio* is create the login accounts needed to access the *Absence Tracking* database through the BCS data connection. This can be done in two ways – either by setting the user credentials for a specific database or setting them at the server level.

> **Important Security Note –** Setting individual user access rights to an application database should never be done in a production environment. This should only be done in a development/testing environment against non-production databases.

To set the user credentials at the individual database level go to the *Security\Users* folder for the *Absence Tracking* database. Right click and choose **New User**. The screen as shown in **Illustration 32** below will display.

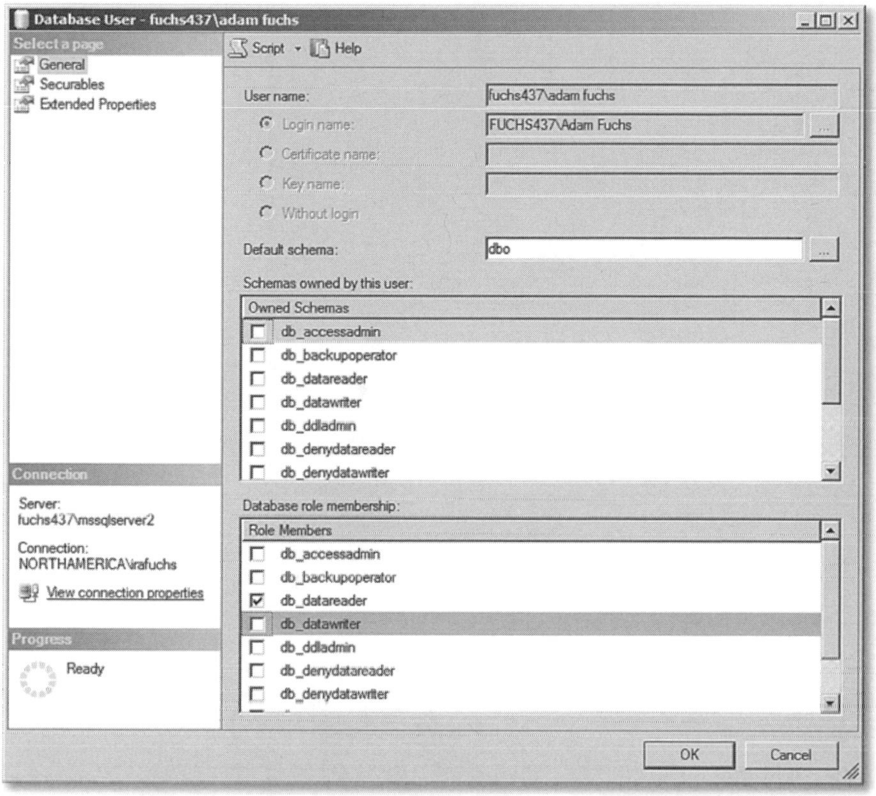

Illustration 32 - Adding security credentials to a database

Enter the *User Name* and the domain qualified *Login name* for the users you just created in *Windows Server* to give them access to the database. Check the database role membership for **db_datareader**.

> **Important Note** – Only provide your user account (that is, the account with all Administrator permissions that you are using to develop this application) with **db_datwriter** role membership to this database. When we create a connection to the *Absence Tracking* database using the *SharePoint Designer External Content Type Wizard* we will configure the connection to support Create, Read, Update and Delete (CRUD) operations on the database that can be executed on a SharePoint *External Content Type* (ECT) list. We will give users read-only access to this information. The information in the database will only be updated programmatically by a workflow

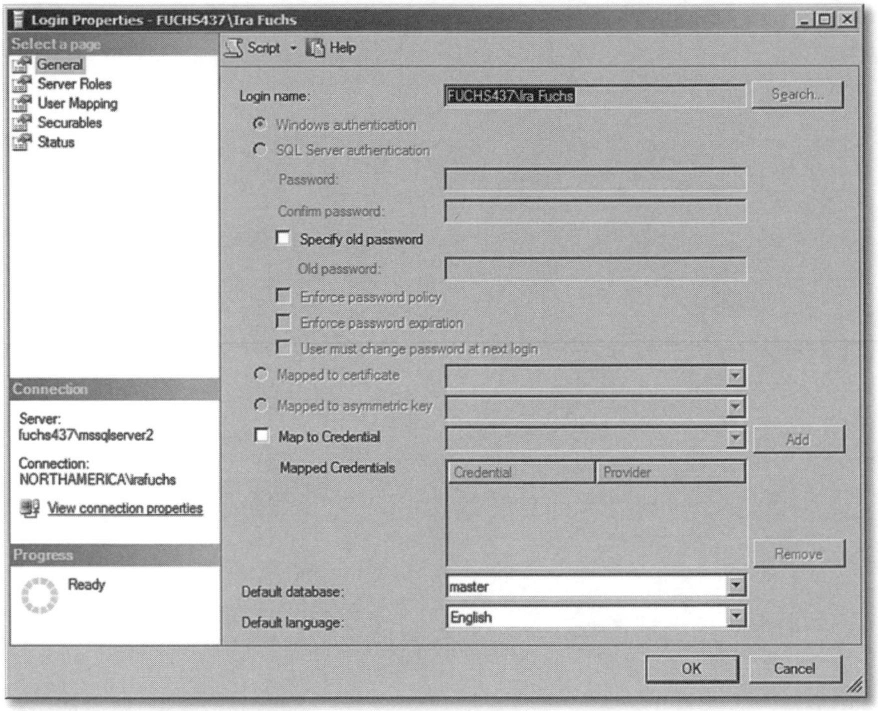

Illustration 33 - Setting security user credentials at the server level

Click **OK** to save. To set the user credentials at the server level go to the top level *Security\Logins* folder for the Server instance. Right click and choose **New Login**. The screen shown in **Illustration 33** at left will display:

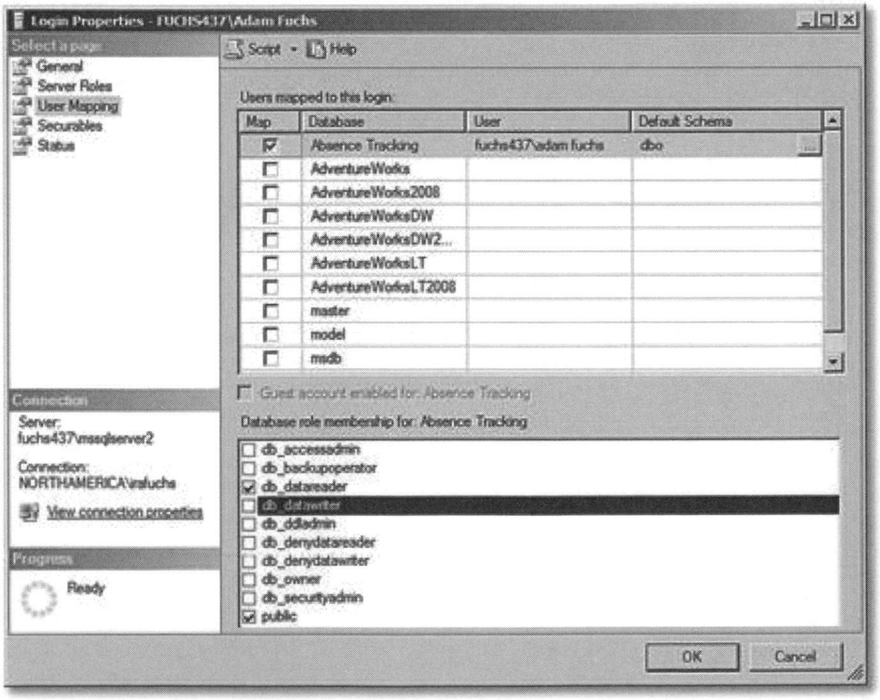

Illustration 34 - Mapping security user credentials to database objects

Enter the domain qualified *Login name*. Next go to *User Mapping* as shown in **Illustration 34** at left.

Check the databases that the user is given access to and for each database check the database membership roles for *db_ datareader*. Click the **OK button** to save and exit.

These same user account credentials will be set for the *BCS External Content Type* for this data source later.

Creating the SharePoint Artifacts and Components – the SharePoint Development Process

Creating applications in *SharePoint* is done in a top-down way. That is, you first create a host site in which you then create the artifacts and components of the application. In this book we use the term artifact to mean the native, out-of-the-box SharePoint objects such as lists, libraries, views, Web Part pages and Web Parts. An artifact starts out in life as an atomic object, a stand-alone unit of functional value. By combining the capabilities of multiple artifacts we create composite functionality, or components. One of the reasons why *SharePoint* is such a promising application development platform is because it facilitates artifact and component reuse. Later on we will demonstrate how to save artifacts and components so that they can be re-used in any *SharePoint* environment.

While we can create and configure most artifacts and some components directly in *SharePoint* we will do much of our work in *SharePoint Designer*. *SharePoint Designer* provides application developers with a more versatile and efficient interaction with *SharePoint* artifacts and components. It is also the tool that exposes *SharePoint* developer capabilities such as workflow authoring, the creation of BCS *External Content Types*, custom list and library actions, as well as the WYSIWYG editing of Web Part pages and the underlying XSLT for list and library views.

We will create the *SharePoint* artifacts and components for this application in the following order:

1. The host site for the application

2. The BCS *External Connection* to the SQL database and the *External Content Type* and list that accesses the information from the database tables created earlier

3. The *InfoPath Absence Request* form that uses the BCS *External Content Type* and list

4. The *Absence Request* form library

5. The workflow for the absence approval process

6. The *InfoPath* form used in a Web Part on the application home page

7. The additional supporting information lists and respective Web Parts for the application home page

8. The *SharePoint Solution Package* (WSP) for the application

Illustration 35 on the next page shows the application home page. On the top left is the *InfoPath Form Web Part* that displays the leave time entitlements and usage from the *Employee Information* database. Directly below it is the *Absence Request* form library Web Part that displays the user's previous absence requests and where a new request can be created. On the right are an *Announcement* Web Part and the Web Part for *the Restricted and Reserved Dates* list. All information on the application home page displays information filtered by the user's identity.

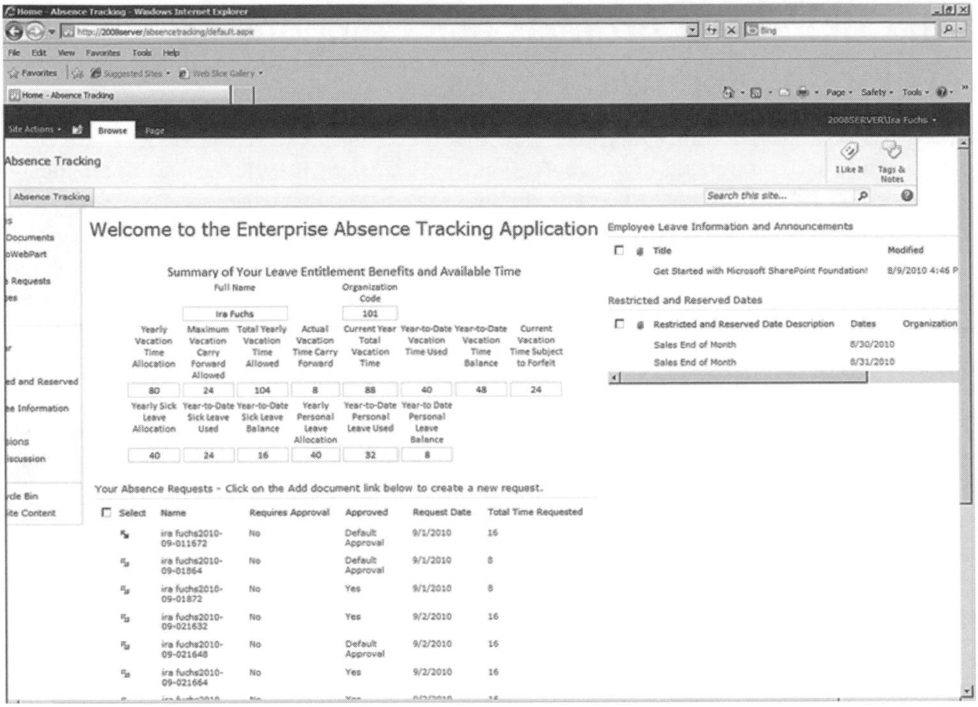

Illustration 35 - Enterprise Absence Tracking Application home page

Creating the Host Site for the Application

Note: The following site creation step assumes that a top-level site collection has been created in *SharePoint Central Administration* under which the host application site will be instantiated.

Open *SharePoint Designer,* which will present you with the *Sites* opening screen as shown in **Illustration 36** below.

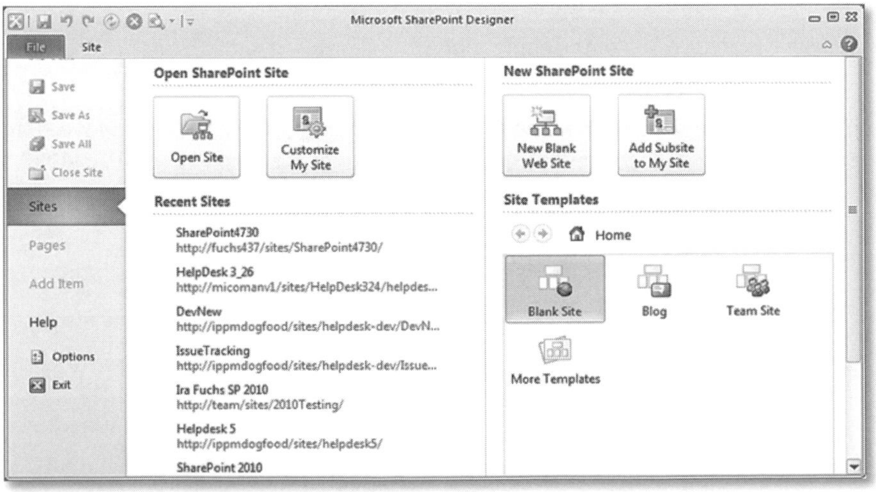

Illustration 36 - SharePoint Designer Sites page

From the *Sites* page you can open existing *SharePoint* sites, create new sites, or add a sub-site to an existing site. We will create a new *Blank Site*. Click on the **Blank Site button** on the right and the *New Blank Web Site* dialogue will appear. Enter "AbsenceTracking" following the name of the site collection you are working with as shown in **Illustration 37** below and click **OK**.

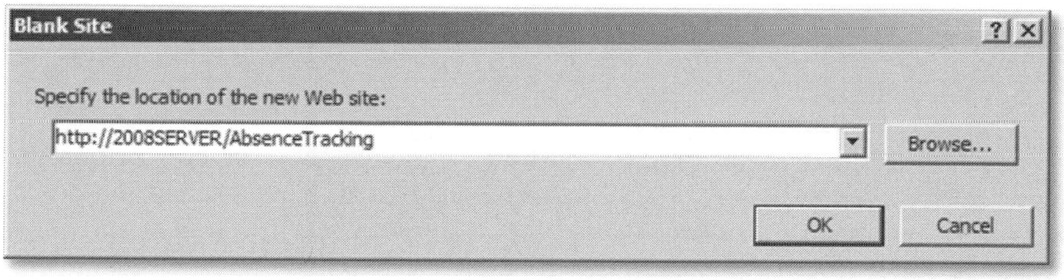

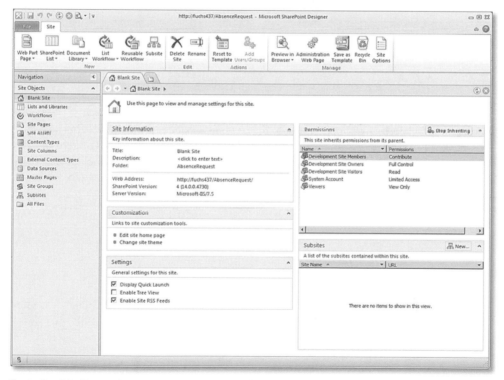

Illustration 37- SharePoint Designer New Site dialogue screen

SharePoint will create the blank site and open it in *SharePoint Designer* to display the summary page for the site as shown in **Illustration 38** below. Click on the *Blank Site* Title and change it to "Absence Tracking".

Illustration 38 - SharePoint Designer summary page for the new site

The summary page allows you to view, create and configure site artifacts and their settings. The *Ribbon* displays the various *New, Edit, Actions* and *Manage* functions that can be executed at the Site level. The summary page tab for *Permissions* displays the *Users and Groups* who have access to the site with their respective permissions while the *Subsites* tab displays all the child sites of the current site with their URL addresses. Clicking on the **Edit site home page** link will open the site's home page in the *SharePoint Designer* page editor where you can modify the underlying web page as shown in **Illustration 39** below.

Illustration 39 - Home page for site opened in Edit mode in SharePoint Designer

Right click on the **Home.aspx tab** and select **Close**. Return to the summary page for the site. Note that by default the new site inherits its permission settings from the parent site collection. Click on the **Permissions** link on the *Permissions* tab to display the users and groups defined for the parent site collection with their attendant permissions. Click on the **Parent Permissions** button on the *Ribbon* to access the *Permissions* page for the top-level site collection as shown in **Illustration 40** below.

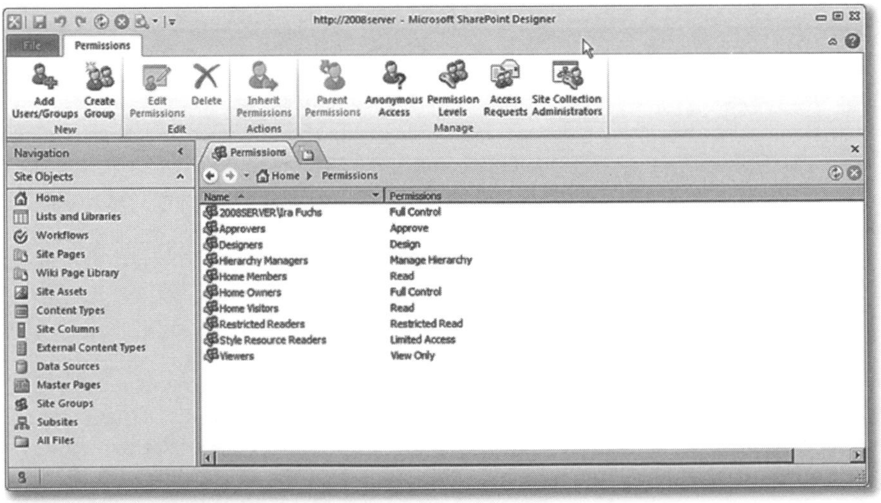

Illustration 40 - Permissions page for the top level site collection in SharePoint Designer

Click on the **Add Users/Groups button** to open the *Add Permissions* dialogue screen as shown in **Illustration 41** below.

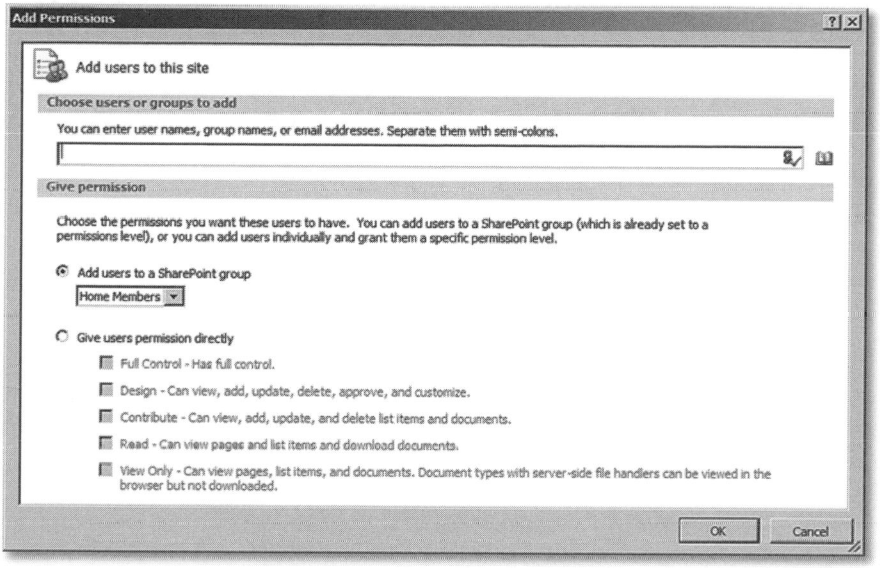

Illustration 41 - Add users dialogue screen in SharePoint Designer

This is where you will add the *Windows Server* user accounts that you created to an existing *SharePoint* group or provide them with permissions directly. Add these new accounts to the *Home Owners* group using the *Add users to a SharePoint group* drop-down list.

Creating the Business Data Connectivity Services Data Connection, External Content Type, and External List

Business Data Connectivity Services is the new version of the *Business Data Catalog* that was introduced in *Microsoft Office SharePoint Server 2007*. It is now provided in *Microsoft SharePoint Foundation 2010* with feature extensions in *SharePoint Server 2010 Enterprise Edition*. BCS enables you to declaratively model external systems so that you can expose external data in *SharePoint Server 2010* and also make it available to *Outlook* and *Microsoft Word*. *SharePoint Designer* provides an easy to use Wizard-like tool for connecting to external systems and identifying the information sets that can be accessed; enabling the operations that can be executed on the information sets; and exposing the information as a list within *SharePoint* and mapped to *Microsoft Office* data types for use in *Outlook* and *Word*.

The steps in creating a BCS *External Content Type* (ECT) in *SharePoint Designer* are as follows:

- Create and name the ECT
- Create a data source connection to the information source for the ECT
- Create the operations (Create, Read, Update and Delete) and pick the data source information set will be available to the operation
- Create an *External List* and *InfoPath* form that displays the information from the data source in a SharePoint list which can be edited by the *InfoPath* list form.

Creating an External Content Type

Click on the **External Content Types** icon on the *Navigation* pane. The main information section will be empty because no *External Content Types* have been created yet, as shown in **Illustration 42** below.

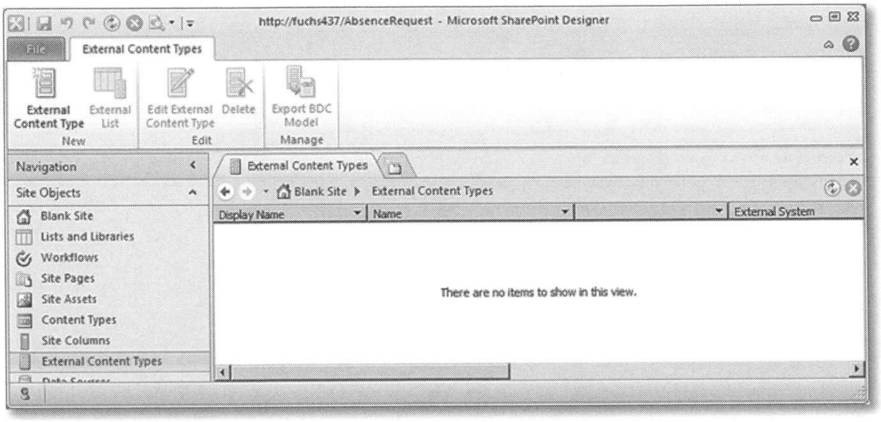

Illustration 42 - External Content Type page in SharePoint Designer

Click on the **New External Content Type button** on the *Ribbon*. The *External Content Type* summary page will display as shown in **Illustration 43** below.

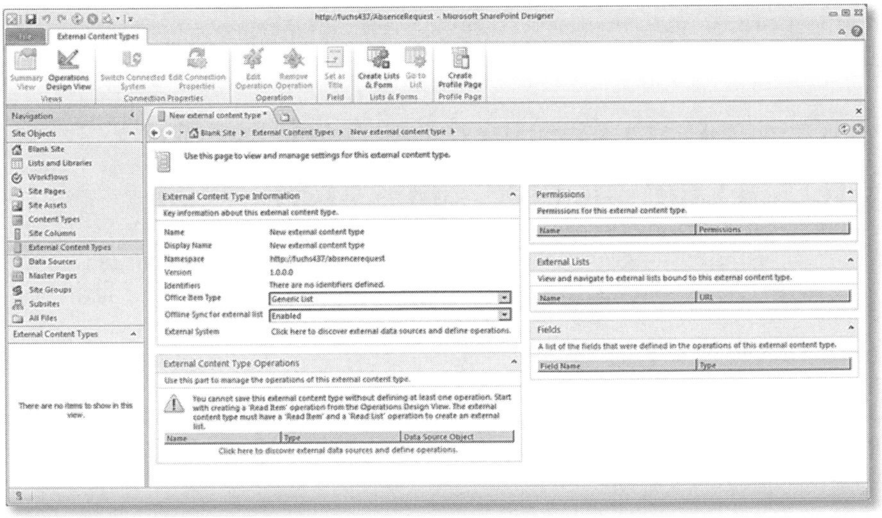

Illustration 43 - SharePoint Designer Summary Page for new External Content Type

Change the *Name* and *Display Name* to "Employee Information". Click on the **Click here to discover external data sources and define operations** link either in the *External Content Type Information* section or the *External Content Type Operations* section. The *Operation Designer* screen will be displayed as shown in **Illustration 44** on the next page.

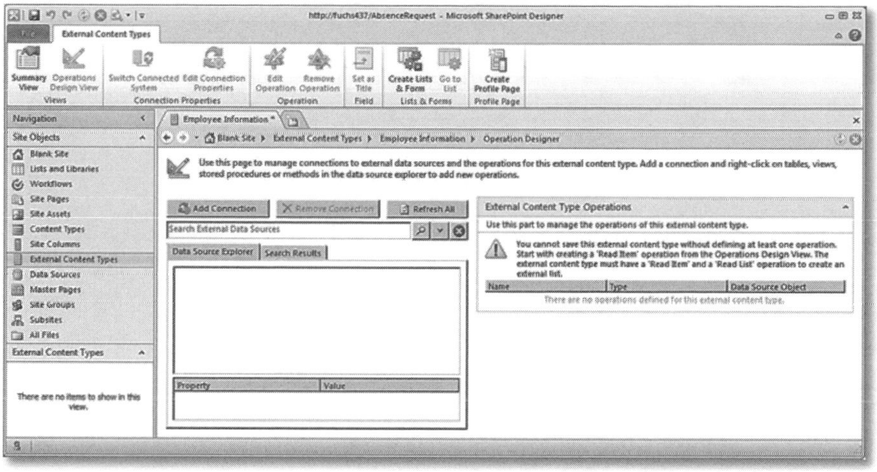

Illustration 44 - ECT Operation Designer main screen in SharePoint Designer

Creating the External Data Source Connection

This page contains the *Data Source Explorer* section and *External Content Type Operations* section. This is where we will create a connection to a data source, in this case to the *SQL Server* database containing the *Employee Information* table that we created earlier. Click on the **Add Connection** button. The following *External Data Source Type Selection* dialogue box will display as shown in **Illustration 45** below.

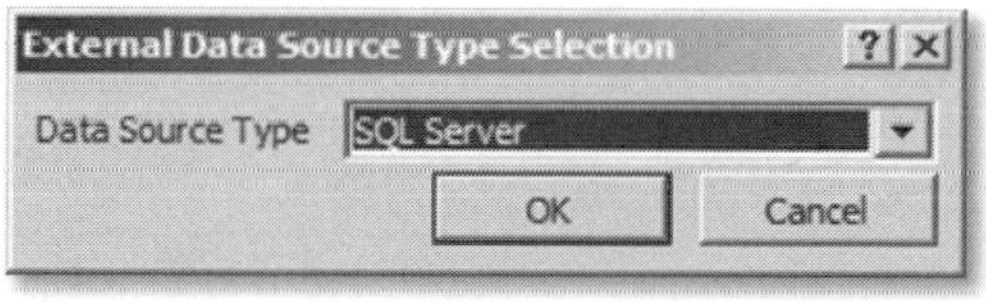

Illustration 45 - External Data Source Type Selection dialogue screen

Choose **SQL Server** and click **OK.** The *SQL Server Connection* dialogue box will appear as shown in **Illustration 46** below. Enter the name of your Database Server and the Database Name which was *Absence Tracking*. Leave the default *Connect with User's Identity* radio button value.

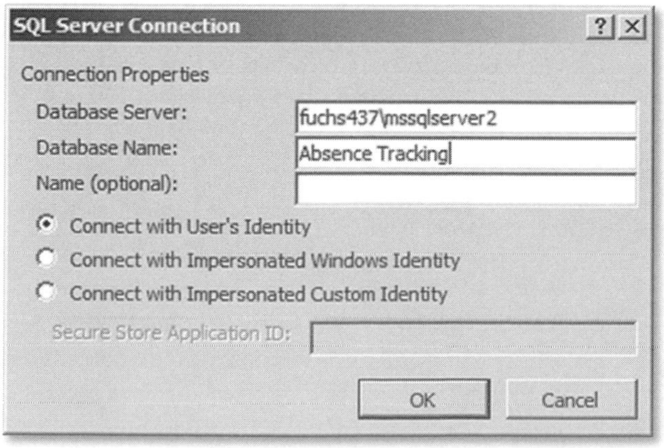

Important Note –We will change the authentication credentials later to **Connect with Impersonated Windows Identity** using a *Secure Store Service* account. We will discuss all the reasons for doing this later in the section on using the *Secure Store Service* with BCS.

Illustration 46 - SQL Server Connection dialogue screen

When the connection is made the *Absence Tracking* database will be displayed in the *Data Source Explorer* panel as shown in **Illustration 47** below. If other data sources were previously created they will be displayed as well.

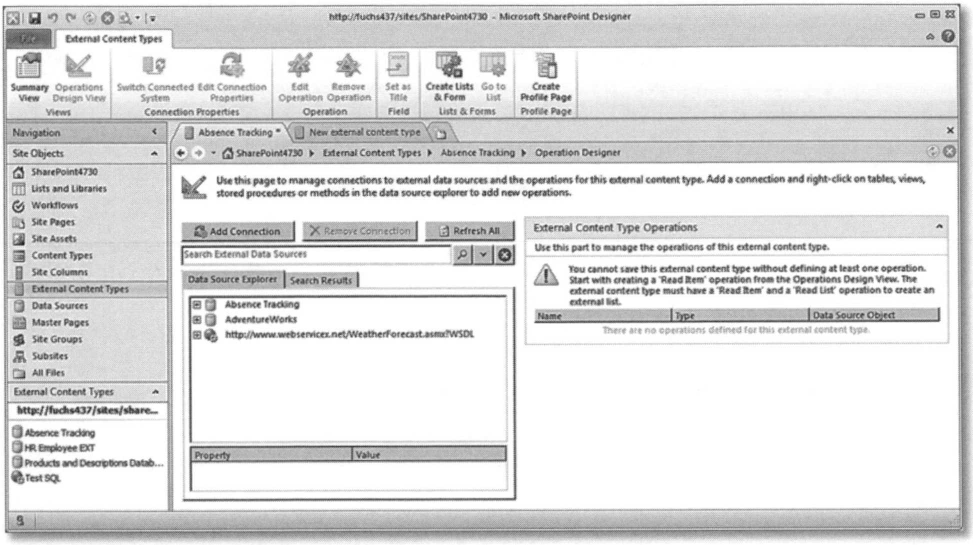

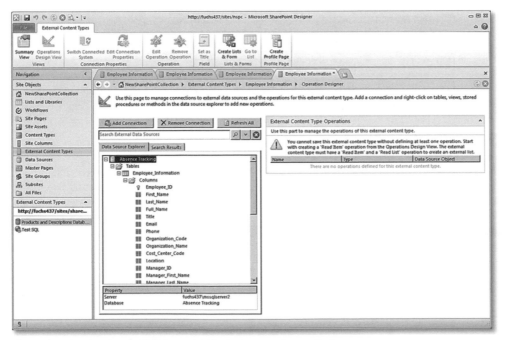

Illustration 47 - Data Source Explorer panel in SharePoint Designer

Expand the *Absence Tracking* database icon in the *Data Source Explorer* to view the Tables, Views and Routines that are exposed. Clicking on the *Tables* or *Views* folder will reveal the database columns for each table or view as shown in **Illustration 48** below.

Illustration 48 - Opening the SQL Server Tables in the Data Source Explorer

Creating the External Content Type Operations

The next step is to create the operations that can be executed on the information in the tables or views and choose what information to make available through the ECT. These operations are the standard Create, Update and Delete (CRUD) functions available in most applications. This is a key enhancement of BCS – enabling the execution of CRUD operations within a *SharePoint* application. In *SharePoint 2007* BDC provided only read-only access to external data sources. Right click on any table or view and the following options will be displayed, as shown in **Illustration 49** below.

- Create All Operations
- New Read Item Operation
- New Read List Operation
- New Create Operation
- New Update Operation
- New Delete Operation
- New Association

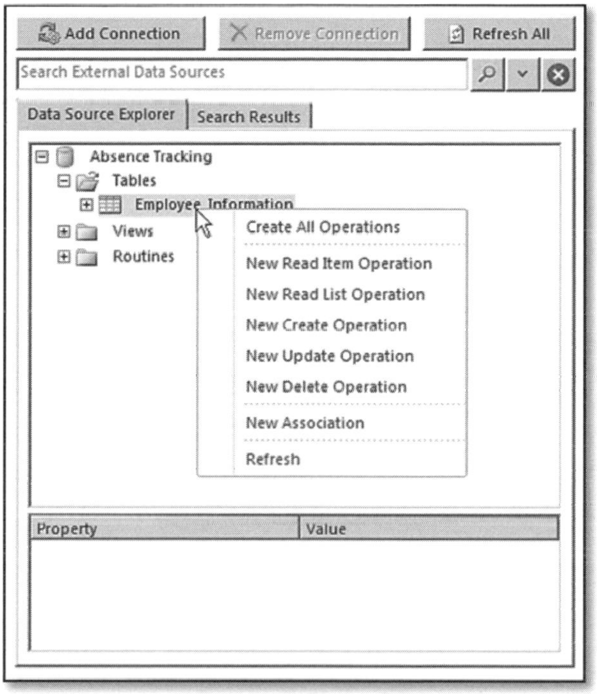

The *SharePoint Designer External Content Type* wizard is decidedly granular about what information you expose and what you can do with that information. The underlying assumption here is that Line of Business information is restricted and privileged and should be exposed as an ECT on an explicit need and use basis. The following is a description of the Operation choices:

Create All Operations – Choosing this option will initiate a Wizard that will create and configure all of the Operations below.

New Read Item Operation – Choosing this option will initiate a Wizard that will allow the ECT List Form to access and display a single record from the data source.

Illustration 49 - ECT Operations that can be created on a data source with SharePoint Designer

New Read List Operation – Choosing this option will initiate a Wizard that will create a data set from the data source that will display as a SharePoint List. This Operation is prerequisite requirement of creating an External Content Type List and Form.

New Create Operation – Choosing this option will initiate a Wizard that will allow a user to create a new record in the data source using the underlying InfoPath form for the ECT List. This is a new write-back capability of BCS.

New Update Operation – Choosing this option will initiate a Wizard that will allow a user to update one or more data source fields with a new value from an ECT List view or from the underlying InfoPath form for the ECT list. This is a new write-back capability of BCS.

New Delete Operation – Choosing this option will initiate a Wizard that will allow a user to delete an entire record. This can be accomplished by deleting a row in an ECT List view or as an item displayed in the underlying InfoPath form for the ECT list. This is a new write-back capability of BCS.

New Association – Choosing this option will initiate a Wizard that is used to link two tables in the same database.

For the *Employee Absence Tracking* application we will *Create All Operations* on the *Employee Information* table that we created in the *Absence Tracking* database earlier.

Right click on the *Employee_Information* table icon in the *Data Source Explorer* and click on **Create All Operations**. The *Operation Properties* Wizard screen will display as shown in **Illustration 50** below.

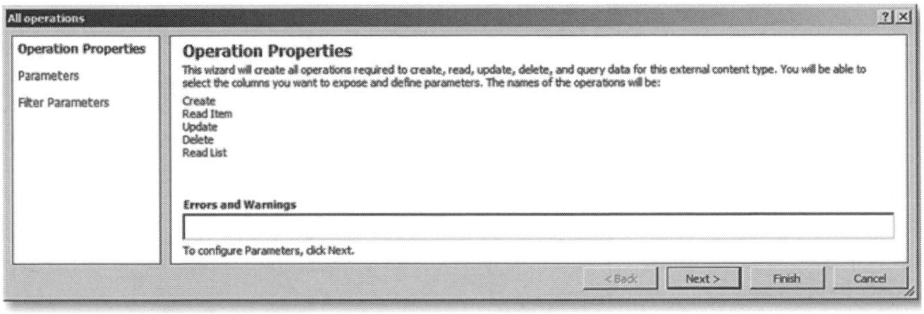

Illustration 50 - Operation Properties page of the ECT Wizard

Click on the **Next button** to display the *Parameters Configuration* page of the wizard as shown in **Illustration 51** below. Four section panels are displayed: the Wizard steps, the *Data Source Elements*, the *Element Properties* and *Errors and Warnings*.

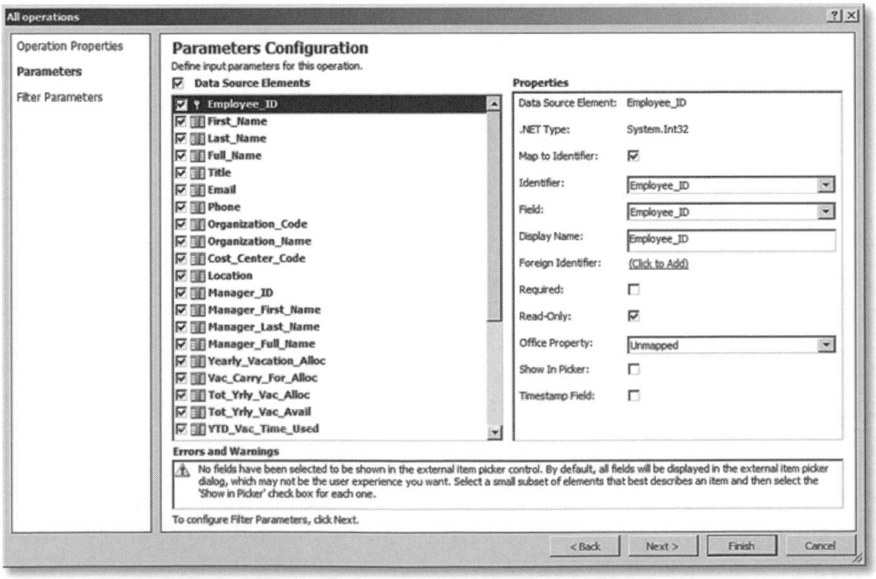

Illustration 51 - the Parameters Configuration page of the ECT wizard

On this Wizard step we can choose the fields from the database table that we want to use in the *External Content Type* and configure settings and properties for the fields. The *Data Source Elements* section displays the available fields from the database table. All fields from the data source are selected for inclusion in the *External Content Type* by default but any field that is not required can be de-selected and omitted from the *External Content Type* record definition. The Wizard accesses the properties defined for these fields in the SQL database and makes sure that any of the choices in this step do not invalidate those properties. For example, if we de-select any of the fields that were set to not nullable (i.e. required) such as the First Name, the Wizard would display an error message in the *Errors and Warnings* panel. An error message is displayed for every instance of an error condition.

Depending upon the operation and data source field selected the *Properties* panel will display different property settings. The following is a description of these property items:

Data Source Element – The name of the field in the data source.

.NET Type – The data type assigned to the field in the data source.

Map to Identifier check box – Used to specify which field will be used as the key (indexed) fields in the External Content Type. At least one field must be specified as the Identifier, typically the same key field defined in the database, such as the *Employee_ID*. You can create multiple key fields by selecting a field in the *Data Source Elements* panel, clicking *Map to Identifier*. The ECT *Identifier* by default will be the same field specified in the database.

Identifier – When a *Data Source Element* is checked to *Map to Identifier* a corresponding ECT field must be identified.

Field – The default mapping of the data source field name to the ECT column name.

Display Name – If you would like to use a friendly or different name for the ECT column it can be specified here. For example, instead of *Yearly_Vacation_Alloc* as the default ECT column name, you can make the Display Name for the column "Yearly Vacation Time Available".

Office Property – Options for mapping an ECT field to Office metadata definitions will be displayed in this drop-down list if an Office Item Type (Appointment, Contact, Task or Post) was set for the ECT on the *External Content Type* Information tab of the summary page. This mapping allows ECT information exposed in *SharePoint* to be used by *Outlook* and *Word*.

Required – A check box setting used in the *Create Read List Operation* to indicate that the field is required. If this property was set in the data source it will be checked here.

Read Only – A check box setting used in the *Create Read List Operation*. This setting allows you to make the ECT field read only.

Show in Picker – A check box setting used in the *Create Read List Operation* that will bind this field to a picker control in the ECT list form.

Time Stamp Field – A check box setting used in the *Create Read List Operation* to time stamp this field.

Default Value   A default value for an ECT field can be specified here. For example if you wanted to set the default value for the Yearly_Vacation_Alloc to be 80 hours you would enter "80" here.

Filter – A context sensitive filter can be applied to any field. We will discuss this in more detail below.

Foreign Identifier – Used to link two database tables in an Association.

With the **Employee_ID** selected check the **Map to Identifier box** and make sure that the Identifier drop-down list displays *Employee_ID*. Click on the **Next button**. The *Parameters Configuration* page of the wizard will display as shown in **Illustration 52** below.

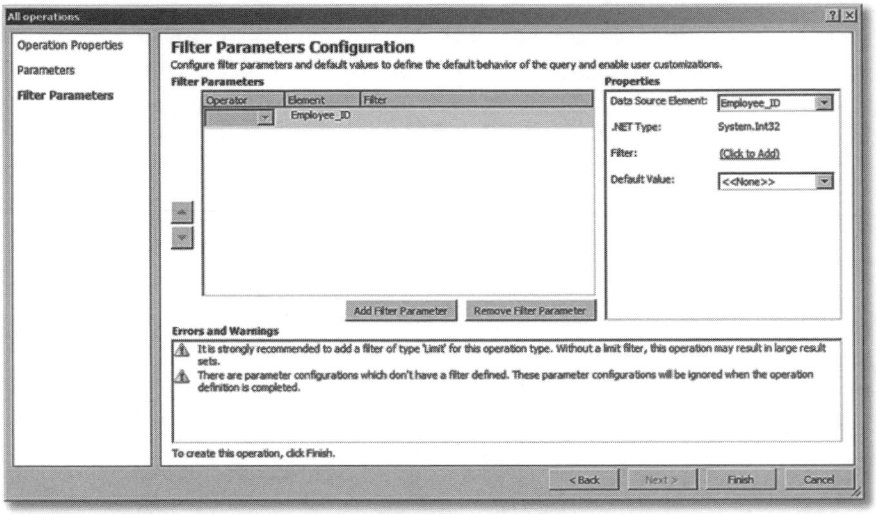

Illustration 52 - the Parameters Configuration page of the ECT wizard

Click the **Add Filter Parameter button**. By default the first field in the data source will display in the *Filter Parameters* panel. Click the **Click to Add** link for Filter in the *Properties* panel. The *Filter Configuration* dialogue box will display as shown in **Illustration 53** below.

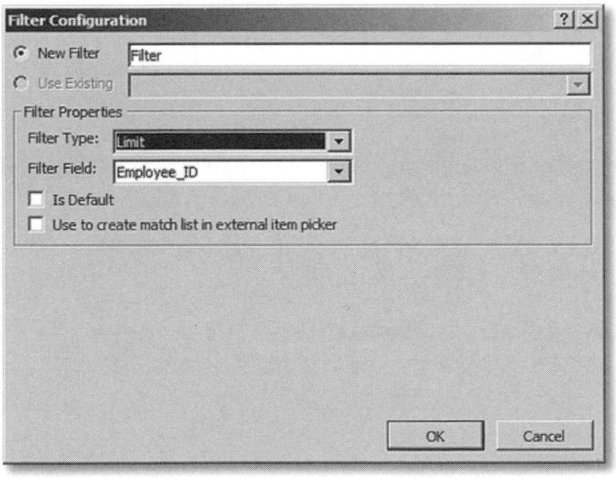

Illustration 53 - The Filter Configuration dialogue box of the ECT wizard

Select the **New Filter radio button** and pick *Limit* for the *Filter Type* and *Employee_Id* for the *Filter Field*.

Click **OK**. For the default value put in a numeric value that will specify the number of rows the ECT list will return on a page, as shown in **Illustration 54** below.

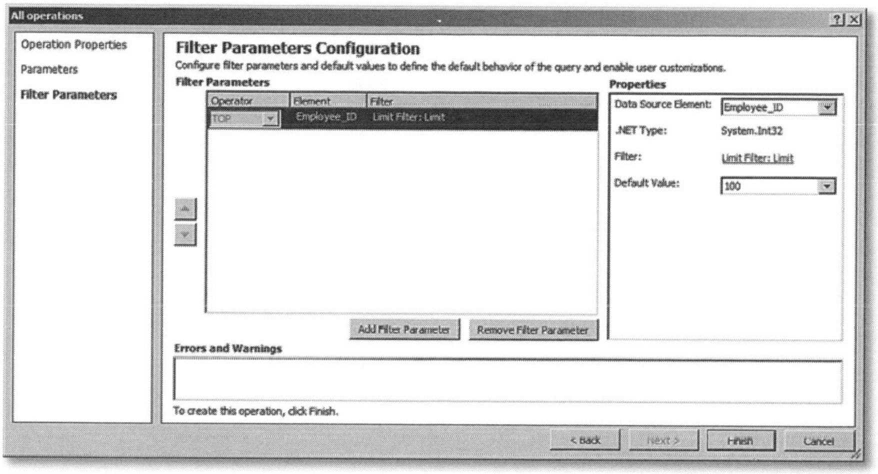

Illustration 54 - Entering the filter value for the number of rows the ECT list will return on a page

Click the **Finish** button. We have completed the step of creating the *Employee Information* ECT operations. If you return to the *Summary Page* by clicking on the **Summary View** Ribbon button you will now see all the operations displayed in the *External Content Type Operations* section as shown in **Illustration 55** below.

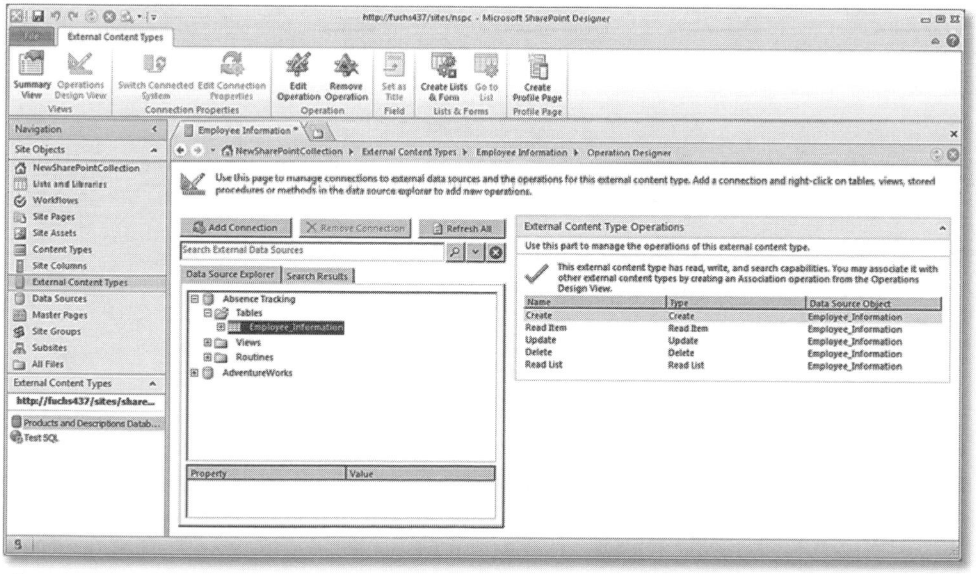

Illustration 55 - Operations Designer main page showing the defined operations

Creating the ECT List and Form

The next step is to create the ECT List and Form for this ECT. Click on the **Create Lists & Form** button on the *Ribbon*. The *Create List and Form* dialogue screen will display as shown in **Illustration 56** below.

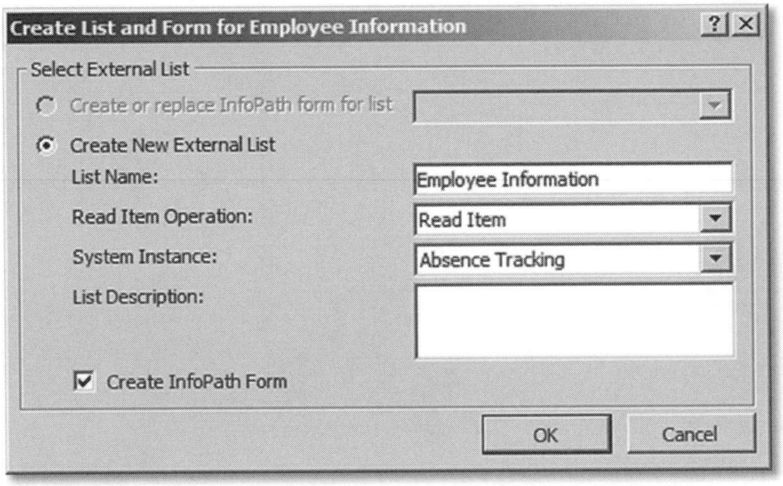

Illustration 56 - Create List and Form dialogue screen for the ECT

The radio button for *Create New External List* will be displayed. Enter a List Name and make sure you **check** the **Create InfoPath Form check box**. You can create multiple external lists for an ECT. Click the **OK** button. *SharePoint Designer* will now generate an *External List* for the ECT. Click on the **Lists and Libraries** icon in the *SharePoint Designer Navigation* pane and you will see the *Employee Information* list under the *External Lists* group as shown in **Illustration 57** below.

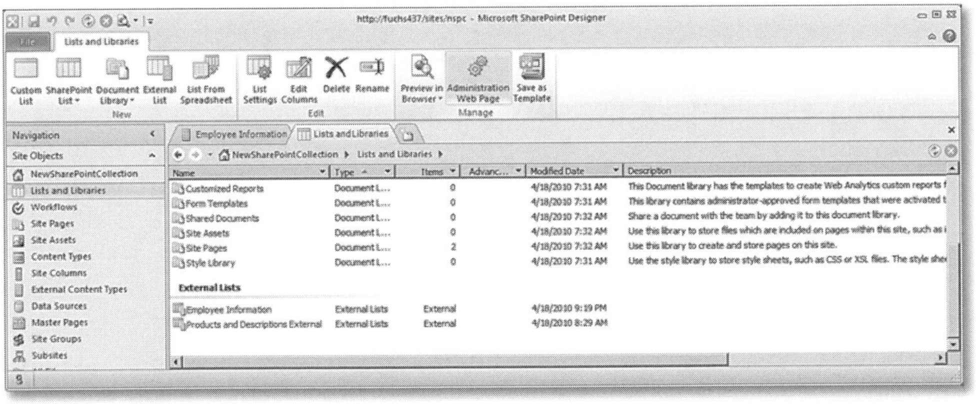

Illustration 57 - External List for ECT displaying in SharePoint Designer List and Libraries page for the site

If you click on the **Employee Information list item**, *SharePoint Designer* will open the summary page for the list as shown in **Illustration 58** on the next page.

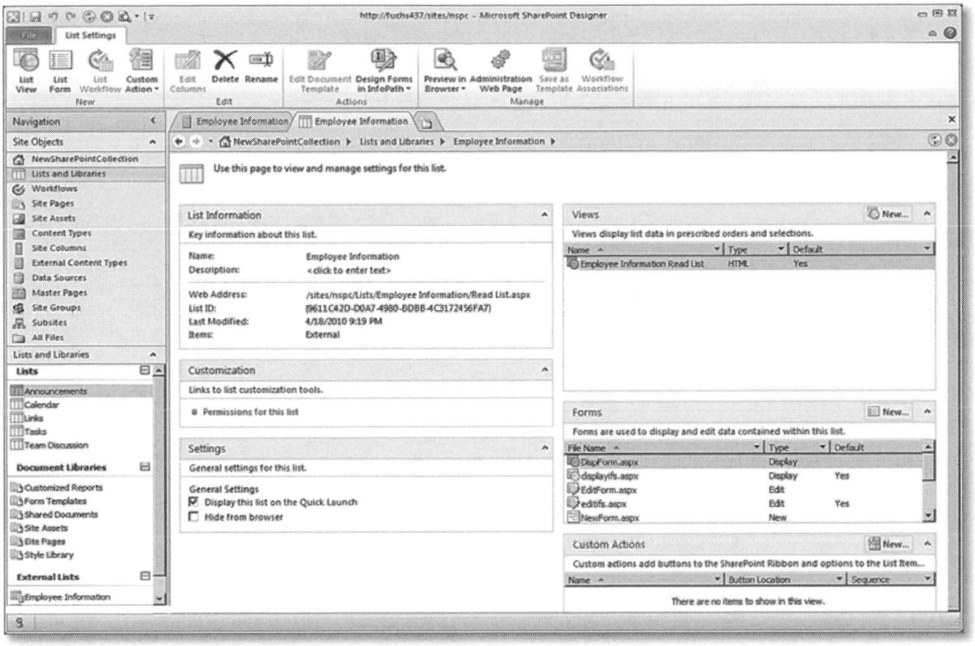

Illustration 58 - Summary page for the Employee Information ECT list

From the summary page you can set the permissions for the list, create custom actions and view and modify the underlying *InfoPath* list form.

Return to the summary page for the *Employee Information External Content Type*. You will now see all the fields listed in the *Fields* tab as shown in **Illustration 59** below.

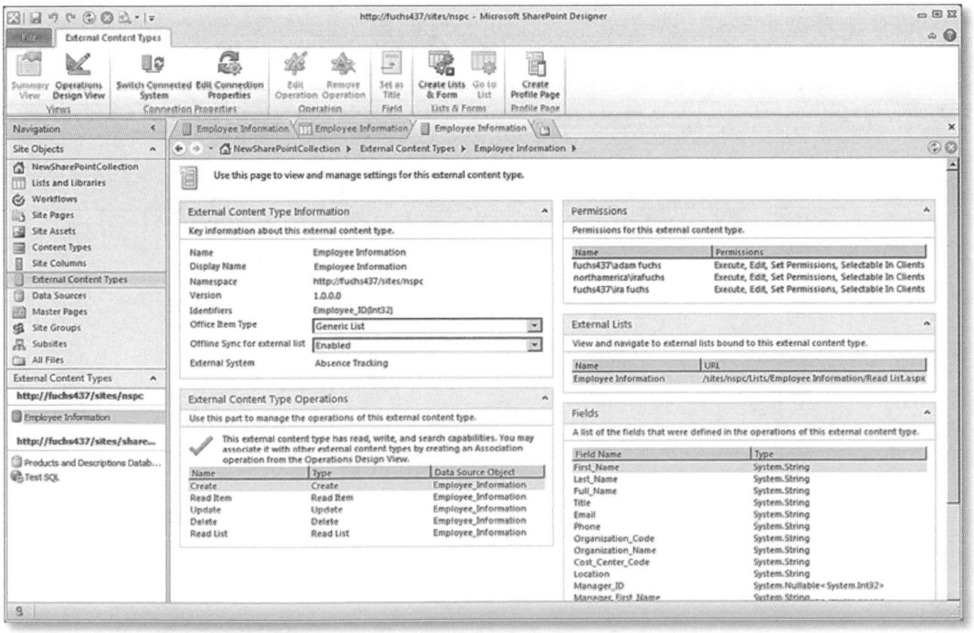

Illustration 59 - Summary page for the Employee Information ECT displaying Fields

Important Note – Configuring *Object Permissions* for *External Content Types* in *SharePoint Central Administration*. The external list that we just created from the *Employee Information ECT* will not be accessible to a user until they are granted permissions to access the *External Content Type*. Accessing the ECT within *SharePoint* requires a separate permission from the permission to access the list itself. Without the ECT permission the following screen message, as shown in **Illustration 60** below will be displayed when a user accesses the *Employee Information* list.

Illustration 60 - How the ECT list will display if access permissions to the ECT are not set

Setting the External Content Type Permissions

Permissions to access the ECT are set in *Business Data Connectivity Services* of *SharePoint Central Administration*. In a production environment the procedure described below would be done by the *SharePoint* farm administrator. Since your development environment is a complete *SharePoint* installation you will be able to do this step directly. In *Central Administration* click **Manage service applications**. The *Service Applications* page will display as shown in **Illustration 61** below.

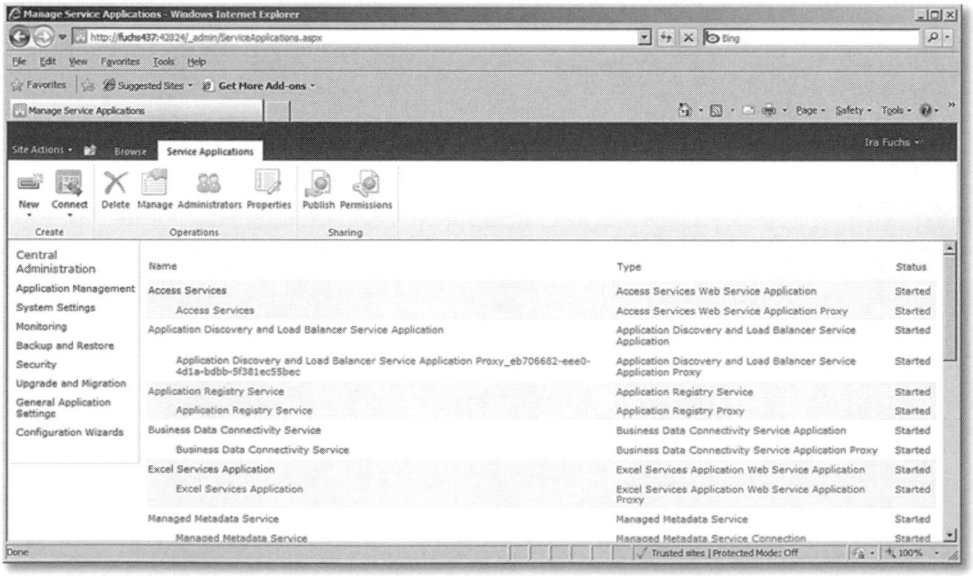

Illustration 61 - SharePoint Central Administration Service Applications page

Click **Business Data Connectivity Services** to display the *External Content Types* that have been created. ECT's are farm level objects and are accessible from any site collection in the farm. In the drop-down list of the *Views* tab on the *Ribbon* make sure that *External Content Types* are selected. The *Employee Information* ECT will be displayed as shown in **Illustration 62** below.

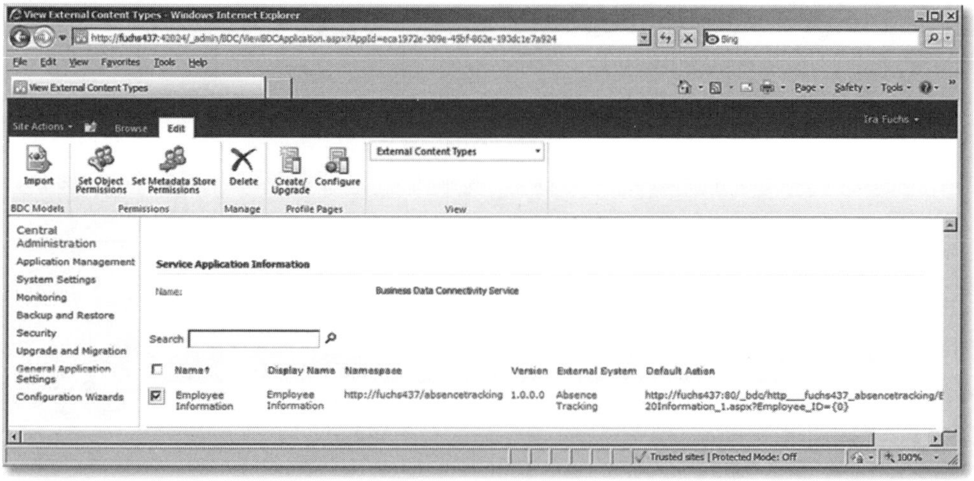

Illustration 62 - Business Data Connectivity Services External Content Types page

Select the *Employee Information ECT* by checking its **checkbox**. Now click the **Set Object Permissions button** on the *Ribbon*. The *Set Object Permissions* dialogue screen will display as shown in **Illustration 63** below.

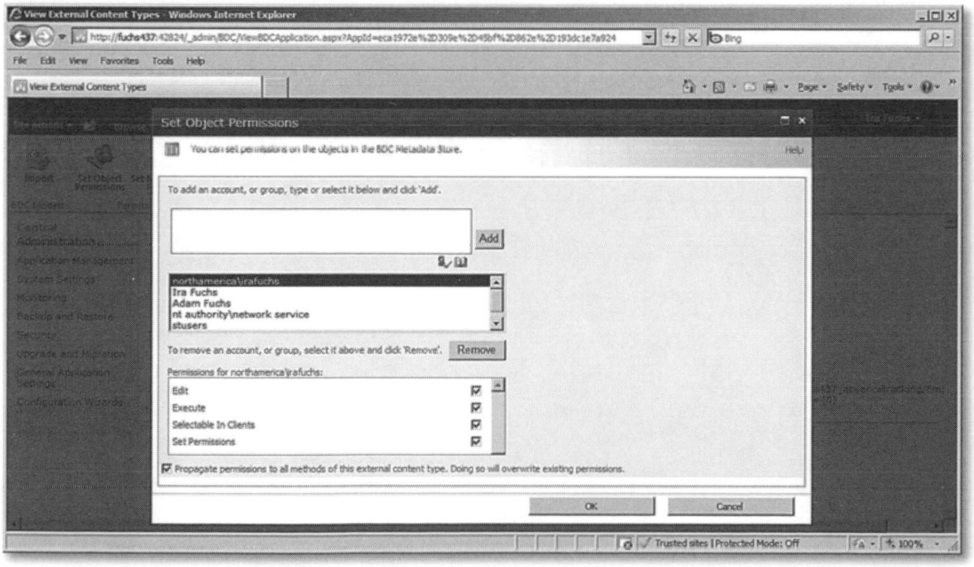

Illustration 63 - The Set Object Permissions screen in Central Administration BCS

Use the *People Picker* control to add the *Windows* user accounts you created including your own user account. For each user select all the permissions in the *Permissions* list and click **OK**.

Adding Records to the Employee Information Database from the ECT List

Now open the *Absence Tracking* site in *SharePoint*. The *Employee Information* list will be found on the *Quick Launch* pane. Click on it to go to the list. The single record that was entered directly in the SQL database table will be displayed as shown in **Illustration 64** below.

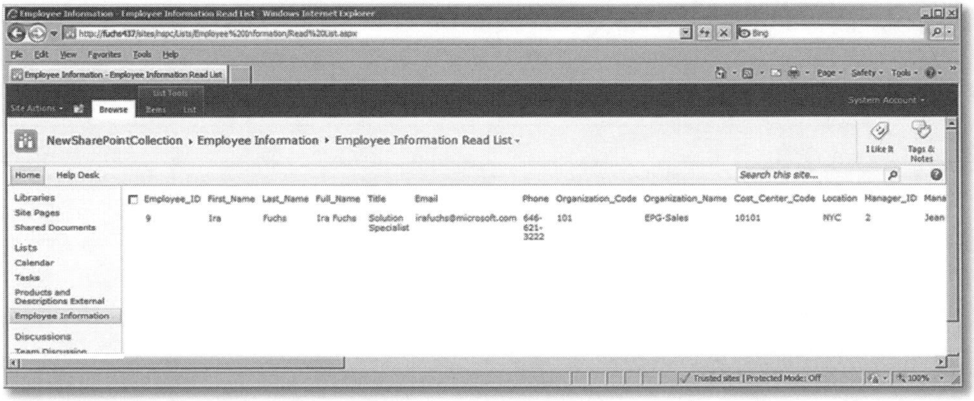

Illustration 64 - Employee Information ECT list

Click the **Items Button** on the *Ribbon* under *List Tools*. Now click on the **New Item Button** on the top left. An empty *InfoPath list form* for the *Employee Information ECT* will display as shown in **Illustration 65** below. This form template was created during the *External Content Type* list creation step. Because all operations were created for the ECT – create, update and delete, we can do all of these from the list form.

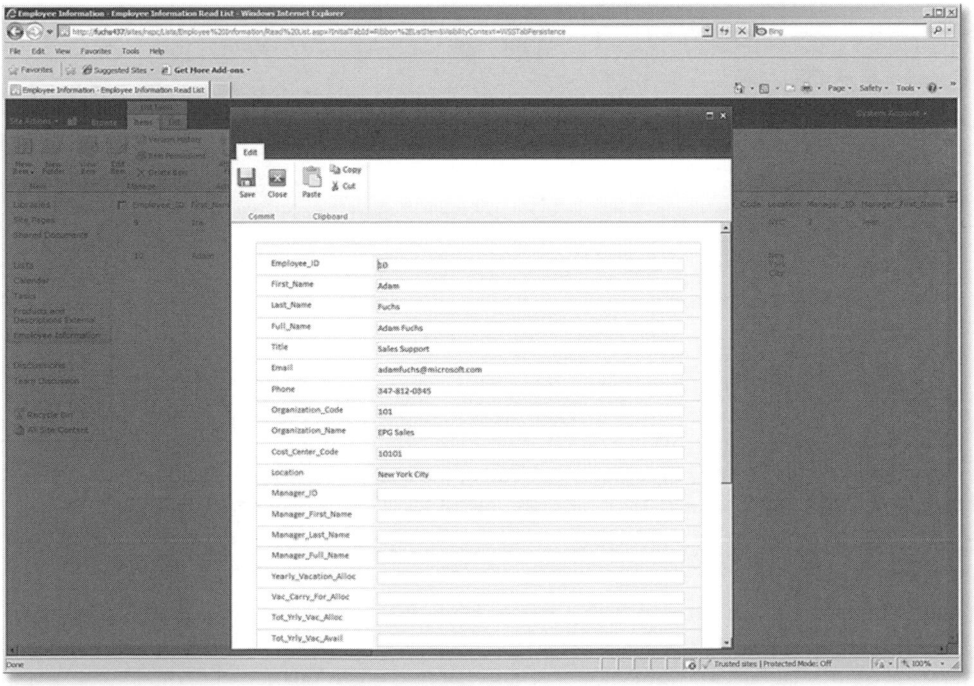

Illustration 65 - InfoPath list form for the Employee Information ECT list

> **Important Development Note –** The business logic that we will create for the *Absence Request* form is driven by the identity of the person creating or opening an *Absence Request* form. The source of the current user's identity in *SharePoint is the Username* of the person who is currently logged on to the *Windows* operating system. For the form logic to work the value entered for the *User_Name* field in the *Employee Information* database must be identical to the value used for the *Windows Username.* You do not have to enter an *Employee_ID*, as this value will be auto-generated when you save the record. For the *Organization_Code* enter "101" as this value will be used later.

Once you have entered the information into the form click on the **Save** button. You will see that this new record been added to the *Employee Information* list and this item has an *Employee_ID* value of "2". The new record information has been written directly into the SQL database table and the *Employee_ID* value was generated there and then displayed in the *SharePoint* list.

Even though the list information resides in an SQL database and not in the list itself all of the *SharePoint* list capabilities and settings are available for an ECT list. The ability to execute write operations to an external data source using *SharePoint* and *InfoPath* opens up numerous options for creating versatile and sophisticated enterprise applications quickly and without writing code. These options will become apparent once we have completed this application.

We have completed the steps of creating a *BCS External Content Type* and its corresponding list and form.

Review and Discussion of Creating BCS Artifacts Using SharePoint Designer

What we have just accomplished with BCS and *SharePoint Designer* deserves some discussion. Let's review the value and benefits that BCS and *SharePoint Designer* offer:

- **Streamlined and simplified integration with external applications** – Prior to BCS and *SharePoint Designer's External Content Type* creation capabilities the effort of creating similar functionality required the painstaking effort of professional programmers who had to invest a sizable amount of time and effort in understanding the arcane intricacies of the BDC specification. Now, connecting to external data sources and implementing the common application operations within SharePoint can be done by any sophisticated user within hours. In large organizations there are typically hundreds if not thousands of legacy applications that could be enhanced and extended simply by making the information in them accessible within *SharePoint*. However the costs and effort to implement application integration on a broad scale has always been prohibitive. Now with BCS and *SharePoint Designer's External Content Type* creation facilities it is well within the realm of the possible to do so. The ability to open up and extend these applications in such a streamlined and simplified way is unprecedented.

- **Enhanced usability of external information** – In addition to streamlining and simplifying the process of accessing the interfaces and operations of external systems, *SharePoint* provides out-of-the box BCS artifacts and capabilities for making external information readily useable and useful to end users. These include the fundamental ECT list that is generated, the use of InfoPath to provide additional functional value, BCS Web Parts, and mapping of ECT fields to *Office* item types allowing Outlook and Word to immediately use the information in external systems. An additional usability benefit of exposing external systems through BCS is that the information in those systems can now be indexed and crawled with *SharePoint* search.

- **Versatility –** Multiple content type definitions as well as multiple list definitions can be generated from the same data source. These can have different properties and settings allowing for a great deal of versatility in addressing specialized functional requirements and access constraints.

- **Reusability** – An external content type is a reusable manifestation of an application's functionality. Once created, it is available to any site collection or site on a farm. Once instantiated it can be modified and extended. Furthermore a BCS profile file for an ECT can be exported and imported for reuse anywhere.

- **Granular security** – External Content Types use the security mechanisms of both the external system and SharePoint allowing for granular access and permission setting not just for the ECT but for the *SharePoint* artifacts that access the ECT information as well.

- **Centralized management and governance** – ECTs are farm level entities that are managed through *SharePoint Central Administration*. Consequently any attributes and properties of an ECT can be efficiently administered.

Creating the Absence Request InfoPath Form

We are now going to get into the heart of the application by creating the *Absence Request* form in *InfoPath*. *InfoPath* has been part of the *Office* application suite since version 2003. It is a tool for creating data entry and information gathering forms, but this is a simplistic description of what *InfoPath* is capable of as we will demonstrate shortly.

We will be creating a document based *InfoPath* form. The information captured in a document based form is represented as an XML document file, and the instances of these files are hosted and stored in a *SharePoint* form library. When we generated the *External List* for the *Employee Information* ECT we also had *SharePoint Designer* generate an *InfoPath* list form which stores the information captured in the form directly in a *SharePoint* list.

Start *InfoPath 2010*. It will display the **New** opening page as shown in **Illustration 66** below.

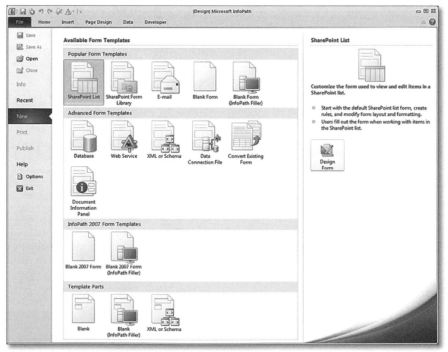

Illustration 66 - The New form screen in InfoPath 2010

With the **SharePoint Form Library Form** template option selected click on the **Design Form** button. A new form template will open. For a new document based form *InfoPath* automatically lays out a single column table with both a four column table and a two column table embedded in it as a placeholder for labels and controls as shown in **Illustration 67** below.

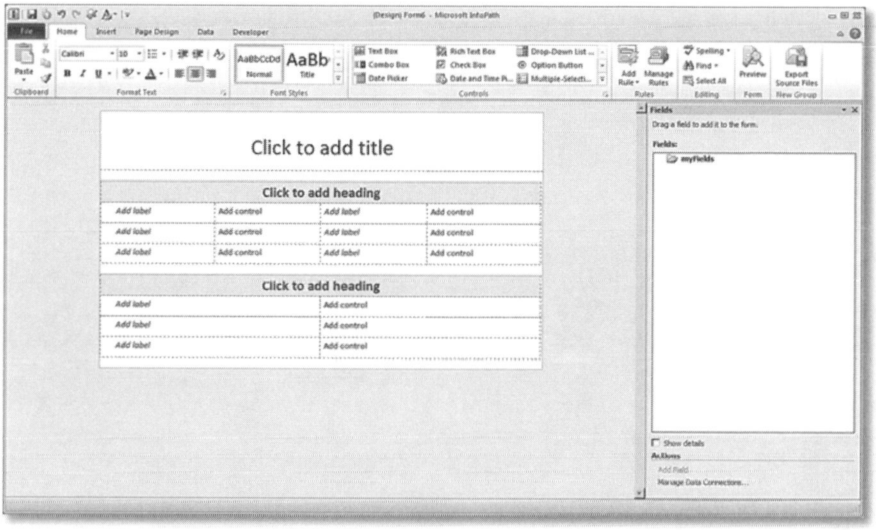

Illustration 67 - New default InfoPath form template

We are not going to use this placeholder table. Place your cursor at the top left of the table. A table selection box will display. Click on this selection box and the entire table will be highlighted. Right click and from the drop-down menu that displays choose **Delete** as shown in **Illustration 68** below.

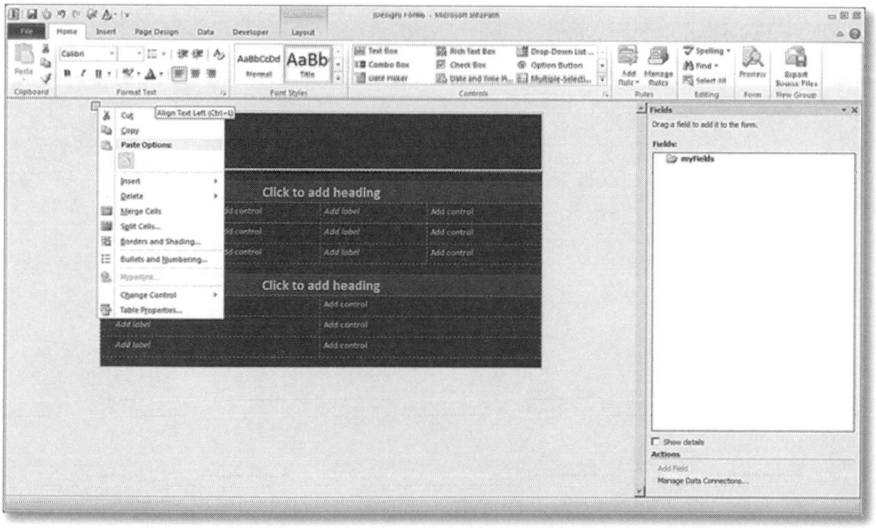

Illustration 68 - Deleting the default table from the form

The *InfoPath* design surface will be completely blank as shown in **Illustration 69** below.

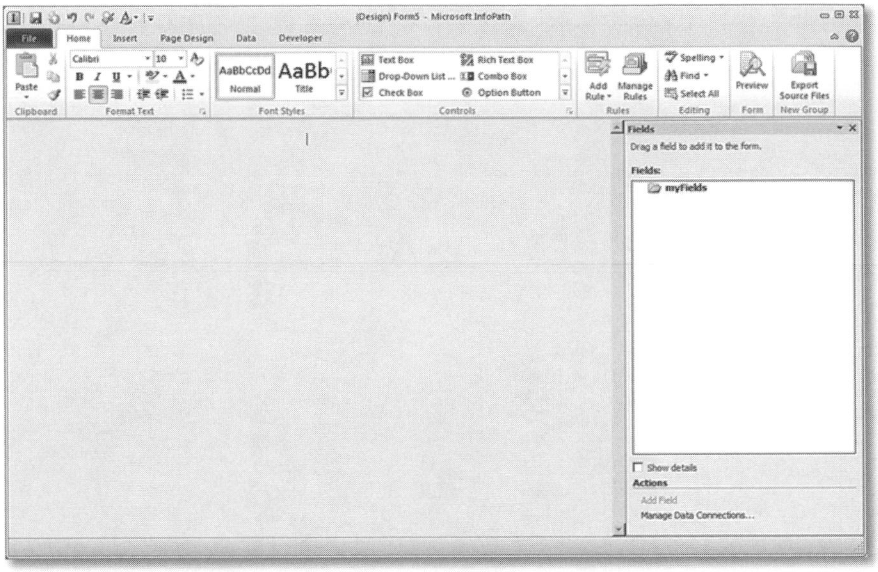

Illustration 69 - InfoPath form template with empty design surface

The fundamental objects that comprise a form are layout tables, controls and fields. Layout tables provide a structured way to design the form as well as organize the placement of controls. Controls are the functional objects placed in the form. Controls capture, display and generate the values that are bound to fields in the form. The form's fields are defined and organized using *XML Schema*, which in turn generates the output data set of the form. Rules comprised of conditional statements and operations provide the form application logic.

Illustration 70 on the next page shows a simple two column table placed on the design surface and a number of different controls that were placed within the table cells. With the placement of each control *InfoPath* automatically created a field node.

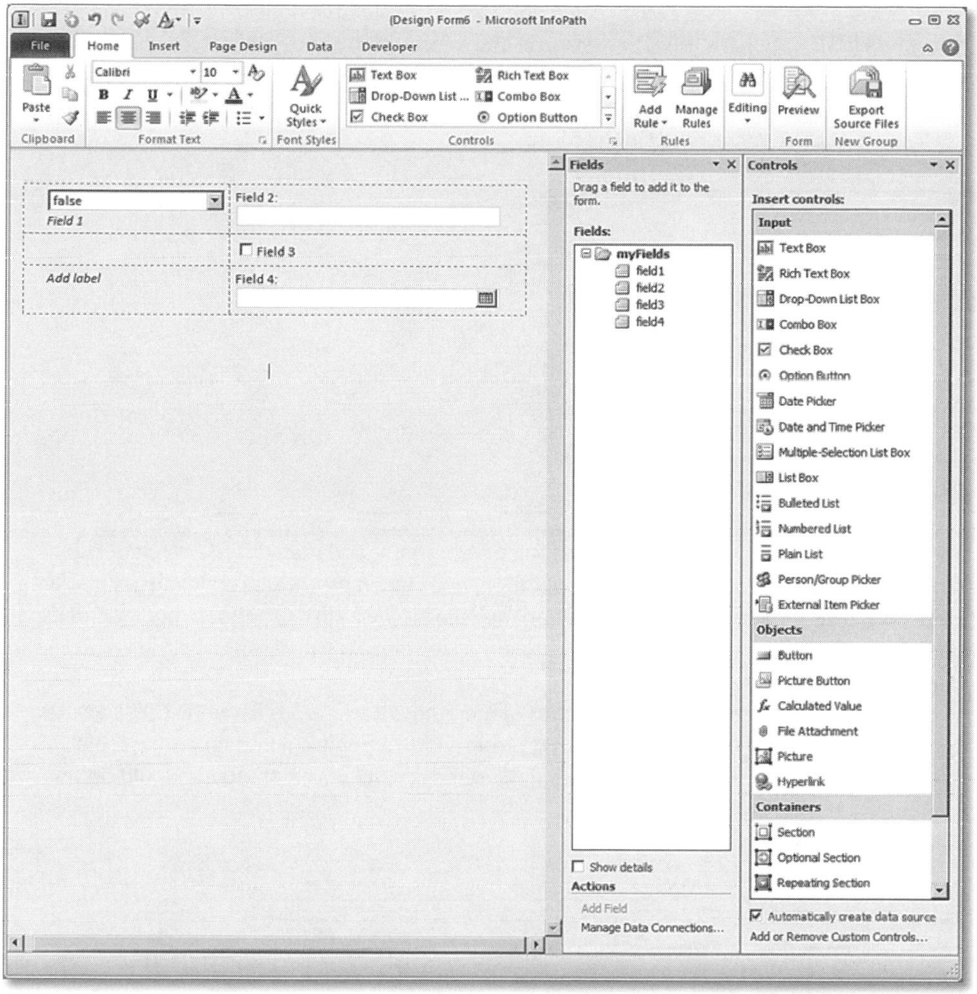

Illustration 70 - InfoPath form template with random controls

With *InfoPath* you can design and develop a form in flexible ways. You can place controls within tables or by themselves. For information sets with complex behavior requirements *InfoPath* can automatically generate sections or tables with embedded controls in them that implement the complex behavior of the information set schema.

Illustration 71 below shows a segment of an *XML Schema* node group (*Organization_Section*) from an *InfoPath* form. The Line of Business (LOB) group is a repeating group as the information about more than one LOB may need to be represented in the form. Furthermore, embedded within the LOB repeating group is another repeating group – the *Initiated_By* group. This indicates the possible existence of multiple LOB entities within any given LOB that may also need to be represented in the form.

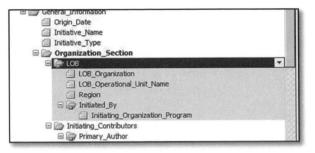

Illustration 71 - XML schema segment with complex behavior

Complex information models that incorporate both repeating one-to-many, and many-to-many relationships such as these can be challenging to implement in any application, even when procedural code is used to create this functionality. However, this type of complex information modeling is *InfoPath*'s strong suit, because of its incorporation of *XML Schema*.

Illustration 72 below shows the repeating table that *InfoPath* generated automatically from the LOB schema node above. Note how the *Initiated_By* repeating group is represented as a single column repeating table embedded in a column of the LOB repeating table. Creating the same control layout manually would be very labor intensive.

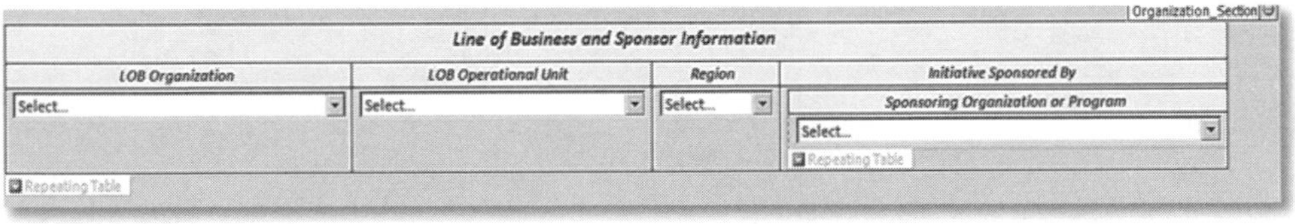

Line of Business and Sponsor Information			
LOB Organization	LOB Operational Unit	Region	Initiative Sponsored By
Select...	Select...	Select...	Sponsoring Organization or Program
			Select...

Illustration 72 - Form section and controls generated from the schema segment in Illustration 71

A defining feature of a document based *InfoPath* form is that it represents information captured in the form as XML tagged data. The organization and structure of this XML is based on *XML Schema*, the specification for defining structured XML metadata. One of the benefits of generating XML tagged information that conforms to a schema is that any *XML Schema* enabled application can read and process the XML tagged information. This is the same mechanism that makes *Web Services* work and it is how *InfoPath* represents information and communicates with external data sources and other applications.

Creating an Information Set Schema in InfoPath

When creating a document based *InfoPath* form, *InfoPath* will automatically build a schema for the information set when controls are placed on the form as shown in **Illustration 70** above, but this will result in an ad-hoc, unstructured schema. Alternatively, an information set based on *XML Schema* can be created in an XML editing tool and imported into *InfoPath*. However, once the schema is imported into *InfoPath* it is locked and cannot be modified. A third option is to define and build the information set schema directly in *InfoPath*.

This is exactly how we will proceed. We will create the information set schema for the form's information set before we design and build the form with layout tables and controls.

> **Best Practice Note** – Creating the information set schema within *InfoPath* first is a best practice for two reasons:
>
> 1. One, *InfoPath* provides an easy way to build a schema for an information set.
> 2. Two, by first designing and implementing the structural and behavioral requirements of the information set within the schema, the subsequent effort of designing the form and laying out the controls will be much more efficient, and the resultant form will be functionally optimized.

Designing the form directly from the schema structure leverages the combined capabilities of *XML Schema* and *InfoPath's* rich library of form controls.

Right click on the **myFields** root node in the *Fields* pane as shown in **Illustration 73** at right and choose the **Properties** option.

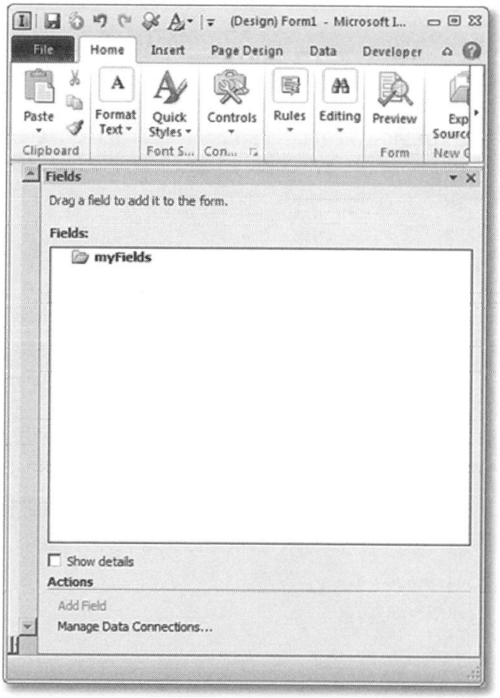

The *Field or Group Properties* dialogue screen will display as shown in **Illustration 74** below. Change the *Name* to "Absence_Request_Form" and click **OK**.

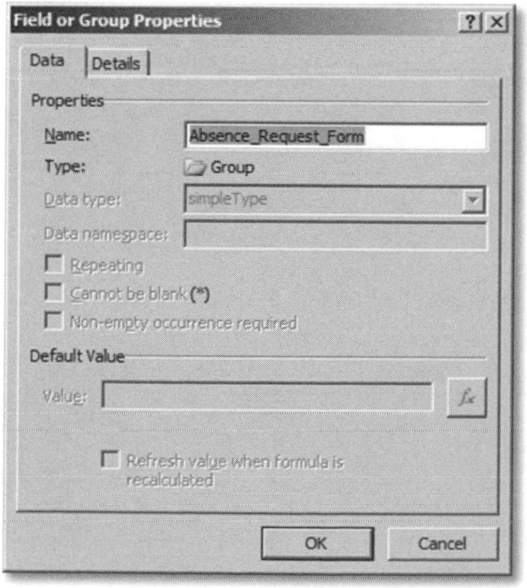

Illustration 73 - InfoPath Fields pane

Illustration 74 - InfoPath Field or Group Properties dialogue screen

Right click on the renamed **Absence_Request_Form root node** and choose the **Add** option. The *Add Field or Group* dialogue screen will display as shown in **Illustration 75** at right.

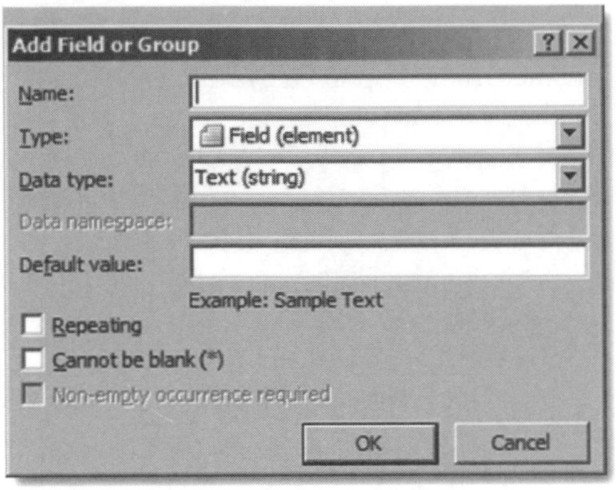

Illustration 75 - InfoPath Add Field or Group dialogue screen

In the *Name* field enter "Current_User". Leave the default *Field (element)* choice in the *Type* drop-down list. In the *Data type* drop-down list choose *Text (string)* from the drop-down list. The *Add Field or Group* dialogue screen will display as shown in **Illustration 76** at right.

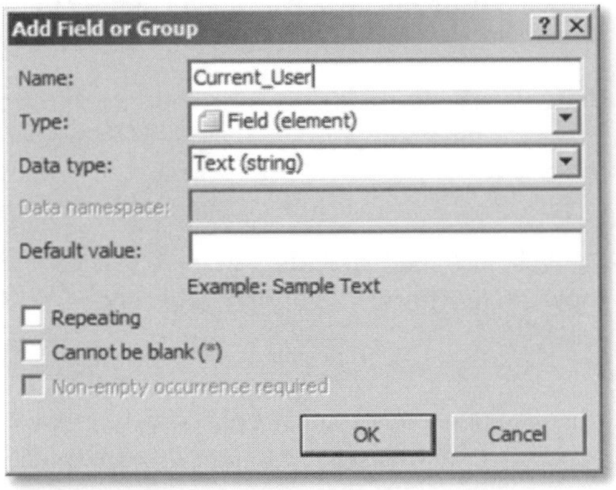

Illustration 76 - Add Field or Group with Name field entered

Click **OK**. The *Fields* pane will now display a *Current_User* child node as shown in **Illustration 77** at right.

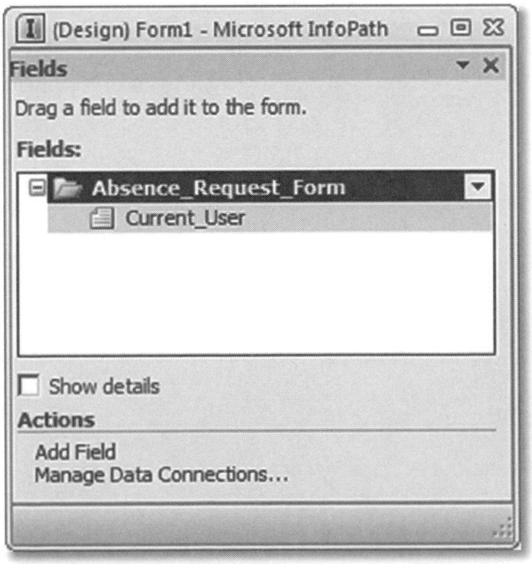

Illustration 77 - Fields pane with Current_User field added

Right click again on the **Absence_Request_Form root node** and select **Add**, or click the **Add Field** link on the bottom of the Fields pane. In the *Add Field or Group* dialogue screen enter "Request_Date" in the *Name* field, leave the *Type* as *Field (element)*, and pick *Date (date)* as the *Data type*. The dialogue screen will look like **Illustration 78** at right.

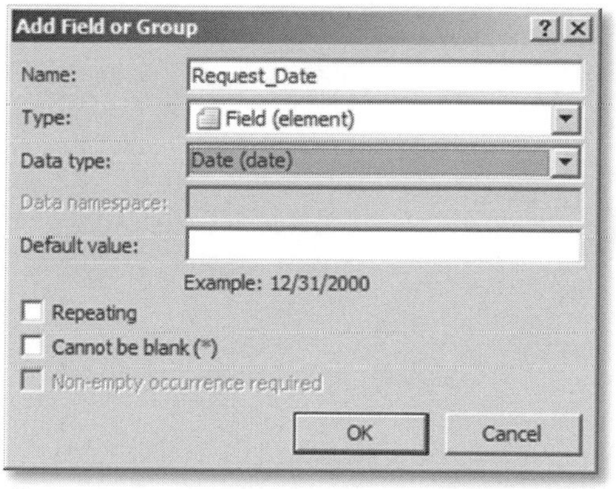

Illustration 78 - Request_Date field added to the information set schema

Click **OK**. Right click again on the **root node** and select **Add**, or click the **Add Field** link on the bottom of the *Fields* pane. In the *Add Field or Group* dialogue screen enter "Submitted" in the *Name* field, leave the *Type* as *Field (element)*, and pick *Text (string)* as the *Data type*. The dialogue screen will look like **Illustration 79** at right.

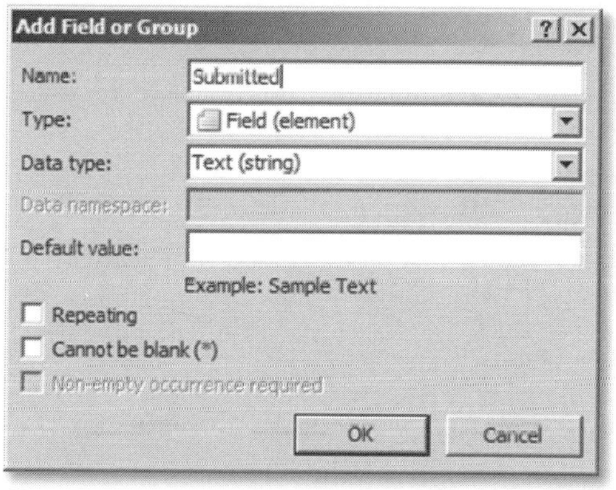

Illustration 79 - Submitted field added to the information set schema

Click **OK** again. The schema information set for the *Main* data source will look like **Illustration 80** at right.

Illustration 80 - Schema information set for the Main data source

With the **root node** selected add another field. Enter "Employee_Information" in the *Name* field. This time choose *Group* from the drop-down list of *Type* choices and click **OK**. The schema will now look like **Illustration 81** at right.

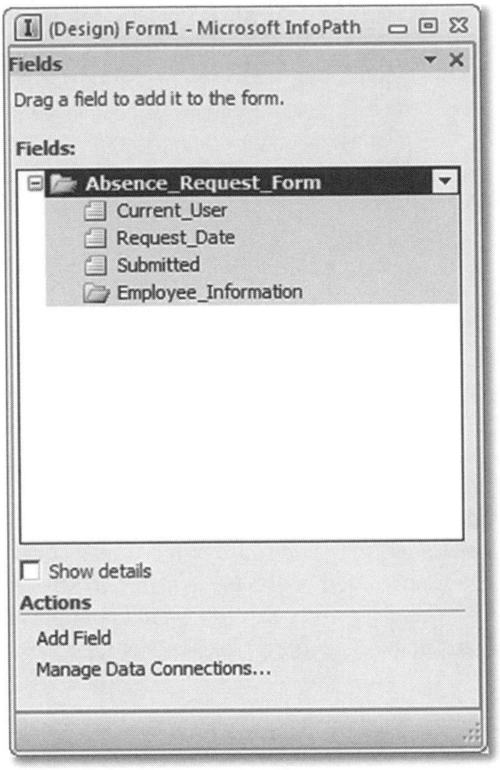

Illustration 81 - Schema with Employee_
Information group added

Click on the **Employee_Information group node** in the schema, right click and choose **Add**. Enter "Employee_ID" in the *Name* field and leave the default values for *Type* and *Data Type* as shown in **Illustration 82** at right.

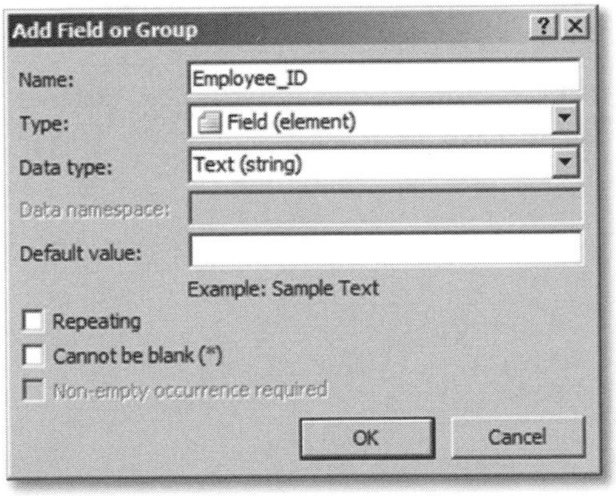

Illustration 82 - Employee_ID field added to
the schema

Click **OK**. The schema will look like **Illustration 83** at right.

With the **Employee_Information group node** selected, repeat the **Add Field** step for the following fields:

> Full_Name
> Email
> Title
> Manager_User_Name
> Manager_Full_Name
> Manager_Email
> Alternate_Approver
> Alternate_Approver_Email
> Organization_Name
> Organization_Code
> Level

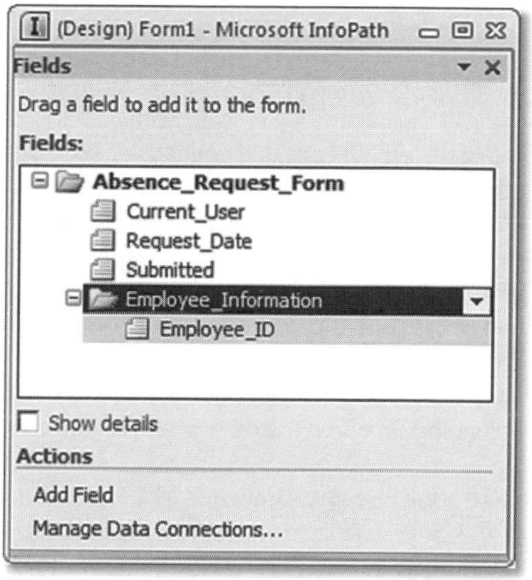

Illustration 83 - Employee_ID child node added to Employee_Information group

All of the fields above are *Field (element)* Types, and *Text (string)* Data types with the exception of the *Level* field. Choose *Whole Number (integer)* for the *Level* Data type. When you are finished the schema for the information set will look like **Illustration 84** at right.

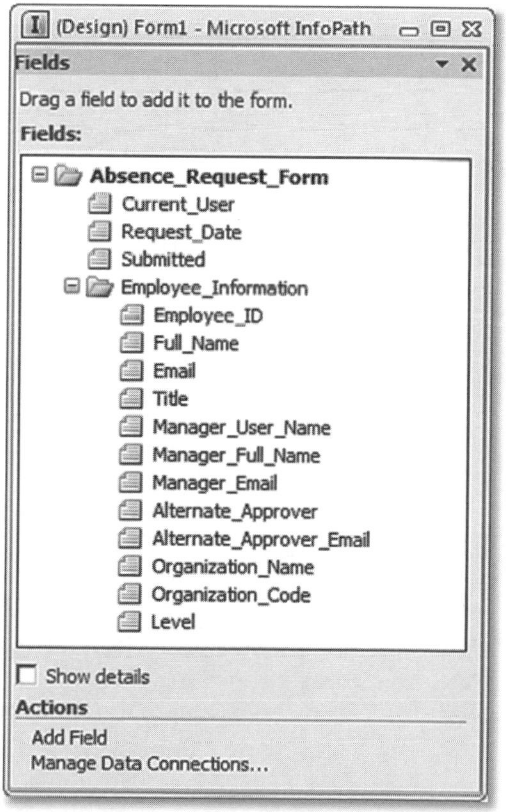

Illustration 84 - Completed Employee_Information group

About XML Schema

Before we continue building out the form schema lets pause to investigate what the underlying schema is and its function and value. *XML Schema* is the *World Wide Web Consortium (W3C)* specification for building an abstract model of a document using metadata (elements, attributes, and groups of these elements and attributes) that defines the organization, structure, and meaning of the document content. The value of creating XML documents that conform to an *XML Schema* is that the meaning, function and use of the information in the document is transparently comprehensible to any XML enabled application that can access the underlying schema for the document. By having access to the *XML schema* for the instance document an application can understand and process the information in it, regardless of how the information was originally generated. This is the mechanism that *Web Services* use to expose an application's methods and allow those methods to be invoked through an XML message exchange, without any knowledge of or consideration for the underlying technology in which the original application was created.

Illustration 85 below shows the *XML Schema* fragment for the *Employee_Information* group nodes that we just created. *InfoPath* creates this automatically and it defines the information set that the form will ultimately generate as an XML document. The BCS ECT profile that *SharePoint Designer* generated earlier is also represented by the definition and structure of an XML schema.

```
<xsd:element name="Employee_Information">
        <xsd:complexType>
            <xsd:sequence>
                <xsd:element ref="my:Current_User" minOccurs="0"/>
                <xsd:element ref="my:Employee_ID" minOccurs="0"/>
                <xsd:element ref="my:Full_Name" minOccurs="0"/>
                <xsd:element ref="my:Email" minOccurs="0"/>
                <xsd:element ref="my:Title" minOccurs="0"/>
                <xsd:element ref="my:Manager" minOccurs="0"/>
                <xsd:element ref="my:Manager_Email" minOccurs="0"/>
                <xsd:element ref="my:Alternate_Approver" minOccurs="0"/>
                <xsd:element ref="my:Alternate_Approver_Email" minOccurs="0"/>
                <xsd:element ref="my:Organization_Name" minOccurs="0"/>
                <xsd:element ref="my:Organization_Code" minOccurs="0"/>
                <xsd:element ref="my:Level" minOccurs="0"/>
            </xsd:sequence>
        </xsd:complexType>
    </xsd:element>
    <xsd:element name="Current_User" type="xsd:string"/>
    <xsd:element name="Employee_ID" type="xsd:string"/>
    <xsd:element name="Full_Name" type="xsd:string"/>
    <xsd:element name="Email" type="xsd:string"/>
    <xsd:element name="Title" type="xsd:string"/>
    <xsd:element name="Manager" type="xsd:string"/>
    <xsd:element name="Manager_Email" type="xsd:string"/>
    <xsd:element name="Alternate_Approver" type="xsd:string"/>
    <xsd:element name="Alternate_Approver_Email" type="xsd:string"/>
    <xsd:element name="Organization_Name" type="xsd:string"/>
    <xsd:element name="Organization_Code" type="xsd:string"/>
    <xsd:element name="Level" nillable="true" type="xsd:integer"/>
```

Illustration 85 - XML Schema representation of Employee_Information information set

The element nodes in the instance document are where the values that are entered into the form are stored. **Illustration 86** on the next page shows a fragment of an empty (because there are no values in any of the field elements) XML instance document that the form will generate based on the *XML Schema* definition above.

```
<my:Employee_Information>
          <my:Current_User></my:Current_User>
          <my:Employee_ID></my:Employee_ID>
          <my:Full_Name></my:Full_Name>
          <my:Email></my:Email>
          <my:Title></my:Title>
          <my:Manager></my:Manager>
          <my:Manager_Email></my:Manager_Email>
          <my:Alternate_Approver></my:Alternate_Approver>
          <my:Alternate_Approver_Email></my:Alternate_Approver_Email>
          <my:Organization_Name></my:Organization_Name>
          <my:Organization_Code></my:Organization_Code>
          <my:Level xsi:nil="true"></my:Level>
     </my:Employee_Information>
```

Illustration 86 – Fragment of XML instance document generated from the Schema definition

Using *InfoPath*'s *Submit* functions we can send this XML document anywhere for consumption by other applications.

Right-click on the **Submitted** field and select **Properties**. The *Field or Group Properties* dialogue screen will display where the functional attributes of the field or group can be set. Default values can be specified using fixed values, variables, formulas or filtered look-ups. Rule-sets can be created and applied to schema fields and groups as well. By applying properties and rule sets to schema objects directly any form control that is bound to the schema object will inherit this logic.

In the **Value** box for *Default Value* enter the text "FALSE" as shown in **illustration 87** below.

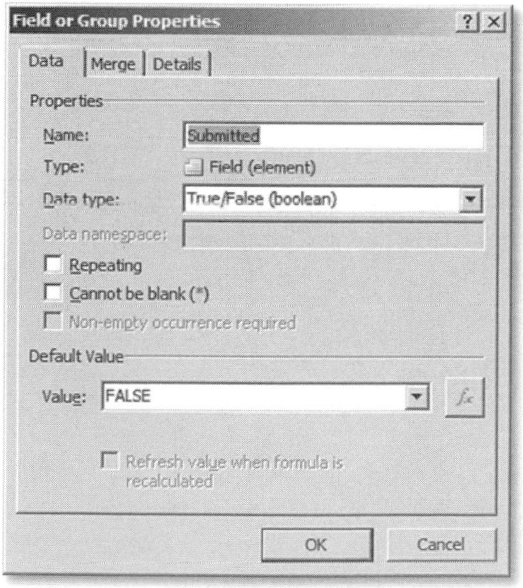

Illustration 87 – Value of FALSE entered as the
default value for the Submitted field

> **Best Practices Note** – Setting the properties, default values, and rules for the form fields first is a best practice for developing *InfoPath* forms. Setting these attributes upfront will drive the form design and the functional behavior of the controls that will be bound to the schema objects.

InfoPath Property Attributes of Information Set Schema Objects

The following is an overview of the *Property* attributes for information set schema objects:

Type – These are the fundamental *XML Schema* building blocks that *InfoPath* implements. The Type choices are *Field Element, Group, Choice Group, Field Attribute, XML Schema* or *Document*.

Data Type – This specifies the content format for the Type. The choices are *Text, Rich Text, Whole Number, Decimal, True/False (Boolean), Hyperlink, Date, Time, Date and Time, Picture* or *File Attachment, Custom*.

Repeating Check Box – Setting this attribute to True will allow the specified field or group item to repeat in the form.

Cannot be Blank Check Box – Setting this attribute to "True" will enforce that a value be present for the specified field.

Default Value – A default value can be set for any field. The default value can be entered directly in the Value field or it can be derived through a look-up to another field or from a formula function. Later we will set the default value for the *Request_Date* to be the current day using the today function as shown in the illustration above.

Rules – Rules are one of the most powerful features of *InfoPath*. We will use rules extensively in this form.

Programming – There will always be the case where some functional requirement just cannot be implemented using the native capabilities of *InfoPath* or by using rule sets. For those situations, *InfoPath* can host custom code directly in the form.

Fields and Groups can be inserted anywhere in the schema tree and reorganized later, using the *Move Up, Move Down* and *Move* options. With the *Move* option you can move a field or a group to any other group, and groups can be nested to any level. At any time we can delete fields and groups and we can change their property attributes as well.

Adding the Absence_Time_Information Group to the Information Set Schema

Let's continue building the rest of the schema objects for the form. With the **Absence_Request_Form** root node selected add a new group and name it "Absence_Time_Information". With this new group selected add the following fields:

> *Yearly_Vacation_Allocation*
> *Vacation_Carry_Forward*
> *Vacation_Carry_Forward_Allowed*
> *Total_Vacation_Allowed*
> *Current_Year_Available_Vac_Time*
> *YTD_Vacation_Time_Used*
> *YTD_Vacation_Time_Balance*
> *Vacation_Time_Forfeit*
> *Yearly_Sick_Leave_Allowed*
> *YTD_Sick_Leave_Used*
> *YTD_Sick_Leave_Balance*
> *Yearly_Personal_Leave_Allowed*
> *YTD_Personal_Leave_Used*
> *YTD_Personal_Leave_Balance*

All of these are defined as *Field (element)* Types and *Whole Number (integer)* Data types.

These fields correspond to the ones that we created earlier in the SQL database table. We will use these fields in the form to capture and display the information from the SQL database brokered through the BCS ECT. When you have completed adding these fields to the *Absence_Time_Information* group your schema should look like **Illustration 88** below.

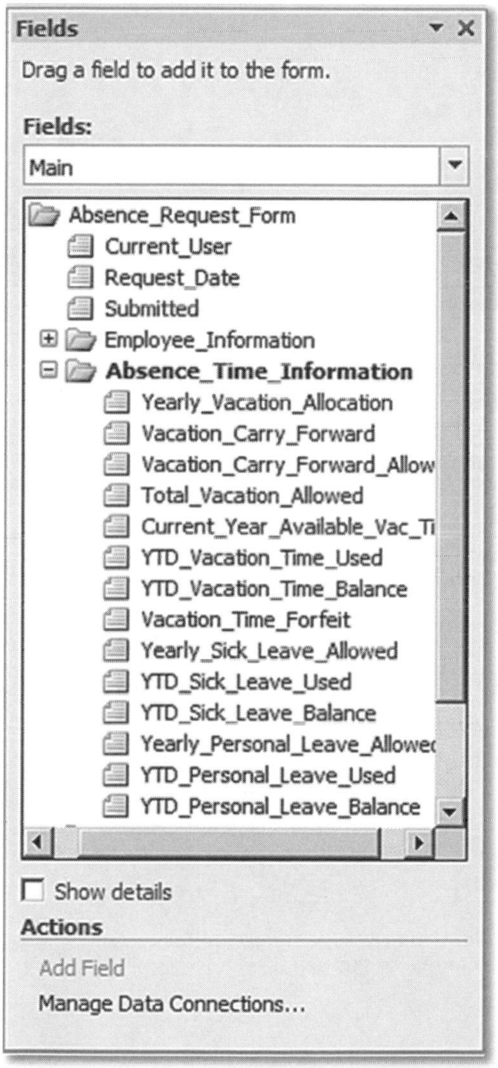

Illustration 88 - Completed Absence_Time_Information group

Adding the Transaction_Information Group to the Information Set Schema

With the **Absence_Request_Form** root node selected add a new group and name it "Transaction_Information". This group will contain the fields for the vacation, sick leave and personal leave dates that a user requests. The finished group will look like **illustration 89** at right.

With the **Transaction_Information** group selected add a new group named "Vacation_Requests" and check the **Repeating check box**.

With the **Vacation_Requests** group selected add a "Vacation_Request_Dates" field element. Set its *Data type* as *Date and Time*.

Now add a "Vacation_ Request_Time" field element and set its *Data type* as *Whole Number*.

Add two more repeating groups to the **Transaction_ Information** group: "Sick_Days_Requests" and "Personal_Leave_Requests".

To the **Sick_Days_Requests** group add a "Sick_Day_ Dates" field element and set its *Data type* as *Date and Time*. Now add a "Sick_ Day_Time" field element to this group and set its *Data type* as *Whole Number.*

Add the corresponding fields "Personal_Leave_Dates" and "Personal_Leave_Time" to the **Personal_Leave_ Requests** group each with their respective *Data types*.

Finally, with the **Transaction_Information** group selected add the following three field elements; all are *Whole Number Data types*:

Total_Vacation_Time_Requested
Total_Sick_Day_Time_Requested
Total_Pers_Leave_Time_Requested

Your *Transaction_Information* group should look exactly as it does in **Illustration 89** at right.

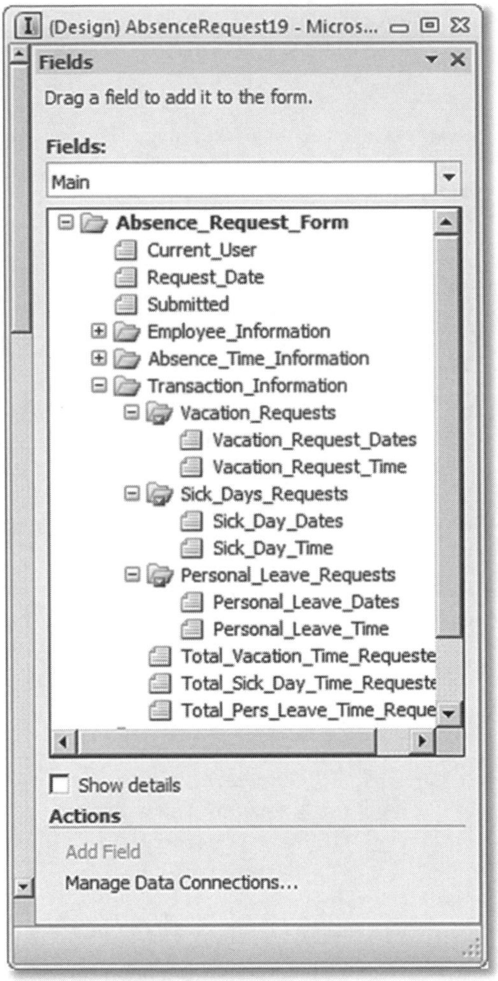

Illustration 89 - The completed Transaction_ Information group

Let's review what we just created. These fields will be bound to form controls that will allow the user to choose the vacation, sick leave and personal leave dates that they wish to take off. Typically people request multiple days and we cannot anticipate how many dates will be requested in any given request form. So we need to accommodate this non-deterministic requirement, and this is a use case that *XML Schema* and *InfoPath* can accommodate readily using the repeating item setting. For each date requested we also want to set and store a value for the number of time-away hours for that date. Consequently, the date and its respective time value should be a repeating unit. We accomplished this simply by creating the structure of repeating groups and then within those groups creating the set of fields that all need to repeat in tandem.

How InfoPath Interprets Schema Structure to Automate Form Design

When laying out form controls *InfoPath* automatically interprets the behavior that this structure will require and provides the developer with a number of control layout options that will implement the behavior defined by the schema structure. Let's see how this works.

Select the **Vacation_Requests repeating group** and drag the group to the design surface. You will be presented with three options: a *Repeating Table*, a *Repeating Section with Controls* and a *Repeating Section*. Choose the *Repeating Table*.

InfoPath will automatically generate a horizontal table that will include all the fields within the group as shown in **Illustration 90** below. It will also generate the appropriate controls that implement the functionality of each field's Data type, as shown by the date picker control that *InfoPath* automatically placed in the table for the *Vacation_Request_Dates* field.

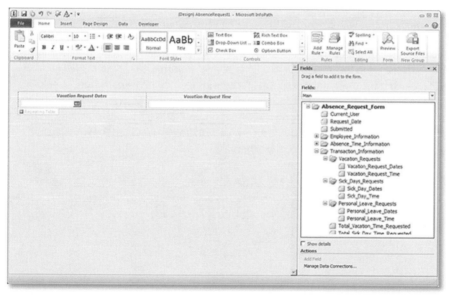

Illustration 90 – The automatic layout of a repeating table to implement the behavior of a repeating group

Select the **Vacation_Requests repeating group** and drag the group to the layout surface again. This time choose **Repeating Section with Controls**, which is exactly what you will get, as shown in **Illustration 91** on the next page.

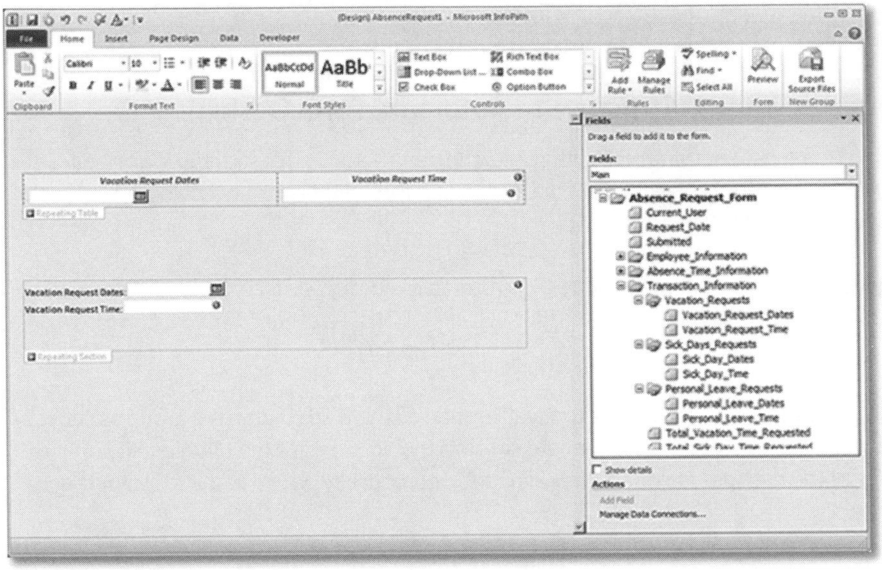

Illustration 91 - Alternative repeating section with controls for the same repeating group

Delete the **Repeating Table** and the **Repeating Section** from the layout surface. Now select the **Transaction_ Information** schema section and drag it to the design surface. *InfoPath* will automatically create a *Section* containing three repeating tables and the three individual Total time fields as shown in **Illustration 92** below.

This is why designing and building the schema for the form's information set first is a leveraged activity and best practice; *InfoPath* will do a substantial amount of the form layout work for you and the form design will correspond to the organization and functions defined by the schema.

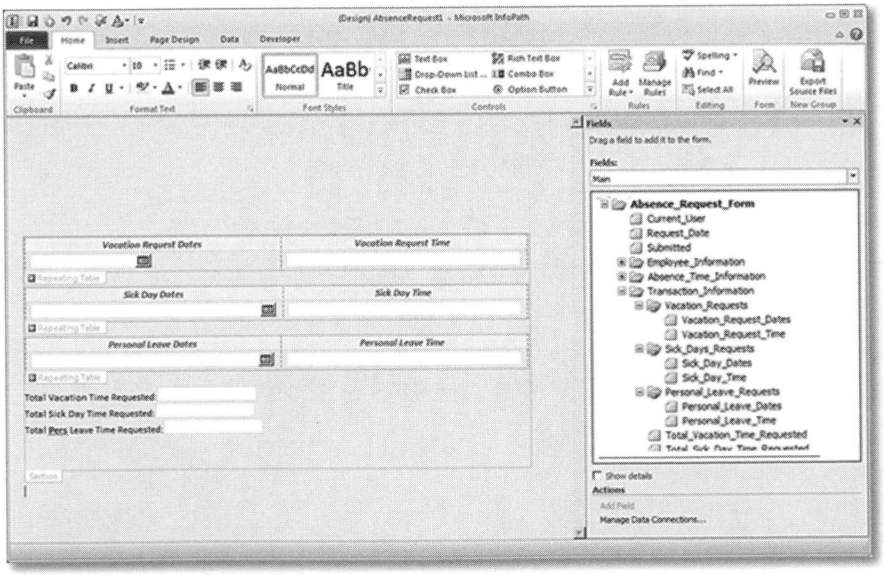

Illustration 92 - Automatic layout of the Transaction_Information group

The final layout design that we will implement for the repeating tables and total time fields is shown in **Illustration 93** below.

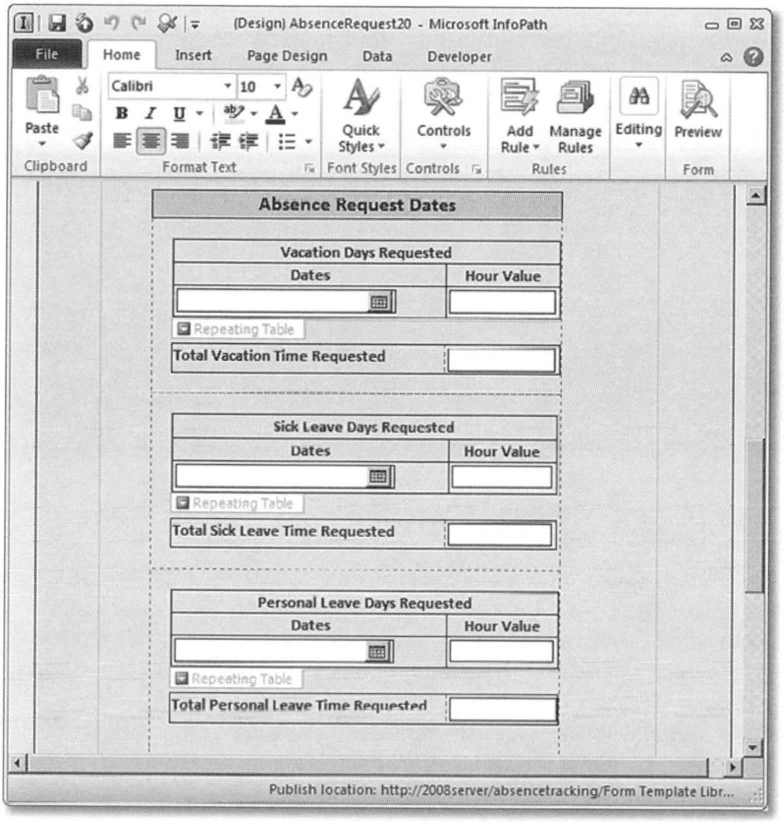

Illustration 93 - Final layout design for the Transaction_Information group

We will be reviewing section and control layout design considerations shortly but we still have some schema related work to do first.

Adding a Secondary Data Source to the Form

The information that will be captured and stored in the form can be acquired in a number of ways: it can be entered into form controls manually, generated from a function or rule, and obtained from secondary data sources. The schema that we have built is also the *Main data source* of the form. It is treated as a data source because any information entered into, or generated for a field can be accessed and used to populate other fields in the *Main data source* as well as fields in secondary data sources. We are now going to add secondary data sources to the form.

The initial secondary data source that we will add to the form is the *Employee Information ECT External List*. We will use the information in this secondary data source to auto-populate its corresponding fields in the *Main* data source.

Click on the *InfoPath* **Data** tab on the Ribbon. Then click on the **Data Connection** button. The *Data Connection* dialogue box will display as shown in **Illustration 94** below.

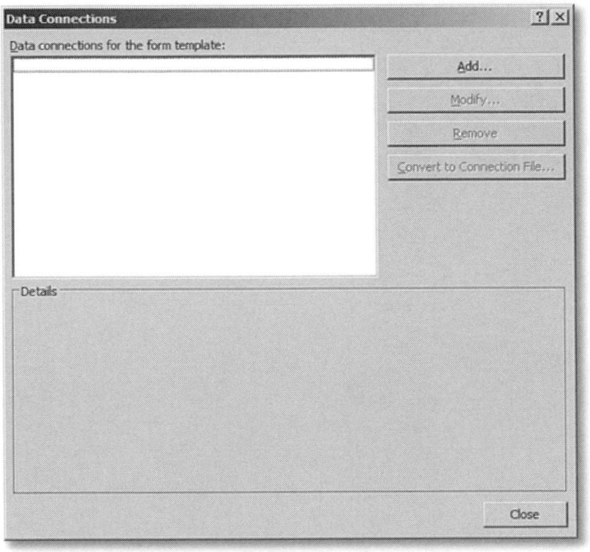

Illustration 94 - InfoPath Data Connections dialogue screen

Click the **Add** button and the first screen of the *Data Connection Wizard* will display as shown in **Illustration 95** below.

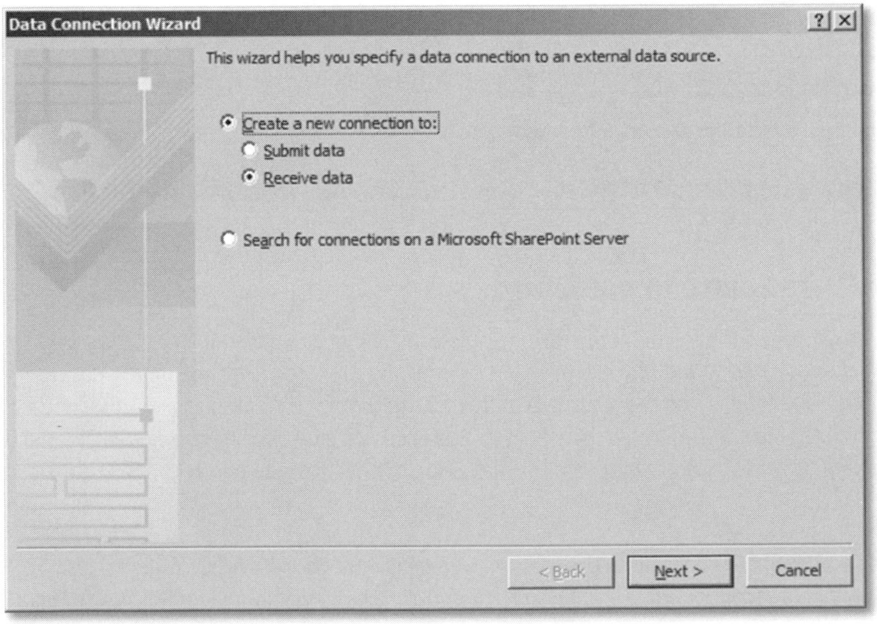

Illustration 95 - The first screen of the Data Connection Wizard

Keep the default values of *Create a new connection to*: *Receive data* and click **Next**. The next screen as shown in **Illustration 96** below allows you to pick the source of the data for the data connection.

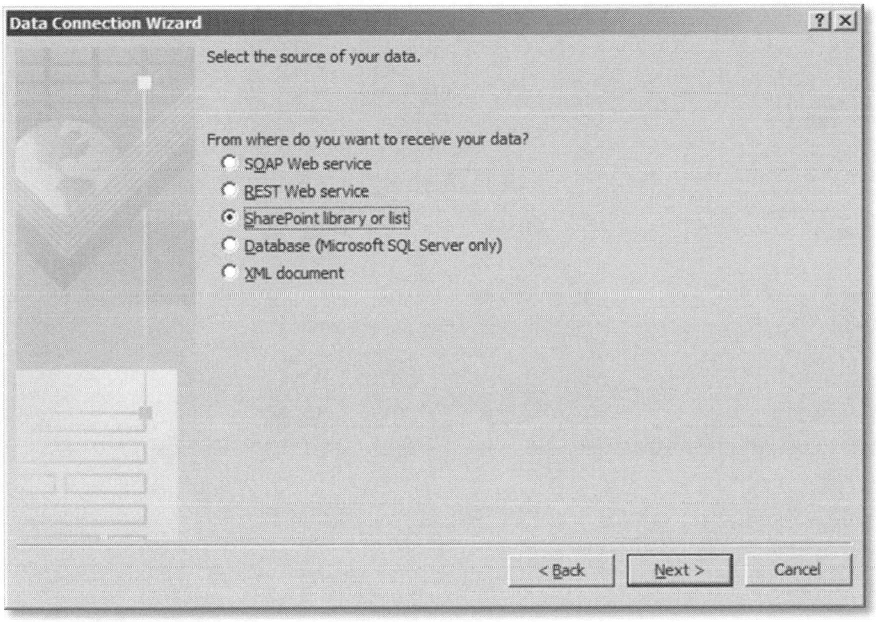

Illustration 96 – The second screen of the Data Connection Wizard

Click the **radio button** for *SharePoint library or list* and click the **Next** button. On the next screen as shown in **Illustration 97** below you will enter the address of the *SharePoint* site that the list resides in.

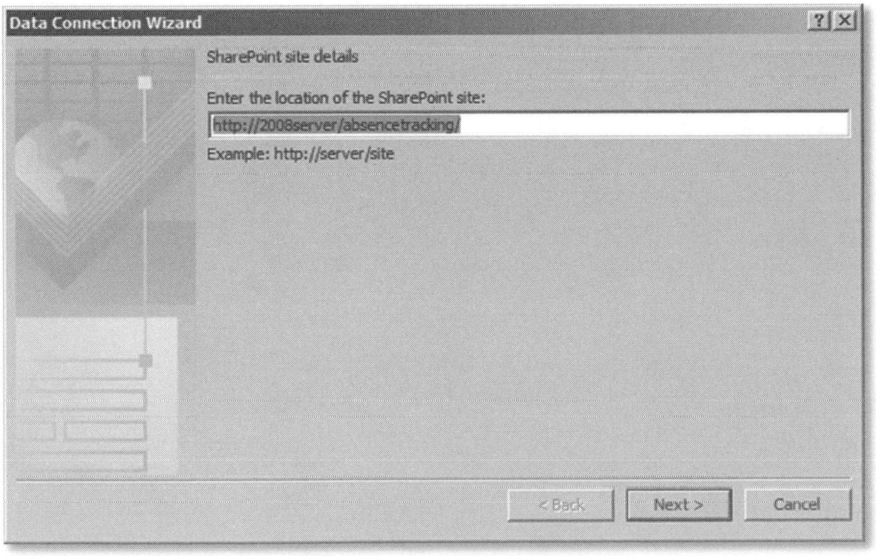

Illustration 97 - The third screen of the Data Connection Wizard

Enter the site address and click the **Next** button. *InfoPath* will now connect to the specified *SharePoint* site and display all of the lists and libraries on that site as shown in **Illustration 98** below.

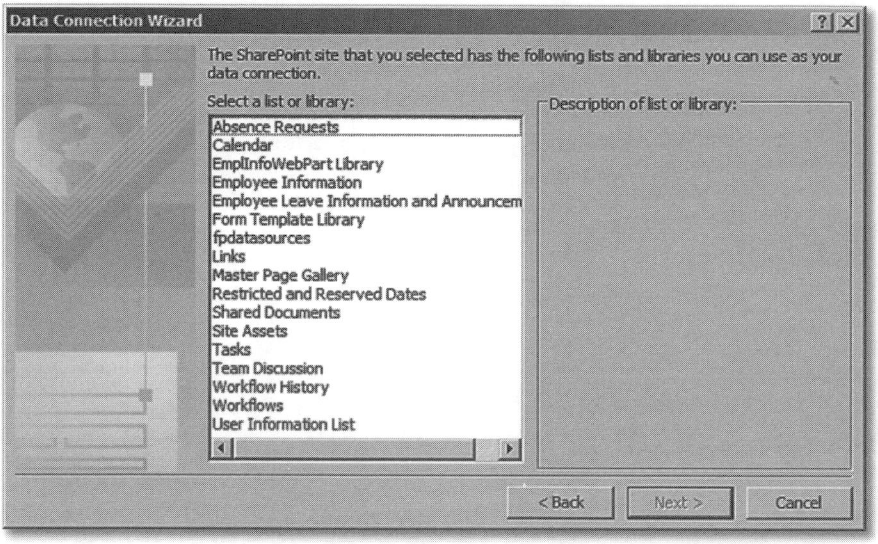

Illustration 98 - The fourth screen of the Data Connection Wizard

Choose the **Employee Information** list and click the **Next** button. On the next screen of the *Data Connection Wizard* as shown in **Illustration 99** below the field columns of the list are displayed and you can select the fields that you want to use in the form as well as the field to sort on.

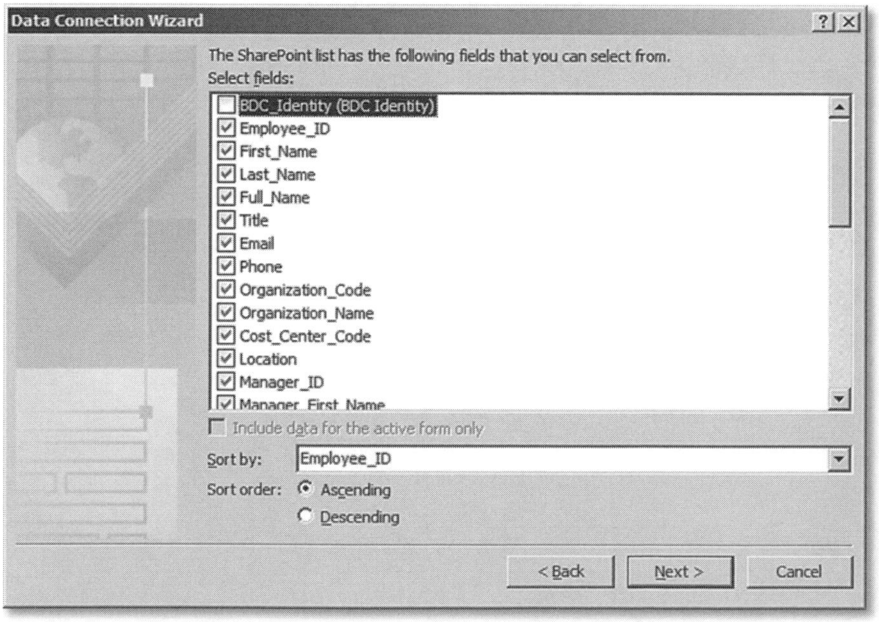

Illustration 99 - The fifth screen of the Data Connection Wizard

Select all the column fields and pick **Employee_ID** for the Sort by value. Click the **Next** button. This screen provides the option of storing the information from the list in the form for offline use as shown in **Illustration 100** below.

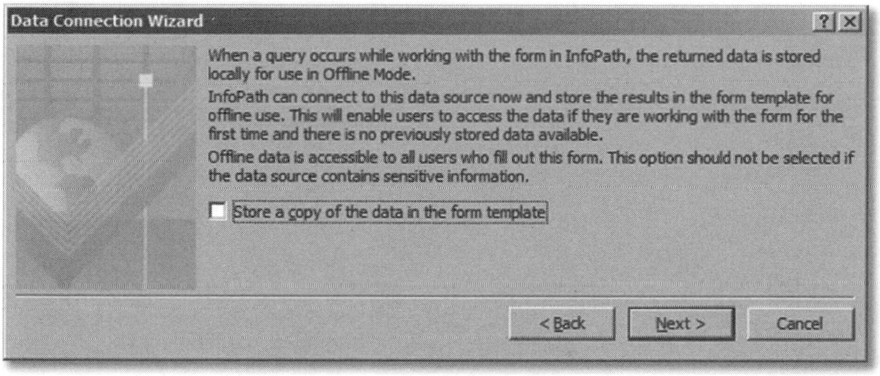

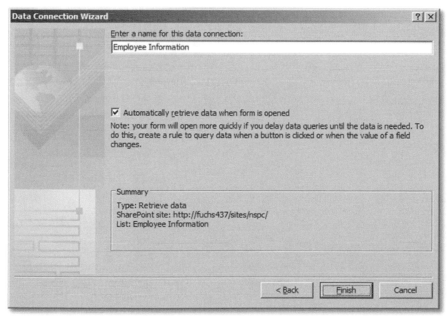

Illustration 100 - The sixth screen of the Data Connection Wizard

Since this is a browser based form and an absence request transaction will only be executed over a network we will *not* choose this option. De-select the **check box** on this screen and click the **Next** button.

On the subsequent screen, as shown in **Illustration 101** below, you can enter a different name for the data connection if you do not want to use the list name. You can also specify if you want the data connection to retrieve information from the list automatically when the form is opened. We will want to do this so select the **check box** for this option and click the **Finish** button.

Illustration 101 - The final screen of the Data Connection Wizard

The *Data Connection* dialogue screen will display again with the new *Employee Information* data connection displayed in the list of connections as shown in **Illustration 102** at right.

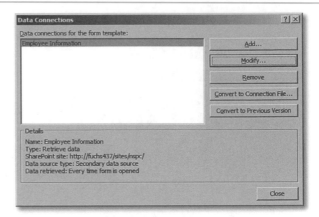

Illustration 102 - Data Connections dialogue screen showing completed Employee Information data connection

You will now see a drop-down icon on the right of the *Fields* pane that displays the additional data sources in the structure of an XML schema. Click on the drop-down and you will see the *Employee Information* data source. Choose it and expand the *dataFields* group to see the fields available as shown in **Illustration 103** at right.

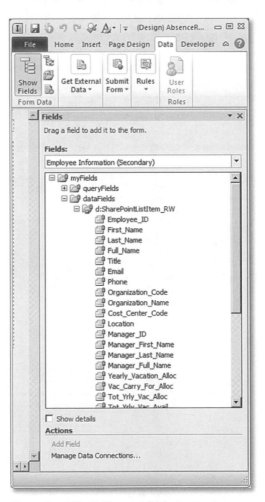

Illustration 103 - Fields pane displaying Employee Information secondary data source

The *Employee Information* data source and all other data sources that we will add to the form will also be displayed in the *Select a Field or Group* dialogue box as shown in **Illustration 104** at right.

The form can now access the *Employee information* table data in the *SQL Server* database through the *Employee Information ECT* list and we will use this information to auto-populate fields in the form.

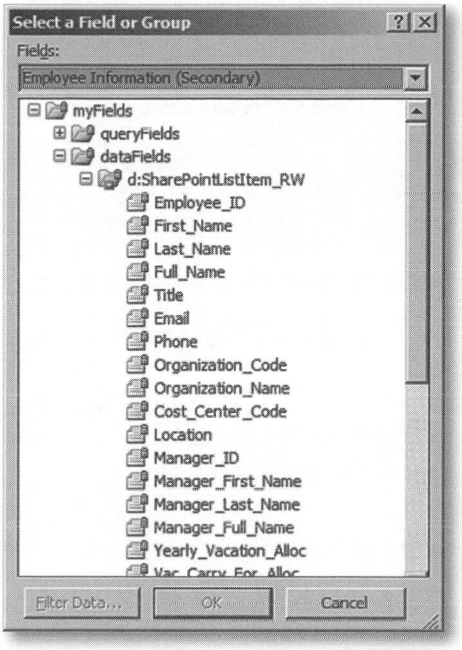

Laying Out Form Controls and Binding Them to the Information Set Schema Fields

We will now start laying out form controls and binding them to schema fields. We will create a temporary layout as shown in **illustration 105** below without spending a lot of time on the design aesthetics of the form.

Our main objective presently is to demonstrate *InfoPath's* sophisticated information handling and form behavior capabilities. As we go along we will demonstrate best practices for form design and ultimately we will render a structurally versatile and well-designed form.

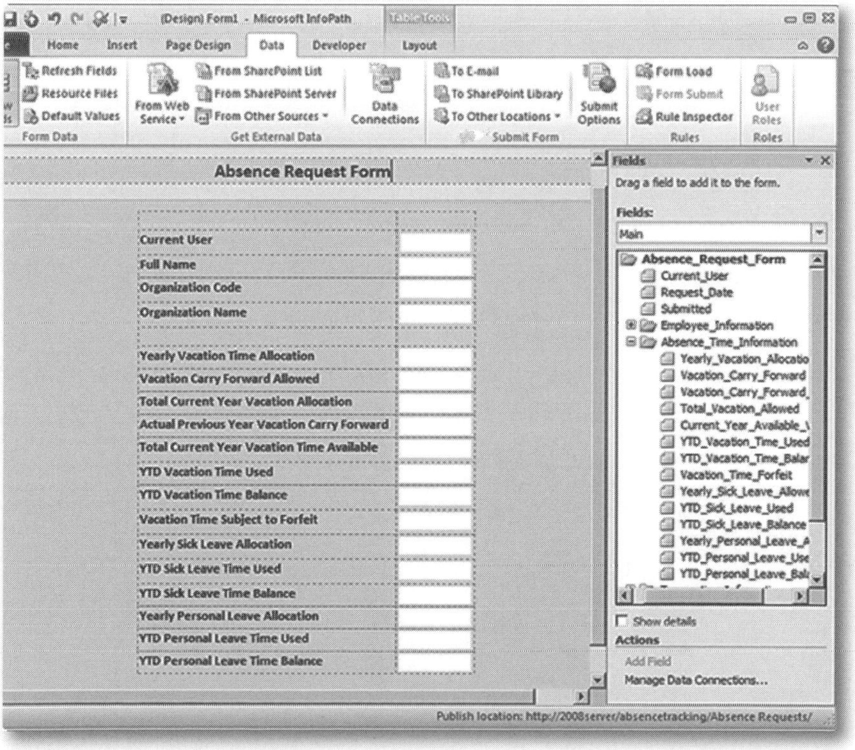

Illustration 104 - Select a Field or Group dialogue screen displaying secondary data sources

Illustration 105 - Temporary form layout of controls

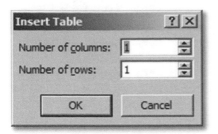

Place your cursor near the top of the layout surface and click the **Insert** tab on the Ribbon. Click **Custom Table** and click the **Layout Table** option. The *Insert Table* dialogue box will display as shown in **Illustration 106** at left.

Illustration 106 - Insert Table dialogue screen

Enter 1 column and 1 row and click **OK**. A one column empty table will appear. With the cursor placed under the first table insert another single column table. Grab the bottom border of the second table and drag it so that the table is about two inches high. Place your cursor in the first table and type "Absence Request Form". Right click with the first table selected to display the drop-down menu of table operation options as shown in **Illustration 107** below.

Illustration 107 - Drop-down menu of table operation options

Choose **Borders and Shading** from the drop-down menu as shown in **Illustration 108**. Click on the **Shading** tab and pick any color from the color palette and click **OK**.

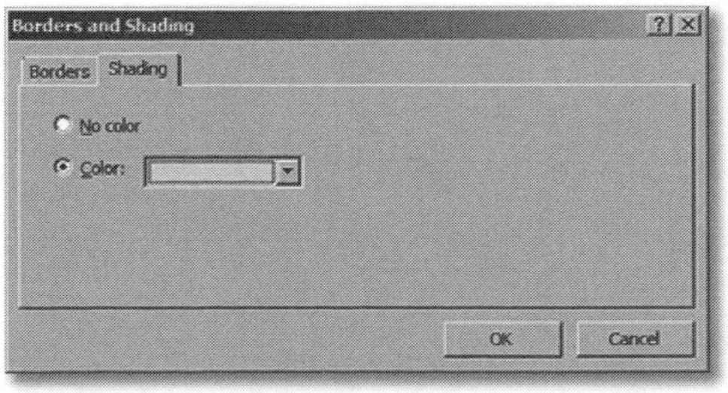

Illustration 108 - Borders and Shading dialogue screen

Apply the same color to the second table so that your form looks like **Illustration 109** below.

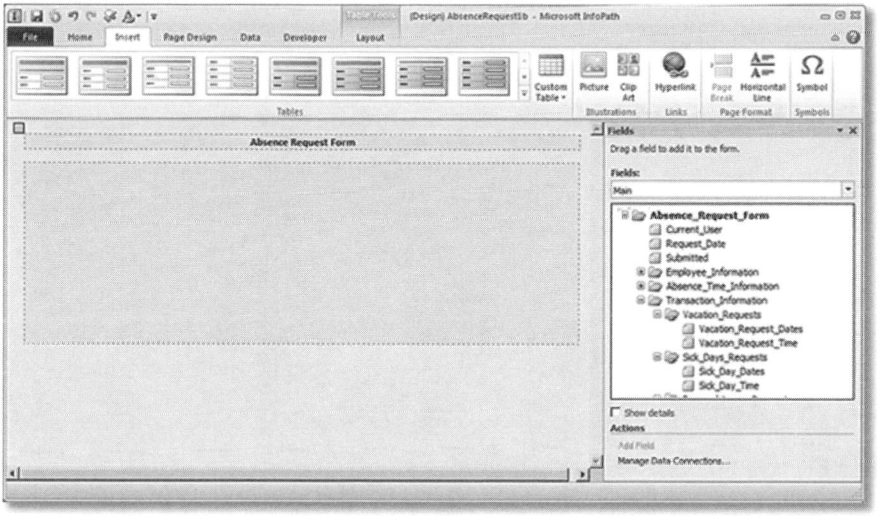

Illustration 109 - Shading applied to the two tables in the form

With your cursor placed in the second table right click again and choose the **Table Properties** option. Click on the **Cell** tab of the *Table Properties* dialogue box. Enter "15" points in the **Top, Bottom, Left** and **Right Cell** padding choice boxes as shown in **Illustration 110** below and click **OK**.

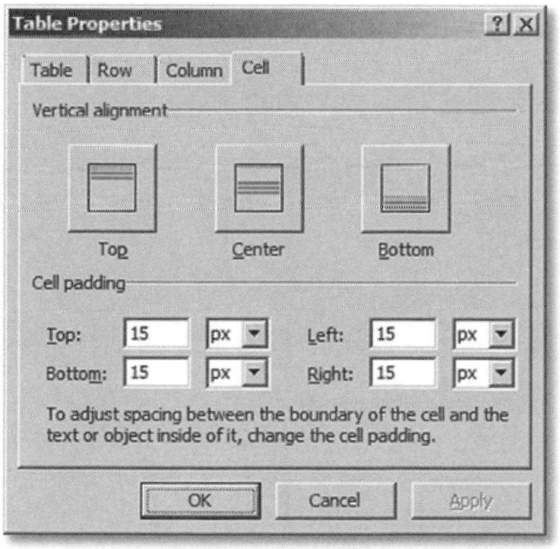

Illustration 110 - Table Properties dialogue screen

With the cursor placed top left **within** the second table, click on the **Custom Table button** on the *Ribbon* and then **Layout Table** to insert another table with **16 rows and 2 columns**. Your design surface should like **Illustration 111** below.

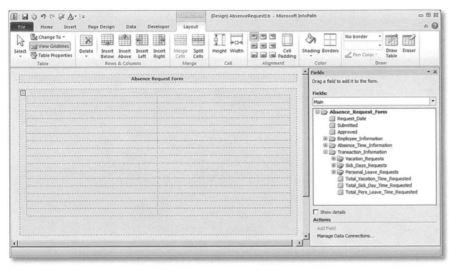

Illustration 111 - Insertion of table with 16 rows and 2 columns within the single column and row table

Grab the right border of the table you just inserted and drag it to the left so that the right column is about an inch wide. Than grab the inner column border and drag that to the left so that the left column is about two inches wide.

Place your cursor in the top right column of this table. Now select and right click on the **Current_User** field. A drop-down menu will display. Choose the first item, **Text Box** as shown in **Illustration 112** below.

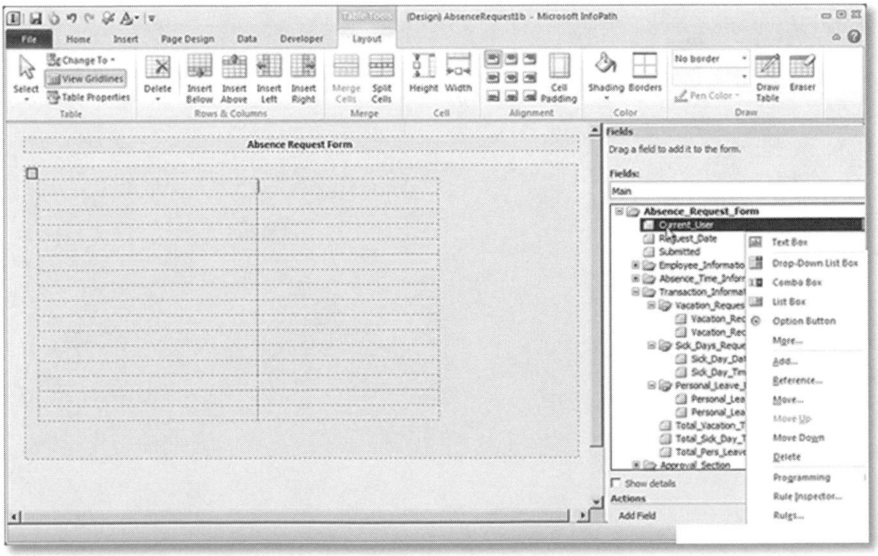

Illustration 112 - Selecting a field and control to be placed at the cursor position in the form

A *Text Box* control will be bound to the *Current_User* field and inserted in the top right column as shown in **Illustration 113** below.

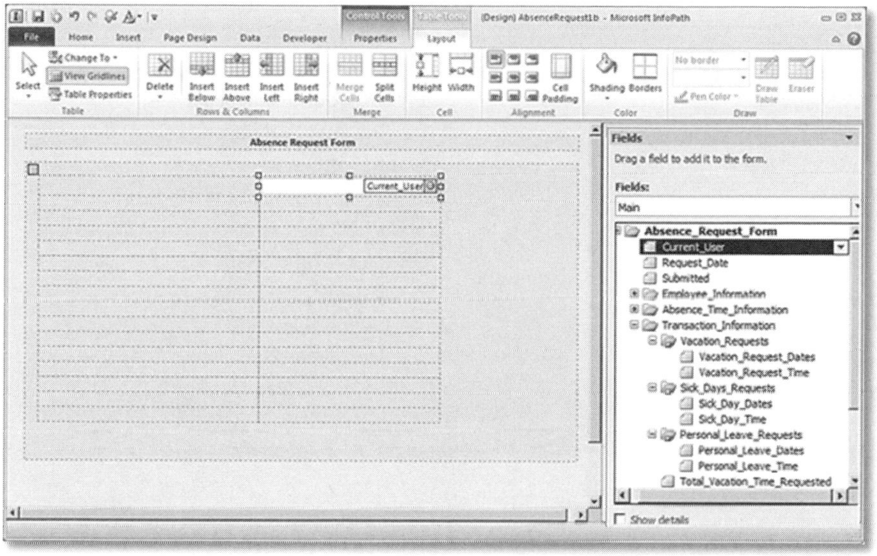

Illustration 113 - Text Box control bound to the Current_User field placed in the table

Place your cursor in the top left column directly to the left of the *Text Box* just inserted and enter the label text "Current User".

Place your cursor In column 2 row 2, click on the **Full_Name** field in the schema, right click and choose **Text Box** again to insert a text box control in that cell. In the column to the left of that cell enter the label text "Full Name".

Do the procedure for the *Organization_Code* and *Organization_Name* fields so that you form looks like **Illustration 114** below.

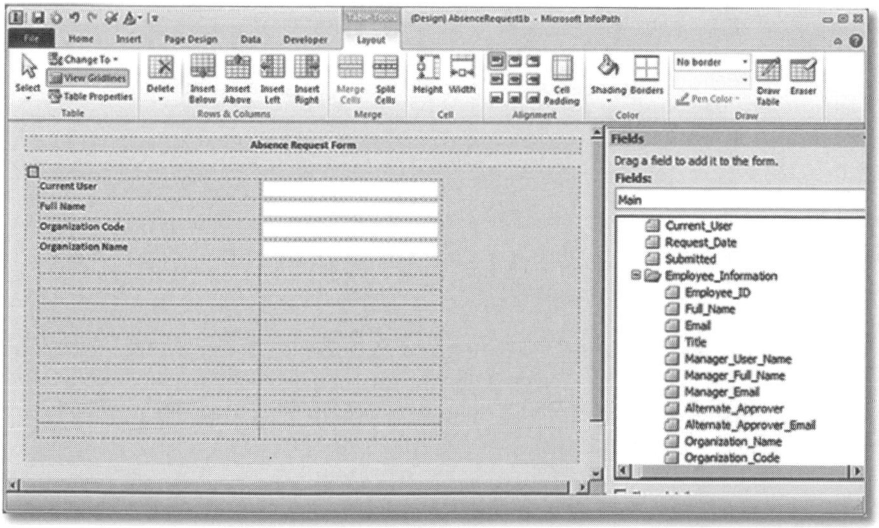

Illustration 114 - Table with Text Box controls and labels

Skip the next row in the form. Expand the *Absence_Time_Information* group and insert **Text Box** controls in the right column using the same procedure described above for the following fields:

Schema Node Name	Text Box Field Label
Yearly_Vacation_Allocation	Yearly Vacation Time Allocation
Vacation_Carry_Forward	Actual Previous Year Vacation Carry Forward *
Vacation_Carry_Forward_Allowed	Vacation Carry Forward Allowed *
Total_Vacation_Allowed	Total Current Year Vacation Allocation
Current_Year_Available_Vac_Time	Total Current Year Vacation Time Available
YTD_Vacation_Time_Used	YTD Vacation Time Used
YTD_Vacation_Time_Balance	YTD Vacation Time Balance
Vacation_Time_Forfeit	Vacation Time Subject to Forfeit
Yearly_Sick_Leave_Allocation	Yearly Sick Leave Allocation
YTD_Sick_Leave_Time_Used	YTD Sick Leave Time Used
YTD_Sick_Leave_Balance	YTD Sick Leave Time Balance
Yearly_Personal_Leave_Allocation	Yearly Personal Leave Allocation
YTD_Personal_Leave_Used	YTD Personal Leave Time Used
YTD_Personal_Leave_Balance	YTD Personal Leave Time Balance

We now have a number of *Text Box* form controls that are bound to schema fields. The information captured by the controls will be stored as values in the fields.

> **Development Note –** The presence of a form control is not necessary to capture and store values. Formulas and rules can set values to schema fields directly. Furthermore these values can also be set for secondary data source fields as well, which we will do later.
>
> Form controls and their labels do not have to be placed in the same order of the schema fields, they can be placed anywhere on the form in any sequence. Note that the *Vacation_Carry_Forward* field and its corresponding *Actual Previous Year Vacation Carry Forward* text box control and label are placed out of sequence on the form.

Your form should look like **Illustration 105** shown on Page 83.

Creating a Form Load Rule

We are now going to create a *Form Load* rule that will populate some of these fields. *Form Load* rules execute immediately upon opening a form, either when a new form instance is created or when an existing, already populated form is subsequently opened.

Click on the **Data** tab on the *Ribbon* and then the **Form Load** button. The *Rules* pane will display. The *Rules* pane can be opened when any schema object or control is selected. Rule sets can then be created that are bound to the schema field or group. Rules are ***not*** bound to the controls themselves except in the case of a Button or for the form itself through the *Form Open* and *Submit* options.

The *New Created Form* rule that we will create will have two conditions and twenty-one actions. When we are finished creating all the actions for the rule, some of which will be added later on in the book, it will look like **Illustration 115** below.

Illustration 115 - Form Load rule for New Created Form

Before we construct this rule let's review the scenario that it will facilitate. We want the following things to happen immediately and automatically when a user creates a new *Absence Request* form instance:

- Upon opening the form determine whether it is a new form instance or an existing instance.

- If it is a new form instance execute the actions for a new form as follows:

  o Capture the Identity of the user opening the form and store that identity for use as a parameter to query the *Employee Information External List* for their time away allocations, time away used, and balance of time remaining for the vacation, sick and personal leave time categories.

  o Display the above values in the form controls and store them in the *Main* data source schema fields.

Click on the **Create a New Rule** button and choose **Action**. Name the Rule "New Created Form". Under *Condition*, click on the **None – Rule runs when form is opened** link. The following *Condition* dialogue box will display as shown in **Illustration 116** below.

Illustration 116 - Rule Condition dialogue screen

Click on the **down arrow** in the first drop-down selector and choose the **Submitted** field that displays. In the second drop-down selector **pick is equal to**. Pick the value **FALSE** in the third drop-down selector. Click the **And** button and a new condition row will display.

A rule can have an arbitrary number of conditional clauses using and/or joining logic. The conditional clauses must resolve to true for the rule actions to fire. Leave the *And* option. In the first drop-down selector of the second conditional clause row pick **Select a field or group**. The *Select a Field or Group* dialogue box will display as shown in **Illustration 117** at right. From here you can select any field or group from any data source. Select the **Current_User** field in the *Main* data source and click **OK**.

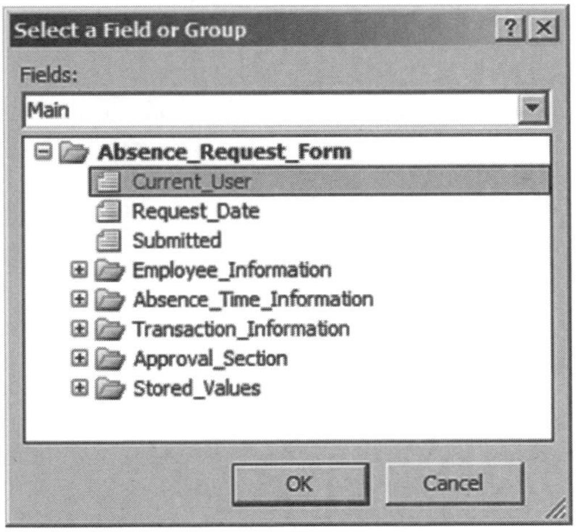

Illustration 117 - Select a Field or Group dialogue screen

In the second drop-down selector choose **is blank**. The third drop-down selector will be grayed out as there is no matching logic for an *is blank* condition. Your *Condition* will look like **Illustration 118** as follows. Click **OK**.

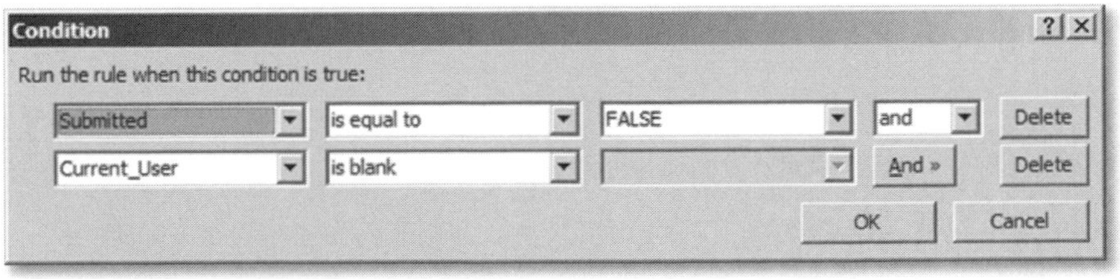

Illustration 118 - Completed Condition statement for New Created Form rule

Let's review what this condition logic will accomplish. Earlier when we created the *Submitted* field we set its *Data type* as *True/False (Boolean)* and we set its *Default Value* to *FALSE*, as shown in **Illustration 119** at right.

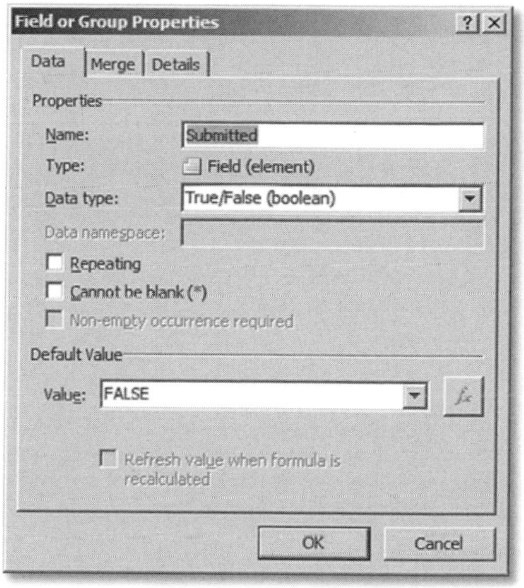

This default value of FALSE for the *Submitted* field provides one of the condition criteria that establishes that this is a new form that has not yet been submitted. We will eventually construct a *Submit data* rule set that will execute a number of actions upon submission of the *Absence Request* form to its host form library. One of the *Submit data* actions will be to set the value of the *Submitted* field to "TRUE". This value will be written to a column in the form library and used by the application workflow and the other *Form Load* rules that we will be creating.

Illustration 119 - Field or Group Properties dialogue screen for Submitted field

Setting the Current User Value for Use with the Form Load Rule Actions

The first action of the *Form Load* rule that we are presently constructing will be to set the value of the *Current_User* field with the *userName* function. Consequently an already submitted form will contain both field values. Since a new form will have neither of these values the condition above will resolve to true and the subsequent rule actions will execute.

When an already submitted instance of the form is opened the *Submitted* field value will have a value of TRUE and the *Current_User* field will be populated. As a result the condition will resolve to false and consequently this rule will not execute.

> **Development Note** - This is a technique that can be used in any *InfoPath* form to determine whether the opened form is a new or existing instance.

In the *Rules* pane click the **Add** button to the right of **Run these actions:** The following choices will display in the drop-down list:

> Switch Views
> Set a field's value
> Query for data
> Submit data
> Send data to Web Part

Pick **Set a field's value**. The *Rule Details* dialogue screen as shown in **Illustration 120** at right will display:

Illustration 120 - Rule Details dialogue screen

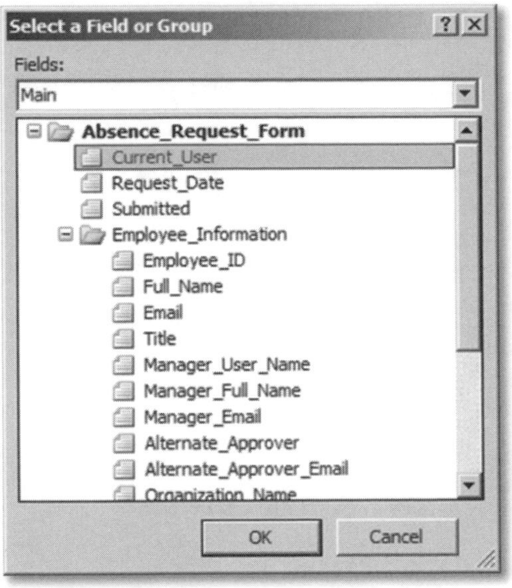

Illustration 121 - Select a Field or Group dialogue screen

Click on the **Select a Field or Group** button to the right of the *Field* box. The *Select a Field or Group* dialogue box will display. Select the **Current_User** field as shown in **Illustration 121** at left. Click **OK**.

Illustration 122 - Insert Formula dialogue screen

Current_User will now be displayed in the *Field* box. Click on the **Formula** button to the right of the *Value:* box. The **Insert Formula** dialogue screen will display as shown in **Illustration 122** at left.

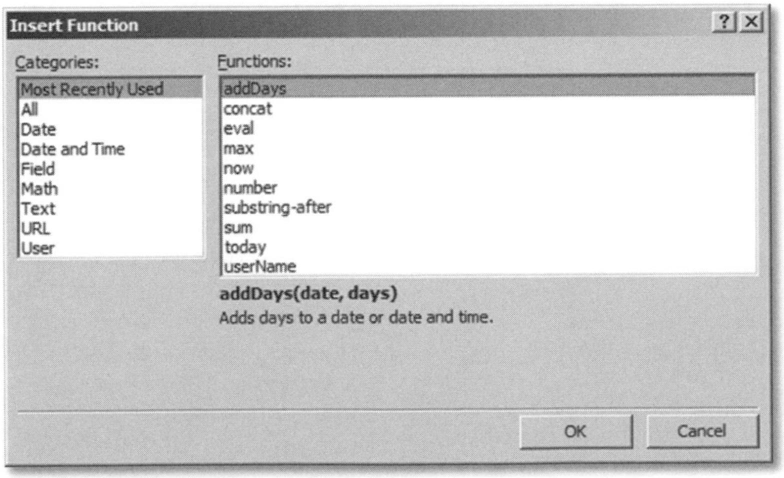

Illustration 123 - Insert Function dialogue screen

Click the **Insert Function** button and the *Insert Function* dialogue screen will display as shown in **Illustration 123** at left.

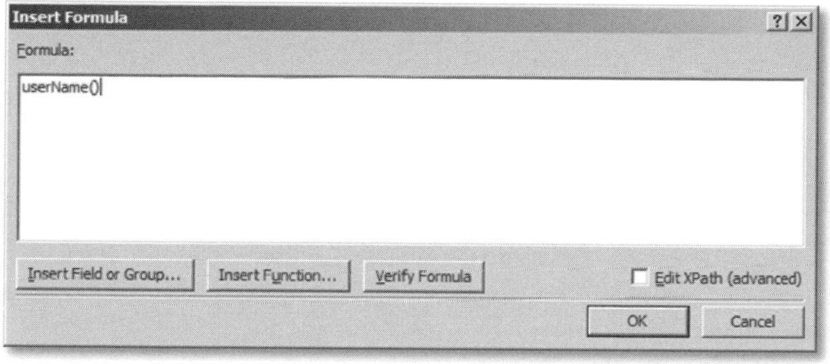

Illustration 124 - userName() function selected for use in a formula

Click **User** in the *Categories* box on the left. The *userName* function will appear in the box on the right. Select the **userName** function and click **OK**. The *Insert Formula* dialogue box will look like **Illustration 124** at left. Click **OK**.

Illustration 125 - Completed set a field's value action

The completed *Rule Details* dialogue box will now look like **Illustration 125** at left. Click **OK** to complete this rule action.

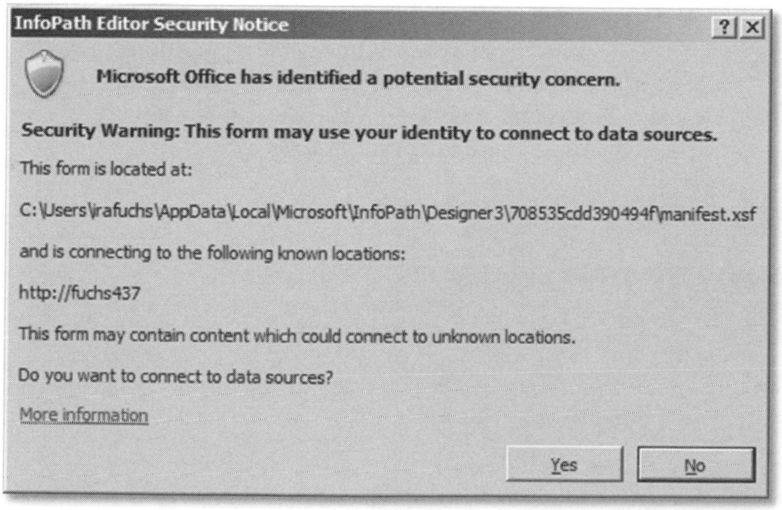

Illustration 126 - InfoPath Editor Security Notice

The first action for the *Form Load* Rule 1 rule is now *Set a field's value: Current_User = userName*. Why did we do this first and what does the action do? Let's do a preview of the form to see the results of this action. Click on the **Home** tab of the Ribbon and then click the **Preview** button. You will get the security notice shown in **Illustration 126** at left. Click **Yes**.

The following preview of the run-time form will display as shown **in Illustration 127** below. The *Current User* field control should be populated with *your username*. The *InfoPath userName* function returns the user name of the person who is currently logged on to the *Windows* operating system. With the *userName* value captured in the *Current_User* field we can now use this value to query the *Employee Information* ECT to return the current user's specific database record containing the information that we need for this application. This is exactly what we will do in constructing the subsequent fifteen actions of this rule.

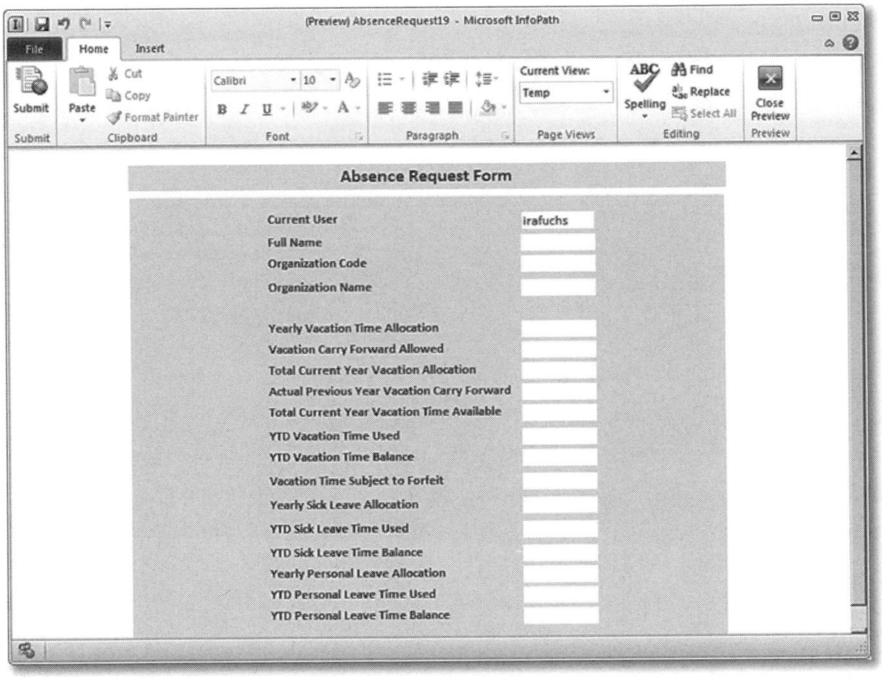

Illustration 127 - Preview of the run-time form

Querying the Employee Information Secondary Data Source

Close the form preview and return to the *Form Load* rule panel. click the **Add** button to the right of **Run these actions:** and select **Query for data**. The *Rule Details* dialogue screen **in Illustration 128** below will display. The *Employee Information* data connection will automatically display because it is the only data connection that we have created so far. We will be creating additional data connections later. Click **OK**.

Illustration 128 - Query for data Rule Details dialogue screen

Now click the **Add** button to the right of **Run these actions:** and select **Set a field's value.** Once again, the *Rule Details* dialogue screen for this action will display as shown in **Illustration 129** below.

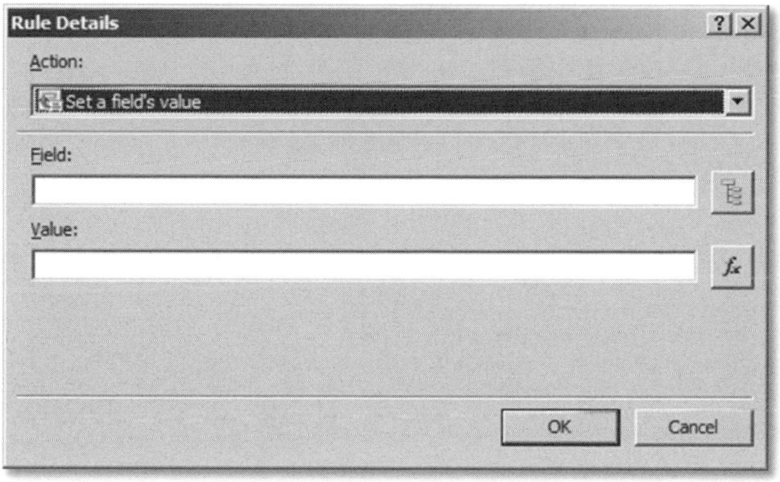

Illustration 129 - Rule Details dialogue screen

Click on the **Select a Field or Group** button on the right of the *Field* box. Expand the *Employee_Information* group from the *Main* data source and select the **Organization_Code** as shown in **Illustration 130** below. Click **OK**.

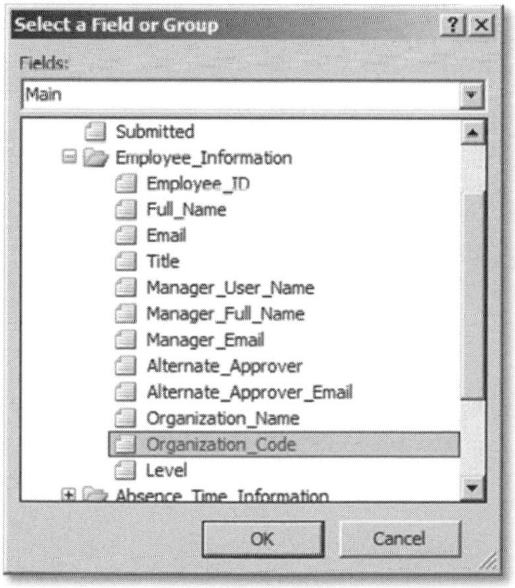

Illustration 130 - Select a Field or Group dialogue screen

On the *Rule Details* dialogue screen click the **Formula** button to the right of the *Value* box. The *Insert Formula* dialogue screen will display as shown in **Illustration 131** below. Click on the **Insert Field or Group** button.

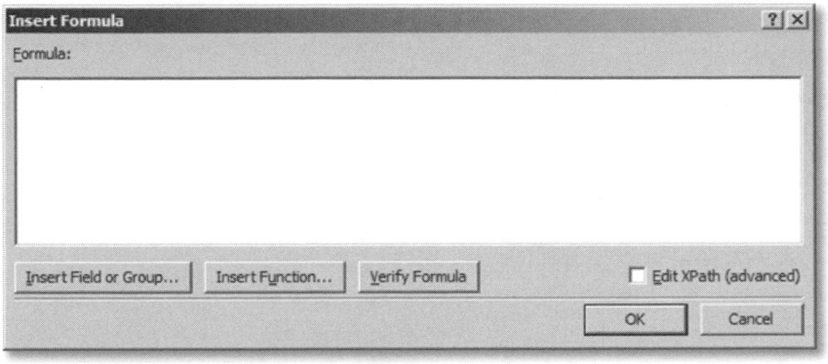

Illustration 131 - Insert Formula dialogue screen

Choose the **Employee Information** secondary data source from the *Fields* drop-down selection box. Select the **Organizaton_Code** field as shown in **Illustration 132** below.

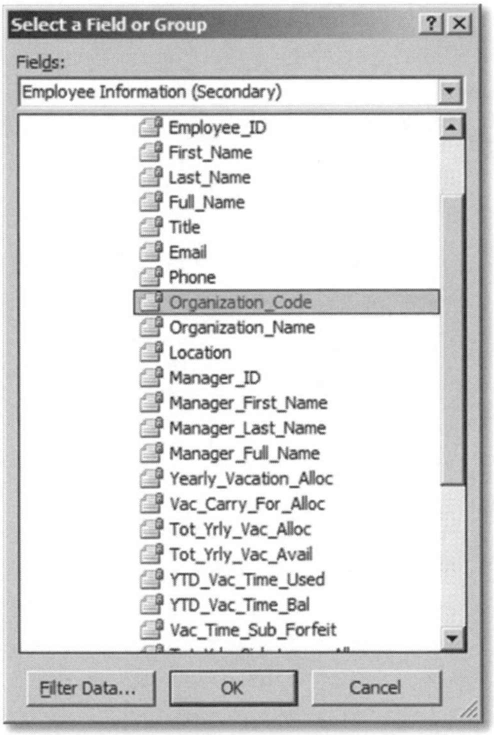

Illustration 132 - Select a field from the Employee
Information secondary data source

Important— do not click OK yet.

Adding the Current User Filter Parameter to Find a Value from a Specific Record

What we need to do now is provide the query filter parameter that will be used to look-up the value for the *Organization_Code* in the *Employee Information* ECT for the corresponding value of the *Current_User* that we set earlier. The returned *Organizaton_Code* value from the *Employee Information* ECT query will be used to set the *Organization_Code* value in the *Main* data source.

To accomplish this click the **Filter Data** button. The *Filter Data* dialogue screen will display as shown in **Illustration 133** at right.

Illustration 133 - Filter Data dialogue screen

Click the **Add** button. The *Specify Filter Conditions* dialogue screen will display as shown by **Illustration 134** below. This is where we will specify the query filter parameter.

Illustration 134 - Specify Filter Conditions

In the first drop-down selection box scroll to the bottom of the list and choose **Select a field or group**. Pick the **Main** data source from the *Data source* drop-down list. The *Main* data source will display as shown in **Illustration 135** at right.

Select the **Current_User** field. Click **OK**. Leave the *is equal to* argument in the second drop-down selection box of the *Specify Filter Conditions* dialogue screen. In the third drop-down selection box again choose **Select a field or group**.

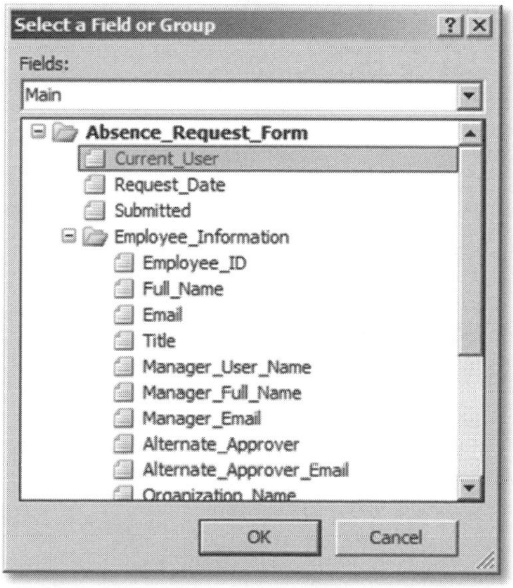

Illustration 135 - Select a Field or Group dialogue screen

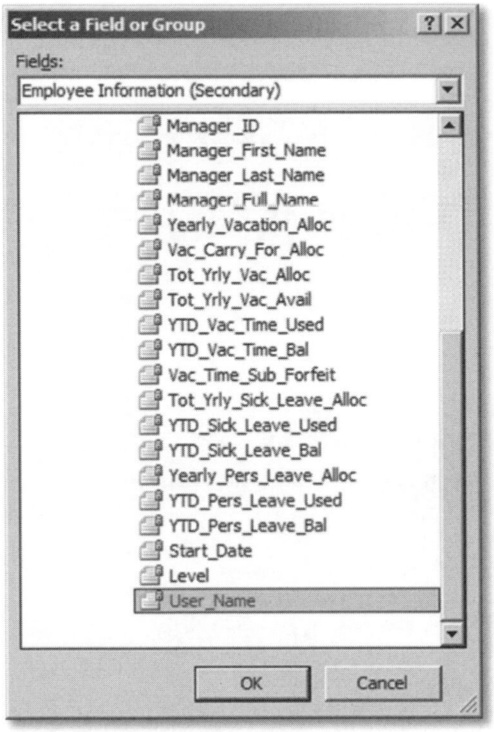

Now choose the **Employee Information** secondary data source. Scroll down to the bottom and select the **User_ Name** field as shown in **Illustration 136** at left. Click **OK**.

Illustration 136 - Select User_Name field from Employee Information secondary data source

The *Specify Filter Conditions* screen will now look like **Illustration 137** below.

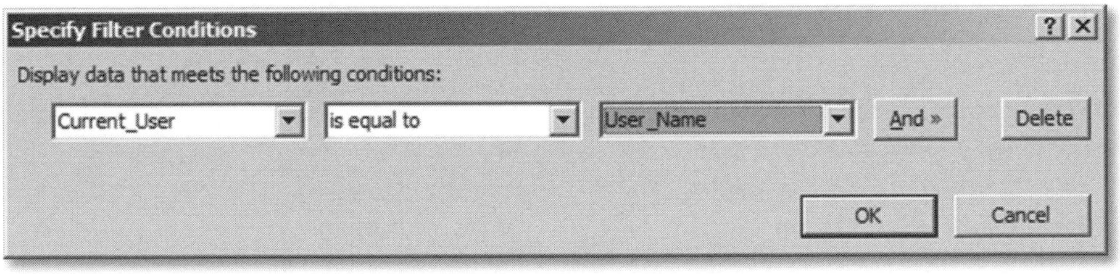

Illustration 137 - Completed Specify Filter Conditions statement

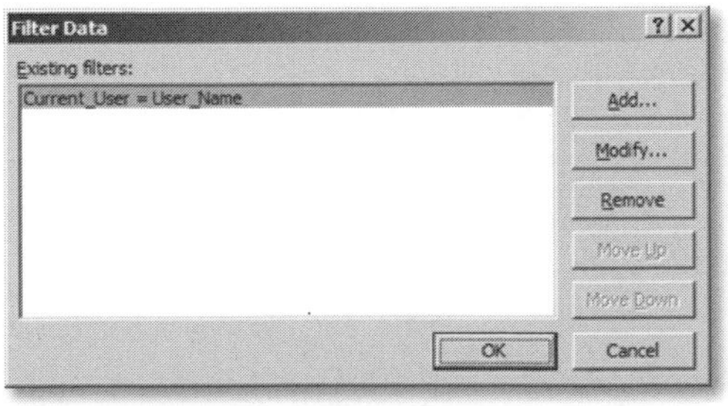

Click **OK**. The *Filter Data* screen will look like **Illustration 138** at left. Click **OK**.

Illustration 138 - Completed Filter for look-up selection

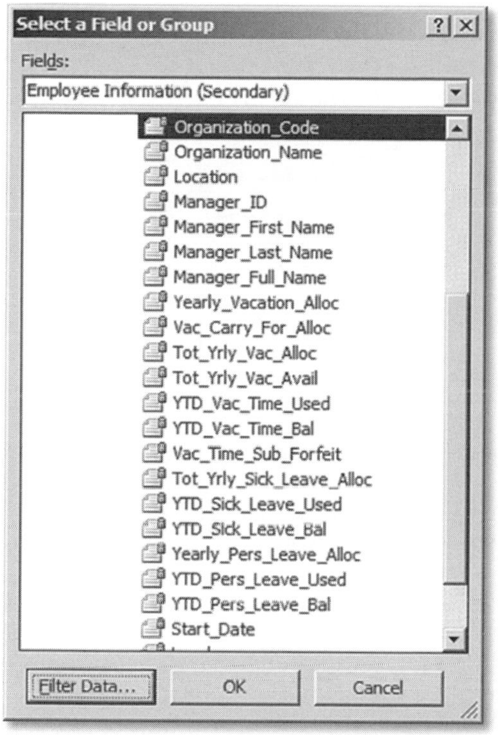

Now that the filter for the query parameter is defined click **OK** on the *Select a Field or Group* dialogue screen as shown in **Illustration 139** at left.

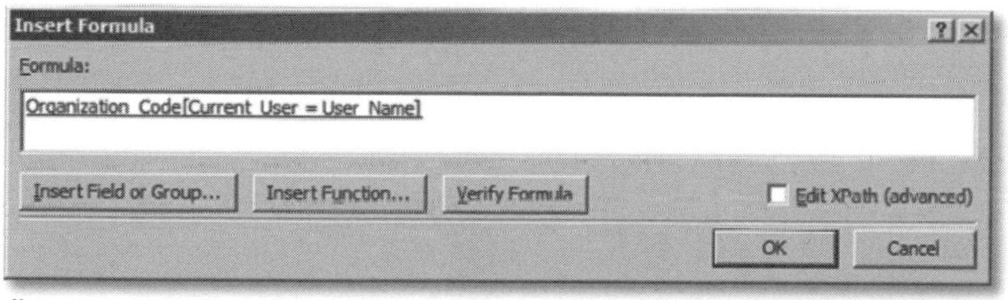

Illustration 139 - Filtered Organization_Code selection

The *Insert Formula* dialogue screen will now display the formula *Organization Code[Current_User = User_Name]* as shown in **Illustration 140** at left. Click **OK**.

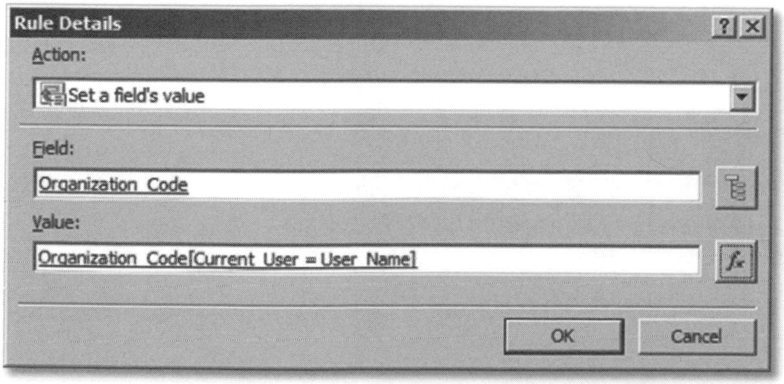

Illustration 140 - Completed filtered look-up formula for Organization_Code

The completed *Rule Details* dialogue screen will now look like **Illustration 141** at left.

Illustration 141 - Completed rule action for setting a filtered field value

Click **OK**. Congratulations! You have just taken advantage of one of *InfoPath*'s most powerful features. Using the same *[Current_User = User_Name]* query filter parameter we are going to repeat these steps to create the rest of the *Set a fields value* actions for the following fields in the form that have corresponding fields in the *Employee Information* database:

> *Organization_Name*
> *Full_Name*
> *Yearly_Vacation_Allocation*
> *Vacation_Carry_Forward*
> *Vacation_Carry_Forward_Allowed*
> *Total_Vacation_Allowed*
> *Current_Year_Available_Vac_Time*
> *YTD_Vacation_Time_Used*
> *YTD_Vacation_Time_Balance*
> *Yearly_Sick_Leave_Allowed*
> *YTD_Sick_Leave_Used*
> *YTD_Sick_Leave_Balance*
> *Yearly_Personal_Leave_Allowed*
> *YTD_Personal_Leave_Used*
> *YTD_Personal_Leave_Balance*
> *Email*

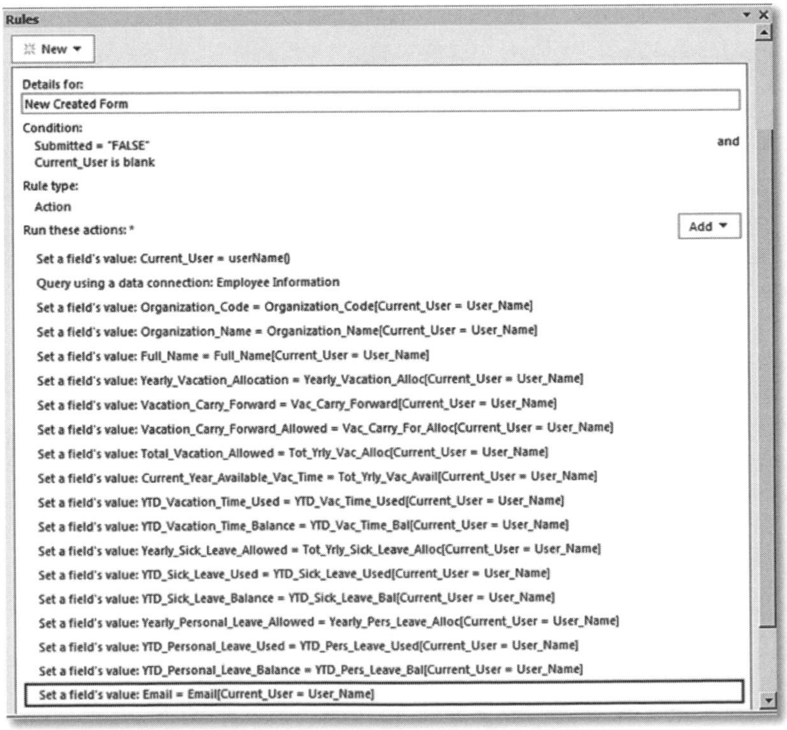

Illustration 142 - Completed set of actions for the Form Load rule

When you are finished the *Rules* panel for the *New Created Form* rule will look like **Illustration 142** on the previous page. Preview the form after all the actions have been implemented to see what the *Form Load* behavior for this rule is. As shown in **Illustration 143** below the fields that we have set values for have been auto-populated with the data from the *Employee Information* external list based on the user's identity.

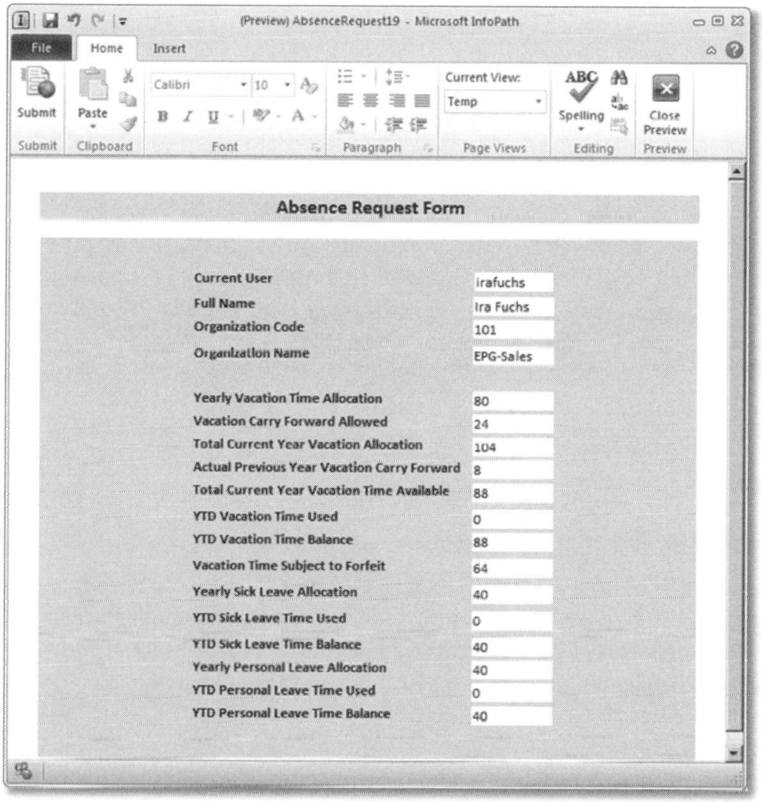

Illustration 143 - Preview of form after all Form Load actions have been implemented

Review of What We Have Accomplished So Far in InfoPath

Let's review what we have just accomplished using *InfoPath*. We created a structured schema for the information set that will be captured in the form. We added a secondary data source to the form that allowed the form to access information from the *Employee Information* external list. We bound fields from the schema to controls in the form. We used a *Form Load* rule condition to determine whether the form being opened was a new or existing instance. If the form instance was new we used the built-in *userName* function to capture the identity of the person creating the form. We then queried the *Employee Information* external list and used the value of the *userName* as a query filter parameter to return the relevant record information for the user which we then captured in the fields of the *Main* data source and displayed in the controls bound to those fields.

These initial form creation steps demonstrate what the more sophisticated capabilities of *InfoPath* are, and what the art-of-the-possible is for creating complex, rigorous applications using declarative development techniques. It should be apparent that an *InfoPath* form is much more than just a data-entry tool. An *InfoPath* form should be thought of as a smart and versatile integration tool capable of aggregating, manipulating, presenting, and generating information to and from any number of data sources. We will continue to add secondary data sources to the form and use formulas and rule sets to enforce validation requirements, execute business logic and drive form behavior.

> **Development Note** – In the *Employee Information* database we created a field that stores the employee's *User_Name* that corresponds to their Windows login credentials, which is in turn used to look-up additional information about the employee in the external application. This identifying information may not always be available in a Line of Business (LOB) application. In that case we would need an alternative mechanism to map the identity provided by the InfoPath userName function to information in the database. The *SharePoint User Profile* Web Service can be queried using the *userName* value to return another identifying value, which can be used as the query parameter to the external data source. The *SharePoint User Profile* data store contains fields for *AccountName*, *FirstName, LastName, UserName* and *Manager*. If the User Profile database is populated with this information from Active Directory then these values can be obtained through the *User Profile Service* and used to query the external application through BCS. See the section **Accessing SharePoint User Profile Service Information** on page 371 for more information on this topic.

The values now displayed in the form's field controls were **physically** copied from the *Employee Information* external list using the *Set a field's value* action and are now stored in the schema fields. Changing any of this information in the form will not affect the external list.

Making InfoPath Controls Read-only

The auto-populated values that display in the field controls can be changed by the user and we want to prevent this from happening as the information in these fields will be used later to update the *Employee Information* external list. If a user can change the values in these fields they will have completely compromised the integrity of the application. We must be able to make this information read-only. Once again, this is something that *InfoPath* handles easily.

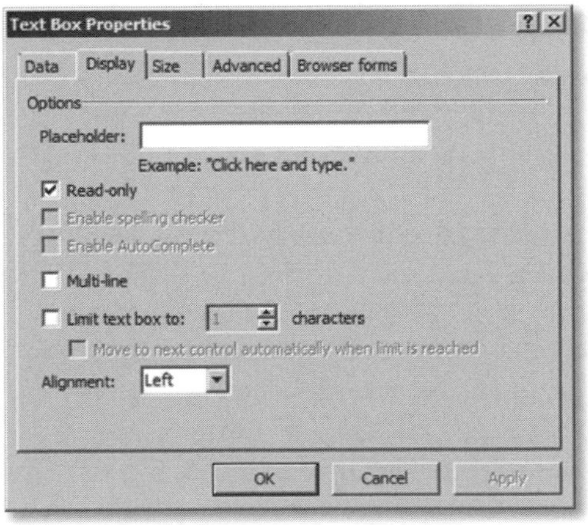

Select the **Text Box** control for the **Current_User** field and right click. Choose **Text Box Properties** to display the *Text Box Properties* dialogue screen. Select the **Display** tab to display the dialogue screen shown in **Illustration 144** at left.

Illustration 144 - Text Box Properties dialogue screen

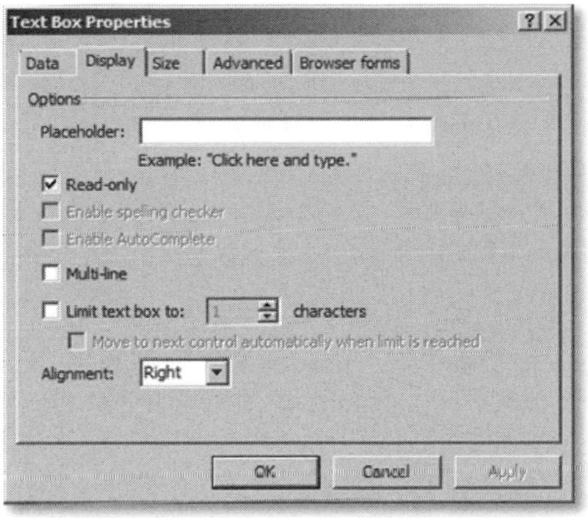

Illustration 145 - Text Box Properties Alignment setting in the Display tab

Select the **Read-only** check box and make sure it is checked. Click **OK.** Now do the same for all of the *Text Box* field controls. For all the time-away fields that store a *Whole Number* Data type change the *Alignment* in their *Text Box* controls from *Left* to *Right* as shown in **Illustration 145** at left.

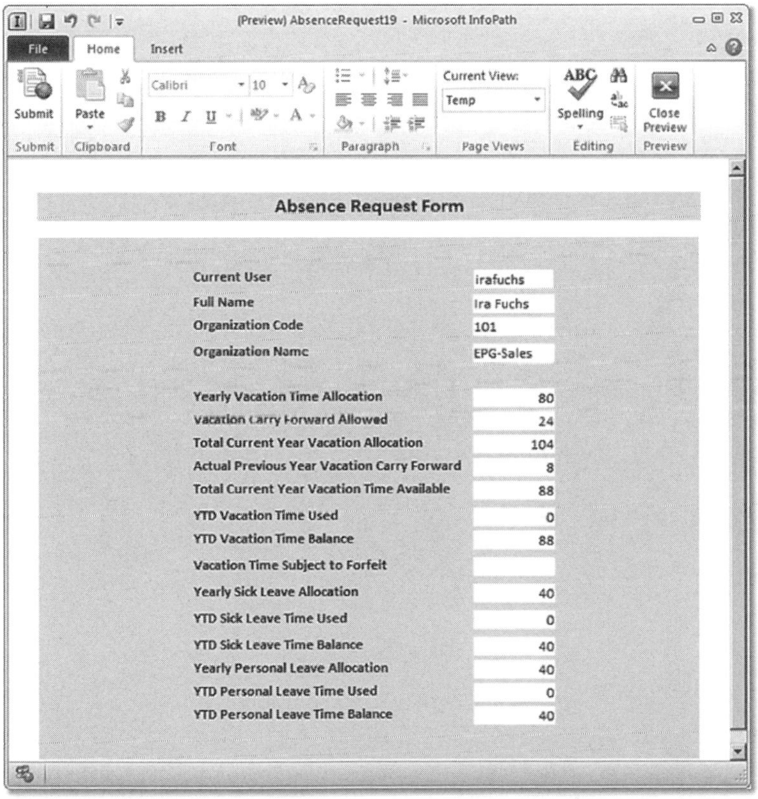

Illustration 146 - Preview of form after fields have been set to read-only and right aligned

Preview the form again. You will find that all of the fields are locked and the information in the time-away fields is right aligned as shown in **Illustration 146** at left.

Development Note – Setting the controls to read-only does not affect setting the value for the fields with the *Form Load* rule action. The read-only setting only prevents the user from changing the values in the control. The form developer can use formulas and rules to set values programmatically on any control (not just on Form Load) even when it is set to read-only.

Setting a Field's Value with a Formula Calculation

Notice that the *Vacation_Time_Forfeit* control is blank in the form preview as shown in **Illustration 146** on the previous page. This field will store a calculated value for the amount of vacation time that the user will not be able to carry forward into the next year based on the following formula:

(YTD_Vacation_Time_Balance) - (Vacation_Carry_Forward_Allowed)

We will create this formula now. Right click on the **Vacation_Time_Forfeit** field or control. Select **Properties**. In the **Properties** dialogue screen click the **Formula** button to the right of *Value*. The *Insert Formula* dialogue screen will display. Click the *Insert Field or Group* button. Select **YTD_Vacation_Time_Balance** from the **Main** data source as shown in **Illustration 147** at left.

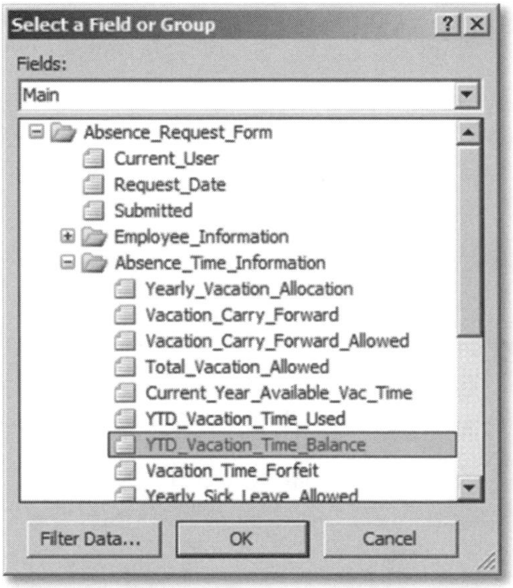

Illustration 147 - Select a Field or Group selection for field calculation

Click **OK**. Directly after *YTD_Vacation_Time_Balance* enter a **minus (-) sign.** Click the **Insert Field or Group** button again. Select the **Vacation_Carry_Forward_Allowed** field and click **OK**. The *Insert Formula* dialogue screen should look like **Illustration 148** below.

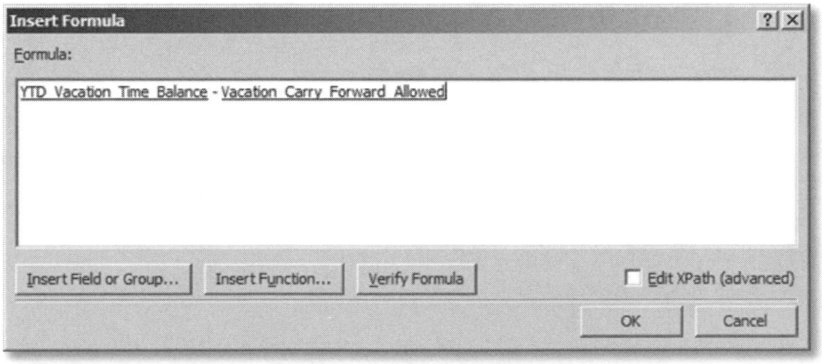

Illustration 148 - Formula for Vacation_Time_Forfeit value

Click **OK** on the *Insert Formula* dialogue screen and the *Properties* screen. Let's test the formula by previewing the form. From the *Home* tab on the *Ribbon* click the **Preview** button. The *Vacation_Time_Forfeit* control now displays the calculated value as shown in **Illustration 149** below.

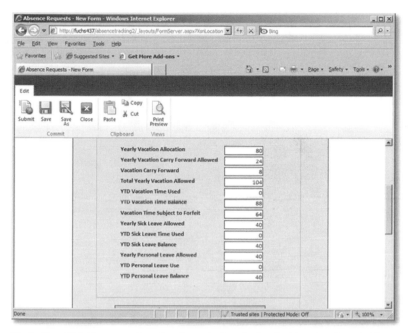

Illustration 149 - Form preview showing calculated value for Vacation Time Subject to Forfeit

This formula works properly when the *YTD_Vacation_Time_Balance* value is greater than or equal to the *Vacation_Carry_Forward_Allowed* value. When the *YTD_Vacation_Time_Balance* value is less than the *Vacation Carry Forward_Allowed* value the formula that we just created would result in a negative number displaying in the *Vacation_Time_Forfeit* control. The value that should be displayed in this situation is "0".

Using a Rule to Correct the Generation of an Incorrect Value

To accomplish this we will create a rule with an action that sets the value of *Vacation_Time_Forfeit* to "0" if the *YTD_Vacation_Time_Balance* value is less than or equal to the *Vacation_Carry_Forward_Allowed* value.

With the *Vacation_Time_Forfeit* field or control selected click on the **Manage Rules** button on the *Ribbon*. Click the **New** rule button and select **Action**. Name the rule "Negative Vacation Time Forfeit Adjustment". Click on **Condition: None** and create the following condition statement as shown in **Illustration 150** below.

Illustration 150 - Condition statement for 0 or negative number YTD_Vacation_Time_Balance

Click **OK** then **Add** the action **Set a field's value**. From the *Main* data source select the *Vacation_Time_Forfeit* field. Enter "0" for the *Value*. The *Rule Details* dialogue screen will look like **Illustration 151** below.

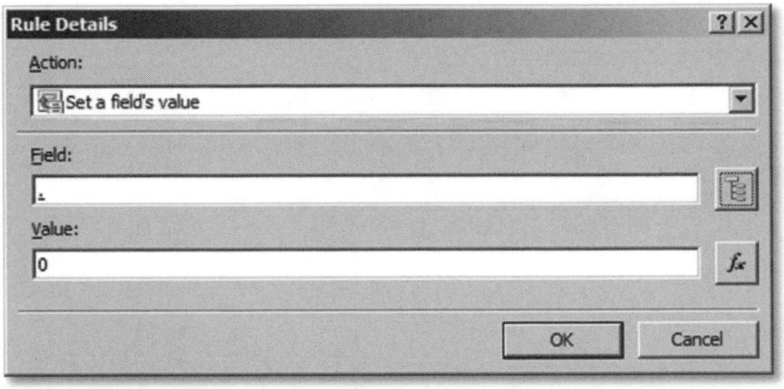

Illustration 151 – Rule action to set the field value to 0

The completed rule will look like **Illustration 152** below.

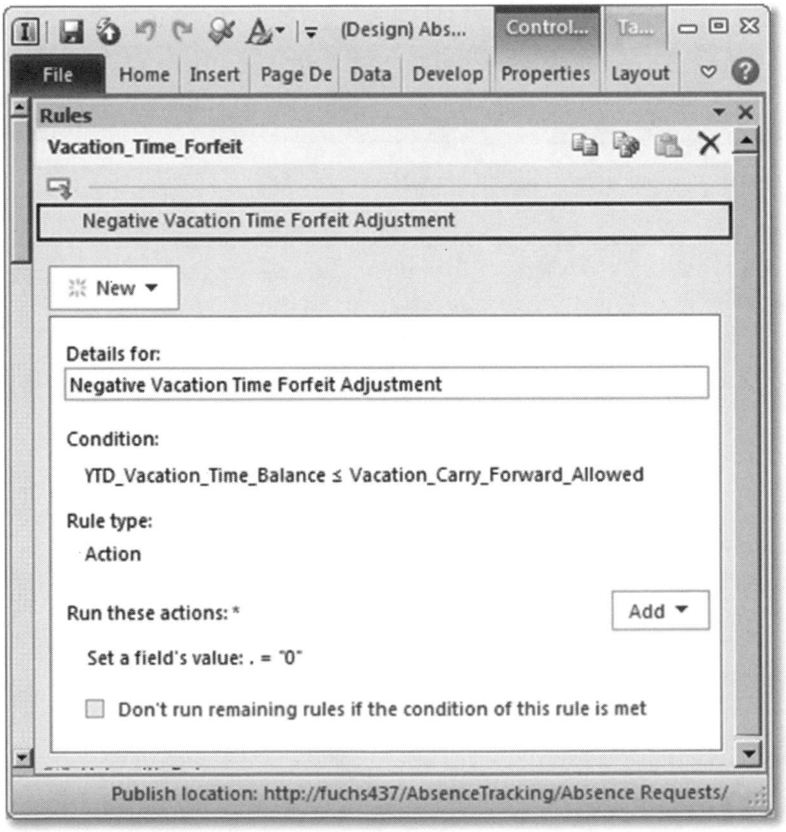

Illustration 152 – Completed Negative Vacation Time Forfeit Adjustment rule

Creating a Repeating Table for the Vacation_Requests Group and Fields

Let's continue building out the form by laying out the controls for the *Transaction_Information* groups and fields. Place your cursor on the design surface a half inch below the table for the *Employee Information* controls. Insert a table with a single row and column.

Expand the table so that it is approximately 4 inches wide and two inches high. Open the **Table Properties** dialogue screen and on the **Cell** tab set the **Cell padding** for the *Top, Bottom, Left* and *Right* inside margins to 10 points. Click **OK**.

Select the **Vacation_Requests** repeating group in the *Transaction_Information* group. Drag it to the table you just inserted. Select the **Repeating Table** option.

InfoPath will automatically insert a repeating table containing field controls for the *Vacation_Request_Dates* and *Vacation_Request_Time* fields as well as column headings. Note that for the *Vacation_Request_Dates* field there are two controls as shown in **Illustration 153** below.

The first is a date-picker control and the second is a text box that displays the time. This is because when we defined the field in the schema we set its *Data type* as *Date and Time*. We are not going to display the time in the form so we are going to delete this control. However, the field was deliberately defined as a *Date and time Data type* for a reason and we will explain why shortly.

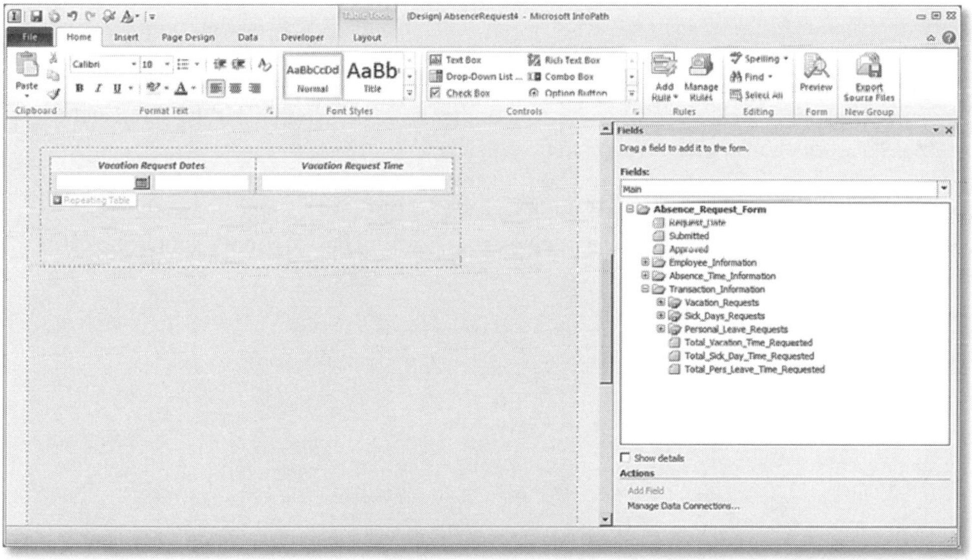

Illustration 153 - Repeating table for Vacation_Requests group showing date and time fields

Select the **Time** control for *Vacation_Request_Dates*, right click and choose **Cut**. Delete the words "Vacation Request" over the data picker control and replace "Vacation Request Time" with "Hour Value" over the *Time Text Box*.

Select the **data picker** control. Grab the right border and elongate it so that it fits the cell. Grab the right side of the table and drag it to the left so that the *Vacation_Request_Time* field is approximately one inch wide.

Illustration 154 - Borders and Shading dialogue screen

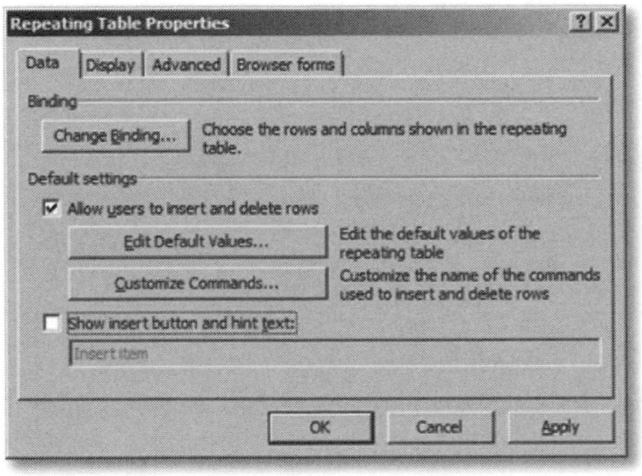

Illustration 155 - Repeating Table Properties dialogue screen

Select the row containing the column labels. Right click and choose **Borders and Shading.** Click on the **Shading** tab, the following screen as shown in **Illustration 154** at left will appear:

Select the **No color** radio button and click **OK**. With the titles row selected right click and choose **Insert>Rows Above.** The new row will be selected. Right click and choose **Merge Cells**. Place your cursor in the row and press the **delete key** to remove the extra vertical space. Type "Vacation Days Requested" in the row.

Select both title rows. Click on the **Home** tab. Select the **Quick Styles** drop-down arrow. Choose the **Normal** style and then click **B** (for Bold) on the Ribbon section for **Format Text.**

Select the **Repeating Table**. Right click and choose **Repeating Table Properties**. The dialogue screen shown in **Illustration 155** at left will display.

De-select the **Show insert button and hint text check box**. Click **OK**. Place your cursor directly below the repeating table. Insert a row with two columns. Drag the right border to the left so that it is the same width as the repeating table. Place your cursor in the right column cell.

Select the **Total_Vacation_Time_Requested** field in the *Main* data source. Right click and choose **Text Box**. In the column cell to the left type "Total Vacation Time Requested". The form design surface should look like **Illustration 156** below.

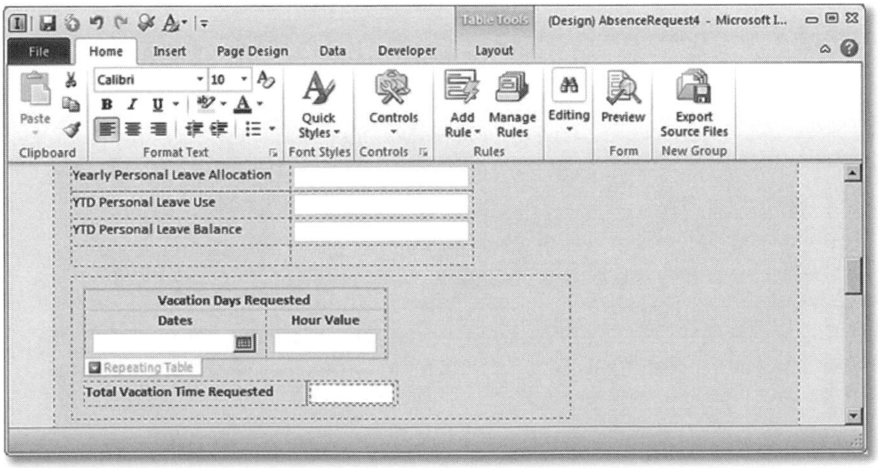

Illustration 156 - Layout of section and controls for the Vacation_Requests group fields

Description of the Rule Logic for Vacation Requests

Our next steps are to compose six rules; two validation rules that will constrain the dates that can be picked with the date picker control, and four action rules that will provide the logic for generating or removing a value in hours in the *Vacation_Request_Time* text box for each vacation day picked. These rules can be seen in **Illustration 157** below.

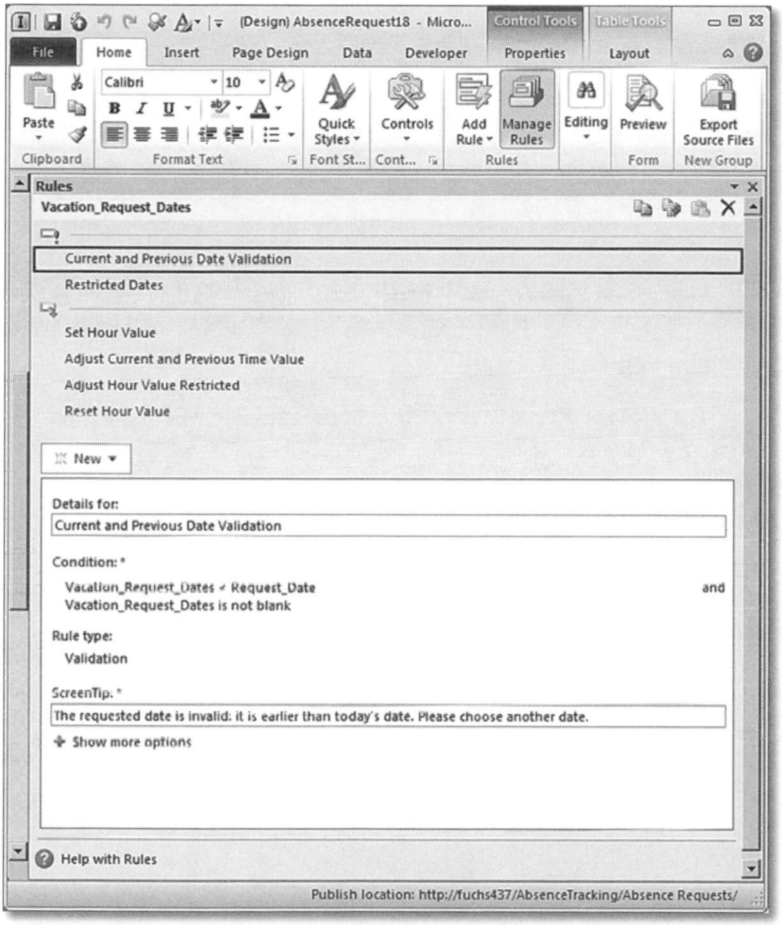

Illustration 157 - Rule set for the operational policy logic applied to vacation requests

These rules enforce the operational policies required to ensure the orderly running of a business or organizational entity as it relates to employee absence management.

In the first rule, *Current and Previous Date Validation*, we will create logic that prevents a user from requesting vacation time off for days prior to the current date. In many organizations a vacation day is considered planned time away and operational policy requires that it be requested ahead of time, so that it can be managed. A vacation request may also require approval from management depending upon the number of days requested and other criteria. Taking vacation time and retroactively documenting it circumvents the ability to manage this benefit. This rule will not be applied to sick leave, as sick leave occurrences are not planned and an employee must be able to subsequently document the time away.

The second rule, *Restricted Dates*, is also a validation rule and it prevents a user from requesting vacation time for days that have been identified as restricted or reserved dates. In any operational group of an organization there are typically periods where an intense effort is required. In finance and sales the weeks before the end of a fiscal quarter, and certainly before the end of the year are crush times and taking time off during those periods is discouraged if not actually prohibited. Special events are also typically scheduled in advance so that people will plan around them. This rule will check requested vacation dates against a list of restricted and reserved dates in real-time and not allow the conflicting choice to be made. The secondary data source that we will create for this will be a custom *SharePoint* list.

The third rule is an action rule that sets a value of "8" (representing hours) to the *Vacation_Request_Time* field in the repeating table for each vacation date picked. For the purposes of calculating the amount of time away a leave day is converted into an hour equivalent representation. This rule provides this mechanism. The sum of the values of all the *Vacation_Request_Time* instances will be written to the *Total_Vacation_Time_Requested* field and used in subsequent processing steps.

The fourth and fifth rules reverse the third rule and set the value of a *Vacation_Request_Time Text Box* to "0" if the user picks an invalid date or changes a valid date to an invalid one (i.e. a date prior to the current date or a restricted date).

The sixth rule is required to reset the value of *Vacation_Request_Time* to "8" in the situation where the user picks an invalid date and then changes it to a valid one.

Creating the Restricted and Reserved Dates List

This list will have four columns: *Restricted Dates Description, Dates, Organization Code and Organization Name*. Open *SharePoint Designer* and connect to the *Absence Tracking* site. Click on **Lists and Libraries** in the **Navigation** pane. Click the **Custom List** button on the *Lists and Libraries* tab. In the *Create list or document library* dialogue screen enter "Restricted and Reserved Dates" for the name of the list and click **OK** as shown in **Illustration 158** below.

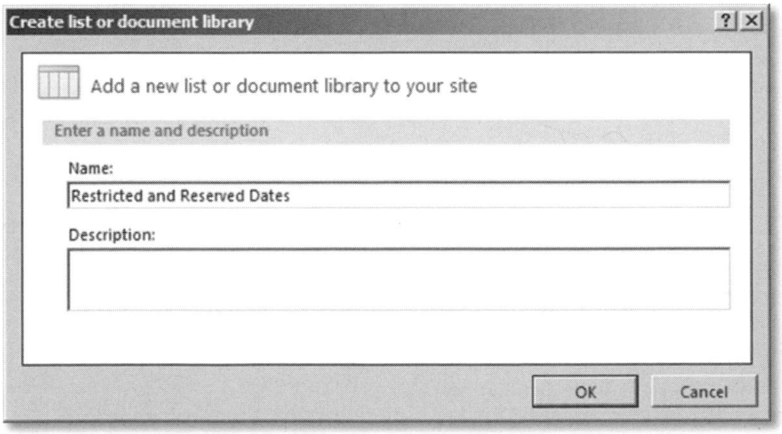

Illustration 158 - SharePoint Designer Create list or document library dialogue screen

The *Restricted and Reserved Dates* list will display in the main section. Click on it to display the *Summary Page* for the list as shown in **Illustration 159** below.

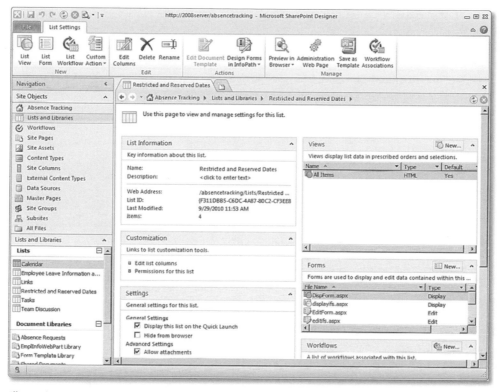

Illustration 159 - Summary page for new Restricted and Reserved Dates list

Click **Edit Columns** on the *Ribbon*. The *List Editor* will appear. Right click on the default **Title** column and choose **Rename**. Change the name to "Restricted Dates Description". Right click again and choose **Column Settings**. Change the **Maximum number of characters allowed** to 100.

Click the **Add New Column button** on the *Ribbon*. Select **Date & Time** from the drop-down selection list. Name the new column "Dates". Right click on the **Dates** column and choose **Column Settings**. The *Column Editor* will display as shown in **Illustration 160** at left.

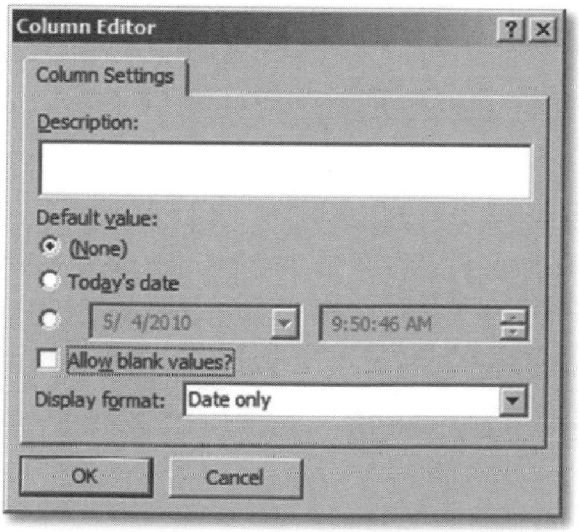

Illustration 160 - SharePoint Designer list Column Editor

For the *Default value* choose the **(None)** radio button. De-select the **Allow blank values** check box. In the *Display format* drop-down list select **Date only**. Click **OK**. Set the Required attribute for the *Dates* column to **Yes**.

Add the "Organization Code" column; set its Data type to **Single line of text,** set the **maximum number of characters** to 20 and make it **Required**.

Add the "Organization Name: column; set its Data type to **Single line of text**, set the **maximum number of characters** to 100 and set it as **Required**. Click **Save** from the File menu.

Now let's go to this list in *SharePoint* and add some items. Create four items with the following values for *Restricted Dates Description*, *Dates*, *Organization Code* and *Organization Name* respectively:

End of Year Financial Statement Closing	6/23/2011	101	EPG Sales
End of Year Financial Statement Closing	6/24/2011	101	EPG Sales
Risk and Compliance Conference	7/14/2011	102	ISU
Risk and Compliance Conference	7/14/2011	102	ISU

The *Restricted and Reserved Dates* list should like **Illustration 161** below.

Illustration 161 - Restricted and Reserved Dates list in SharePoint

> **Important Note** — *SharePoint* supports a *Date and Time Data type* format **only**, not *Date* by itself. You can set the option of not displaying the *Time* information in a column but it is still stored in the list. We will be accessing this information as a secondary data source in *InfoPath* and the time information will be present in the value for this field. In order to compare the values of date fields in the *InfoPath Main* data source with dates in *the Restricted and Reserved Dates* list (which we will do shortly) **we need to use the same** *Date and Time* format for the date fields in **both** places. *InfoPath* allows hiding the *Time* information in a control as well.

Let's go back to our *InfoPath* form and add this list as a secondary data source.

Adding the Restricted and Reserved Dates List as a Secondary Data Source to the Absence Request Form

Click on the **Data** tab and the **Data Connections** Ribbon button. Click the **Add** button in the *Data Connections* dialogue screen. Keep the selection for the **Receive data** radio button on the first *Data Connection Wizard* screen. Click Next. Select **SharePoint library or list** as the source of the data. Click **Next.** Enter the URL address of the *Absence Tracking* site containing the *Restricted and Reserved Dates* list as shown in **Illustration 162** below.

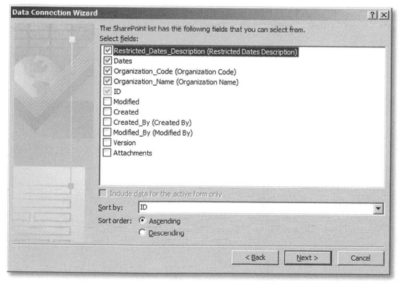

Illustration 162 – The first screen of the Data Connection Wizard

Click **Next**. Select the **Restricted and Reserved Dates** list from the list of libraries and lists. Click **Next**. Select the **Restricted_Dates_Description, Dates, Organization_Code and Organization_ Name** fields as shown in **Illustration 163** below. Click **Next**.

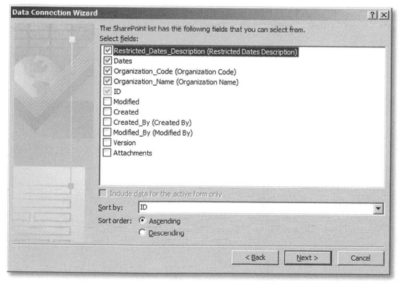

Illustration 163 – The third screen of the Data Connection Wizard

Important – In the next screen of the *Data Connection Wizard* you must check **Store a copy of the data in the form template** as shown in **Illustration 164** below.

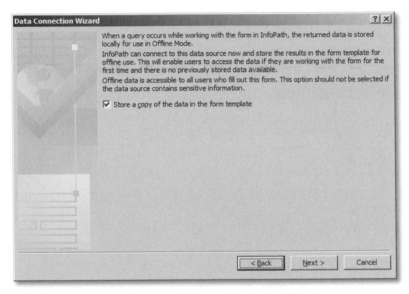

Illustration 164 - The fourth screen of the Data Connection Wizard

Click **Next**. In the last *Data Connection Wizard* screen check the **Automatically retrieve data when form is opened check box.**

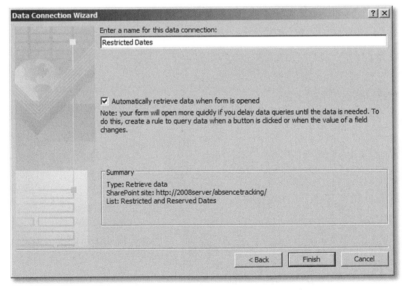

Illustration 165 - The last screen of the Data Connection Wizard

Click the **Finish** button to conclude the steps of adding the new *Data Connection*.

Using an InfoPath Function to Set the Request_Date to the Current Date

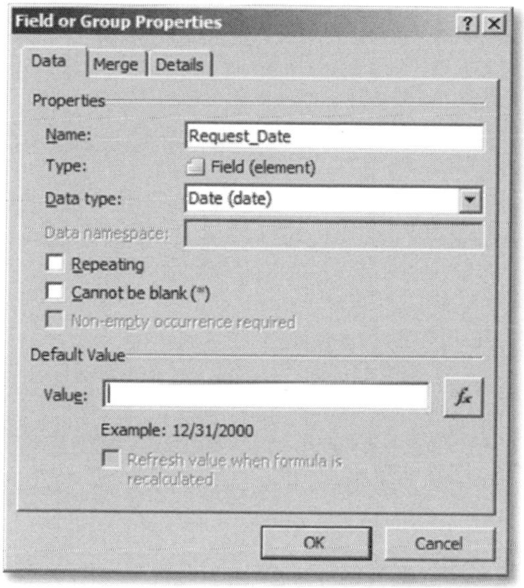

There is one more thing that we have to do before we can create the rule set for *Vacation_Request_Dates*. Right click on the **Request_Date** field in the *Main* data source and choose **Properties**. The *Field or Group Properties* dialogue screen will appear as shown in **Illustration 166** at left.

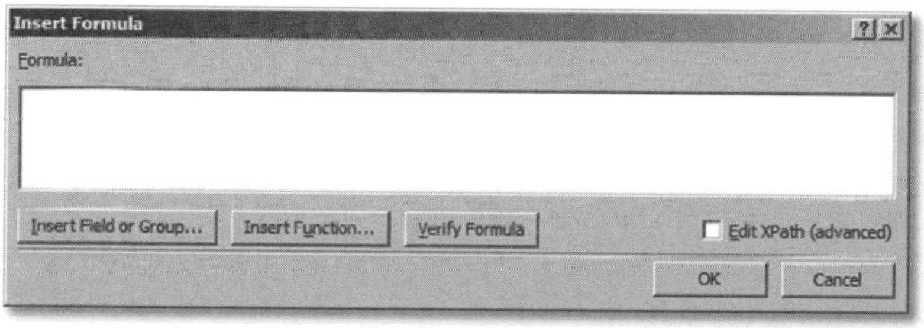

Illustration 166 - Field or Group Properties dialogue screen for the Request_Date field

Click on the **Formula** button to the right of the *Value* box. Once again, the *Insert Formula* dialogue screen will appear as shown in **Illustration 167** at left. Click the **Insert Function** button.

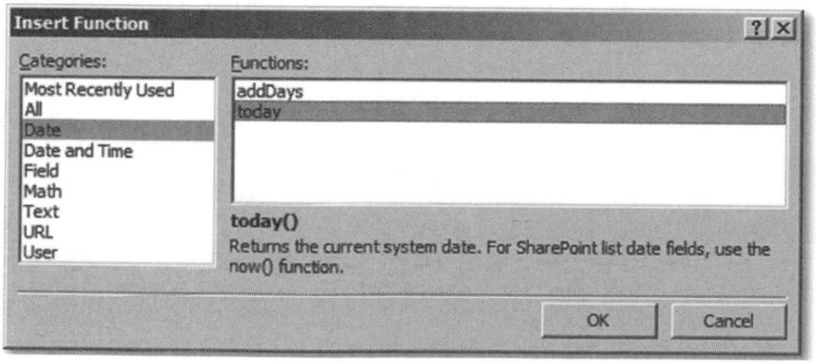

Illustration 167 - Insert Formula dialogue screen

In the *Categories* box on the left side of the *Insert Function* dialogue screen select **Date**. In the *Functions* box select **today**, as shown in **Illustration 168** at left. Click **OK.**

Illustration 168 - Insert Function dialogue screen with Date functions displayed

Click **OK** back through all the open dialogue screens. The *today* function, which returns the current system date and time, will now be the default value of the *Request_ Date* field as shown in **Illustration 169** below.

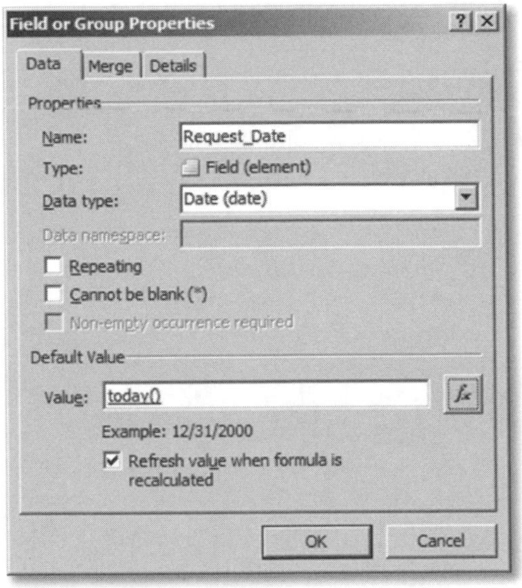

Illustration 169 - Properties dialogue screen for Request_Date field with today() function as the default value

> **Special Note** — the value that is set for a field through a formula or rule can be accessed by other formulas and rules **without being displayed in a control**, which we will do now in building the rule set for *Vacation_Request_Dates*.

Creating the Current and Previous Date Validation Rule for Vacation Request Dates

Select the schema **field** or **date picker** control for *Vacation_Request_Dates*, right click and choose **Rules**. Click the **Add** button and select **Validation**. Name the rule "Current and Previous Date Validation".

Click on **None** under *Condition* and the *Condition* dialogue screen will display. Leave the *Vacation_Request_Dates* value in the first drop-down list. In the second drop- down list select the **is less than or equal to** statement. In the third drop-down click on **Select a field or group** and from the *Main* data source choose the **Request_Date** field. The completed *Condition* will look like **Illustration 170** below.

Illustration 170 – the first Condition statement for the Current and Previous Date Validation rule

Now add a second condition statement that is joined to the first by an **and** operator as shown in **Illustration 171** below.

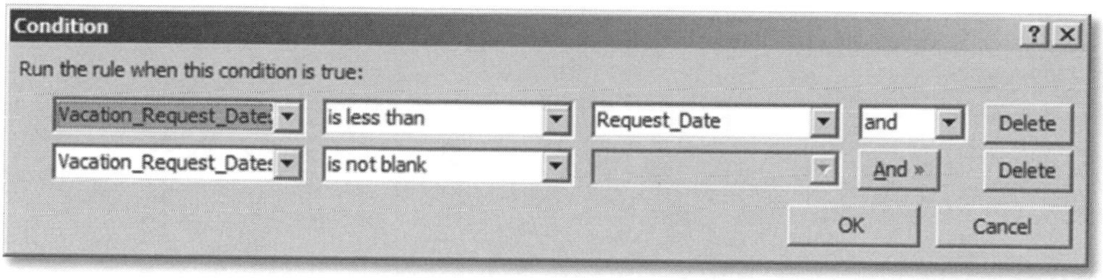

Illustration 171 - the second Condition statement for the Current and Previous Date Validation rule

> **Important Note** – The reason for this second condition statement is to prevent the situation of no date selected (i.e. blank) being evaluated by the first condition as false and preventing the form from being submitted.

This rule will constrain a user from picking a *Vacation_Request_Date* that is earlier than the *Request_Date*. Let's see what the form behavior for this rule will be like. Click on the **Preview button** on the *Home* tab of the *Ribbon*. In the **date picker** choose a date any time in the future as displayed below in **Illustration 172**.

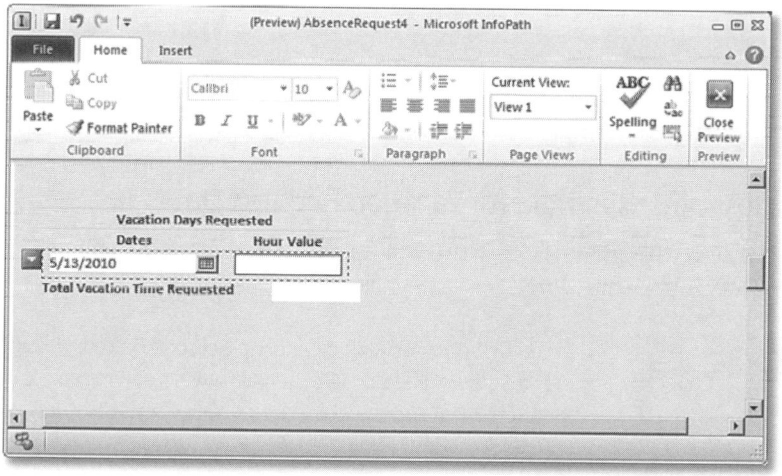

Illustration 172 - Preview of the form displaying Vacation_Requests controls

Now select the **repeating item insertion** icon to the left of the date picker. A drop-down menu will appear. Select **Insert Vacation_Requests after**. An additional table row will display. In the second date picker control enter any date in the past.

You will see a red dotted line around the control, as shown in **Illustration 173** below, which is the *InfoPath* convention for indicating a validation error. When the user hovers their cursor over the control they will also see a screen tip message which we will add now. The form will not be able to be submitted until the validation error is corrected.

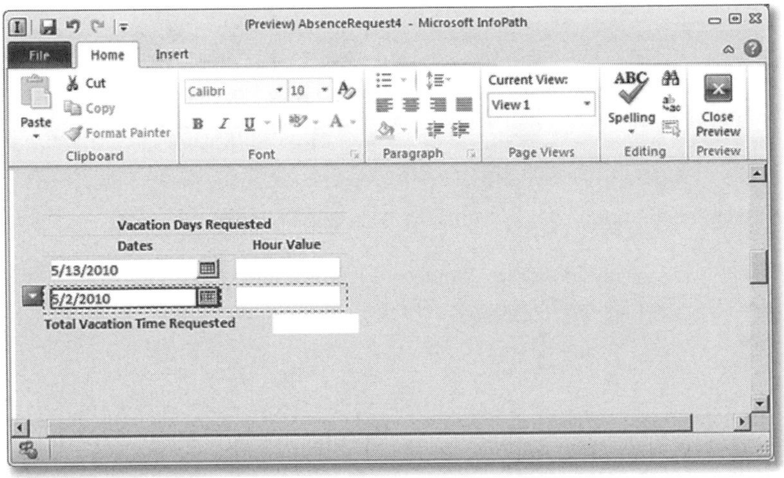

Illustration 173 - Preview of the form demonstrating the behavior of the Current and Previous Date Validation rule

Close the form preview. For the *Vacation_Request_Date* rule *ScreenTip* enter "Requested date is invalid: it is the same as or earlier than today's date. Please choose another date." This completes the first rule.

Creating the Restricted Dates Validation Rule for Vacation Request Dates

Click the **New** rule button again and choose **Validation**. Name this rule "Restricted Dates". Click **None** under **Conditions** to display the Conditions dialogue screen.

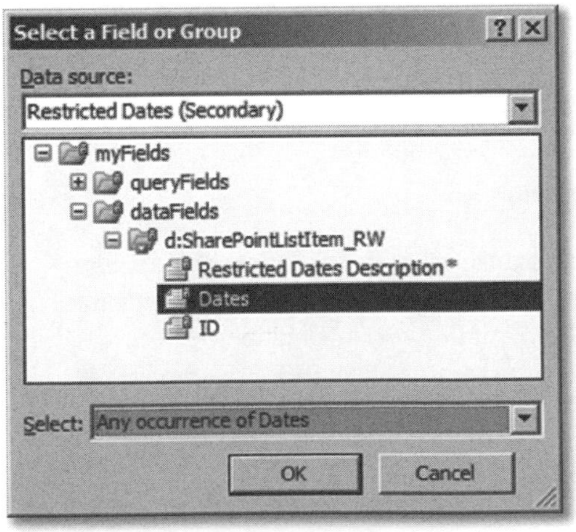

Illustration 174 - Select a Field or Group for the Restricted Dates secondary data source

In the first drop-down box choose **Select a field or group**. In the **Select a Field or Group** dialogue screen choose the **Restricted Dates** secondary data source from the **Data source** drop-down box.

Expand the *dataFields* group and the embedded *SharePointListItem_RW* group. Choose the **Dates** field. In the **Select** drop-down box on the bottom choose **Any occurrence of Dates**. The dialogue screen should look like **Illustration 174** at left.

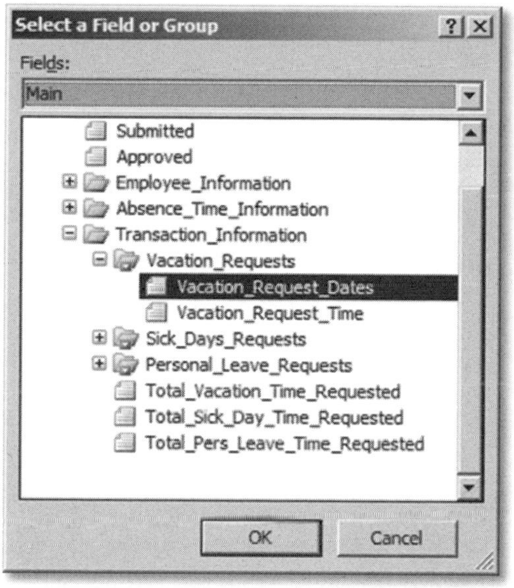

Illustration 175 - Select a Field or Group for the Main
data source for Vacation_Request_Dates field

Click **OK**. Leave the **is equal to** statement in the second
drop-down box. In the third drop-down box choose
Select a field or group. In the **Select a Field or Group**
dialogue screen choose the **Main** data source and select
the *Vacation_Request_Dates* field as shown in **Illustration
175** at left.

Click **OK**. The *Condition* dialogue screen will look like **Illustration 176** below.

Illustration 176 - Condition statement for the Restricted and Reserved Dates rule

Click **OK**. For the *ScreenTip* for this rule enter "This is a restricted date that cannot be taken off".
We have now completed the second validation rule.

> **Special Note** — the syntax of the condition statement that we just constructed for the *Restricted Dates*
> rule is different from all of the other conditions we have created. In a typical condition expression the
> target field (i.e. the field that will store a value) is selected in the first drop-down box and a conditional
> statement is applied to it, or a comparison is made to a source value. In this case we did the opposite.
> We specified the values from a source in the first drop-down box and made a comparison to the
> target value in the third drop-down box. The reason for this is that in this condition we need to check
> the target value against multiple source values. We need to iterate through all of the rows in the
> *Restricted and Reserved Dates* list and compare them to the date picked in the form. InfoPath provides
> a very nice facility for doing just this, as well as the variations of *All occurrences of Dates*, and *Number
> of occurrences of Dates*. Consequently, the syntax for an iterative value comparison requires that the
> source with multiple values be specified first.

Let's test this rule. Click the **Preview button** on the *Ribbon* to open a preview of the form. Use the **date picker** to pick one of the restricted dates in the *SharePoint Restricted and Reserved Dates* list. As shown in **Illustration 177** below the date picker control is now surrounded by a red dotted-line, indicating a validation error. Place the cursor over the **date picker** and the screen tip will appear.

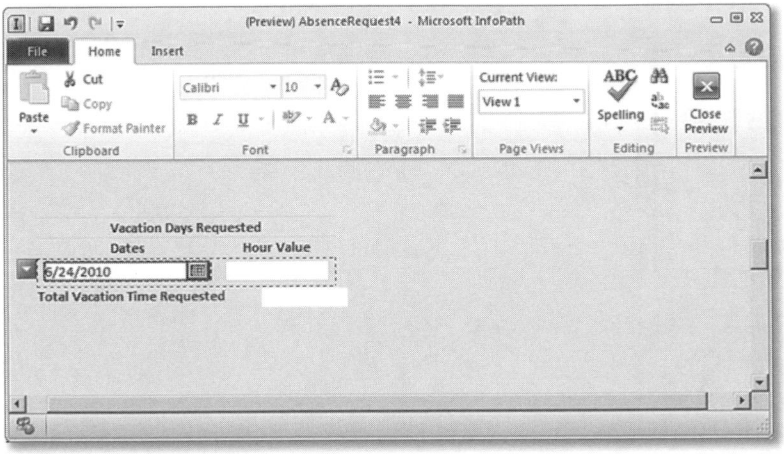

Illustration 177 - Preview of the form showing behavior of Restricted and Reserved Dates validation rule

> **Important Development Note** – this ability of *InfoPath* to execute an ***iterative rule evaluation on multiple values*** enables the deployment of sophisticated business logic that can be implemented for numerous use cases.

Creating the Set Hour Value Rule to Generate an Hour Value Equivalent for Each Vacation Date Requested

The third rule we will create is *Set Hour Value*. This *Action* rule sets a value of "8" (for hours) to each itemization of the *Vacation_Request_Time* fields and displays it in the *Text Box* control of the repeating table. Click the **New** rule button and choose **Action**. Name this rule "Set Hour Value". Click **None** under **Conditions** to display the *Condition* dialogue screen. Create the rule condition statement shown in **Illustration 178** below.

Illustration 178 - Condition statement for the Set Hour Value rule

This rule condition requires that a vacation date be later than the current date set in the *Request_Date* field in order for the *Vacation_Request_Time* field to be set with the value of "8".

Click the **Add** action button and select **Set a field's value**. The *Rule Details* dialogue screen will appear. For the *Field* value select the **Vacation_Request_Time** field in the *Vacation_Requests* group. In the *Value* box enter "8". The *Rule Details* dialogue screen will look like **Illustration 179** below.

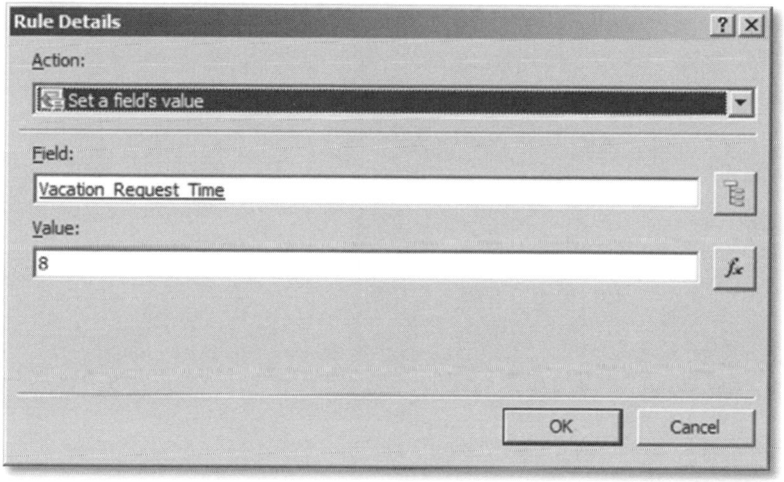

Illustration 179 - Setting the value of the Vacation Request Time field with a value of 8

Click **OK.** This completes rule three.

Creating the Adjust Current and Previous Time Value Rule for Invalid Date Requests

The fourth and fifth rules reverse the third rule and set the value of a *Vacation_Request_Time Text Box* to "0" if the user picks an invalid date or changes a valid date to an invalid one (i.e. a date prior to the *Request_Date* or a restricted/reserved date).

Click the **New** rule button and select **Action**. Name the rule "Adjust Current and Previous Time Value". Create the condition shown in **Illustration 180** below.

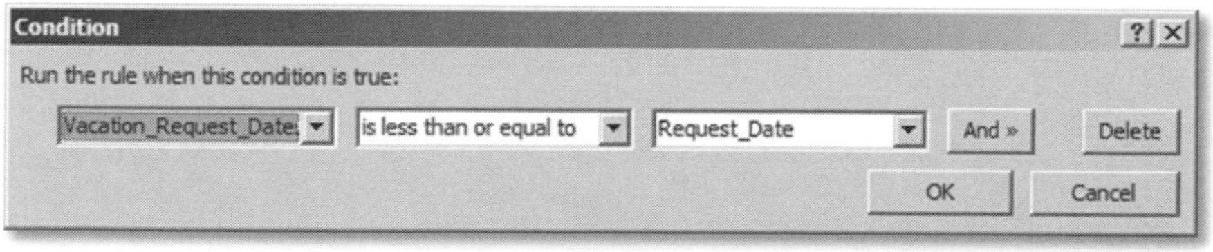

Illustration 180 - Condition statement for Adjust Current and Previous Time Value rule

Click the **Add** action button and select **Set a field's value**. The *Rule Details* dialogue screen will appear. For the *Field* value select the **Vacation_Request_Time** field in the *Vacation_Requests* group. Leave the *Value* box empty. The *Rule Details* dialogue screen will look like **Illustration 181** below.

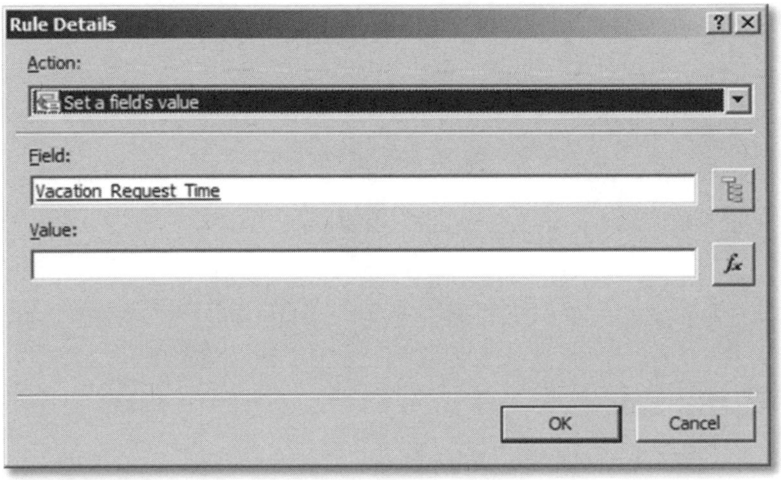

Illustration 181 - Setting the Vacation Request Time field with an empty value for an invalid date

Click **OK**. For this rule check the **Don't run remaining rules if the condition of this rule is met** checkbox as shown in **Illustration 182** below. This is required to make sure that the rule executes properly in a browser form.

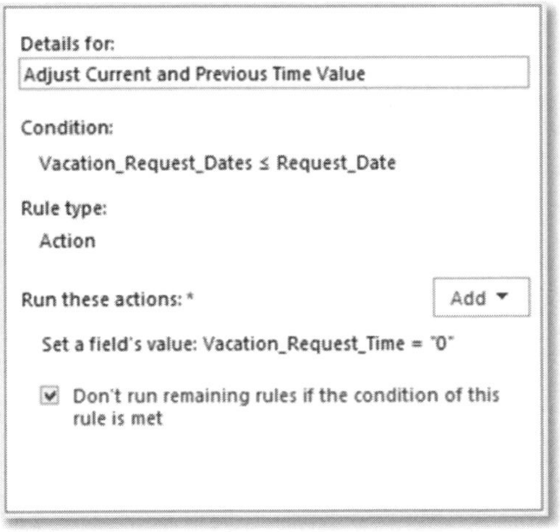

Illustration 182 - Adjust Current and Previous Time Value rule

This completes rule four.

Creating the Adjust Hour Value Restricted Rule

Again, click the **New** rule button and select **Action**. Name the rule "Adjust Hour Value Restricted". Click on **None** under Conditions to display the *Condition* dialogue screen.

In the first drop-down box choose **Select a field or group**. Pick the **Restricted Dates** secondary data source from the **Data source** drop-down box. Expand the **dataFields** and **SharePointListItem_RW** groups and select the **Dates** field.

In the *Select* box choose **Any occurrence of Dates** as shown in **Illustration 183** below.

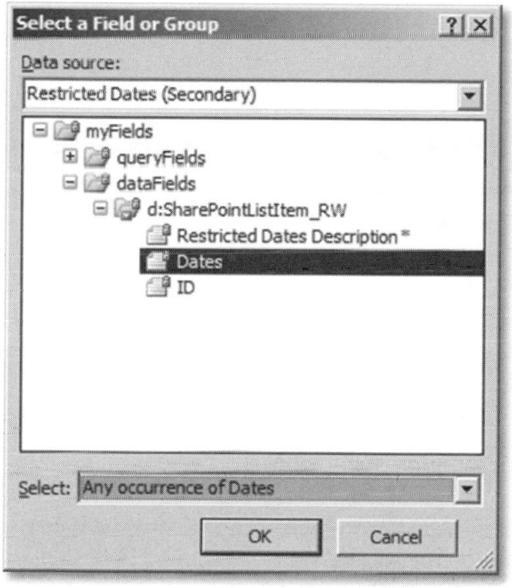

Illustration 183 - Select a Field or Group for Restricted Dates list

Click **OK**. Leave the **is equal to** statement in the second *Condition* drop-down list box. In the third drop-down list box also choose **Select a field or group** and pick the **Vacation_Request_Dates** from the *Main* data source. The *Condition* dialogue screen should look like **Illustration 184** below. Click **OK**.

Illustration 184 - Condition for Reset Hour Value rule

Click the **Add** action button and select **Set a field's value**. The **Rule Details** dialogue screen will appear. For the *Field* value select the **Vacation_Request_Time** field in the *Vacation_Requests* group. Leave the *Value* box empty. The *Rule Details* dialogue screen will look like **Illustration 185** below.

Illustration 185 - Setting the Vacation Request Time field with an empty value for a Restricted and Reserved date selection

Click **OK**. For this rule also check the **Don't run remaining rules if the condition of this rule is met checkbox**. This completes the fifth rule.

The sixth and last rule is required to reset the value of *Vacation_Request_Time* to "8" in the situation where the user picks an invalid date first and then changes it to a valid one. Name this rule "Reset Hour Value".

Leave the **None – Rule runs when field changes** condition. Click the **Add** action button and select **Set a field's value**. For the *Field* value select the **Vacation_Request_Time** field in the *Vacation_Requests* group. In the *Value* box enter "8". The *Rule Details* dialogue screen will look like **Illustration 186** below. Click **OK**.

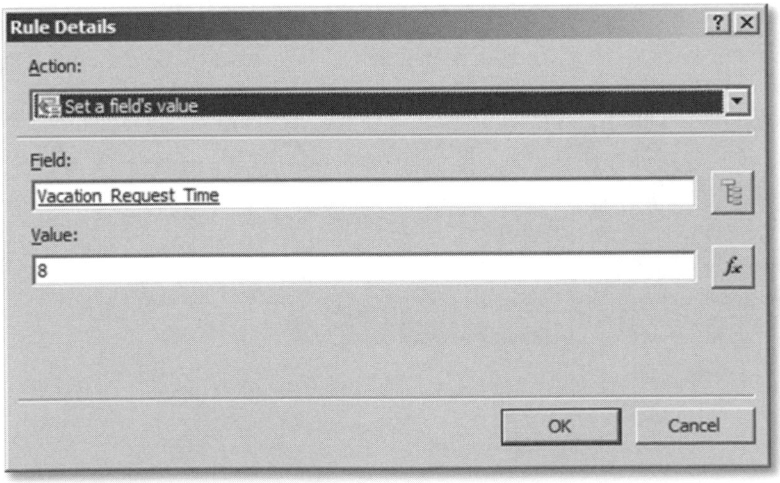

Illustration 186 - Reset value of Vacation Request Time field to 8

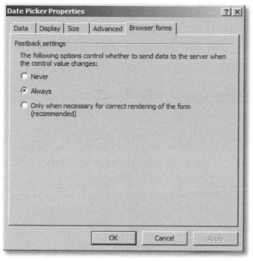

Illustration 187 – Setting the Postback settings for the Vacation_Request_Dates Date Picker control so that the Reset Hour Value rule executes properly.

Important Note – the *Reset Hour Value* rule action is not driven by a condition value; it is driven entirely by the action of changing an invalid vacation date to a valid one. For the *Reset Hour Value* rule action to work properly in a browser form the *Form Server* rule engine must be aware of the date change, even if there is no rule condition logic being triggered. To accomplish this select the **Date Picker Properties** for the *Vacation_Request_Dates date picker* and select the **Browser forms tab** as shown in **Illustration 187** at left. Select the **Always radio button** for the *Postback settings*. This will cause the *Form Server* rule engine to recognize a change in value for the date picker.

This completes rule six and the complete set of rules that implements the application logic relating to vacation date requests.

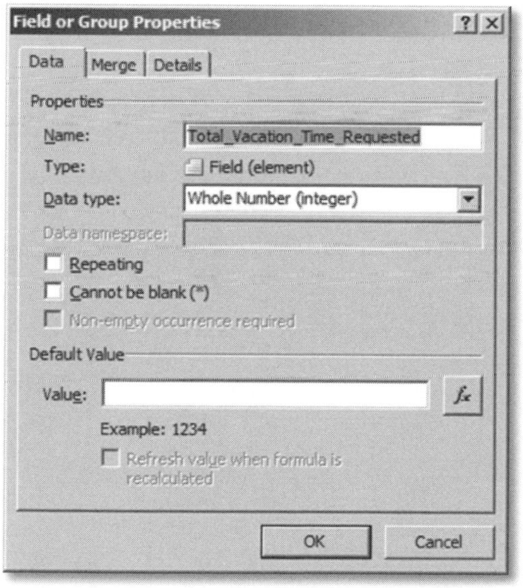

Using the Sum Function to Implement a Running Total of Repeating Item Values

Our next task is to set the value of the *Total_Vacation_Time_Requested* field so that it is the sum of all the *Vacation_Request_Time* itemizations. Right click on the **Total_Vacation_Time_Requested** field and choose **Properties** to display the *Field or Group Properties* dialogue screen as shown in **Illustration 188** at left.

Illustration 188 - Properties dialogue screen for the Total_Vacation_Time_Requested field

Click on the **Formula** button to the right of **Value** box. In the *Insert Formula* dialogue screen click the **Insert Function** button. In the **Insert Function** dialogue screen select **Math** in the *Categories* box on the left and select **sum** in the *Functions* box on the right. Click **OK**. The *Insert Formula* dialogue screen will look like **Illustration 189** below.

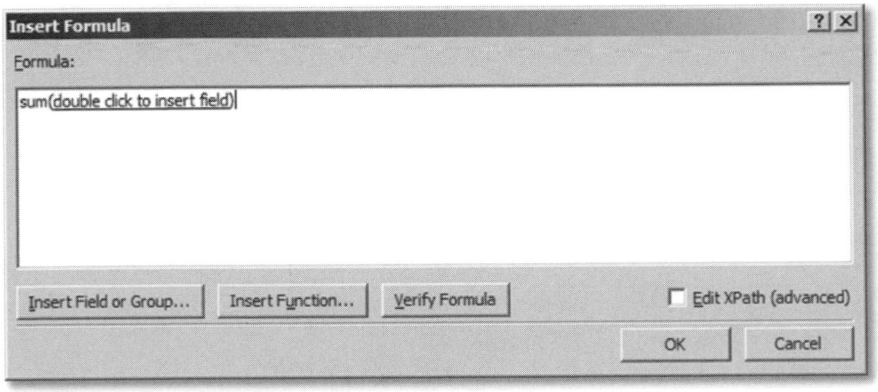

Illustration 189 - Insert Formula dialogue screen displaying sum function

Double click on the **(double click to insert field)** formula clause. The *Select a Field or Group* dialogue screen will display. Select the **Vacation_Request_Time** field as shown in **Illustration 190** below.

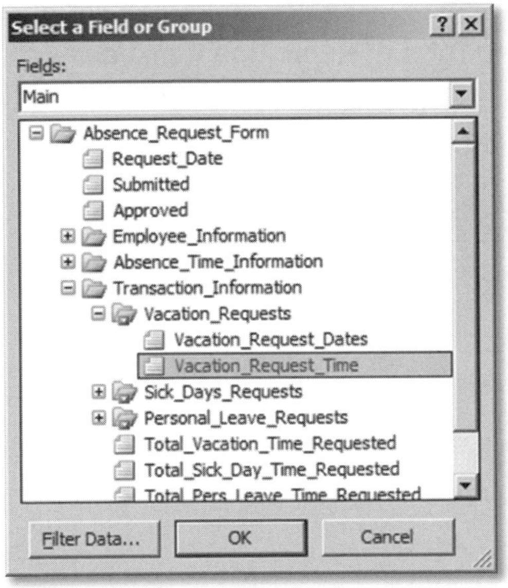

Illustration 190 - Select a Field or Group for
Vacation_Request_Time field

Click **OK**. The *Insert Formula* dialogue screen will look like **Illustration 191** below.

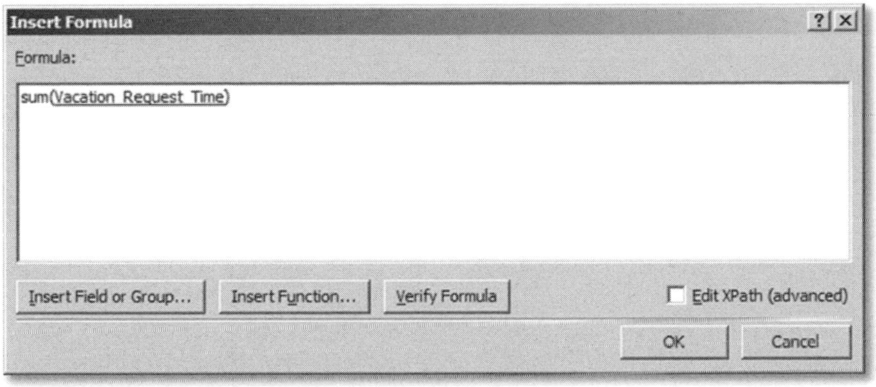

Illustration 191 - The sum function applied to the Vacation_Request_Time field to generate a running total for the Total_Vacation_Time_Requested field

Click **OK**. The *Field or Group Properties* dialogue screen will look like **Illustration 192** below.

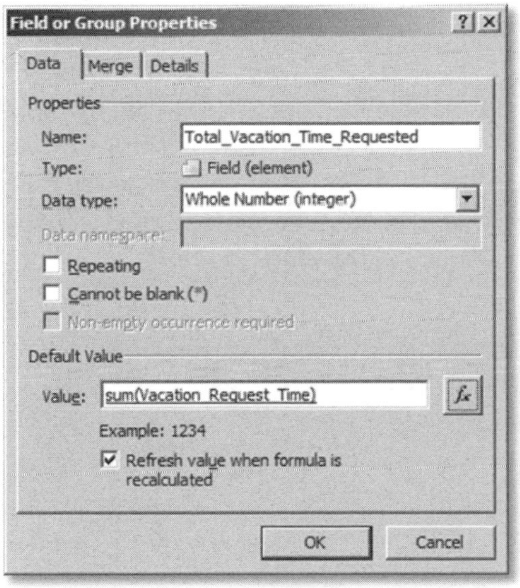

Illustration 192 - Completed formula for running total value for Total_Vacation_Time_Requested field

Click **OK** to finish. Let's test this out. Click on the **Preview** button from the *Ribbon*. The preview of the form will display. Select several vacation dates. The *Total Vacation Time Text Box* control will increment with each additional vacation date added as shown in **Illustration 193** below.

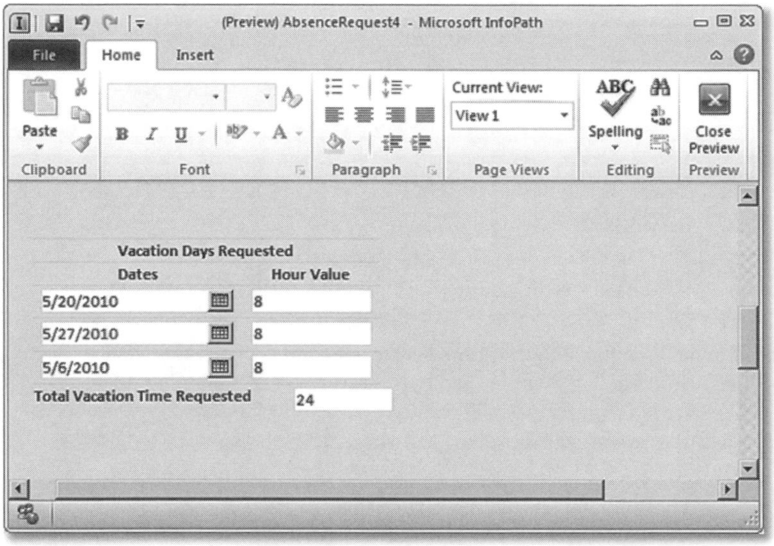

Illustration 193 - Preview of the form showing the running total for the Total_Vacation_Time_Requested field

With the addition of each vacation date the cumulative value of the *Total_Vacation_Time_Requested* field increments accordingly. Close the preview. Right click on the **Total_Vacation_Time_Requested control** and go to the *Display* tab of the *Text Box Properties* dialogue screen as shown in **Illustration 194** below.

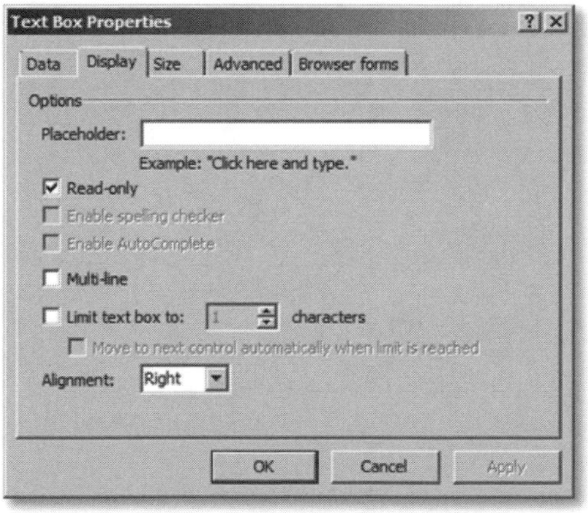

Illustration 194 - Text Box Properties Display tab for Total_Vacation_Time_Requested field

Check **the Read-only** check box. In the *Alignment* drop-down box select **Right** and click **OK**.

Using a Query Parameter to Filter Rule Criteria

Let's go back to one of our rules – the *Restricted Dates* validation rule that prevents a user from requesting a vacation day on a date that has been specified as restricted or reserved in a *SharePoint* list. The only criterion that identifies a date as being restricted or reserved is the date's presence in the list. Suppose we wanted to use additional criteria to specify a restricted date and at the same time have restricted dates made applicable to different situations. For example, certain dates may be restricted to only certain organizational groups – sales and finance are affected by quarterly and year-end financial closing dates, but not customer service. We are going to implement this expanded criteria business logic now.

> **Development Note** – We are going to bind a rule with two actions to the *Organization_Code* field; the purpose of which is to use the value that populated the *Organization_Code* in the *Main* data source (from a lookup in the *Employee Information* secondary data source) to query the *Restricted_Dates* secondary data source in order to select those records in that list that have the same organization code. We will then use that subset of records in the *Restricted Dates* validation rule.

Click on the **Organization_Code** field or control. Click on the **Manage Rules button** on the *Ribbon* to open the *Rules* panel. Click the **New** button and choose **Action**. Name the rule "Set Organization Code query parameter". Click on **None** under **Condition** and add the following condition statement as shown in **Illustration 195** below.

Illustration 195- Condition statement for organization code query action

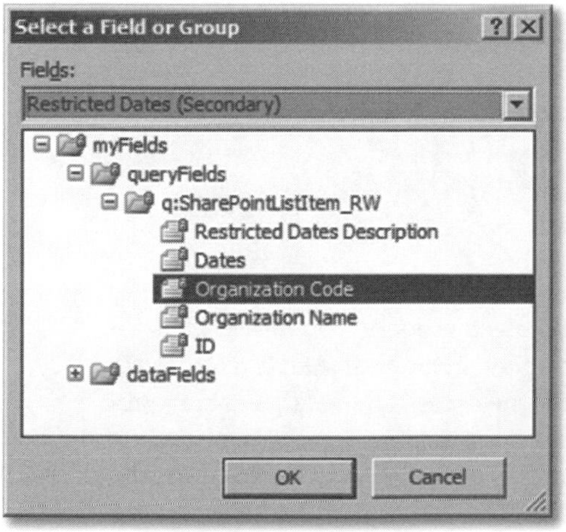

Illustration 196 - Setting the queryFields
Organization Code value

For the rule action click **Add** and choose **Set a field's value**. In the *Rule Details* dialogue screen click the **Field** button and select the **Restricted Dates** secondary data source. Expand the **queryFields** group and select the **Organization Code** field as shown in **Illustration 196** at left.

Important - make sure that you do *not* select the *Organization Code* field in the **dataFields** group

For the *Value*, click on the **Formula** button to open the *Insert Formula* dialogue screen; then click the **Insert Field or Group button**. From the **Main** data source select the **Organization_Code** field. Click **OK**. The *Rule Details* dialogue screen will look like **Illustration 197** below.

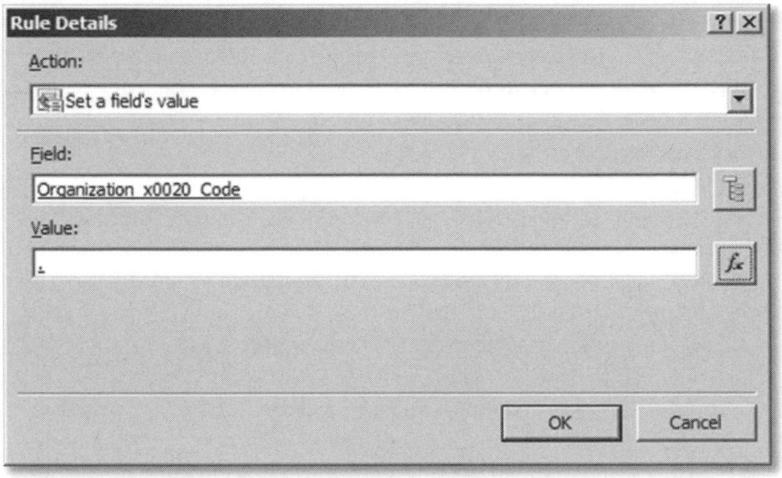

Illustration 197 - Rule Details for setting the queryFields Organization Code value

Click **OK**. Click **Add** again and choose the **Query for data action**.
Select **Restricted Dates** for the *Data connection* as shown in **Illustration 198** below.

Illustration 198 - Query on Reserved and Restricted Dates list filtered by Organization Code

Click **OK**. Now let's preview the form to see what the effect of this selective query is on the *Restricted Dates* rule logic. Previously, if we selected any of the four dates itemized in the *Restricted and Reserved Dates* list using the *Vacation_Request_Dates* date picker control the form would throw a validation error. Now, it only throws a validation error for the two dates where the corresponding *Organization Code* in the list is the same as the value (101) that is displayed in the *Organization Code Text Box* control in the form.

In this way you can build complex rule logic that can selectively use information from multiple data sources. Alternatively you can use a single list with multiple fields all of which can be used as the criteria to drive logic in a form.

Using a Formatting Rule to Hide Controls

We are going to add one more business logic rule for vacation day requests. We don't want users to be able to request vacation time if they have already consumed the maximum amount of time that is allocated to them. This rule will check if the value for the *YTD_Vacation_Time_Used* field is equal to the value of the *Total_Vacation_Allocation* plus the *Vacation_Carry_Forward* field. If it evaluates to true than the *Vacation_Requests* repeating table control will be hidden so that the user cannot request any additional vacation days.

Select the **Vacation_Requests Repeating Table** control in the form. Right click and select **Rules** and **Manage Rules** to open the *Rules* panel. Click the **New** rule button and select **Formatting**. Name the rule "Maxxed out vacation days". Click on **None** under **Condition** and create the following condition statement as shown in **Illustration 199** below.

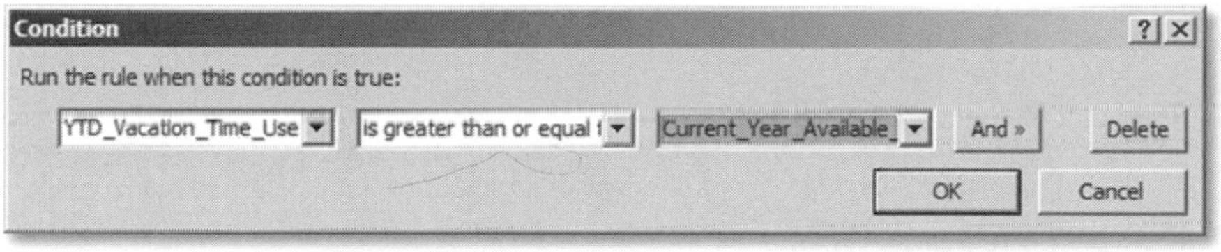

Illustration 199 - Condition to hide the Vacation_Request_Dates date picker control when vacation time is maxxed out

Click **OK** and select the **Hide this control** check box under *Formatting*.

To test this rule go to the *Employee Information* ECT list in the *SharePoint Absence Tracking* site. Select the record you created for yourself and edit the item so that the value for *YTD_Vac_Time_Used* is "88". Click the **Save** button.

Click the **Preview** button for the form. Now, although the repeating table labels are present the controls are hidden and cannot be accessed because the *YTD_Vacation_Time_Used* value is equal to or greater than the *Current_Year_Avail_Vac_Time* value as shown in **Illustration 200** below.

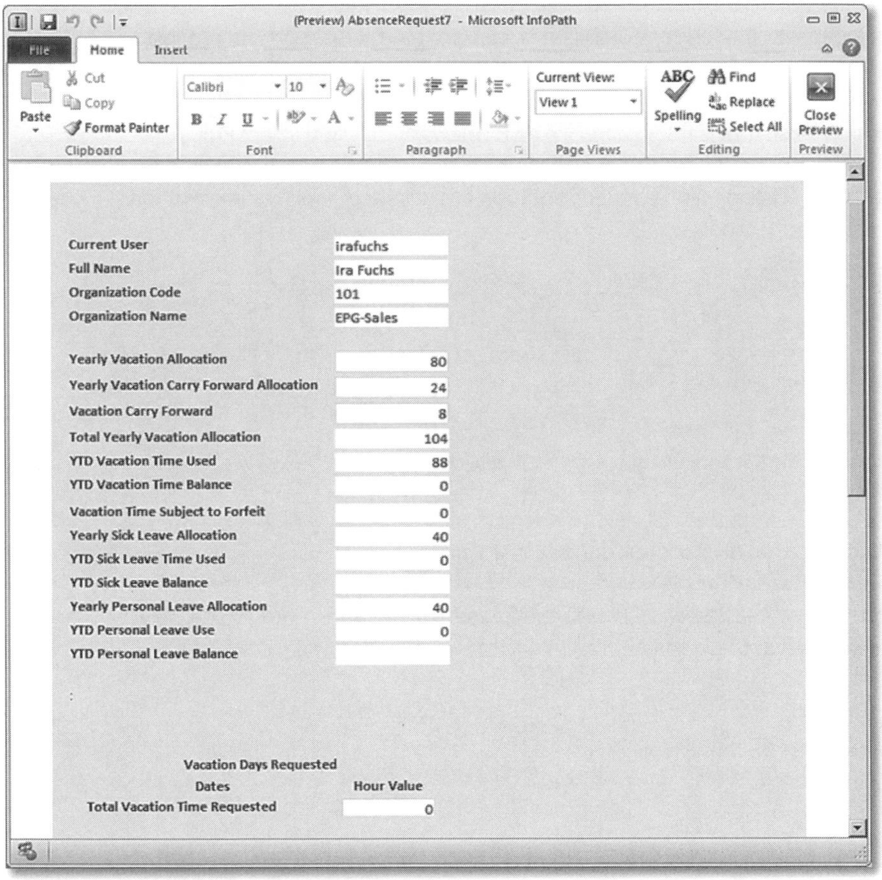

Illustration 200 - Preview of form when vacation time consumed is equal to or greater than the vacation time available

> **Note** –This rule could also be added to the Form Load rule set.

Go back to the *Employee Information* ECT list. Select the record you created for yourself and edit the record so that the value for *YTD_Vac_Time_Used* is less than "88". Click the **Save** button.

Copying Controls and Rules for Re-Use in the Form

We have completed creating the business logic, configuring the properties, and laying out the fields and controls for the *Vacation_Requests* section. Our next tasks are to do the same things for the *Sick_Days_Requests* and *Personal_Leave_Requests* sections. The layout and configuration steps for these sections will be the same as the *Vacation_Requests* section; however the applied rules will be slightly different. Once we have finished laying out these sections the form template will look **like Illustration 201** on the next page.

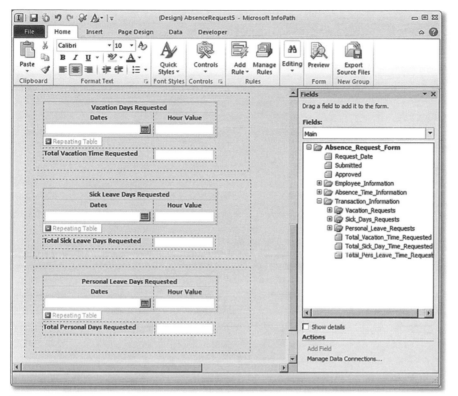

Illustration 201 – Layout of Absence Request Dates sections

Fortunately, we will not have to manually go through all of layout steps that we went through for the *Vacation_Requests* section. InfoPath allows us to copy and paste controls with their accompanying field logic.

Copying Controls

Select the table that contains the *Vacation_Requests* controls as shown in **Illustration 202** below.

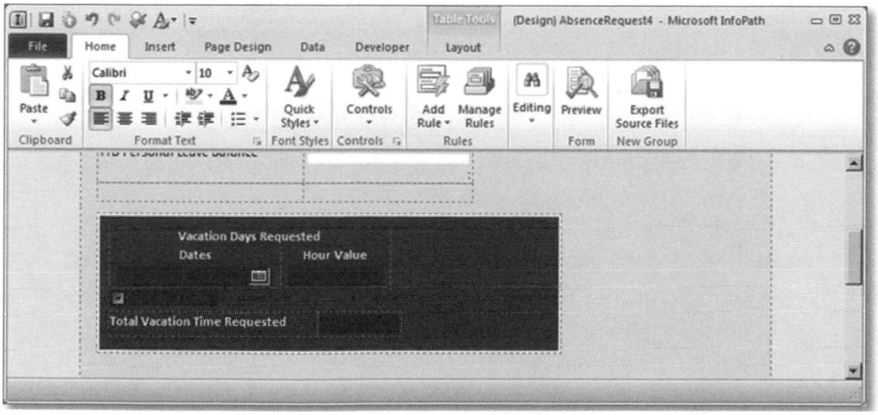

Illustration 202 - Selecting the table containing the Vacation_Requests controls

Right click and select **Copy**. Place your cursor directly beneath the table you just selected and right click again. Select the first **Paste** option (*Keep Source Formatting*) as shown in **Illustration 203** below.

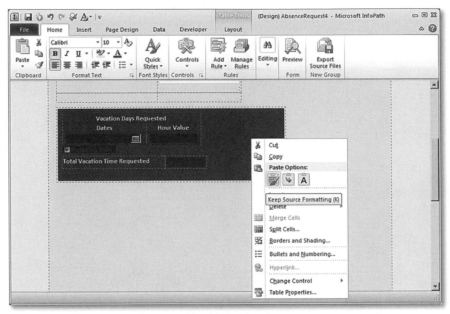

Illustration 203 - Copying and pasting the table for the Absence Requests controls

Your form will now have a duplicated table for the *Vacation_Requests* controls as shown in **Illustration 204** below. Note that all of the controls display a warning icon. If you place your cursor over any of the controls a screen tip will display that says *Control stores duplicate data*. This is an error condition that will go away once we change the field binding of the duplicated controls.

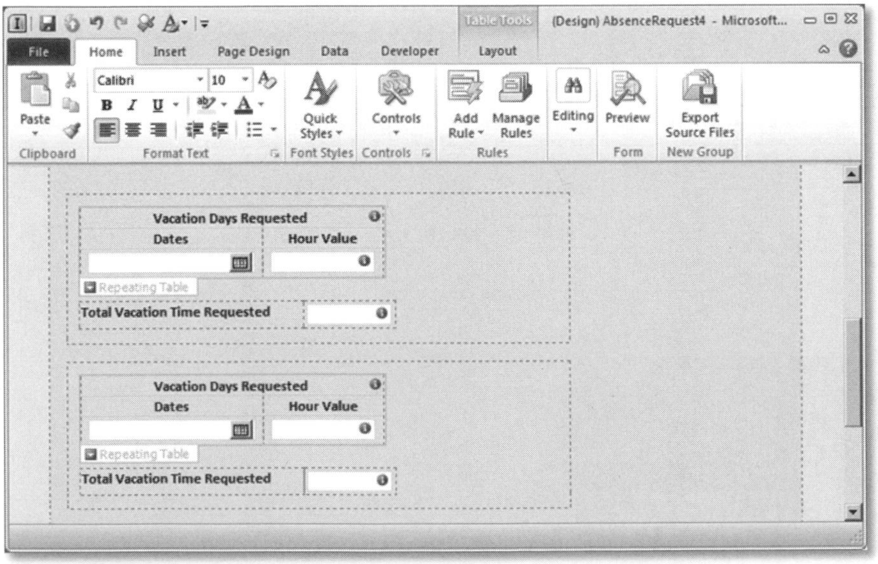

Illustration 204 - Form template with duplicate controls

Select the duplicate *Vacation_Requests* repeating table. Right click and select **Change Binding**. The first **Repeating Table Binding** dialogue screen will display as shown in **Illustration 205** below.

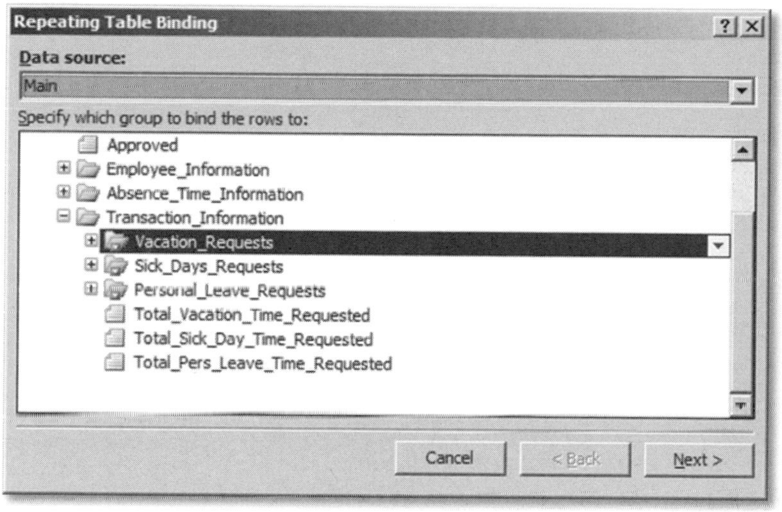

Illustration 205 - The first Repeating Table Binding dialogue screen

Click on the **Sick_Days_Requests** group and click the **Next** button. The second *Repeating Table Binding* dialogue screen will appear as shown in **Illustration 206** below.

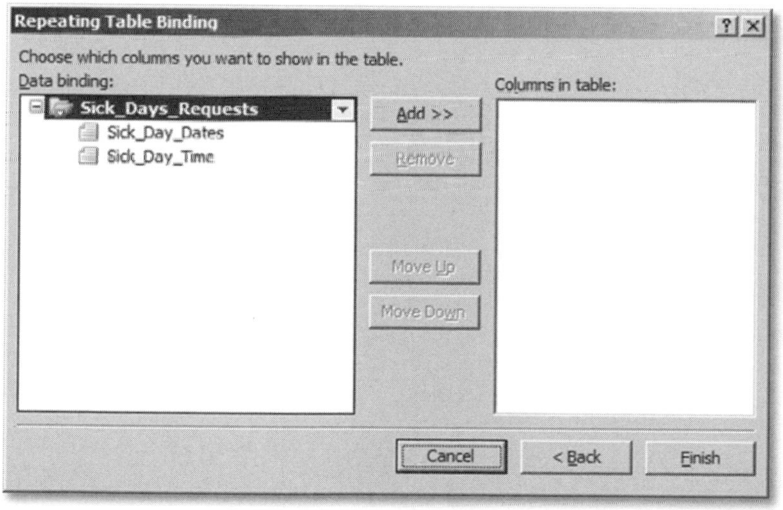

Illustration 206 - The second Repeating Table Binding dialogue screen

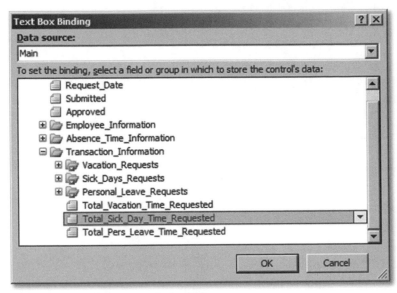

Illustration 207 - The Text Box Binding dialogue screen

Add the **Sick_Day_Dates and Sick_Day_Time** fields and click the **Finish** button. Select the duplicate **Total_Vacation_Time_Requested Text Box** control. Right click and choose **Change Binding**. The *Text Box Binding* dialogue screen will display as shown in **Illustration 207** at left.

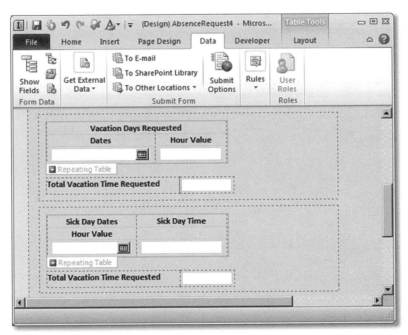

Illustration 208 - Form template after the duplicate table controls have been bound to the new fields

Select the **Total_Sick_Day_Time_Requested** field and click **OK**. The two tables in the form will now look like **Illustration 208** at left.

The controls in the copied section are now bound to their appropriate fields. The labels and table cells need to be edited so that the finished version looks like the following **Illustration 209** below.

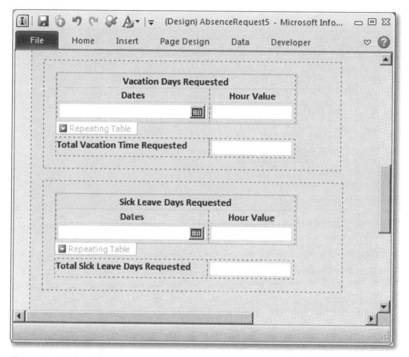

Illustration 209 - Sick Leave Days Requested section with correct labels

Copying Rules

Our next step is to copy the appropriate rule from the *Vacation_Request_Dates* field to the *Sick_Day_Dates* field. We will not be copying the *Current and Previous Date Validation* rule for vacation dates in as much as people take sick days unexpectedly and they need to record them later. We also will not be copying the *Restricted Dates* rule as people do not typically plan sick days, on restricted dates or otherwise. The only rule we will copy is the *Set Hour Value* rule.

Select the **Sick_Day_Dates** field or control and click on the **Manage Rules** button to display the *Rule* pane. Click on the **New** rule button and select **Action**. A blank *Rule 1* will appear. Now select the *Vacation_Request_Dates* field or control and select the **Set Hour Value** rule. Right click and choose **Copy Rule** as shown in **Illustration 210** on the next page.

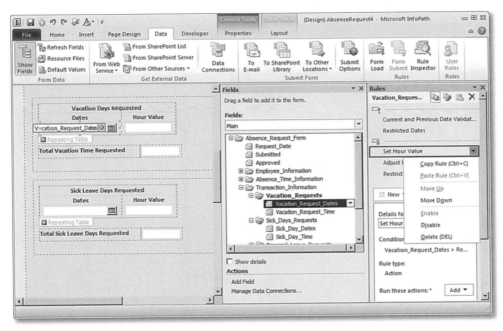

Illustration 210 - Copying the Set Hour Value rule

Select the **Sick_Day_Dates** field or control. Select **Rule 1**, right click and choose **Paste Rule**. The *Set Hour Value* rule will now appear below *Rule 1* as shown in **Illustration 211** below.

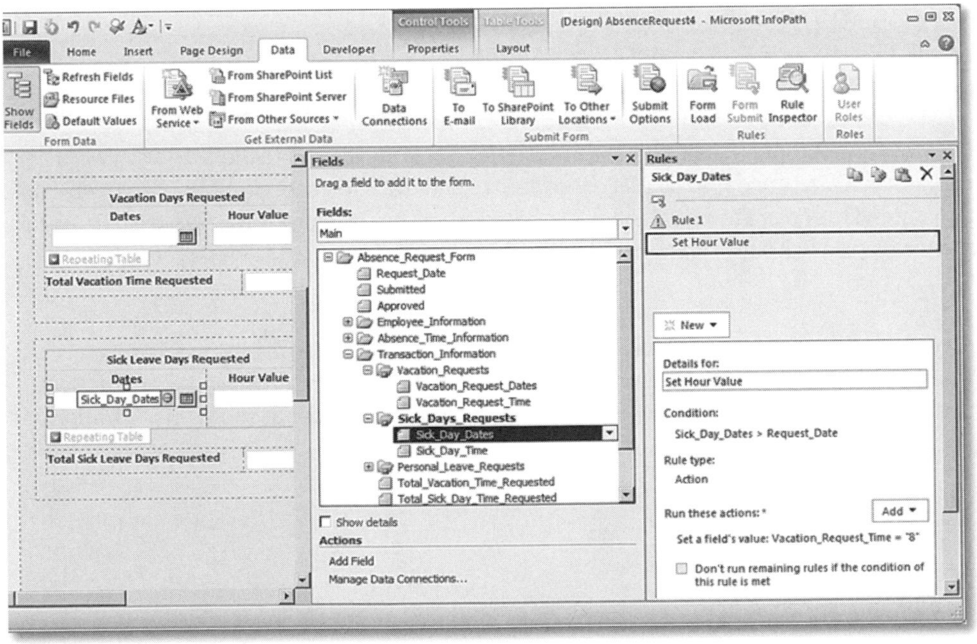

Illustration 211 - Pasting the Set Hour Value rule

Select **Rule 1**, right click and choose **Delete**. Click **OK** to confirm that you want to delete it. Notice that the rule condition references *Sick_Day_Dates* and not *Vacation_Request_Dates*, but the *Set a field's value* action still references *Vacation_Request_Time*. Click on the **action** to display the *Rule* details dialogue box as shown in **Illustration 212** below.

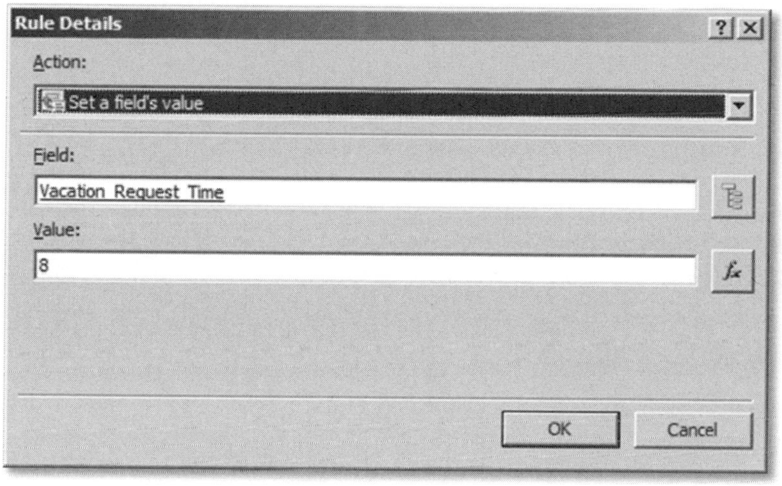

Illustration 212 - Change the Set a field's value action to use the correct field

Click on the **Field button** and change the **Field** value to **Sick_Day_Dates** in the *Main* data source. Leave "8" for the **Value** and click **OK**.

To create the *Personal_Leave_Requests* section repeat all the steps that we just completed of copying the *Vacation_Requests* section controls and rules to create the *Sick_Days_Requests* section. Repeat all the steps from page 133 to 139. The layout, configuration settings and all the rules for the *Personal_Leave_Requests* section will be the same as those for the *Vacation_Requests* section.

You will also want to apply the formatting rule logic to the *Sick_Day_Requests* repeating table and the *Personal_Leave_Requests* repeating table that we applied to the *Vacation_Requests* repeating table control for hiding these controls when the user has already taken the maximum amount of time allocated to them in these leave categories. The instructions for creating this rule logic are found on page 131.

> **Note** – Since there is no yearly carry-forward time for sick leave or personal leave, the condition statement for hiding the repeating tables for *Sick_Day_Requests* and *Personal_Leave_Requests* will be "***the time used is greater than or equal to the time allowed***" for each respectively, as shown in **Illustration 213** and **Illustration 214** below.

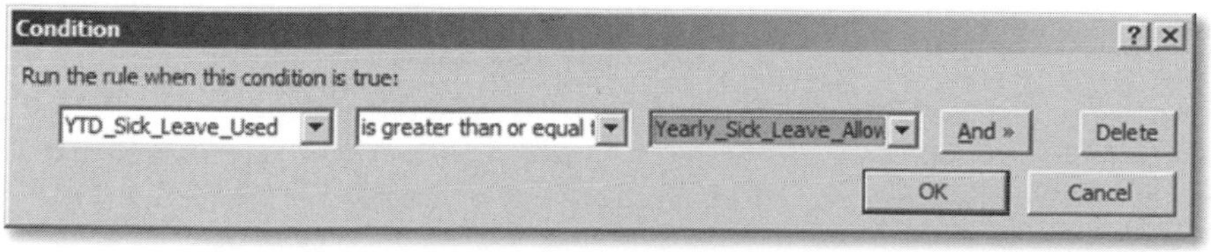

Illustration 213 - Condition for maxxed out sick leave time

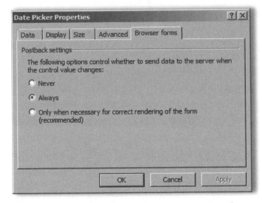

Illustration 214 - Condition for maxxed out personal leave time

Note – copy all the rules from *Vacation_Request_Dates* to *Personal_ Leave_Dates*, as the same business logic for vacation days applies to personal leave days.

Important Note – Make sure that you set the **Postback setting** to **Always** in the *Browser forms tab* of the *Personal_Leave_Dates date picker* control as we did for the *Vacation_Request_Dates data picker* control in order for the *Reset Hour Value* rule action to work properly, as shown in **Illustration 215** below.

Illustration 215 – Setting the Postback settings for the Personal_Leave_Dates Date Picker control so that the Reset Hour Value rule executes properly.

The form template now has the functionality to show the user the allocated, available and used leave time in each category and to request vacation, sick days and personal leave time for which an hour equivalent value will be generated and totaled. The subsequent steps of the absence request process are as follows:

The user will submit the absence request. The instance of the request is stored in the host form library. Once submitted, absence request form instances become read only. They can be opened by the user who created the request but they cannot be edited and re-submitted. Values in the form (e.g.: *Requires_Approval, Approved, Request_Date* etc.) will populate the columns of the form library for each request submission.

A *SharePoint* workflow will start when the form is saved to the form library. If no approval is required the workflow will update the relevant fields in the *Employee Information* database. Once this database update is completed the user will be sent a confirmation email of the transaction. The user's manager is copied on this email. If approval is required the workflow will generate an email to the user's manager indicating that an absence request requires approval and directs the manager to the submitted form instance.

The manager will open the form and review it. If they approve the request they will set the Approved field value to "Yes". If they do not approve the request they will set the Approved field value to "No" and enter a required rejection explanation in the *Rejection_Reason* field. In either case they will click on the *Manager's Submit* button to re-submit the form back to the form library. The Approved column will be updated with the values entered in the form.

If the request was approved the workflow will update the relevant fields in *the Employee Information* database and the user will receive an email notification of the approved request. If the request is not approved the user will receive an email notification with the manager's rejection reason and a request to the user to create a new request. If the manager does not approve or reject the request over some duration the request will be automatically approved and the user will be notified by an email.

Adding the Approval Section Schema Fields

Before we can build the workflows for this application there is still work that has to be done in the form template to facilitate the process steps and functional requirements itemized above.

We need to augment the *Main* data source schema to include an *Approval_Section*. Right click on the **Absence_ Request_Form** top level group node and select **Add**. Choose **Group** for the Type. Name it "Approval_Section".

Select the *Approval_Section* group and add the following fields:

Requires_Approval – with a *Data type* of Text (string)
Approved – with a *Data type* of Text (string)
Approved_By – with a *Data type* of Text (string)
Rejection_Reason – with a *Data type* of Text (string)

The completed *Approval_Section* will look like **Illustration 216** below.

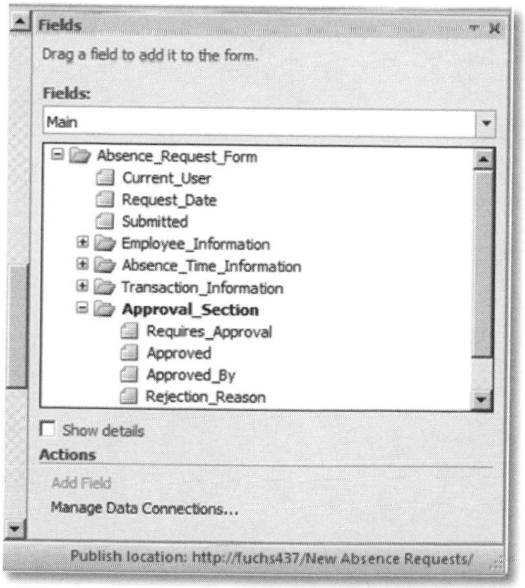

Illustration 216 - Completed Approval Section

Adding the Approval Section to the Form Layout

In the next steps we are going to lay out a section and controls for the *Approval_Section* so that the entire section is only displayed to a manager after the form has been submitted, or to the request initiator in order to see the reason entered by their manager if the request was rejected.

> **Important Note** – While we have not as yet given form layout and design best practices much attention (but we will), the layout technique that we will implement here is important because it facilitates form behavior that addresses a functional requirement.

Insert a single column table directly below the table that contains the *Personal Leave* controls. Drag the right border of the table to the left so that it is the same width as the other tables. Select the table. Right click and choose **Table Properties**. Click the **Row tab** and select the **radio button** for **Row height is at least:** and enter 136 points. Click on the **Column** tab and enter 390 points for the **Column width**. Click on the **Cell** tab and enter 15 points for the Top, Bottom and Left margins. Click **OK**.

With the cursor placed in the table select the **Approval_Section** and right click. Select **Section**. The design surface will look like **Illustration 217** below.

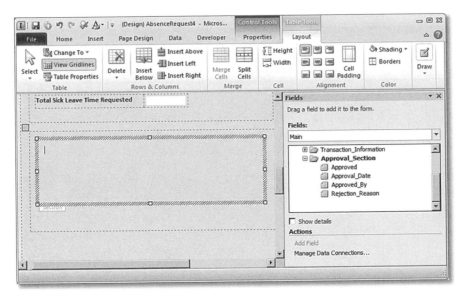

Illustration 217 - Section control for the Approval group

With the inserted section still selected right click and choose **Section Properties** and select the **Size** tab. In the **Padding** section enter 10 points in the Top, Bottom, Left and Right borders as shown in **Illustration 218** below.

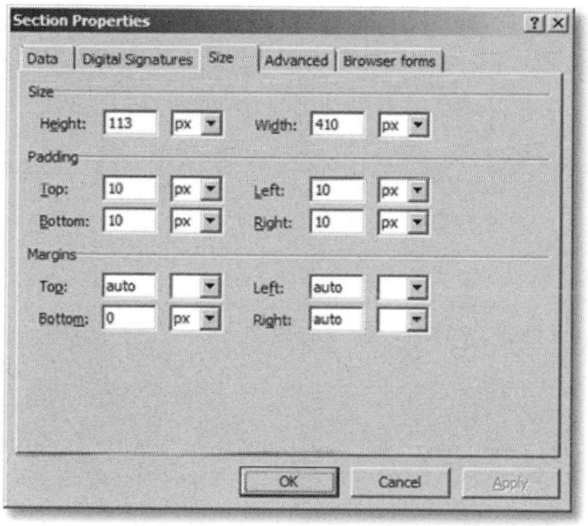

Illustration 218 - Size tab for the Section Properties dialogue screen

Click **OK**. With your cursor positioned in the **Section**, insert a single column and single row table. Grab the right border of the section and drag it to the left so that the right *Section* border is inside the parent table. Grab the right border of the table that was just inserted in the section and drag it to the left so it is inside the section. Enter "Approval Section" in this table and center the text. Your layout surface will look like **Illustration 219** below.

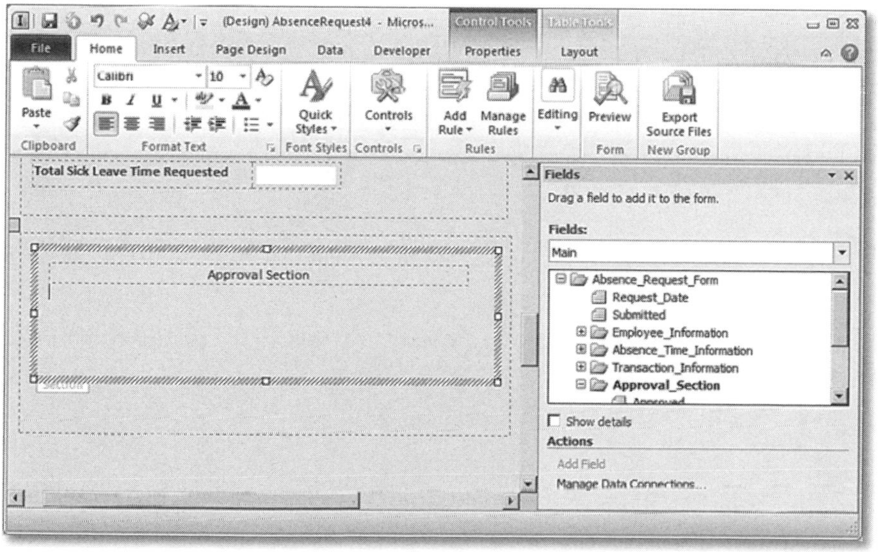

Illustration 219 - Single column and row table placed inside a section control

Position the cursor under this table and insert a table with two columns and three rows. Directly below this table add another table with one two columns and one row. Below this table insert a last table with one column and one row so that your layout surface looks like **Illustration 220** below.

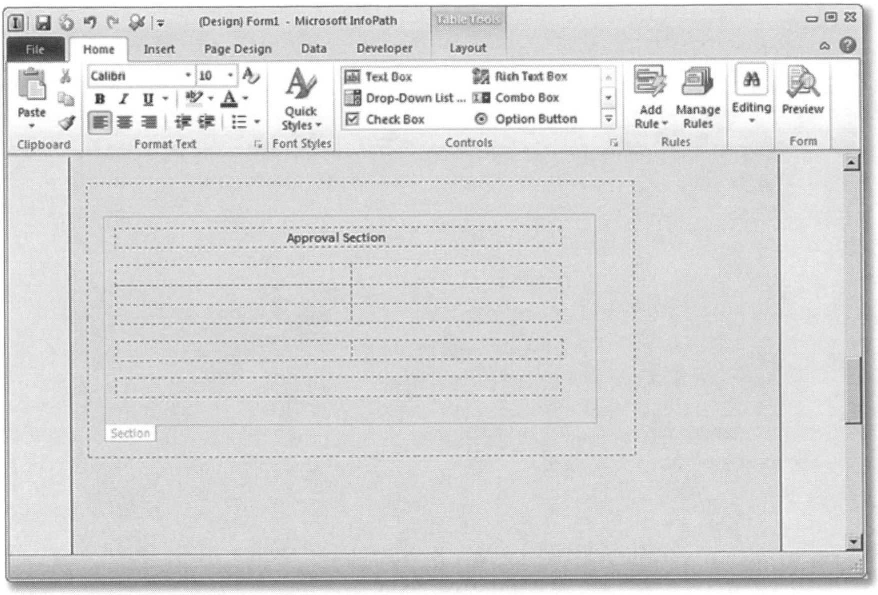

Illustration 220 - Additional tables placed inside a section control

Place your cursor in the top right column cell of the second table. Select the **Approved** field; right click and choose **Drop-Down List Box**. In the cell to the left of the control enter the label "Approved".

Place your cursor in the column cell directly beneath the *Approved Drop-Down List Box* control. Select the **Aproved_Date** field; right click and choose **Text Box**. Enter the label "Date Approved" in the cell to the left.

Place your cursor in the column cell directly beneath the *Aproved_Date Text Box* control. Select the **Approved_ By** field; right click and choose **Text Box**. Enter the label "Approved By" in the cell to the left.

Place your cursor in the left column of the third table. Select the **Rejection_Reason** field; right click and choose **Text Box**. Enter the label "Rejection Reason" in the cell to the left.

Select the right column and drag it to the left. Select the bottom border of this table and drag it down, making it higher. Select the **Text Box** control and drag it down so that it fills the column cell.

In the last table, insert a **Button** control and center it. The design surface should now look like **Illustration 221** below.

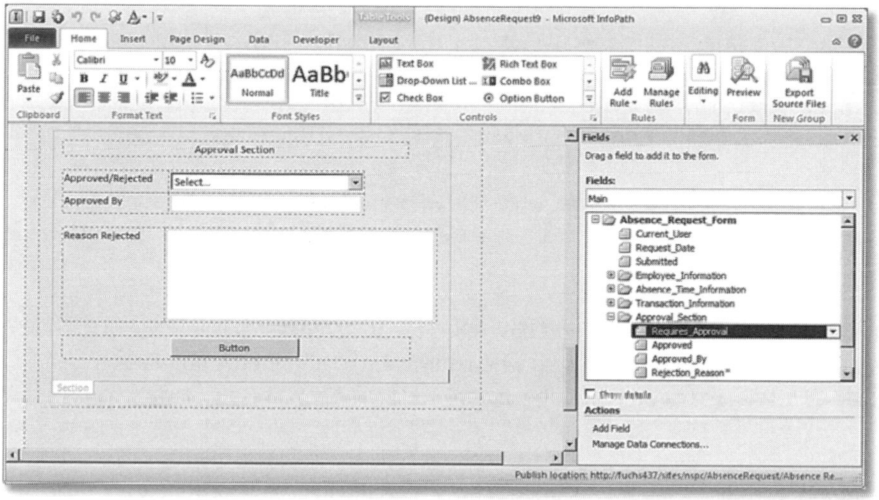

Illustration 221 - Approval Section with controls and labels

Preview the form. The controls will display as shown in **Illustration 222** below.

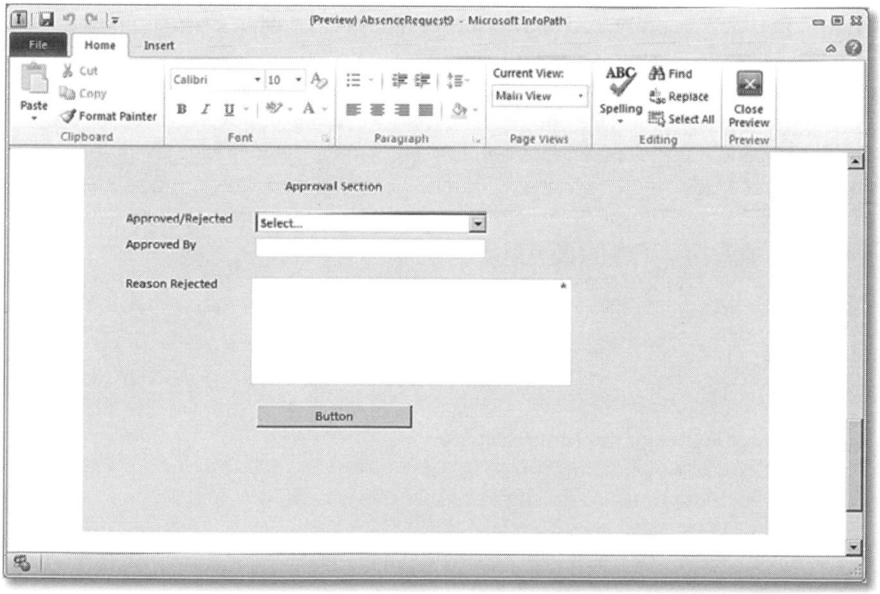

Illustration 222 - Preview of Approval Section

Creating Rules to Hide the Approval Section

We want the *Approval Section* and its respective controls to display only in the following two situations:

- If the request has been **submitted** and the person opening the submitted form is the designated approver. The *Approval Section* should not be displayed to the initiator when it is first created.
- If the request has been rejected by the approver and the initiator of the request opens the form in read-only display mode to review the reason why it was rejected by the designated approver.

Two rules will be created to accomplish this. The first rule, which we will implement now, will be applied to the *Approval Section* on the *Main View* of the form. This rule will hide the *Approval Section* from the initiator when the request is first created.

The second rule will be implemented **later** because it must be applied to the *Approval Section* of the *Main Read-Only View*. This is the view of the form that the initiator sees when they open a submitted request instance. We will create the *Main Read Only View* by copying the entire completed *Main View*, at which time we will create the second rule.

> **Important Development Note** – Rules bound to the controls and sections on a form view are only applicable to the behavior of that view. If you copy the controls and sections from one form view to another the original rules will not be copied. Consequently, any desired functionality for copied controls or sections on a secondary form view must be implemented separately on that view. In addition, different rules can be applied to the copied controls or sections. This allows us to implement different form behavior for the view presented to the initiator after the form has been submitted.

To quickly demonstrate how a *Formatting* rule works let's create a temporary one and test it. Select the **Approval** section in the *Main* data source or on the layout surface and click the **Manage Rules** Ribbon button. Click the **New** rule button and choose **Formatting**. Click **None** under **Condition** and create the following condition statement as shown in **Illustration 223** below.

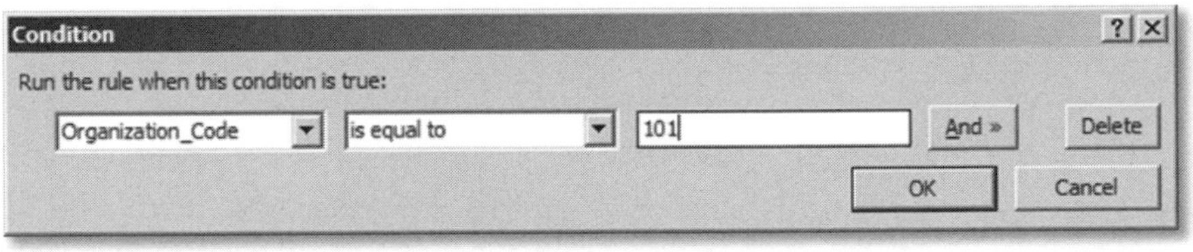

Illustration 223 - Condition statement used in a temporary Formatting rule

Click **OK** and check the **Hide this control check box**. We know that this condition will resolve to true when we preview the form and as a result the *Approval Section* should no longer display. Let's preview the form and test it. As shown in **Illustration 224** below the *Approval Section* is now hidden.

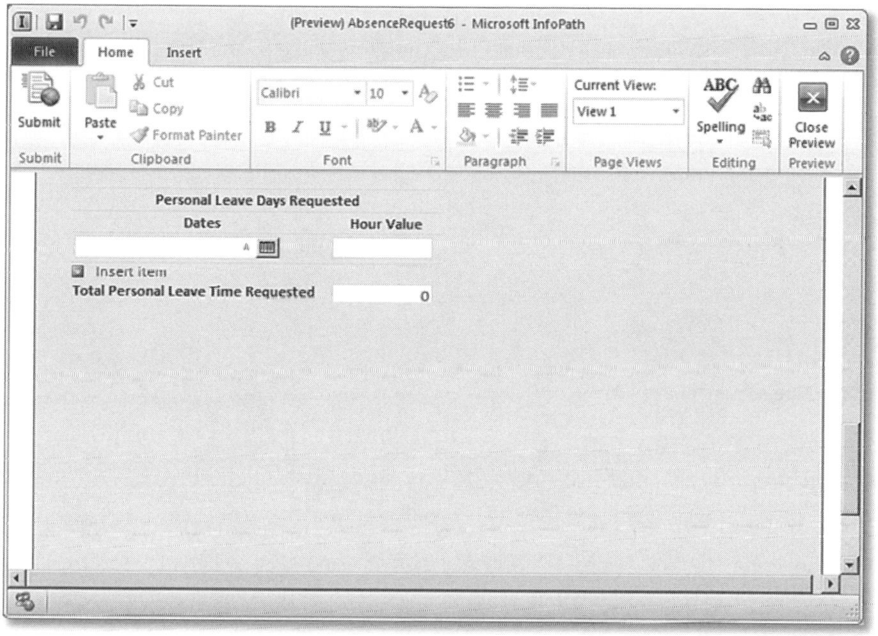

Illustration 224 - Preview of form with Approval Section hidden by Formatting rule

Creating a Rule to Hide the Approval Section to the Initiator When the Request is First Created

Now we will create the actual logic for hiding the *Approval Section* when a request is first generated. Delete the temporary *Formatting* rule. With the *Approval Section* selected click **New** and select **Formatting.** Name the rule "Hide from Initiator upon Creation".

Click **None** under *Condition* and create the condition statement shown in **Illustration 225** below. In the first drop-down box select the **Submitted** field. In the second drop-down box select the **is equal to** operator. In the third drop-down box, enter the text "FALSE".

Illustration 225 - Rule Condition to hide the Approval Section when the request is first created

Click **OK** and check the **Hide this control** checkbox.

Configuring the Property Settings and Creating the Rule Logic for the Approval Section Controls

Right click on the **Approved** drop-down list control and select **Drop-Down List Box Properties**. For **List box choices** select the **Enter choices manually** radio button. Click the **Add** button to display the *Add Choice* dialogue screen. Enter "Yes" for the *Value*. The *Display name* will populate with the same value as the *Value*, but this can be changed. The *Add Choice* dialogue screen looks like **Illustration 226** below.

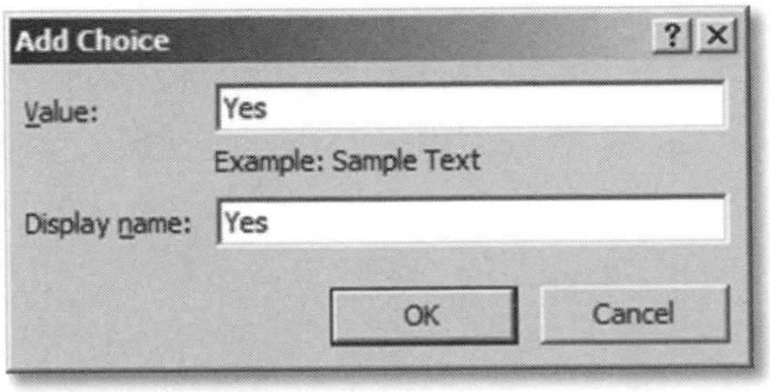

Illustration 226 - Add Choice dialogue screen for drop-down list values

Click **OK,** and then click the **Add** button again. Enter "No" for the *Value* which will default for the *Display Name*. Click the **OK** button.

Once again, click the **Add** button. Enter "Default Approval" for the *Value* and enter "Yes by Default" for the *Display Name*. Click the **OK** button.

Make the first choice item the one with an empty *Value* and a *Display name* of "Select...". The **Drop-Down List Box Properties** dialogue screen should look like **Illustration 227** below.

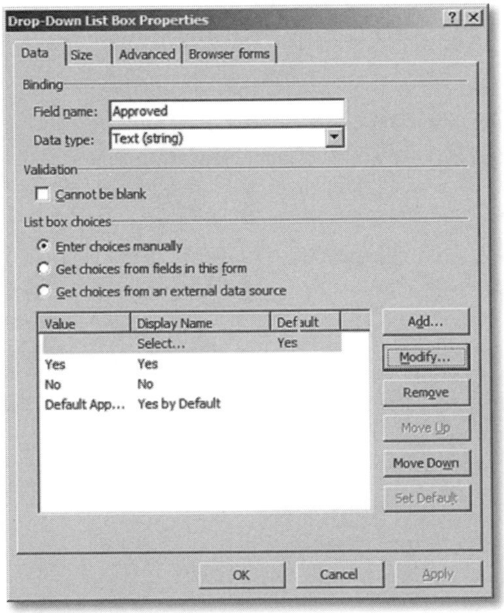

Illustration 227 - Completed set of drop-down list values for Approved control

We will configure the *Approved_By Text Box* control to auto-populate with the *Manager_Full_Name* value. To do this we will add a *Form Load* action to the *New Created Form* rule that will set the value of the *Manager_Full_Name* field in the *Employee_Information* section and then copy that value to the *Approved_By* field.

From the **Data** tab on the Ribbon click **Form Load**. With the **New Created Form** rule selected, click **Add** and choose **Set a field's** value. In the **Select a Field or Group** dialogue screen choose **Manager_Full_Name** in the *Main* data source for the field to set.

For the **Value**, select the **Employee Information** secondary data source and choose the **Manager_Full_Name**. Click the **Filter Data** button and add the same **[Current_User = User_Name]**filter criterion that we used previously for all the **Set a field's value** actions in the *New Created Form* rule as shown in **Illustration 228** below.

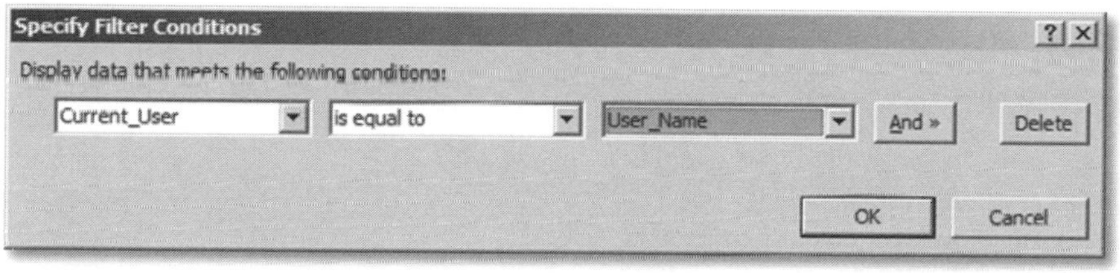

Illustration 228 - Current_User = User_Name Filter Condition

The completed *Rule Details* dialogue screen will look like **Illustration 229** below.

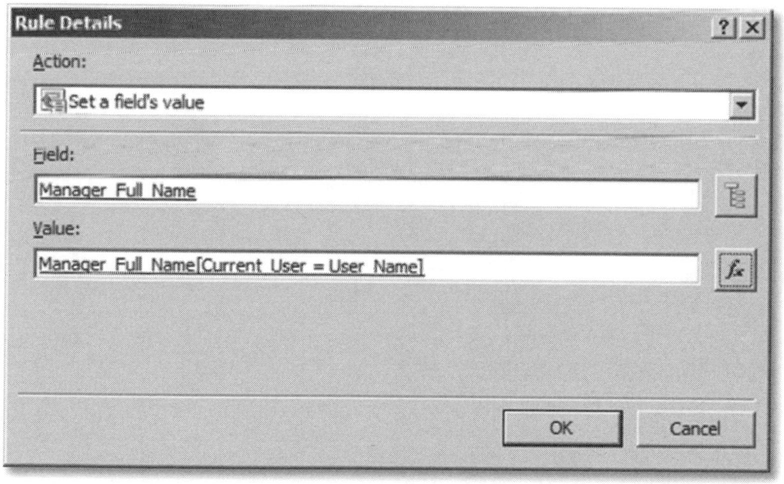

Illustration 229 - Completed Set a field's value action for Manager_Full_Name

Create two additional **Set a field's** actions for *Manager_User_Name* and *Manager_Email* that use the same **[Current_User = User_Name]** look up logic. The completed *Rule Details* dialogue screen will look like **Illustration 230** and **Illustration 231** below.

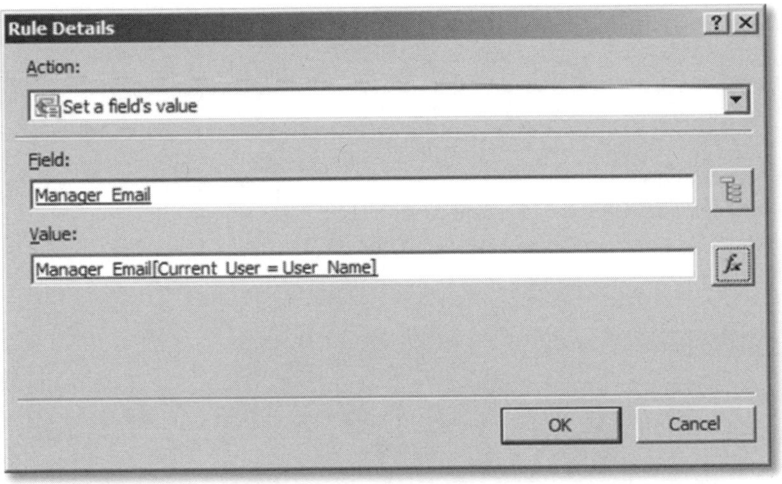

Illustration 230 - Completed Set a field's value action for Manager_Email field

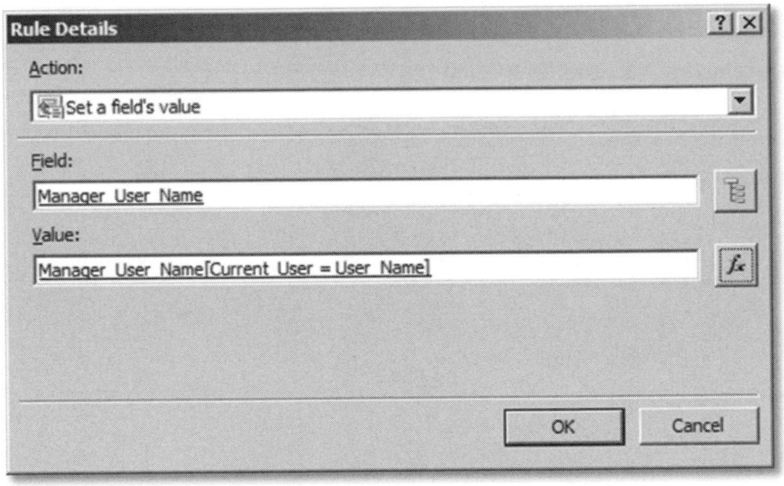

Illustration 231 - Completed Set a field's value action for Manager_User_Name field

Now add the **Set a field's value** action to set the value of the *Approved_By* field with the value from the *Manager_Full_Name* field as shown in **Illustration 232** below.

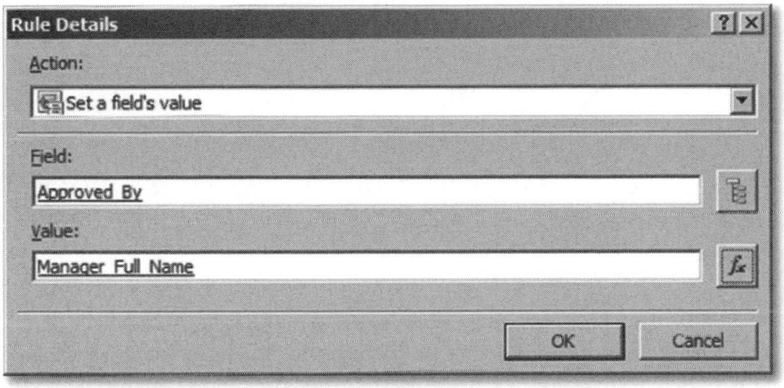

Illustration 232 - Completed Set a field's value action for Approved_By field

To test that these rule actions are working drag the *Manager_User_Name* and *Manager_Email* fields anywhere on the design surface and preview the form. Remove these text box controls when you have finished testing.

Creating Form Load Rules for Existing Instances of an Absence Request

We now need to create additional *Form Load* rules that address the behavior of absence request forms that have already been created. These rules should not be run when a new absence request is first created.

Conversely, the **New Created Form** rule should not execute when an existing absence request form is being open. This can be accomplished by checking the **Don't run remaining rules if the condition of this rule is met** on the bottom of the list of actions as shown in **Illustration 233** below. Check this **box** now for the **New Created Form** rule.

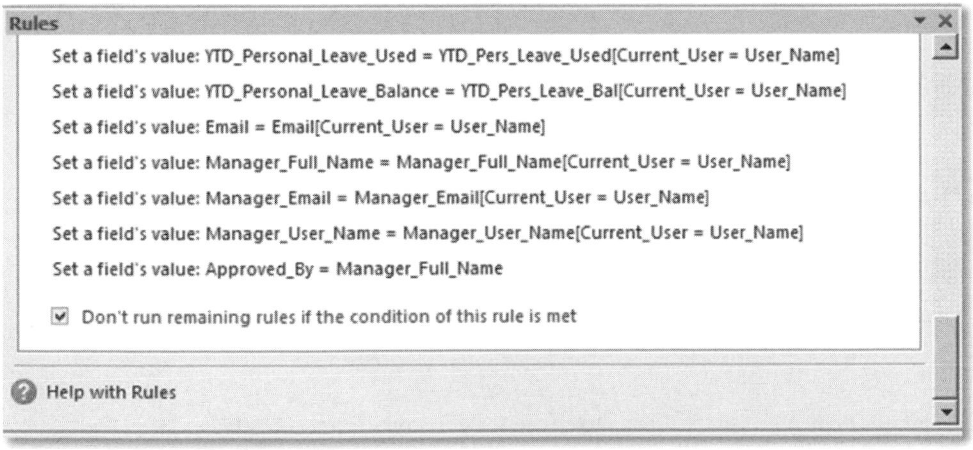

Illustration 233 - Check box setting for Don't run remaining rules if the condition of this rule is met

We will need three new *Form Load* rules, each for the different form behavior required when an existing form is opened by one of three individuals: by the original initiator, the manager responsible for approving the request, or a person who is neither the initiator nor the designated approval manager. Two of the rules will require additional *Form Views*, which we will create now.

Adding Additional Form Views

The first of these *Form Views* will be called "Main Read Only" and will be identical to the default *Main View* except that it will be entirely read only. This is the view that the Initiator of the form can see after they have created and submitted a request. The reason for this is that in this application we only want a request to be submitted once and we want to maintain an unaltered record of the original request.

> **Note** – Until we finish building the form logic and designing the form layout we will not have a completed *Main Read Only* view, but we need a placeholder for the purpose of creating the additional *Form Load* rule for the situation where the Initiator opens a form that they previously created.

Click on the **Page Design** tab of the Ribbon and click the **New View** button. Name the *View* "Main Read Only". A blank design surface will display. Leave this view empty for now.

Click the **New View** button again. Name the second View "Not Authorized to View". On the blank design surface for this view add a table with a single row and column. Enter "Not Authorized to View" in the table row. The *Not Authorized to View "View"* will look like **Illustration 234** below.

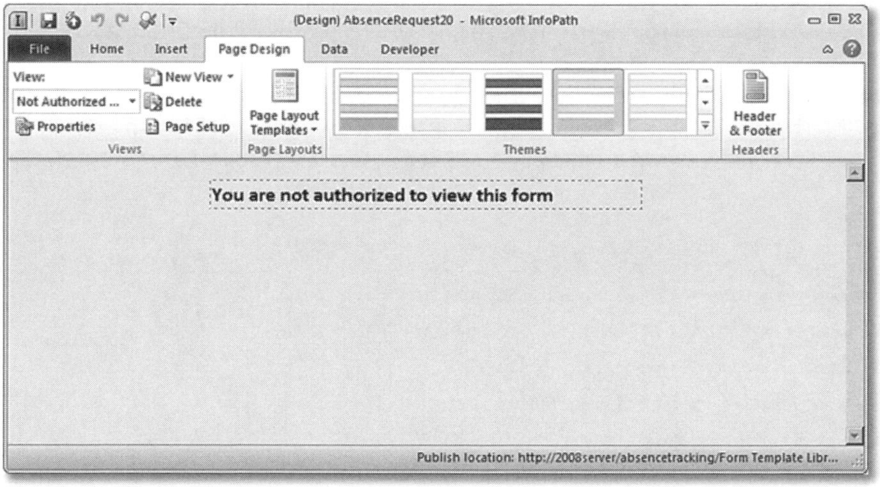

Illustration 234 - Not Authorized to View "View"

This is the view that will be displayed to anyone who is ***not*** the initiator of a request ***or*** the person responsible for approving it. The default *Main View* will be presented to the approving manager.

With these two additional *Form Views* we are ready to create the additional *Form Load* rules.

Creating the "Opener is Initiator" Form Load Rule

Click the **Data** tab on the *Ribbon* and the **Form Load** button. Select the **New Created Form** rule. Click the **New** button and select the default **Action** rule. Name the rule "Opener is Initiator". Click **None** under the *Condition* to open the *Condition* dialogue screen. Create the condition statement shown in **Illustration 235** below.

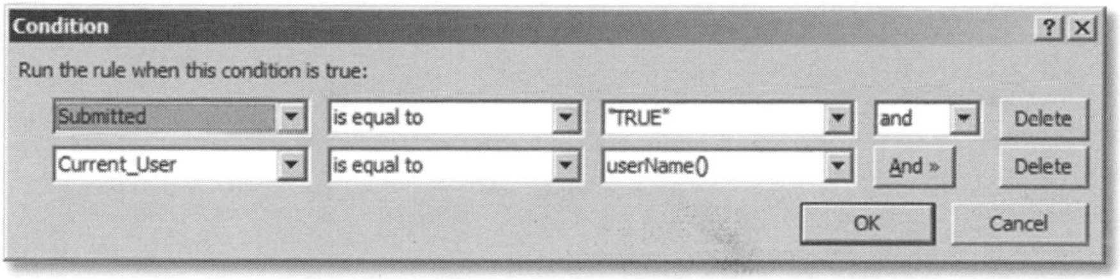

Illustration 235 - Condition statement for Opener is Initiator Form Load rule

The *userName()* function shown in the second statement is accessed by choosing **Use a formula** from the drop down box and selecting the **userName** function from the **Formula** dialogue screen. Note that there is an **and** operator that connects the two statements.

The first *Submitted is equal to TRUE* statement evaluates the *Submitted* value in the form. When the form is submitted a rule will set this field's value to "TRUE", changing its default value of FALSE. As a result when an existing instance of an absence request form is opened the *New Created Form* rule set will not execute. The second statement compares the *userName* value of the person opening the form to the value stored in the *Current_User* field, which is how the rule identifies that the person opening the form was the initiator of the form.

For the action, click **Add** and choose **Switch views**. In the *Rule Details* dialogue screen select the *Main Read Only View* as shown in **Illustration 236** below.

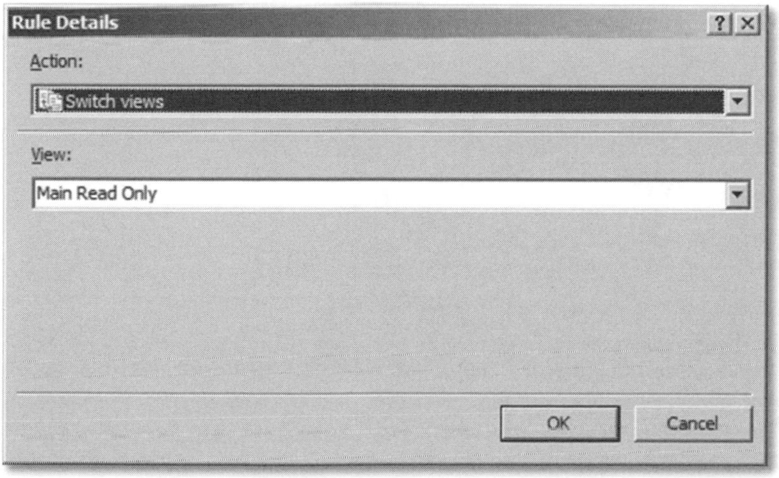

Illustration 236 - Switch views actin for Opener is Initiator rule

Click **OK** to complete this rule.

Creating the "Opener is Manager" Form Load Rule

Click **New** again and select the default **Action** rule. Name the rule "Opener is Manager". Click **None** under the *Condition* to open the *Condition* dialogue screen. Create the condition statement shown in **Illustration 237** below.

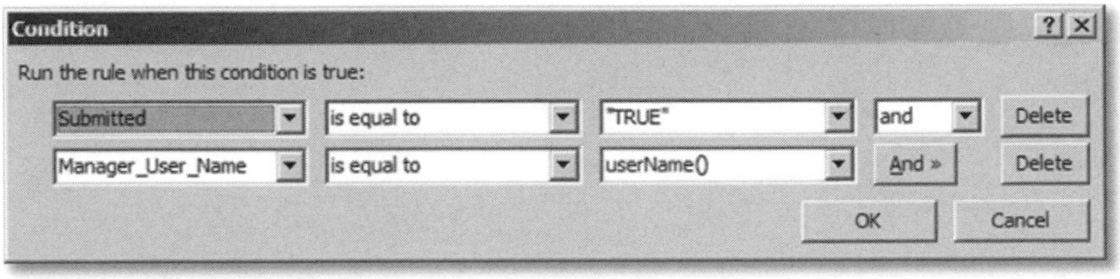

Illustration 237 - Condition statement for Opener is Manager rule

Again, the *Submitted is equal to TRUE* statement establishes that the form in not a new form and as a result the *New Created Form* rule set will not execute. The second statement compares the *userName* credentials of the person opening the form to the value stored in *the Manager_User_Name* field. If it is the same value then the form will open in the default *Main View* allowing the approver to approve or reject the request.

For the rule action, click **Add** and choose **Switch views**. In the *Rule Details* dialogue screen select the *Main View* as shown in **Illustration 238** below and click OK.

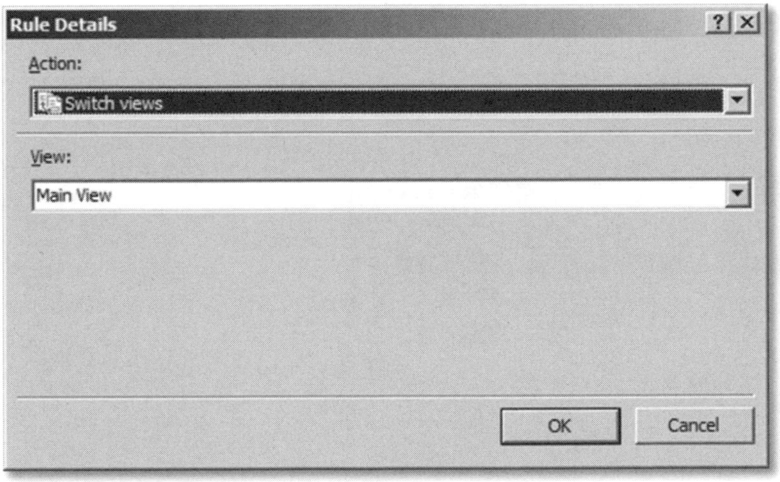

Illustration 238 - Switch views action for Opener is Initiator rule

Click **OK** again to complete this rule.

Creating the "Opener is Not Initiator" Form Load Rule

Select the default **Action** rule again. Name the rule "Opener is not Initiator". Click **None** under the *Condition* to open the *Condition* dialogue screen. Create the condition statement shown in **Illustration 239** below.

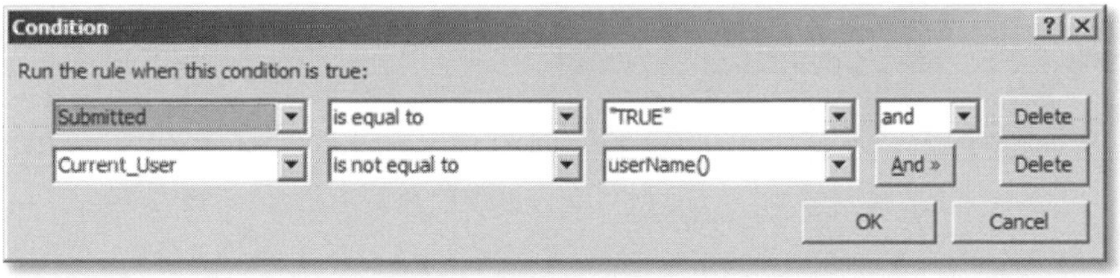

Illustration 239 - Condition statement for Opener is not Initiator rule

The second condition statement uses the **is not equal to** operator to compare the *userName* credentials value of the person opening the form to the value stored in the *Current User* field. If this condition statement resolves to true than the *Not Authorized to View* "View" will be displayed to the person attempting to open the form.

For the rule action, click **Add** and choose **Switch views**. In the *Rule Details* dialogue screen select the **Not Authorized to View** as shown in **Illustration 240** below and click **OK**.

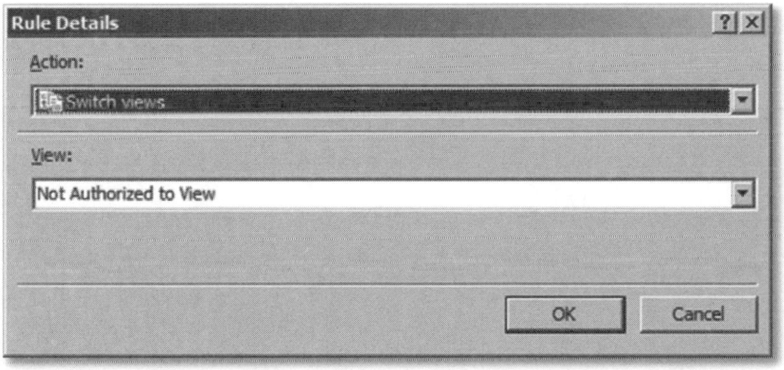

Illustration 240 - Switch views action for Opener is not Initiator rule

We will test all of these rules shortly but in the interim let's see what the form behavior looks like by simply testing the first condition in each rule. Add a new *Form Load* rule with one condition statement as shown in **Illustration 241** below.

Illustration 241 - Temporary rule condition

Click the **Add** action button and choose **Switch views**. Choose the **Not Authorized to View** "View" as shown in **Illustration 242** below.

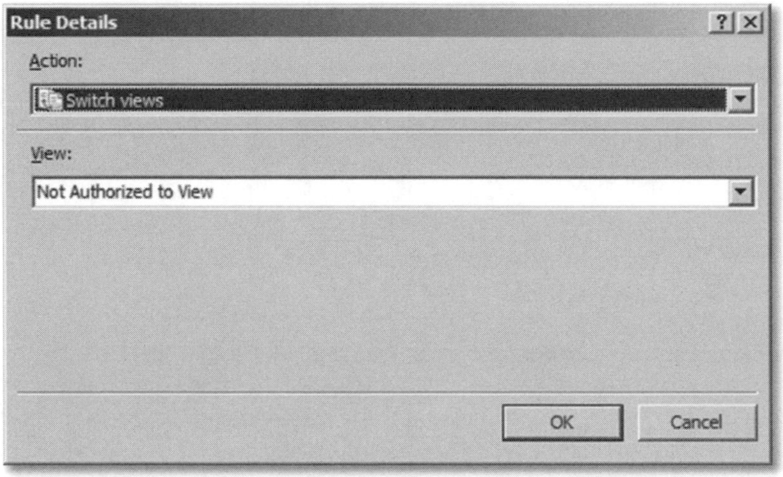

Illustration 242 - Temporary Switch views action

Select the **Submitted** field and right click; choose **Properties**. In the **Field or Group Properties** dialogue box set the Value to "TRUE" as shown in **Illustration 243** below.

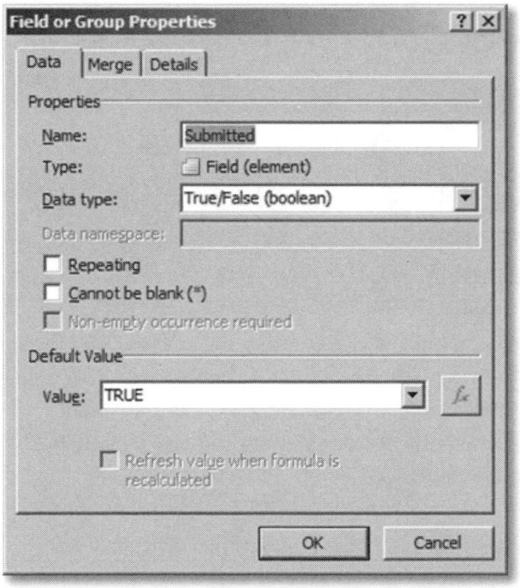

Illustration 243 - Temporary TRUE value setting for Submitted field

Now preview the form. It should look like **Illustration 244** below.

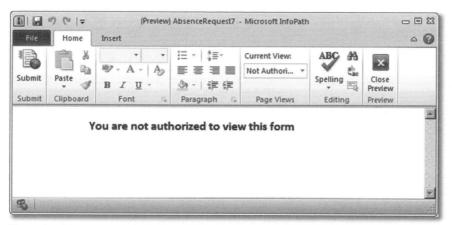

Illustration 244 - Form preview presenting View based on Submitted value set to TRUE

Open the **Field or Group Properties** dialogue box for the *Submitted* field and set the **Value** back to "FALSE". Delete the temporary *Form Load* rule.

Adding the Stored Values Group and Fields

We will use a two-step process to update the *Employee Information* database with the new used and balance available leave time values in each category, as well as the new vacation time forfeit balance. The form will calculate and store these values and when the form is submitted to the form library these values will be written to columns for these fields in the form library. Workflow actions that we will be creating will update the *Employee Information* database with the values written to the form library when the request is approved.

Select the **Absence_Request_Form root node** in the **Main** data source. Right click and select **Add**. Name the new group "Stored_Values" as shown in **Illustration 245** below.

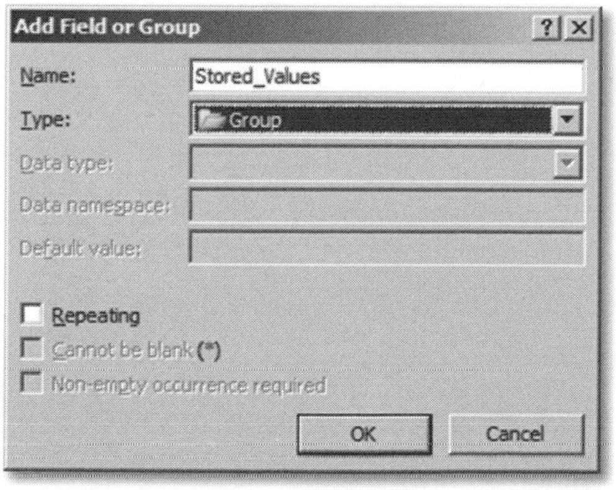

Illustration 245 - New Stored_Values group

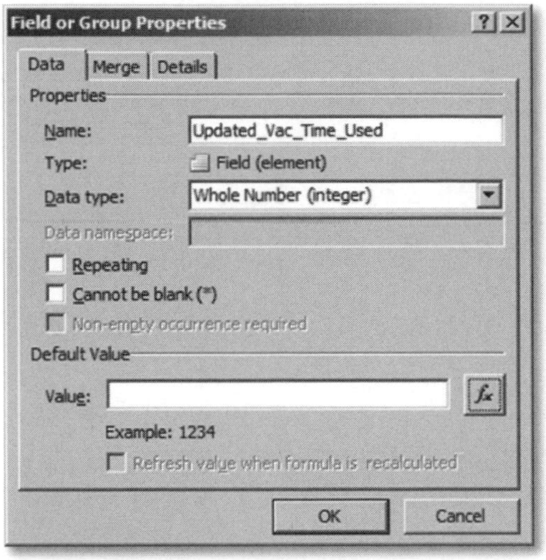

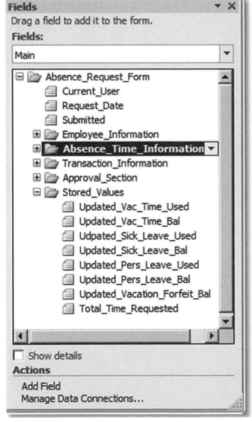

Illustration 246 - Updatad_Vac_Time_Used
Property screen

Select the **Stored_Values** group, right click and **Add** a new *Field (element)* of the Type *Whole Number (integer)* as shown in **Illustration 246** at left.
Repeat this step for the following Field items.
All are *Whole Number (integer)* Types.

Updated_Vac_Time_Bal
Updated_Sick_Leave_Time_Used
Updated_Sick_Leave_Time_Bal
Updated_Pers_Leave_Time_Used
Updated_Pers_Leave_Time_Bal
Updated_Vacation_Forfeit_Bal
Total_Time_Requested

When you have finished the *Main* data source schema will look like **Illustration 247** at left.

Illustration 247 - Main data source with completed
Stored_Values group fields

Creating the Formula Calculations for the Stored Values Fields

Right click on the **Updated_Vac_Time_Used** field and select **Properties**. Click the **Formula** button to the right of **Value**. Click the **Insert or Group** button.

From the **Select Field or Group** dialogue screen select the **YTD_Vacation_Time_Used** field in the *Absence_ Time_Information* group. Add a **plus sign (+)** after this item and then select the **Total_Vacation_Time_Requested** field from the *Transaction_Information* group.

The *Insert Formula* dialogue screen will now look like **Illustration 248** below.

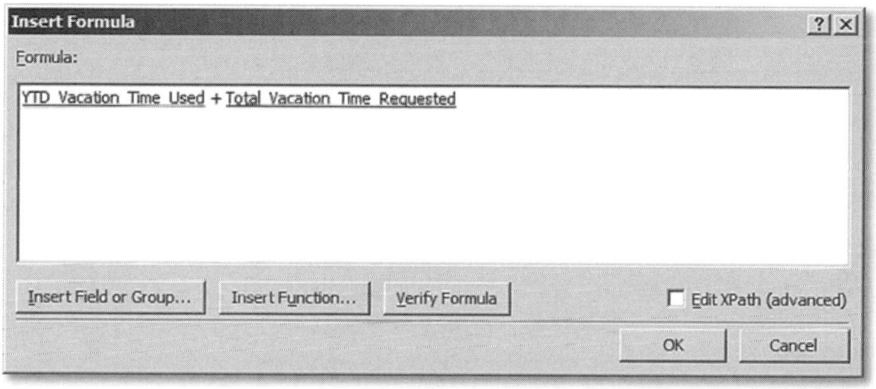

Illustration 248 - Formula for calculated value of Updated_Vac_Time_Used field

Click **OK**. The *Field or Group Properties* dialogue screen for the *Updated_Vac_Time_Used* field will look like **Illustration 249** below.

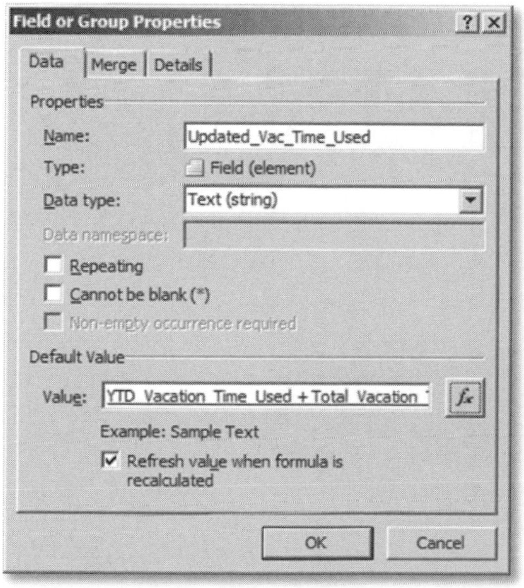

Illustration 249 - Properties screen for Updated_Vac_Time_Used field

To test that the formula logic is working correctly drag the **Updated_Vac_Time_Used** field anywhere on the design surface. Preview the form and use the date picker control to pick vacation days. The *Updated_Vac_Time_Used* field will increment the summed value appropriately. Delete the text box control.

Now create the same formula for the *Updated_Sick_Leave_Time_Used* and *Updated_Pers_Leave_Time_Used* stored values using the corresponding fields in the formula to generate their updated values.

For the *Updated_Vac_Time_Bal* stored value **subtract** the *Total_Vacation_Time_Requested* field from the *YTD_Vacation_Time_Balance* field in the *Insert Formula* dialogue screen as shown in **Illustration 250** below.

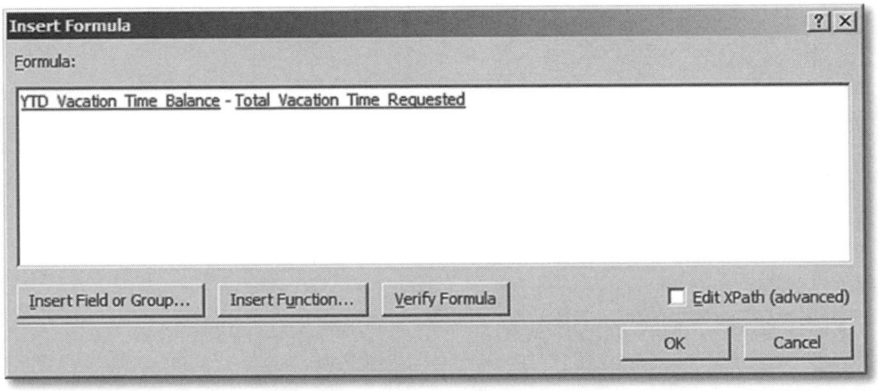

Illustration 250 - Formula for calculated value of Updated_Vac_Time_Bal field

Now create the same formula for the *Updated_Sick_Leave_Time_Bal* and *Updated_Pers_Leave_Time_Bal* stored values using the corresponding fields in the formula to generate their updated values.

For the *Updated_Vacation_Forfeit_Bal* stored value create the following formula as shown in **Illustration 251** below.

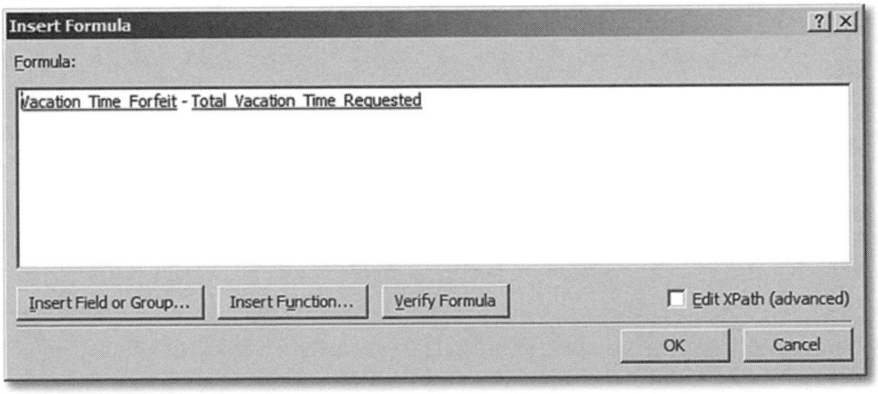

Illustration 251 - Formula for calculated value of Updated_Vacation_Forfeit_Bal field

Creating a Rule to Offset Calculations Resulting in Negative Numbers

The formula for *Updated_Vacation_Forfeit_Bal* will work properly up until the point that the *Vacation_Time_Forfeit* value is greater than or equal to the *Total_Vacation_Time_Requested* value. When the *Vacation_Time_Forfeit* value is less than the *Total_Vacation_Time_Requested* value the formula that we just created would generate a negative number for the *Updated_Vacation_Forfeit_Bal* stored value. The value that should be stored in this situation is "0". To accomplish this we will create a rule action that sets the value of *Updated_Vacation_Forfeit_Bal* to "0" if its calculated value is less than "0".

With the **Updated_Vacation_Forfeit_Bal** field selected right click and choose **Rules**. Click **New** and select the **Action** rule. Name it "Updated Vacation Forfeit Balance Adjustment". Click on **Condition: None** and create the following condition statement as shown in **Illustration 252** below.

Illustration 252 - Condition statement for rule to offset negative number value calculation in Updated_Vacation_Forfeit_Bal field

Click **OK** then **Add** the action **Set a field's value**. From the *Main* data source select the **Updated_Vacation_Forfeit_Bal** field. Enter "**0**" for the Value. The *Rule Details* dialogue screen will look like **Illustration 253** below.

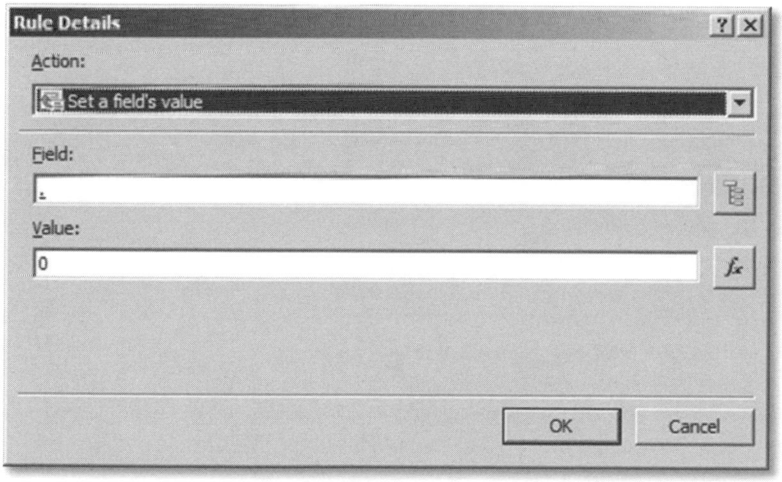

Illustration 253 - Rule action rule to offset negative number value calculation in Updated_Vacation_Forfeit_Bal field

The completed rule will look like **Illustration 254** below.

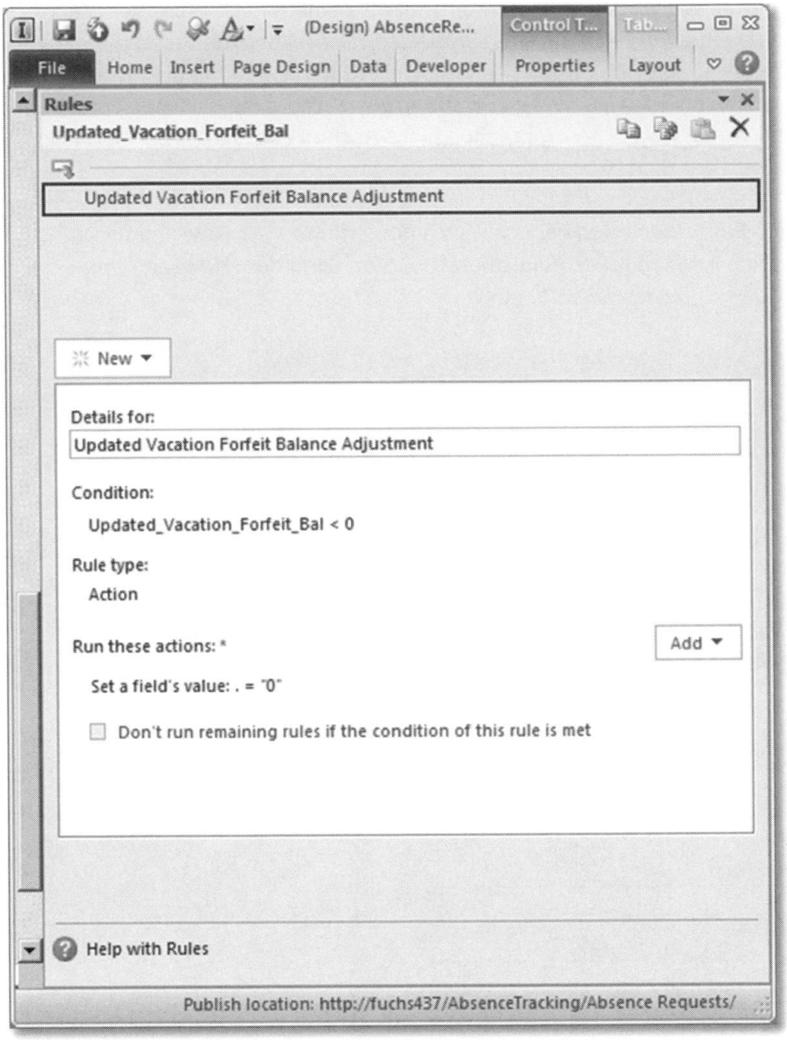

Illustration 254 - Completed Updated Vacation Forfeit Balance Adjustment rule

For the *Total_Time_Requested* stored value, we will add up the values of the *Total_Vacation_Time_Requested*, *Total_Sick_Day_Time_Requested* and *Total_Pers_Leave_Time_Requested* fields in the *Transaction_Information* group.

Create this formula as the *Default Value* of the *Total_Time_Requested* field in the *Insert Formula* dialogue screen as shown in **Illustration 255** on the next page. This stored value will be used in a submit rule to determine if the absence request requires approval from a manager.

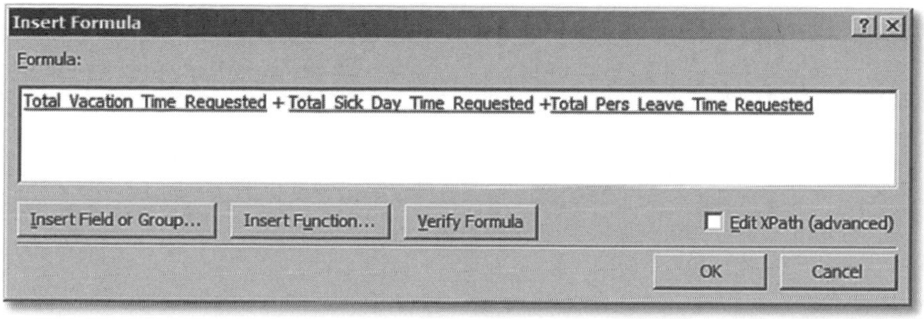

Illustration 255 - Formula for the Total_Time_Requested stored value

Using the addDays Function to Calculate an Employee Tenure Value

We will be creating a rule set that executes when the absence request is submitted as shown in **Illustration 256** below. This rule set establishes the conditional criteria and sets the field values that will be used by the workflow to determine if the request requires a manager's approval.

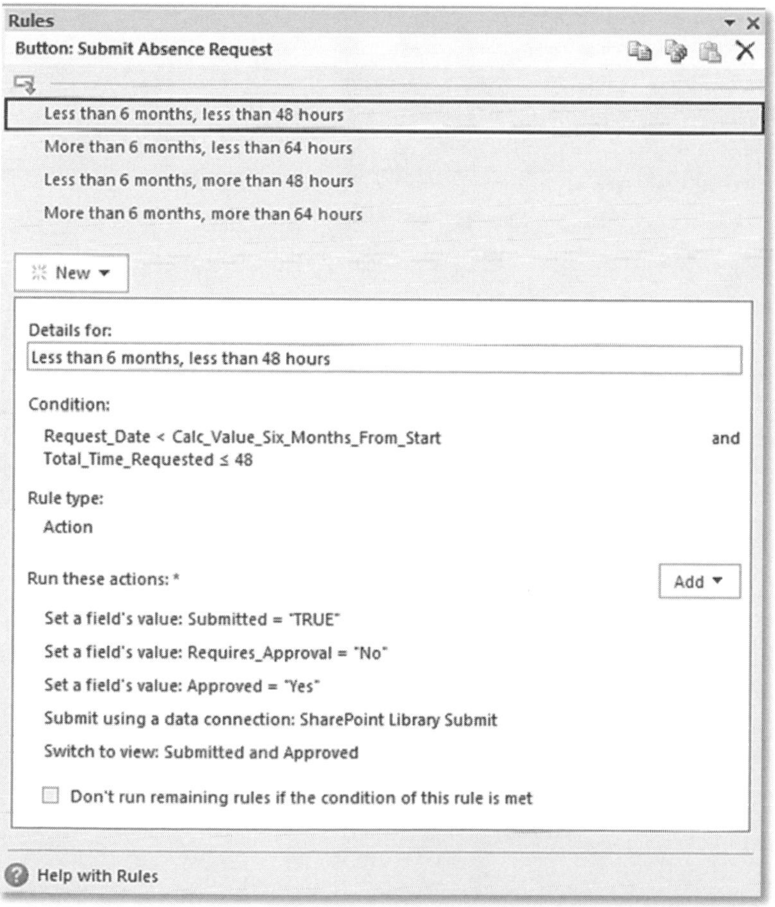

Illustration 256 - Form submit rule set determining if request requires a
manager's approval

The criteria for approval that we will use in this rule set is a combination of the employee's tenure and the number of leave days requested in the form. In the following steps we will create a stored field value that uses a formula to calculate the six month anniversary of an employee's start date, which will then be used in the approval rule set.

Click on the **Stored_Values** group, right click and select **Add**. Add a Field (element) named *Calc_Value_Six_Months_From_Start*. Choose **Date and Time** for the Data type. Click on the **Formula** button to the right of the **Value** box. The *Insert Formula* dialogue screen will display.

Click the **Insert Function** button. Click the **Date** Category and select the **addDays** function. The *Insert Formula* dialogue screen will look like **Illustration 257** below.

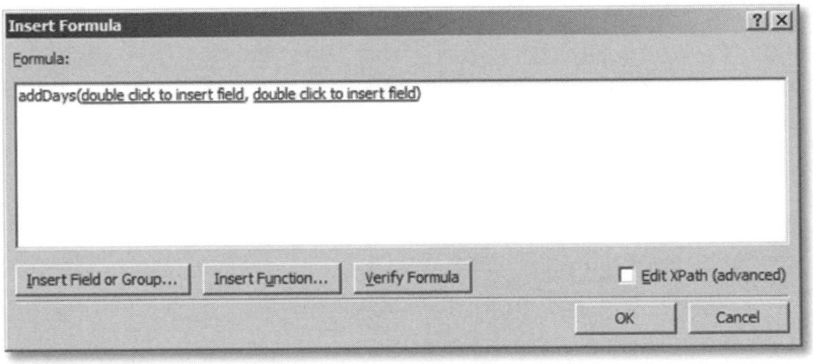

Illustration 257 - addDays function selected for Calc_Value_Six_Months_From_Start field default value formula

Double click the **first double click to insert** field. Choose the *Employee Information* secondary data source. Select the *Start_Date* field and click the **Filter Data** button. In the *Filter Data* dialogue screen create the **[Current_User = User_Name]** look-up filter. The *Insert Formula* dialogue screen will look like **Illustration 258** below.

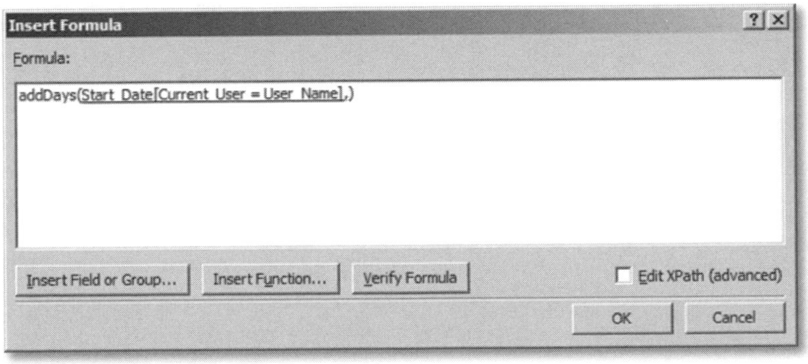

Illustration 258 - Filtered Start_Date value used in addDays formula function

After the comma (,) in the formula, enter the number "183" so that the completed formula looks like **Illustration 259** below.

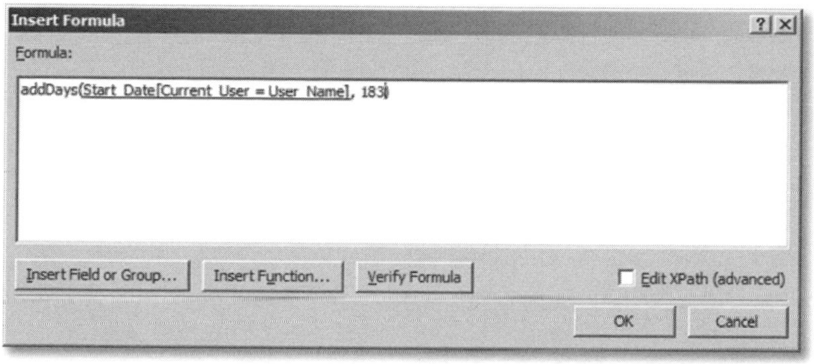

Illustration 259 - Completed formula for Calc_Value_Six_Months_From_Start field

Click **OK**. The *Properties* dialogue screen for the *Calc_Value_Six_Months_From_Start* field will look like **Illustration 260** below.

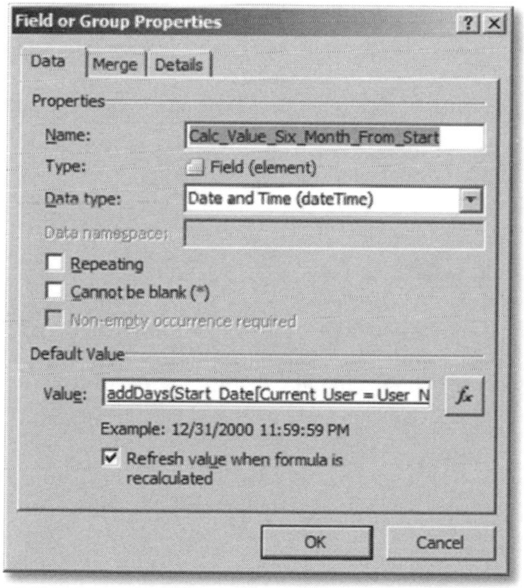

Illustration 260 - The Properties dialogue screen for the Calc_Value_Six_Months_From_Start field

This formula calculates the date value of the six month anniversary of an employee's start date which will be one of the rule condition criteria for determining whether a request requires approval by a manager.

Adding a Submit Button and Reviewing the Submit Rule Set Logic

Add a table with a single column and row between the *Personal Leave Days Requested* section and the *Approval Section*. Insert a **Button** control in this table and center it so that the design surface looks like **Illustration 261** below.

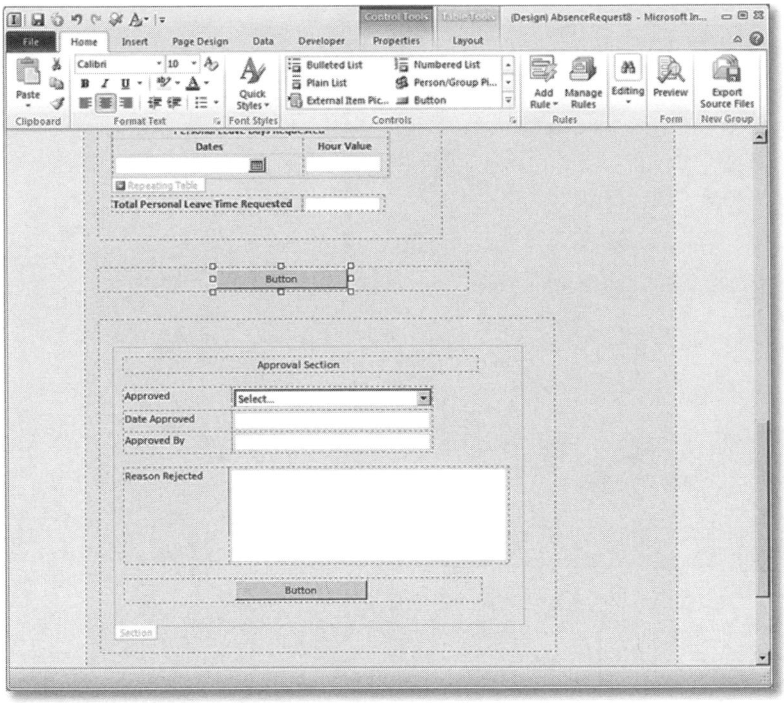

Illustration 261 - Table with Button control added to the form

Right click on the **Button** and select **Button Properties** to display the *Button Properties* dialogue screen as shown in **Illustration 262** below.

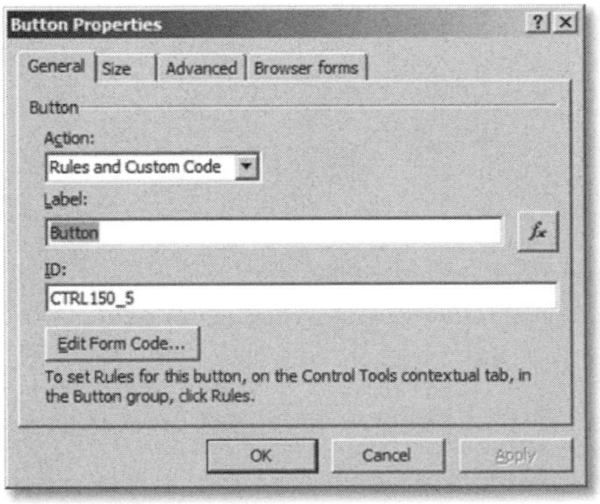

Illustration 262 - Button Properties dialogue screen

Change the **Label** from "Button" to "Submit Absence Request". Leave *Rules and Custom Code* as the setting for the **Action**.

We will create four rules for the *Submit Absence Request* button that implement the following rule conditions:

- If the employee has been employed for less than six months prior to the request date, and the total number of hours requested for all leave categories combined is equal to or less than 48 hours, than no approval of the request is required.

- If the employee has been employed for six months or more prior to the request date, and the total number of hours requested for all leave categories combined is equal to or less than 64 hours, than no approval of the request is required.

- If the employee has been employed for six months or less prior to the request date and the total number of hours requested for all leave categories combined is more than 48 hours, than approval of the request is required.

- If the employee has been employed for six months or more prior to the request date and the total number of hours requested for all leave categories combined is more than 64 hours, than approval of the request is required.

For the two rule conditions where no approval is required, the following actions will be executed:

- The value for the *Submitted* field will be set to "TRUE"
- The value for the *Approved* field will be set to "Yes"
- The completed form will be submitted to a SharePoint Library. The metadata columns of the library will be populated by a row of values from the corresponding form fields.
- A form *View* will be presented to the user that states: "Your request has been submitted and the Employee Information database is being updated. No approval of this request is required".

For the two rule conditions where approval is required, the following actions will be executed:

- The value for the *Submitted* field will be set to "TRUE"
- The value for the *Requires_Approval* field will be set to "Yes"
- The completed form will be submitted to a SharePoint Library. The metadata columns of the library will be populated by a row of values from the corresponding form fields.
- A form *View* will be presented to the user that states: "Your request has been submitted for approval by your Manager (with Manager's name)".

Publishing the Form and Creating the Host Form Library

Before we create the *Submit Absence Request* rule set and the *Submit data connection* for submitting the form to the *SharePoint* library we will publish the form template and simultaneously create the *SharePoint* form library that will host the form. This form library is where new instances of the form are created and completed instances will be submitted.

Click on the **File Menu button** from the *Ribbon*. The *Form Information* screen will display as shown in **Illustration 263** below.

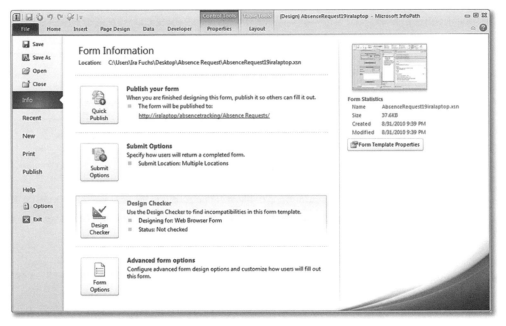

Illustration 263 - File Menu Form Information screen

Click the **Publish** button under the *File* options. The *Publish* options will display as shown in **Illustration 264** below.

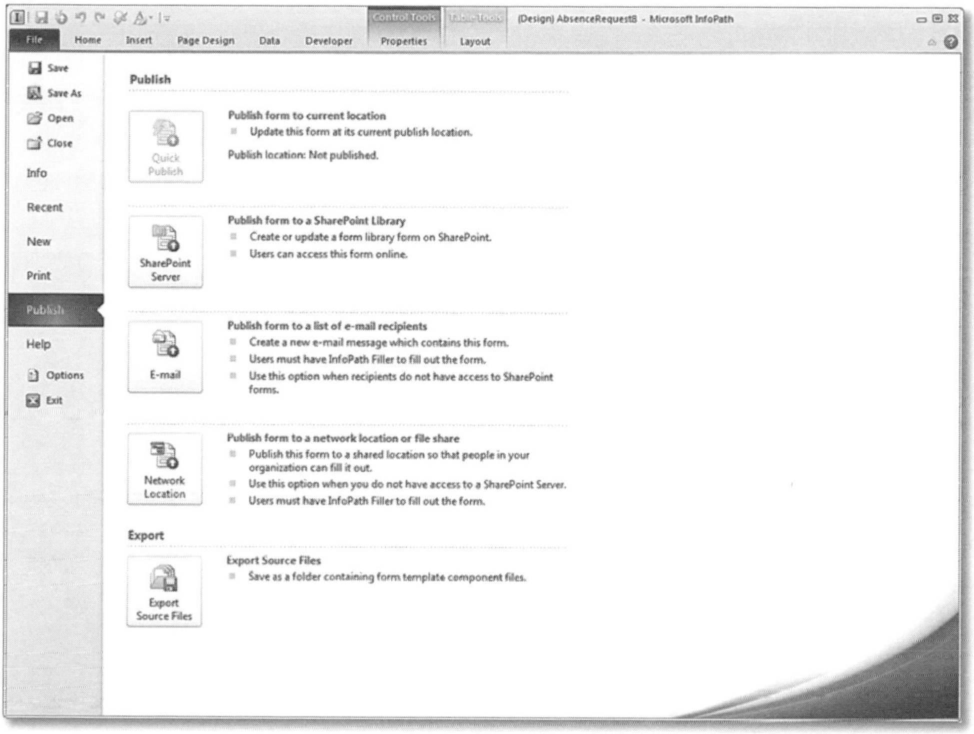

Illustration 264 - The Publish options under the File menue

Click the **SharePoint Server button** to **Publish form to a SharePoint Library.** The first screen of the *Publishing Wizard* will display. Enter the URL location of the *Absence Tracking* site that you created on your server as shown in **Illustration 265** below.

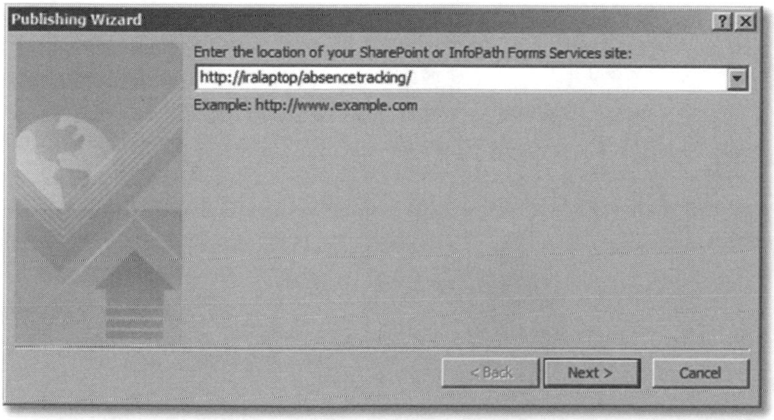

Illustration 265 - The first screen of the Publishing Wizard

Click **Next**. The second screen of the *Publishing Wizard* will appear. Make sure that the **checkbox** for **Enable this form to be filled out by using a browser** is checked, and the **radio button** for **Form Library** is selected as shown in **Illustration 266** below. As this form does not contain any code it does not need to be prepared for Farm Administrator approval processing.

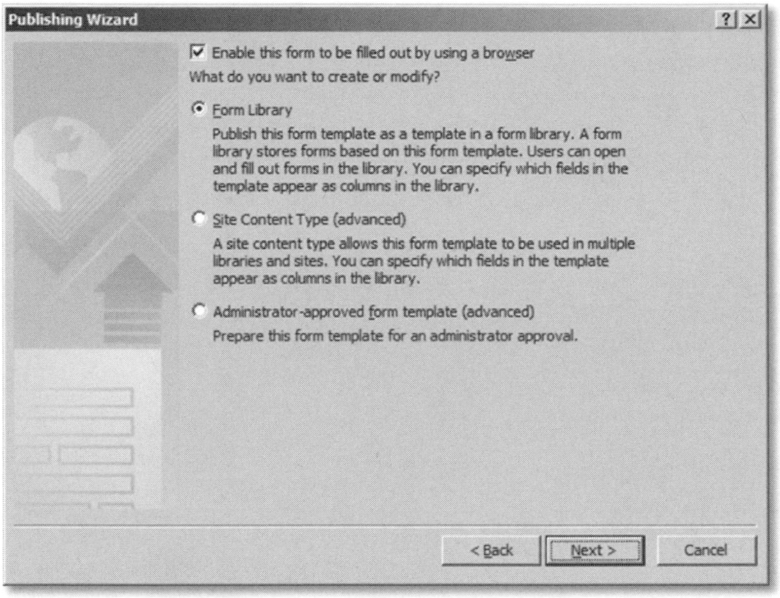

Illustration 266 - The second screen of the Publishing Wizard

Click **Next**. The third screen of the *Publishing Wizard* will display. Make sure that the **radio button** for **Create a new form library** is selected as shown in **Illustration 267** below.

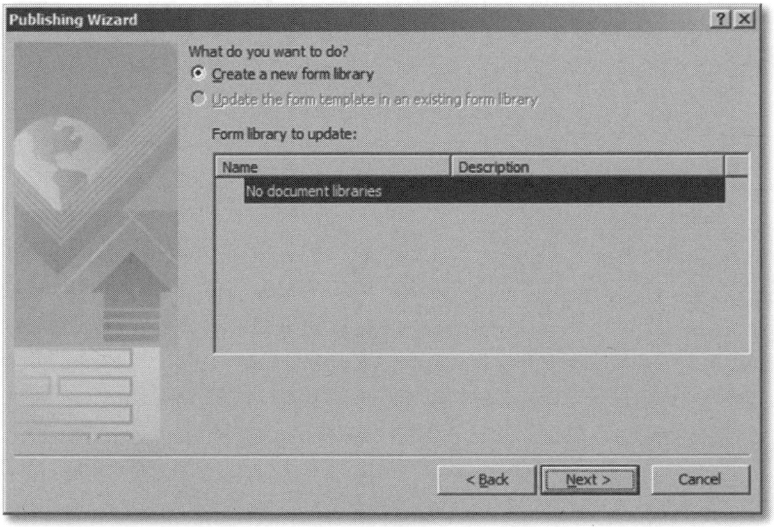

Illustration 267 - The third screen of the Publishing Wizard

Important – We will be re-publishing the form template a number of times. When we re-publish it we will be updating the same form library that we are creating now, **not creating a new one.** You can publish a form template to the same or a different form library any number of times.

Click **Next**. In the fourth *Publishing Wizard* screen name the form library "Absence Requests" as shown in **Illustration 268** below.

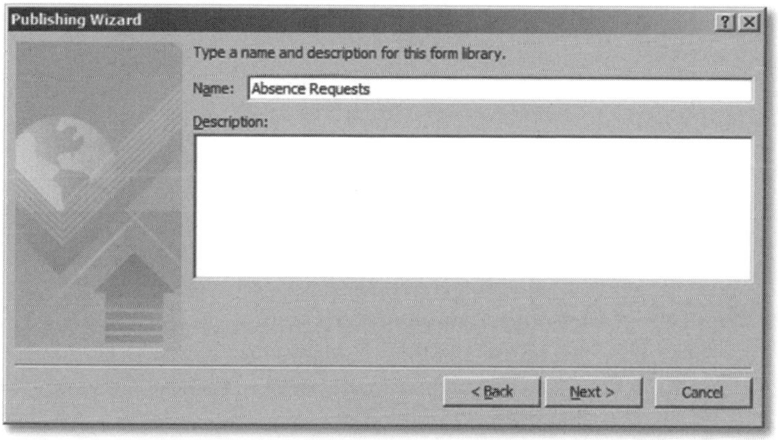

Illustration 268 - The fourth screen of the Publishing Wizard

In the fifth *Publishing Wizard* screen as shown in **Illustration 269** below we will choose the fields in the form that will be used to create the metadata columns in the form library and whose respective values will populate a row each time an *Absence Request* form is submitted.

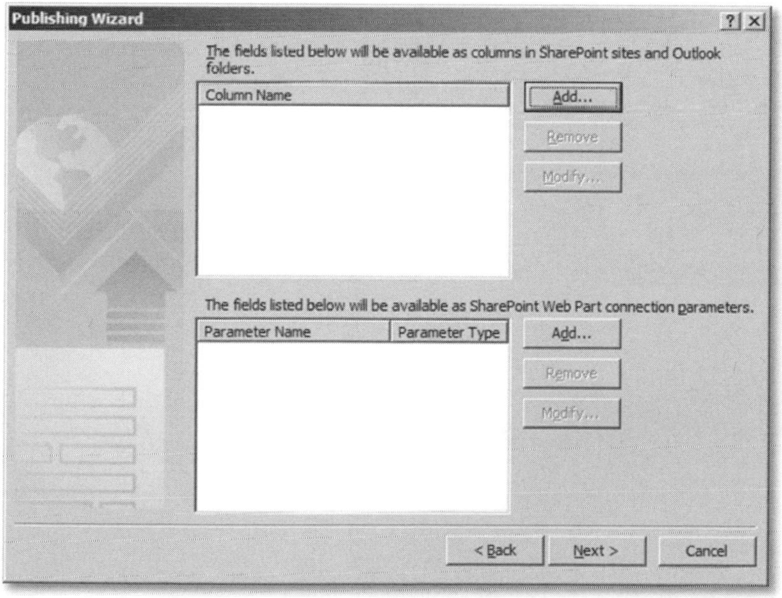

Illustration 269 - The fourth screen of the Publishing Wizard

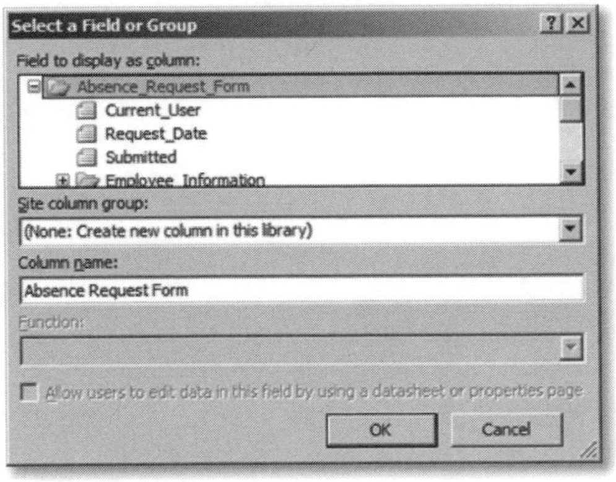

Illustration 270 - Select a Field or Group screen for
fields to populate the form library columns

Click the **Add** button to choose the fields that will display
as form library columns. The **Select a Field or Group**
dialogue screen will display as shown in **Illustration 270**
at left.

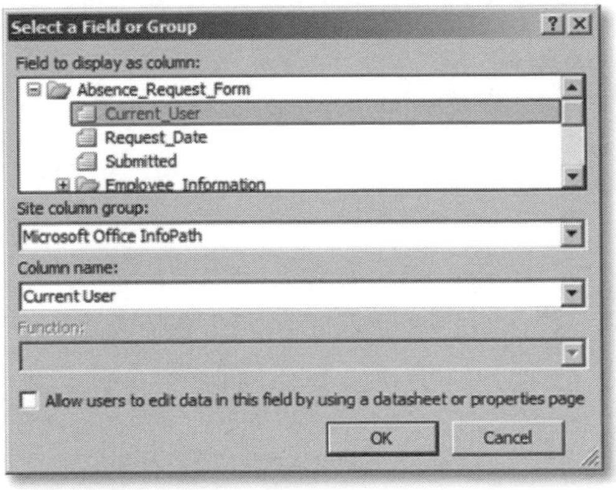

Illustration 271 - Selecting the fields to populate
the form library columns

Select the **Current_User** field. Leave the **Site column
group** value of *(None: Create a new column in this library)*.
Leave *Current User* for the **Column name** as shown in
Illustration 271 at left.

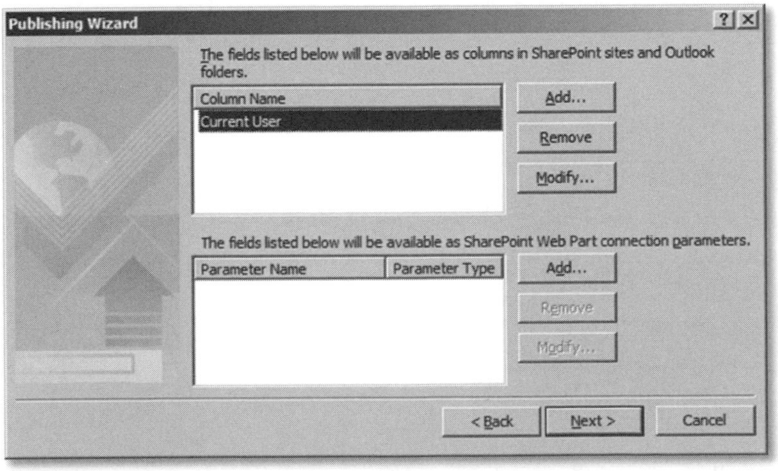

Illustration 272 - The fourth screen of the Publishing Wizard

Current User is now selected
to be a column in the library
as shown in **Illustration 272**
at left.

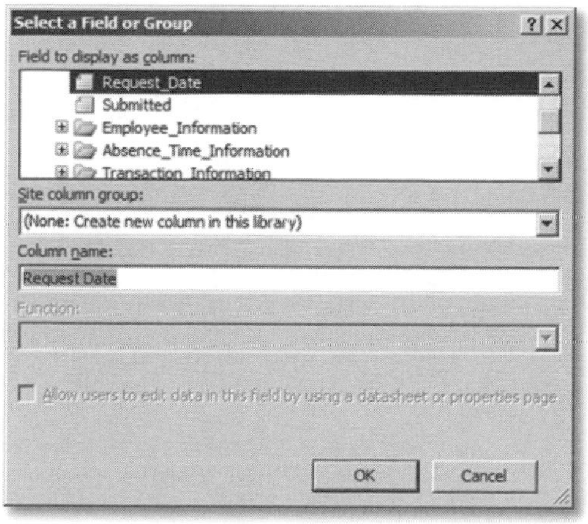

Illustration 273 - Request_Date selected to populate a library column

Click the **Add** button again. Select the **Request_Date** field. Leave the default **Site Column group** and **Column name** values. The *Select a Field or Group* dialogue screen will look like **Illustration 273** at left.

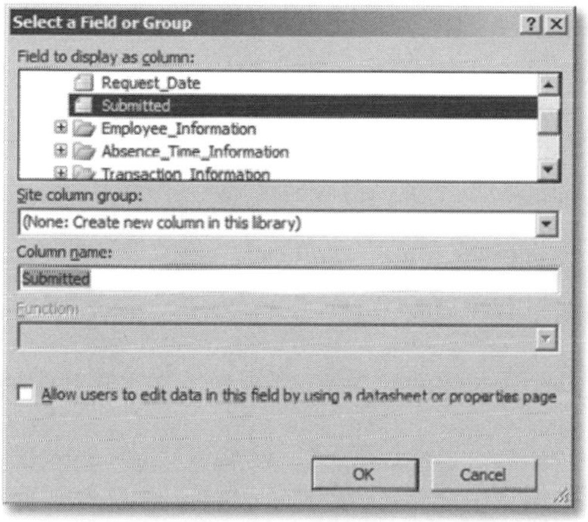

Illustration 274 - Submitted field selected to populate a library column

Click the **Add** button on the *Publishing Wizard* screen again to select additional fields to display as columns. Select the **Submitted** field from the *Select a Field or Group* dialogue screen as shown in **Illustration 274** at left. Leave the default **Site Column group** and **Column name** values.

Important Note – Do not check the **Allow users to edit data in this field by using a datasheet or properties page checkbox** as shown in **Illustration 274** above, for any of the fields *with the exception of* the *Approved* field. Not checking this box will make the information populating the form library read only when the form is submitted, *with the exception of the* Approved field, which will be *editable as a result of checking this option*. We need to make this field editable because one of the workflow actions will be to set the value of the *Approved* field in the library to "Yes".

Click **OK**. Continue adding the following fields:

> *Full_ Name*
> *Email*
> *Manager_User_Name*
> *Manager Email*
> *Organization_Code*
> *Total Vacation_Time_Requested*
> *Total Sick Day_Time_Requested*
> *Requires_Approval*
> *Approved*
> *Approval_Date*
> *Updated_Vacation_Time_Used*
> *Updated_Vacation_Time_Bal*
> *Updated_Sick_Leave_Used*
> *Updated_Sick_Leave_Bal*
> *Updated_Pers_Leave_Used*
> *Updated_Pers_Leave_Bal*
> *Total_Time_Requested*

When you are finished adding these fields the *Publishing Wizard* will look like
Illustration 275 below

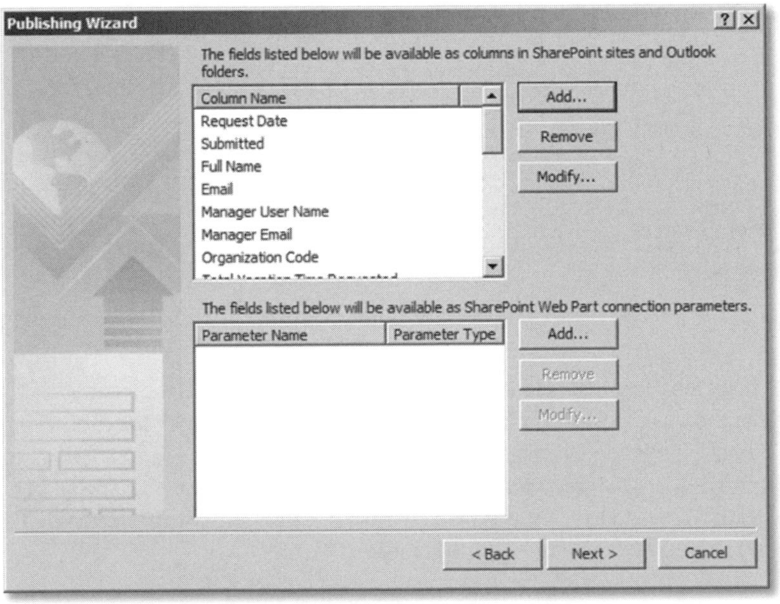

Illustration 275 - Publishing Wizard with all fields selected to be library columns

Click **Next** to display the final confirmation screen before publishing as shown in **Illustration 276** below.

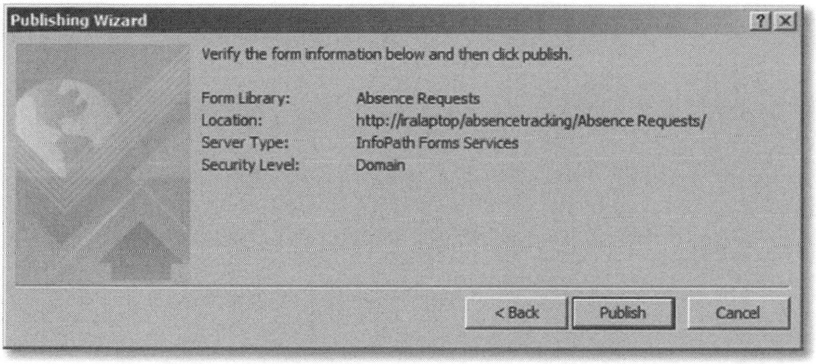

Illustration 276 – Final page of Publishing Wizard

Click the **Publish** button. The Publishing Wizard will connect to the site, create the library with the specified column metadata and publish the form template to *InfoPath Form Services* so that the form can be rendered in a browser. This process will take several minutes and will display the screen shown in **Illustration 277** below.

Illustration 277 - Publishing to InfoPath Forms Service message

Let's see what we have just accomplished. Go to the *Absence Tracking* site where you will now see than an *Absence Request* library has been created. Click on the link for the library to navigate to it as shown in **Illustration 278** below.

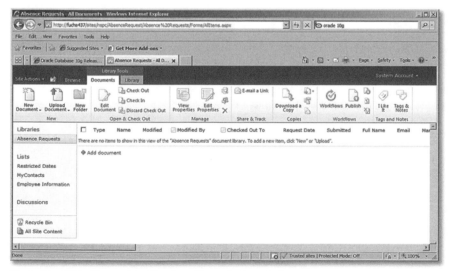

Illustration 278 - Absence Tracking form library just created

You will see that the library columns are the form fields that were specified in the *Publishing Wizard*. Note that there are also default columns that *SharePoint* automatically generates such as *Type, Name, Modified, Modified By* and *Checked Out*. The columns that are displayed and their order can be adjusted on the *Library Settings* page of *SharePoint* or in *SharePoint Designer*. We will do this, in addition to creating custom views of the library later.

Click on the **Add document** link, or with the **Documents** tab selected on the **Library Tools** Ribbon, click the **New Document** button. The *Absence Request* form will load for the current user logged in to *SharePoint*. **Illustration 279** below shows the new *Absence Request Form* for the logged in user Ira Fuchs.

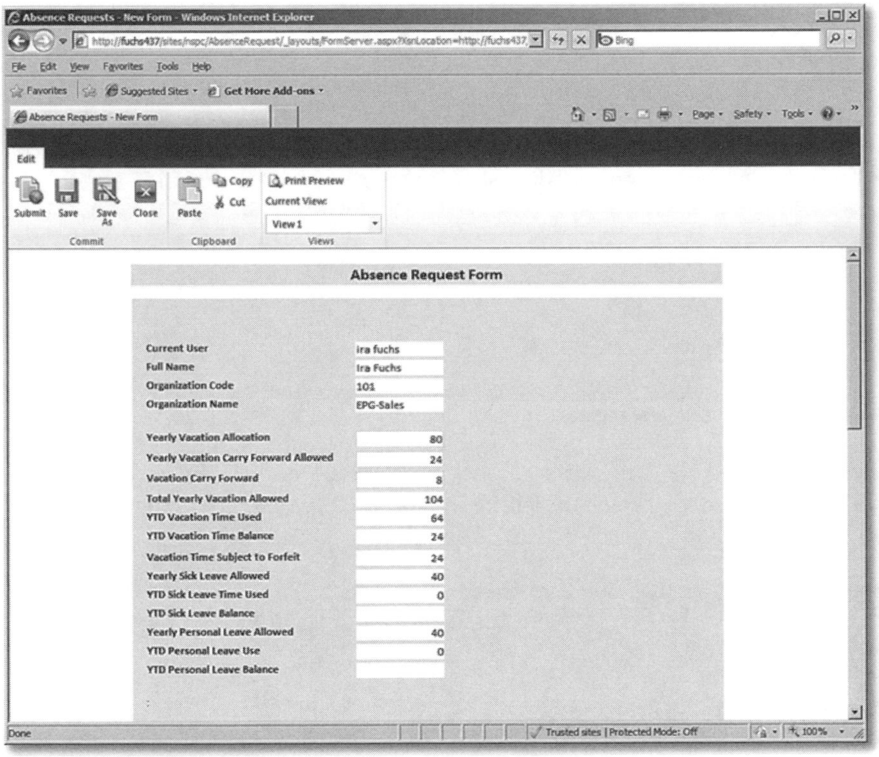

Illustration 279 - New Absence Request Form created when Ira Fuchs is logged in

Illustration 280 below shows a new *Absence Request Form* for Adam Fuchs when he logs onto the site.

Illustration 280 - a new Absence Request Form for Adam Fuchs

Notice that the *Ribbon* menu for the form allows the different *Views* that were created to be selected by the user. We will change the settings in the form so that only the *Close* option is available on the run-time form. We only want users to be able to submit using the buttons that we placed in the form in order to execute all the necessary submit logic that we will be creating shortly.

> **Development Note** – Although we published the *Absence Request* form template to a form library (also named *Absence Request*), instances of the form initiated from this host form library do not have to be submitted back to the same form library where the template was published. Any number of *Submit to SharePoint Library* data connections can be created and a form can be submitted to any one of these generic document libraries using rule logic as well as content in the form to facilitate content based routing. The fields in the form that were designated to display as metadata columns with a corresponding row of values for each form submitted will apply to all of the document libraries submitted to. There is no functional requirement in this application to submit form instances to a separate library so we will be submitting instances of the form back to the form library hosting the template.

Important Note – When we have completed developing the form and before we start development of the application workflow we will publish the *Absence Request Form* as a *Site Content Type*. The *Publishing Wizard* option for this is shown in **Illustration 281** below.

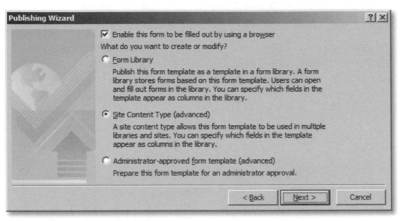

Illustration 281 - Publishing Wizard page where publishing form as a Site Content Type is specified

Publishing the *Absence Request* form as a *Site Content Type* allows the form to be re-used in other sites and libraries. This is an important feature of *Content Types* in general and we will discuss this later. However, the more important reason why we will publish the form as a *Content Type* is that we will be able to create a reusable workflow that we can bind to this *Form Content Type* that will provide *Current Item* context. *Current Item* context is the ability of the workflow to correlate its activities to each unique request instance automatically. We will also discuss this in more detail later when we create the workflow component of the application.

Creating the Submit Data Connection and Using a Formula to Generate a Unique File Name for the Submitted Form

The next step is to create the data connection for submitting completed instances of the form to the form library we just created. On the **Submit Form** Ribbon tab click on the **To SharePoint Library** button. The *Data Connection Wizard* screen shown in **Illustration 282** below will display.

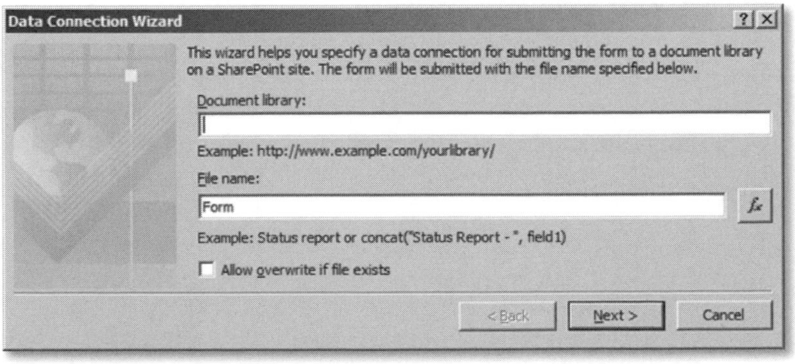

Illustration 282 - First page of Data Connection Wizard to submit to a library

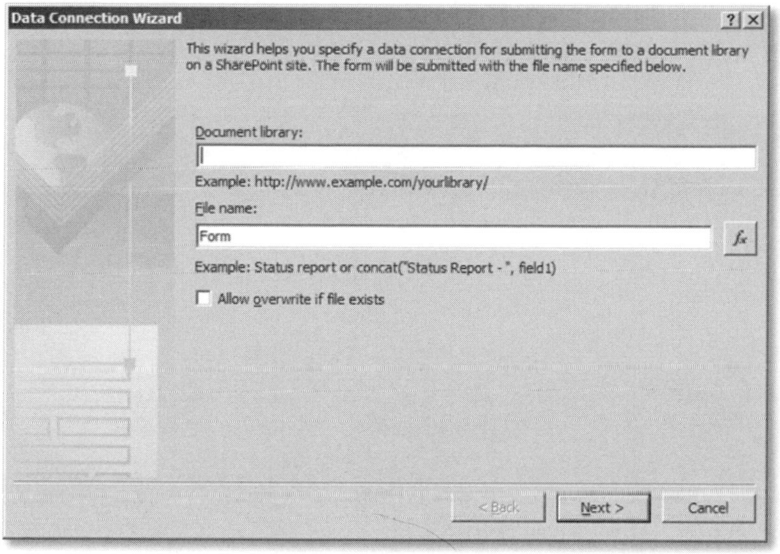

Illustration 282 - First page of Data Connection Wizard to submit to a library

Enter the URL address of the Document (or Form) Library that form will be submitted to as shown in **Illustration 283** below.

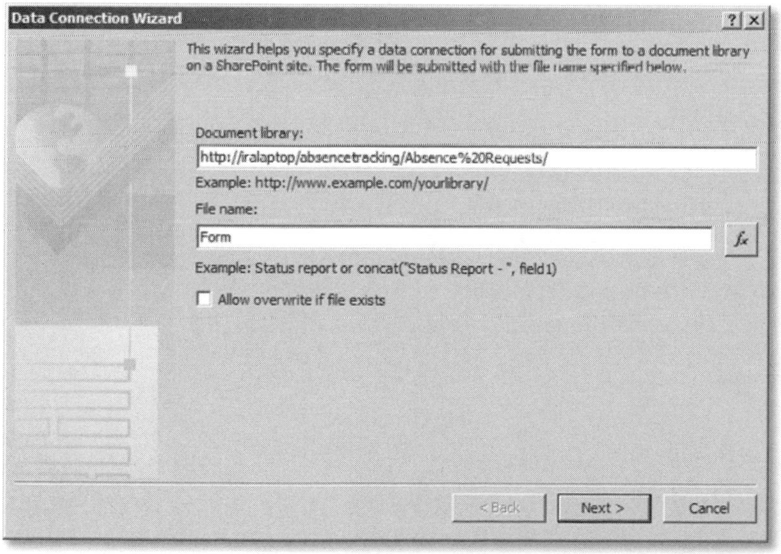

Illustration 283- Second page of Data Connection Wizard identifying the address of the library to be submitted to

Click on the **Formula** button for the **File Name** field. The **Insert Formula** dialogue screen will appear. Click on the **Insert Function** button to display the **Insert Function** dialogue screen as shown in **Illustration 284** below.

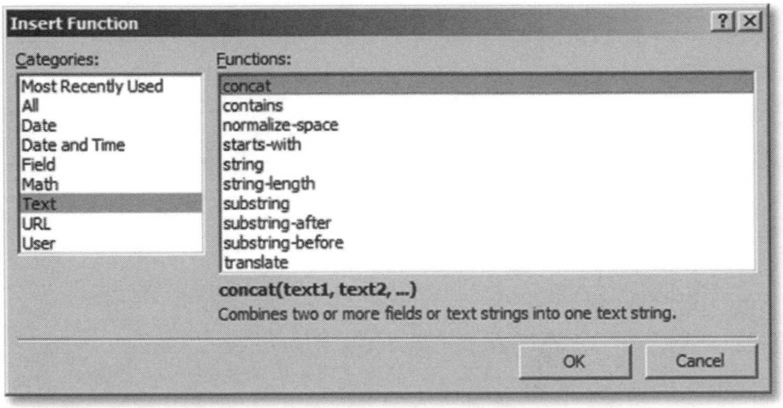

Illustration 284 - Insert Function dialogue screen with concat function selected

Click **Text** in the *Categories* list and select **concat** in the *Functions* list. The *Insert Formula* dialogue screen will look like Illustration **285** below.

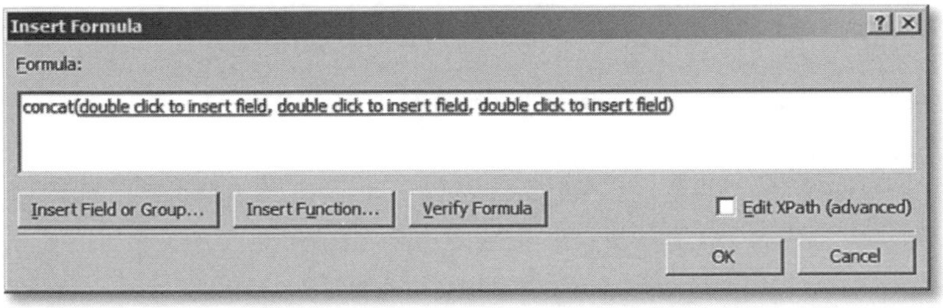

Illustration 285 - Insert Formula dialogue screen with concat function

Double click on the first **double click to insert field** instance and select the **Current_User** field from the *Main* data source. Double click again on the second **double click to insert field** instance and select the **Request_Date** field. Double click the third **double click to insert field** and select the **Total_Time_Requested** field.

Add a comma (**,**) and add as the fourth field the **Updated_Vac_Time_Used** field. Add the closing right parenthesis (**)**) so that the formula looks like **Illustration 286** below.

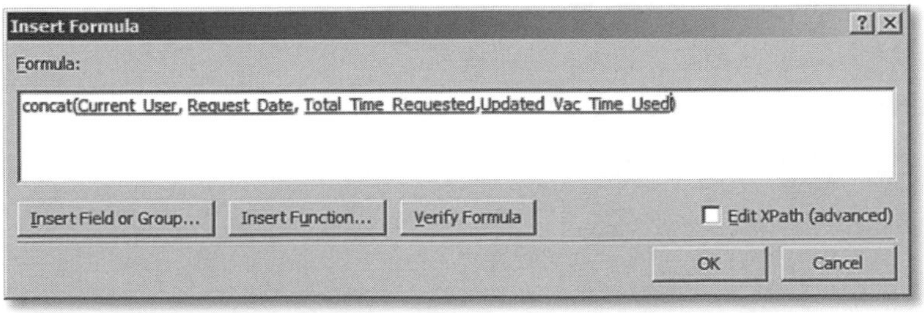

Illustration 286 - Insert Formula dialogue screen with completed formula

Click **OK**. Select the check box for **Allow overwrite if the file exists**. The *Data Connection Wizard* screen will now look like **Illustration 287** below.

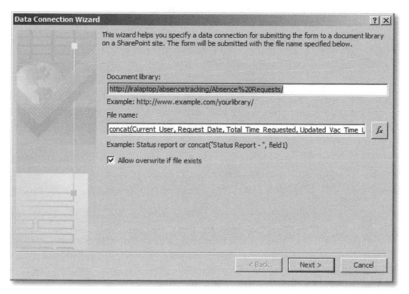

Illustration 287 - Data Connection Wizard with library and File name specified

The **File name**, which will display in the *Name* column of the *Absence Request* form library, will be a combination of the *Current_User*, the *Request_Date*, the *Total_Time_Requested* and the *Updated_Vac_Time_Used* values in the form.

> **Important Note** – The choice of these concatenated values is designed to generate a unique value for the name of the submitted form. The *Updated_Vac_Time_Used stored* value will be used to update the *YTD_Vac_Time_Used* value in the *Employee Information* database by the workflow. Since this new value will be displayed and used the next time an absence request is created this recursive mechanism gives us the means to generate a unique name for each submitted instance of the form.

> **Important Note** – This application is designed so that once a request is submitted by an initiator it cannot be opened, edited and re-submitted. It can only be opened by the initiator in read-only mode. If the request requires a manager's approval, the manager will be able to open the form, approve or reject it, and then re-submit it. Hence the requirement for allowing overwrites of the form instance if the file exists.

Click **Next**. The *Data Connection Wizard* will connect to the *Absence Request* form library.
In the final screen of *the Data Connection Wizard* leave the default name, *SharePoint Library Submit*
for the data connection name as shown in **Illustration 288** below. Click the **Finish** button.

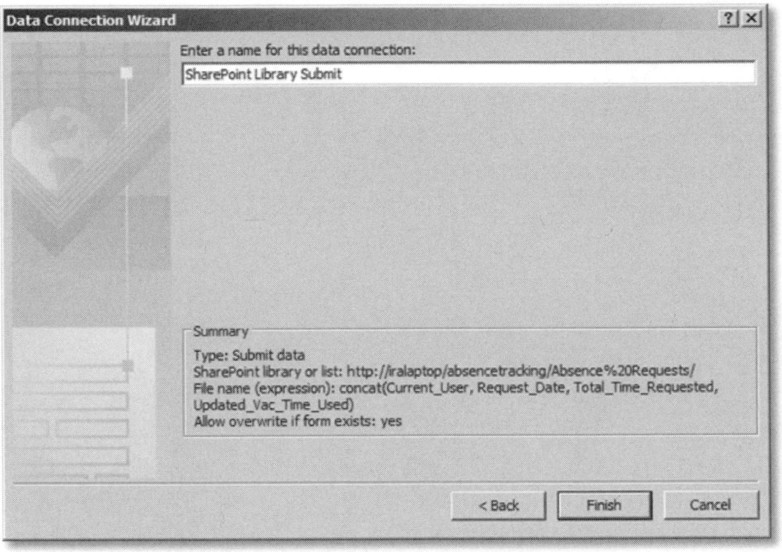

Illustration 288 - Final screen of the Data Connection Wizard

Click on the **Data Connections** tab on the *Ribbon* to display *the Data Connections* for the form template.
The *SharePoint Library Submit* data connection will be listed as shown in **Illustration 289** below.

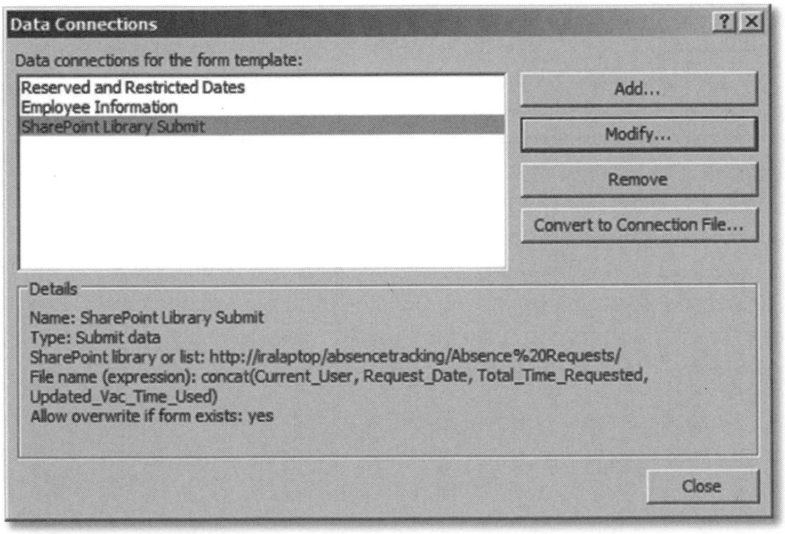

**Illustration 289 - SharePoint Library Submit Data Connection in Data Connections
dialogue screen**

Creating the Submit Rule Set

We will now create the submit rule set that that implements the following conditional criteria:

- If the employee has been employed for six months or less prior to the request date, and the total number of hours requested for all categories combined is equal to or less than 48 hours, than no approval of the request is required.

- If the employee has been employed for at least six months prior to the request date, and the total number of hours requested for all categories combined is equal to or less than 64 hours, than no approval of the request is required.

- If the employee has been employed for six months or less prior to the request date and the total number of hours requested for all categories combined is more than 48 hours, than approval of the request is required.

- If the employee has been employed for at least six months prior to the request date and the total number of hours requested for all categories combined is more than 64 hours, than approval of the request is required.

The actions that will be executed for the two rules where no approval is required are:

- The value for the *Submitted* field will be set to "TRUE"
- The value for the *Requires_Approval* field will be set to "No"
- The value for the *Approved* field will be set to "Yes"
- The completed form will be submitted to the *SharePoint* library.
- A form View will be presented to the user that states: "Your request has been submitted and the Employee Information database is being updated. No approval of this request is required".

The actions that will be executed for the two rules where an approval is required are:

- The value for the *Submitted* field will be set to "TRUE"
- The value for the *Requires_Approval* field will be set to "Yes"
- The completed form will be submitted to a *SharePoint* library.
- A form View will be presented to the user that states: "Your request has been submitted for approval by your Manager (with Manager's name)".

With the **Submit Absence Request** button selected click on the **Manage Rules** Ribbon button to open the **Rules** panel. Click **New** and choose **Action**. Name the rule "Less than 6 months, less than 48 hours".

Click **None** under **Condition** to display the *Condition* dialogue screen. Create the condition statement shown in **Illustration 290** below.

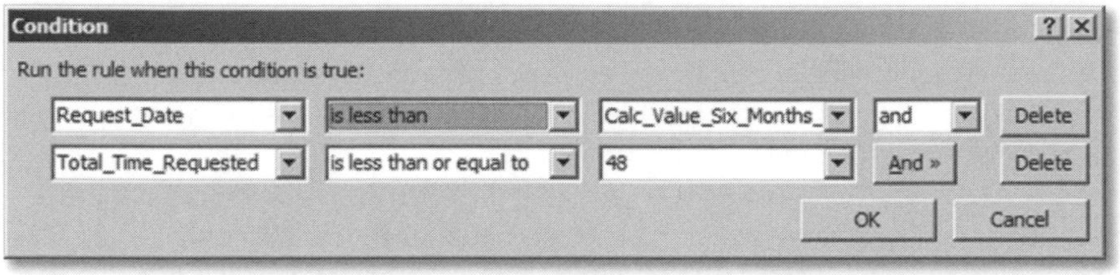

Illustration 290 - Condition statement for Less than 6 months, less than 48 hours rule

The *Calc_Value_Six_Months_From_Start* field stores a calculated date value that is equal to the employee's start date plus six months. The first condition clause evaluates if the request date is less than six months from the employee's start date.

Click **Add** to select the **Set a field's value** action. In the *Rule Details* dialogue screen select the **Submitted** field from the **Main** data source for the **Field** value and enter "TRUE" for the **Value** as shown in **Illustration 291** below.

Add another **Set a field's value** action to set the value of the **Requires Approval** field to "No".

Add a last **Set a field's value** action to set the value of the **Approved** field to "Yes".

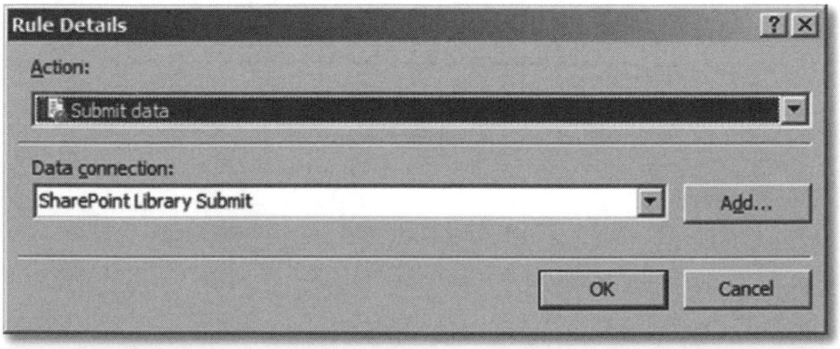

Illustration 291 - Set the Submitted field value to TRUE action

Add a **Submit data** action and select **SharePoint Library Submit Data** connection as shown in **Illustration 292** at left.

Illustration 292 - Submit data action to submit using the SharePoint Library Submit Data connection

Click on the **Page Design** tab on the *Ribbon* and click on **New View**. Name the View "Submitted and Approved". Create a single row and column table with the text shown in **Illustration 293** below.

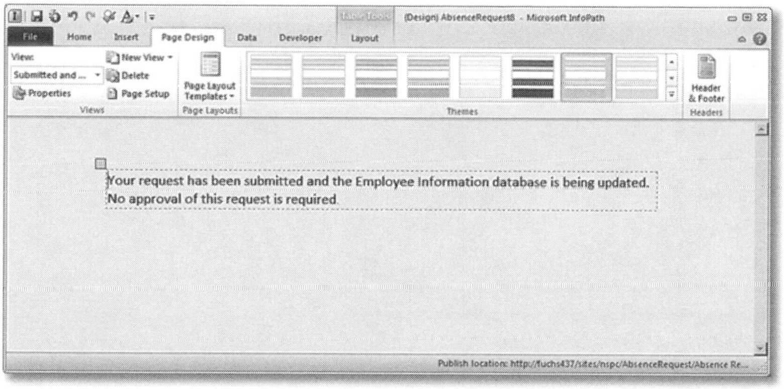

Illustration 293 - New "Submitted and Approved" View

Click on the **Properties** button to display the **View Properties** dialogue screen. De-select the **Show on the View menu when filling out this form check box** so that it is not checked as shown in **Illustration 294** below.

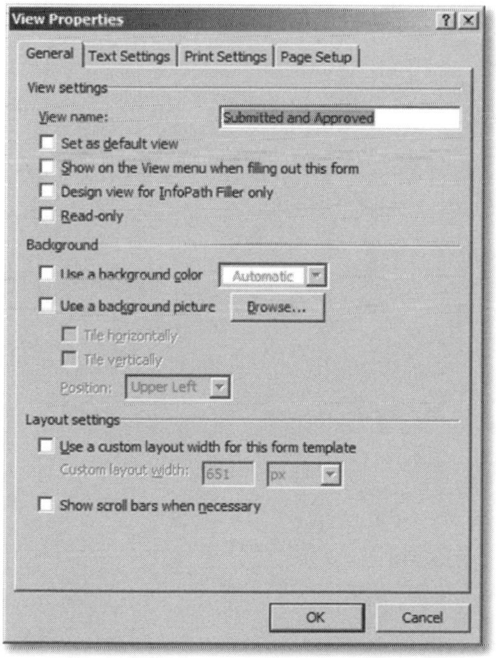

Illustration 294 - View Properties dialogue screen with Show on the View menu when filling out this form de-selected

Click **OK**. Select the **View 1 (default)** View. Click the **Properties** button. Change the **View Name** to "Main View". Click **OK**.

Select the **Submit Absence Request button** and open the *Rules* panel.
Add a **Switch views** action and select the **Submitted and Approved View** as shown in **Illustration 295** below.

Illustration 295 - Switch views action added to the first submit rule

Click **OK**. The completed *Less than 6 months, less than 48 hours* rule should look like **Illustration 296** below.

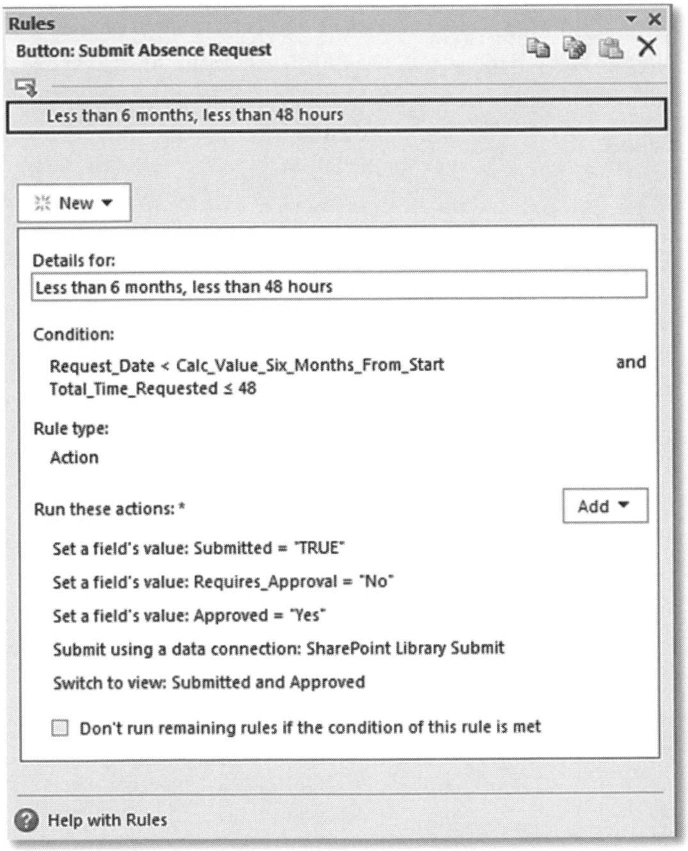

Illustration 296 - The completed Less than 6 months, less than 48 hours rule

Now we will add the second rule. Click **New** and select **Action**. Name the rule "More than 6 months, less than 64 hours". Click **None** under **Conditions** and create the condition statement shown in **Illustration 297** below.

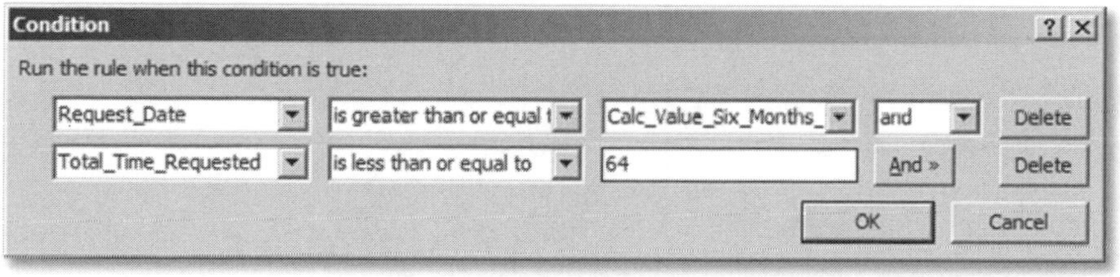

Illustration 297 - Condition statement for the More than 6 months, less than 64 hours rule

Click **Add** to select the **Set a field's value** action. In the **Rule Details** dialogue screen select the **Submitted** field from the **Main** data source for **Field**, and enter "TRUE" for the **Value**.

Add another **Set a field's value** action to set the value of the field **Requires_Approval** to "No".

Add a last **Set a field's value** action to set the value of the field **Approved** to "Yes".

Add a **Submit data** action and select **SharePoint Library Submit Data** connection.

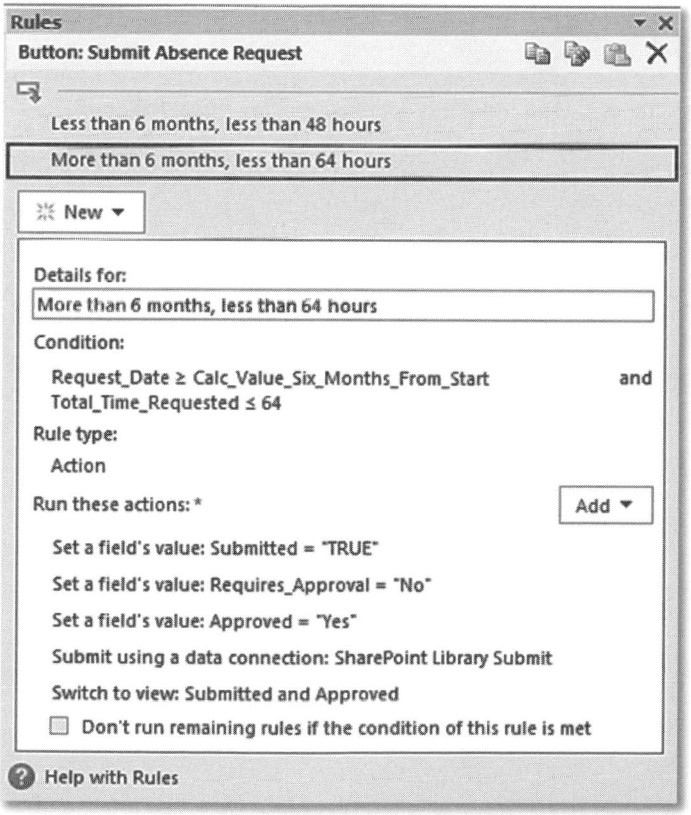

Add a **Switch views** action and select the **Submitted and Approved View.** The completed *More than 6 months, less than 64 hours* rule will look like **Illustration 298** at left.

Illustration 298 - The completed More than 6 months, less than 64 hours rule

Now we will add the third rule. Click **New** and select **Action**. Name the rule "Less than 6 months, more than 48 hours".

Click **None** under **Conditions** and create the condition statement shown in **Illustration 299** below.

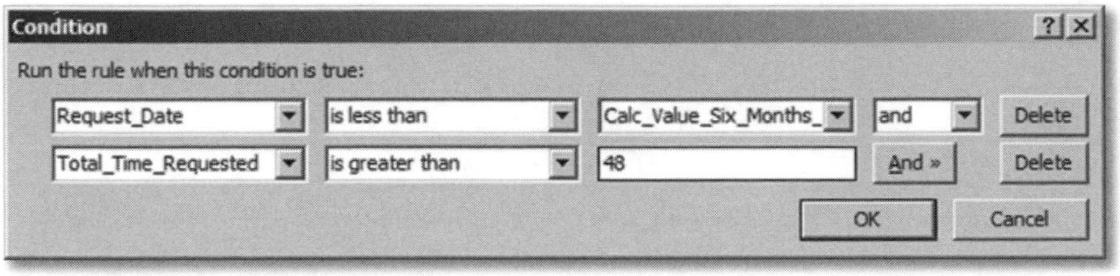

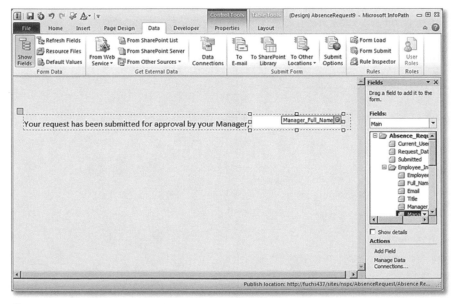

Illustration 299 - Condition statement for the Less than 6 months, more than 48 hours rule

Click **Add** to select the **Set a field's value** action. In the **Rule Details** dialogue screen select the **Submitted** field from the **Main** data source for **Field**, and enter "TRUE" for the **Value.**

Add another **Set a field's value** action to set the value of the field **Requires_Approval** to "Yes". Add a **Submit data** action and select **SharePoint Library Submit Data**.

Click on the **Page Design** Ribbon tab and click on **New View**. Name the *View* "Submitted for Approval". Create a single row and column table with the following text: "Your request has been submitted for approval by your Manager".

Place a **Text Box** control for the *Manager_Full_Name* field after the text as shown in **Illustration 300** below.

Illustration 300 - New Submitted for Approval View

Select the **Text Box**, right click and choose **Properties**. Select **Borders and Shading**. Select the **Shading tab** and choose the **No color** radio button. Click **OK**.

View Properties dialogue screen

General | Text Settings | Print Settings | Page Setup |

View settings

View name: Submitted for Approval

☐ Set as default view
☐ Show on the View menu when filling out this form
☐ Design view for InfoPath Filler only
☐ Read-only

Background

☐ Use a background color   Automatic
☐ Use a background picture   Browse...
   ☐ Tile horizontally
   ☐ Tile vertically
   Position: Upper Left

Layout settings

☐ Use a custom layout width for this form template
   Custom layout width: 651   px
☐ Show scroll bars when necessary

OK   Cancel

Illustration 301 - View Properties dialogue screen with "Show on the View menu when filling out this form de-selected

Click on the **Page Design** Ribbon tab and click the **Properties** button to display the **View Properties** dialogue screen. De-select the **Show on the View menu when filling out this form** check box so that it is not checked as shown in **Illustration 301** at left.

Return to the **Main View**. Select the **Submit Absence Request button** and open the **Rules** panel. Select the **Less than 6 months, more than 48 hours** rule.

Add a **Switch views** action and select the **Submitted for Approval** view.

The completed *Less than 6 months, more than 48 hours* rule will look like **Illustration 302** at left.

Rules

Button: Submit Absence Request

Less than 6 months, less than 48 hours

More than 6 months, less than 64 hours

Less than 6 months, more than 48 hours

⁂ New ▾

Details for:

Less than 6 months, more than 48 hours

Condition:

Request_Date < Calc_Value_Six_Months_From_Start   and
Total_Time_Requested > 48

Rule type:

Action

Run these actions: *   Add ▾

Set a field's value: Submitted = "TRUE"

Set a field's value: Requires_Approval = "Yes"

Submit using a data connection: SharePoint Library Submit

Switch to view: Submitted for Approval

☐ Don't run remaining rules if the condition of this rule is met

❓ Help with Rules

Illustration 302 - The completed Less than 6 months, more than 48 hours rule

Now we will create the fourth and last rule. Click **New** and select **Action**. Name the rule "More than 6 months, more than 64 hours". Click **None** under **Conditions** and create the condition statement shown in **Illustration 303** below.

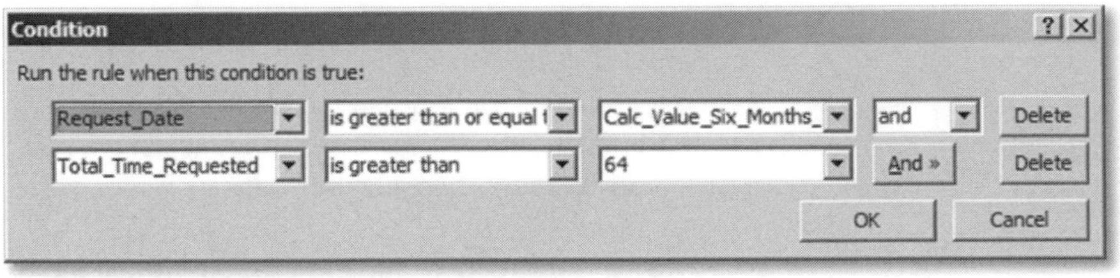

Illustration 303 - Condition statement for the More than 6 months, more than 64 hours rule

Add the same actions used in the *third* rule. The completed *More than 6 months, more than 64 hours* rule will look like **Illustration 304** below.

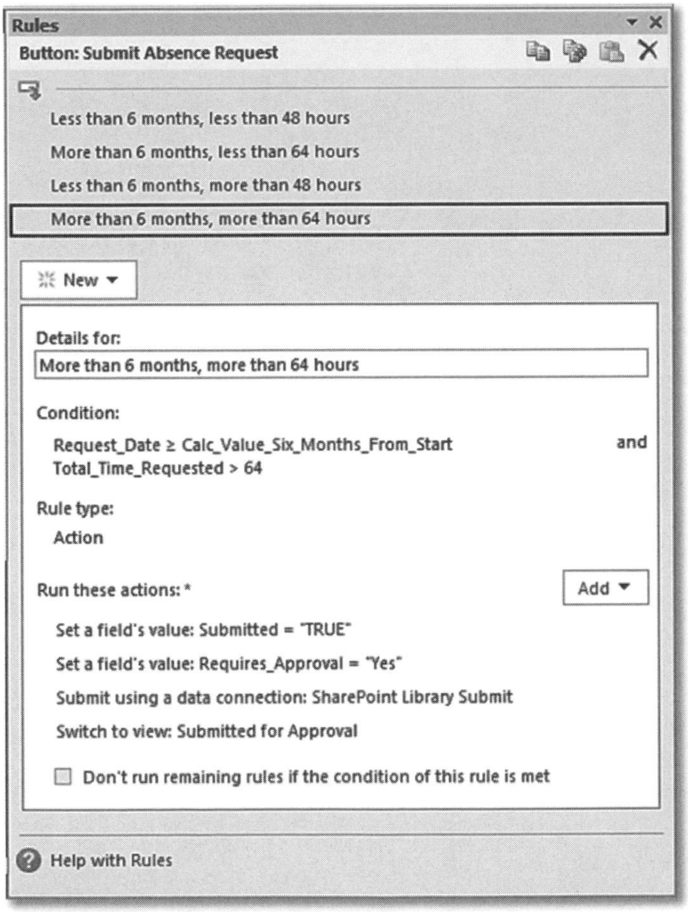

Illustration 304 - The completed More than 6 months, more than 64 hours rule

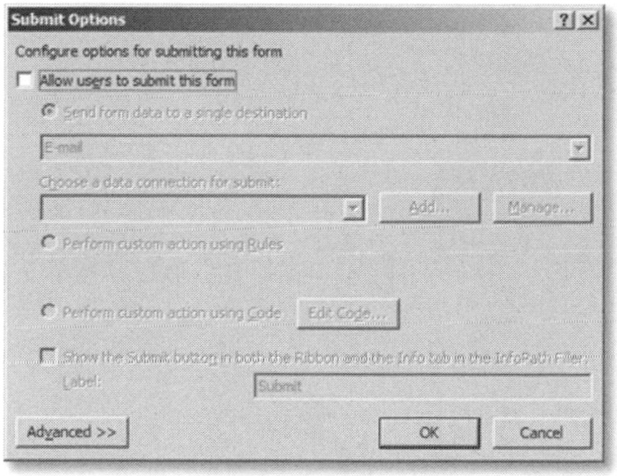

Illustration 305 - The Submit Options dialogue screen

Before we test these rules and the submit behavior of the *Submit Absence Request button* we should check the settings of the *Submit Options* for the form. Click the **Data** tab on the *Ribbon* and click the **Submit Options** button. The *Submit Options* dialogue screen will display as shown in **Illustration 305** at left.

Make sure that the checkbox for **Allow users to submit this form** is *not* checked. The *Submit Options* settings are used when the form is being designed to be submitted by clicking a *Submit* button on the Ribbon. Since we are using a custom button embedded in the form we want to disable all other submit options.

Testing the Submit Rules

We are now ready to test the **Submit Absence Request** logic. If you want to see the values for *Start_Date* and *Calc_Val_Six_Months_From_Start* that drive the rule logic drag these fields temporarily to the design surface of the form.

Go to the *Employee Information* ECT list and change the *Start Date* for the *Current User* so that it is less than six months from the *Current Date*.

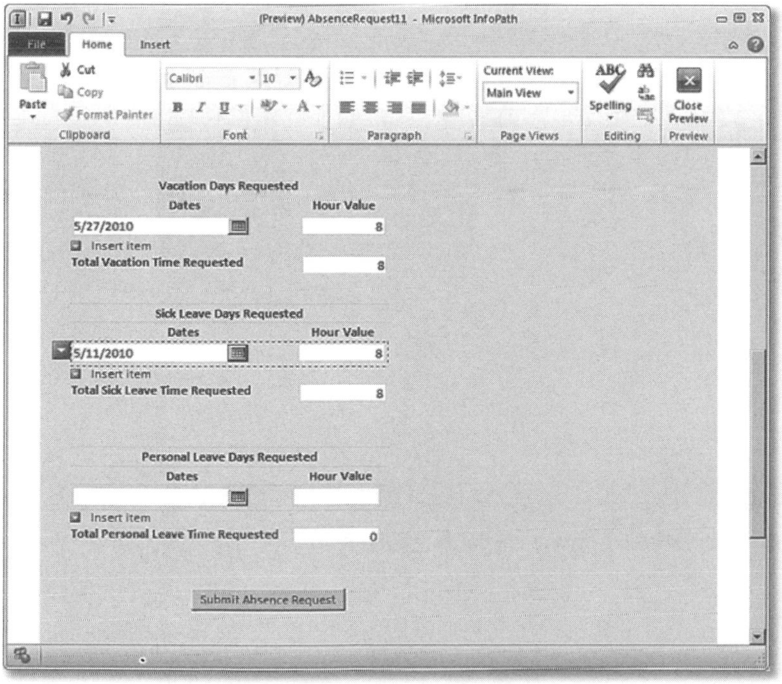

In the form click the **Preview button** on the **Ribbon**. Make two date selections in any leave category so that the combined number of hours is 16 as shown in **Illustration 306** at left.

Illustration 306 - Preview of the form with two leave dates requested

Click the **Submit Absence Request button**. Once the form has been submitted the *Submitted and Approved* view is displayed as shown in **Illustration 307** below, which is the action specified for the form rule *Less than 6 months, less than 48 hours*. Close the form preview.

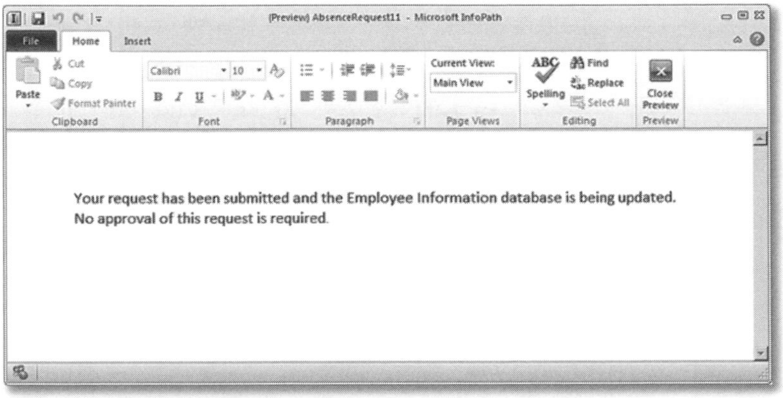

Illustration 307 - Form view displayed for Less than 6 months, less than 48 hours rule

Go to the *Absence Request* form library. You will see an absence request instance posted as shown in **Illustration 308** below. Note that for the new form instance there is a value of TRUE in the *Submitted* column, No in the *Requires Approval* column and Yes in the *Approved* column.

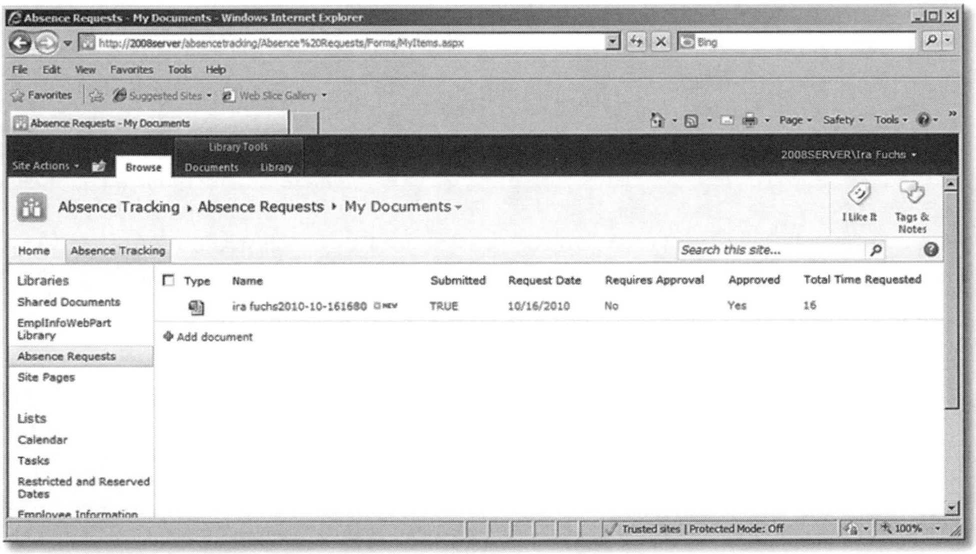

Illustration 308 - Absence Requests form library showing instance of the form submitted

Click the **Preview button** of the form template again. Now we want to test what happens when the number of leave hours requested is more than 48 hours and the employee has been on the job for less than six months. Choose any combination of leave dates so that the total hours requested exceeds 48 hours as shown in **Illustration 309** below.

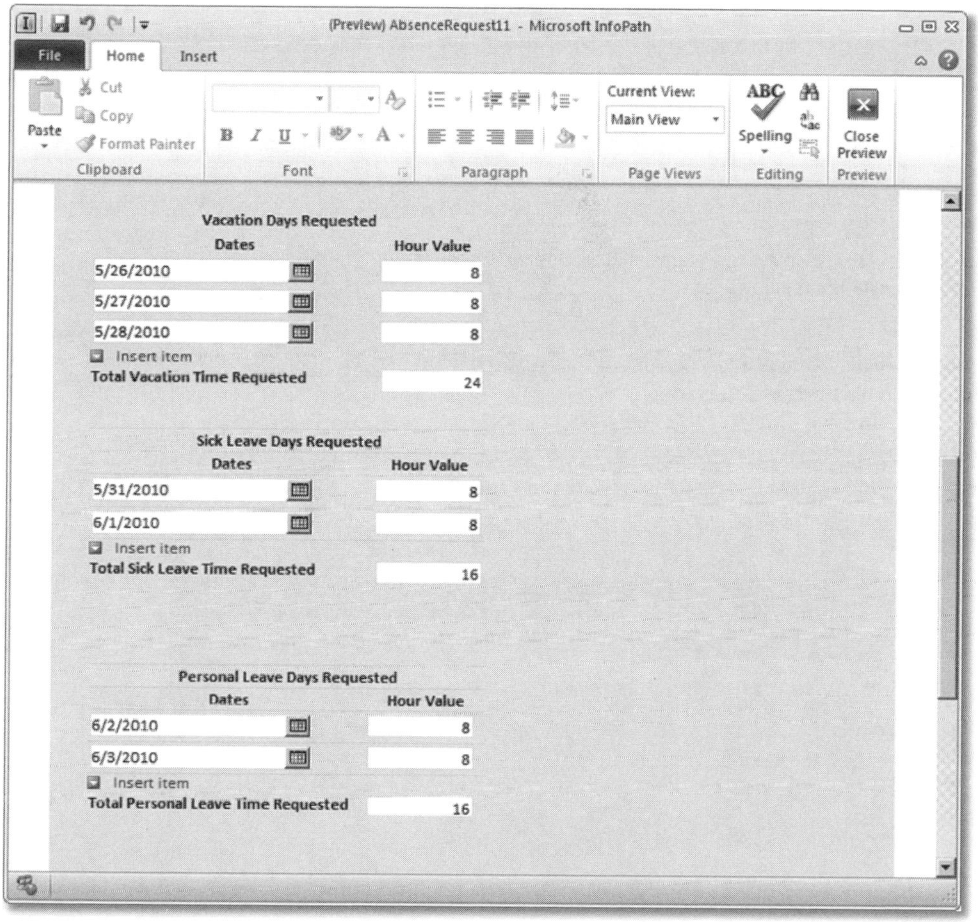

Illustration 309 - Preview of the form with 7 leave dates requested

Click the **Submit Absence Request button**. When the form has been submitted to the *Absence Request* form library the *Submitted for Approval View* will display as shown in **Illustration 310** below.

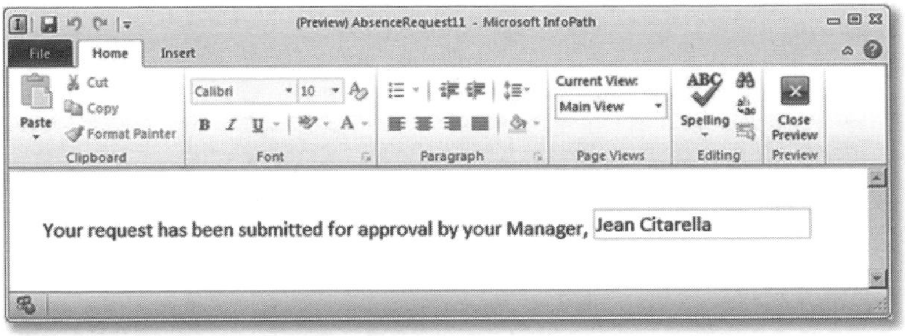

Illustration 310 - Form view that displays for request submission where the Less than 6 months, more than 48 hours rule applies

Go to the *Absence Requests* form library. You will see that a new instance of an absence request form has been posted as shown in **Illustration 311** below.

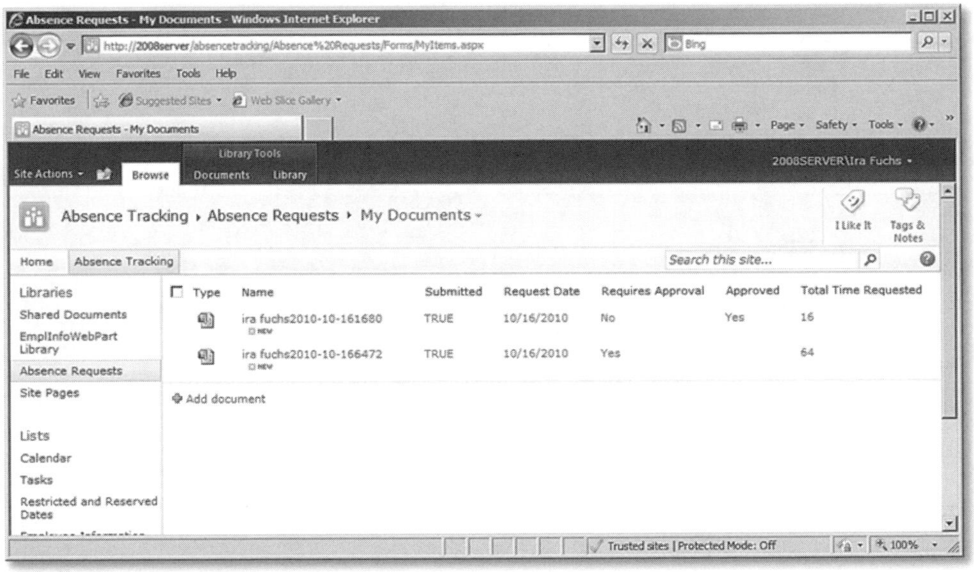

Illustration 311 - Absence request form submitted to the form library requiring a manager's approval

Note that there is a value of *Yes* in the *Requires Approval* column for this form instance and the Approved field is empty. We now have tested the *Less than 6 months, more than 48 hour rule* and it is working as specified.

To test the two remaining submit rules, *More than 6 months, less than 64 hours* and *More than 6 months, more than 64 hours* go back to the *Employee Information* ECT list and change the *Start Date* for the *Current User* so that it will be more than six months from the *Request Date*.

Now generate two additional form submissions, one where the total number of leave hours is less than 64 hours and the other where the total number of leave hours is more than 64 hours. You should get the same results as in the first two form submission tests and the form library should look like **Illustration 312** below.

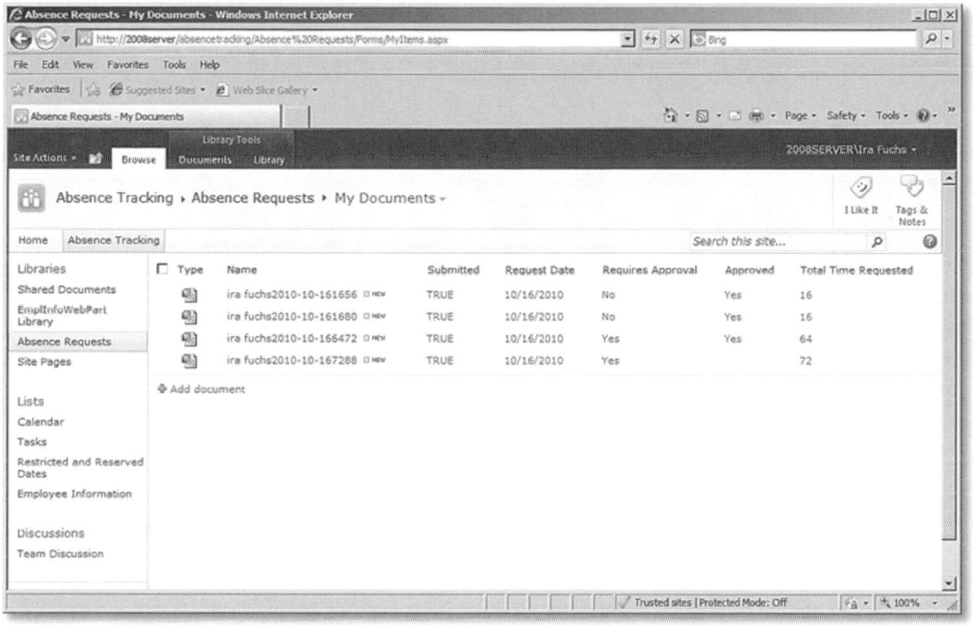

Illustration 312 - Form library showing form submissions for all four test cases

Development Note – One of the truly compelling reasons to build applications on the *SharePoint* platform, and particularly using *InfoPath* and *SharePoint Designer* workflows is that almost all of the application's functional logic is defined and executed as rules.

Business processes are driven by business rules but in traditional application development the rules are first defined as conditional statements similar to what we have been working with but are then re-written as procedural code that is compiled into run-time assemblies. The greater majority of lifecycle modifications to business process applications are business rule centric (as opposed to technology related modifications). However because business rules in conventional applications are embodied in programming code, they cannot be accessed or modified easily, and without risk of effecting the code base in unintentional ways.

With *InfoPath* rules and *SharePoint Designer* workflows the business logic remains in an accessible form that is self-documenting, transparent and loosely-coupled from other functional aspects of the application. A rule set incorporated within *InfoPath* can be viewed and modified with confidence that the changes will not affect other functions of the application. We could easily add conditional statements to the form submit rules governing request approval that incorporated the position level of the employee. The *Restricted Dates* rule could be readily modified to include a geographic component.

InfoPath treats rules as first class objects and it provides a *Rule Inspector* that documents all of the rules in a form as well as their multiple dependencies.

About the InfoPath Rule Inspector

Select the **Data tab** on the Ribbon and click on the **Rule Inspector button**. The *Rule Inspector* organizes the rules by their type – Validation, Action and Formatting, as well as Calculated Default Values as shown in **Illustration 313** and **Illustration 314** on the next page.

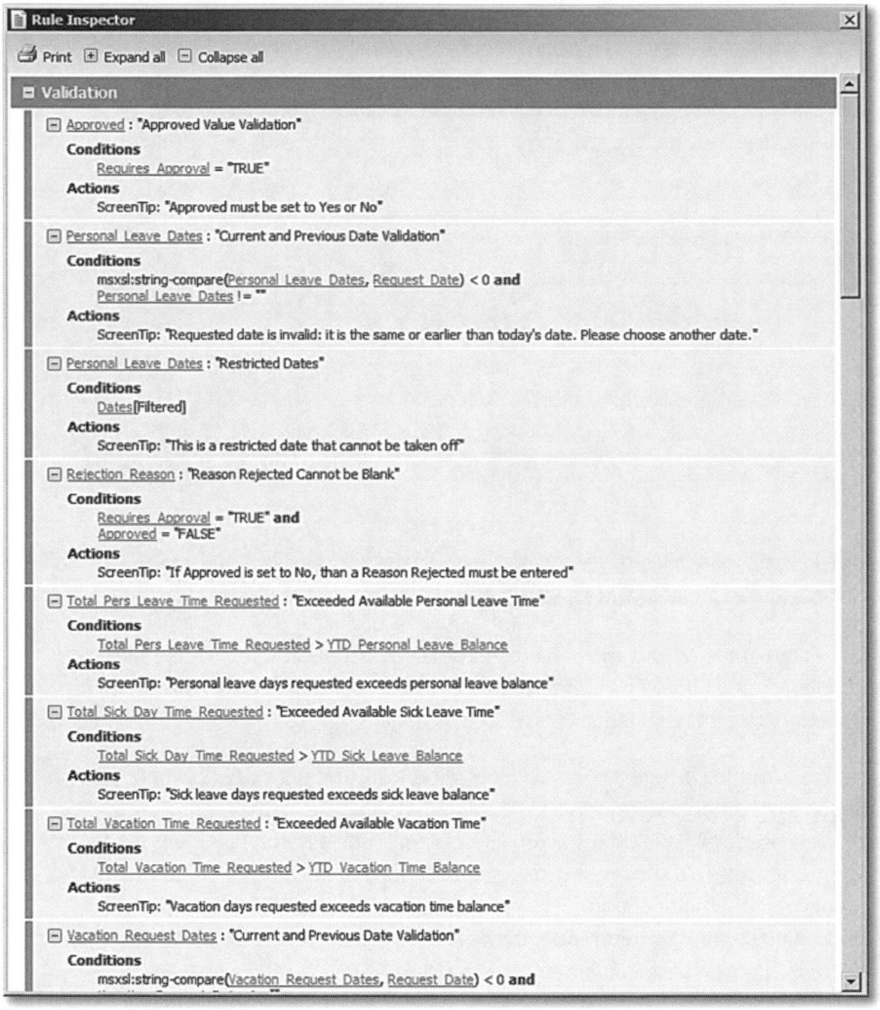

Illustration 313 - Rule Inspector 1

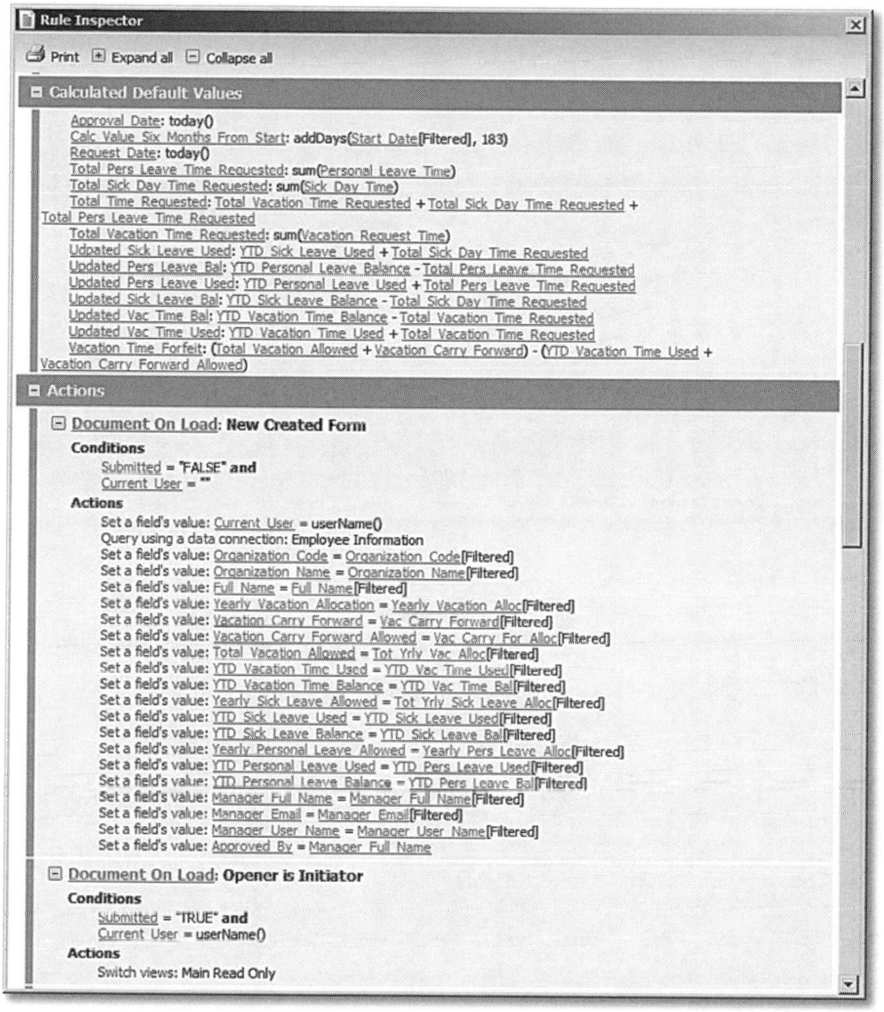

Illustration 314 - Rule Inspector 2

All of the rule objects in the *Rule Inspector* – the referenced groups and fields, condition statements, actions and validation *ScreenTips* are hyperlinked. By clicking on any link *InfoPath* will display all of the dependencies relating to that object as shown in **Illustration 315** below for "Approved".

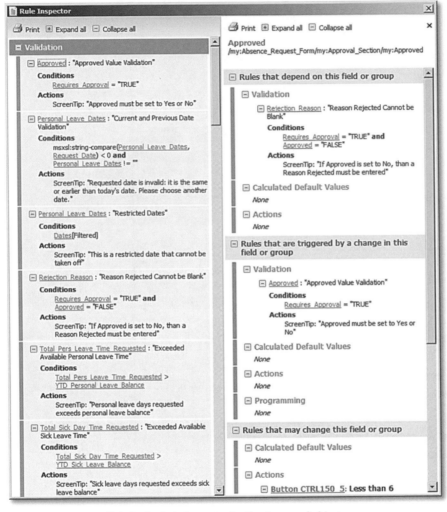

Illustration 315 - Hyerlinks in the Rule Inspector for the Approved object

Approaching application development from a rule-centric methodology is enabling, efficient and enlightening. The capabilities that *InfoPath* provides for creating and documenting rule logic are robust enough to accommodate almost any business process contingency making it a truly viable platform for Enterprise application development.

Best Practices for Designing InfoPath Form Layouts

We are now ready to work on the design aspects of the form and discuss best practices for working with sections, controls and fields. The first thing we are going to do is re-create the layout for the user information and historic leave information fields. While there is nothing functionaly wrong with what we did originally, it is not the optimal form design. So why didn't we create it the best possible way the first time? Because we wanted to focus on the logic implementation aspects and capabilities of InfoPath first, rather than form design. Now that you have a good appreciation of the depth and breadth of *InfoPath*'s capabilities for addressing sophisticated functional requirements, the amount of time required to rework the form layout is nominal and this is a more appropriate point in the application development process to examine this aspect of *InfoPath* application development .

Add a new single row and column table above the table containing the *Vacation Days Requested* table. Enlarge its height by dragging the bottom border so that it looks like **Illustration 316** below.

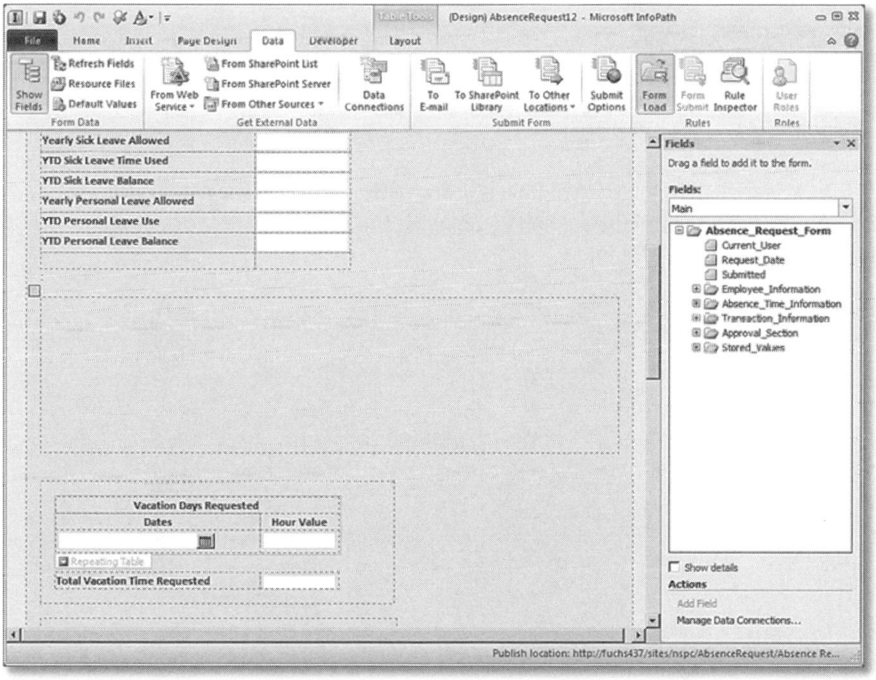

Illustration 316 - Single row and column table added to the form

Right click on the table and select **Table Properties**. On the **Cell** tab add 15 points of padding to the Top and Left borders as shown in **Illustration 317** below.

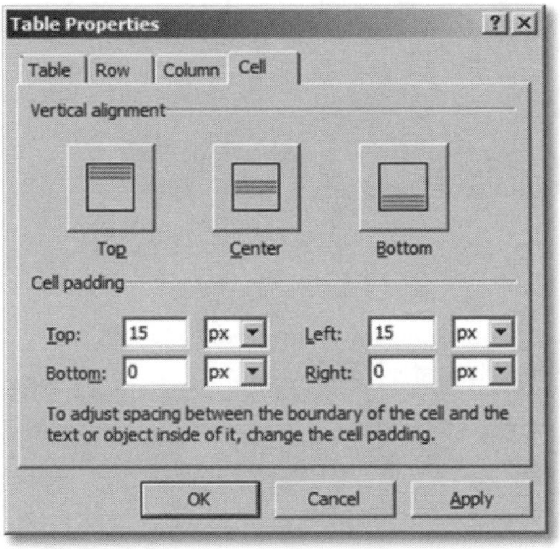

Illustration 317 - Table Properties dialogue screen

With your cursor placed in the table, right click on the **Employee_Information** group in the **Main** data source and choose **Section**. Enlarge the height of the section by dragging the bottom border down so that your design surface looks like **Illustration 318** below.

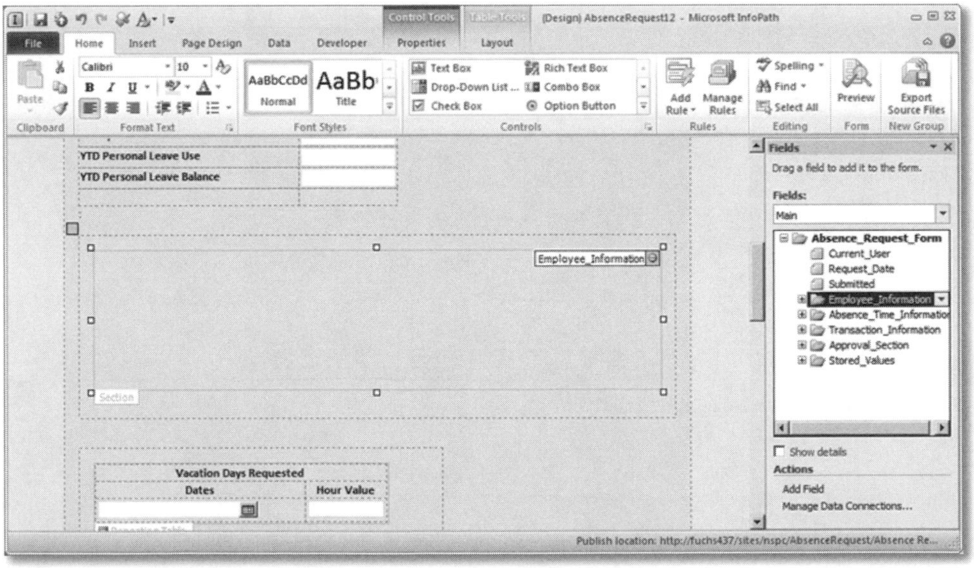

Illustration 318 - Employee_Information section placed in the table

Select the **Employee_Information** section, right click and choose **Section Properties**. Click on the **Size** tab and add 10 points of padding to the Top and Left borders as shown in **Illustration 319** below.

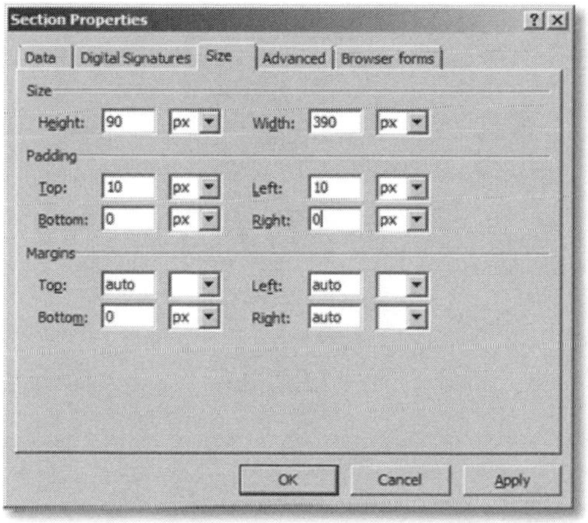

Illustration 319 - Section Properties dialogue screen

With your cursor positioned in the *Employee_Information* section, insert a table with two columns and four rows. Adjust the size of this table, as well as the *Employee_Information* section, and the host table for the section so that it looks like the design surface in **Illustration 320** below.

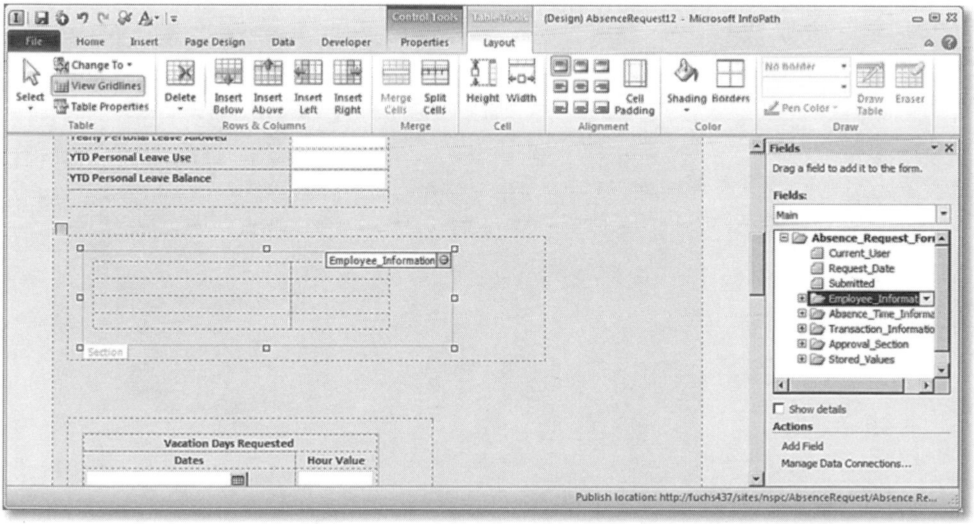

Illustration 320 - Insertion of table with 2 columns and 4 rows in the Employee_Information section

Merge the two columns in the first row of the table you just inserted and enter the text "Employee Information". Center the text and make it bold.

Now select the **Text Box** control for *Full_Name* in the original table. Right click and select **Cut**.

Place your cursor in the right column of row two, right click and select **Paste**. Enter the text "Employee Name" in the column to the left of the **Text Box** so that your design surface now looks like **Illustration 321** below.

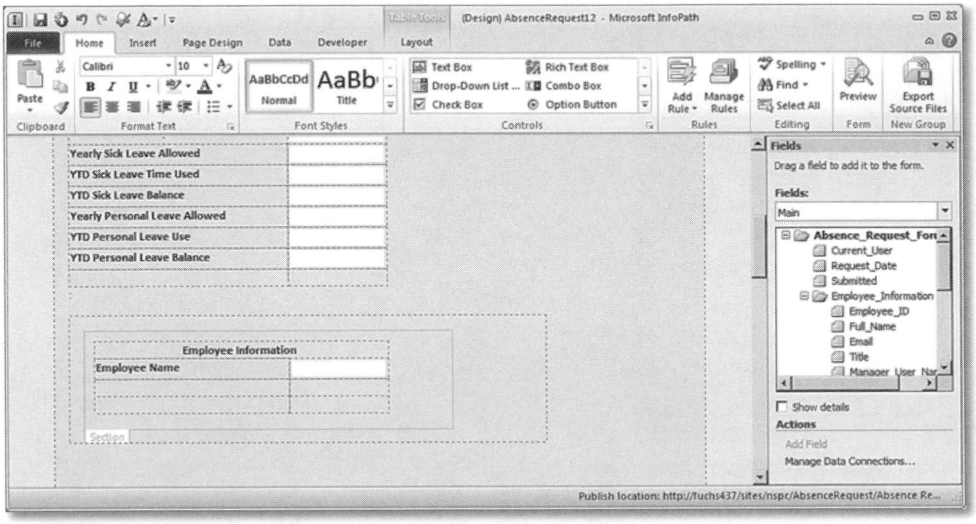

Illustration 321 – Cut and Paste of Text Box control from one table cell to another

Now do the same cut and paste procedure for the **Text Boxes** and labels for the *Organization_Code* and *Organization_Name* fields. Your finished table will look like **Illustration 322** below.

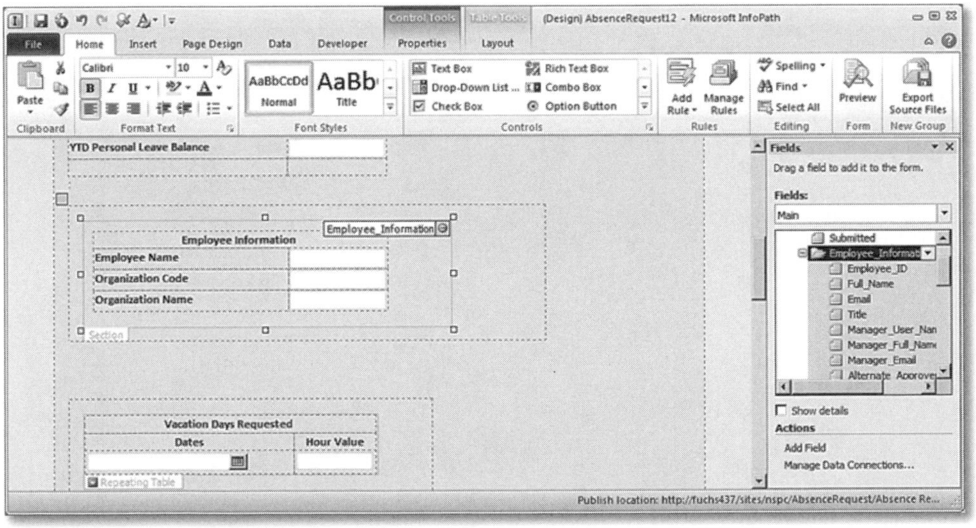

Illustration 322 - Completed Employee_Information section

Working with Tables and Schema Group Sections to Optimize Form Layout

Let's review these layout steps and the reasons for designing the form in this way.

When creating an *InfoPath* form layout the first thing to start with is a table. The entire form should be encapsulated in a table and logically related sections and controls should always be embedded in tables.

As soon as you place any table, set the padding for the top and left margins. The padding does two things: it makes it easy to see how the form is organized and it allows the tables, sections and controls placed in it to align consistently. Objects (sections, tables and individual controls) will automatically align within a table and among multiple tables if you simply add the padding consistently. Never hesitate to use a table as an organizing design structure.

We then embedded an *empty* schema group section (*Employee_Information*) in the host table before we placed any of the fields that are members of the schema group. This is a best practice that should always be observed. Doing so tightly couples the organization of the schema with the organization of the form, establishing structural coherency between the information set and the form layout. Once again, we added padding for the top and left margins. Using the padding settings everywhere allows you to easily reposition all of the embedded objects in a table or section.

The next step is to insert the table for the individual controls and placing the controls and labels in the table cells. You have a lot of flexibility to arrange the controls and labels in this way. We simply used two columns and arranged the labels and fields horizontally along rows. You can use as many columns as you wish in order to set up a varied spacing or hierarchical layout, or use horizontal labels above or below the controls. It is also very easy to rearrange the size and position of an entire set of columns or rows when you use a tabular format, as well as apply shading and border lines.

Using Borders and Shading

Select the three **Text Box** controls for *Employee_Name, Organization_Code* and *Organization_Name* while holding the **Shift key** down and clicking on each control. They will all be selected. Now right click and select **Borders and Shading**. The *Borders and Shading* dialogue screen will display as shown in **Illustration 323** below.

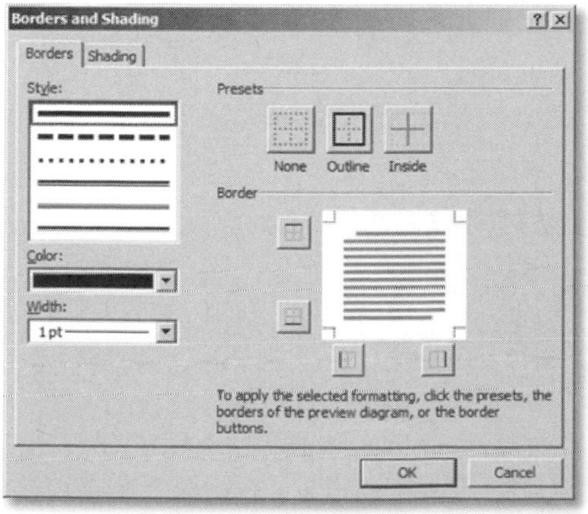

With the **Borders** tab selected click on the **Outline** button then the **OK** button. You will see that the three **Text Box** controls now have a 1 point black border around them. You can apply any color or width to the border. You can simultaneously apply shading to the controls as well. You can apply separate **Border and Shading** settings to the table for the controls, the section container and the host table. If you select the three **Text Box** controls again you can also apply any text attributes such as alignment or color to all three controls.

Illustration 323 - Borders and Shading dialogue screen

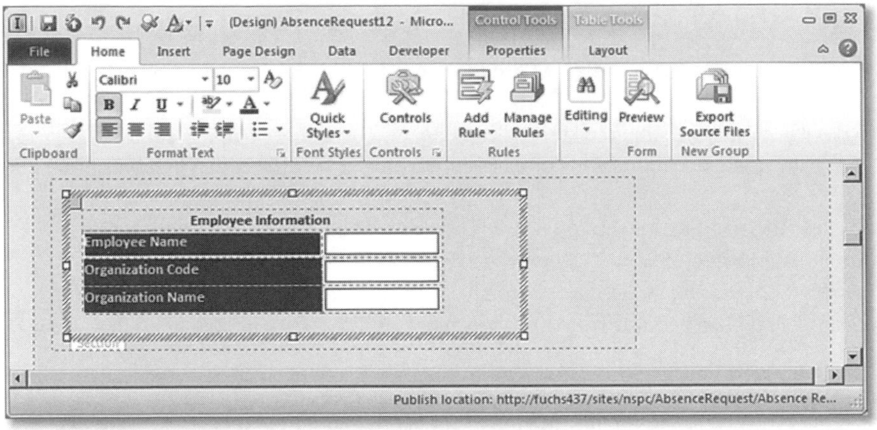

Illustration 324 - Labels in multiple cells simultaneously selected

Place your cursor on the top left column of the **control table** and with the left mouse button held down move the mouse down so that the three labels are highlighted as shown in **Illustration 324** at left.

You can apply any formatting to multiple labels separately from the controls that they are associated with.

Reconstructing the Absence_Time_Information Section

Create a new single column and row table to host the empty section for the *Absence_Time_Information* group. Place this below the new *Employee Information* table we just created. Add 15 points of padding to the top and left borders of the table.

With the cursor positioned in the table right click on the **Absence_Time_Information** group and select **Section**. The *Absence_Time_Information* section will be inserted in the table. Drag the bottom border of the section down to increase its height. Add 10 points of padding to the top and left borders of this section.

With the cursor placed in the section insert a table with two columns and one row by selecting the **Insert** tab on the Ribbon and clicking the **Custom Table** button. Drag the right border of this table to the left. Your design surface will look like **Illustration 325** below.

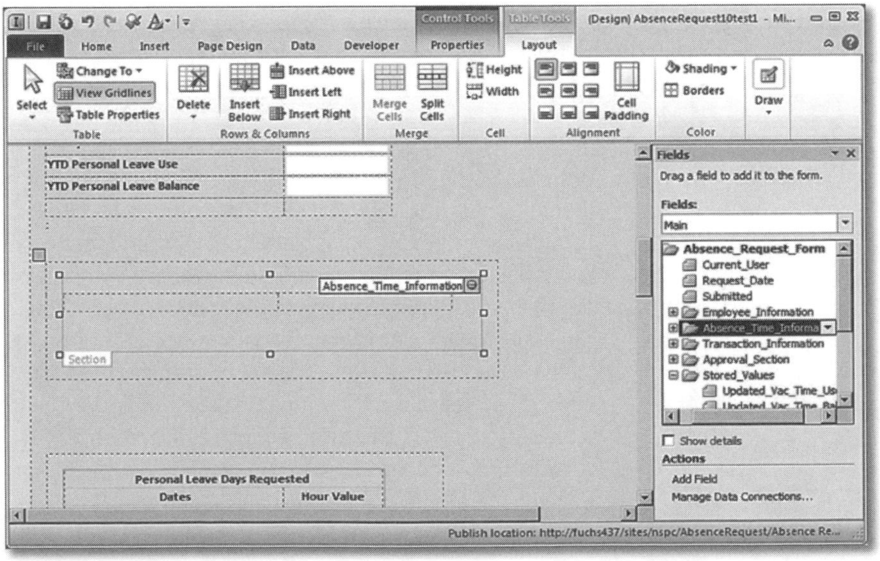

Illustration 325 - Absence_Time_Information section placed in a host table and a table inserted within the section

Copying Multiple Control and Label Cells

With your left mouse button pressed down highlight the original cells containing the labels and controls for **Yearly Vacation Allocation** down to **YTD Personal Leave Balance** as shown in **Illustration 326** below.

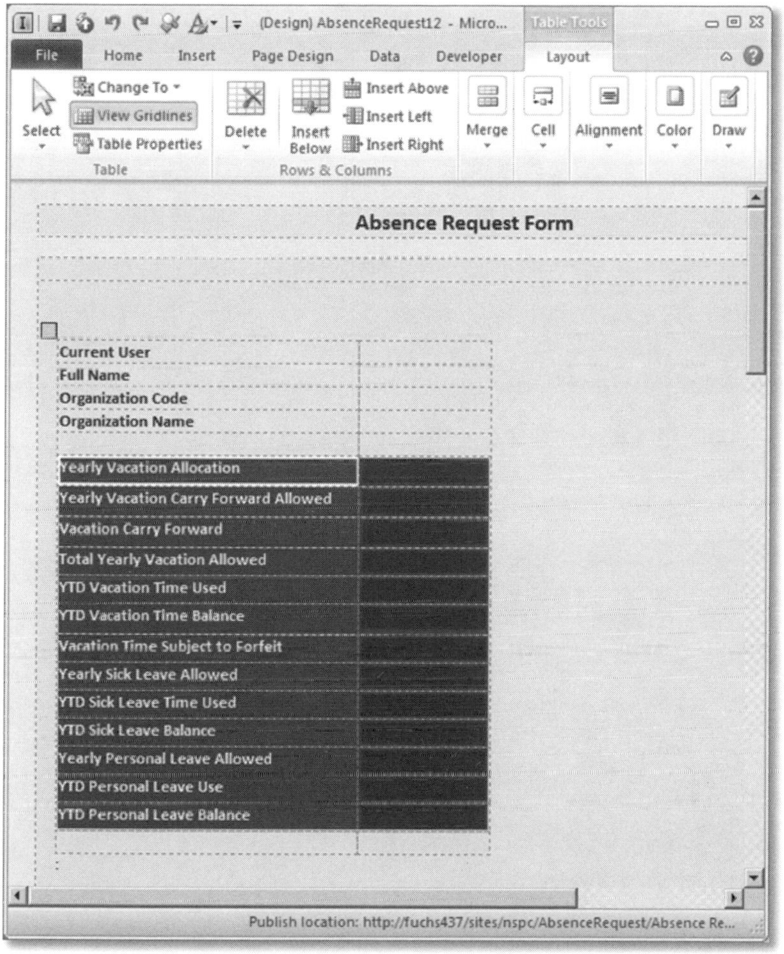

Illustration 326 - Selecting multiple cells containing labels and controls

Right click and select **Cut**. Now position your cursor in the top left cell of the ***new table*** we just inserted into the *Absence_Time_Information* section; right click and select **Paste**. All of the *Text Box* controls with their labels were moved in bulk as shown in **Illustration 327** below.

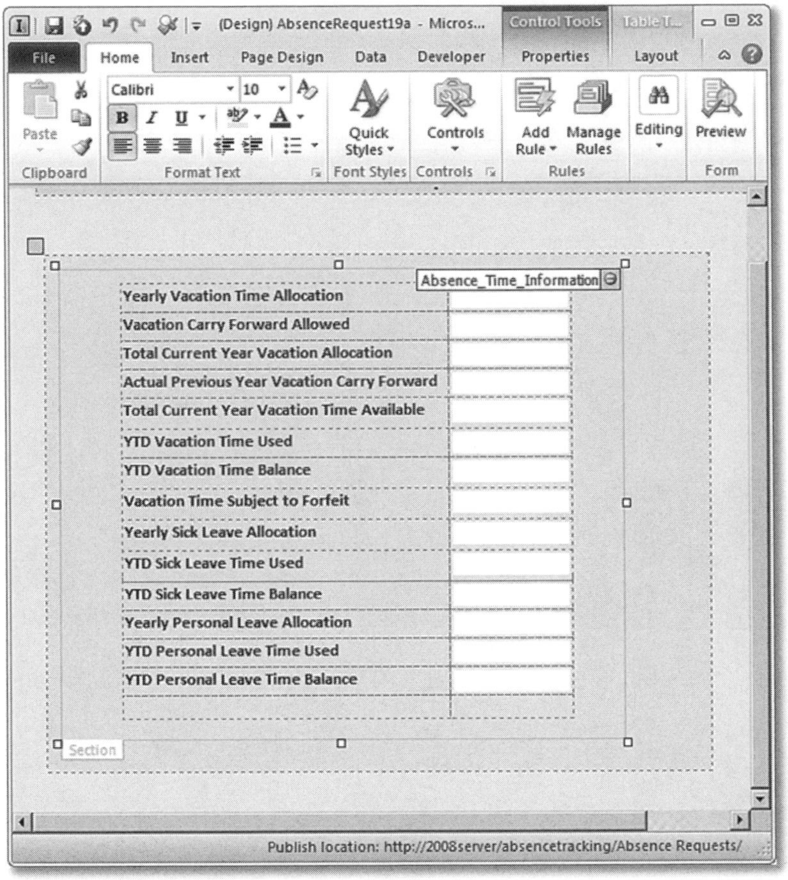

Illustration 327 - Copy and paste of multiple table cells into another table

> **Note** – If we had pasted the cells directly into the *Absence_Time_Information* **section** instead of the embedded section ***table*** the row and column size settings would have changed and we would have to manually adjust each row. Pasting into the new table preserves the size and format settings.

> **Important Note** – If the controls were laid out free form on the design surface instead of this tabular structure we wouldn't have the flexibility and efficiency of being able to restructure and reorganize the form this way.

Add two rows to the top of the table. Merge the cells in the top row and enter the text "Current Year Leave Information" and center the text.

Align the horizontal width of the control tables, group sections and host tables for the *Employee Information* and *Current Year Leave Information* sections so that they line up and look like **Illustration 328** below.

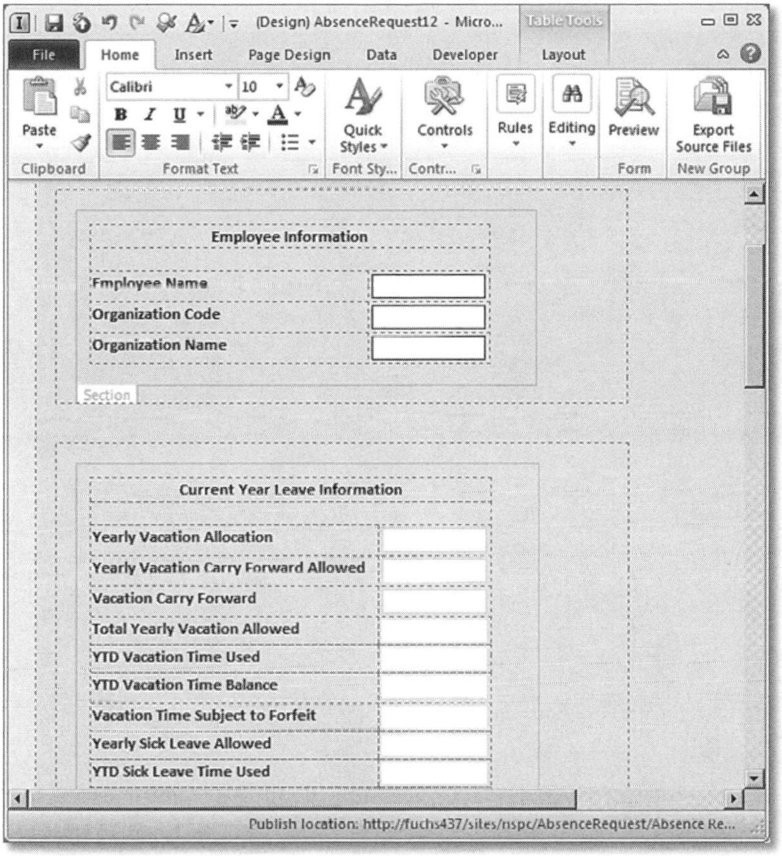

Illustration 328 - Cell columns in the two form sections aligned with each other

Select all the **Text Box** controls in the *Current Year Leave Information* table. Right click and choose **Borders and Shading**. With the **Border** tab selected set the color as **black** and click on the **Outline** button.

Delete the **Text Box** control and label for *Current_User* as we will not be displaying that information in the finished form.

Reconstructing the Absence Request Dates Sections

Insert a single column, single row host table below the *Current Year Leave Information* table and above the *Vacation Days Requested* table. Add 15 points of padding to the left and top borders.

Now insert a table with one column and six rows in this host table so that your design surface looks like **Illustration 329** below.

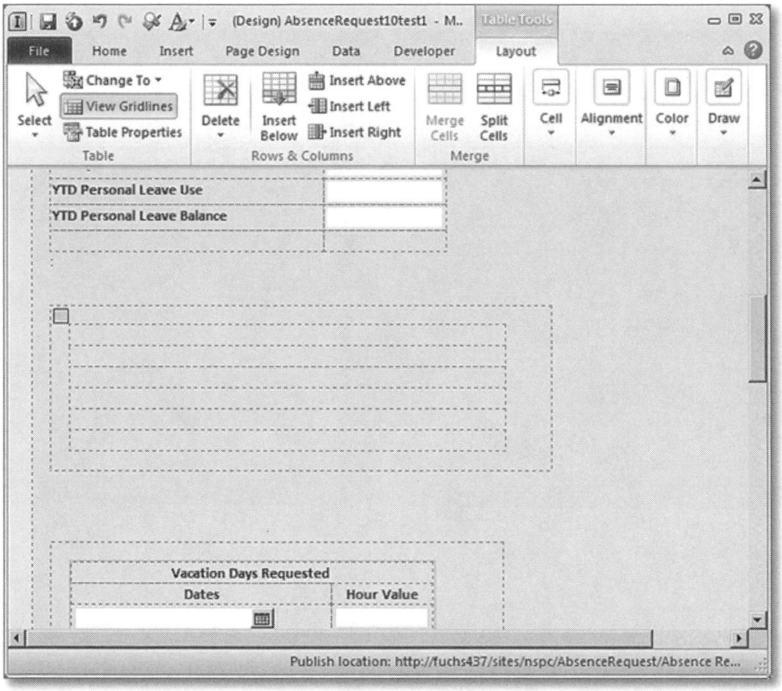

Illustration 329 – A single row and column table with a six row table placed inside it

Select the host table containing the *Vacation_ Requests* repeating table and *Total_Vacation_Time_Requested Text Box* as shown in **Illustration 330** below.

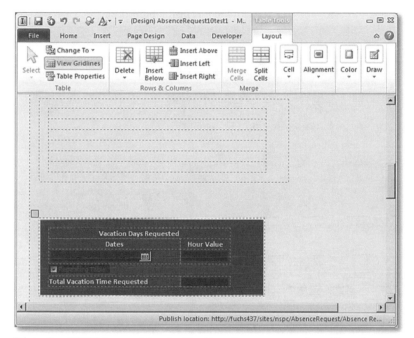

Illustration 330 Table containing the Vacation_ Requests repeating table and Total_Vacation_Time_Requested Text Box control selected

Right click and select **Cut**. Place your cursor in the **second row** of the six row table we just created; right click and select **Paste**. The design surface will look like **Illustration 331** below.

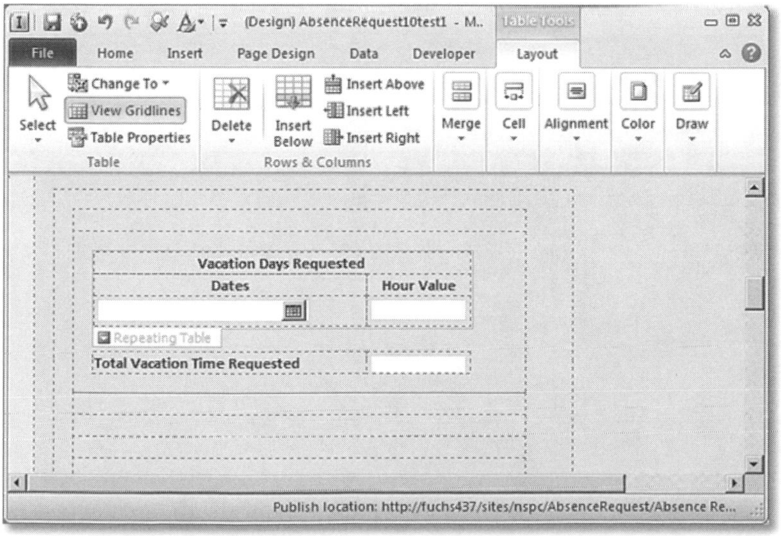

Do the same cut and paste procedure for the host tables containing the *Sick Leave* and *Personal Days Requested* controls and labels, skipping a row between insertions.

Illustration 331 - Copy and paste of table with labels and controls into the new table

Adding Borders and Shading to the Repeating Tables

Select the repeating table for *Vacation_Days_Requested*; right click and choose **Borders and Shading**. With the **Borders tab** selected set the color to **black** and click the **Outline** and **Inside** buttons.

Select the table containing the *Total Time Requested* label and *Text box*, again right click and choose **Borders and Shading**. With the **Borders tab** selected set the color to black and click the **Outline button**.

Repeat this procedure for the *Sick Leave Days Requested* and *Personal Leave Days Requested* repeating tables and their respective total time requested tables. Select all the D**ate Picker** and **Text Box** controls and apply a black **Outline** border. The design surface now looks like **Illustration 332** below.

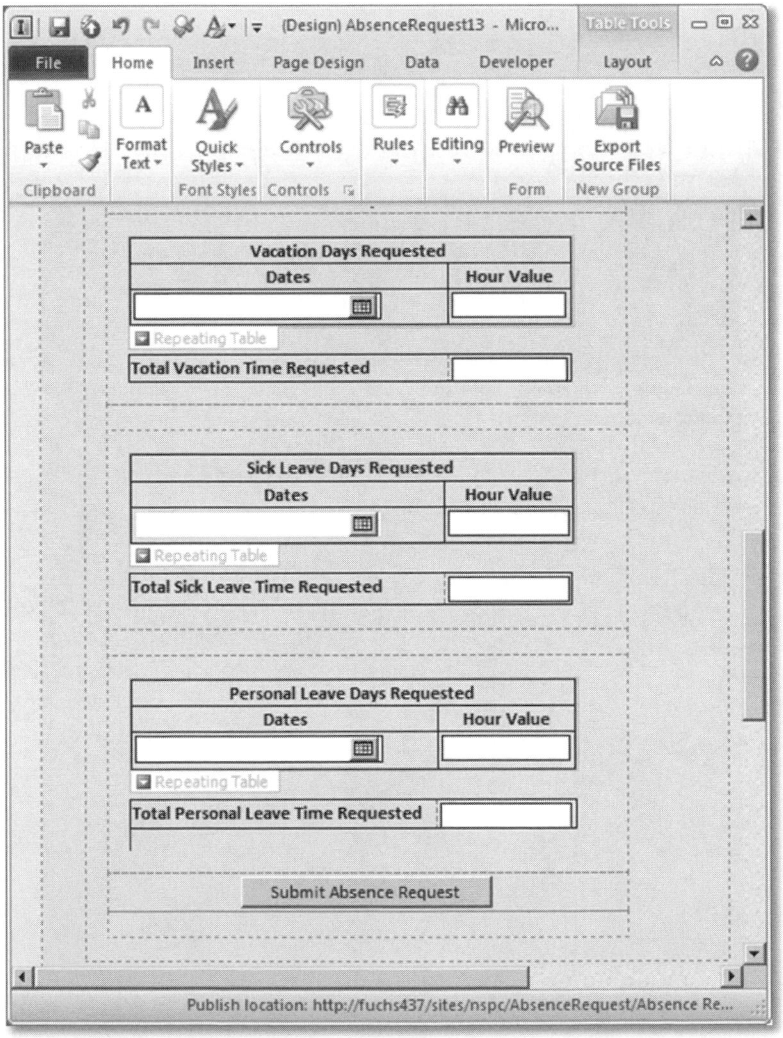

Preview the form. It is beginning to have a more consistent, polished look. We will remove the excess table rows and spacing between tables at the very end of the design process.

Illustration 332 – Re-structured Absence Request Dates section

Cut and paste the text "Absence Request Form" from the table at the top of the form into the top row of the primary form table. Delete the empty table at the top. Highlight the "Absence Request Form" text and choose the **Accent 5, Darker 50%** color setting from the text color palette as shown in **Illustration 333** below.

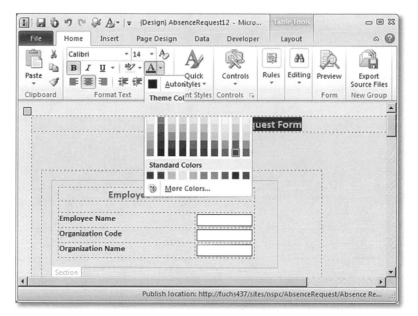

Illustration 333 - Cutting and pasting the Absence Request Form table label

Select the row containing the "Absence Request Form" text. Right click and choose **Borders and Shading**. Click the **Shading tab** and using the color selection palette choose **Accent 5, Lighter 60%.**

Select the **Employee Information** table label. Change the font size to 12 points and apply the same **Accent 5, Darker 50%** color setting we just used. Select the row containing this text and choose **Borders and Shading**. Click the **Shading tab** and using the color selection palette and again choose **Accent 5, Lighter 60%.**

Apply the same settings to the text and rows for *Current Year Leave Information, Absence Request Dates,* and *Approval Section*. Your form should look like **Illustration 334** below.

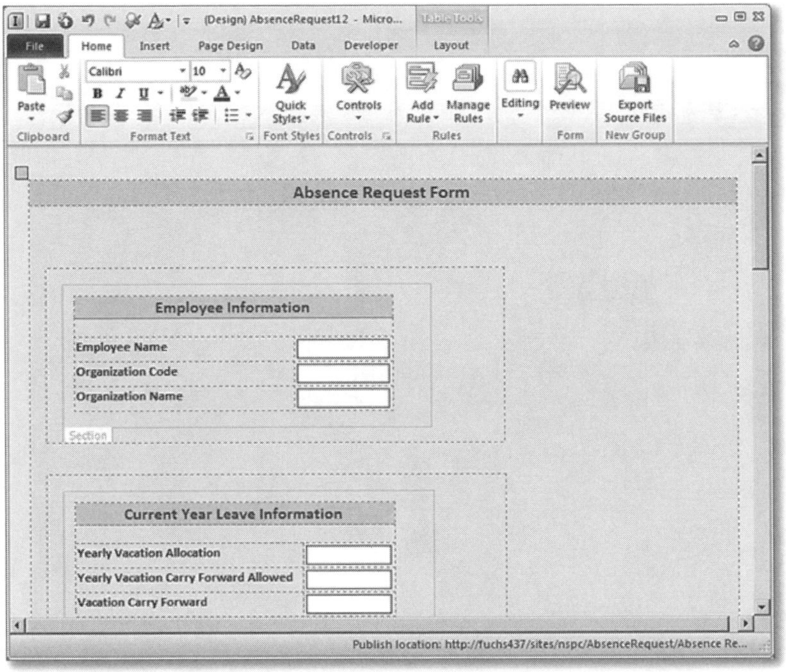

Illustration 334 - Applying text formatting and shading

Select the host table for the *Employee Information* section as shown in **Illustration 335** below.

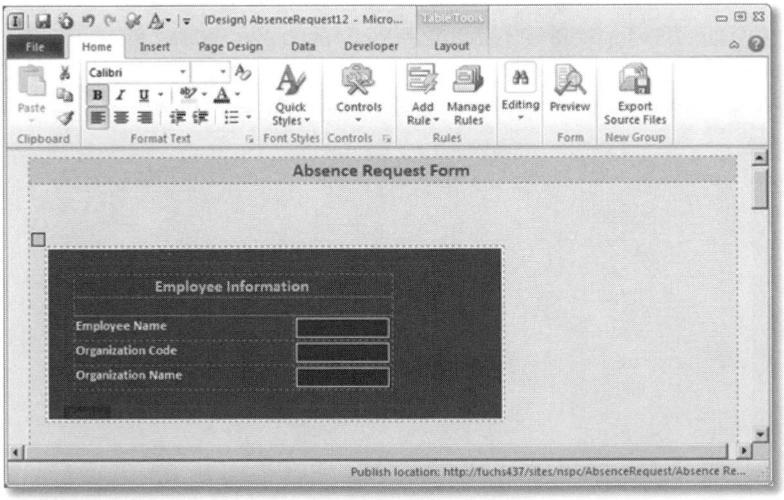

Illustration 335 - Table for the Employee Information section selected

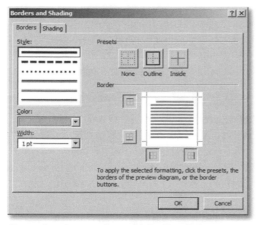

Illustration 336 - Borders and shading dialogue screen

Right click and choose **Borders and Shading**. With **the Borders tab** selected change the color to **Accent 5, Lighter 40%**. Click the top, left and right border buttons to apply the colored border as shown in **Illustration 336** at left.

Now apply same border to the tables for *Current Year Leave Information* and *Absence Request Dates* with the following modifications:

For the **Current Year Leave Information** table apply the border setting to the left, right and bottom border. For the **Absence Request Dates** table click the **Outline** button to apply the setting to all the borders.

Select the form's main host table. In **Borders and Shading** select the **Accent 5, Lighter 40%** Color and choose **2 1/4** points for the Width. Click the **Outline button**.

Now click the **Preview button** to see what the run-time form will look like as shown in **Illustration 337** at left.

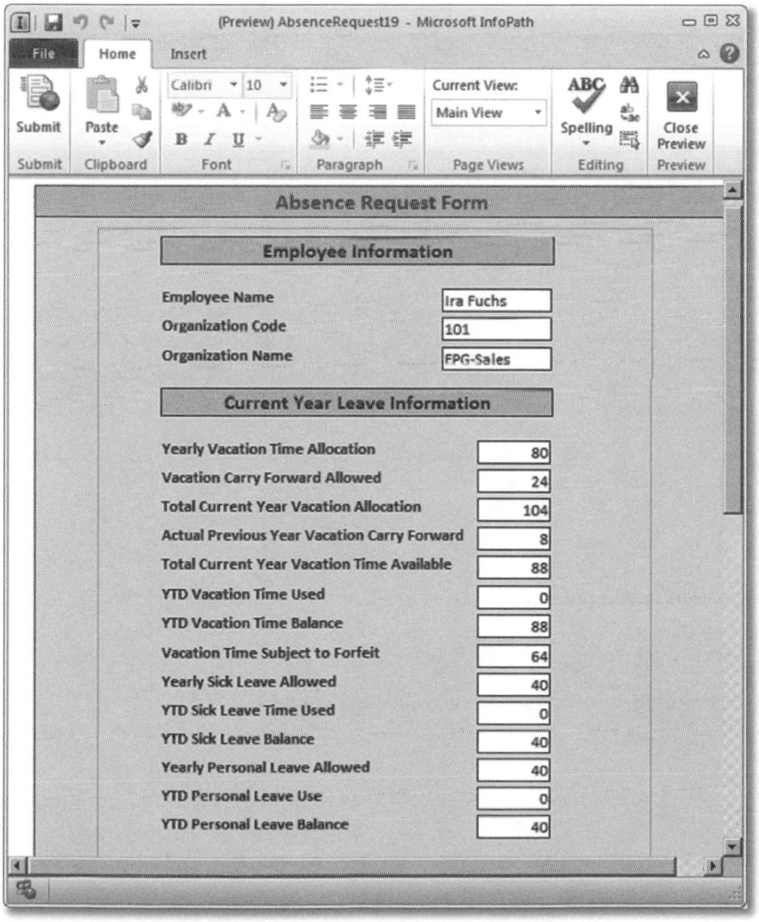

Illustration 337 - Preview of the formatted form

Layout Considerations for Hidden Sections

Note – We are going to deviate from embedding the *Approval Section* in a host table. Instead we are going to align the right border of the *Approval Section* with the borders of the host tables for the other form sections and apply the **Accent 5, Lighter 40%** Color to the outline border of the **section** itself.

The reason for this is that the *Approval Section* is hidden except when accessed by the approver or the form initiator when viewing the reason for a rejected request. However we can only apply the conditional formatting rule to **hide a section, not a table**. So if we embed a section that is meant to be hidden in a table, the section will indeed be hidden but the space (and border outline) taken up by the host table will display in the form as shown in **Illustration 338** below. This would not look right so we can prevent this from happening by **not** embedding a section that is meant to be hidden in a host table.

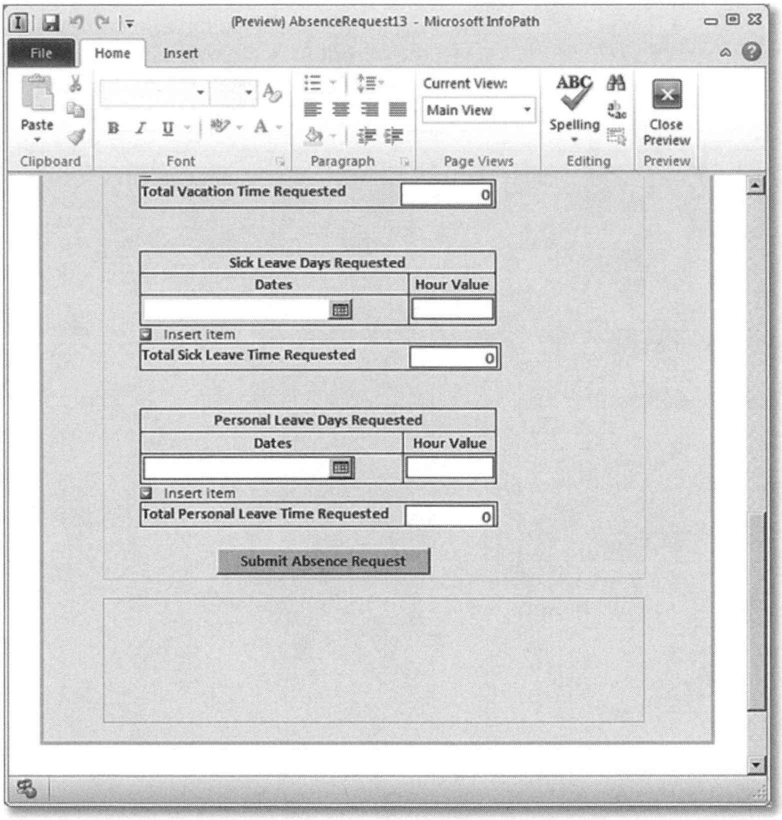

Illustration 338 – Display behavior of a hidden section when it is embedded in a table

Centering the Tables in the Form

Now let's center the tables in the form. Select the **main host** table. Right click and choose **Table Properties**. Click the **Cell tab** of the **Table Properties** dialogue screen. Set the **Cell padding** for the left border to **50 points** as shown in **Illustration 339** below.

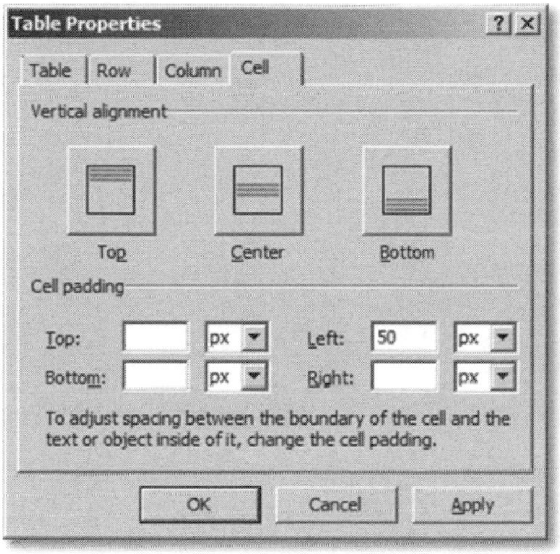

Illustration 339 - Centering the main host table using cell padding in Table Properties

Now select the tables for *Employee Information, Current Year Leave Information, Absence Request Dates,* and *Approval Section* and set the left cell padding for each of these tables to **40 points** as shown in **Illustration 340** below.

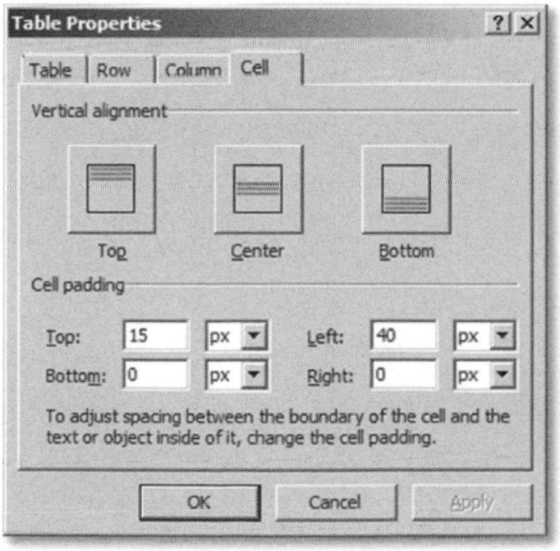

Illustration 340 - Setting the cell padding for the section tables in Table Properties

Your form should look like **Illustration 341** below.

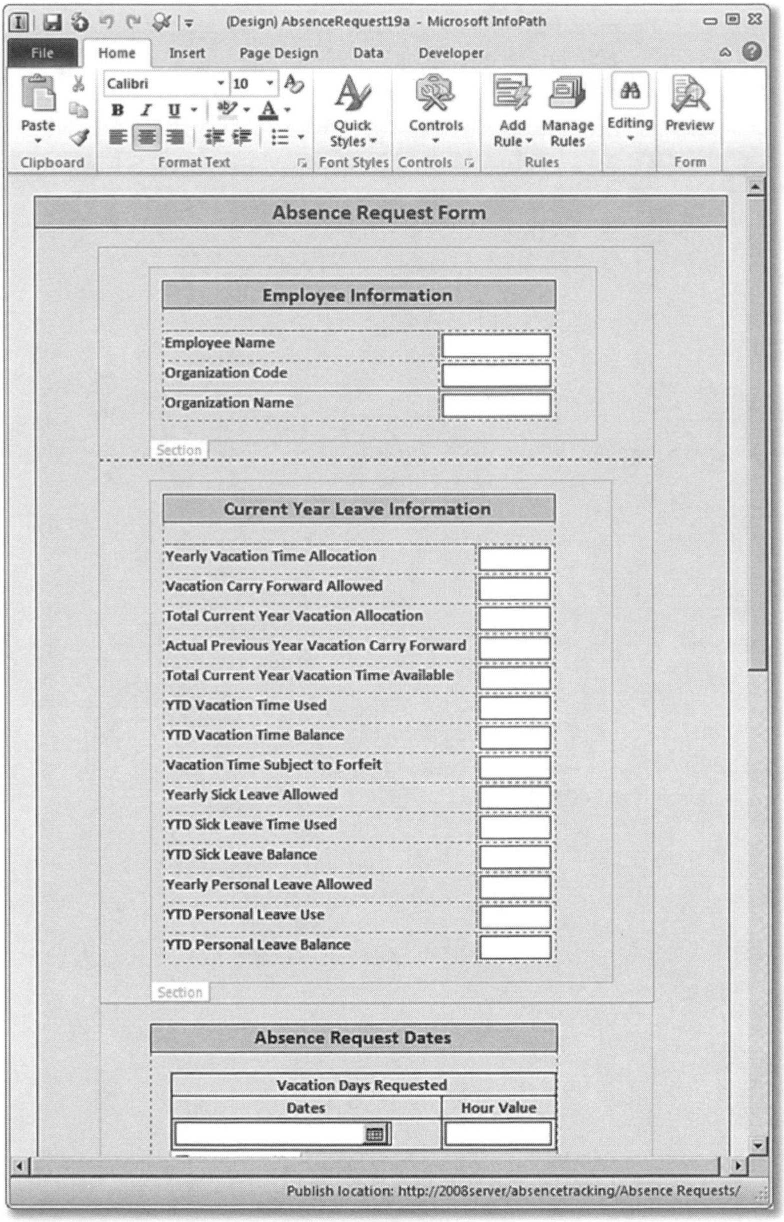

Illustration 341 – Form with centered tables

Again, note how easy it is to modify the layout of the form when it is organized using tables and sections.

Select the **Submit Absence Request button**. Right click and choose **Borders and Shading**. Select **Accent 5, Lighter 40%** for the color.

In the *Approval Section* select all the controls and apply a black, **1 point Outline** border to them. Select the **button** and rename it "Manager Submit". Apply the **Accent 5, Lighter 40%** color.

Final Form Layout Adjustments

Adjust the control tables so that they right align with the control tables in the other sections. Adjust all the section host tables so that they right align.

Illustration 342 - Setting the row height for the main form table

Remove any empty rows in tables, and spaces between tables. Finally, select the host table for the entire form.

Right click and choose **Properties**. In the **Table Properties** dialogue screen click on the **Row** tab. Select **the Row height is at least radio button** and clear out any value in the box, so that it is empty as shown in **Illustration 342** at left.

Setting the row height for the entire table in this way forces *InfoPath* to *not render* empty vertical space in the form.

Design Layout Best Practices Review

Let's review the form design best practices that we employed in creating this form:

- Build the schema for the information set first. Consider the hierarchical structure of the information and use groups to organize information logically.

- Apply rule logic and default values to groups and fields as much as possible before placing controls on the design surface.

- Use tables everywhere, except with sections that have conditional formatting rules to hide them. Build the form within a primary host table and always use tables to host sections and controls.

- When working with fields that are part of a group, always insert a blank section for the group in a host table and then insert a table in the section for placement of the individual fields.

By observing these four form design principles, you will have a well-designed form where the relationships between your information set and the form controls are well-understood, and you have maximum flexibility and efficiency in extending, modifying and re-using any components of the form.

Configuring the User Interface Options for a Browser Form

By default, when an *InfoPath* browser form opens it will display the commands to *Save, Save As, Close, Views* and *Print Preview*. These user interface options for a browser form can be found and modified in the *Form Options* screen. Click on **File** on the *Ribbon* and then click on the **Form Options** button as shown in **Illustration 343** at left.

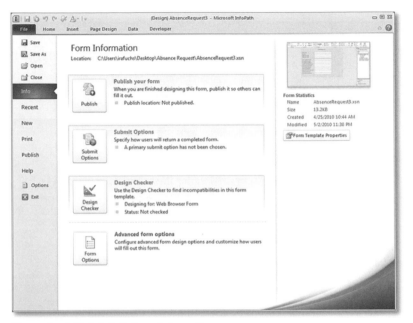

Illustration 343 - InfoPath Form Information page

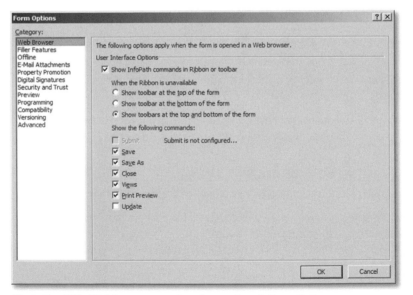

Illustration 344 - Web browser user interface options in Form Options

The *Form Options* page will open with the *Web Browser* selected in the Category list with the default settings as shown in **Illustration 344** below.

The only command that we want the user to have access to is *Close*. We do not want the user to be able to save the form instance or see the *Views* that we have created. De-select all the default command options *except* Close and select the **Show toolbar at the top of the form radio button** and click **OK**.

We are almost finished building the *Absence Request* form. There are two things left to do: implement rule logic for the *Approval Section* and copy the entire *Main* form view to a read-only view of the form.

Adding a Validation Rule for the Reason_Rejected Text Box in the Approval Section

Click on the **Reason_Rejected Text Box** control. Click **Manage Rules** on the **Ribbon**. Click **New** and **Validation**. Name the rule "Reason Rejected Cannot be Blank". Click **None** under and create the condition statement in **Illustration 345** below.

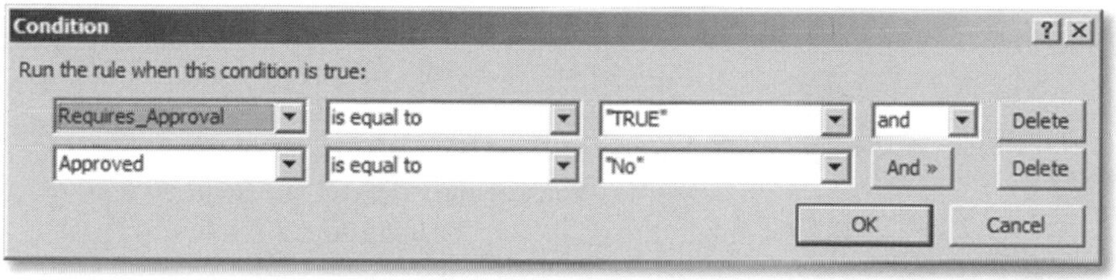

Illustration 345 - Condition statement for Reason Rejected Cannot be Blank rule

For the **ScreenTip** enter "If Approved is set to No, than a Reason Rejected must be entered".

Illustration 346 - Adding a new View to close the form after the manager's review

From the **Page Design** tab on the *Ribbon* create a **New View** and name it "Close After Manager Review" as shown in **Illustration 346** below.

The new *View* will appear. Delete the default table and add a table with three rows and one column. In the first row enter the text "An email will be sent to the initiator informing them that you have reviewed this request".

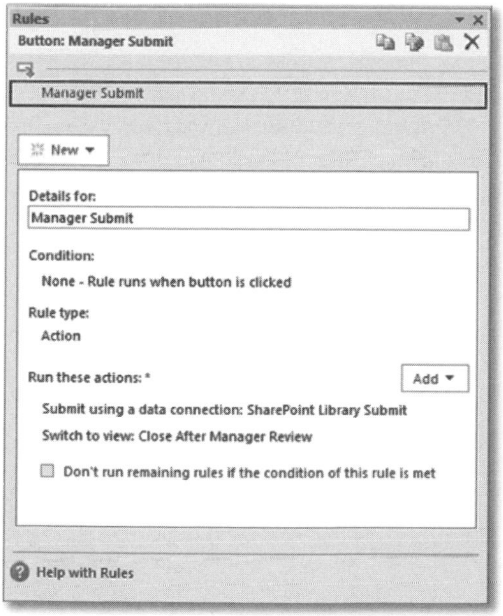

Return to the *Main View* and select the **Manager Submit** button. Click **Manage Rules** on the *Ribbon*.

Click **New** and then **Action**. Name the rule "Manager Submit". Leave **None** under **Condition**. Add a **Submit data** action and choose **SharePoint Library Submit**. Add a **Switch views** action and choose **Close After Manager Review**. The *Manager Submit* rule will look like **Illustration 347** at left.

Illustration 347 - The Manager Submit rule

Copying and Pasting the Main View of the Form to the Main Read Only View

Now that we have finished the *Main View* of the form, we can copy it to the *Main Read Only View*. Select the main host table for the form. Right click and choose **Copy**.

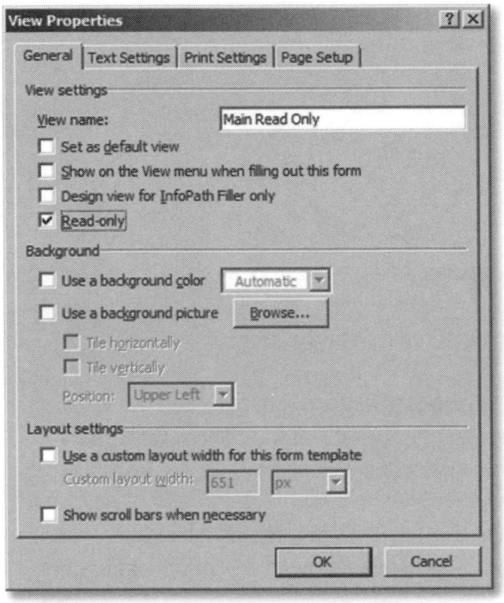

Click **Page Design** from the Ribbon. Select the **Main Read Only** view. Place your cursor at the top of the design surface, right click and select **Paste**.

Click the **Properties button**. In the **View Properties** dialogue screen check the **Read-only checkbox** as shown in **Illustration 348** at left.

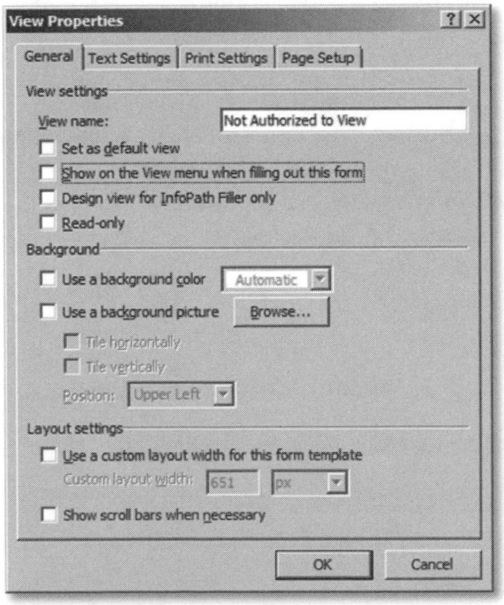

Illustration 348 - Setting the Main Read Only View to Read-only in the View Properties dialogue screen

Also check that none of the *Views* with the exception of the **Main** default View has the checkbox for **Show on the View menu when filling out this form** checked, also shown in **Illustration 349** at left.

Illustration 349 - All Views with the exception of the Main View should have the checkbox for "Show on the View menu when filling out this form" de-selected

Creating a Formatting Rule to Hide the Approval Section in the Main Read-Only View

Recall earlier that we created a rule to hide the *Approval Section* and its respective controls from the initiator when the form is initially created. We now will create the second rule that applies to the *Main Read Only View* of a submitted request. This rule hides the *Approval Section* from the initiator if the request has been approved by a manager or approved by default by the workflow.

With the *Main Read Only View* open and the *Approval Section* selected, click on the **Manage Rules** button from the *Home* tab on the *Ribbon*. In the *Rules* pane click **New** and select **Formatting.** Name the rule "Hide from Initiator after Submit". Click **None** under *Condition* and create the condition statement shown in **Illustration 350** below.

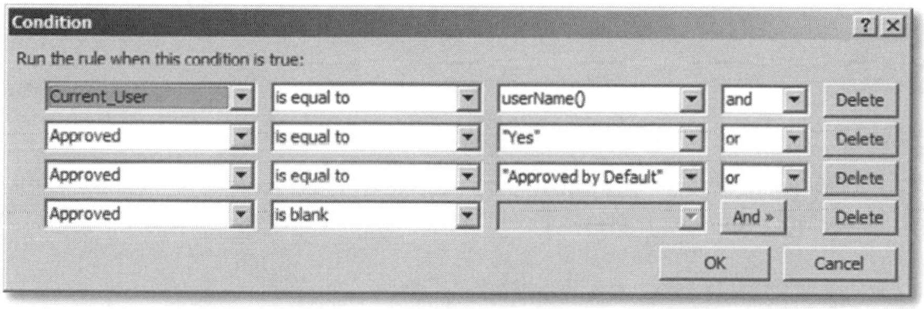

Illustration 350 - Condition statement for Hide from Initiator after Submit rule

In the first drop-down box select the **Current_User** field. In the second drop-down box choose the **is equal to** operator. In the third drop-down box select **Use a formula**. The *Insert Formula* dialogue screen will display. Click the **Insert Function** button and select the **userName** function. The *Insert Formula* dialogue screen will look like **Illustration 351** below.

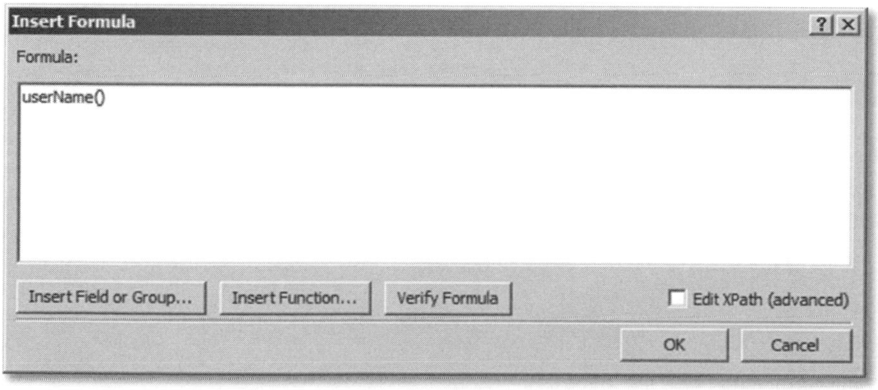

Illustration 351 - The Insert Formula dialogue screen with userName() function selected

Click **OK**. Click the **down arrow** to the right of the third drop-down box. Leave the **and** operator. The second conditional statement will be inserted.

Select the **Approved** field in the first drop-down box and leave the **is equal to** operator in the second drop-down box. Enter the text "Yes" in the third drop-down box (without quotation marks). Add the **or** operator to add the third conditional statement.

Select the **Approved** field in the first drop-down box and leave the **is equal to** operator in the second drop-down box. Enter the text "Approved by Default" in the third drop-down box. Add the **or** operator to add the fourth conditional statement.

Select the **Approved** field in the first drop-down box and choose the **is blank** operator in the second drop-down box. Then click **OK** to finish.

This rule establishes the condition for hiding the *Approval Section* when the submitted request has been approved by a manager, approved by default by the workflow, or is empty because it has not been approved or rejected. The only other value that can be set for the *Approved* field is "No", which is the only condition where the *Approval Section* should be displayed to the request initiator. This completes the logic required for displaying or hiding the *Approval Section*.

Adding a Close the Form Button to the Submit Message Views

Display the *Submitted and Approved* View. Add a single column and single row table below the first table. Insert a **button** and name it "Close the Form" and apply the **Accent 5, Lighter 40%** shading.

Add an *Action* rule named "Close Form" that has no conditions and a single action – *Close the form*. Your design surface will look like **Illustration 352** below.

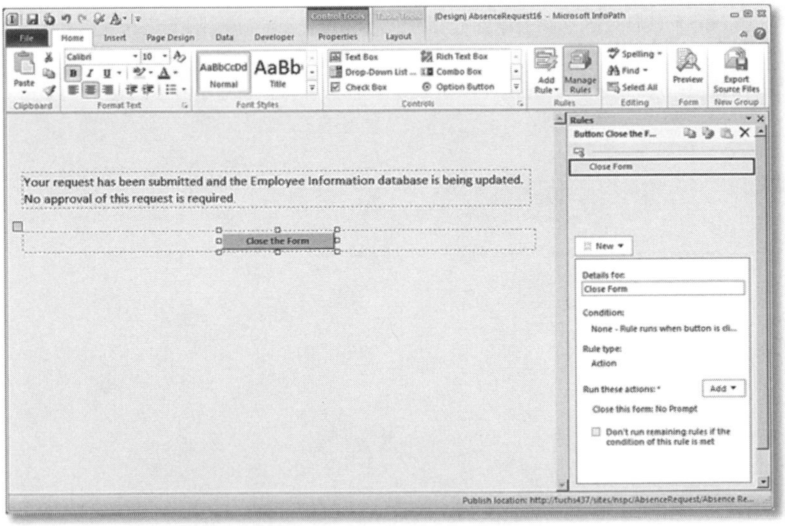

Illustration 352 - New Close the Form button and rule

Important Note – The reason why we are adding a Close the Form button and rule to each submit message View is because the rule action *Close the Form* does not work after a **Switch Views** action. If we were to make *Close the Form* the last action for each of the *Submit Absence Request button* rules, they would not execute; so this is the work around to close the form after switching views.

We want the form to be closed from a button rule rather than from the *InfoPath* browser *Close* button because the browser *Close button* will display a *Close dialogue screen* as shown in **Illustration 353** below that is confusing to the user, and will provide additional save options that are not necessary.

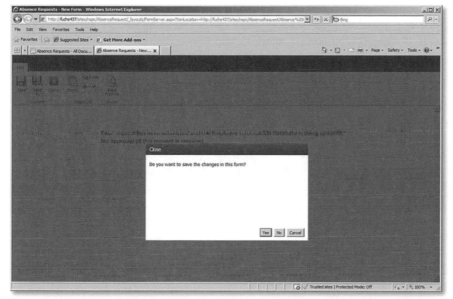

Illustration 353 – Using a form button to avoid displaying the browser Close button that will display a confusing Close dialogue screen

Copy the table with the **Close the Form button**. Go to the *Submitted for Approval View*. Paste the table beneath the first table so that the *Close the Form* button is now on this view.

Open the **Rules** for the pasted button. You will see that the *Close Form* Rule for the button was copied as well as shown in **Illustration 354** below.

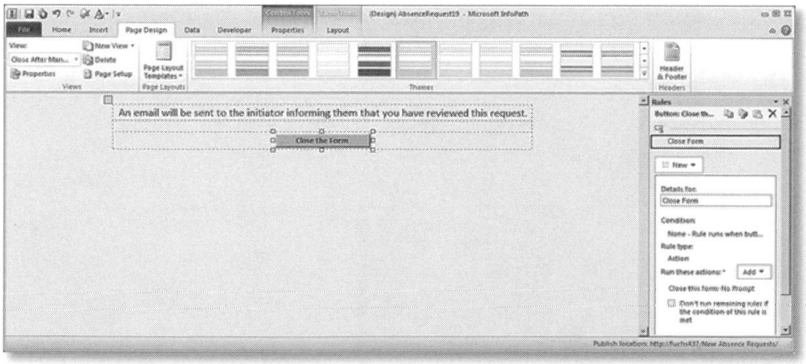

Illustration 354 – Close Form rule copied with the Close the Form button to the Close After Manager Review "View"

Go to the *Submitted and Approved View*. Copy the table with the **Close the Form** button again. Go to the *Close After Manager Review "View"* and paste the table.

Publishing the InfoPath Form as a Content Type

Content Types are the DNA of *SharePoint*. Practically everything in *SharePoint* is defined as a content type, from which all other *SharePoint* artifacts are created and assembled into components. A content type is the abstract representation of a *SharePoint* artifact combined with its respective property settings. A content type is conceptually analogous to an XML schema that defines the content, structure and attributes of an object or function and is used to generate an actual usable instance of the object or function. The abstract representation of a content type can also be copied and extended to create its derivatives.

We are going to generate a content type from the *Absence Request* form so that in the next section where we build the application workflow we can utilize *a Reusable Workflow* that will be bound to the *Absence Request Form Content Type*. The reason for doing this will be discussed in more detail when we create the workflow.

> **Note** — an *InfoPath Form Content Type* can be published at the site collection level or to a specific site. If it is published at the site collection level it will be available to any site in the entire site collection. If it is published to a specific site it will be available only to that site and any child sites of that site.

> **Important Note** — when an *InfoPath Form Content Type* is created its form template must also be stored in a document library *separate* from the form library where instances of the form are instantiated and stored. As such, create a *Document Library* and name it "Absence Request Form Content Type Library". Do not display it on the navigation pane.

In the *Absence Request* form click on **File** from the *Ribbon* and then **Publish**. Click the **SharePoint Server Publish** button. The *Publishing Wizard* will start and will prompt you to enter the location of the *SharePoint* site as shown in **Illustration 355** below. Enter the location for your site and click **Next**.

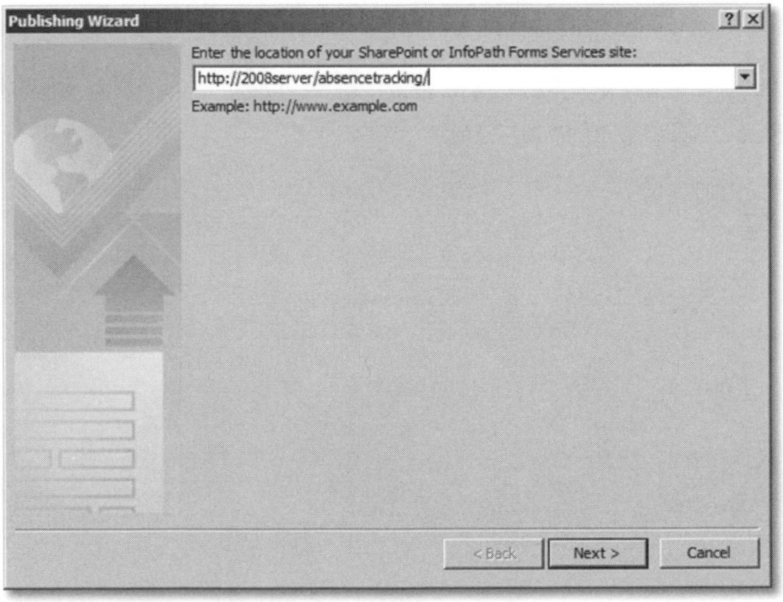

Illustration 355 - The first screen of the Publishing Wizard

In the following screen select the **Enable this form to be filled out by using a browser check box** and select the **Site Content Type radio button** as shown in **Illustration 356** below.

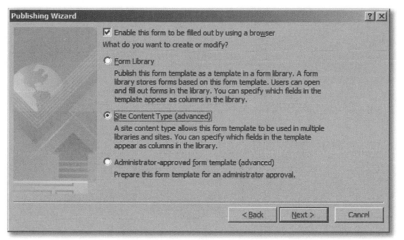

Illustration 356 - The second screen of the Publishing Wizard where publishing the form as a Site Content Type is specified

Click **Next**. In the subsequent screen leave the default *Create a new content type radio button* selection. Every content type created must be based on an existing content type. As this is the first form content type being created its base content type is the *Form* content type, and this will display by default as shown in **Illustration 357** below.

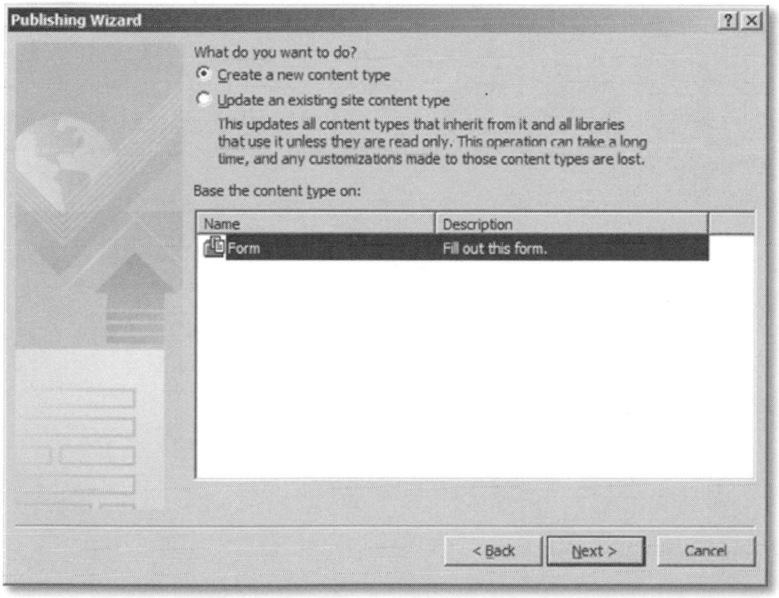

Illustration 357 – Click the radio button to Create a new content type on the third Publishing Wizard screen

Click **Next**. In the subsequent screen enter "Absence Request Form Content Type" as the name for this content type and enter a description as shown in **Illustration 358** below.

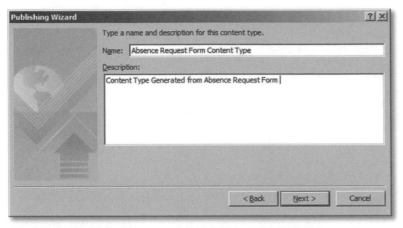

Illustration 358 - The fourth screen of the Publishing Wizard where a name is entered for the content type

Click Next. In the subsequent screen you enter the location and name of document library that will host the form template for the *form content type*. Enter the address of the *Absence Request Content Type Library* you just created and name the template "Absence Request Form Content Type" as shown in **Illustration 359** below.

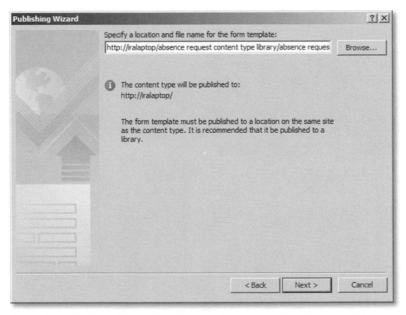

Illustration 359 - The address of the library and the name of the form template are specified in the fifth screen of the Publishing Wizard

Click **Next**. In the subsequent screen of the Publishing Wizard as shown in **Illustration 360** below, you are prompted for the fields in the form that will be display as columns when this form content type is attached to a form library, as will be seen shortly. Since we already published this form to a form library in an earlier step the previously selected fields will be displayed by default. We will want the form content type to surface the same fields and settings.

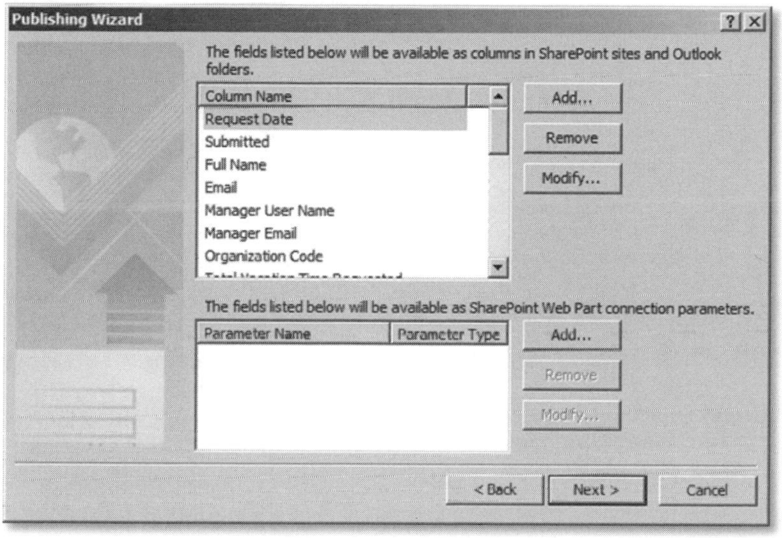

Illustration 360 - The sixth screen of the Publishing Wizard where fields to be displayed as columns are specified

Click **Next**. The verification screen will display. Click **Next**. *InfoPath* will now go through the process of generating the form content type and will display a completion screen when it is done.

Go to the *Absence Request Content Type Library.* You will see that the template for the form content type has been added as shown in **Illustration 361** below.

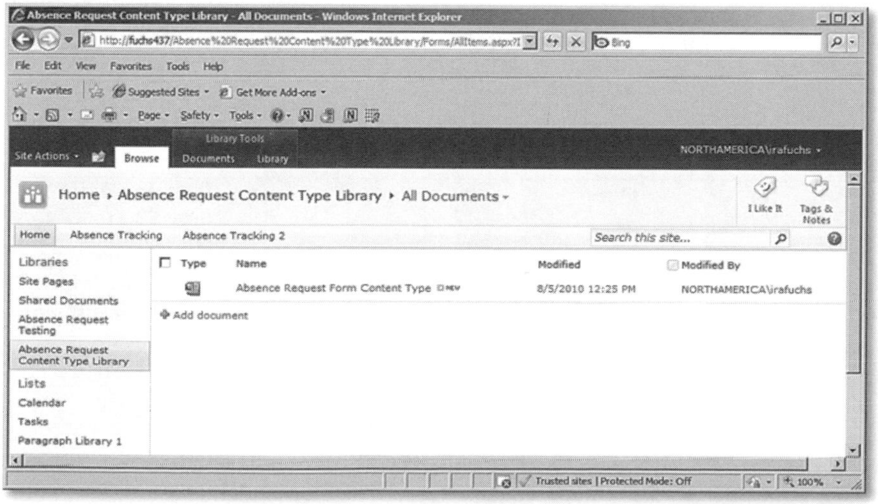

Illustration 361 - The hidden document library that stores the form content type template

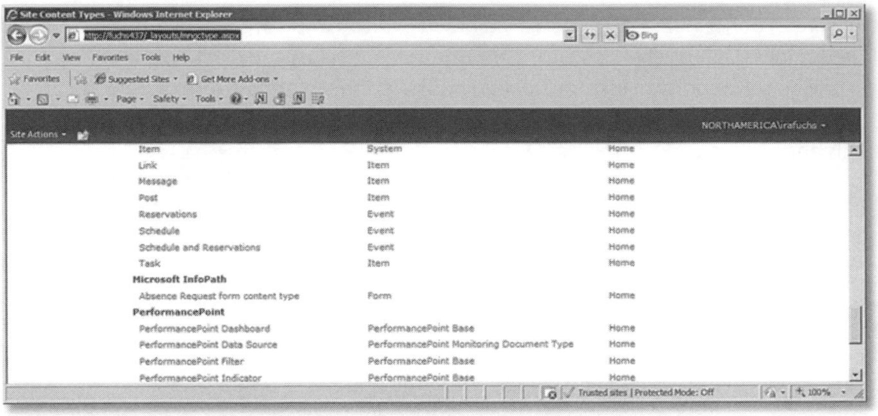

Illustration 362 - Absence Request form content type found in the Gallery for Site content types

From the *Site Actions* drop-down menu select **Site Settings**. Under *Galleries* select **Site content types**. Scroll down the list of content types. Under the *Microsoft InfoPath* group you will find the *Absence Request form content type* as shown in **Illustration 362** at left.

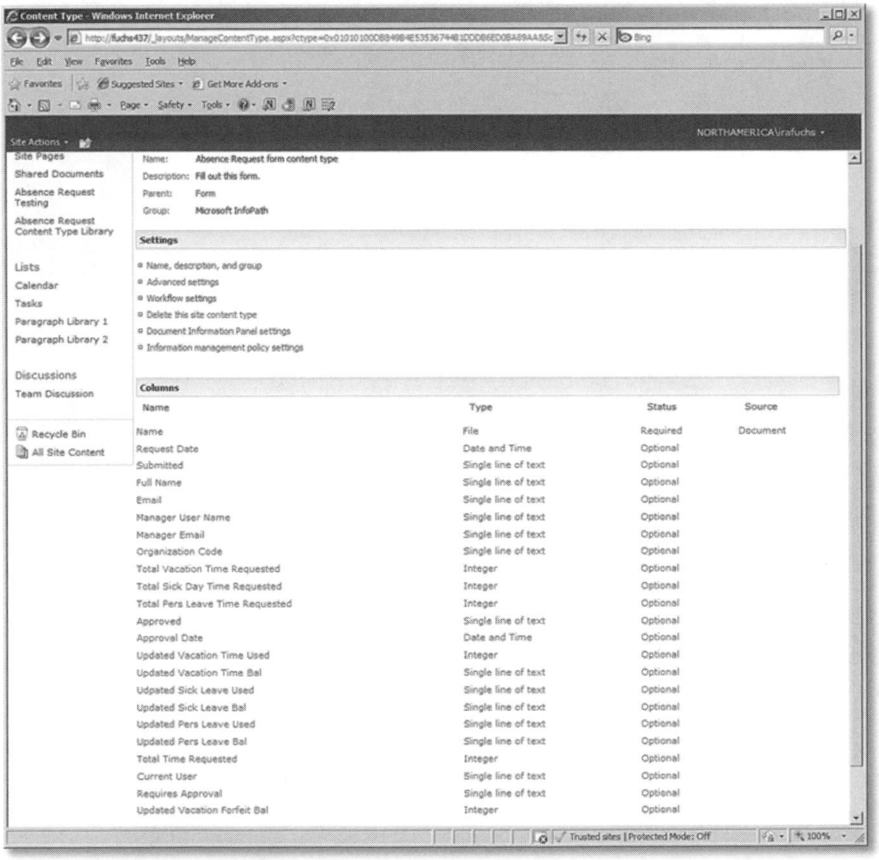

Click on the **Absence Request form content type** to display its settings page as shown in **Illustration 363** at left. The columns generated from the fields in the form are shown and the common Settings applicable to any list, library or content type are available. Additional columns can be added and the column order can be modified just as can be done for any list or library.

Important Development Note – A key value of content types is that they provide a mechanism for defining and applying complex functional attributes to the abstract entity, such as a workflow, and then

Illustration 363 - Settings page for the Absence Request form content type

any actual deployment of the content type instantiates these functional attributes. This is one of the important ways that *SharePoint* as an application development platform enables component re-use and extensibility. By binding a workflow to a content type the workflow will be implemented on the list or library that the content type is attached to, or to a new content type derived from it.

Another value of content types is the ability to automatically propagate changes made to the content type to all the instantiated instances of it as well as to content types that are derived from the content type. This means that if we make a change to the workflow that is bound to the content type, those changes can be automatically propagated to any list or library that the content type is attached to or to a derived content type. This is the default behavior that SharePoint sets for content types.

Click on **Advanced settings**. As shown in **Illustration 364** below, the *Update all content types inheriting from this type radio button* is set to Yes by default.

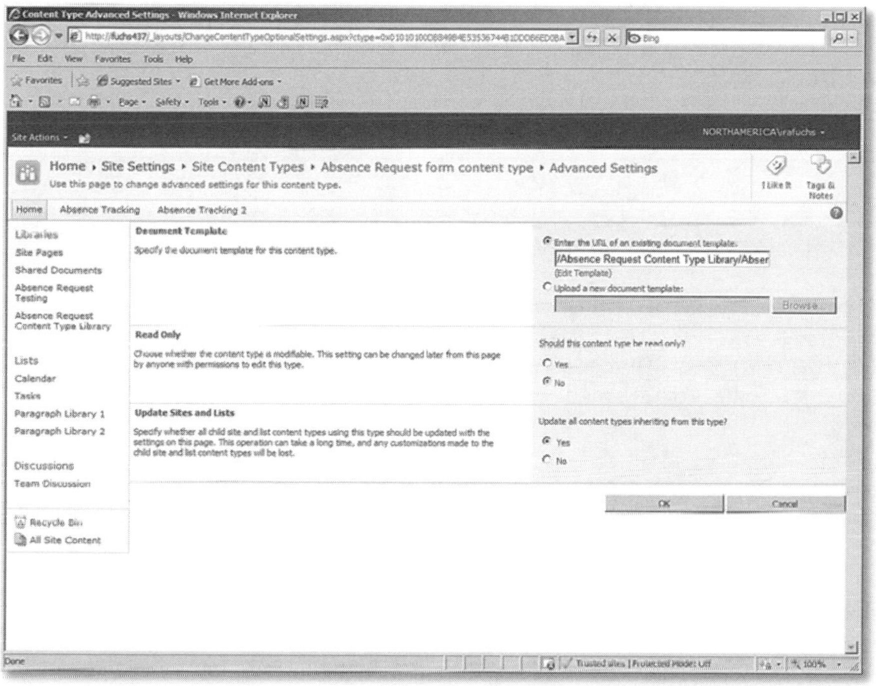

Illustration 364 - Advanced Settings page for the Absence Request form content type

Creating a Form Library Configured to Support Content Types and Binding the Absence Request Content Type to the Form Library

Now that we have created the *Absence Request form content type* we will create a new *Absence Requests* form library that will host the content type and will be the new repository for actual instances of the requests.

> **Important Note** – The new form library that we create here should not be confused with the ***document library*** that was created to store the ***template*** for the form content type.

Create a new form library and name it "New Absence Requests". Click on **Library Settings** and then **Advanced Settings.** On the *Advanced Settings* page select the **Yes radio button** for *Allow management of content types?* as shown in **Illustration 365** below.

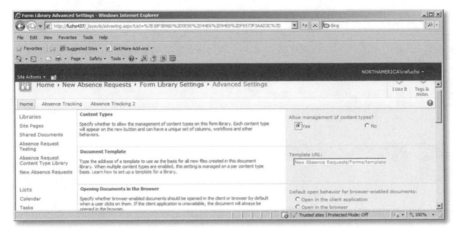

Illustration 365 - Advanced Settings page for the new form library

Click **OK**. On the *Form Library Settings* page you will now see a section for *Content Types* as shown in **Illustration 366** below. Note that a content type named *Form* is set as the default content type, as this was created as a form library.

Illustration 366 - Content Types section on the settings page for the form library

Click on **Add from existing site content types**. On the *Add Content Types* screen that displays as shown in **Illustration 367** on the next page you can choose one or more content types to attach to this form library. Choose the **Absence Request form content type** and click **OK**.

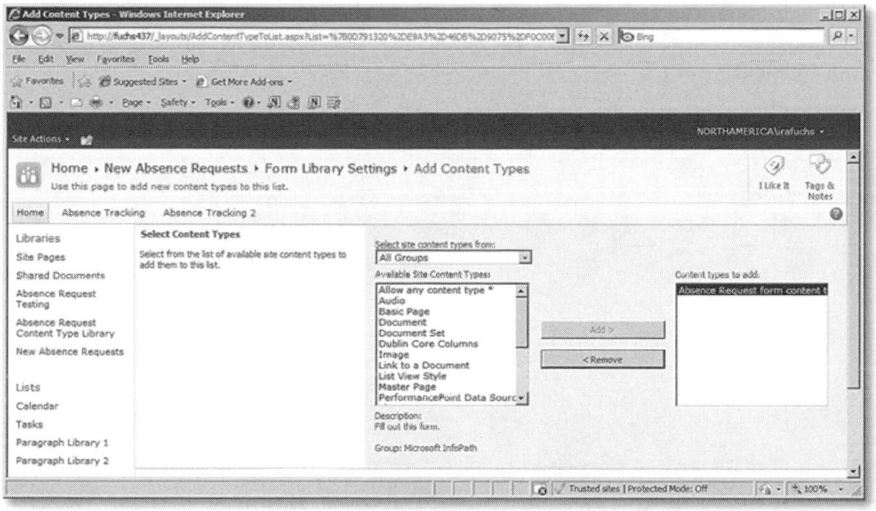

Illustration 367 - Adding the Absence Request form content type to the form library

Note that the *Form Library Settings* page now displays the *Absence Request Form content type* as well as the *Form* content type, and the form fields specified to be library columns in the *Publishing Wizard* display as well as shown in **Illustration 368** below.

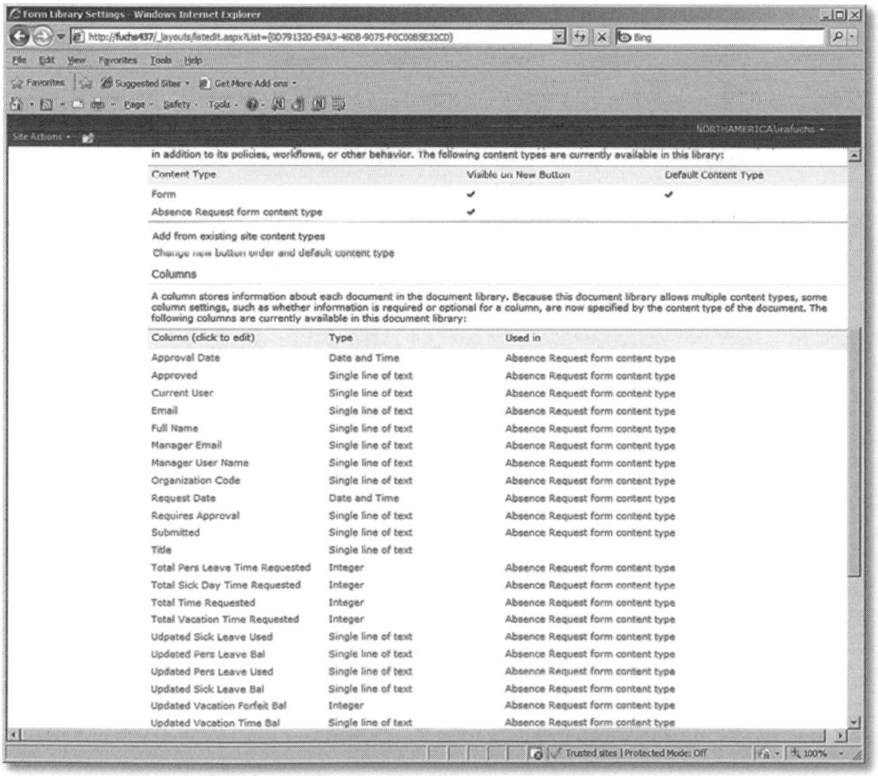

Illustration 368 - Content type columns available for use in the library

Click on **Change new button order and default content type**. On the *Change New Button Order and Default Content Type* page de-select the *Visible* check box for the *Form* content type and set the *Position from Top* setting for the *Absence Request form content type* to **1** as shown in **Illustration 369** below.

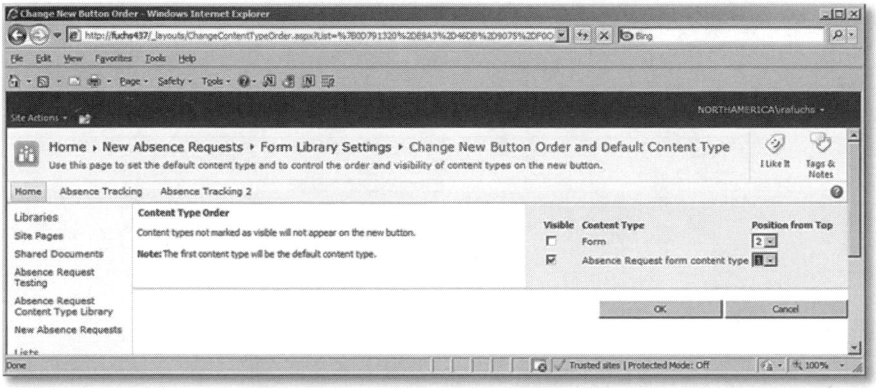

Illustration 369 – Turn on/off the display of the library content types and change their button order

Return to the *Form Library Settings* page. Note that the *Absence Request form content type* columns ***are not*** displaying; only the default fields for the *Form* content type are showing. This is because they have not yet been selected to display in the default *All Documents* view.

From the *Library Tool\Library Ribbon* menu select **Modify View**. The *Edit View* of the *All Documents* view will display as shown in **Illustration 370** below and **Illustration 371** on the next page.

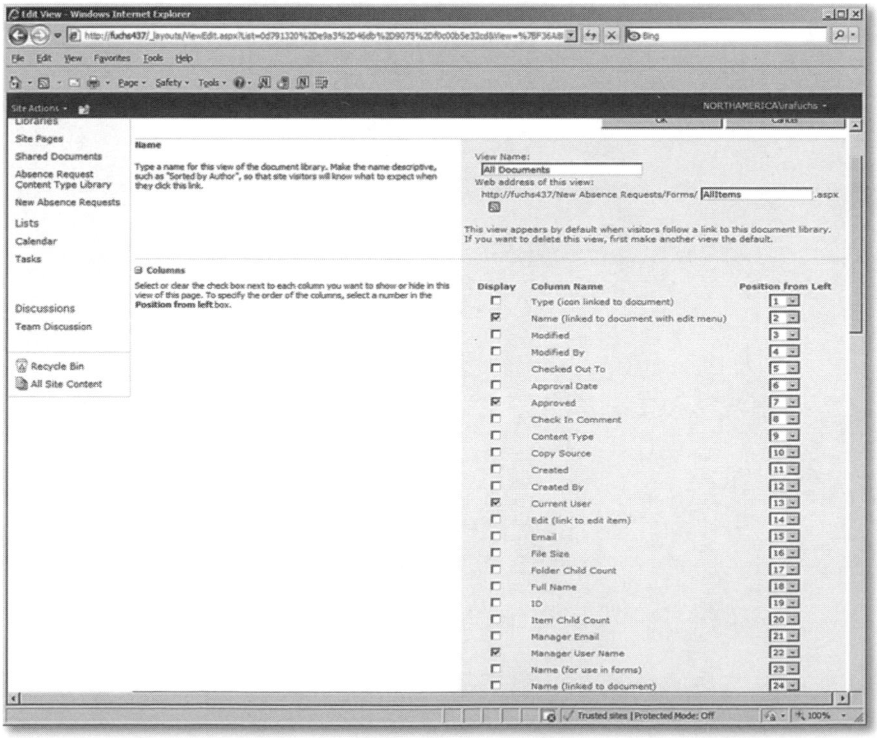

Illustration 370 – Top of the Edit page for the All Documents View of the form library

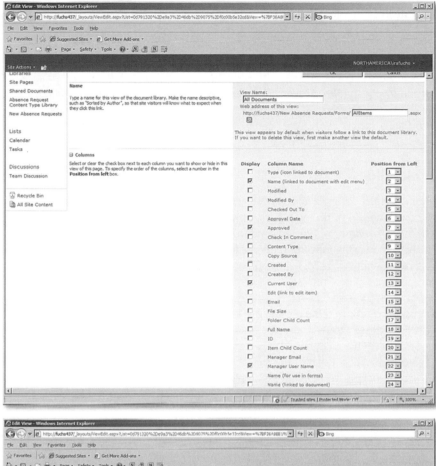

Illustration 371 - Bottom of the Edit page for the All Documents View of the form library

Deselect the *Type, Modified, Modified By and Checked Out to* columns and select all the columns checked in **Illustration 370** and **Illustration 371** above. You can iterate through this column selection process to refine the display order of the columns, which will now display in the *All Documents* view of the library.

Return to the *New Absence Requests* form library and click **Add** document or select the **New Document** button from the *Ribbon,* which will display the *Absence Request* form content type form. The *Absence Request* form will open.

> **Important Note** – If you were to create and submit a new absence request form the new instance would ***not show up*** in the *New Absence Requests* library. Recall that the *SharePoint Library Submit* data connection that we originally created was configured to submit the form to the original *Absence Requests* form library. We need to change this setting so that the form is submitted to the *New Absence Requests* form library.

Form Publishing Considerations

> **Important Development Note** – When a *form content type* is deployed in a solution there are two ways to modify the underlying form template for any form library: publish a revised form template ***directly*** to the **form library** where you want to instantiate the changes or publish the revised form template to modify the **form content type** for the site collection or site. There are different use cases that are appropriate for each approach and there will be different results for each. The following is a description of the ramifications and considerations for each approach:

You can make changes to any aspect of a form template (i.e. rule logic, presentation design, data connectivity, etc.) and publish it directly to a form library. The instances of the form generated will reflect those changes. However the settings for the content type, specifically the workflow attached to the form content type, will still be in effect. In addition, the columns available for display in the library and their order are also governed by the content type. You can have multiple form libraries in a site collection or site, each with a variant of the form template, but all executing the same workflow.

If you want to change he workflow settings for all form libraries for which the same content type has been deployed it is simply a matter of modifying and publishing the revised workflow; you do not have to change or republish the content type. If you want to change the columns that display or their order then you will publish the revised form to modify the original form content type. For these changes to be propagated to all deployments of the content type the *Update all content types inheriting from this type* must be set to Yes on the *Advanced Setting* page.

A third option is to create multiple form content types. You would do this if you want to have different workflows implemented but did not want to keep track of multiple form templates associated with different form libraries. Of course now you would be keeping track of multiple form content types.

The ability to modify a specific library form template yet still maintain the workflow implementation of the content type allows for significant deployment flexibility in an Enterprise. As we stated in the very beginning of this book, one of the key design aspects of this Enterprise application is the ability to easily and readily instantiate distributed instances of the application, each with its own custom logic, and have all of them update the same data store.

Modify the SharePoint Library Submit Data Connection to Submit to the New Form Library

Click on **Data Connections** on the *Ribbon* to open the *Data Connections* screen as shown in **Illustration 372** below.

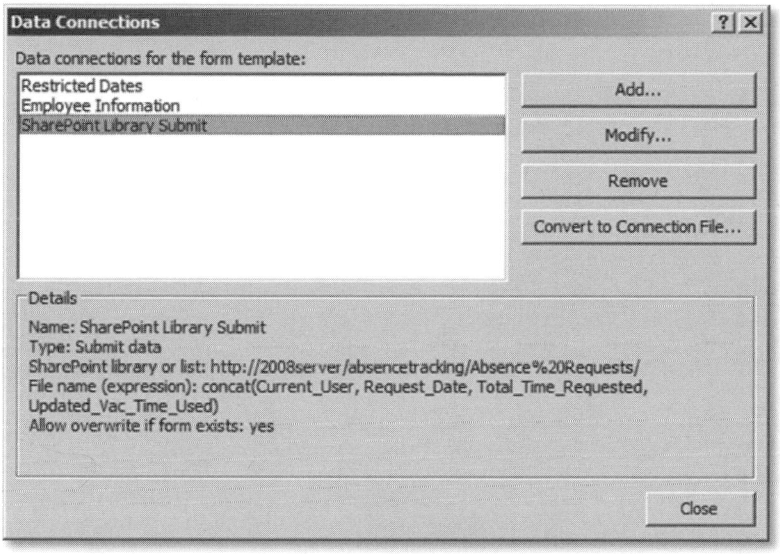

Illustration 372 - Data Connections screen showing all data connections

Select the **SharePoint Library Submit** data connection and click the **Modify** button. The *Data Connection Wizard* will begin as shown in **Illustration 373** below.

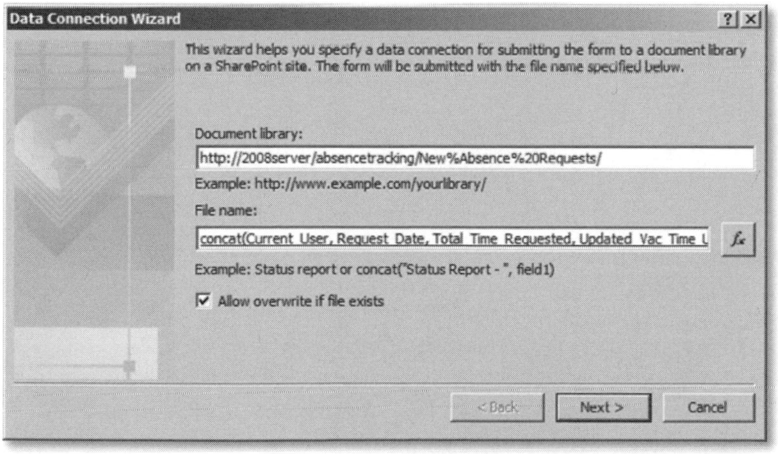

Illustration 373 – Modification screen of the Data Connection Wizard changing the form library or file name of the submitted forms

Enter the address for the *New Absence Requests* library for the *Document library* and leave the *File name* setting. Click **Next** to finish.

Publishing the New Absence Request Form to the New Form Library

Now that we have a revised form template the next step is to publish it to the *New Absence Requests* form library. Click **File** from the *Ribbon* and **Publish**. Click the **SharePoint Server** button to **Publish form to a SharePoint Library** as shown in **Illustration 374** below. *Do not* select the *Quick Publish* button.

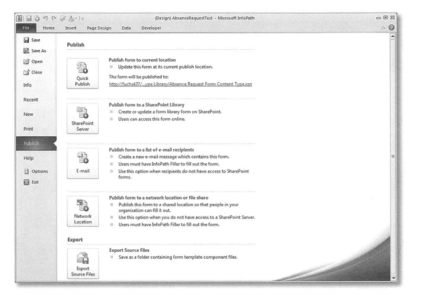

Illustration 374 - Publish options from the File menu

The first screen of the *Publishing Wizard* will display. Leave the **Enable this form to be filled out by using a browser check box** checked and select the **Form Library radio button** as shown in **Illustration 375** below.

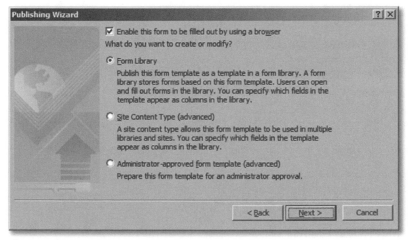

Illustration 375 - First screen of the Publishing Wizard

Click **Next**. In the next *Publishing Wizard* screen select the **Update the form template in an existing form library radio button** and choose the **New Absence Requests** library as shown in **Illustration 376** below.

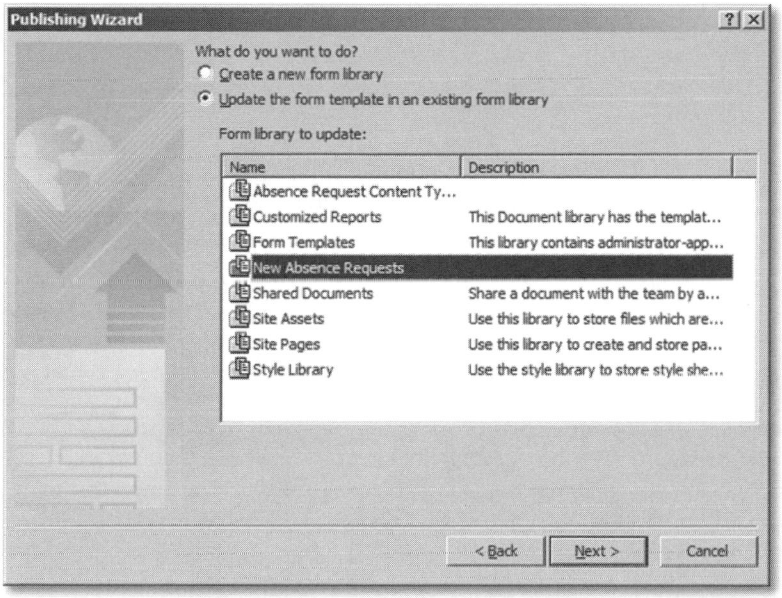

Illustration 376 - Choosing to "Update the form template in an existing library" in the second screen of the Publishing Wizard

Click **Next**. The *Publishing Wizard* page for promoting the form fields to library columns will display. Click **Next** to display the verification page. Click **Next** to complete publishing the revised form template to the *New Absence Requests* form library.

> **Note** – There are a number of fields in the *Employee Information* FCT as well as the *Absence Request* form (e.g.: *Title, Alternate_Approver, Location, Level*) that are not used in the application. This is not an oversight; these fields are part of the information set for which application functionality was anticipated but the final set of functions to be implemented changed. One example of this was to have the workflow route a request requiring approval to a delegate approver if the manager was not available. This is part of the development process; the specification will change for any number of reasons. However it doesn't hurt to have these artifacts present and they provide an opportunity for the reader to experiment creating additional functionality in the application that addresses requirements that they will encounter.

> **Note** - Delete the original *Absence Requests form library* as it will no longer be used.

We have now completed the form creation part of the application. We are now ready to create the workflow component of the application.

Creating the Application Workflow

We designed the application so that the *Absence Request* form generates the new values for the year-to-date time used, and the year-to-date time balances in each leave category. It does this by adding the existing year-to-date values from the *Employee Information* database with the total leave time in each category requested in the form and storing these values in the *Stored Value* fields. These new year-to-date values are written to the form library columns when the form is submitted.

This serves as the interim record of the transaction prior to updating the permanent employee record in the *Employee Information* database. The workflow will update the *Employee Information* database with the new values as well as execute the rule logic for the approval contingencies. Below is a description of the steps in the workflow process logic:

1. If the submitted request does not need approval (status of *Requires_Approval* equals No) then the new year-to-date values are updated in the *Employee Information* database and the request initiator is sent a confirmation email of this.

2. If the submitted request requires approval (status of *Requires_Approval* equals Yes) then an email is sent to the approval manager informing them of a pending approval. The workflow calculates a duration of two days from the workflow start date during which one of the following events are anticipated:

   a. If the value of *Approved* in the form library column for the request instance is changed to "Yes", indicating that the manager has approved the request, then the new year-to-date values are updated in *the Employee Information* database and the request initiator is sent a confirmation email of this.

   b. If the value of *Approved* in the form library column for the request instance is changed to "No", indicating that the manager has rejected the request, then an email is sent to the request initiator informing them of the request rejection.

   c. If the value of *Approved* in the form library column remains empty, indicating that no action has been taken by the manager, the workflow sends a follow-up email to the manager and an additional three hours are added to the approval period time during which one of the following events will take place:

      i. The value of *Approved* in the form library column for the request instance is changed to "Yes", indicating that the manager has approved the request, then the new year-to-date values are updated in *the Employee Information* database and the request initiator is sent a confirmation email of this.

      ii. The value of *Approved* in the form library column for the request instance is changed to "No", indicating that the manager has rejected the request, then an email is sent to the request initiator informing them of the request rejection.

      iii. If the value of *Approved* in the form library column remains empty, indicating that no action has been taken by the manager, then the *Approved* status is set to *Yes by Default*, the new year-to-date values are updated in the *Employee Information* database and the request initiator is sent a confirmation email of this.

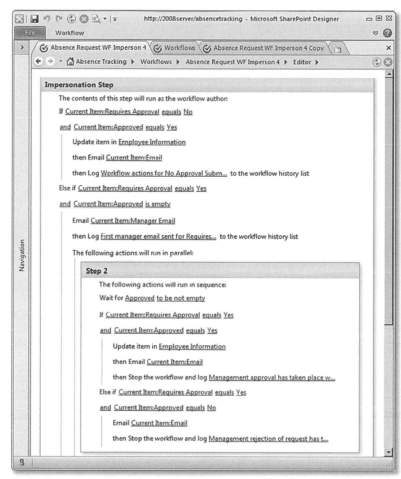

Illustration 377 and **Illustration 378** at left show the completed workflow in the *SharePoint Designer Workflow Editor*.

Once again, a fundamental design and development principle of this book is to demonstrate a viable rule-driven paradigm for Enterprise class application development. The *SharePoint Designer 2010 Workflow Editor* has been dramatically improved over the 2007 version. The *SharePoint Designer 2010 Workflow Editor*, in conjunction with *InfoPath 2010*, delivers the robust declarative, rule-based development capabilities to the *SharePoint* platform that can accommodate almost any functional and operational requirements.

Illustration 377 - Completed workflow template

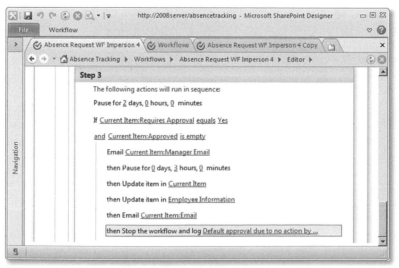

Illustration 378 - Completed workflow template

Introduction to SharePoint Designer Workflows

Open *SharePoint Designer* and connect to the *Absence Tracking* site. Click on **Workflows** in the *Navigation* pane. The *Workflow Ribbon* and the three built-in *SharePoint* workflows will display as shown in **Illustration 379** below.

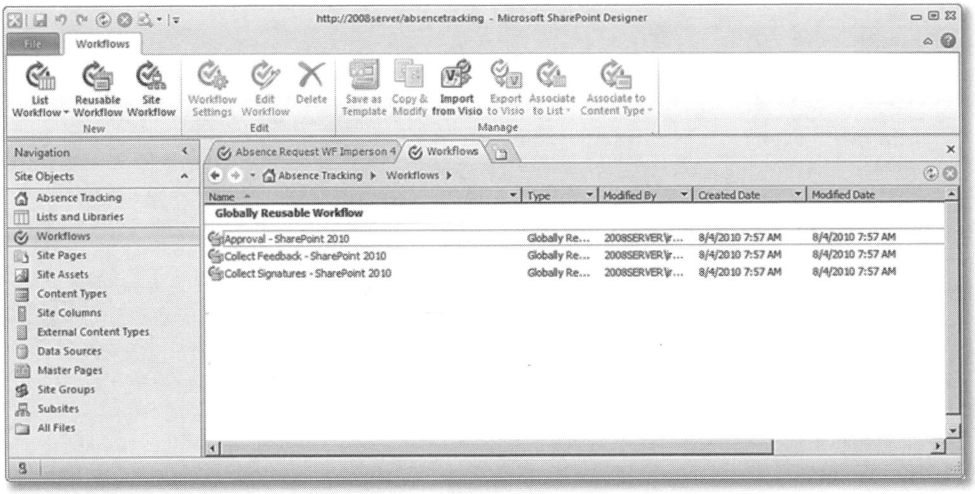

Illustration 379 - Workflow main screen in SharePoint Designer 2010

In *SharePoint Designer 2010* you can create *List Workflows*, *Reusable Workflows* and *Site Workflows*. *List Workflows* are bound to a specific *SharePoint* list and are not reusable. *Reusable Workflows* can be designed and created independently of any *SharePoint* artifacts and can be later associated to lists, libraries and content types, and will run in the context of the items that they are associated to. *Site Workflows* do not require the context of a list, library or content type item to run.

The primary reason why we created a content type for the *Absence Request* form is so that we could bind a *Reusable Workflow* to it. The substantial value that we derive from doing so is the automated correlation management of workflow instances to the requests that triggered them, or what is known as "current item context". A workflow process as described above is triggered automatically when a new request is submitted to the form library. There could be hundreds of workflow instances running at any given time as a result of hundreds of absence requests being submitted. Each workflow instance must be directly bound to the request that spawned it and execute its specific processing details.

Note the *Current Item* prefixes for the column items referenced in the workflow as shown in **Illustration 377** on the previous page. In addition, the *Update item in Employee Information* action implies that the unique *Employee Information* record for the initiator of the request will be updated, and not someone else's.

Creating the correlation mechanism for "current item" context is one of the challenges of workflow development as a unique identifier for each request must become part of the workflow context and this is not trivial to implement. *SharePoint Designer* workflows that are bound to lists, libraries and content types will automatically manage current item context for workflow instances. There are some limitations to binding a workflow to a list or library however:

- The workflow cannot be re-used – you cannot save a *SharePoint Designer* list/library workflow, modify it and then apply it to another list or library. You have to create a new workflow from scratch.

- The workflow is not saved with the list or library when saved as a template – Often after modifying and configuring a list or library you would like to reuse it by saving it as a template. Unfortunately the workflow attached to a list or library is not saved with the template for a list or library (although workflows are saved when you save a site as a *SharePoint Solution Package*).

- The current item context of the workflow often breaks when modifications to the list or library are made. Creating additional views or rearranging column order will sometimes break the workflow connection.

Fortunately, *SharePoint Designer* workflows that are based on a content type provide current item context, and are completely reusable and transportable by attaching the content type with its accompanying workflow to any appropriate list or library.

Getting Familiar with the SharePoint Designer Workflow Editor

We are ready to get an object lesson in how this all works. Open *SharePoint Designer* and connect to the *Absence Tracking* site. Select *Workflows* on the *Navigation* pane. Click the **Reusable Workflow button** on the *Ribbon*. The *Create Reusable Workflow* dialogue screen will appear as shown in **Illustration 380** at left. Name the workflow "Absence Request Workflow" and from the *Content Type* drop-down list select the *Absence Request form content type*.

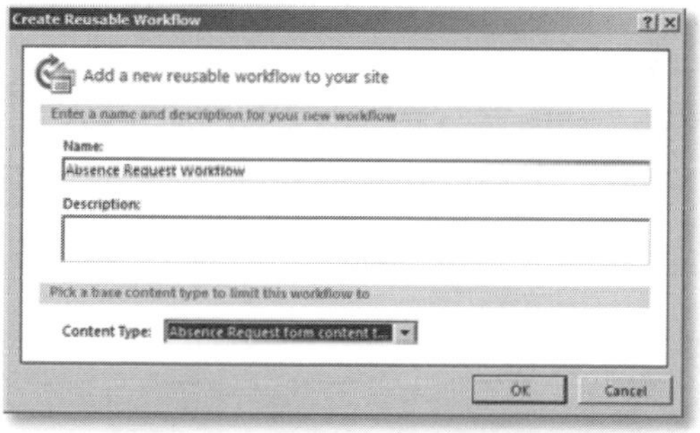

Illustration 380 - Create Reusable Workflow dialogue screen where the content type that the workflow will be based on is specified

The workflow editor will open and an initial step will be displayed as shown in **Illustration 381** below.

Notice the horizontal line under the text "*Start typing or use the Insert group in the Ribbon.*" This is a visual cue that this is a hierarchical "positional region" where a workflow operative function – a *Condition, Action, Step* or *Parallel Block* can be inserted. The hierarchical positional regions are a key aspect of the workflow editor and understanding how the positional regions work with operative functions is fundamental to constructing workflows. As such we are going to review it in depth here.

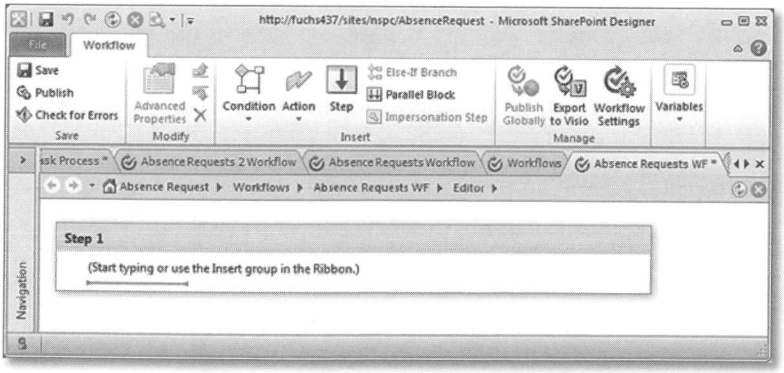

Illustration 381 - Workflow editor displaying a new workflow template

Right click on the **horizontal line**. A drop-down list of insertion options will display as shown in **Illustration 382** below.

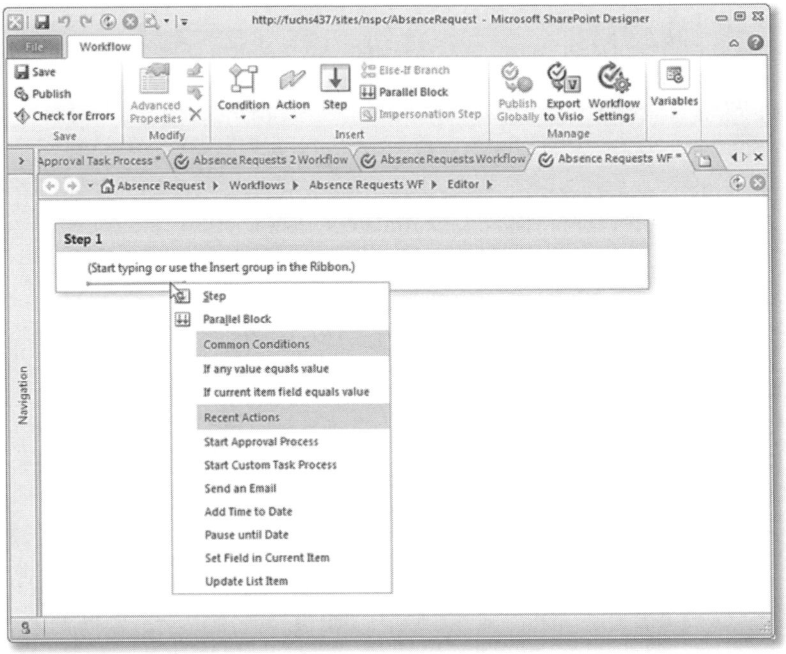

Illustration 382 - Steps, conditions and actions available by right-clicking at this insertion point

Alternatively, you can type directly at a workflow editor position. If a word is recognized as being part of a *Condition* or *Action* statement *SharePoint Designer* will display the insertion options that are available, as shown in **Illustration 383** below.

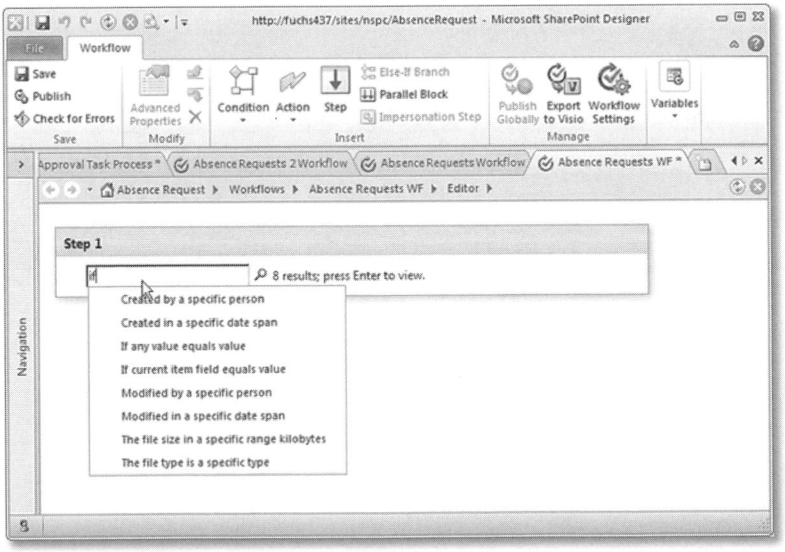

Illustration 383 - Steps, conditions and actions available by typing at the insertion point

Illustration 384 below shows the drop-down list that displays the *Conditions* that are available out of the box from the *SharePoint Designer Workflow Editor*. The two *Common Conditions* are similar to *InfoPath* conditions and implement various operators that can define almost any type of conditional statement.

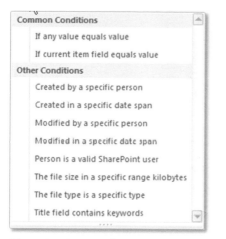

Illustration 384 - Conditions available out
of the box from SharePoint Designer

Illustration 385 below shows the drop-down list that displays some of the *Actions* that are available out of the box from the *SharePoint Designer Workflow Editor*. Additional *Actions will* display in the context of working with specific workflow features and functions.

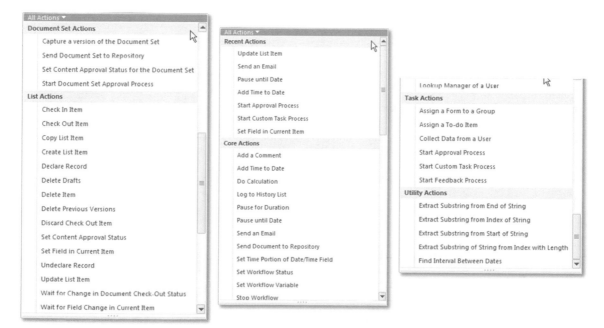

Illustration 385 - Actions available out of the box in SharePoint Designer

In addition to *Steps, Conditions, Actions* and *Parallel Blocks,* the workflow editor provides the ability to create *Local Variables* and *Association Parameters* that store information used by a workflow. Some sample *Local Variables* are shown in **Illustration 386** below.

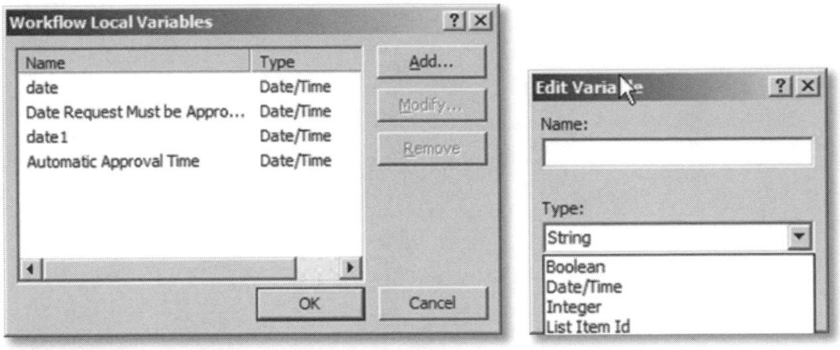

Illustration 386 - Workflow local variables dialogue screens

Select **the If any value equals value Condition**. The condition will be inserted as shown in **Illustration 387** below.

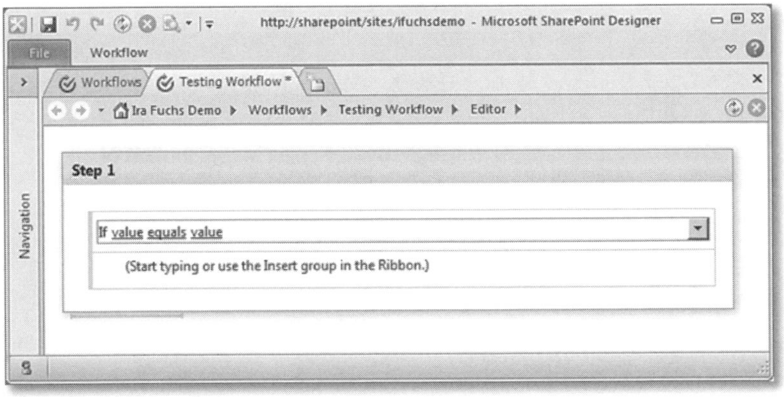

Illustration 387 - Selecting the "If any value equals value" Condition for insertion into the workflow

Place your cursor directly above the condition and click. Now move the cursor up higher and click again. Note how the delineated positional region changes as shown in **Illustration 388** and **Illustration 389** on the next page.

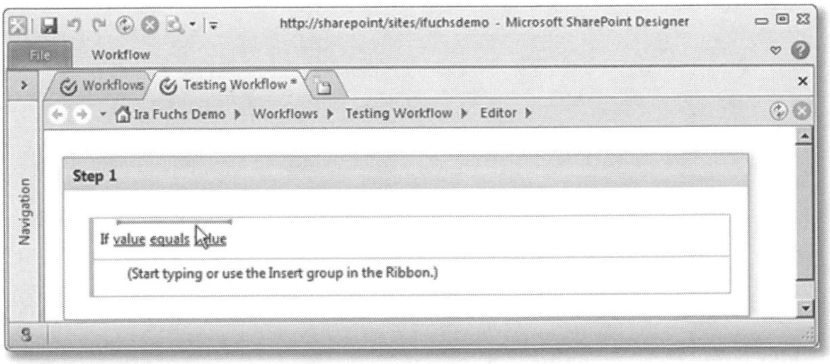

Illustration 388 - Moving the cursor to delineate a positional region currently available in the workflow

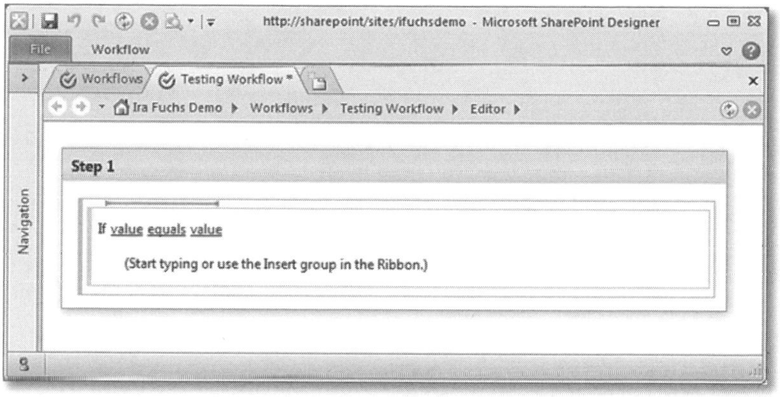

Illustration 389 - Moving the cursor again to delineate another currently available positional region

Place your cursor directly below the condition statement and click as shown in **Illustration 390** below.

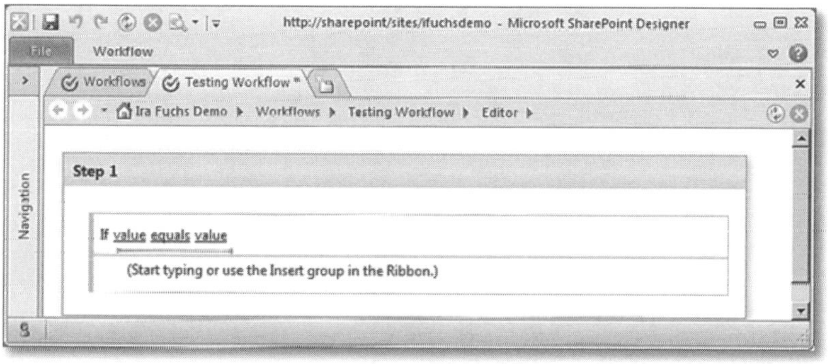

Illustration 390 - Placing the cursor directly below the condition statement

Now move the cursor to the next level down and click as shown in **Illustration 391** below.

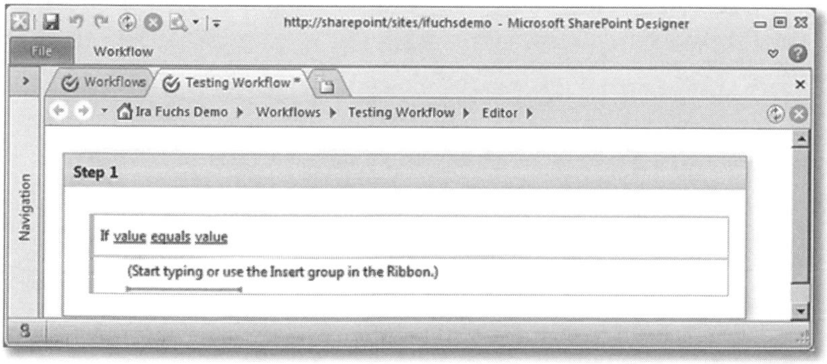

Illustration 391 - Moving the cursor another level down from the condition statement

The cursor can be moved two more levels down and you can see, as shown in **Illustration 392** and **Illustration 393** below, how the positional region changes each time you move the horizontal line with your cursure.

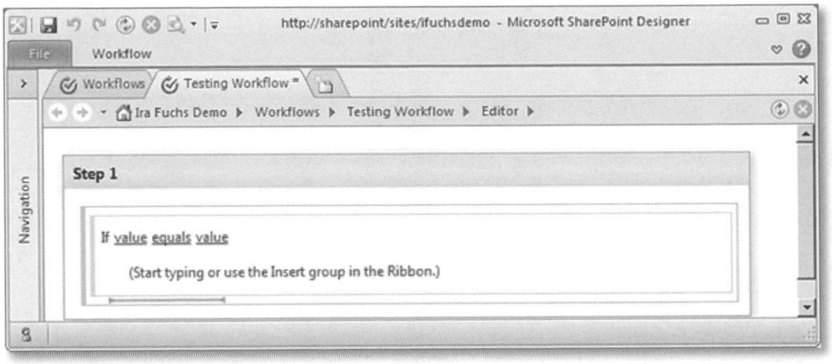

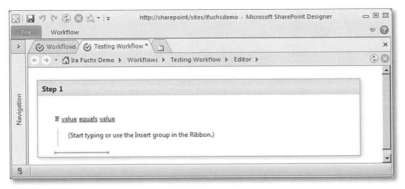

Illustration 392 - Moving the cursor down further to delineate a positional region

Illustration 393 - Moving the cursor down once again to delineate another available positional region

Now place your cursor above the *Step* region and right click. The available operative functions that can be inserted at that regional position are presented as shown in **Illustration 394** below. A *Step* or *Impersonation Step* can be inserted at this hiearchical level.

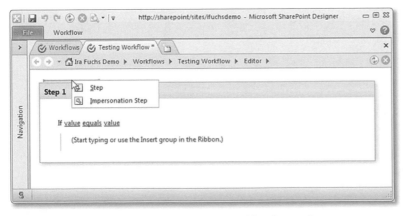

Illustration 394 - Available operative functions outside a Step region

Place your cursor directly below the *Step 1* label inside the *Step* region as shown in **Illustration 395** below and right click. The operative functions that can be inserted at any given hierarchical regional position are presented by the workflow editor.

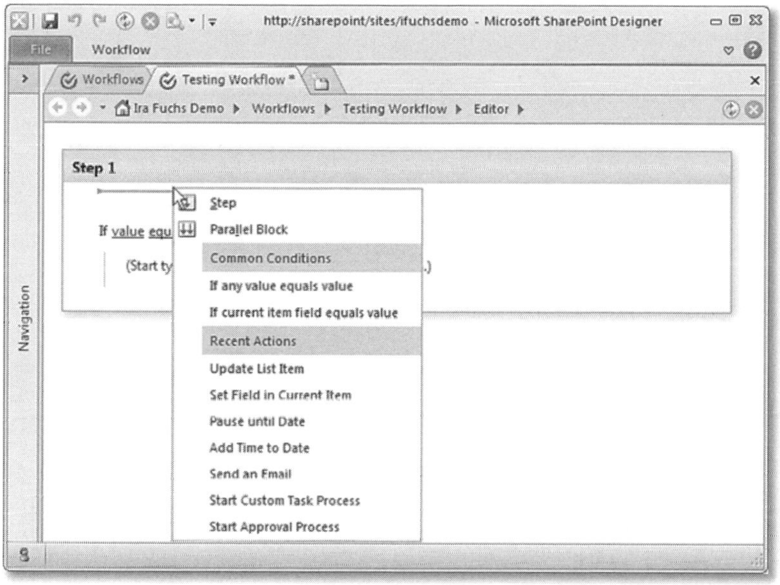

Illustration 395 - Operative functions in the positional region directly below a Step

Inserting a **Step** at this position creates a child *Step* region embedded in the first *Step,* and the new *Step* is at the same hierarchical level as the conditional statement that we initially inserted as shown in **Illustration 396** below.

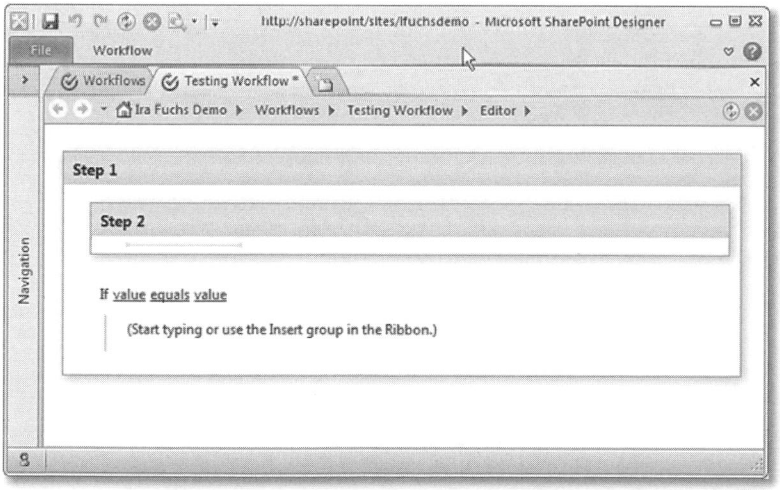

Illustration 396 - Embedding a Step directly below an existing Step

In this manner the *SharePoint Designer Workflow Editor* guides and constrains the implementation of the process logic for a workflow. The visual placement of operative functions in the context of hierarchical regions allows the workflow developer to conceptualize and build the workflow in a logically intuitive way.

Note the choice of operative function insertion options at each positional region as shown in **Illustrations 397 through 401** below and the next two pages. The nesting of operative functions and regions allows for the creation of modular logic that visually represents the overall process organization and structure while providing the granular details about the artifacts that implement the execution of the process.

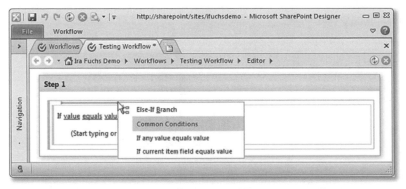

Illustration 397 - Available operative functions at different positional regions

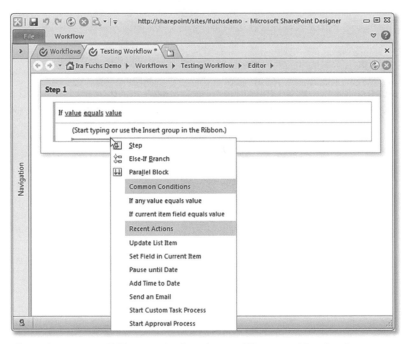

Illustration 398 - Available operative functions at different positional regions

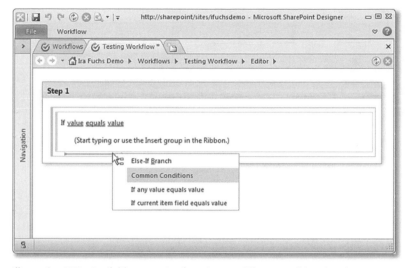

Illustration 399 - Available operative functions at different positional regions

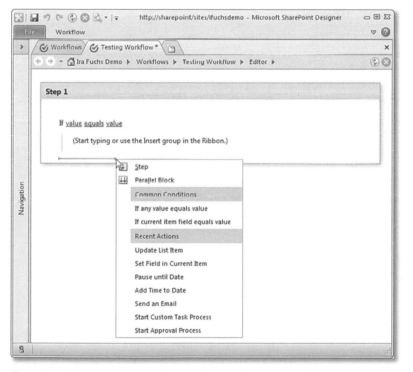

Illustration 400 - Available operative functions at different positional regions

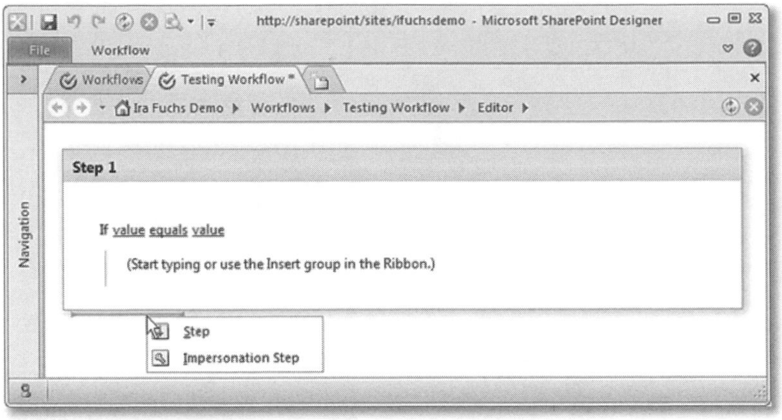

Illustration 401 - Available operative functions at different positional regions

Discussion of Important Security Considerations When Creating Workflows that Interact with External Content Types

Before we commence building the absence request workflow there are several inter-dependent security and operational factors that need to be understood about how a *SharePoint Designer* workflow interacts with an *External Content Type* as this one will.

- The first factor is that *SharePoint* workflows run under a system account and that system account must have object permissions assigned to it for the *External Content Type* in the *Business Data Connectivity Service* of *Central Administration*.

- The second factor is that *SharePoint* workflows will only work with an *External Content Type* if the connection to the external system is configured to use *Impersonation credentials* created in the *SharePoint Secure Store Service*. The *system account* under which a *SharePoint* work flow runs must be an "owner" of these Impersonation credentials.

- The third factor is that *SharePoint Designer* workflow actions are security trimmed at run-time to use the permissions of the logged-in user. ***This means that irrespective of the system account and impersonation credential settings above, the permissions of the user submitting the absence request govern what the workflow is allowed to do.***

When we have completed creating all the artifacts and components of the application we will want to set the most restrictive permissions to the entire site for all users and then apply custom permissions to site artifacts according to functional need and role. We don't want any user to have direct access to the *Employee Information* ECT list and we will hide it. In addition, as a best practice, we will create unique permissions for this list that are read-only for everyone.

However, this across the board read-only permission setting for the *Employee Information* ECT list will also ***prevent the workflow from being able to update the list values***. There is a workaround for this matter, which is to encapsulate the entire workflow in an *Impersonation Step*. An *Impersonation Step* runs under the identity of the person who authored the workflow, who will inherently have higher level permissions to access and execute operations on the application artifacts. By making the first step in the workflow an *Impersonation Step* and having all subsequent steps run under it we can empower the workflow to access and update the ECT list irrespective of the logged-in user's permissions. Because the update list action occurs in all of the workflow steps we will want the entire workflow to run within an *Impersonation Step*.

> **Important Note** – If a workflow containing an *Impersonation Step* is deployed through a *SharePoint Solution Package* the contents of the impersonation step will run under the permission settings of the user who ***activates the workflow solution package***. Creating, deploying and activating a workflow solution package is described in the section **Re-Using a SharePoint Designer Workflow** on pages 382 to 385.

We will set the object permissions in BCS for the system account and create SSS *Impersonation Credentials* after we create the workflow.

Creating the Absence Request Workflow

Encapsulating the Workflow in an Impersonation Step

Place your cursor below **Step 1** as shown in **Illustration 402** below and click on the **Impersonation Step** button.

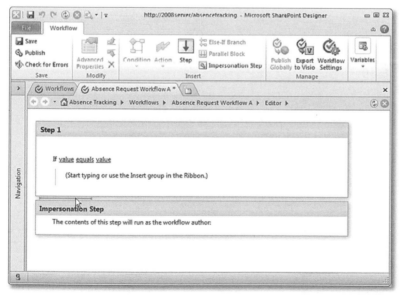

Illustration 402 - Inserting an Impersonation Step

An *Impersonation Step* will appear. Select **Step 1** and click the **Delete** button. *Step 1* will disappear. Now place your cursor within the **Impersonation Step**. Right-click and select **Step** as shown in **Illustration 403** below.

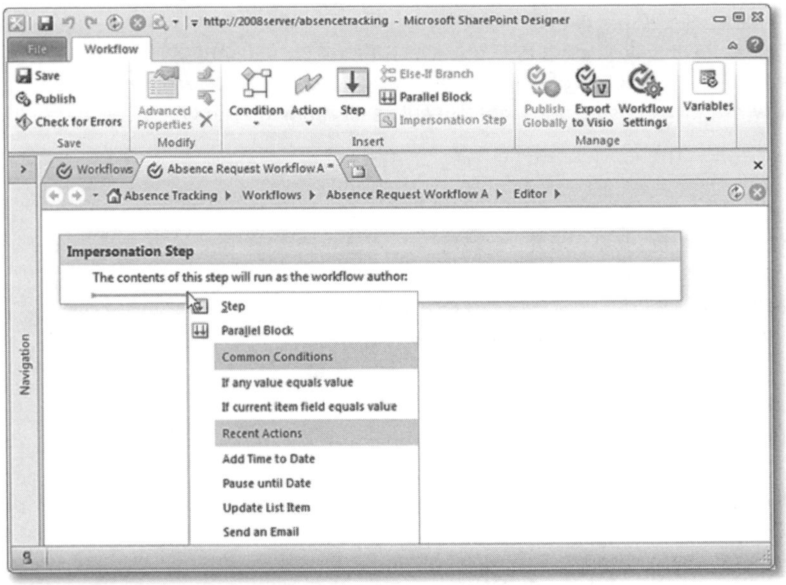

Illustration 403 - Inserting a Step within the Impersonation Step

A new step will be created that is encapsulated within the *Impersonation Step*. The new step will be named *Step 2*. Click on the name *Step 2* and rename it *Step 1* as shown in **Illustration 404** below.

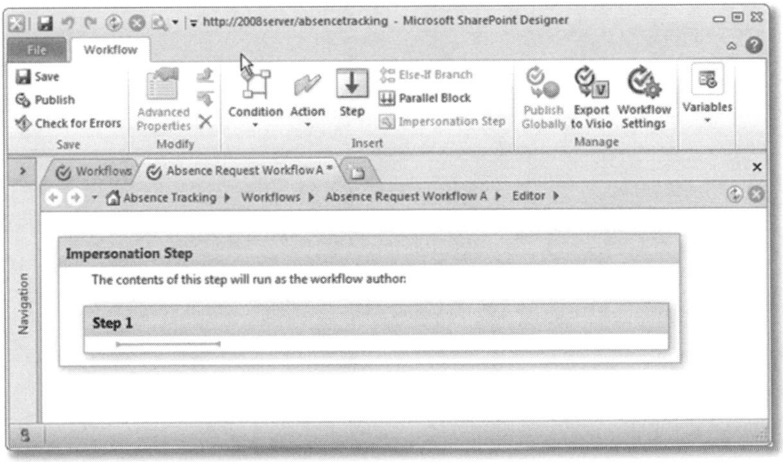

Illustration 404 - Renaming the new Step

What we have just done is create an *Impersonation Step* that will "host" all the workflow steps that will follow.

Inserting a Condition Statement

With your cursor directly under *Step 1* as shown in **Illustration 402** above, click the **Condition** button on the *Ribbon* and choose the **If current item field equals value** condition.

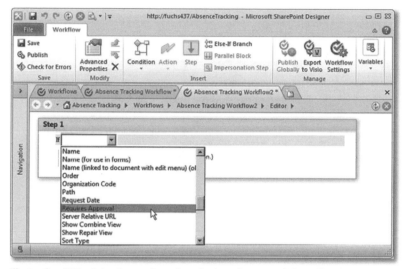

Illustration 405 – Selection options that display when you click on "field" in the condition statement

Click on **field** in the *If condition* statement. A drop down list of the *Current Item* fields will display. Scroll down and choose the **Requires Approval** field as shown in **Illustration 405** at left.

Important Development Note – In a list based workflow or *Reusable Workflow* based on a content type, *SharePoint Designer* automatically manages the workflow correlation to the "*Current Item*"; the Current Item being the object of the workflow process. In this case the workflow object is the instance of a new form submitted to the *Absence Request* form library and the corresponding row of column information that was generated from the form. *SharePoint* will create a specific instance of a workflow for each instance of a new submitted form. Neither the developer of the workflow, nor the end user submitting the form need to do anything to relate the new workflow to the unique instance of the form. Later, we will set the workflow to start upon the creation of a new form instance.

The workflow editor will look like **Illustration 406** at left.

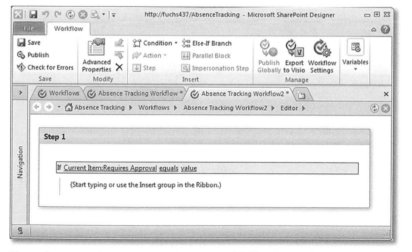

Illustration 406 - Selecting the Requires Approval field in the Condition statement

Click on the **equals** operator. A drop down list of operators will display as shown in **Illustration 407** below.

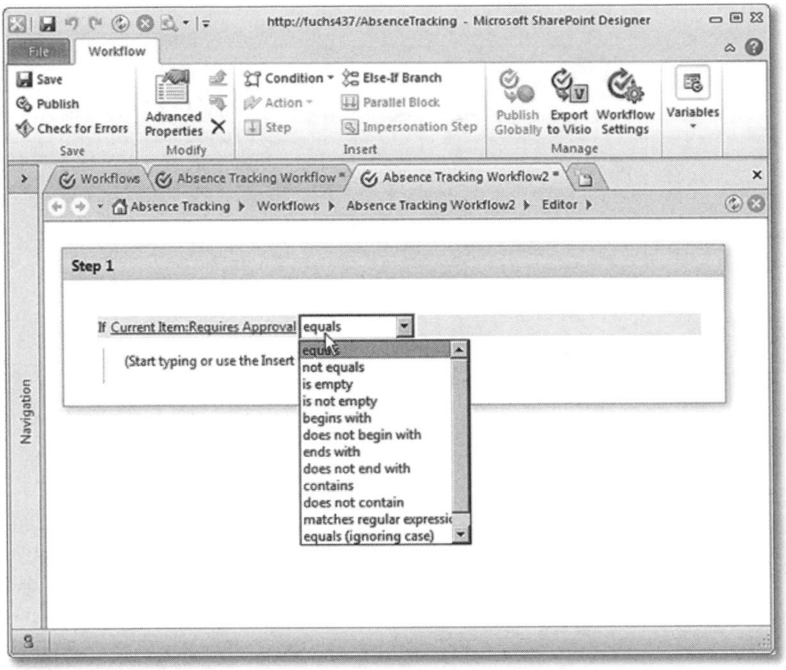

Illustration 407 - Operator options available in a Condition statement

Leave the *equals* operator. Click on **"value"** to display the value options as shown in **Illustration 408** below.

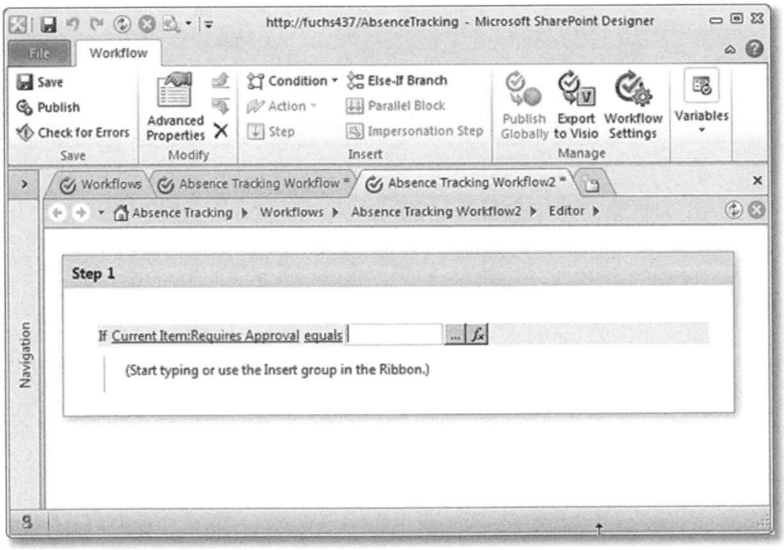

Illustration 408 - Clicking on "value" in the Condition statement

You can enter a text string directly in the box shown; build a complex string using the *String Builder* as shown in **Illustration 409** below; or lookup a value from another data source or variable as shown in **Illustration 410**.

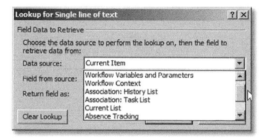

Illustration 409 - The workflow editor String Builder

Illustration 410 - The workflow editor lookup dialogue screen

Enter "No" in the string entry box so that the condition statement looks like **Illustration 411** below.

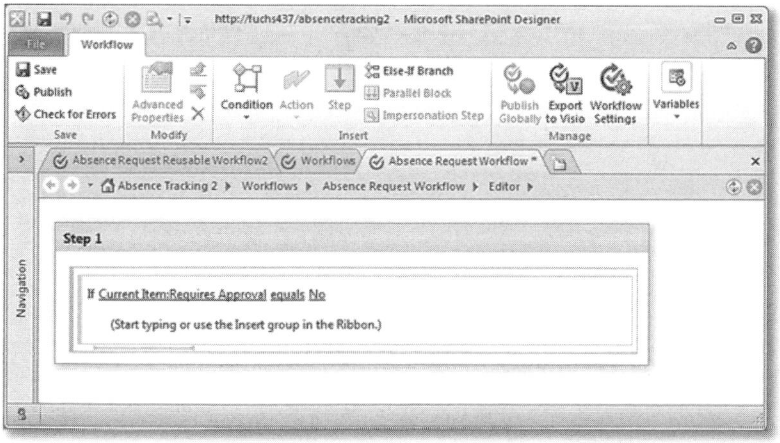

Illustration 411 – A single clause Condition statement

Recall that the *Submit* rules for the form set the value of the *Requires_Approval* field to either Yes or No and these values populate the corresponding columns in the form library.

Development Note – A workflow authored in *SharePoint Designer* can access values from any list or library within the site that the workflow is authored in including ECT lists; information generated by the workflow framework as shown in **Illustration 412** below; or local variables. A workflow, no matter where it is authored, cannot directly access the information in an *InfoPath* form itself. The information in a form that needs to be accessed by a workflow has to be exposed through the form library columns.

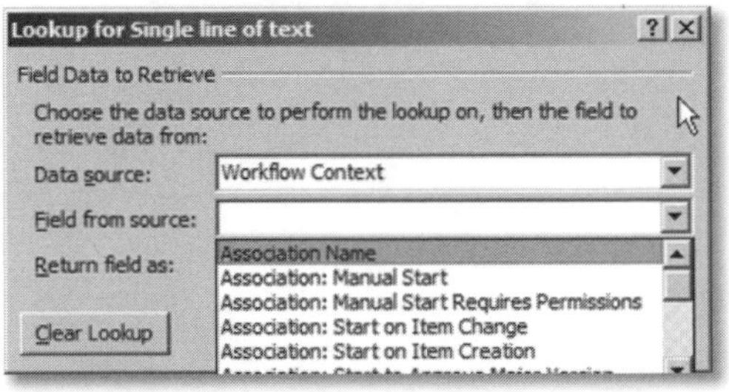

Illustration 412 - Workflow Context lookup items

Adding a Clause to the Condition Statement

Position the **horizontal line** directly below and to the right of the first condition statement. Click the **Condition** button on the *Ribbon* and select the **If current item field equals value** condition as shown in **Illustration 413** below.

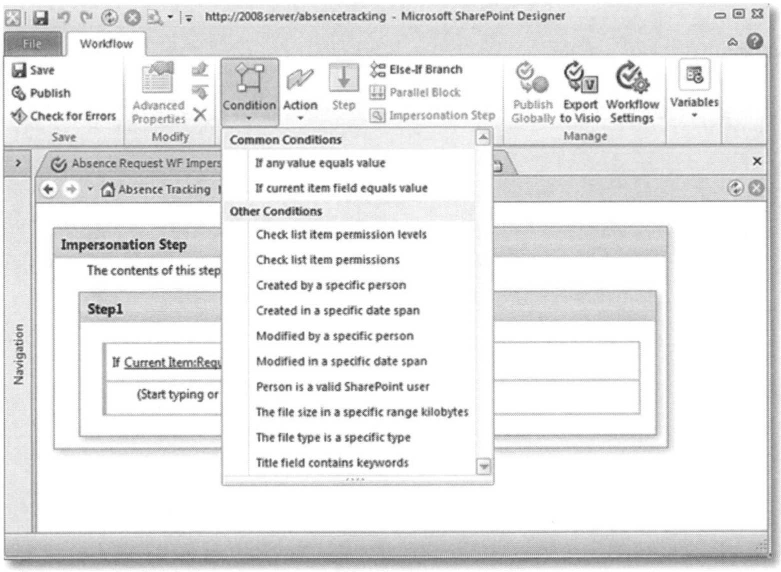

Illustration 413 - Adding a clause to the Condition statement

A second condition statement clause as shown in **Illustration 414** below will display. Note that it is joined to the first statement by an *and* operator. Clicking on the operator will toggle it between **or** and **and**. Leave the *and* operator.

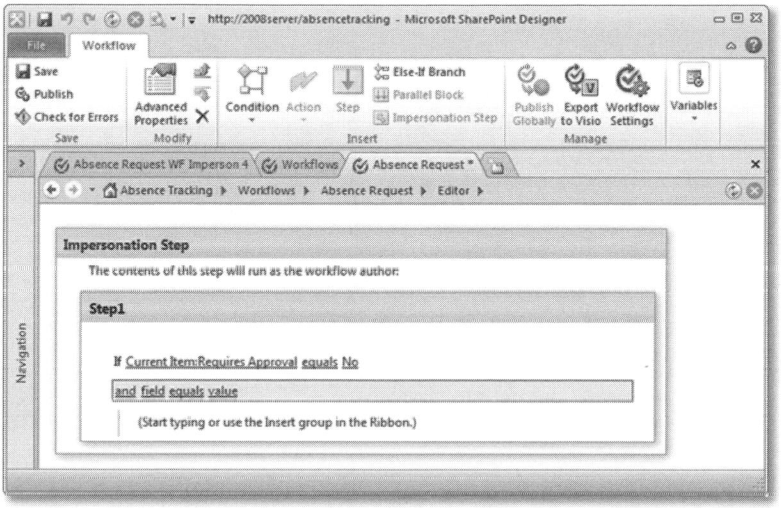

Illustration 414 –The Condition statement with the second clause added

Click on the **field** link and select the **Approved** field. Note how this field is automatically prefixed with *Current Item*. Leave the *equals* operator. Click on the **value** link and enter the text "Yes" (without the quotation marks). The workflow editor will look like **Illustration 415** below.

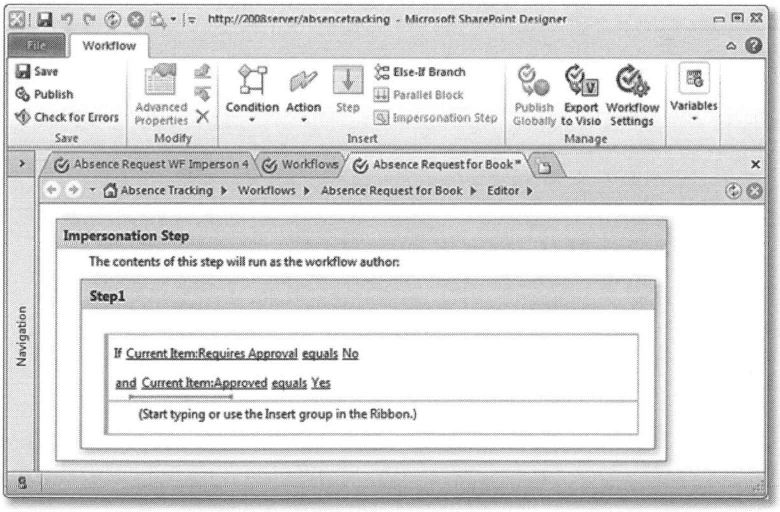

Illustration 415 - The completed Condition statement

We now have the first workflow condition statement that corresponds to the form submission rule criteria where no approval of the request is required and we can add the attendant actions that follow: we will update the *Employee Information External Content Type* list and send an email to the initiator of the form.

Creating the Workflow Action for Updating the Employee Information Database

Position the **horizontal line** directly below and to the right of the condition statement. Click and choose **Update List Item** from the drop-down list of options. The workflow editor will look like **Illustration 416** below.

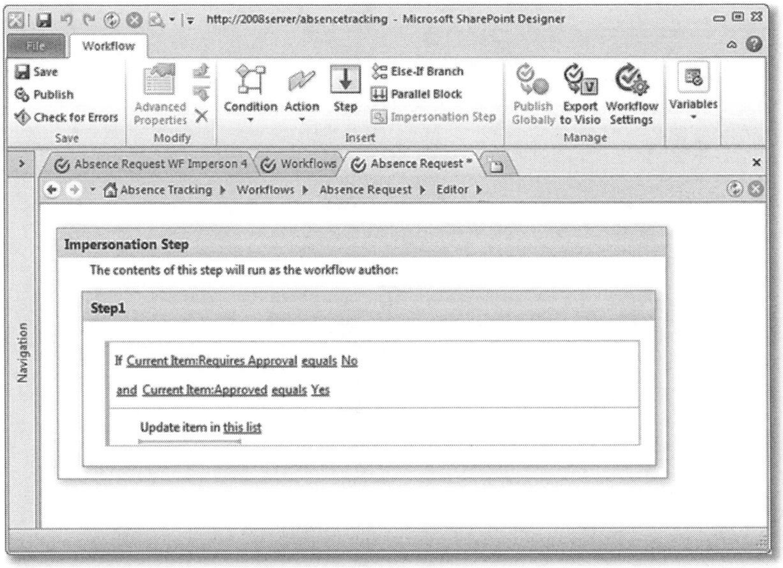

Illustration 416 - Inserting the "Update List Item" action in the workflow

Click on **this list** and the *Update List Item* dialogue screen will display as shown in **Illustration 417** below.

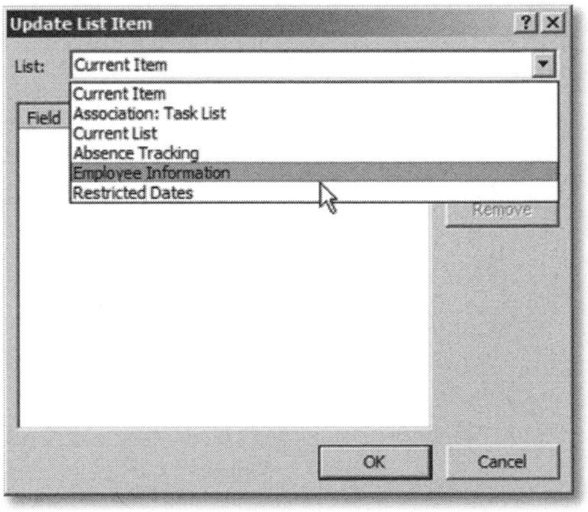

Illustration 417 - Update List Item dialogue screen

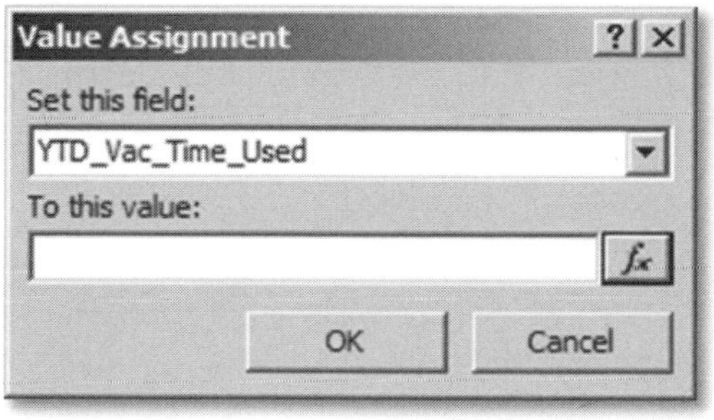

Select the **Employee Information** ECT list. Click the **Add** button to display the *Value Assignment* dialogue screen. The *Set this field* drop-down list will display the column fields of the *Employee Information ECT* list. Select the **YTD_Vac_Time_Used** field as shown in **Illustration 418** at left.

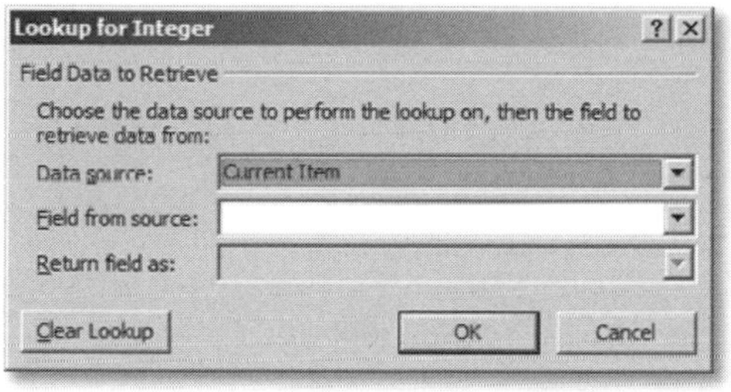

Illustration 418 - The Value Assignment dialogue screen

Now click the **To this value formula button**. The *Lookup for Integer* dialogue screen will display as shown in **Illustration 419** at left.

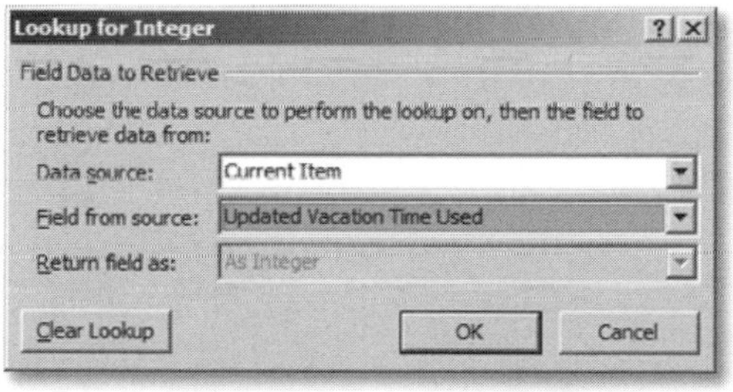

Illustration 419 - The Lookup for Integer dialogue screen

Leave the **Current Item** in the **Data source**. In the **Field from source** drop-down list select the **Updated Vacation Time Used** field as shown in **Illustration 420** at left.

Illustration 420 - Selecting the Updated Vacation Time Used field from the Current Item source

Click **OK**. The completed *Value Assignment* dialogue screen will look like **Illustration 421** at left.

Illustration 421 - Completed Value Assignment dialogue screen

Click **OK**. The *Update List Item* dialogue screen will now look like **Illustration 422** below.

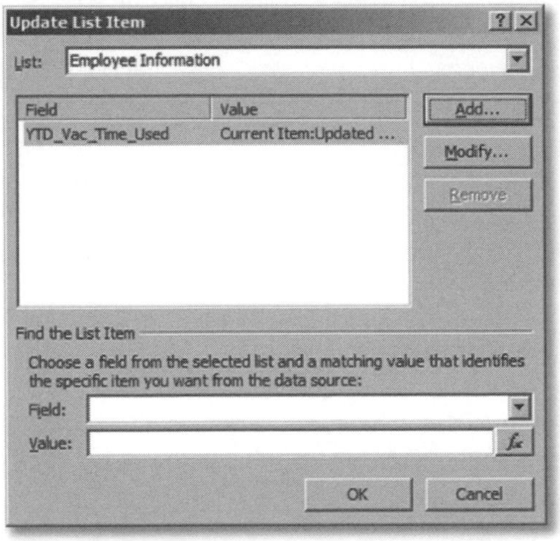

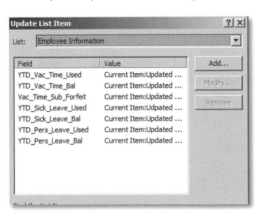

**Illustration 422 - First value assignment for
Update List Item action**

Repeat the *Update List Item* steps above to update the following *Employee Information* fields with their corresponding *Current Item* field values:

Employee Information fields	Current Item fields
YTD_Vac_Time_Bal	Updated Vacation Time Bal
YTD_Sick_Leave_Used	Updated Sick Leave Used
Vac_Time_Sub_Forfeit	Updated Vacation Forfeit Bal
YTD_Sick_Leave_Bal	Updated Sick Leave Bal
YTD_Pers_Leave_Used	Updated Pers Leave Used
YTD_Pers_Leave_Bal	Updated Pers Leave Bal

The completed *Update List Item* dialogue screen will look like **Illustration 423** below.

**Illustration 423 - Update List Item dialogue screen
with all value assignments**

Click the **OK** button. Note that you *cannot* save your settings. The reason for this is that the workflow editor needs additional information to properly match the list item in the *Employee Information* that will be updated by the *Current Item* fields. But didn't we just say that in a *SharePoint Designer* list or content type based workflow the *Current Item* correlation is automatically managed for us? Yes, *but only for the current item context in which the workflow is running*, which is the currently submitted form and its corresponding library columns. In order for the workflow to operate on any other *SharePoint* content that content must be explicitly identified.

SharePoint Designer does not know anything about the *Employee Information* list that is an ancillary participant in the workflow process. The implicit question here is "what Employee Information list item should be updated?"

We know that in the *Employee Information* database there is a unique record for every employee, consequently we can use the same **User_Name = Current_User** selection technique that we employed in the *InfoPath* rules.

In the *Field* drop-down list select the **User_Name** field.

For the *Value* click the **Formula button** and select the **Current User** field from the *Current Item Data source* as shown in **Illustration 424** below.

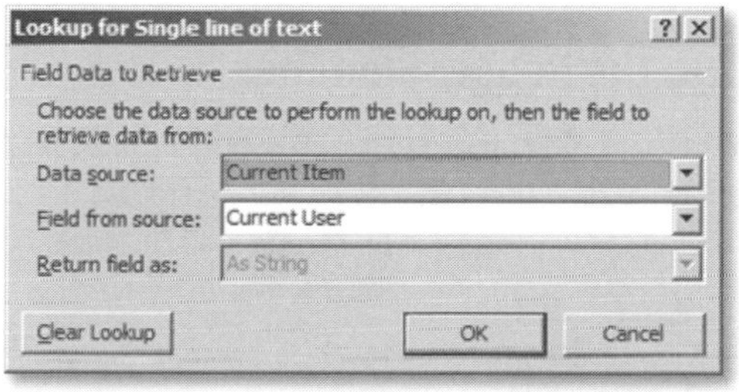

Illustration 424 – Lookup for the Find the List Item correlation value

Illustration 425 - The completed Update List Item dialogue screen

The completed *Update List Item* dialogue screen will now look like **Illustration 425** on the previous page.

Click **OK**. The message in **Illustration 426** below will display.

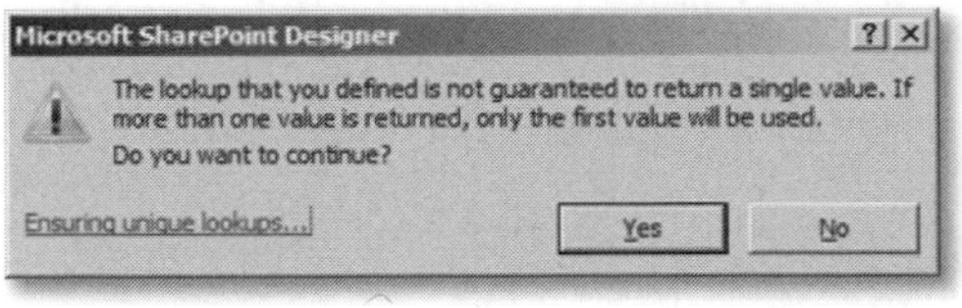

Illustration 426 - Unique value lookup warning

This is a warning that the correlation information provided will not guarantee a unique match. This is because the only way to guarantee a unique correlation between two list items is if there is a unique value common to both lists, such as an ID key value. However, because we know there is a unique list item for each employee in the *Employee Information* database and *SharePoint Designer* manages the *Current Item* context for the submitted request we have a high degree of confidence that the update will work correctly. Click the **Yes** button.

As you can see the process of creating the workflow logic is nearly identical to working with rules in *InfoPath*.

Creating a Workflow Action that Sends an Email to the Request Initiator

The next action that executes under the first conditional statement is sending an email to the request imitator. Place your cursor directly under the *Update item* action and click. The *orange horizontal line* will indicate the insertion point. Right click and select **Send an Email**. The workflow editor will look like **Illustration 427** below.

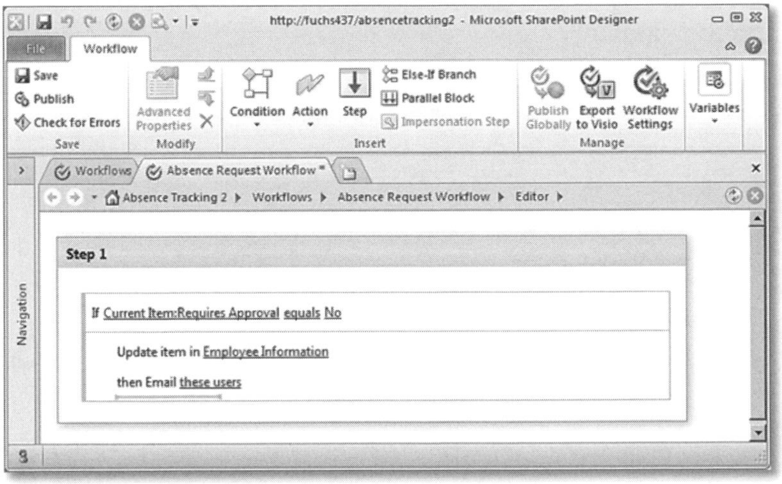

Illustration 427 - Inserting a "Send an Email" action

Click on **these users**. The *Define E-mail Message* dialogue screen, which logically resembles an email message will appear as shown in **Illustration 428** below.

Illustration 428 - Define E-mail Message dialogue screen

Click on the look-up button to the right of the **To:** field. The *Select Users* dialogue screen as shown in **Illustration 429** will appear. Choose **Workflow lookup for a User** and click the **Add** button.

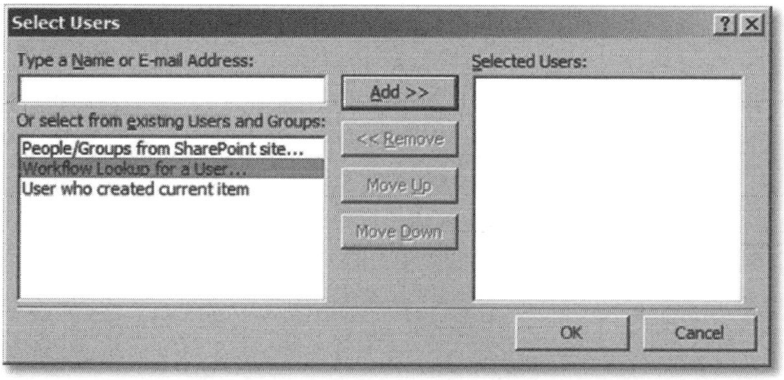

Illustration 429 - The Select Users dialogue screen for lookups

The Lookup for Person or Group dialogue screen will appear. Leave **Current Item** for the **Data source** and choose the **Email** field as shown in **Illustration 430** below.

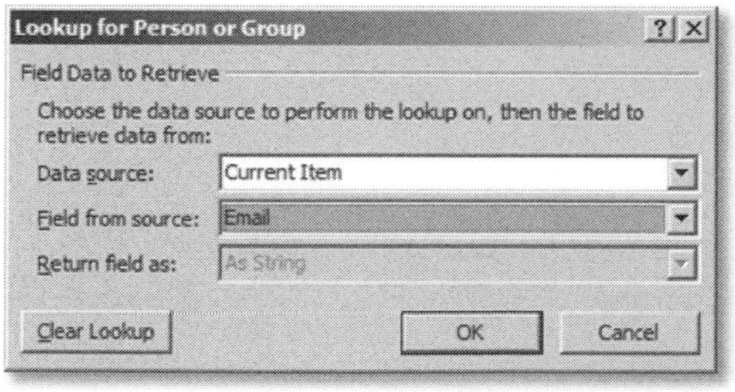

Illustration 430 - The Lookup for Person or Group dialogue screen

Click **OK**. Why didn't we select the *User who created current item option*? Because this selection would have returned the *userName* value, not the user's email address.

Now click on the look-up button for the **CC:** field in the email template. The *Select Users* dialogue screen will appear again. Select **Workflow Lookup for a User** and click the **Add** button. The *Lookup for Person or Group* dialogue screen will display as shown in **Illustration 431** below. Leave **Current Item** for the **Data source** and choose the **Manager Email** field.

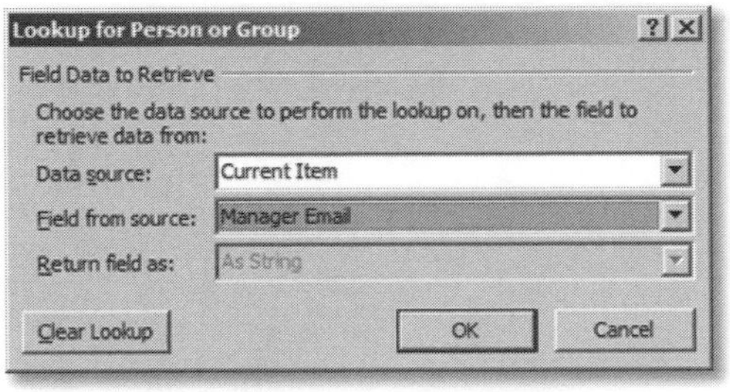

Illustration 431 - The Lookup for Person or Group dialogue screen

Click **OK** and **OK** again for the *Select Users* dialogue screen. Click on the **String Builder button** to the right of the **Subject** field to display the *String Builder* dialogue screen.

In the *String Builder* dialogue screen type "Your absence request" and then click the **Add or Change Lookup button**.

In the *Lookup for String* dialogue screen as shown in **Illustration 432** below choose the *Name (for use in forms)* field for the *Field from source* with the *Current Item* default selection for the *Data source*.

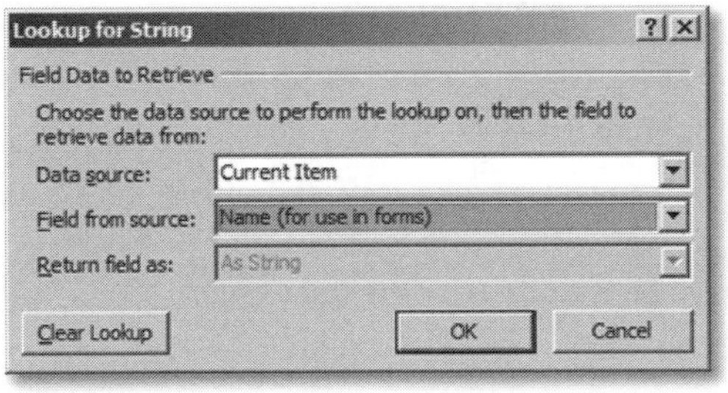

Illustration 432 - Lookup for String dialogue screen

Click **OK**. Directly after the *Name* look up string enter the text "has been approved". The *String Builder* will look like **Illustration 433** below.

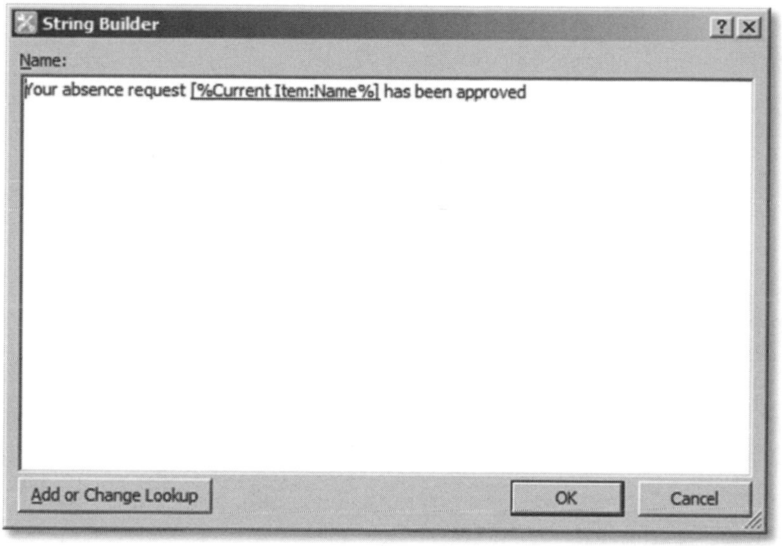

Illustration 433 - Completed String Builder for the Subject line of the E-mail message

Click **OK**. Now place the cursor in the body of the E-mail message. For the salutation click the **Add or Change Lookup button** and select *Full Name* from the *Current Item* source. Enter the text as shown in **Illustration 434** below and use the look-up procedure described above to embed the *Current Item:Name* of the request in the body of the email.

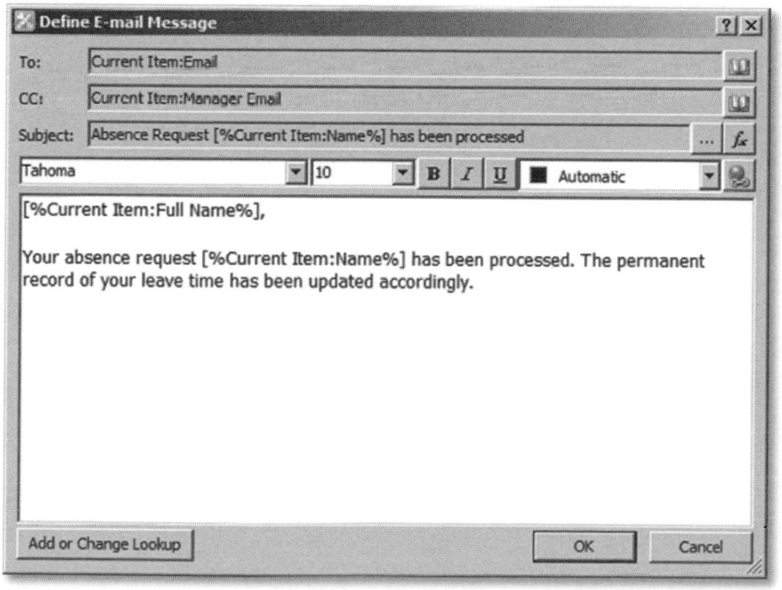

Illustration 434 - Completed Define E-Mail Message dialogue screen

Click **OK**. Now place your cursor directly below the *then Email Current Item:Email* action. Click the **Action** button from the *Ribbon* or right-click and select **Log to History List**. The workflow editor will look like **Illustration 435** below.

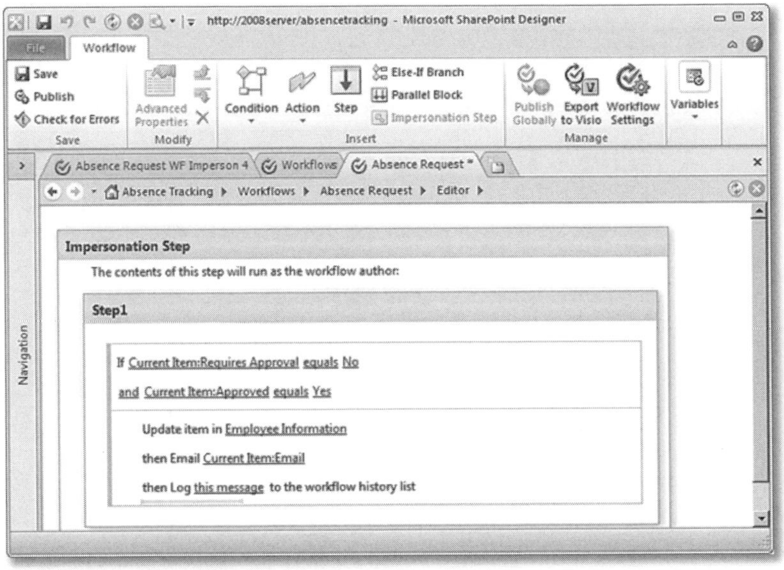

Illustration 435 – The Log to History List action added to the workflow

Click on **this message** and select **the String Builder**. In the *String Builder* enter the text: "Workflow actions for No Approval Submission executed" and click **OK**.

This log message and the other log messages that we embed in the workflow will display in the runtime *Workflow History* list for each instance of the workflow as shown in **Illustration 436** below.

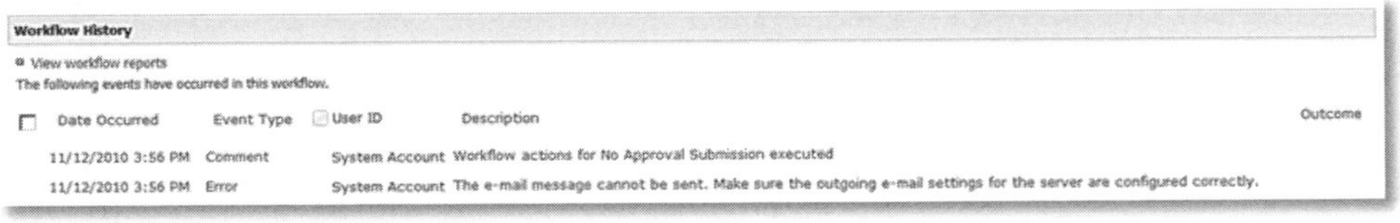

Illustration 436 - Workflow History list for each instance of the workflow

We have now completed the workflow actions for the first condition where no approval is required. Click the **Save** button on the **Ribbon**. Save often as you continue to build the workflow.

Creating the Second Workflow Condition and Respective Actions

Now we will create the second workflow condition and respective actions where a manager's approval is required. Place your cursor directly beneath the **Log to History List** action. Right click and select the **Else-If-Branch**.

The workflow editor will look like **Illustration 437** below.

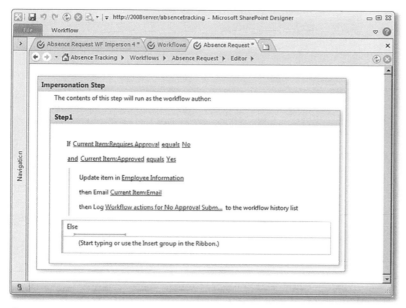

Illustration 437 – Insertion of Else-If-Branch for second Condition

At the **horizontal line position** click the **Condition button** from the *Ribbon* or right click and select the **If current item field equals value** condition. Set the **field** to **Requires Approval**, leave the **equals** operator and enter "Yes" for the **value**.

Place the cursor directly below this condition and again select the **If current item field equals value** condition. Set the **field** to **Approved**, and change the operator to **is empty**.

Creating a Workflow Email Message to Send to the Approving Manager

Directly under this condition insert the **Send an Email** action. The workflow editor will look like **Illustration 438** below.

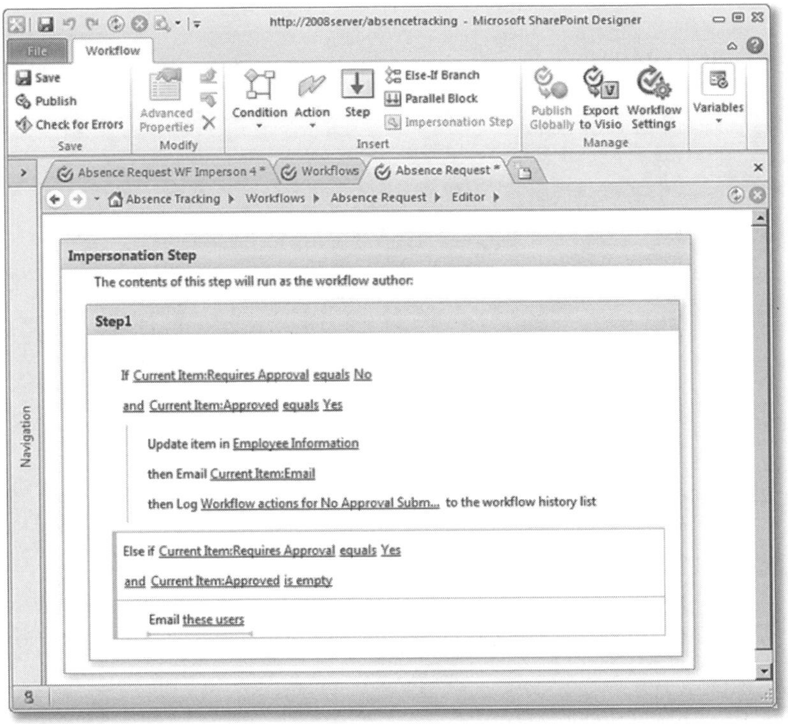

Illustration 438 – Inserting a Send an Email action after the second Condition statement

Click on **these users** to display the **Define E-mail Message** screen.
The completed Email message will look like **Illustration 439** below.

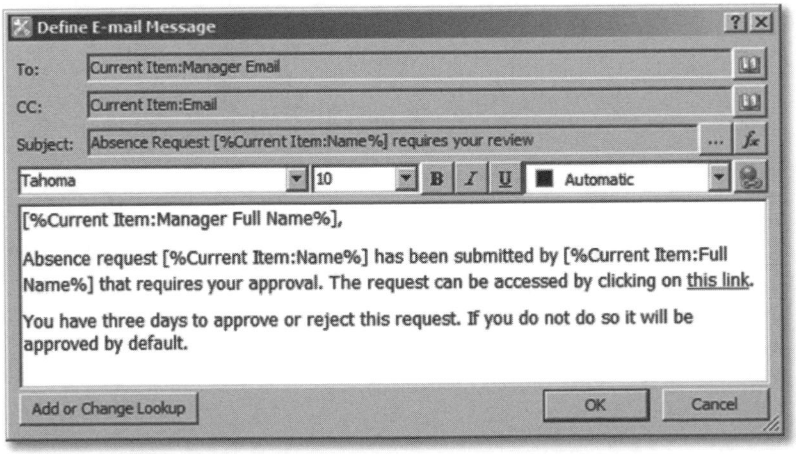

Illustration 439 - The completed Define E-mail Message dialogue screen

Set the values for the **To:** and **CC:** fields by clicking on the **Select Users button** and choosing **Workflow Lookup for a User.** Pick **Manager Email** and **Email** respectively from the **Current Item** *Data source.*

Use the **String Builder** to enter the text for the **Subject** field and use the **Add or Change Lookup** button to embed the **Name (for use in forms)** field from the **Current Item** *Data source.*

In the email body use the **Add or Change Lookup button** to embed the **Manager Full Name, Name (for use in forms),** and **Full Name** from the **Current Item** *Data source.*

After typing the text "The request can be accessed by clicking on" click the **Link Editing button** . The *Edit HyperLink* dialogue screen will display as shown in **Illustration 440** below.

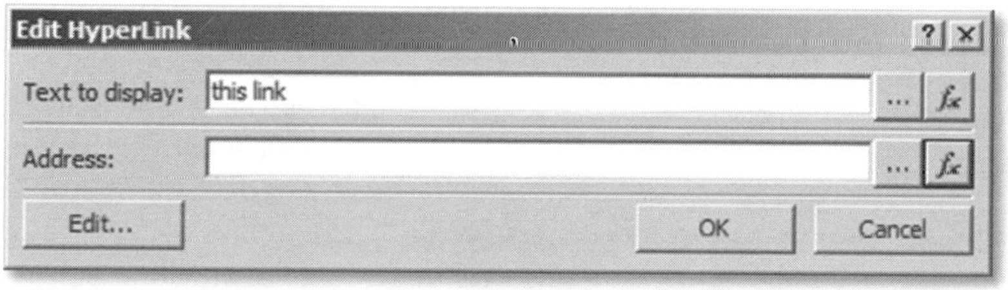

Illustration 440 - Edit HyperLink dialogue screen

Enter "this link" in the **Text to display:** field. Click on the **function button** to the right of the **Address:** field to display the *Lookup for String* dialogue screen. Select **Workflow Context** for the *Data source* and **Current Item URL** for the *Field from source* as shown in **Illustration 441** at left.

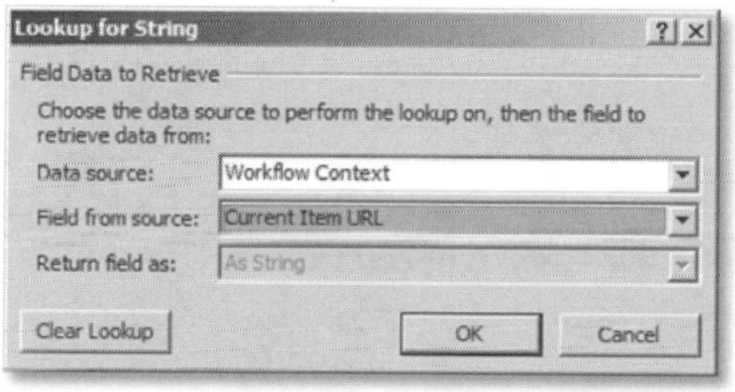

Illustration 441 - Lookup for String dialogue screen for HyperLink

Click **OK**. The completed **Edit HyperLink** dialogue screen will look like **Illustration 442** below.

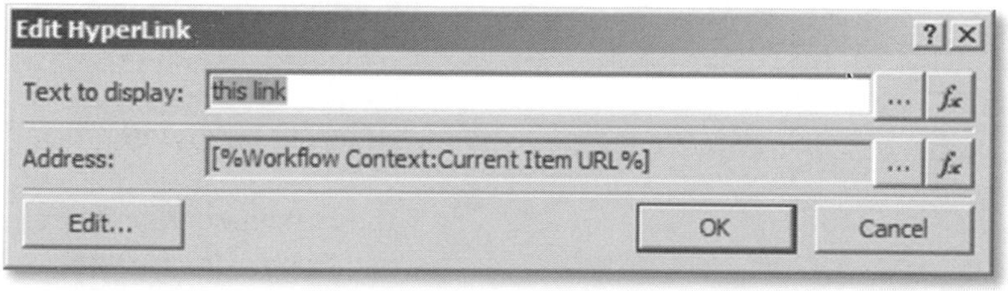

Illustration 442 - The completed Edit HyperLink dialogue screen

Click **OK**. This HyperLink will open the current item instance of the absence request that requires approval.

In the workflow editor insert a **Log to History List** action directly under this **Send an Email** action. Click on the **String Builder** to enter the text "First manager email sent for Requires Approval request submission".

Using a Parallel Block to Create a Race Condition

Place your cursor directly under the **Log to History List** action and insert a **Parallel Block** by clicking the **Parallel Block button** on the *Ribbon* or right clicking. A line that states "The following actions will run in parallel:" will display. The workflow editor will now look like **Illustration 443** below.

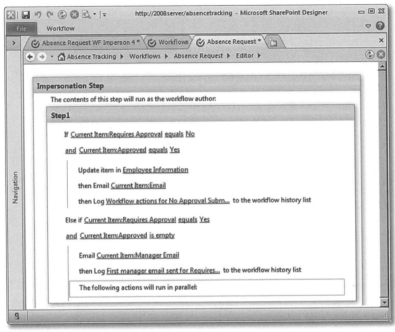

Illustration 443 – A Parallel Block inserted inside the positional region of the second Condition

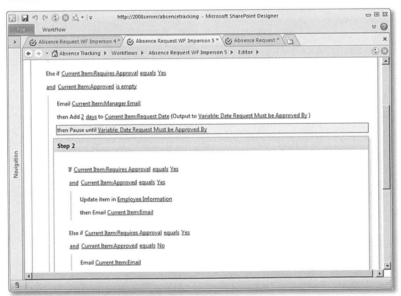

Illustration 444 – A workflow that implements an action to pause the workflow for two days

The second condition addresses an absence request that requires a manager's approval. We want to impose a timeframe in which the manager either approves or rejects the request, say within two days; otherwise the workflow will approve the request by default.

Pausing the workflow for two days while waiting for the manager to take the required actions would appear to be the most obvious method of accomplishing this and the workflow in **Illustration 444** below shows how this could be constructed.

The problem with this approach is that the manager's actions of approving or rejecting the request, which in turn changes the value of the *Approved* field in the form library from empty to Yes or No respectively, does not cause the workflow to automatically resume.

The workflow only resumes *at the end of the two day duration*, at which time it executes the respective actions for the Yes or No *Approved* value or executes an alternate course of action. The workflow editor does not provide an explicit action for terminating a pause state and resuming the workflow. Consequently, even if the manager should approve the request within minutes after being submitted the initiator would have to wait two days to be informed of this. As such, this approach to setting a timeframe for an event to take place is not a viable option.

What we want to implement is known as a "race condition" where a number of events execute in parallel but once one of the events completes successfully (i.e. wins the race) the other events terminate. **Illustration 445** below shows the workflow method that we will use to implement a race condition for all possible workflow outcomes within a finite period of time.

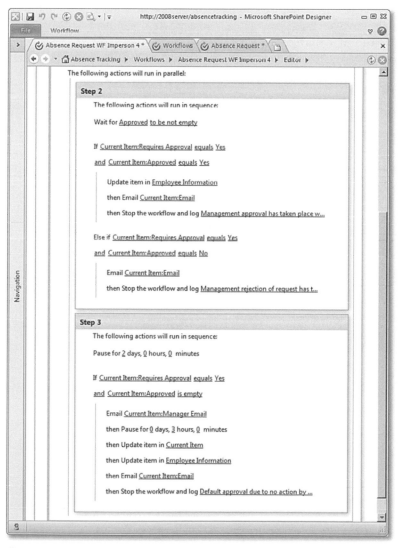

Illustration 445 - the workflow method that implements a race condition for all possible manager action outcomes within a finite period of time

Step2 and *Step 3* of the workflow are embedded in a *Parallel Block*. Both of these steps will execute simultaneously but only one will complete successfully.

The two conditions and their respective actions within *Step 2* can execute over an indefinite period of time, as facilitated by the *Wait for Approved to be not empty* action. When either condition in *Step 2* evaluates to true the respective actions for the condition will execute immediately and both events have a final action instructing the workflow to stop. If either of the *Step 2* events takes place in less than two days from the start of the workflow, *Step 3* will not complete because *Step 2* will have run the race.

However, we don't want to wait an indefinite period of time for the manager to approve or reject the request. Consequently the first action of *Step 3* is to pause for two days from the start of the workflow. If at the end of two days neither of the events defined in *Step 2* takes place the subsequent actions specified in *Step 3* will execute: a second reminder email will be sent to the manager and the workflow will pause for three more hours. After three hours if there is no change to the *Approved* field value (during which time *Step 2* is still running), it will be set by the workflow to "*Approved by Default*" and the remaining actions will execute including stopping the workflow. *Step 3* wins the race if after two days and three hours neither of the *Step 2* events takes place.

> **Development Note** – This *Parallel Block* construct that uses one step to pause for a specific duration before stopping while the other steps can run over an indefinite period of time can be applied to any race condition use case.

Creating the First Parallel Block Step

Let's continue building out this workflow. Place your cursor directly after **The following actions will run in parallel** line and insert a new *Step*, so that the workflow editor looks like **Illustration 446** below.

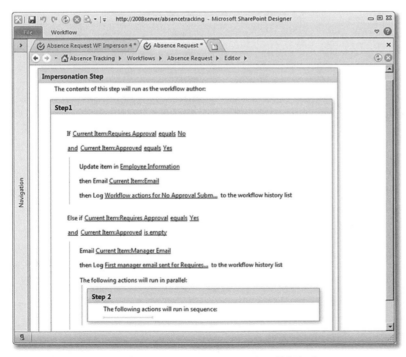

Illustration 446 - Insertion of the first step within the Parallel Block

Step 2 will display the message that *The following actions will run in sequence*. With the **horizontal line** positioned directly under this text insert the **Wait for Field Change in Current Item** action. Click on **field** and choose the **Approved** field. Change the **equal** operator **to be not empty**.

Creating the First Condition Statement and Actions for Step 2

With your cursor positioned directly under the **Wait for Approved to be not empty** action, insert the **If current item field equals value** *Condition*.

Click on **field** and select the **Requires Approval** field from the **Current Item** Data source. Leave the equals operator and enter "Yes" for the value.

Place your cursor directly below this condition and insert another **If current Item field equals value** condition. The workflow editor will append an "**and**" to the beginning of the condition statement.

Select the **Approved** field from the **Current Item** Data source. Enter "Yes" for the value. The workflow editor will look like **Illustration 447** below.

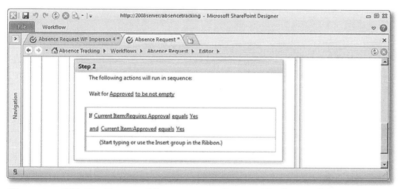

Now place your cursor directly below this condition statement and insert an **Update List Item** action. Click on **this list** to display the **Update List Item** dialogue screen. Select **Employee Information** for the list to be updated.

Illustration 447 - The first condition statement for step 2 in the parallel block

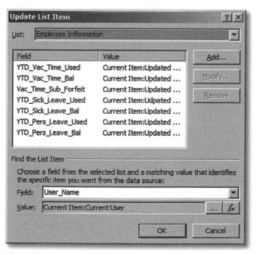

Illustration 448 - Update List Item dialogue screen showing fields updated in the Employee Information database

You are now going to update the same set of YTD fields as described earlier on pages 258 to 262. The completed *Update List item* dialogue screen for this action will look like **Illustration 448** at left.

Note – The *SharePoint Designer Workflow Editor* does not have the capability to copy and paste operative functions. Even if it is an identical function it must be manually constructed. This functionality will most likely be added in the next version.

After you have completed creating the **Update List Item** action insert a **Send an Email** action directly below it. Click on **these users** to edit the **Define E-Mail Message** screen so that it contains the information shown in **Illustration 449** below.

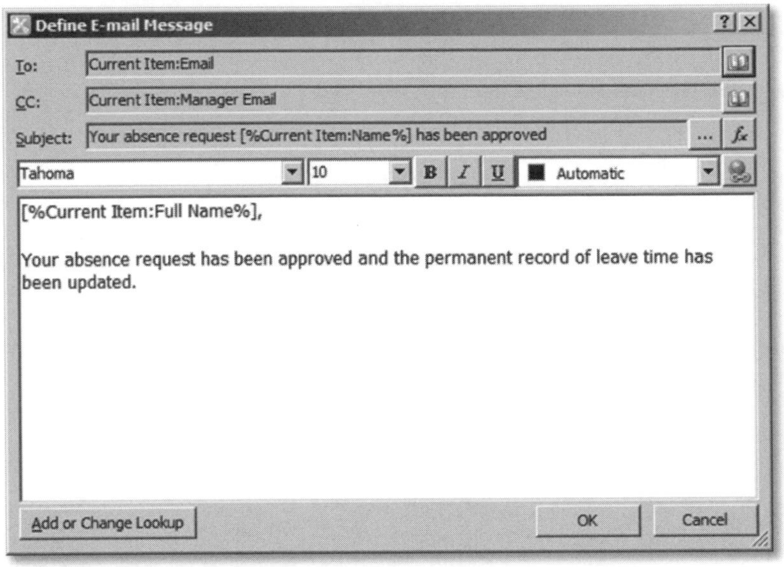

Illustration 449 - Define E-mail Message dialogue screen for an approved request

Finally, add a **Stop Workflow** action. Click on the **this message** link in the action and select the *String Builder* to enter the text "Management approval has taken place within 3 days of submission, Employee Information database updated and initiator sent an email" as shown in **Illustration 450** below.

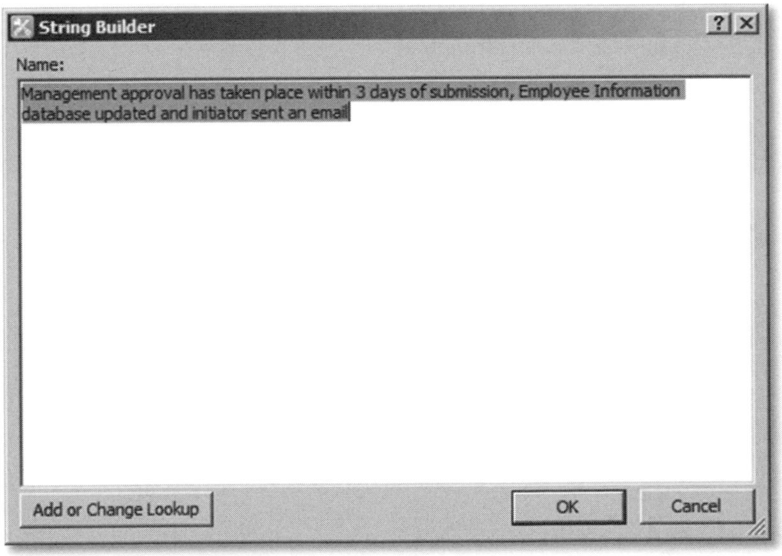

Illustration 450 - String Builder showing Stop workflow action log message for approved condition

The first conditional statement and its respective actions for **Step 2** are now complete. The workflow editor will look like **Illustration 451** below.

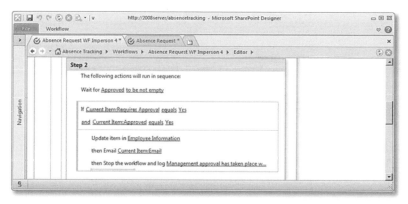

Illustration 451 – The completed first condition statement and actions in Step 2

Creating the Second Conditional Statement and Actions for Step 2

Place your cursor below the "**then Stop the workflow and log Management approval has taken place. . .**" action and insert an **Else-If Branch**. Insert an **If current Item field equals value** condition.

Select the **Requires Approval** field from the **Current Item** Data source. Enter "Yes" for the value.

Place the cursor directly below this condition statement and again select the **If current item field equals value** condition. Set the **field** to **Approved**, leave the **equals** operator and change the **value** to "No".

Insert a **Send an Email** action. Click on **these users** to edit the **Define E-Mail Message** screen so that it contains the information shown in **Illustration 452** below.

Define E-mail Message	
To:	Current Item:Email
CC:	Current Item:Manager Email
Subject:	Absence Request [%Current Item:Name%]

Tahoma | 10 | **B** *I* <u>U</u> | Automatic

[%Current Item:Full Name%],

Your absence request [%Current Item:Name%] has been rejected by your manager. You can view the reason why the request was rejected by accessing the the request at this link. The permanent record of your leave time has not been updated.

Please submit a new absence request.

Add or Change Lookup   OK   Cancel

Refer to page 269 for instructions how to use the *Edit HyperLink* function to embed a link to the *Current Item:URL* of the absence request in the body of the email.

Illustration 452 - Define E-mail Message dialogue screen for rejected request

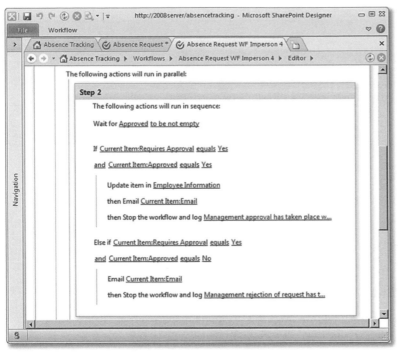

Illustration 453 - The completed first Step in the Parallel Block

Finally, add a **Stop Workflow** action. Click on the **this message** link in the action and select the *String Builder* to enter the history message log text "Management rejection of request has taken place within 3 days and initiator sent an email".

Step 2 is now complete and will look **like Illustration 453** at left.

Creating the Second Parallel Block Step

Place your cursor so that **the horizontal line** is positioned under and ***outside*** of *Step 2*. Insert a **Step** so that it is at the same hierarchical position as *Step 2* and will become the second set of parallel events in the *Parallel Block* as indicated by **Illustration 454** at left.

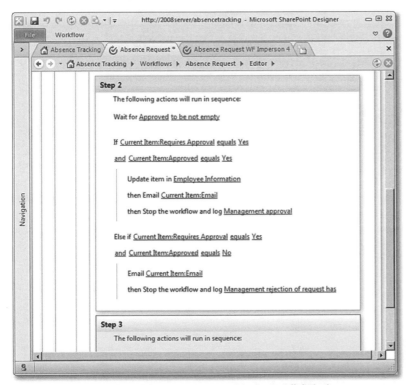

Illustration 454 - Insertion of the second Step inside the Parallel Block

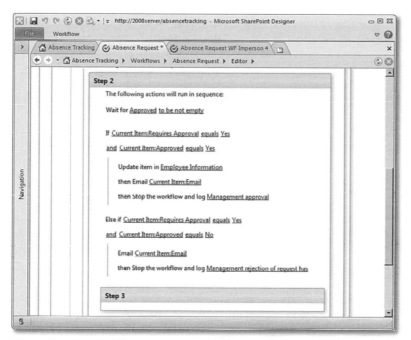

Note - if you insert the new step *inside* of *Step 2* your workflow will look like **Illustration 455** at left. Embedding *Step 3* within *Step 2* would make it a contingency of the conditional statement of *Step 2*. While the conditional logic and actions of an embedded *Step 3* would still execute properly, the parallel relationship of the two steps is obscured by this construction.

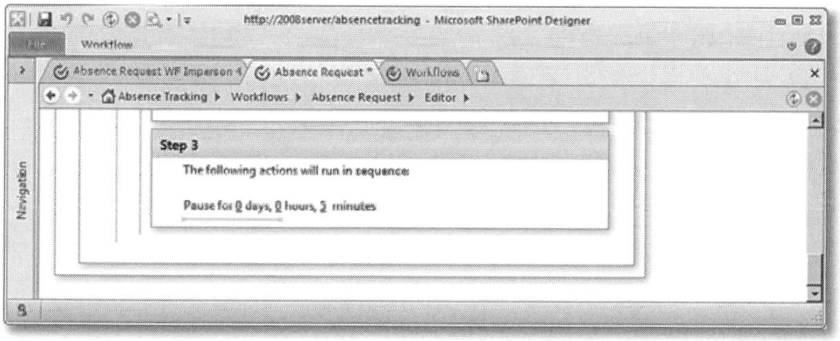

Illustration 455 - Workflow construction if Step 3 was inserted inside the Step 2 positional region

Now insert a **Pause for Duration** action in *Step 3* as shown in **Illustration 456** at left.

Note that at a minimum the workflow sets a 5 minute duration for the action. Click on the "**0**" in front of **days** and change the value to "**2**". Click on the "**5**" in front of **minutes** and change the value to "**0**".

Illustration 456 – The insertion of a Pause for Duration action at the beginning of Step 3

Below the *Pause for Duration* action insert an **If current Item field equals value** condition. Click on the **field** link and select the *Requires Approval* field. Leave the **equals** operator and enter "Yes" for the **value**.

Directly below this condition statement insert another **If current Item field equals value** condition. Select the **Approved** field from the **Current Item** Data source. Change the **equals** operator to **is empty.** The workflow editor will look like **Illustration 457** below.

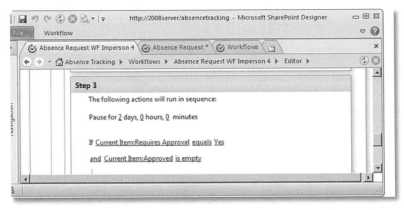

Illustration 457 – The only condition statement in the second Step of the Parallel Block

Insert a **Send an Email** action directly below the conditional statement. Click on **these users** to edit the **Define E-Mail Message** so that it contains the information shown in **Illustration 458** below.

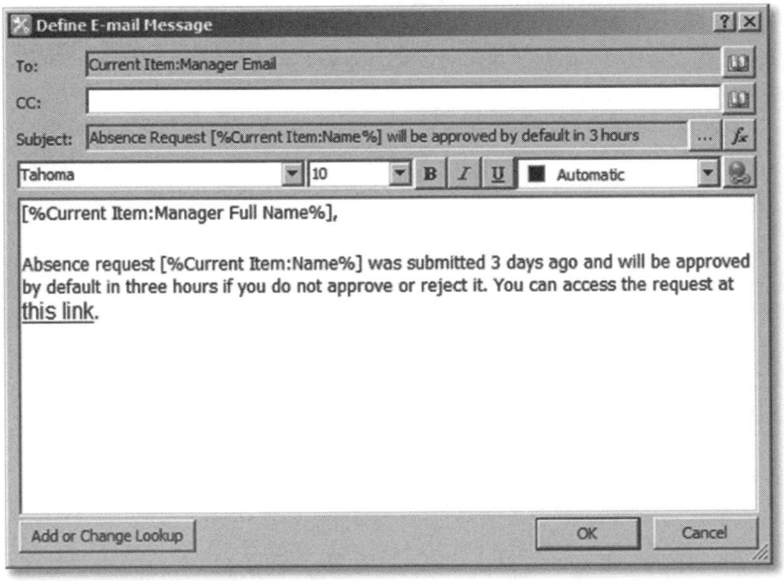

Illustration 458 - Define E-mail Message dialogue screen for second email to Manager

Directly below the *Send an Email* action insert a **Pause for Duration** action. The workflow editor will place the prefix *"then"* in front of the action. Click on the *"0"* in front of **hours** and change the value to *"3"*. Click on the *"5"* in front of **minutes** and change the value to *"0"*.

Now insert an **Update List Item** action directly after the **Pause for Duration** action. Click on **this list** to display the *Update List Item* dialogue box. Select the **Approved** field in the **Current Item** list and set its value to "**Approved by Default**" as shown in **Illustration 459** below.

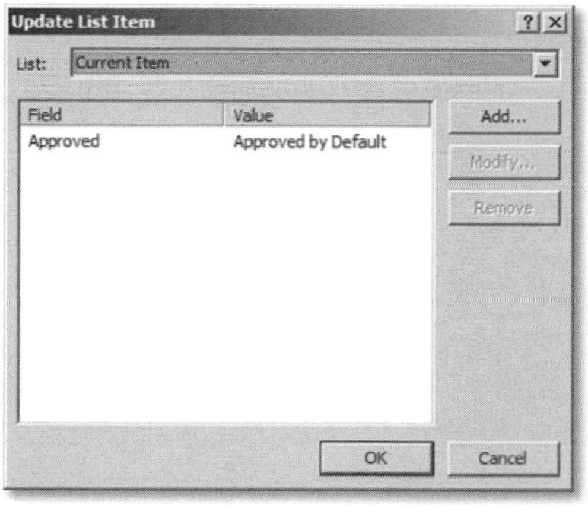

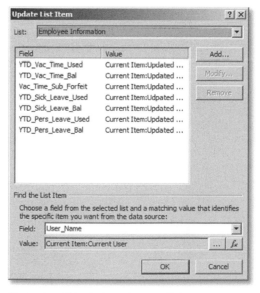

Illustration 459 - Update List Item dialogue screen to set Approved field to "Approved by Default" value

Click **OK**. Now insert and re-create the **Update item in Employee Information** and **Email Current Item: Email** actions used when the *"Current Item: Approved equals Yes"* condition is true.

The completed *Updated List Item* dialogue screen for the *Update item in Employee Information* action will look like **Illustration 460** below.

Illustration 460 - Update List Item dialogue screen showing fields updated in the Employee Information database

The completed *Define E-Mail Message* will look like **Illustration 461** below.

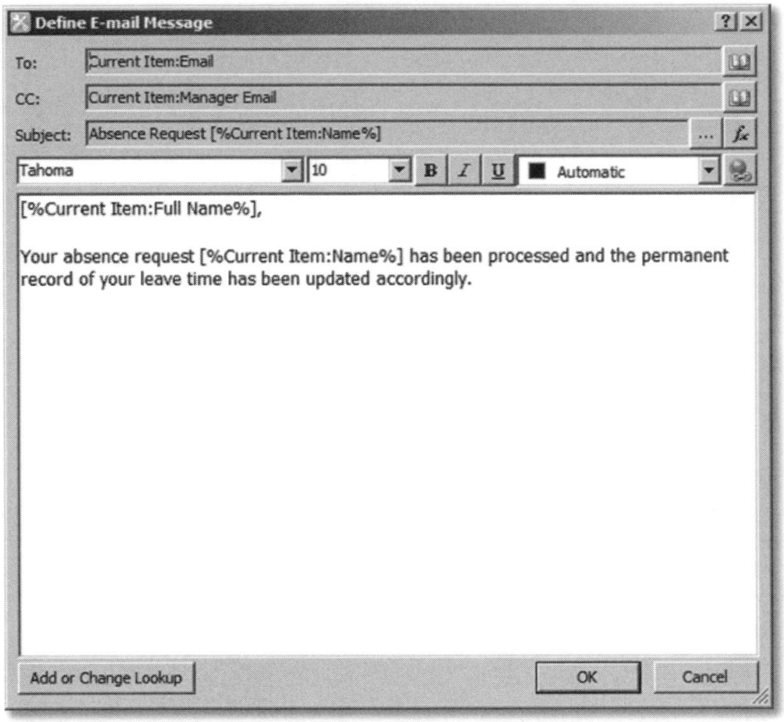

Illustration 461 - The Define E-mail Message dialogue screen for the "Approved by Default" message

Finally add a **Stop Workflow** action and use the *String Builder* to enter the history log message "Default approval due to no action by manager after 3 days and 3 hours. Employee Information database updated and email sent to initiator" as shown in **Illustration 462** below.

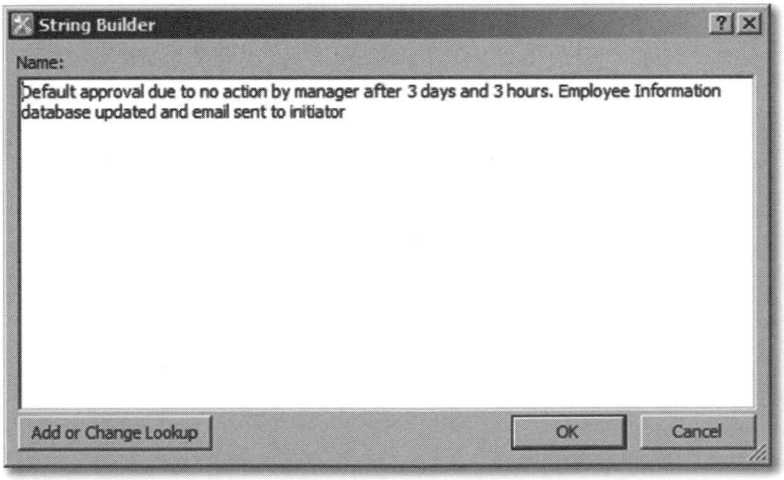

Illustration 462 - Stop workflow history log message for default approval

The completed *Step 3* will look like **Illustration 463** below.

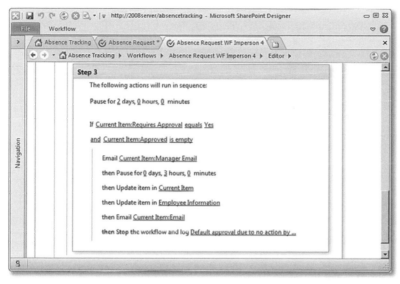

Illustration 463 – The completed second Step of the Parallel Block

We have completed building the workflow for this application! Click the **Save** button on the *Ribbon*.

The workflow still needs to be published and tested but before we can do that we first have to create and configure the necessary authentication mechanisms that will allow the workflow to interact with the Employee Information External Content Type.

Setting the Security Settings for Running a Workflow that Interacts with an External Content Type

Prior to creating the application workflow we identified three security setting factors (see page 250) that must be implemented for a *SharePoint Designer* workflow to work with an *External Content Type*. We implemented one of these, the *Impersonation Step* directly in the workflow.

We now need to identify the service account that the workflow runs under and set its object permissions in the *Business Data Connectivity Service* of *Central Administration*. Secondly, we will create and configure the *Impersonation Credentials* in the *SharePoint Secure Store Service* that the system account will use to connect to the external data source.

Identifying the System Account under which SharePoint Workflows Run

The system account under which *SharePoint* workflows run is the same account that the *SharePoint* application pool runs under. To determine this system account open *Internet Information Services Manager* and click on the *Application Pool* node for the web server as shown in **Illustration 464** below.

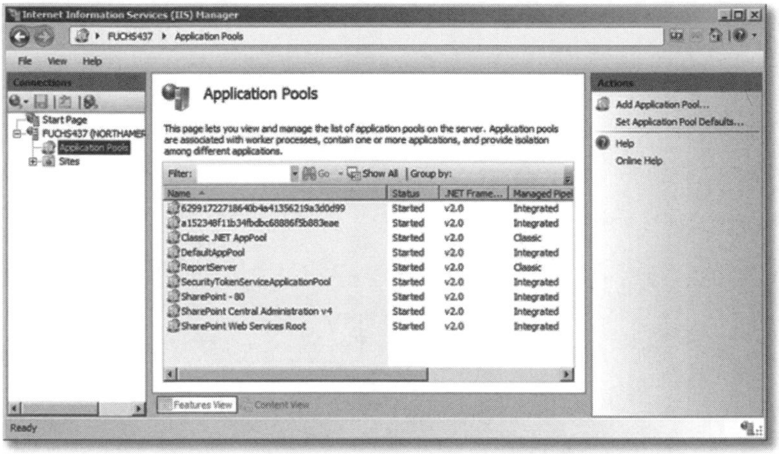

Illustration 464 - Application Pools in Internet Information Services Manager

Select the **SharePoint – 80 Application Pool**, which is the default application pool for *SharePoint*. If another application pool is running the *SharePoint* web application select that one.

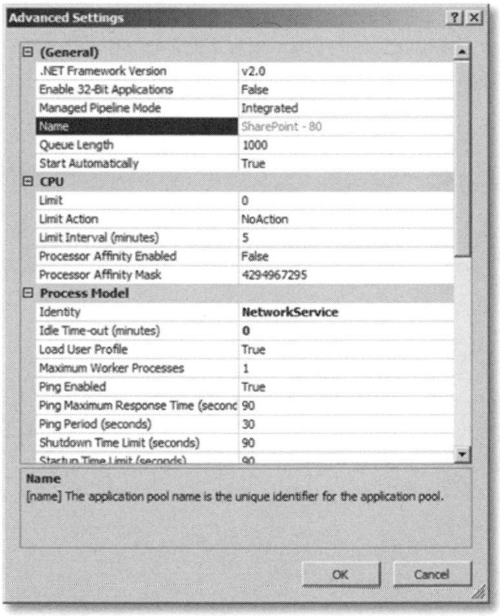

Illustration 465 - Advanced Settings screen for an Application Pool

Right click and select **Advanced Settings**. The *Advanced Settings* screen will display as shown in **Illustration 465** below.

The service account that this installation of *SharePoint* is running under is the **NetworkService** Identity.

Assigning the Service Account Permission to Interact with the Employee Information ECT

To give this service account permission to interact with the *Employee Information ECT*, which will confer the same permission to the *SharePoint* workflow engine, open *SharePoint 2010 Central Administration* and click on **Manage Service Applications** in the *Application Management* section as shown in **Illustration 466** below.

Illustration 466 - SharePoint Central Administration console

The *Manage Service Applications* screen will display as shown in **Illustration 467** below.

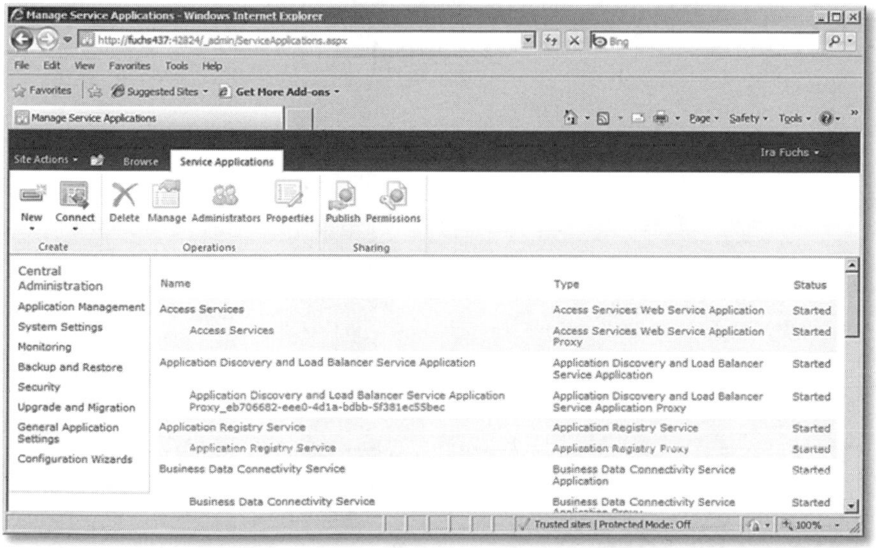

Illustration 467 - The Manage Service Applications screen in SharePoint Central Administration

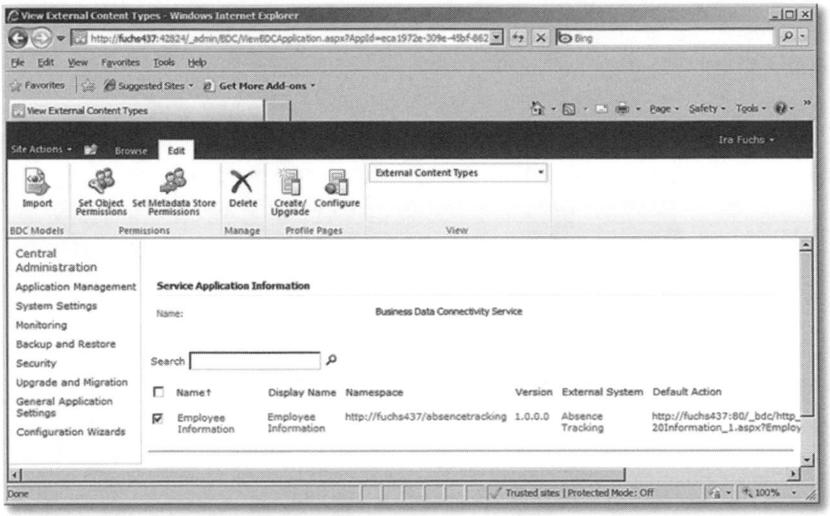

Illustration 468 - The Service Application page for the Business Data Connectivity Service

Click on the **Business Data Connectivity Service** link. The *Service Application* page for the *Business Data Connectivity Service* will display as shown in **Illustration 468** at left. Make sure that **External Content Types** are selected from the drop-down list on the *Ribbon*.

Check the **Employee Information** checkbox and click on the **Set Object Permissions button** on the *Ribbon*. The *Set Object Permissions* screen will display. Type "NetworkService" in the **account to add box** and click on the **People Picker** icon to resolve the name. Once resolved it will display as "*nt authority\ network service*".

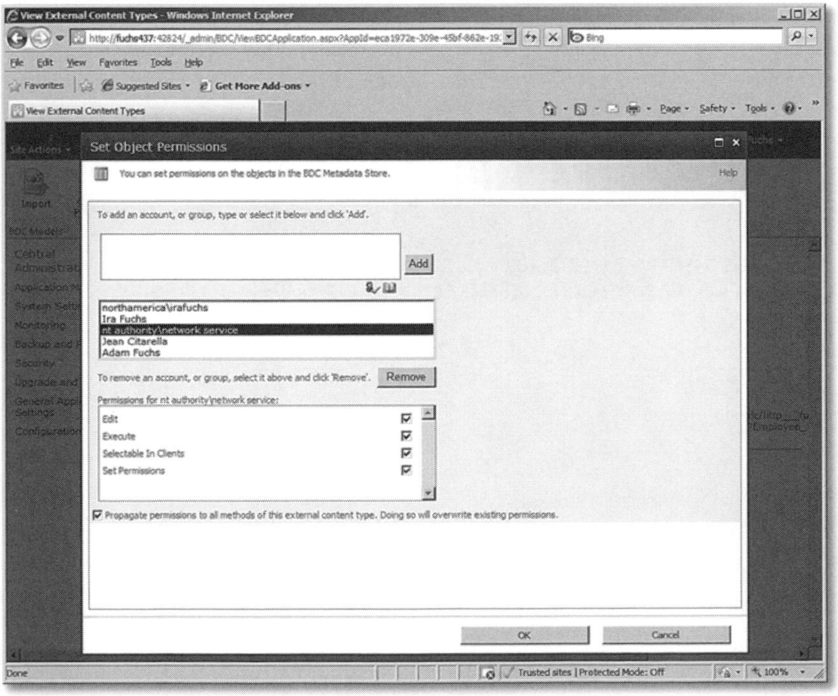

Illustration 469 - The Set Object Permissions dialogue screen

Click the **Add** button to add this service account to the permissions group. Now check the **checkboxes** for the permissions to *Edit, Execute, Selectable in Clients,* and *Set Permissions*. The *Set Object Permissions* screen will look like **Illustration 469** at left.

Click **OK**. This completes the procedure of assigning BCS permissions to the workflow service account. The next step is to set up and configure *Secure Store Services* to provide the credentials used to access the *SQL Server* database for the *Employee Information ECT*.

Creating Impersonation Credentials in Secure Store Service for the ECT Data Connection to SQL Server

Because this is a user-context driven application we needed to create user accounts as a pre-requisite to developing and testing this application, including one for the developer creating the application. These accounts were first created in *Windows Users and Groups* and we then gave these user accounts access permissions to the *Absence Tracking* database directly within *SQL Server*. We added these user accounts to *SharePoint* artifacts as users or within groups, and subsequently we configured the *Connection Properties* for the *Employee Information ECT* data connection in *SharePoint Designer* to connect to the database using the *User's Identity*, which is the *Windows Username* and *Password*, as shown in **Illustration 470** below.

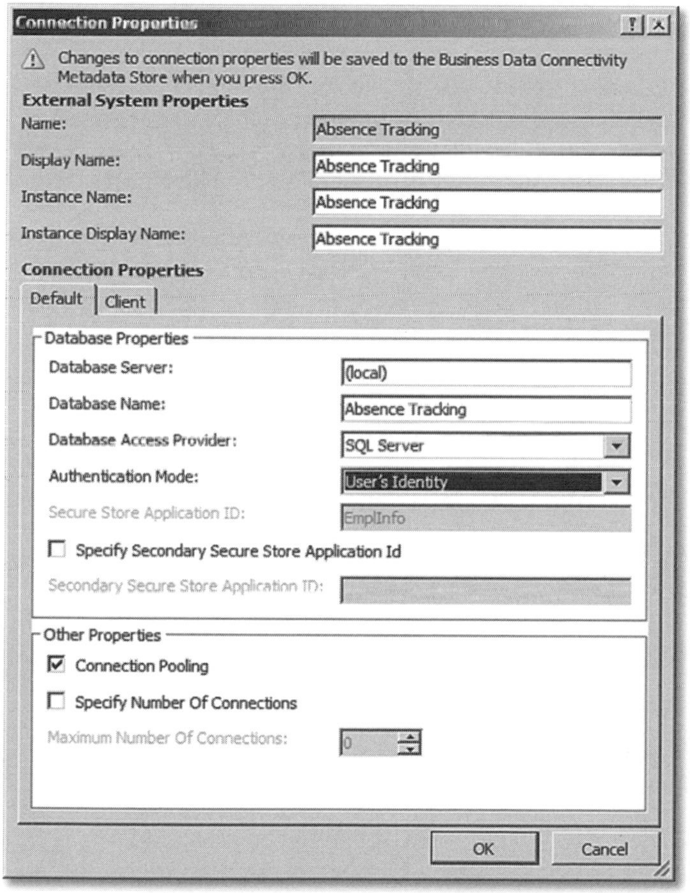

In a production environment it is not practical to provide individual accounts with the permissions to access and use application resources. Instead users are assigned to groups in a directory service, typically *Active Directory*. The directory groups are meant to have specific access to and use of application resources and they are then used by target applications, such as *SharePoint* and *SQL Server*, to provide access to and use of those resources to the users in the directory groups. When configured to use *Windows Integrated* security credentials, these applications authenticate a user in a group through their *Windows Username and Password*.

Illustration 470 - Connection Properties for the Absence Tracking database in SharePoint Designer

However, there are situations where it is not possible or practical to use individual user credentials to access and use an application. Examples of these situations are:

- When one application accesses another application on behalf of users. While the users may be authenticated by the first application they may not have authentication credentials established in the second application. This could be due to the substantial administrative overhead of creating user credentials in any given application or because it is not always possible to know who the users of the first application are at any given time.

- When there are heterogeneous authentication methods and credentials used by multiple systems. It is very common that the numerous systems and applications in an enterprise use different authentication and credential schemes and managing and mapping of individual credentials of a large number of users against hundreds if not thousands of applications is not practical.

- When functions in one application run under system accounts that do not have authentication credentials. Numerous application functions, such as *SharePoint* workflows, run under system accounts that do not have user credentials. In order for these functions to access an external application that requires credentials, they need to be provided with impersonation credentials.

All three of these situations will frequently turn up when attempting to utilize *SharePoint External Content Types*. A *SharePoint ECT* list is acting as an intermediate application providing *SharePoint* users access to information in an external system. An ECT list can be created on any site collection or site and the users/groups assigned permission to access the ECT list will not be known to the administrator of the external system; and it is very possible that the external system may not use *Windows* credentials for authentication. Furthermore if an automated process such as a workflow is implemented that accesses an ECT list, the service account for the workflow will need to be provided with impersonation credentials as well.

Understanding the SharePoint 2010 Secure Store Service

The *SharePoint 2010 Secure Store Service* (SSS) was created to address these authentication contingencies. The fundamental idea behind SSS is to allow multiple users to authenticate themselves to an application by impersonating the credentials of another user account. This is accomplished in SSS by creating a "target application" that contains the following information in an encrypted data store:

- The definition of the authentication and credential scheme used by an application.

- An actual user account of the target application, with their respective credentials, that serves as the Impersonation account that will be used by other users and groups to access an application.

- The *Members* using the Impersonation credentials; that is the users and groups assigned to the target application that can use the Impersonation account credentials to access the application. These *Members* are also deemed the "*Credential Owners*".

Once the target application is created we use *SharePoint Designer* to configure the *Connection Properties* of an *External Content Type* to use it, allowing any of the "owners" of the impersonation credentials to access the external information from within *SharePoint*.

Let's go through the process of creating and configuring all the necessary artifacts to use SSS for authenticating users with impersonation credentials.

Create the Windows User Account

We will first create the *Window's* user account that will be impersonated. From the **Task Bar** in *Windows Server 2008* choose **Administrative Tools** and then **Computer Management**. Select **Local Users and Groups**. Right click on the **Users** folder and choose **New User**. Enter the *User name* "sssproxy", a *Full name* and a *Password* as shown in **Illustration 471** below and click the **Create button**.

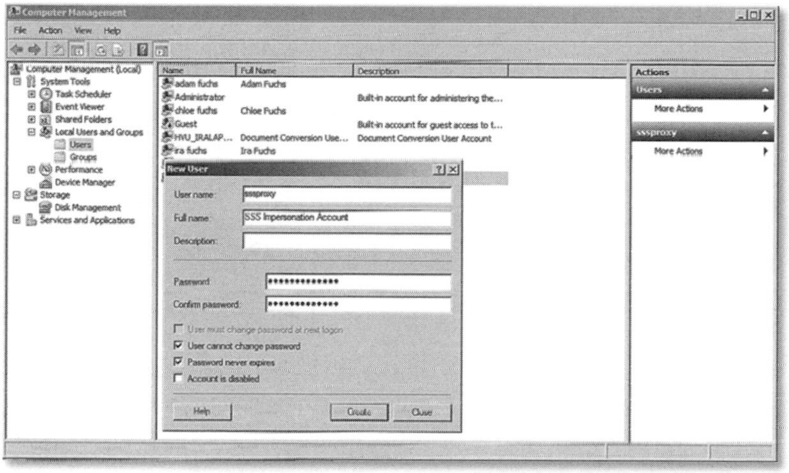

Illustration 471 – Creating the Impersonation User in Windows Server 2008 Computer Management console

Now open *SQL Server Management Studio* and connect to the database server. Select the **Security** folder and expand it. Select the **Logins** folder and right click. Choose **New Login**. The *Login-New* dialogue screen will appear as shown in **Illustration 472** below. Leave the **Windows authentication radio button** checked and for the *Default database* choose **Absence Tracking** from the drop-down list.

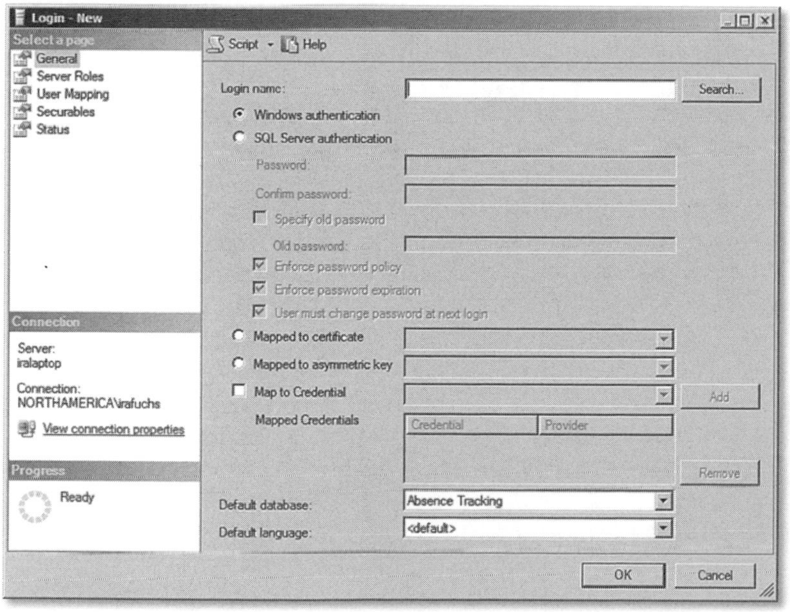

Illustration 472 - New Login account dialogue screen in SQL Server

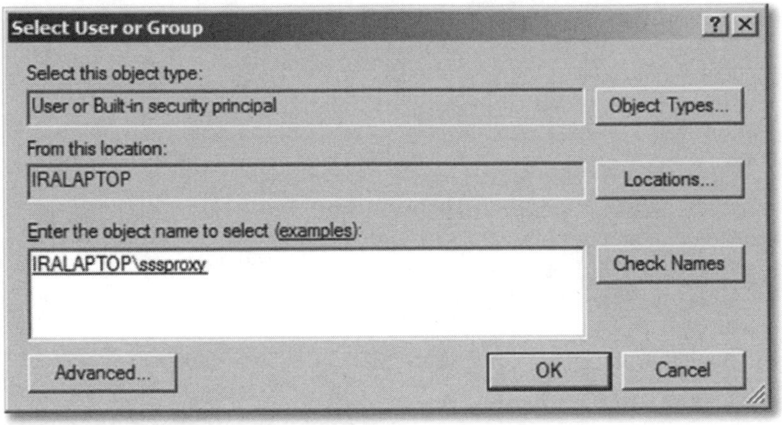

Illustration 473 - Select User or Group dialogue screen for finding a user account

Click the **Search** button and enter the domain qualified name for "sssproxy" and click the **Check Names button** to resolve the name as shown in **Illustration 473** at left.

Click **OK**. Leave the **Windows authentication radio button** checked and for the *Default database* choose **Absence Tracking** from the drop-down list. Click **OK**.

Now select the **Databases** folder and expand it. Choose the **Absence Tracking** database and expand it. Select the **Security** folder and expand it. Choose the **Users** folder and right click on it to select **New**.

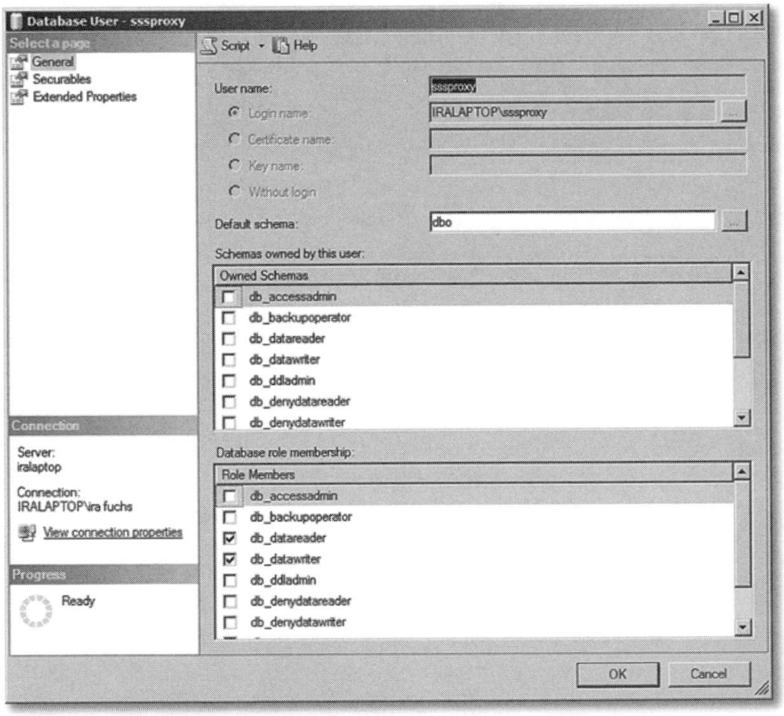

The *New User* dialogue screen will appear. Enter "sssproxy" for the *User name*. Click on the search box to the right of the Login name radio button to open the *Select Users and Groups* dialogue box as shown in **Illustration 473** above. Enter "sssproxy" for the *object name* and click the **Check Names button**. Click **OK**.

Illustration 474 - Setting the Impersonation account security credentials to the Absence Tracking database

In the *Database role membership* window on the bottom select the **db_datareader** and **db_datawriter** checkboxes as shown in **Illustration 474** at left.

Click **OK**. Now that we have created the impersonation user account in *Windows Server* and given it the necessary permissions in *SQL Server,* we are ready to create the target application in the *Secure Store Service*.

Using the Secure Store Service

Open *SharePoint 2010 Central Administration* again. Click on **Manage Service Applications** in the *Application Management* section. Click on **Secure Store Services**. The following screen will appear as shown in **Illustration 475** below.

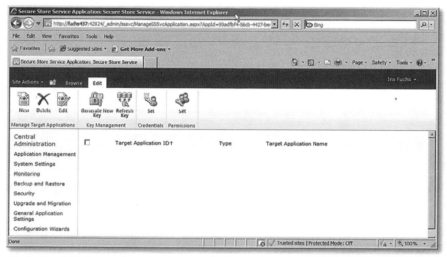

Illustration 475 - Secure Store Services page in SharePoint Central Administration

Initializing the Secure Store Service

Before a target application can be created we need to initialize an instance of the *Secure Store Service* which essentially creates an encrypted store of the target application information. To do this click on the **Generate New Key button** on the *Ribbon*. The *Generate New Key* dialogue screen will display as shown in **Illustration 476** below.

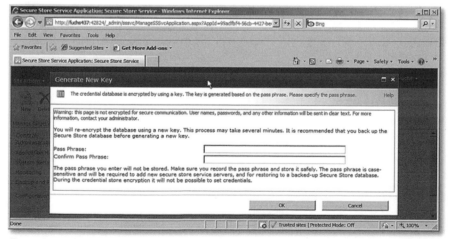

Illustration 476 - The Generate New Key dialogue screen to initialize an instance of the Secure Store Service

Enter a *Pass Phrase* and confirm it. Click **OK**. Store this *Pass Phrase* in a safe place.

Creating a Secure Store Service Target Application

Click on the **New button** on the *Ribbon*. The first page of the *Create New Secure Store Target Application* will display as shown in **Illustration 477** below.

Illustration 477 – The Create New Secure Store Target Application page

For the *Target Application ID* enter any arbitrary unique ID. Enter a *Display Name* and *Contact Email* for the individual who owns the management of the *Target Application*.

For *Target Application Type* choose *Group* from the drop-down list. Click the **Next** button. The second page of the *Create New Secure Store Target Application* will display as shown in **Illustration 478** below.

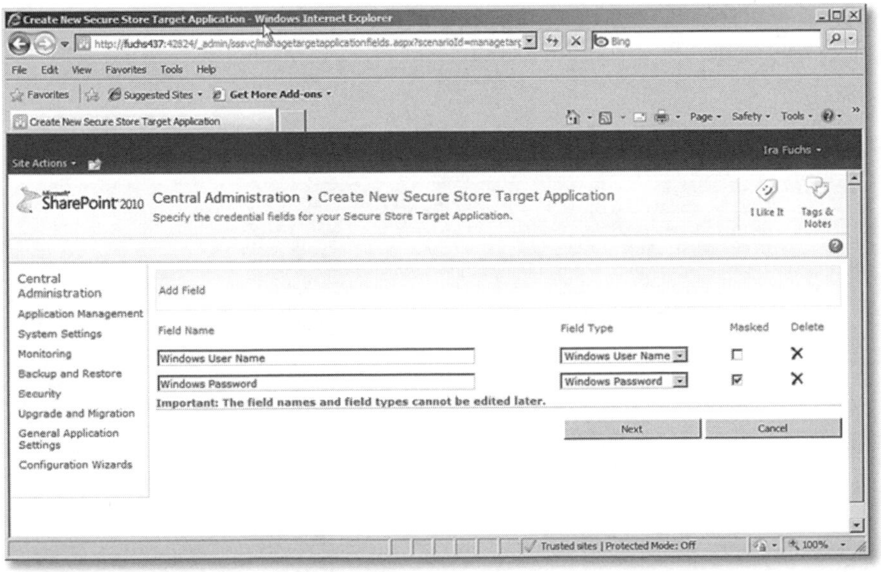

Illustration 478 - The second page of the Create New Secure Store Target Application

On this page the authentication and credential scheme used by the *Target Application* is created. By default the *Windows Authentication* scheme is presented, which deploys a *Username* and *Password*. Other authentication schemes may require additional credential information and on this page you can add the additional credential fields that define these authentication schemes. The *Field Names* can be edited to describe the name for any credential component as shown in **Illustration 479** at left. The drop-down selection box for the *Field Type* will display the component credential types. Leave the default *Windows Authentication* settings and click **Next**.

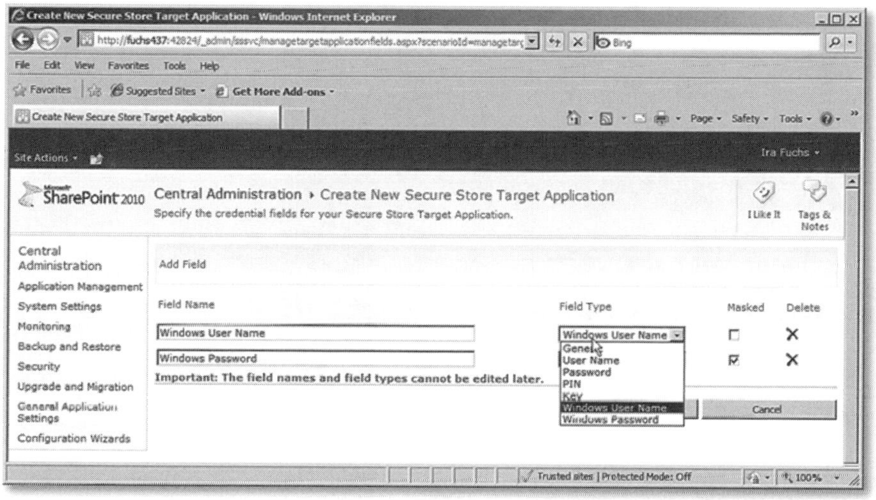

Illustration 479 – Credential types and components can be flexibly defined for an SSS target application

The *Specify the membership* settings page will display as shown in **Illustration 480** below. On this page you use the *People Picker* control to specify the users who are the *Target Application Administrators*, those people who can modify the settings of a *Target Application*; and the users and groups who are the *Members* (or *Credential Owners*) of the *Target Application* who will use the *Impersonation Credentials* to access the external application through *SharePoint*.

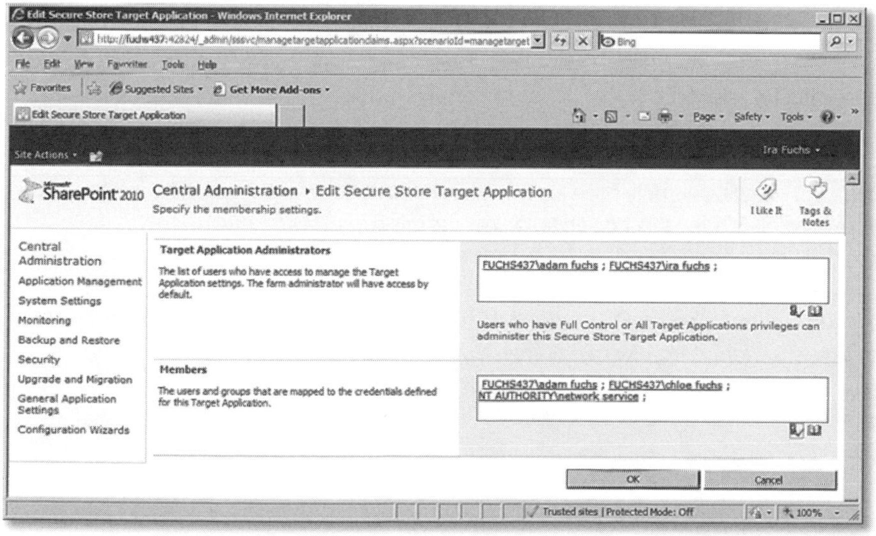

Important Note – The service account running the workflow that we identified earlier (*NetworkService*) must be added to the list of *Members* that will use the *Impersonation user account*. If the workflow service account is not made a *Member* then the workflow will not work.

Click **OK**. The *Target Application* will now be listed in the SSS home page. The next step is to specify the *Impersonation user account* for the *Target Application*.

Illustration 480 - The Specify the membership settings page where owners of the Impersonation account are specified

Select the **check box** for the *Target Application ID* and click on the **Set Credentials** button on the *Ribbon*. The *Set Credentials for Secure Store Target Application* dialogue screen will display as shown in **Illustration 481** below. The users and groups assigned to use the *Impersonation user account* in the previous step will be listed in the *Credential Owners* box.

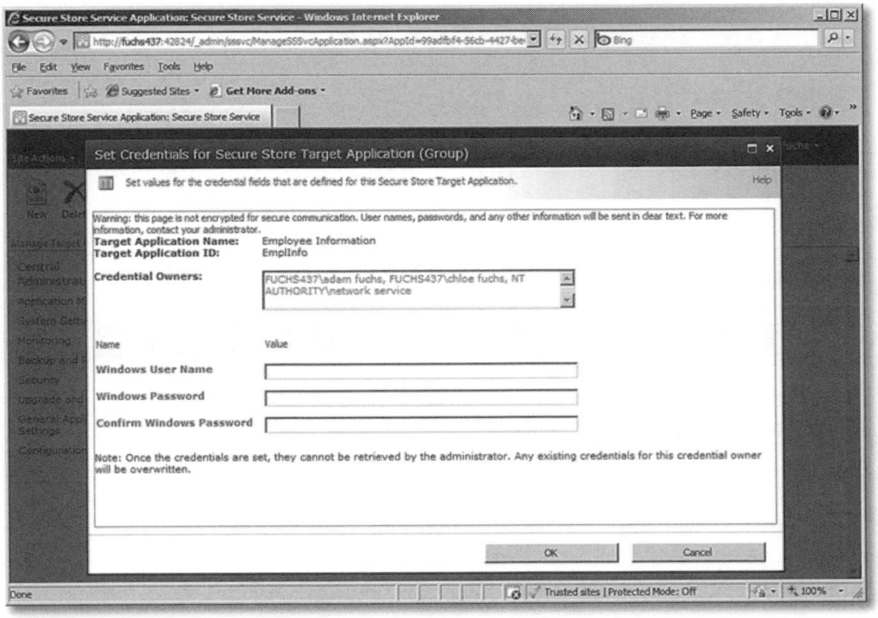

Illustration 481 - The Set Credentials for Secure Store Target Application dialogue screen

In the *Windows User Name* box enter the fully qualified name (2008SERVER\sssproxy) of the *Impersonation account*. In the *Windows Password* box enter the password created for this account and confirm the password. Click **OK**.

This completes the process of setting up *Secure Store Service* as the proxy credentials provider.

> **Important Note** – *SharePoint External Content Type Lists* are created at the site collection and site level and administrators at those levels only have access to *SharePoint* users and groups. However any user or group accessing an ECT list must be given object permissions in BCS, and if *Target Applications* are used, they must be assigned credential impersonation privileges in SSS. Because BCS and SSS are *Farm* level services they do not have access to *SharePoint* groups. When using the *People Picker* to assign BCS permissions or SSS credential impersonation rights to any user or group, those users or groups must be found from within *Active Directory.* Consequently any deployment of BCS and SSS requires careful planning around the process of managing and coordinating permission and rights requests that originate at the *SharePoint* site collection level but can only be addressed by accessing *Active Directory.*

Changing the Connection Properties for the ECT in SharePoint Designer to use the Impersonation Account Credentials

The final step is to modify the connection properties of the *Employee Information ECT* to use the *Target Application* to authenticate to the *SQL Server* database. Open *SharePoint Designer* and connect to the *Absence Tracking* site. Click on **External Content Types** in the *Navigation pane,* and then click on the **Employee Information ECT** to open its *Summary Page* as shown in **Illustration 482** below.

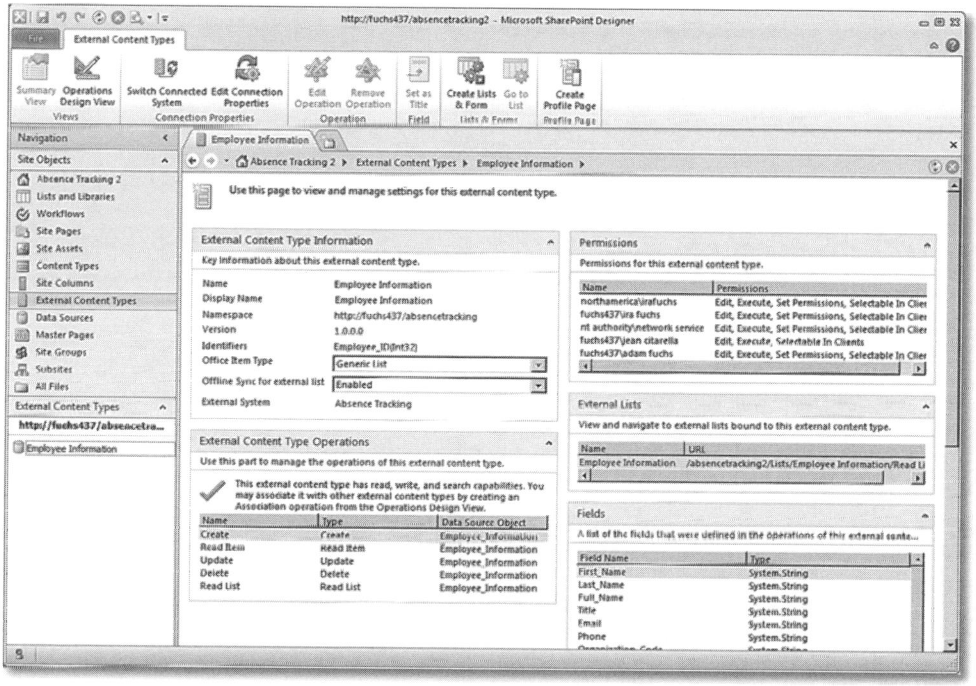

Illustration 482 - Employee Information ECT Summary Page in SharePoint Designer

Click the **Edit Connection Properties button** on the *Ribbon*. The *Connection Properties* dialogue screen will display as shown in **Illustration 483** below.

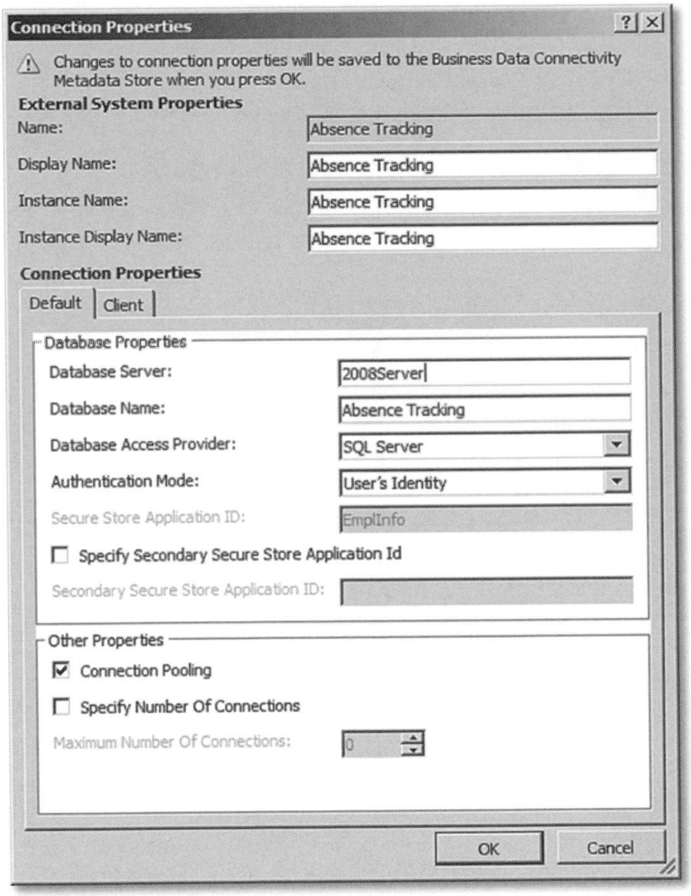

Illustration 483 - The Connection Properties dialogue screen for the Absence Tracking database

In the *Authentication Mode* drop-down list change the value from **User's Identity** to **Impersonate Windows Identity**. In the *Secure Store Application ID: box* enter the **ID** of the *Target Application* that was just created.

We have now bound a specific *SharePoint* ECT to a *Target Application* that specifies both the credentials used to authenticate to the database server and the users and groups who can access the database by impersonating those credentials. A secondary *Secure Application ID* can be specified here as well as one that can serve as a backup *Target Application* or contains different credentials and user/groups depending upon need.

> **Note** – The users and groups assigned to impersonate the *Target Application* authentication credentials do not need to be added to the *Security Login* accounts or database users in *SQL Server*.

Summary of Required Settings When Using Workflows to Access External Content Types

The following are the required settings for using workflows to access External Content Types in a SharePoint application:

- The *Connection Properties* for the ECT external system set in *SharePoint Designer* must use the *Impersonate Windows Identity* authentication mode.
- Using the *Impersonate Windows Identity* authentication mode requires the creation of a *Target Application* in *Secure Store Services*.
- The *Service Account* running the workflow must be assigned all *Object Permissions* in *Business Data Connectivity Services*.
- The *Service Account* running the workflow must be made an impersonation credentials *Member* (*Credential Owners*) in *Secure Store Services*.
- All user accounts that use the impersonation credentials (*Credential Owners*) in *Secure Store Services* must also be provided with *Object Permissions* in *Business Data Connectivity Services*.

Important Security Note – Even though the *User Accounts* created in *SQL Server* for the *Absence Request* database were assigned *db_datareader* role membership privileges, this restriction is over-ridden by the *Object permissions* set in *Business Data Connectivity Services*. Unfortunately at this time, if full create, read, update and delete (CRUD) operations are created for the *External Content Type*, the default *Execute permission* assigned in BCS to access the ECT list confers editing capabilities to all users. The only way to prevent users from being able to edit the items in the ECT list when Create, Update and Delete operations have been implemented is to set the permissions to the list itself to *Read-Only* for all users. However, the ECT list will be hidden from users and not be directly accessible to them.

The *Impersonation Step* in the workflow and the *Impersonation Credentials* deployed in SSS to allow the workflow to access the *External Content Type* list are two separate setting requirements, both of which **must be implemented in this particular use case** where the workflow updates the *External Content Type* list. By design, a workflow accessing an *External Content Type* must have the service account that it runs under authenticate itself to the external data source using SSS *Impersonation Credentials*. The *Impersonation Step* that we implemented is a workaround to address an unintended permission conflict that prevents the workflow from updating the values in the *External Content Type* list when the default permission to the list is set to *Read-Only*, which is necessary.

Publishing and Associating the Workflow

When you publish a *SharePoint Designer* workflow you make it available to the *SharePoint* workflow engine for execution. The workflow validates the logic and entities referenced by the workflow. After a reusable workflow has been published it can then be associated with a list, library or content type.

Important Note – *Associating* a published reusable workflow with a content type is **not** the same thing as creating a workflow template that is **based** on a content type definition.

When we created the *Absence Request reusable workflow* the first thing that we did was choose a content type on which to base the workflow template. Doing so provided the metadata context of the information that the workflow would be interacting with: that being the *Absence Request form* fields which in turn provided the "Current Item" correlation mechanism. This allowed us to efficiently create a workflow process that is *applicable* to working with an Absence Request content type.

Associating a reusable workflow is the function of binding a *run-time instance* of that workflow to an *instance* of a content type.

When we enabled the *Absence Requests* form library to support content types and then bound the *Absence Request form content type* to it, we created an *instance* of the *Absence Request form content type* for that *specific* library. **Illustration 484** below shows an *Absence Request form content type Settings* page accessed from the *Absence Request Form Library Settings* page that hosts this content type. Note that the *Absence Request form content type* is identified as a *List Content Type,* that is, a *child instance* of the parent *Absence Request form content type* that was created at the site level when the *InfoPath* form is published as a content type.

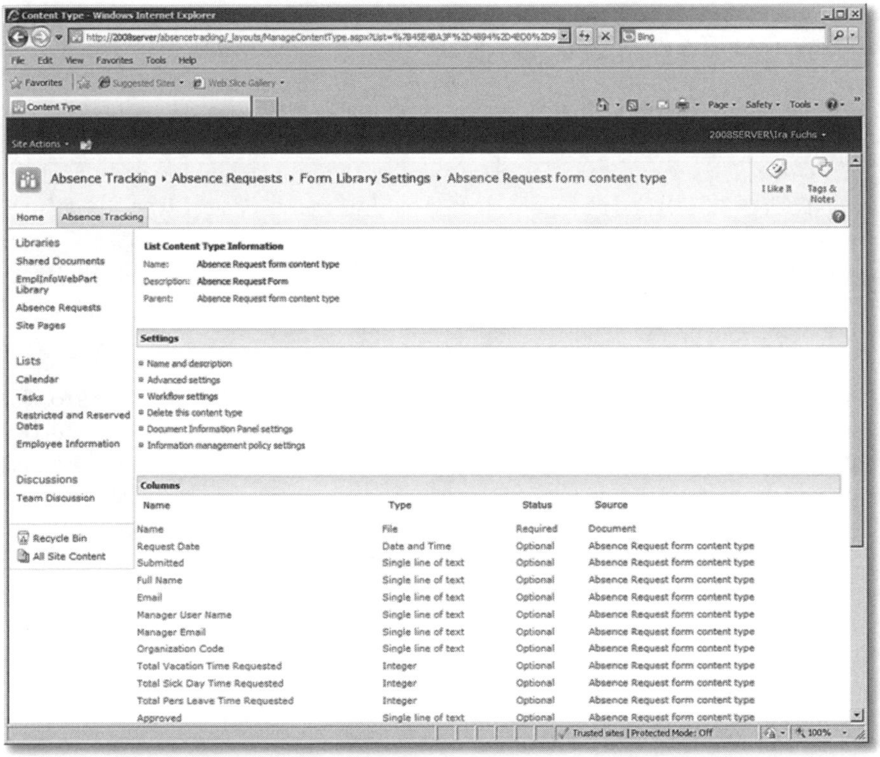

Illustration 484 - The Absence Request form content type Settings page accessed from the Absence Request form library Settings page

The *Workflow settings* page for the *Absence Request form content type **instance*** will show the workflows that have been associated with this ***instance*** of the content type as shown in **Illustration 485** below. Here you can see that a content type can have multiple workflows associated with it.

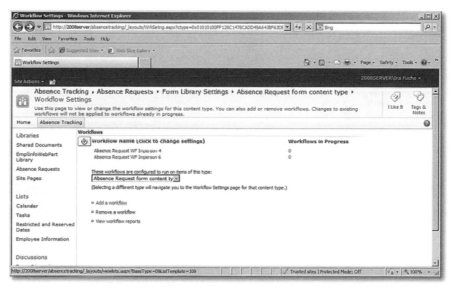

Illustration 485 - The workflows associated with an instance of a content type

There are two ways that workflows can be **associated** with a content type:

You can associate one or more workflows to the site content type. If you associate multiple workflows to a site content type every instance of the content type will have those workflows associated with it.

You can associate one or more workflows to a unique list content type; that is, an instance of the content type that is bound to a library. In this case the workflows associated with the list content type instance can be different from the site content type.

To publish the *Absence Request* workflow click the **Publish Button** on the *SharePoint Designer Ribbon*. The following message as shown in **Illustration 486** will display.

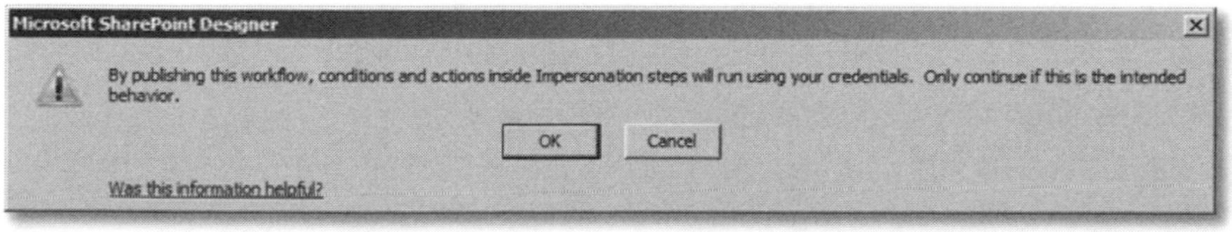

Illustration 486 - Publish workflow message in SharePoint Designer

Click **OK**. To associate the workflow with a site content type you can go to the *Summary Page* for the *Absence Request* workflow in *SharePoint Designer* or go to the *Workflows* page for the *SharePoint* site.

Click on the **Associate to Content Type button** on the *Ribbon*. The content type used to define the workflow template metadata will display below the button as shown in **Illustration 487** below. Select the **Absence Request form content type**.

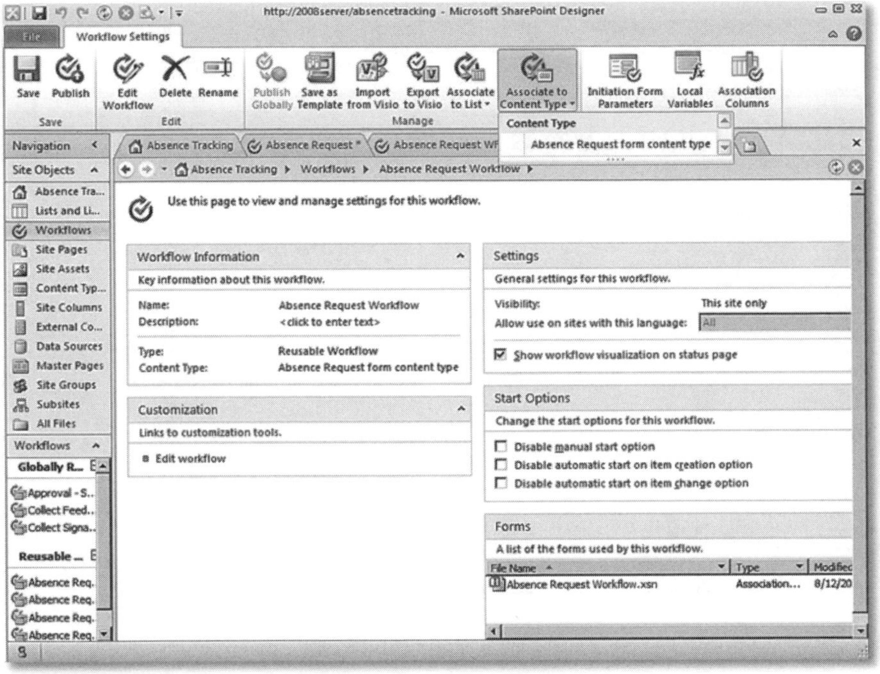

Illustration 487 - Associating a workflow with a content type

Alternatively you can go to the *Site Settings* page for the *Absence Request* site and select **Site Content Types**. On the *Site Content Type* page click the **Absence Request form content type** to display the settings page for this content type as shown in **Illustration 488** below.

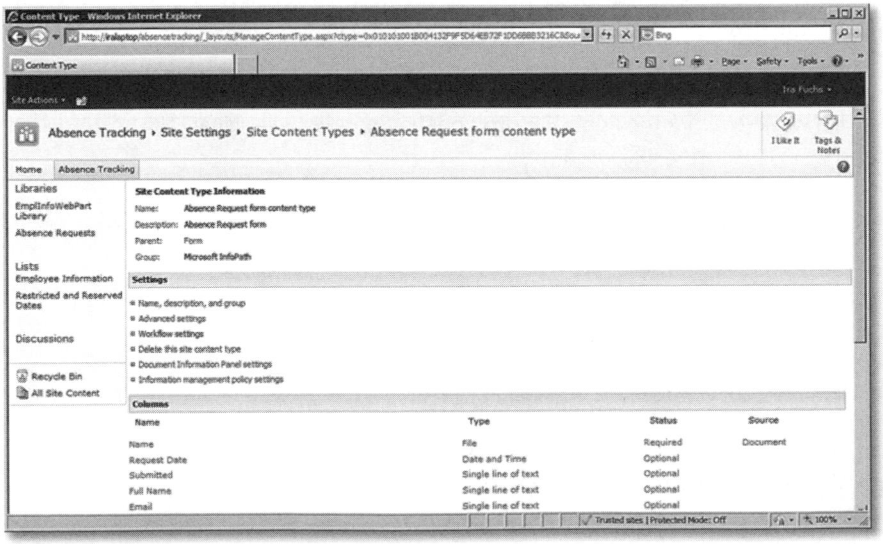

Illustration 488 - Site Content Type Settings page showing the Workflow settings link

Click on **Workflow settings** to display the workflow settings page and click **Add a workflow**. The *Add a Workflow* page will display as shown in **Illustration 488** below. On this page you can associate one or more published workflows to the site content type.

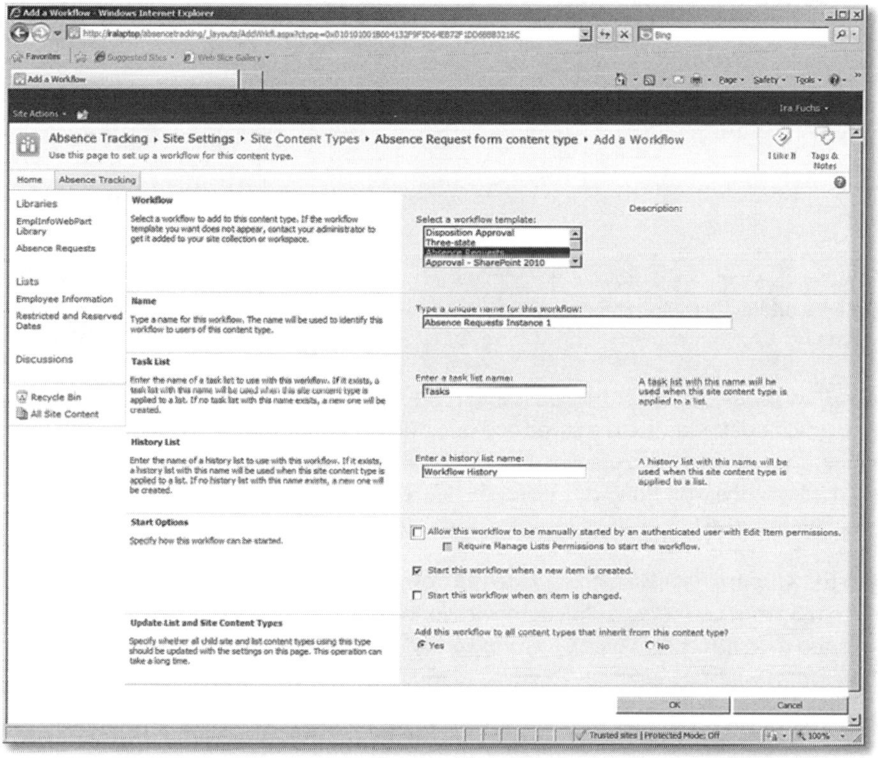

Illustration 489 - Adding a workflow to a content type from the content type Workflow settings page

If you associate the workflow from *SharePoint Designer* the name of the workflow template is automatically used for the workflow instance associated with the content type. If you use the *Add a Workflow* settings page in *SharePoint* you can give the workflow instance a unique name.

If it has not already been selected choose **Absence Request** from the list of available workflows. In the *Name* box enter a name for this instance of the *Absence Request* workflow. Note that you could associate multiple instances of the same workflow, each with a different name.

Leave **Tasks** and **Workflow History** as the list names for the respective *Task List* and *History* lists. These will be used by default as well if the workflow is associated using *SharePoint Designer*.

Select the **Start the workflow when a new item is created check box**; and *deselect* the **Allow the workflow to be manually started by an authenticated user with Edit Item permissions**. Leave the **Yes radio button** selected for *Add the workflow to all content types that inherit from the current type*. Click **OK**. Your completed *Workflow Settings* screen will look like **Illustration 490** on the next page.

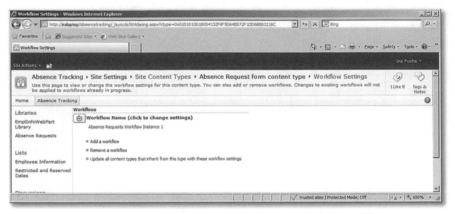

Illustration 490 – The completed Workflow Settings screen showing the workflows
associated with the content type

This step completes the workflow development for this application. You can modify the workflow at any time
and then save and publish it. Any modifications to the saved and published workflow will be propagated to the
unique instances of that workflow that have been associated with the site content type. The previous versions of
the workflow instances will display in the workflow settings for the Site content type as well as the List content
type instances but will no longer be active.

This can be seen by going to the *Absence Request form content type* from either the *Site Settings* or *Library
Settings* pages and then go to the *Workflow settings*. Click **Remove Workflows** to display the active and inactive
associated workflows associated to a ***site*** content type or a ***form library*** content type ***instance*** as shown in
Illustration 491 below.

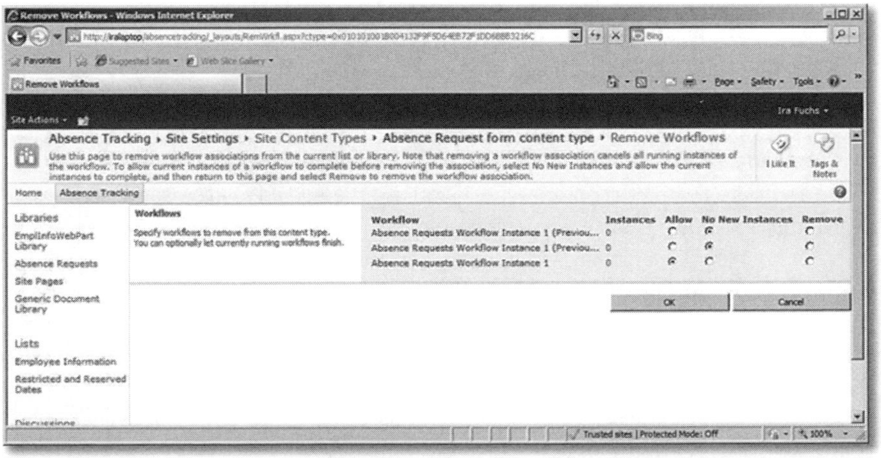

Illustration 491 - Remove Workflows page showing the active and inactive workflows for
a site content type or library content type instance

Each time a workflow is modified, saved and published it propagates the changes to the workflow instances
created from it by generating a new version of that instance. However the previous instance versions of the
workflow are not eliminated, they just are just rendered inactive as shown in **Illustration 491** above. You can
completely remove the inactive workflow instances from this page.

Setting up an SMTP Server to Test Workflow Email

We will test the functional logic of the form and workflow by creating absence requests using different user criteria and input; approving or rejecting requests; and opening request instances using different log-in accounts and under different approval status circumstances. We will want to ascertain that the workflow updates the *Employee Information* database appropriately and generates the specified email messages.

While the execution of the form logic has no dependencies on external systems other than the *Employee Information* external database, the workflow for the application generates email messages and in order to determine that those messages are being generated and contain the correct information we will need a way to capture and examine those email messages.

This can be accomplished by installing and configuring an *SMTP Server* on your *Windows Server 2008* development workstation.

Go to *Administrative Tools* from the *Windows Start* menu and choose **Server Manager**. In *Server Manager* click on **Features** in the hierarchy pane on the left as shown in **Illustration 492** below.

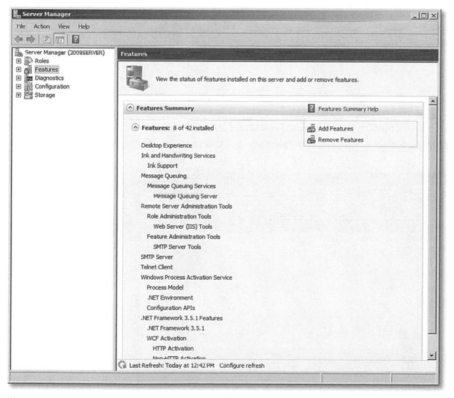

Illustration 492 – Windows Server 2008 Server Manager showing the Features Summary

Click **Add Features**. The *Select Features* screen will display as shown in **Illustration 493** below.

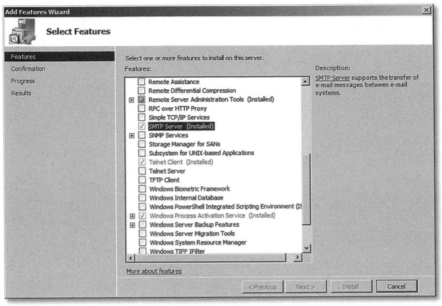

Illustration 493 - The Select Features Wizard screen

Scroll down the *Feature* options and select the **SMTP Server check box** and click **Install**. After the *SMTP Server* has been installed go to *Administrative Tools* from the *Windows Start* menu again and select **Internet Information Services (IIS) 6.0 Manager**, which will open. Expand the server to display the *SMTP Virtual Server* node as shown in **Illustration 494** below.

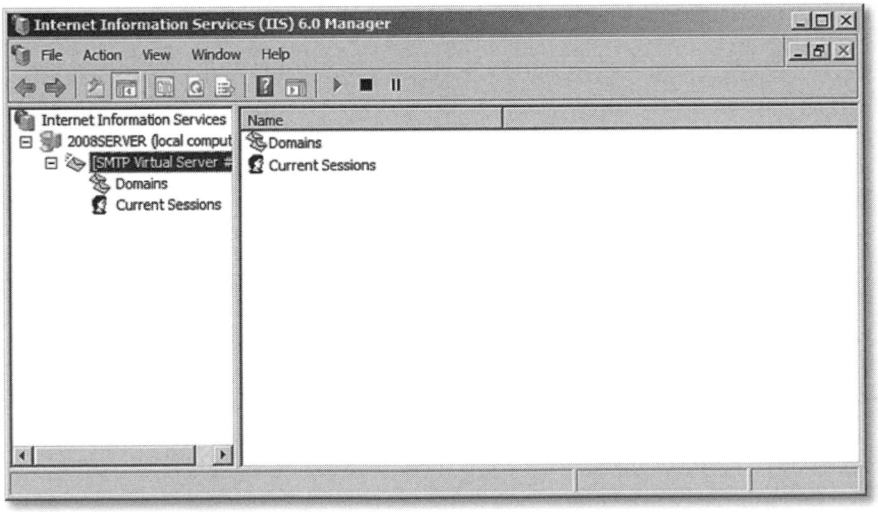

Illustration 494 – Internet Information Services 6.0 Manager with the SMTP Virtual Server node selected

Right click on the **SMTP Virtual Server** and ascertain that it is started. If it is not started, start it now as shown in **Illustration 495** below.

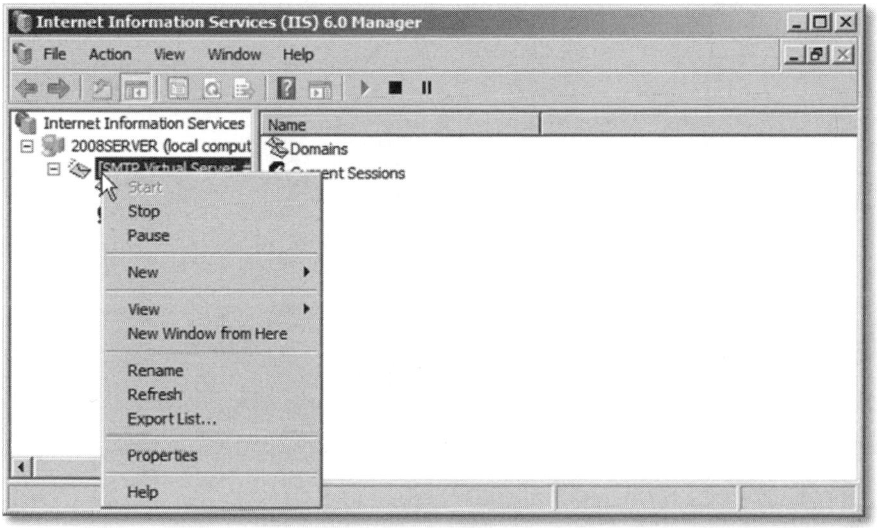

Illustration 495 - Making sure the SMTP Virtual Server is running

Now select **Properties** in order to configure the *SMTP Server*. The *General Tab* will display and the first thing we need to do is identify the Server's IP address as shown in **Illustration 496** below.

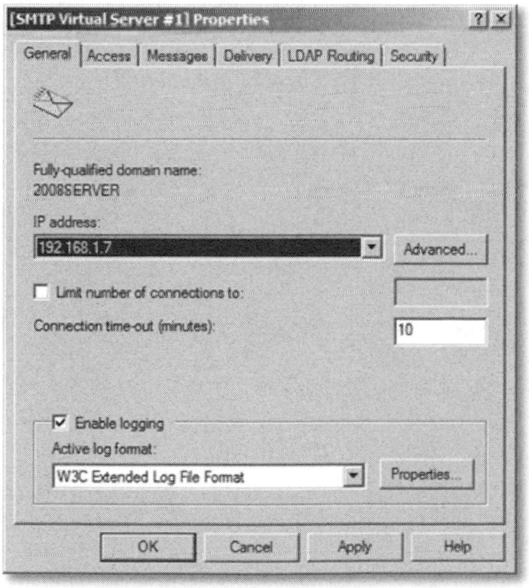

**Illustration 496 - Identifying the Server's IP address
from the General tab of the Properties dialogue screen**

The computer that you are working on most likely does not have a fixed (static) IP address. It obtains an IP address from the *Dynamic Host Configuration Protocol* (DHCP) application running on the wireless router or modem that provides the network connectivity to your computer. To determine your dynamic IP address at any given time open a *Command Prompt* window and type **IPConfig**. The IP address will be indicated as the *IPv4 Address* as shown in **Illustration 497** below.

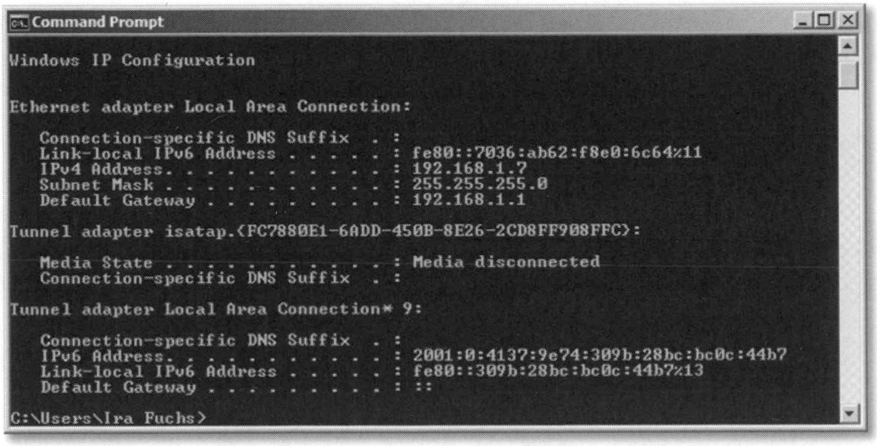

Illustration 497 - Running IPConfig from the Command Prompt to obtain the current IP address

The *SMTP Server* will automatically determine the IP address but sometimes it does not always do so. If the IP address (that matches the one displayed by *IPConfig*) is not shown on the *General Tab* than click the **Advanced Button**. From the *Advanced* screen click the **Add** button and enter your computer's current IP address and "25" for the *TCP Port* as shown in **Illustration 498** below.

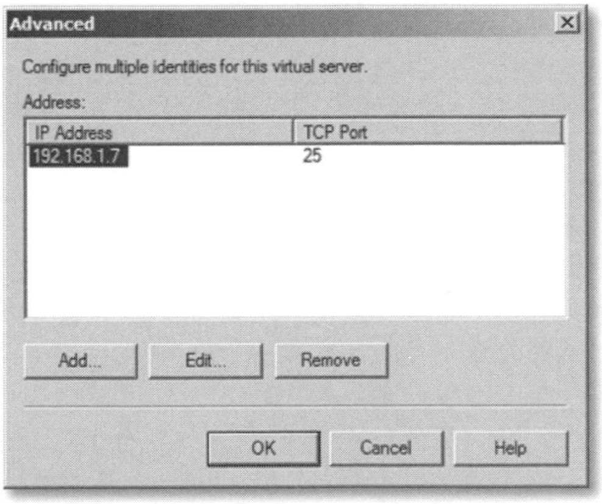

Illustration 498 - Manually entering the IP Address and TCP Port for the SMTP Server

Click **OK** and the **Enable logging check box**.
Click on the **Access Tab** as shown in **Illustration 499** below.

Illustration 499 - The Access tab on the Properties dialogue screen of the SMTP Server

Click on the **Authentication button** and make sure that **Anonymous access** is checked as shown in **Illustration 500** below.

Illustration 500 - The Authentication settings screen on the Access tab

Click **OK** and click the **Connection** button. On the *Connection* screen as shown in **Illustration 501** below select the **All except the list below radio button**.

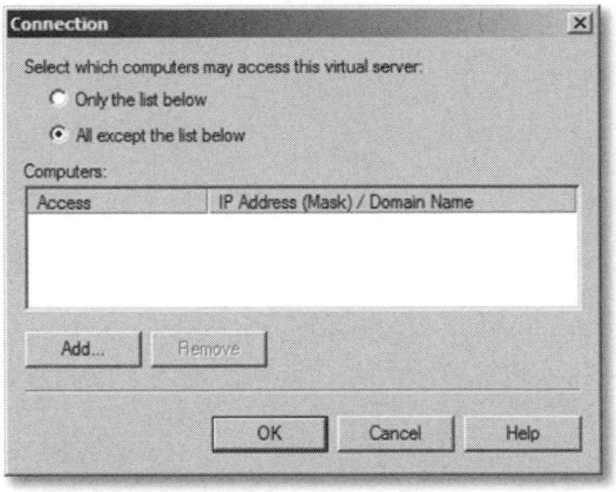

Illustration 501 - The Connection settings screen
on the Access tab

Click **OK** and click on the **Relay** button. Select the **All except the list below radio button** and check the **Allow all computers which successfully authenticate to relay regardless of the list about check box** as shown in **Illustration 502** below.

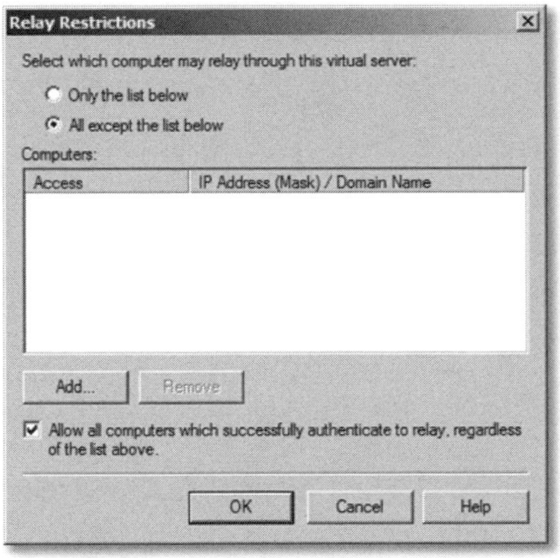

Illustration 502 - The Relay Restrictions setting
screen on the Access tab

Click **OK**. We have finished configuring the *SMTP server*. We now have to configure *SharePoint's* outgoing mail settings. Open *SharePoint Central Administration* and click on **System Settings** as shown in **Illustration 503** below.

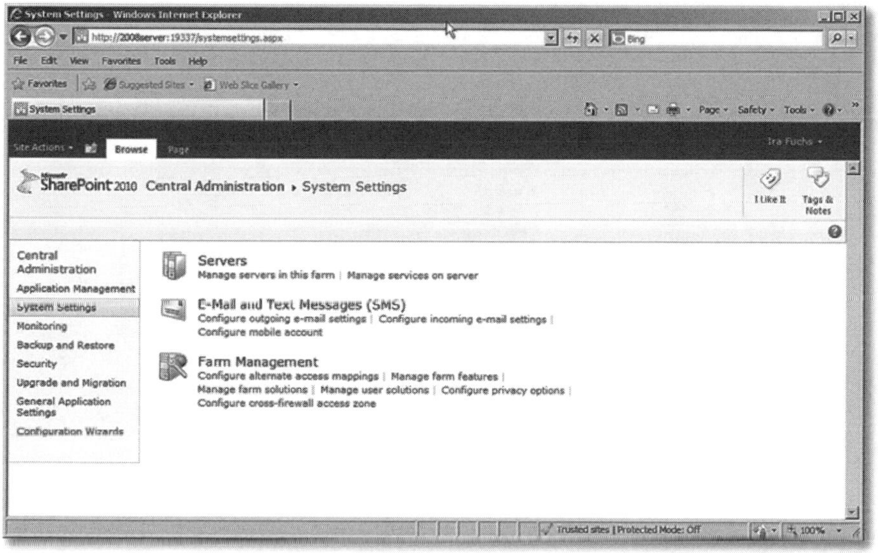

Illustration 503 - System Settings page in SharePoint Central Administration

Click **Configure outgoing e-mail settings** under *E-Mail and Test Messages (SMS)*. In the screen that displays as shown in **Illustration 504** below enter the same IP address of your computer as you used for the *SMTP Server* above. For *the From and Reply-to-address* enter an arbitrary email address. The emails generated by the workflow will use the *From* address specified here.

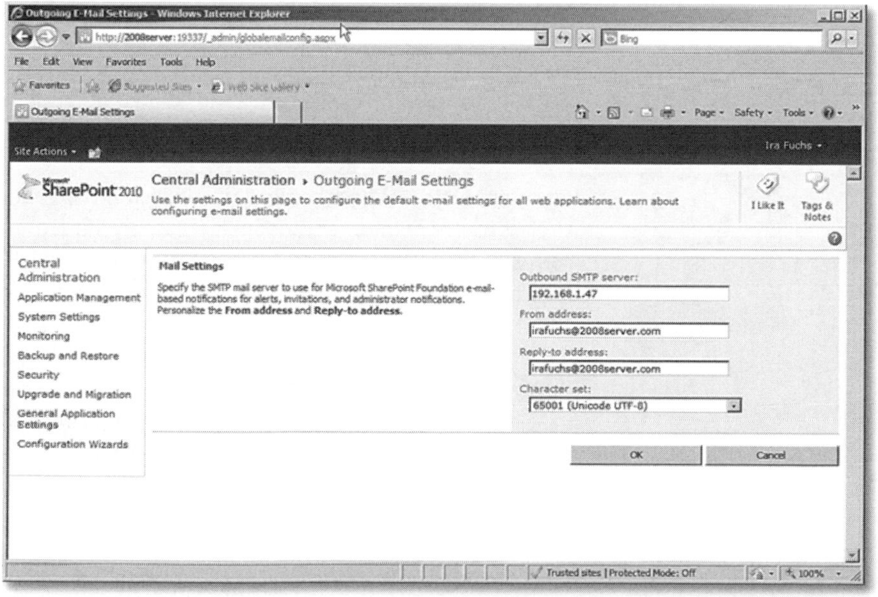

Illustration 504 - Outgoing E-Mail Settings page in SharePoint Central Administration

You will want to make sure that the *SMTP Server* starts automatically when you boot up your computer. To accomplish this choose **Administrative Tools** from the *Windows Start* menu and select **Services**. The *Services* screen will display as shown in **Illustration 505** below.

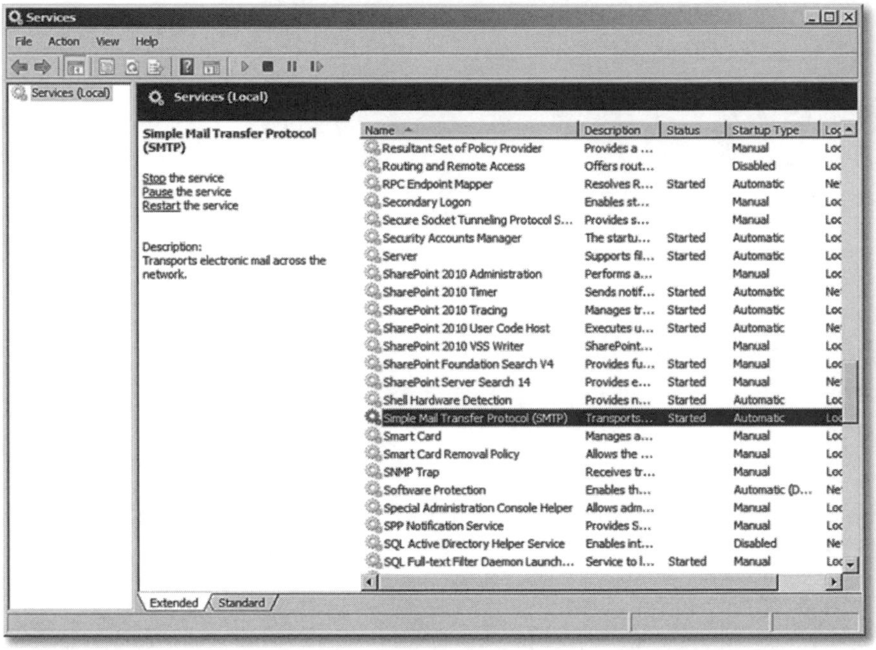

Illustration 505 - The Services screen accessed from Windows Server Administrative Tools

Select **Simple Mail Transfer Protocol** and right click to open the **configuration settings** dialogue screen as shown in **Illustration 506** below.

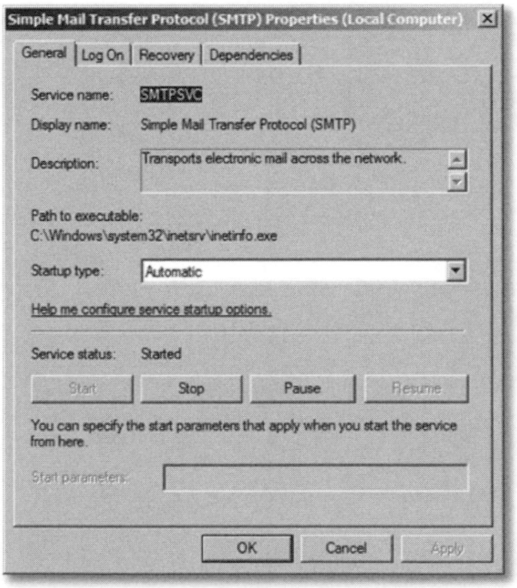

Illustration 506 - SMTP Services Properties screen

From the *Startup type* drop-down list select **Automatic** and click **OK**. This completes the setup and configuration of the outgoing mail services needed to test the workflow process.

Important Note – While the IP address allocated by your wireless router or Internet modem is dynamic, the same IP address is typically cached by the client computer and DHCP application. This means that if you turn your computer on and off when it connects again to the router or modem it will obtain the same IP address, and consequently you do not have to re-enter a new IP address for the *SMTP Server* and *SharePoint*. However, this is not always the case and periodically you should use *IPConfig* in a *Command Prompt* to ascertain what your current IP address is. If it changes you will have to set this address in *SMTP Server* and *SharePoint Central Administration*. This will also need to be done if you connect your computer to another network.

How to View Emails Generated by the Workflow

The function of an *SMTP Server* is to route outgoing emails to external *SMTP servers* that can ultimately deliver mail to the intended recipients. We did not configure *SMTP Server* to do this; we only configured it to accept incoming email from an application, in this case *SharePoint*. Consequently any email messages that are generated will end up sitting in a *Queue* folder used by the *SMTP Server* and will then be moved into another folder for undeliverable items. The *Queue* folder and *Badmail* folders used for these purposes can be seen in **Illustration 507** below.

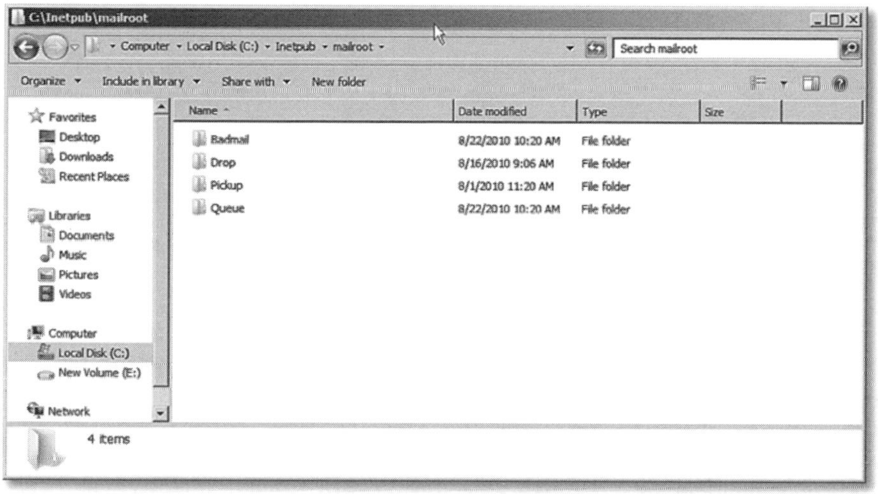

Illustration 507 - The mailroot folder under the InetPub folder

These folders can be found in the *Server\Local Disk\Inetput\mailroot* folder. The emails generated by the workflow will be deposited into the *Queue* folder as shown in **Illustration 508** below.

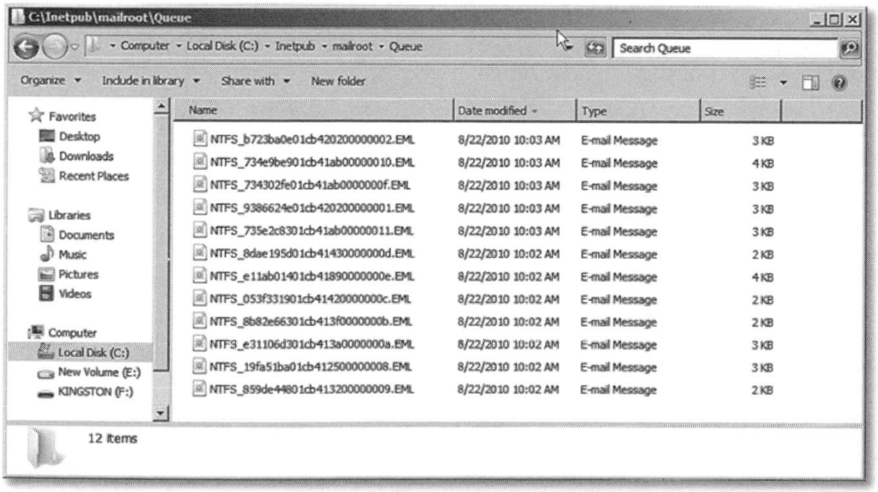

Illustration 508 - The Queue folder showing email messages queued to be forwarded

If you copy and paste one of the .EML email messages to your desktop and click on it, it will open in *Outlook* as shown in **Illustration 509** below.

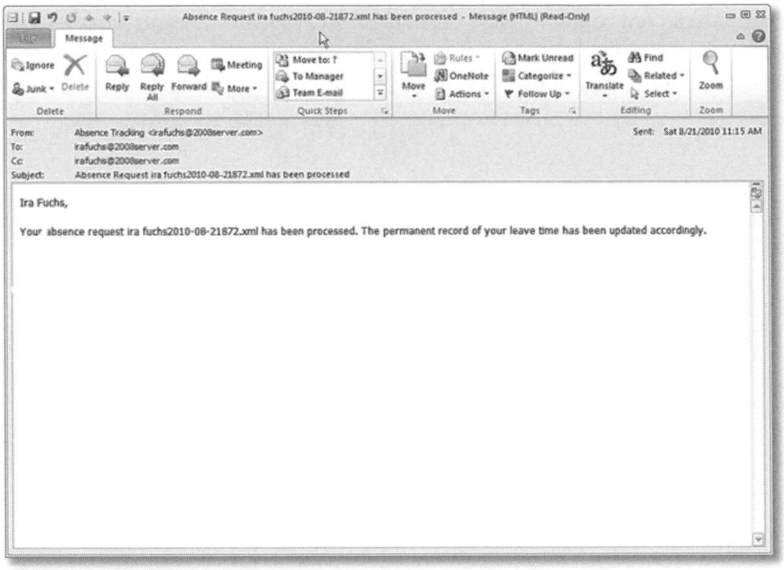

Illustration 509 - An email message in the Queue folder generated by the Absence Request workflow

This is how we can determine if the emails in the workflow are being sent and generated with the values that we used in them. Because these email messages have no place to go they will ultimately be moved into the *Badmail* folder which will also generate other files as well as shown in **Illustration 510** below. These files, as well as the email messages in the *Queue* folder can be deleted at any time.

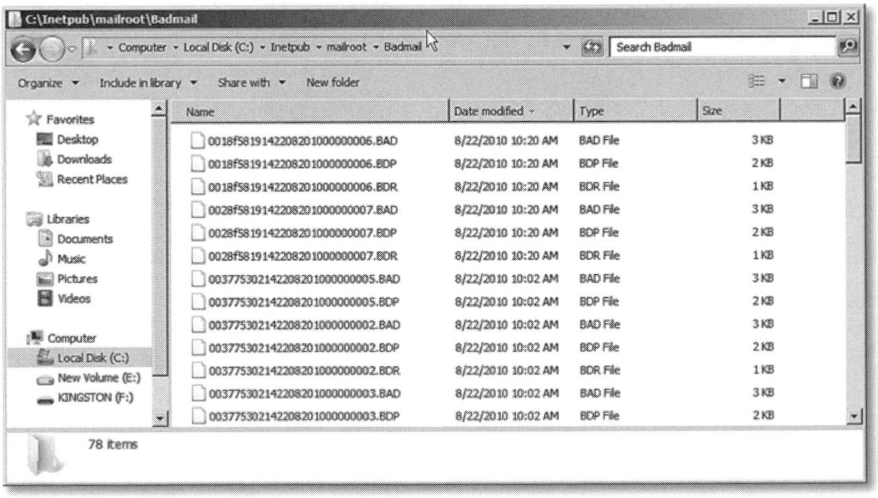

Illustration 510 – Unsent emails transferred from the Queue folder into the Badmail folder

Testing the Application Logic

We can now systematically test the *InfoPath Absence Request* form and the corresponding workflow for the application. We will accomplish this by:

- Creating and submitting multiple absence requests under the same user account
- Creating new absence requests logged-in as different users
- Opening submitted requests that require approval and approving or rejecting them by logging in using the account of the designated approving manager as indicated in the Employee Information database
- Open submitted requests logged in as the user who created the requests as well as by other users
- Viewing the workflow visualization page
- Inspecting the emails generated by the workflow process
- Checking that the *InfoPath Web Part* on the application home page is updated by the workflow process
- Viewing the application's lists and libraries under different accounts to

The following table itemizes the full suite of functions and conditions to test with the expected application behavior.

Test/Condition (Prerequisite Set-Up)	Expected Application Behavior
New Request - Date Entry Tests	
Enter multiple valid vacation dates	Each additional item sets Hour Value field to 8 and increments Total Vacation Time Requested field
Enter vacation dates prior to current date	Validation error displays on date field with cursor hover message and Hour Value field set to 0. Total Vacation Time Requested field not incremented. Cannot submit form. Delete item to correct
Enter vacation dates that are restricted dates	Validation error displays on date field with cursor hover message and Hour Value field set to 0. Total Vacation Time Requested field not incremented. Cannot submit form. Delete item to correct
Delete vacation dates	Item is removed successfully and Total Vacation Time Requested field is decreased
Enter multiple sick leave dates	Each additional item sets Hour Value field to 8 and increments Total Sick Leave Time Requested field
Enter sick leave dates prior to current date	Each additional item sets Hour Value field to 8 and increments Total Sick Leave Time Requested field
Enter sick leave dates that are restricted dates	Each additional item sets Hour Value field to 8 and increments Total Sick Leave Time Requested field

Test/Condition (Prerequisite Set-Up)	Expected Application Behavior
New Request - Date Entry Tests	
Delete sick dates	Item is removed successfully and Total Sick Time Requested field is decreased
Enter multiple valid personal leave dates	Each additional item sets Hour Value field to 8 and increments Total Personal Leave Time Requested field
Enter personal leave dates prior to current dates	Validation error displays on date field with cursor hover message and Hour Value field set to 0. Total Personal Time Requested field not incremented. Cannot submit form. Delete item to correct
Enter personal leave dates that are restricted dates	Validation error displays on date field with cursor hover message and Hour Value field set to 0. Total Personal Time Requested field not incremented. Cannot submit form. Delete item to correct
Delete personal dates	Item is removed successfully and Total Personal Leave Time Requested field is decreased
Enter vacation dates that exceed available balance (set available vacation time in ECT list to balance of 8 hours)	Hour Value field increases. Validation error displays for Total Vacation Time Requested field with cursor hover message, but value increments. Cannot submit form. Delete item to correct
Enter sick leave dates that exceed available balance (set available sick time in ECT list to balance of 8 hours)	Hour Value field increases. Validation error displays for Total Sick Time Requested field with cursor hover message, but value increments. Cannot submit form. Delete item to correct
Enter personal leave dates that exceed available balance (set available personal time in ECT list to balance of 8 hours)	Hour Value field increases. Validation error displays for Total Personal Time Requested field with cursor hover message, but value increments. Cannot submit form. Delete item to correct
Enter vacation dates when available balance is 0 (set available vacation time in ECT list to 0)	Date picker control will not display. Clicking Insert Item will not work
Enter sick dates when available balance is 0 (set available sick time in ECT list to 0)	Date picker control will not display. Clicking Insert Item will not work
Enter personal dates when available balance is 0 (set available personal time in ECT list to 0)	Date picker control will not display. Clicking Insert Item will not work

Test/Condition (Prerequisite Set-Up)	Expected Application Behavior
Submit Request Tests	
No approval required condition: If an employee has been employed for less than six months and submits an absence request with a total amount of time equal to or less than 48 hours (set the start date in the Employee Information database to a date that is less than six months from the current date. Enter dates for leave time in any category whose total is less than or equal to 48 hours	• Request is submitted to form library and displays View indicating that no approval is required • Form sets Requires Approval field/column to "No", Approved field/column to "Yes", and Submitted field/column to "TRUE" • Workflow updates the Employee Information database with values in Stored Values fields and sends an email to the request submitter.

Approval required condition:
If an employee has been employed for less than six months and submits an absence request with a total amount of time greater than 48 hours (set the start date in the Employee Information database to a date that is less than six months from the current date. Enter dates for leave time in any category whose total is greater than 48 hours
	• Request is submitted to form library and displays View indicating that manager approval is required
	• Form sets Requires Approval field/column to "Yes", and Submitted field/column to "TRUE"
	• Workflow sends an email to manager to approve.
	• Workflow pauses for three days*.
	• If manager approves:
	  o Approved field/column value set to "Yes"
	  o Workflow updates the Employee Information database with values in Stored Values fields
	  o An email is sent to the request submitter.
	• If manager rejects:
	  o Approved field/column value set to "No"
	  o Email sent to submitter informing them of rejected request
	• If manager does nothing:
	  o Workflow send an email to manager
	  o Workflow pauses for three hours*
	• If manager approves:
	  o Approved field/column value set to "Yes"
	  o Workflow updates the Employee Information database with values in Stored Values fields and sends an email to the request submitter.
	• If manager rejects:
	  o Approved field/column value set to "No"
	  o Email sent to submitter informing them of rejected request
	• If manager does nothing – after three hours:
	  o Email sent to submitter informing them of rejected request
	• If manager does nothing:
	  o Approved field/column value set to "Yes"
	  o Workflow updates the Employee Information database with values in Stored Values fields.
	  o An email is sent to the request submitter.
	*See workflow test modification below

No approval required (>6 months≤64 hours)	Same as above
Approval required (>6 months>64 hours)	Same as above

Open Existing Form Tests	
Creator opens form they created/ Approved Creator opens form they created/ Rejected	Form opens in Read Only Main View, Approval section is not displayed. If rejected by manager than form opens in Read Only Main View and Approval section is displayed.
Manager opens form they created/ Approved Creator opens form they created/ Rejected (Same as Creator)	Form opens in Read Only Main View, Approval section is not displayed. If rejected by manager than form opens in Read Only Main View and Approval section is displayed.
Manager opens form of direct report	Form open in editable Main View.
Not creator or manager opens form	Form displays Not Authorized to View View

Approval Tests	
Manager approves request	• Manager opens submitted form of direct report and sets Approved field to Yes and clicks Manager Submit. • Form is saved to form library. o Approved field/column value set to "Yes" o Workflow updates the Employee Information database with values in Stored Values fields o An email is sent to the request submitter.
Manager rejects request	• Manager opens submitted form of direct report and sets Approved field to No with reason and clicks Manager Submit. • Form is saved to form library. o Approved field/column value set to "No" o Email sent to submitter informing them of rejected request
Manager ignores request	• Manager does nothing: o Approved field/column value set to "Yes by Default" o Workflow updates the Employee Information database with values in Stored Values fields. o An email is sent to the request submitter.

User/Role Access Behavior Tests	
Home Page artifact access (Log-in as different users)	For all users/roles: • InfoPath Form Web Part displays read-only view of logged-in user's record only • Absence Request library Web Part displays logged-in user's requests in My Documents view. Existing requests can be opened in read-only mode and new requests can be created • Restricted and Reserved date list displays those dates for the organization that the logged-in user is a member
Absence Request Form Library	Accessible to managers only and displays the My Documents View by default showing requests submitted by themselves and a Managers View displaying requests submitted by their direct reports
Restricted and Reserved Dates List	Accessible to designated users only and displays only dates for organization that logged-in user is a member of.
Employee Information ECT List	Should not be made accessible to anyone, and if it must, in read-only mode and displays only the logged-in user's record.
EmployeeInfoWebPart Library	No access to library except to application manager

Things to Note When Testing the Application

In the workflow that we created for the application the workflow pauses for two days unless the manager approves or rejects the request. After two days the workflow sends a follow-up email to the manager and pauses for two more hours. Then it approves the request by default. These durations obviously do not facilitate efficient testing of the application. As such these variables should be modified to 15 minutes and 5 minutes respectively while testing.

The hidden library that will store the *InfoPath* form that will be displayed as a Web Part on the application home page will be created in the next chapter.

Before and during testing of the application you will have to make sure that the records in the *Employee Information* database contain the information necessary to test correctly and you will have to reset the leave time available and balance values in order to test the different behavior itemized in the test table above.

Make sure that each of the records that you created in the *Employee Information* database contains *User_Name* and *Manager_User_Name* values, and these are identical to the User names created in the *Computer Management Local Users and Groups* function as shown in **Illustration 511** below.

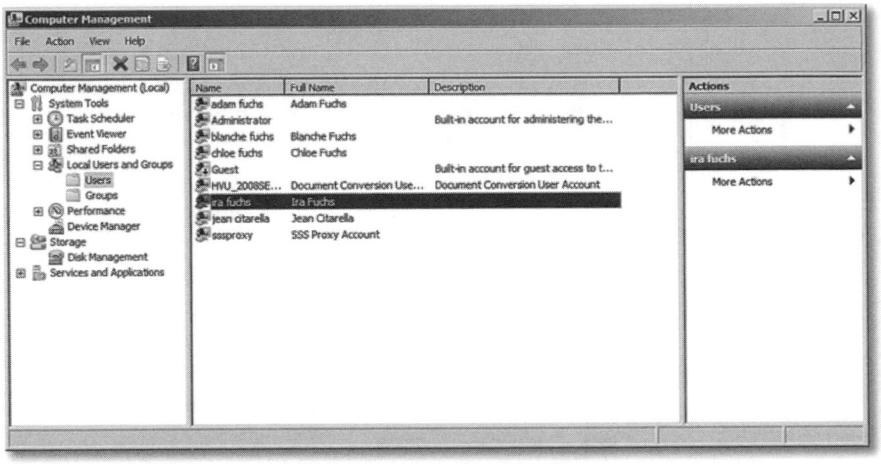

Illustration 511 - User accounts in Computer Management Local Users and Groups

Make sure that at least one of the *Employee Information* records has an employment start date that is greater than six months from the current date and another record has an employment start date that is less than six months from the current date. These variables are necessary to display different form views and trigger different conditional actions of the workflow.

Also make sure that there is an Email address and a Manager Email address value in each *Employee Information* record used in testing.

Implementing a SharePoint Develop, Test and Deploy Staging Process

A process for moving an application from its development environment to a testing environment and ultimately to production is a necessary consideration of creating applications that will be deployed widely in an Enterprise. Formal development platforms such as *Team Foundation Server* provide comprehensive methodologies and tools for managing the end-to-end lifecycle process of developing, testing, deploying and maintaining code based applications where different people are responsible for the respective development, testing and deployment tasks. While a great deal of *SharePoint* development will be done on a tactical ad-hoc basis without a formal develop, test and deploy process, a formal methodology and infrastructure will be a requirement once *SharePoint* application development becomes more prevalent and the applications created in SharePoint become more business critical.

One of the key enhancements in *SharePoint 2010* that facilitates the implementation of a formal develop, test and deploy staging process is the ability to easily package up all the artifacts, as well as the content of an application, into a *SharePoint Solution Package*, known as a WSP. A WSP is a single file containing all the artifacts and components of a site, including content types, workflows, code and optionally the contents of lists and libraries. The WSP can be copied anywhere and uploaded to the *Solution Gallery* of any site collection as shown in **Illustration 512** below.

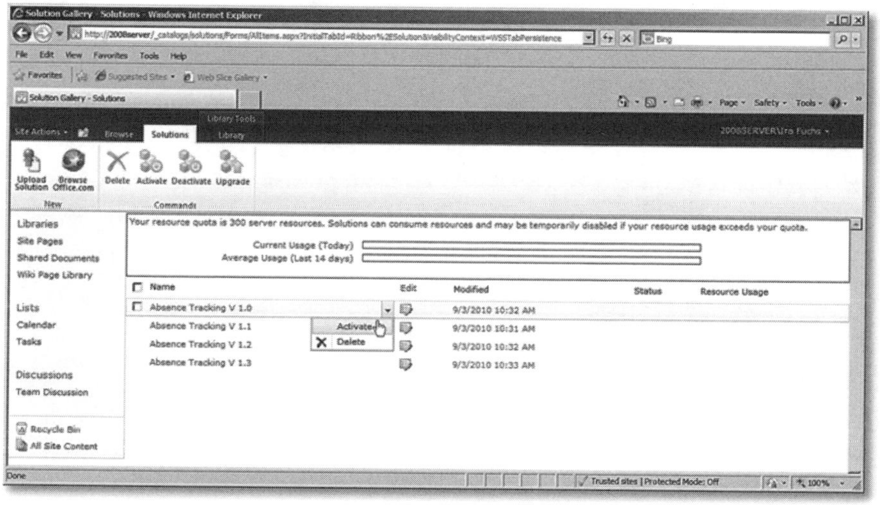

Illustration 512 - Solution Gallery page of a site collection

Once the WSP is uploaded the application can be *Activated* and instantiated as a site. Different versions of the same application can be instantiated on the same site collection or on different ones. If changes are made to these sites they can then be saved again as WSPs.

This straightforward way to package and deploy a site based application provides the mechanism for implementing a formal methodology and environment for developing, testing and deploying *SharePoint* applications. Furthermore, the *Solutions Gallery* is a *SharePoint* library that can be configured using all the *SharePoint* library features and functions, such as versioning and workflow, to implement formal deployment governance controls. The *Library Tools Ribbon* can be seen in **Illustration 513** below.

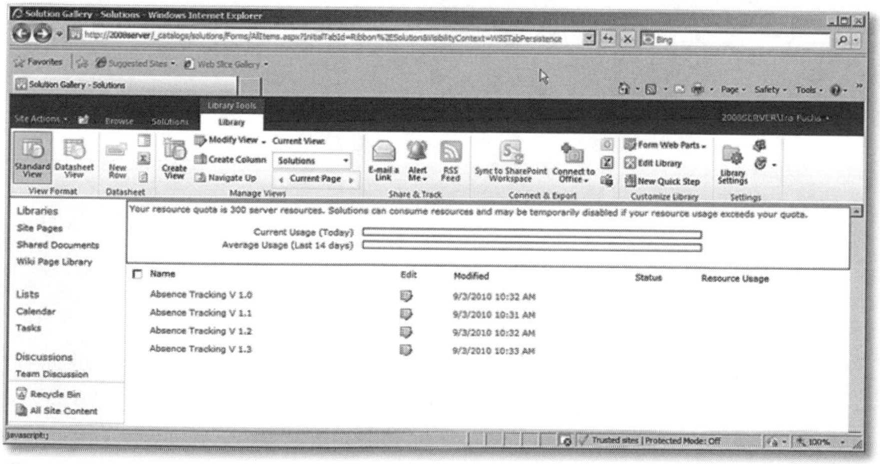

Illustration 513 - The Library Tools Ribbon for the Solution Gallery

After we have completed the creation of the application home page and related artifacts we will save the application as a *SharePoint Solution Package*.

Walkthrough of a Test

Note the values displayed for available and balance leave time in the *Employee Information* database for the logged-in user.

Absence Request Dates

Vacation Days Requested	
Dates	Hour Value
9/2/2010	8
9/3/2010	8

☐ Insert item

Total Vacation Time Requested	16

Sick Leave Days Requested	
Dates	Hour Value
8/17/2010	8

☐ Insert item

Total Sick Leave Time Requested	8

Personal Leave Days Requested	
Dates	Hour Value

☐ Insert item

Total Personal Leave Time Requested	0

Submit Absence Request

Create an absence request and choose dates for any of the leave categories as shown in **Illustration 514** at left.

Submit the request. Depending upon the number of leave days requested and the duration of employment either the *Submitted for Approval* or the *Submitted and Approved* view will display upon submission as shown in **Illustration 515** below.

Illustration 514 - Sample leave dates selected in an absence request

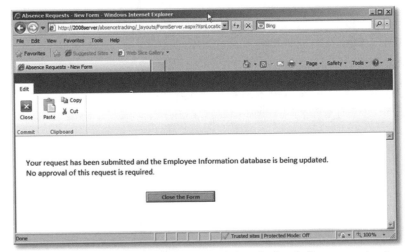

Illustration 515 - The Submitted and Approved view displayed after a request not requiring approval has been submitted

Go to the *Absence Request* library. The absence request submitted will display in the library as shown in **Illustration 516** below. There will also be a column for *Absence Request Workflow Instance 1* and it will show a value of *In Progress* which will change to *Completed* if everything is working correctly.

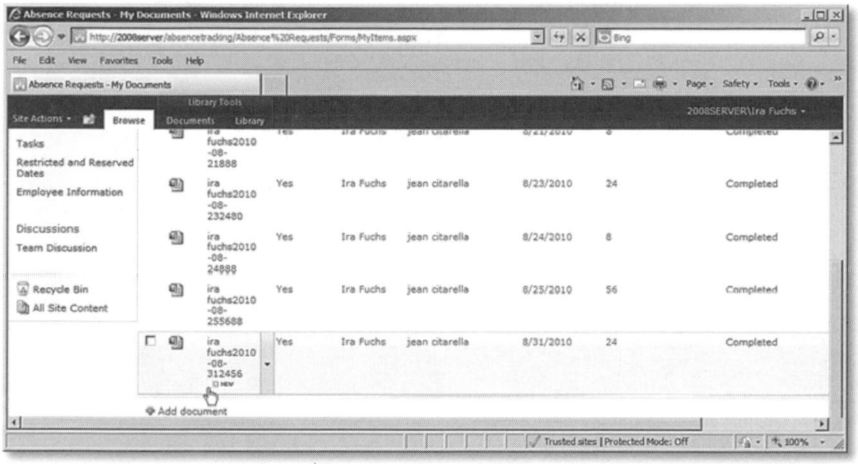

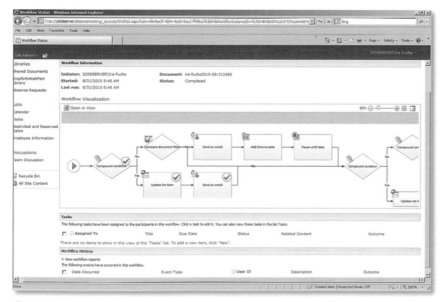

Illustration 516 - The Absence Request library showing the absence request instance submitted

Click on the **In Progress** or **Completed** hyperlink to go to the *Workflow Visualization* page as shown in **Illustration 517** below. Drag the workflow image to the right in order to display the visualization of *Step 1* of the workflow. If the request did not require approval than the *Update List Item* and *Send an email* action boxes will be checked and there will be no error messages in the *Workflow History* as shown in **Illustration 517** below. If the workflow fails to execute properly an *Error* value will display in the form library and in the *Workflow Visualization* page. The action boxes in the visualization will not be checked and the *Workflow History* will provide some indication of what failed.

Illustration 517 - the Workflow Information page for a running workflow with the runtime visualization and Workflow History

If the workflow completed successfully then the used and available leave time values, as well as the vacation time subject to forfeit value will be updated in the *Employee Information* database. These updated values will also display in an *InfoPath form Web Part* (that we will create shortly) that displays this information on the home page of the application as shown in **Illustration 518** below.

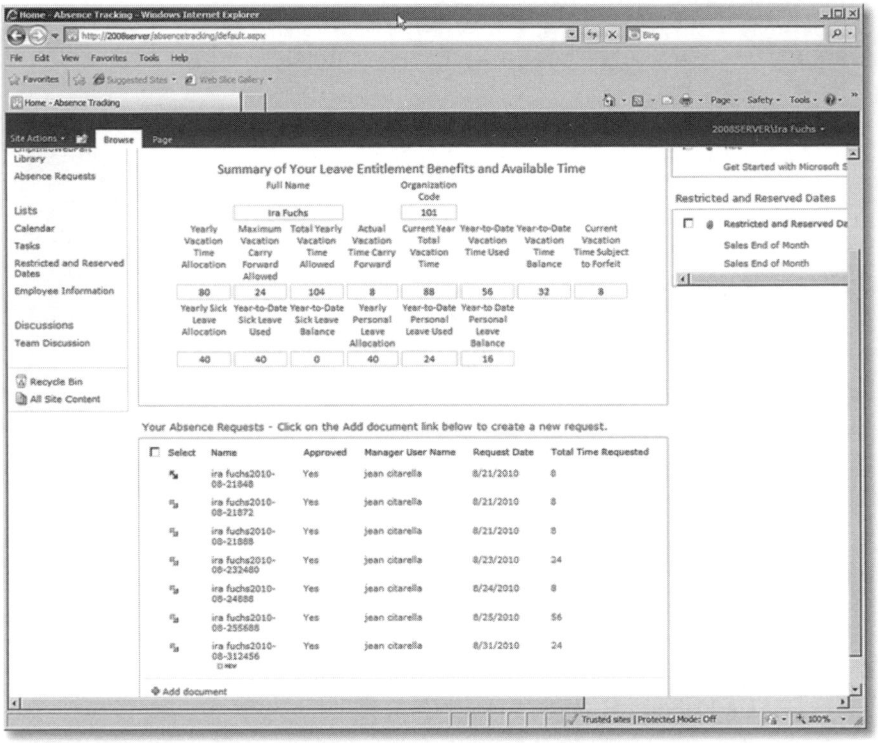

Illustration 518 - The Home Page for the application (to be created)

Open the C:\Inetpub\mailroot\Queue folder. If the workflow completed successfully there will be an email message in the folder as shown in **Illustration 519** below.

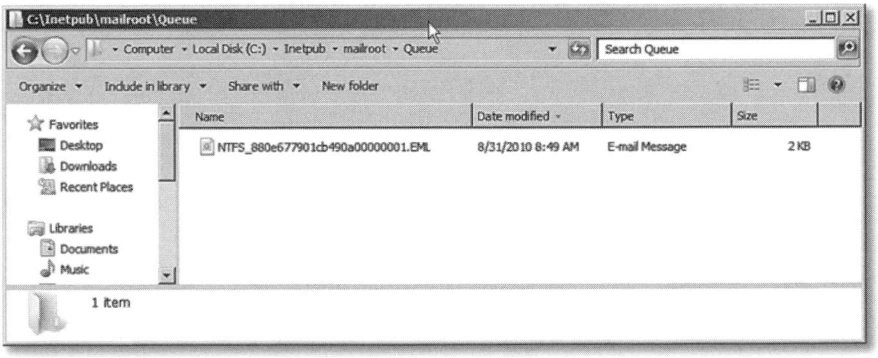

Illustration 519 - Email message generated by the workflow in the SMTP Queue folder

Double-click on the email message to open it in *Outlook* as shown in **Illustration 520** below to see that the values specified in the workflow are present in the email message.

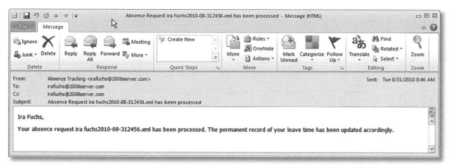

Illustration 520 - The email message generated by the workflow opened in Outlook

Creating the Home Page for the Application

Creating and Configuring the Library, List and Form Components to be Used in the Home Page Web Parts

Now that we have tested the functional logic of the application the last part of our work is to insert and configure Web Parts on the home page so that the application has a portal look and feel to it as shown in **Illustration 518** on the previous page. The design objective here is to create a single page where all the relevant information and transactional functions regarding an employee's leave time entitlements are available.

The following is a description of the Web Parts to be placed on the home page with their respective configuration settings:

> **Content Editor Web Part** – Used to place and format text on a page. No special configuration settings are required for this Web Part.
>
> **Announcement List Web Part** – A Web Part pointing to a standard *Announcements* list with attachments.
>
> **Absence Request Form Library Web Part** – A Web Part displaying a custom list view of the *New Absence Requests* form library that displays only those absence requests created by the current user. The user can create a new absence request directly from this Web Part.
>
> **Restricted and Reserved List Web Part** – This Web Part uses the organization code from the *Absence Request* library Web Part as a filter to display only those restricted and reserved dates applicable to the current user based on the organizational unit they are part of.
>
> **Employee Information InfoPath Web Part** – This is an *InfoPath* Web Part created to display the current user's leave time information and is dynamically updated by the application workflow.

Before we can place these Web Parts we need to first create and configure the *New Absence Requests* form library view that we will use in the home page Web Part as well as the *InfoPath* form used in the Web Part that displays the *Employee Information* ECT list data.

Create and Configure Views for the New Absence Requests Form Library

Configuring the My Documents View

We will remove the link to the *New Absence Requests* form library on the *SharePoint Navigation* pane as we want users to create new requests and access their previously created requests from the application home page. However, managers will have access directly to the form library in order to review those requests that require approval, and in workflow generated emails a link to the request instance is embedded in the body of the email. Consequently although the form library will not be linked to the navigation pane, it will still be indirectly accessible to users. As such we will implement two views of the library, a *My Documents* view and a *Managers View*. The *My Documents* view is a built in view of any list or library and it is simply a view that is filtered using the *[Me]* function. The *My Documents* view will also be used in the Web Part on the home page.

The *Manager's View* filters the library to display only those request where the *User name* of the logged-in user, obtained from the *User Profile Service*, matches the *Manager_User_Name* found in that library column, thus displaying only those requests requiring approval from the logged-in manager.

Go to the *New Absence Requests* form library and click on the drop-down arrow to the right of the breadcrumb link for *All Documents* as shown in **Illustration 521** below.

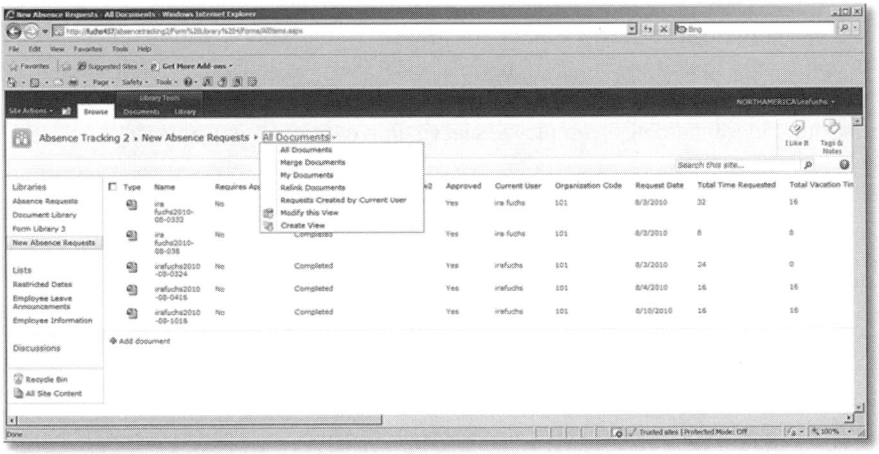

Illustration 521 - Right clicking on the breadcrumb link of the New Absence Request form library

A drop down list of available views will appear. Select **My Documents**. Click on **My Documents** then the **Library tab** and then **Modify View** to display the settings page for the *My Documents* View as shown in **Illustration 522** below.

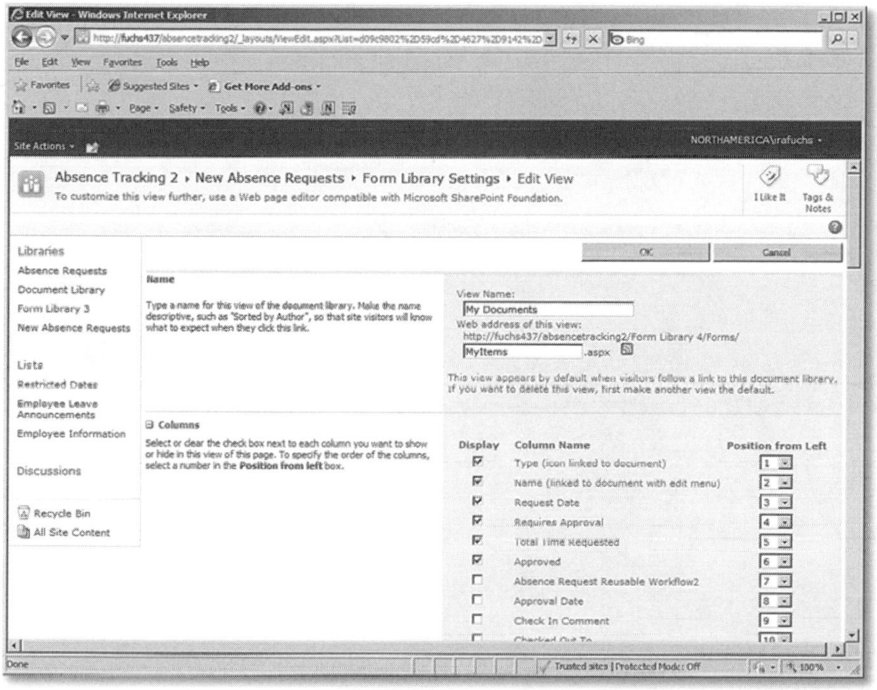

Illustration 522 - The My Documents View edit page of the New Absence Request form library

Select the **Make this the default view check box** and select the **Display check boxes** for the following columns:

> *Type*
> *Name (linked to document with edit menu)*
> *Request Date*
> *Requires Approval*
> *Total Time Requested*
> *Approved*
> *Absence Request Workflow*

You will have to select the *Position from Left* settings and click **OK** more than once to get the column order right.

> **Note** – SharePoint automatically creates a library column for the status of the workflow instance that is associated with the content types bound to the list or library. The name of the column is the same as the workflow instance. If you have more than one workflow associated with a content type a column for each workflow instance will be created.

Scroll down to the *Filter* section of the library settings page and note that the *Created By* field is filtered by the *[Me]* function as shown in **Illustration 523** below.

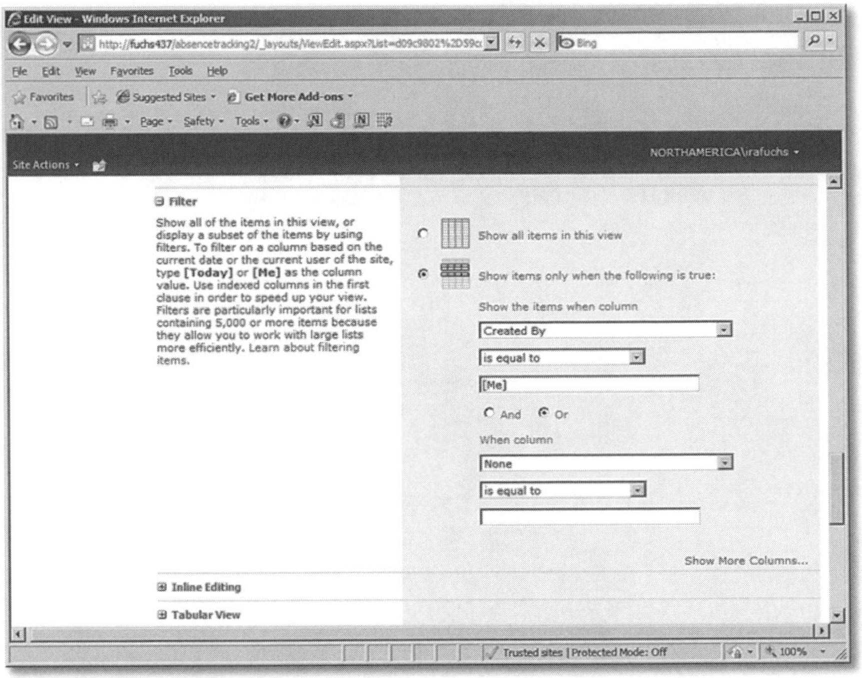

Illustration 523 - Applying the [Me] filter to the Created By column

> **Note** - The *[Me]* function can be applied to any column that uses a *People Picker* control. However, the *[ME]* function will not work on a column containing a string value for the *User Name*.

Click **OK**. The *My Documents* view of the library will display (or select it from the *Current View* drop-down list) as shown in **Illustration 524** below. As you can see only the requests of the current logged-in user are displayed as well as the columns that were selected for this view.

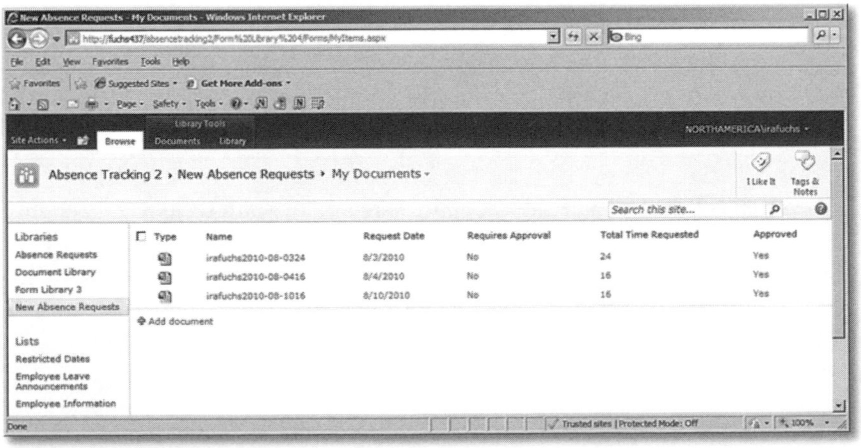

Illustration 524 - The My Documents view now filtered by the current user's identity

Configuring the Managers View of the New Absence Requests Form Library

Click on **Library** from the *Ribbon* and then **Create View**. The *Create View* page will display as shown in **Illustration 525** below.

Illustration 525 - The Create View page

Select **Standard View**. In the *Create View* page enter "Managers View" for the *View Name* and select the following columns to appear in the same order:

> *Type*
> *Name (linked to document with edit menu)*
> *Full Name*
> *Request Date*
> *Requires Approval*
> *Total Time Requested*
> *Approved*
> *Manager User Name*
> *Absence Request Workflow*

Click **OK** when finished. The *Manager' View* page will display as shown in **Illustration 526** below. Note that the requests for all users are displayed as this view is not yet filtered and will display all items in the library.

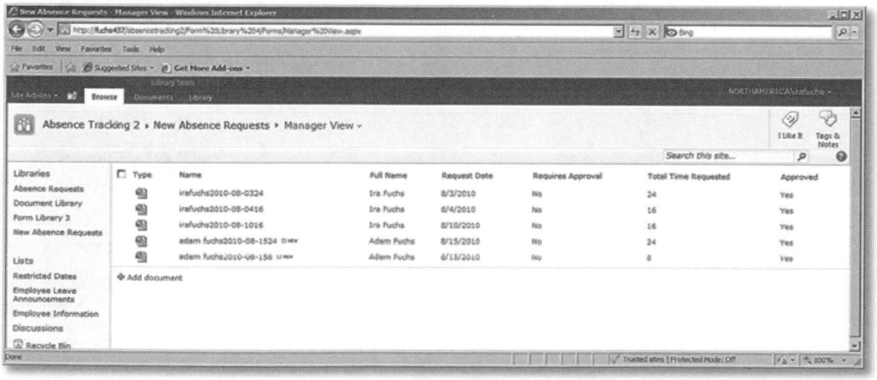

Illustration 526 - The Managers View of the New Absence Requests form library

Using the Current User Filter Web Part on the Managers View

Now we will apply a filter to this view in order to display only those items where the value for *Manager_User_Name* is the same as the *userName* of the current logged-in user. Select **Edit Page** under *Site Actions*. In Edit mode the Web Parts that comprise the page will display as shown in **Illustration 527** below.

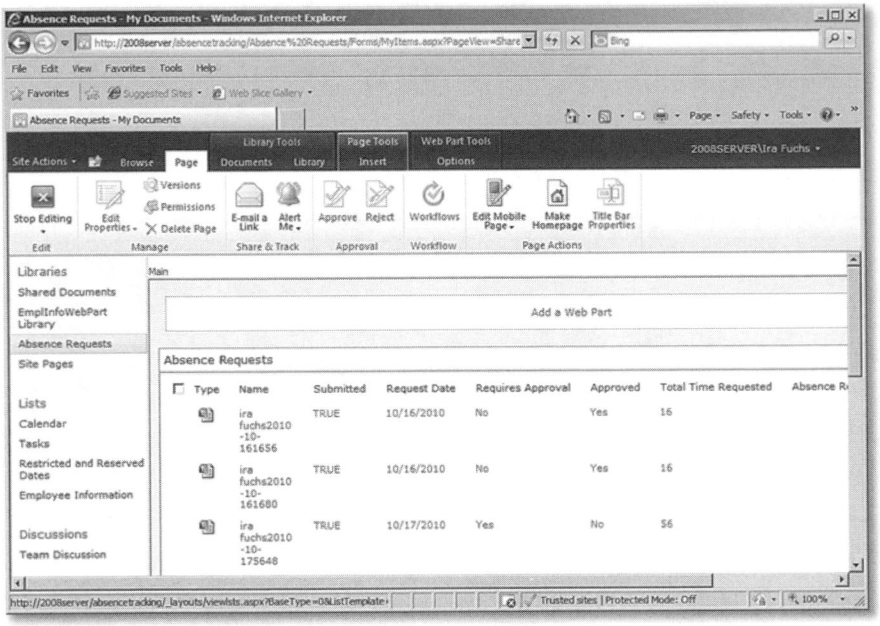

Important Development Note – Every *SharePoint* page is a Web Part page. This includes the *View* pages for any list and library pages. This feature provides a great deal of versatility for building application user interfaces. Any page can be modified directly in the *SharePoint* user interface or in *SharePoint Designer.*

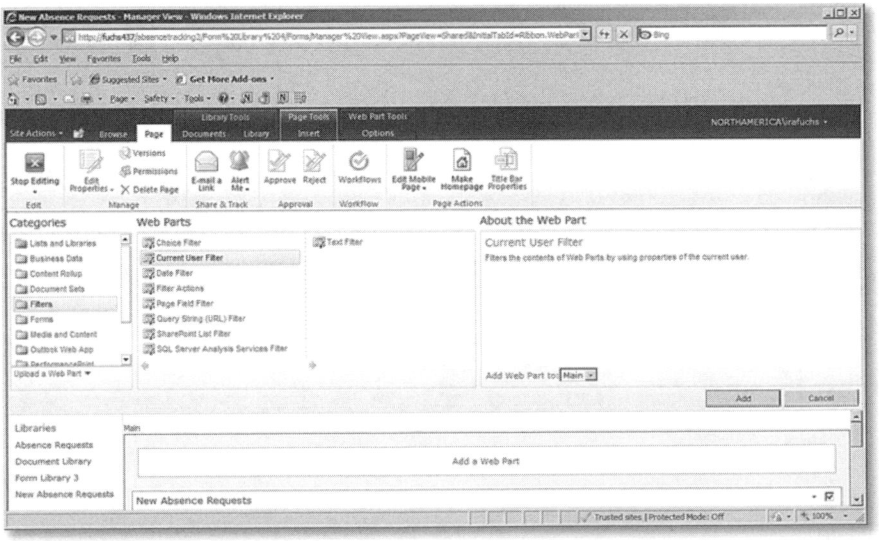

Illustration 527 - The Managers View in Edit mode displaying the underlying page's Web Parts

Click on the **Add a Web Part** link on the top of the page. The *Insert Web Parts View* of the page will display and the *Ribbon* will display the *Web Part Tools tab*. From the *Categories* list select **Filters**. From the *Web Parts* list choose **Current User Filter** and click **Add** as shown in **Illustration 528** at left.

Illustration 528 - Adding the Current User Filter Web Part to the Managers View page

The *Current User Filter* will be inserted on the page. Place your cursor at the top right corner of the Web Part.

The *Web Part Menu icon* [▼] will display. Select it to display the menu as shown in **Illustration 529** below.

Illustration 529 - Clicking on the Web Part Menu icon for a Web Part

Select **Edit Web Part** from the drop-down menu. The *Current User Filter* configuration pane will display as shown in **Illustration 530** below.

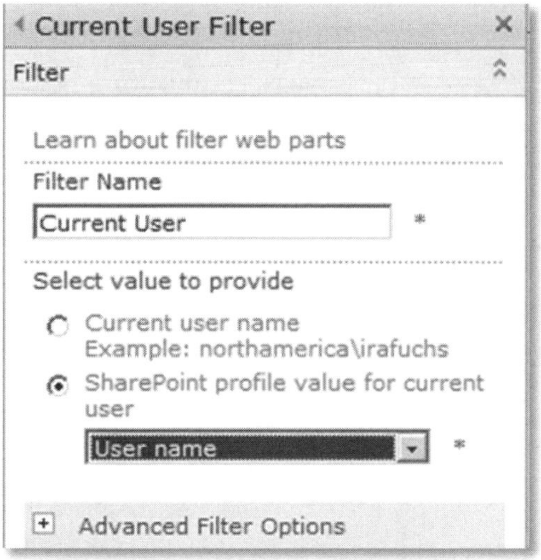

The default value that the *Current User* filter uses is a fully qualified name as in "domain name\username". However the values for *User_Name* and *Manager_User_Name* in the *Employee Information* ECT list, as well as the value produced by the *InfoPath userName* function do not use the domain prefix. Consequently this filter value will not work. Fortunately *SharePoint* provides the option of using additional values from the *SharePoint User Profile Service*. In the beginning of this book we created *SharePoint User Profiles* and this service automatically generates a *User name* value which is only the *username* suffix part of the fully qualified name.

Illustration 530 - The Current User Filter configuration pane

> **Note** – In the section **Accessing SharePoint User Profile Information** starting on page 371 we discuss how to use this service to obtain user context information in different scenarios.

Select the **SharePoint profile value for current user radio button** and from the drop-down list choose **User name**. Click **OK** to close the Web Part configuration pane.

Connecting the Web Parts to Pass Parameters

Click the **Web Part Menu** icon for the *Current User Filter* Web Part again. Choose **Connections**, and then **Send Filter Value To**. The *New Absence Requests* Web Part will display by default as it is the only other Web Part on the page as shown in **Illustration 531** below.

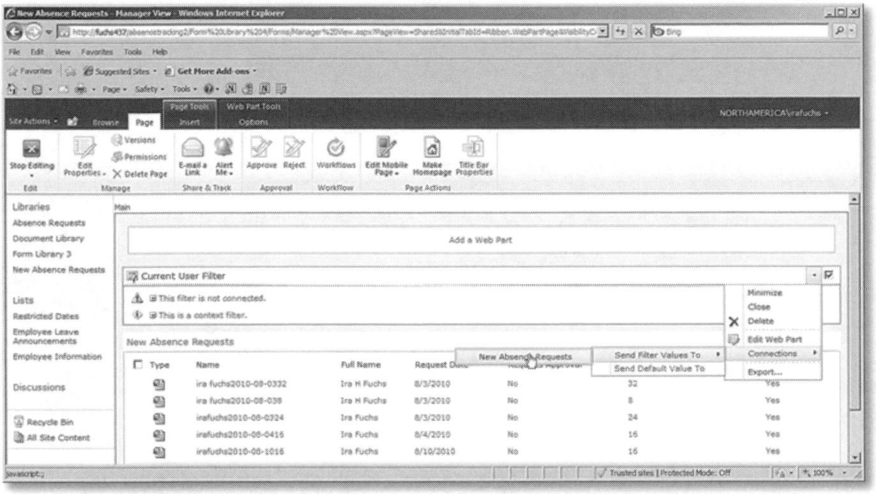

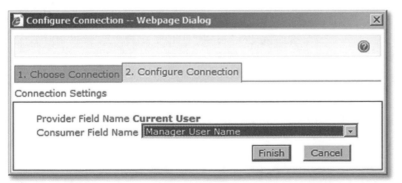

Illustration 531 - Selecting Connections from the Web Part drop-down menu and choosing "Send Filter Value To"

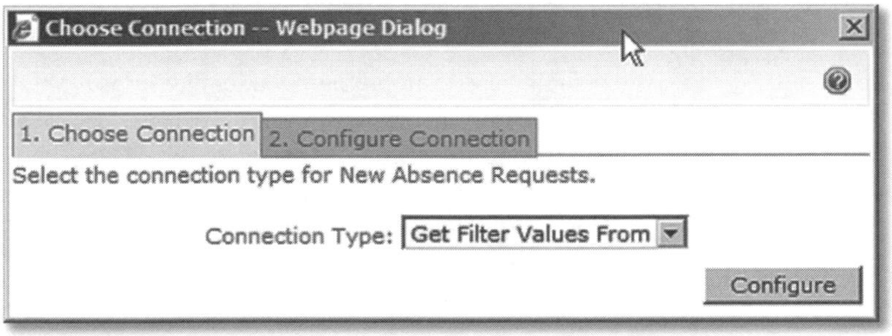

The first screen of the *Choose Connection Wizard* will display as shown in **Illustration 532** at left.

Illustration 532 - The first screen of the Choose Connection Wizard

Select **Get Filter Values From** the *Connection Type* drop-down list. Click the **Configure Button**. The second *Configure Connection* screen will display where you identify the *Consumer Field Name*; that is, the column value in the library that you want to filter with the *User name* value. **Choose Manager User Name** from the drop down list as shown in **Illustration 533** at left.

Illustration 533 - The second screen of the Configure Connection Wizard

Click **Finish** and then **Stop Editing** from the *Ribbon*. Note that now the *Managers View* displays only those absence requests where the logged-in user is the specified *Manager* responsible for approving those requests, as shown in **Illustration 534** below.

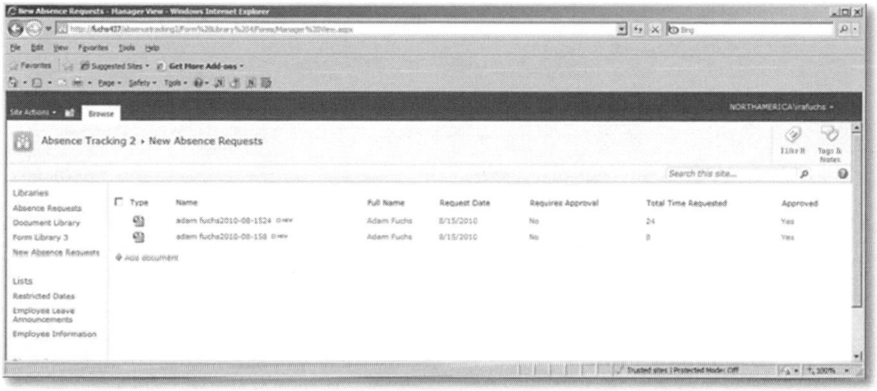

Illustration 534 - The Managers View filtered by the Current User Filter Web Part

Creating a Two-Part Filter for the Restricted and Reserved Dates List to Display Dates Relevant to the Current User

We will be placing a Web Part for the *Restricted and Reserved Dates* list on the application home page and we will also keep the *Navigation pane* link to the list itself. The reason for this is that the Web Part will be configured to display items only; we will disable it from being able to add or modify list items. However we do need to provide editable access to the list to those people authorized to maintain and update it.

Consistent with the overall user-context driven behavior of the application we only want the items relevant to the user to be displayed in this Web Part. To facilitate the selective display of information we will modify the Web Part page for the *Restricted and Reserved Dates* list in the following ways:

- Add a List Web Part to it for the *Employee Information ECT* list. The records in this list identify the *Organization Code* and *User Name* for any given employee.

- Add a *Current User Filter* Web Part. We will use the *User Name* value to filter the Web Part for *the Employee Information ECT* list to display only the record for the current logged in user.

- We will use the *Organization Code* value from the filtered *Employee Information* record to filter the items to display in the *Restricted and Reserved Dates* list.

- We will minimize the *Employee Information ECT List* Web Part and the *Current User Filter* Web Part so they do not display.

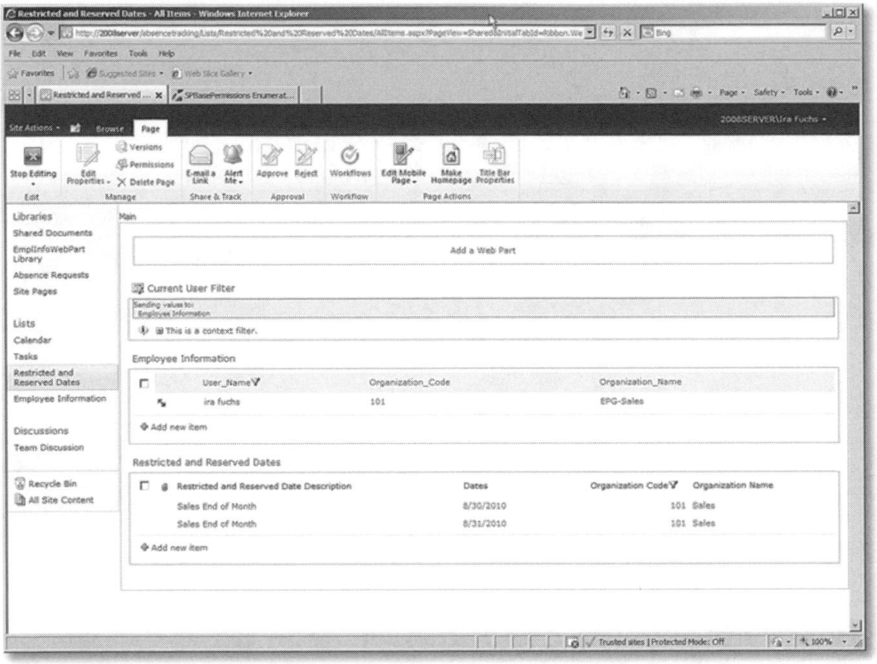

Illustration 535 - the Restricted and Reserved Dates list in Edit mode with the inserted Web Parts

Illustration 535
at left shows the
*Restricted and
Reserved Dates*
list in Edit mode
with the inserted
Web Parts.

Go to the *Restricted
and Reserved
Dates* list and from
Site Actions click
Edit Page. Add
the *List Web Part*
for the *Employee
Information ECT* list.

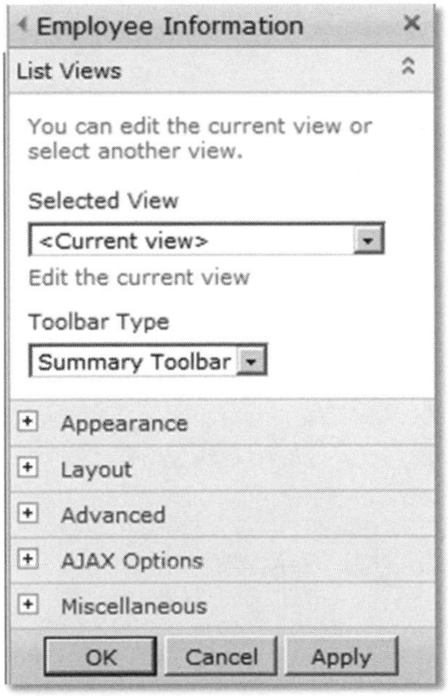

**Illustration 536 - the Employee
Information Web Part configuration pane**

Click on the ⌄ icon and select **Edit Web Part** to display the
Employee Information Web Part configuration pane as shown in
Illustration 536 at left.

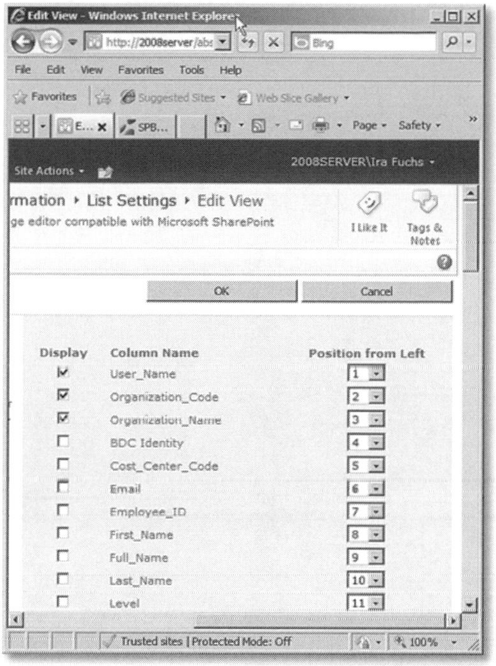

Illustration 537 - The column selection and order for the Web Part Current View for Employee Information ECT list

With the default <*Current view*> selected, click **Edit**. From the list of columns to display select **User_Name, Organization_Code** and **Organization_Name** only and deselect all other columns. **Illustration 537** at left shows the column selection and order for the resultant *Current view* for this Web Part.

Now add the *Current User Filter* Web Part to the page.

Click on the icon and select **Edit Web Part** to display the *Current User Filter* Web Part configuration pane. As we did earlier select **User name** for the *SharePoint profile value* for the current user as shown in **Illustration 538** below.

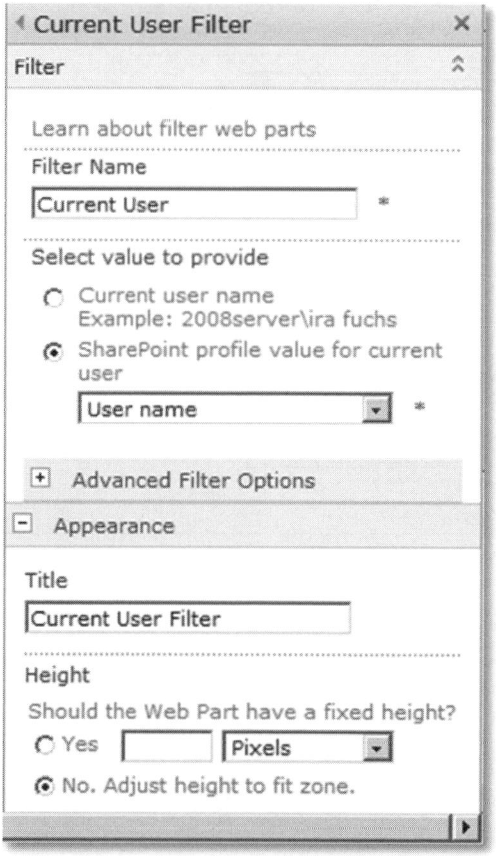

Illustration 538 - Configuration pane for the Current User Filter Web Part with User name selected for the filter value

Select the **Employee Information list Web Part Connections** option and select **Get Filter Values From** and then **Current User Filter** as shown in **Illustration 539** below.

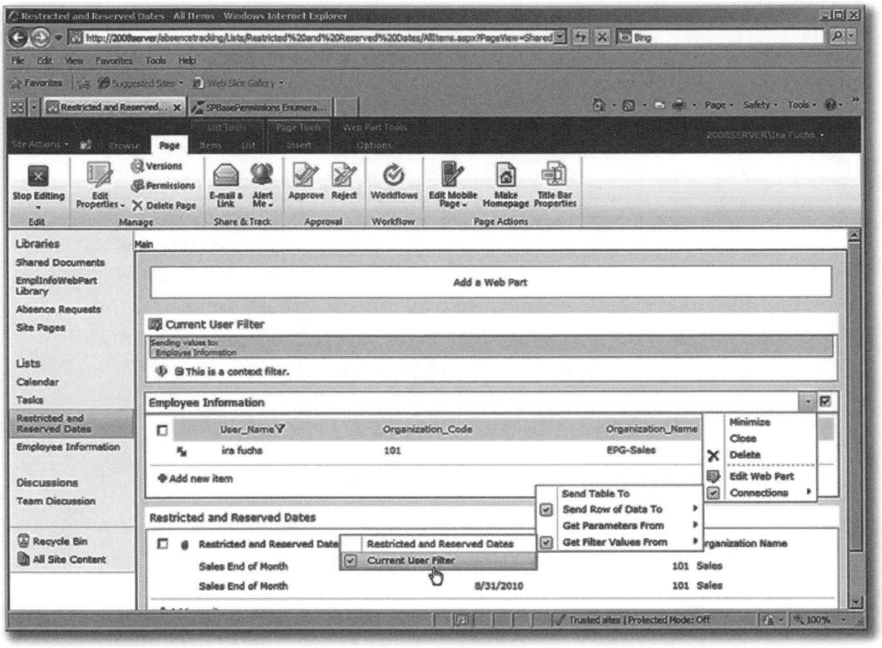

Illustration 539 - Selecting Web Part Connections from the Employee Information list Web Part

In the *Configure Connection* dialogue screen select **User_Name** for the *Consumer Field* as shown in **Illustration 540** below and click **Finish**.

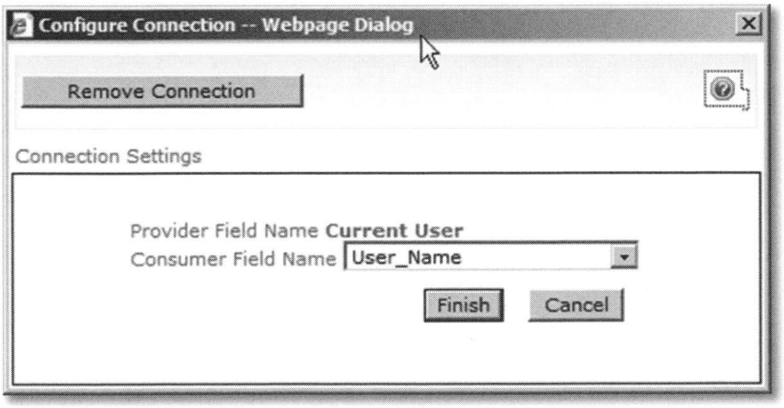

Illustration 540 - Connecting the Current User Provider Field Name with the
User_Name Consumer Field Name

Now select the **Restricted and Reserved Dates list Web Part Connections** option.
Select **Get Filter Values From** and then **Employee Information** as shown in **Illustration 541** below.

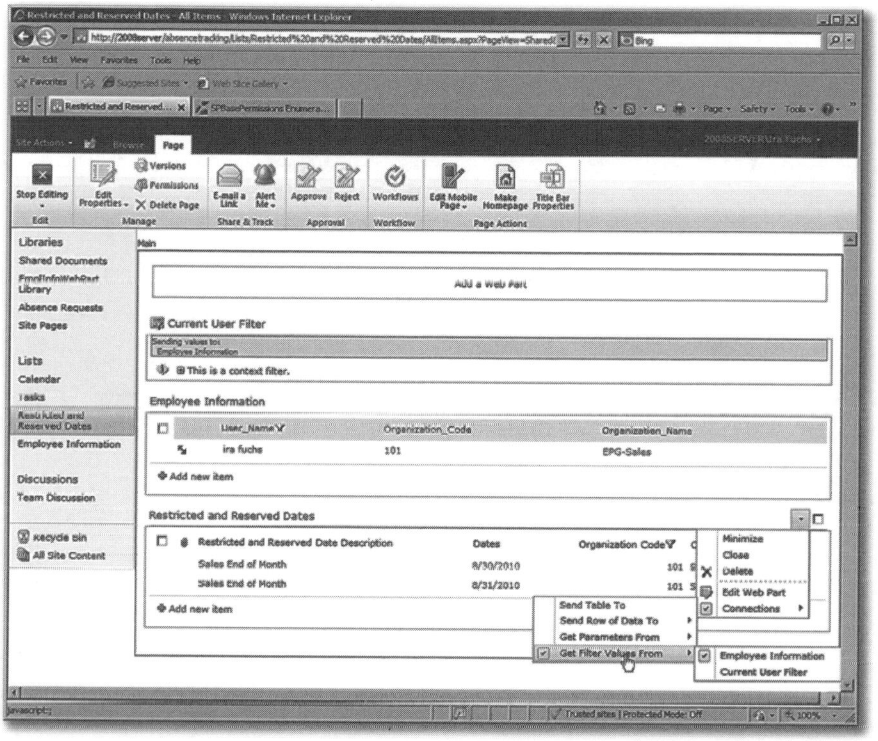

Illustration 541 - Connecting the Restricted and Reserved Dates list Web Part to the
Employee Information list Web Part

In the *Configure Connection* dialogue screen select **Organization_Code** for the *Provider Field* and
Organization Code for the *Consumer Field* as shown in **Illustration 542** below and click **Finish**.

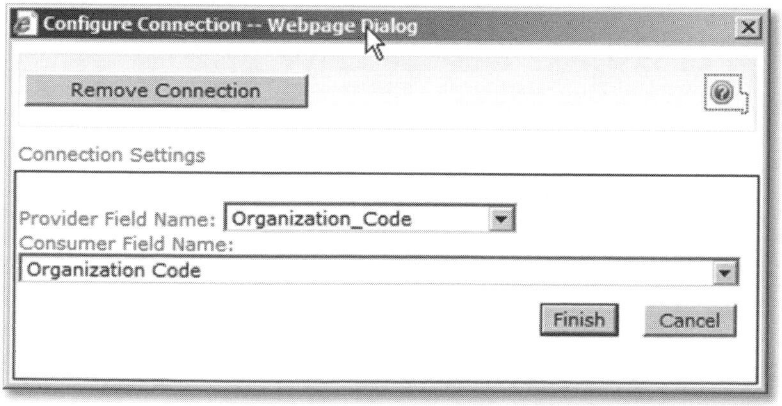

Illustration 542 - Connecting the Organization_Code Provider Field Name
with the Organization Code Consumer Field Name

Now click the **Minimize** option for both the *Current User Filter* and *Employee Information* list Web Parts. Minimizing a Web Part hides it on the page. Click **Stop Editing** from the *Ribbon*. The *All Items* default view of the list will now only display those dates applicable to the organization that the current logged-in user is a member of as shown in **Illustration 543** below.

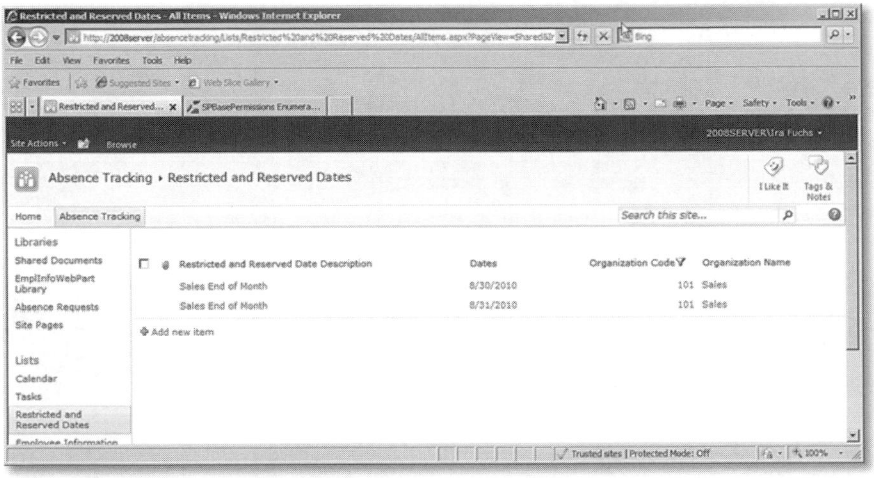

Illustration 543 - The All Items default view displaying those dates applicable to the organization of the current logged-in user

Creating an InfoPath Form to Use as a Web Part to Display Leave Time from the Employee Information ECT List

We are going to return to *InfoPath* now to create the form Web Part for the application home page. This form Web Part will display the information in the *Employee Information ECT* list for time entitlements, time used, and balance of time available in each leave category. The completed design view of the form will look like **Illustration 544** below.

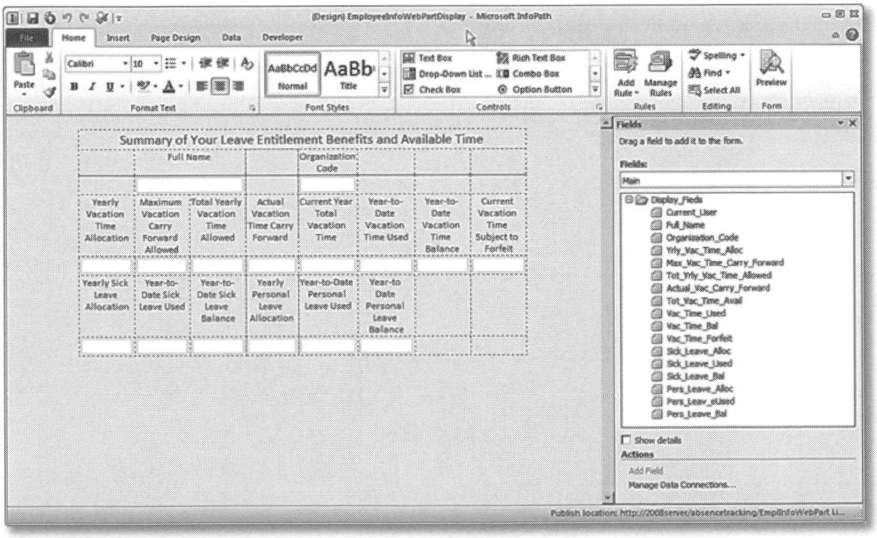

Illustration 544 – The InfoPath form used to display information from the Employee Information database on the application home page

There are three reasons why we want to use an *InfoPath Form Web Part* on the application home page to display this information:

- One, a form allows us to organize and present the information anyway that we want to. If we used a list Web Part to display this information we could create a View for the field-columns we wanted to show, but it would be displayed as a single, long row of information, which is not visually elegant.

- Two, when we created the *Employee Information ECT* we implemented all operations – Create, Read, Update and Delete. We wanted the Create and Update operation in order to create the user records as well as change the values in the records for testing purposes. The Update operation is also a function of the application, but it is executed by the workflow exclusively, not through any user interaction. We do not want any users, including managers, to have access to the *Employee Information* list and as such we will remove it from the navigation pane. The only access to the information in the *Employee Information* list will be through the *InfoPath* form Web Part on the application home page. We will make the form read-only, on the field or view level, and disable all of the *User Interface Options* for the form Web Part.

  Development Note - In anticipation of the possibility that someone inadvertently gets access to the *Employee Information* list we can do two things to limit what they can see and do: assign all users to a group with Read permissions only at the site level, so that they can only view the list, and apply the *[Me]* filter to the default view of the list so that they will only be able to see their own record.

- Three, an *InfoPath Form Web Part* is automatically "opened" when a page loads, no user interaction is required. Combining this feature with *Form Load* rules to auto-populate the form provides a very powerful and versatile information presentation mechanism.

  Development and Pattern Note – Because an *InfoPath* form can aggregate and manipulate information from any number of data sources, an *InfoPath Form Web Part* using *Form Load* rules provides extraordinary opportunities for presenting complex information sets in visually sophisticated ways on a *SharePoint* page.

Creating the Information Set Schema Fields

Open *InfoPath* and create a new blank form. Display the schema *Fields* pane. Right click the **MyFields** root node and select **Properties**. Change the root node name to "Display_Fields" and then add the fields shown in **Illustration 545** at right.

Set the *Data types* for *Current_User* and *Full_Name* to **Text**. Set the *Data types* for the rest of the fields to **Whole Number (Integer)**.

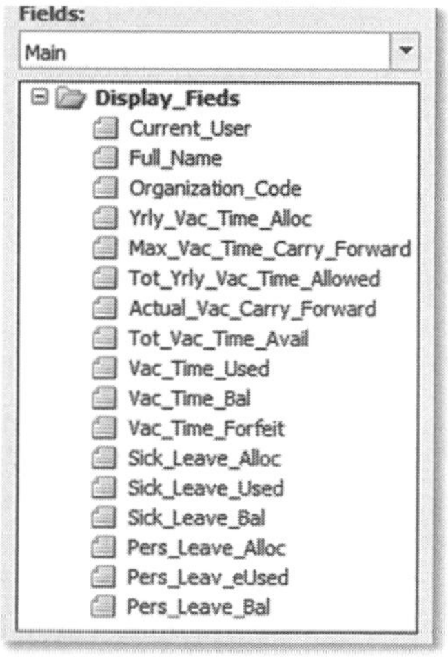

Illustration 545 - The completed information set for the Main data source of the form

Creating the Form Load Rule

The next step will be to create the *Form Load* rule set as shown in **Illustration 546** below.

Illustration 546 - The Form Load rule set that auto-populates the form

This *Form Load* rule set will capture the identity of the current user using the *userName* function and use that identity to set the values in the form fields with the information for *the Employee Information ECT* list for the current user. This is the same rule set we created for the *Absence Request* form.

> **Note** – In the *Set a field's value* actions in the *Absence Request* form we used a filtered lookup that compared the *Current_User* field in the *Main Data Source* to the *User_Name* field in the *Employee Information ECT* list. In this form we have just reversed the syntactic order: the *User_Name* field in the *Employee Information ECT* list is compared to the *Current_User* field of the *Main Data Source*. The logic and result is identical and it was done this way for the purpose of demonstrating the fact that there is flexibility in the rule grammar.

We will walk-through creating the first three actions of the rule set as a refresher to using this technique. There is no condition that has to be evaluated so leave the *Condition* as is.

The first thing we want to do is capture the current user identity and store that in the form. Click **Add** and choose **Set a field's value**. Select the **Current_User** field in the *Main Data source*. For the *Value* select **Insert Function** and choose **userName**. The completed *Rule Details* dialogue screen will look like **Illustration 547** below.

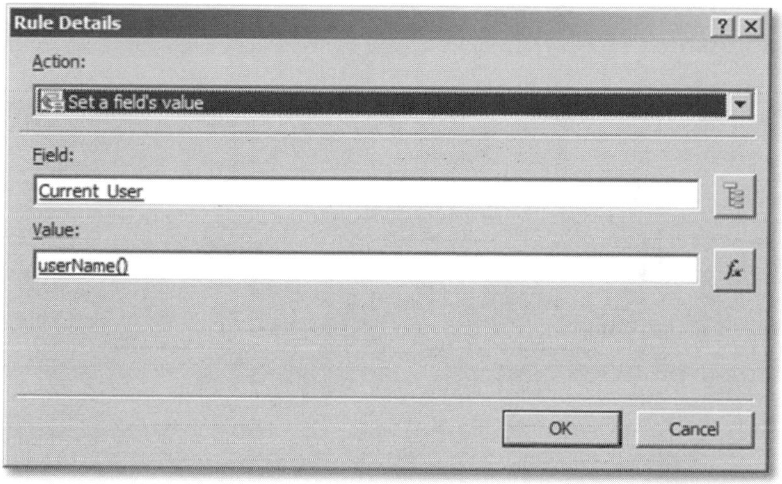

Illustration 547 - Setting the Current_User value using the userName function

Click **OK**. Click **Add** again and choose **Query for data**. In the *Data connection* drop-down list select **Employee Information**. The completed *Rule Details* dialogue screen will look like **Illustration 548** below.

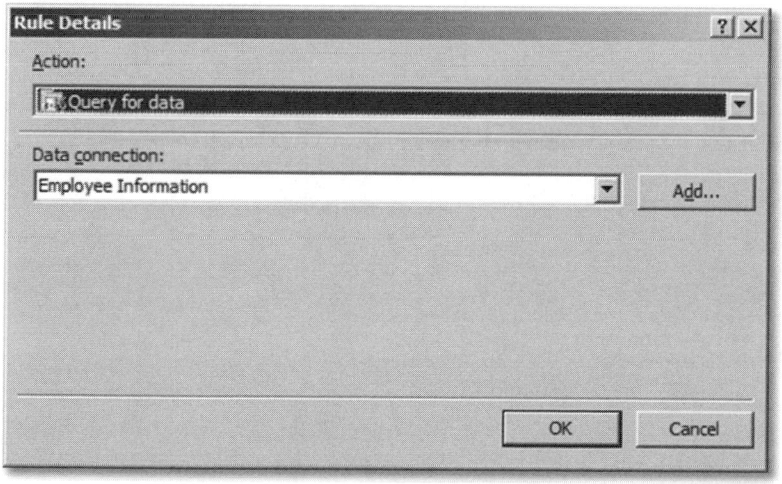

Illustration 548 - Querying the Employee Information database

Click **OK**. Click **Add** and choose **Set a field's value**. Select **Full_Name** in the *Main Data* source for the *Field*. Click the **Formula button** to the right of the *Value* field. In the *Select a Field or Group* dialogue screen choose **Full_Name** from the *Employee_Information Secondary* source as shown in **Illustration 549** below.

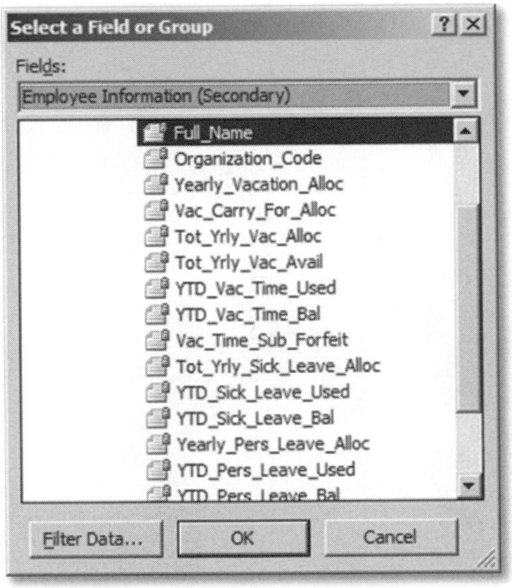

Illustration 549 – Selecting the corresponding field from the Employee Information secondary data source

Click the **Filter Data button** and then the **Add** button. The *Specify Filter Conditions* dialogue screen will display. In the first box select **User_Name** as shown in **Illustration 550** below. This field is coming from the current context data source – the *Employee Information* database. Leave **is equal to** in the operator box.

Illustration 550 - Applying the User_Name = Current_User filter to the lookup

In the third box choose **Select a field or group** and from the *Main Data* source and select the **Current_User** field as shown in **Illustration 551** below.

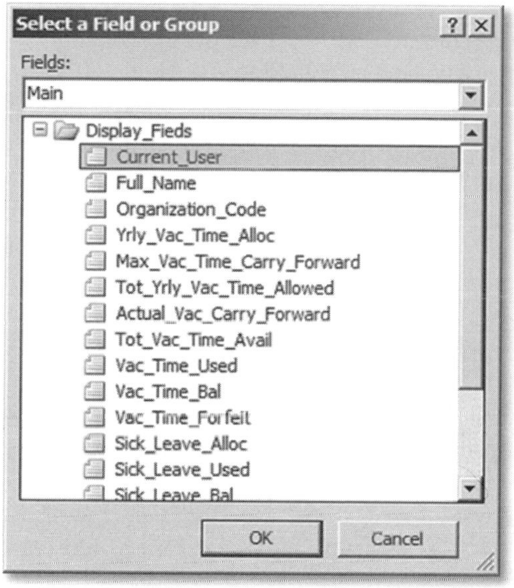

Illustration 551 - Completing the filter condition statement

Click **OK** back four times to go back to the *Rule Details* screen which will look like **Illustration 552** below.

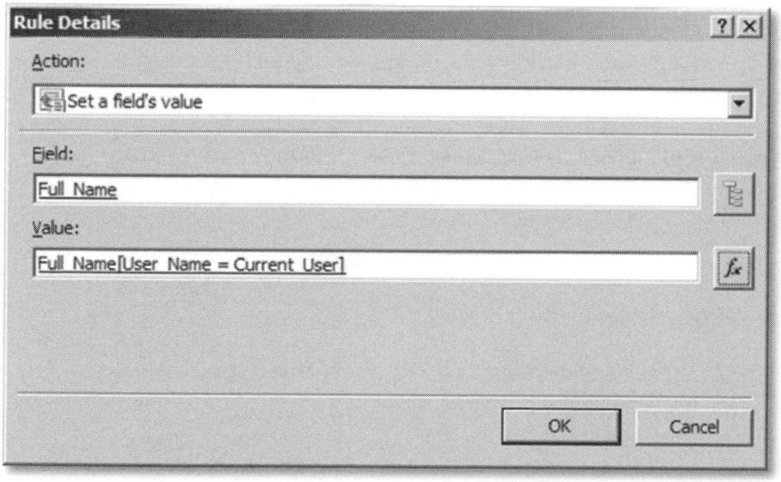

Illustration 552 - Completed Set a field's value Rule Details for Full_Name

Now add a **Set a field's value** action for each of the remaining fields in the form using the same filtered value logic.

Laying Out the Form Table and Controls

When you have finished creating the rule set create a table with 7 rows and 8 columns.

Highlight all of the cells in the first row; right click and select **Merge Cells**. You will now have a single column row. Enter the text "Summary of Your Leave Time Entitlement Benefits and Available Time.

In each of the cells in the fourth and sixth rows enter the field names as shown in **Illustration 553** below.

Summary of Your Leave Entitlement Benefits and Available Time							
	Full Name			Organization Code			
	[ ]			[ ]			
Yearly Vacation Time Allocation	Maximum Vacation Carry Forward Allowed	Total Yearly Vacation Time Allowed	Actual Vacation Time Carry Forward	Current Year Total Vacation Time	Year-to-Date Vacation Time Used	Year-to-Date Vacation Time Balance	Current Vacation Time Subject to Forfeit
[ ]	[ ]	[ ]	[ ]	[ ]	[ ]	[ ]	[ ]
Yearly Sick Leave Allocation	Year-to-Date Sick Leave Used	Year-to-Date Sick Leave Balance	Yearly Personal Leave Allocation	Year-to-Date Personal Leave Used	Year-to-Date Personal Leave Balance		
[ ]	[ ]	[ ]	[ ]	[ ]	[ ]		

Illustration 553 - Layout of the table cells and Text Box controls for the form

Center all the field label text. Make the heading text 14 points, bold and blue. Make the label titles 10 points and blue. Select the entire table; right click and choose **Properties**. Set the width for each column to .75 inch. Set this value once and click **Next Column** to set the same value for all columns.

Highlight the second and third cells in row two; right click select **Merge Cells**. Enter the field name "Full Name". In row three, column five enter the field name "Organization Code". Highlight the second and third cells in row three; right click and select **Merge Cells**.

Binding the Fields to Text Box Controls

Now that we have laid out the structure of the table and entered the field label names we will bind the schema fields to *Text Box* controls and place them in the table cells.

Place the cursor in the merged cell in row three directly below the *Full Name* field title. Now select *Full_Name* in the schema pane, right click on it and choose **Text Box**. The *Text Box* control will automatically be inserted in that cell. Do the same procedure for the remaining fields in the form.

Now select each **Text Box** control that you inserted in the form, right click on it and choose **Text Box Properties**. On the *Text Box Properties* dialogue screen select the **Display Tab**. Select the **Read-only check box** and for *Alignment* choose **Center**. The *Text Box Properties* screen for each Text Box should look like **Illustration 554** below.

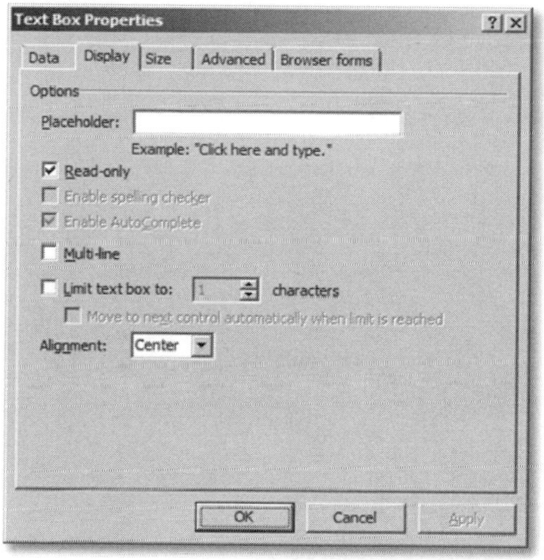

Illustration 554 - The Text Box Properties Display tab

> **Note** – instead of setting each *Text Box* control to *Read-only* you could do the same to the entire View of the form.

Preview the form. It should now display the information from the *Employee Information ECT* list as shown in **Illustration 555** below.

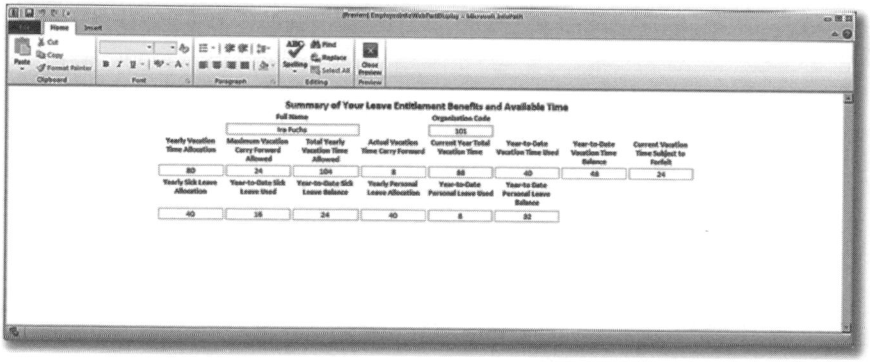

Illustration 555 - Preview of the form successfully auto-populating the fields

Disabling the Form User Interface Options

Important Step – We want to disable all of the *User Interface Options* for the form Web Part. Click on **File** and the **Form Options button**. In the *Web Browser* screen *de-select* the **Show InfoPath commands in Ribbon or tool bar** as shown in **Illustration 556** below.

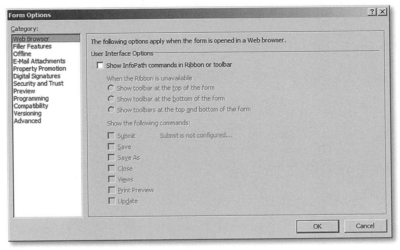

Illustration 556 - Web Browser setting screen in Form Options where Browser user interface options are disabled

Click **OK**. This completes the form and the next step is to publish it to a form library. Save the form template with the name "EmployeeInfoWebPartDisplay".

Publishing the Form to a Form Library

We will have *InfoPath* create the form library for us using the *Publishing Wizard*. From the **File** menu select **Publish** and choose the **SharePoint Server button**. In the first *Publishing Wizard* screen enter the address of the site as shown in **Illustration 557** below.

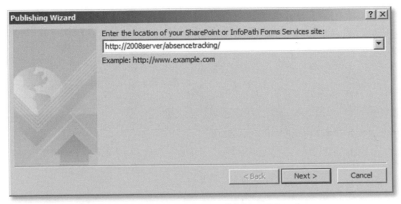

Illustration 557 - The first screen of the form Publishing Wizard

Click **Next** to go to the next page of the *Publishing Wizard* as shown in **Illustration 558** below. Check the **Enable this form to be filled out by using a browser check box**. Select the **Form Library radio button**.

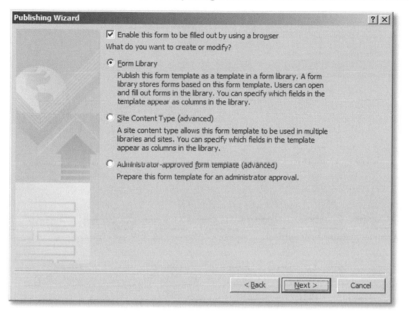

Illustration 558 - The second screen of the form Publishing Wizard

Click **Next** to go to the next page of the *Publishing Wizard*.
Select the **Create a new form library radio button** as shown in **Illustration 559** below.

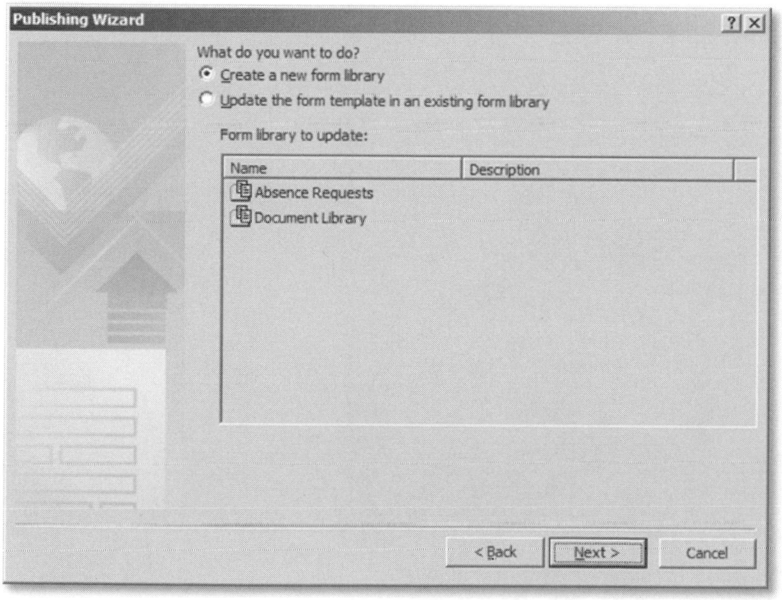

Illustration 559 - The third screen of the form Publishing Wizard where a new form library is created

Click **Next** for the screen where you will enter a *Name* for the library as shown in **Illustration 560** below. Name the form library "EmployeeInfoWebPartDisplay Form Library – Do Not Delete".

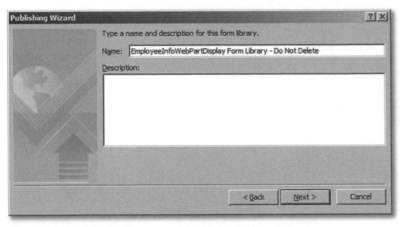

Illustration 560 - The fourth screen of the form Publishing Wizard

Click **Next** again to go to the final *Publishing Wizard* screen where you specify which fields in the form will be used to populate the library's columns.

We are not using this library for any functional purpose other than as a location where the form template is stored. As such *we do not want to display* any information in this library so *no* fields are selected to display as columns as shown in **Illustration 561** below.

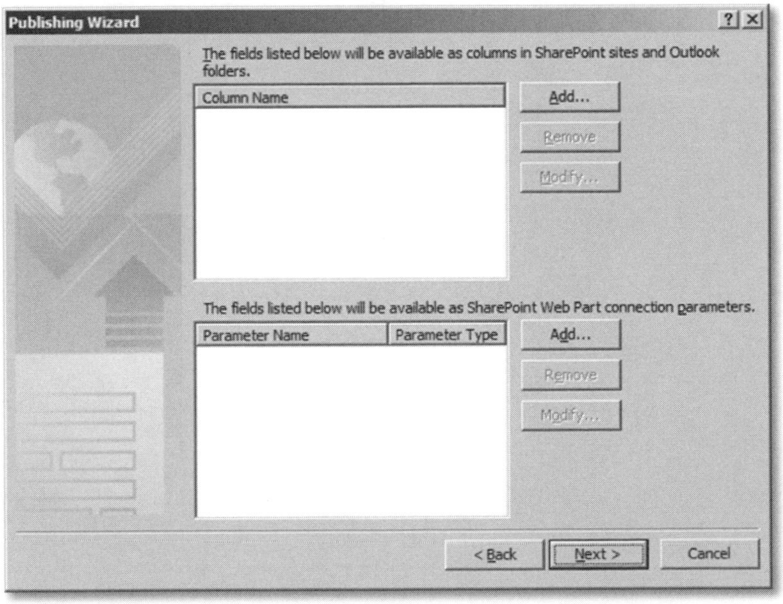

Illustration 561 - The fifth screen of the form Publishing Wizard where no fields are selected to become form columns

Click **Next** to finish the process of publishing the form template and creating the form library.

When the *Publishing Wizard* completes open the form library which will look like **Illustration 562** below.

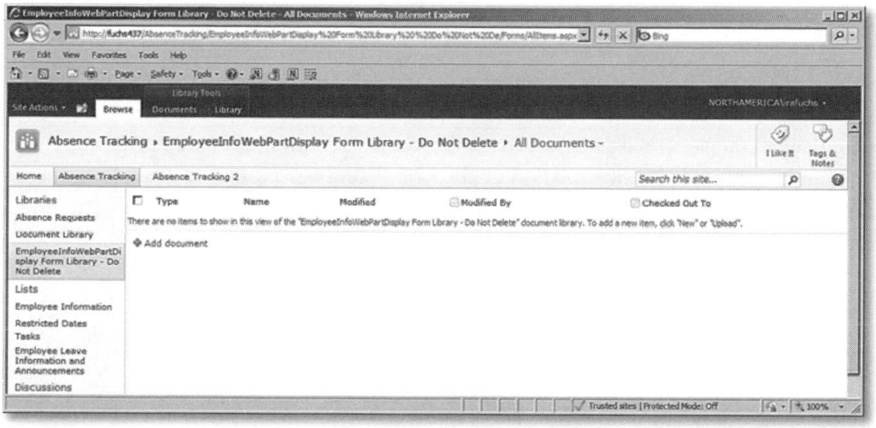

Illustration 562 - The EmployeeInfoWebPartDisplay form library

Click on the **Library button** on the *Ribbon* and then click on the **Library Settings button**. Click on the **Title, description and navigation** link on the *Form Library Settings* page to display the *General Settings* page for the library. Select the **No radio button** for the *Display this document library on the Quick Launch* setting.

Creating and Configuring the Application Home Page Web Parts

Now that we have created and published the *InfoPath* form and configured the views for the *Absence Requests* library and *Restricted and Reserved Dates* list we can insert and configure the corresponding Web Parts for these on the application home page.

Go to the *Absence Tracking site home page*. Click on **Site Settings** on the top left of the page and choose **Edit Page.** The *Site home page* will display in Edit mode as shown in **Illustration 563** below. Clicking on **Page** on the *Ribbon* will also display the *Page Edit Ribbon* menu where you can click **Edit Page** to work in Edit mode.

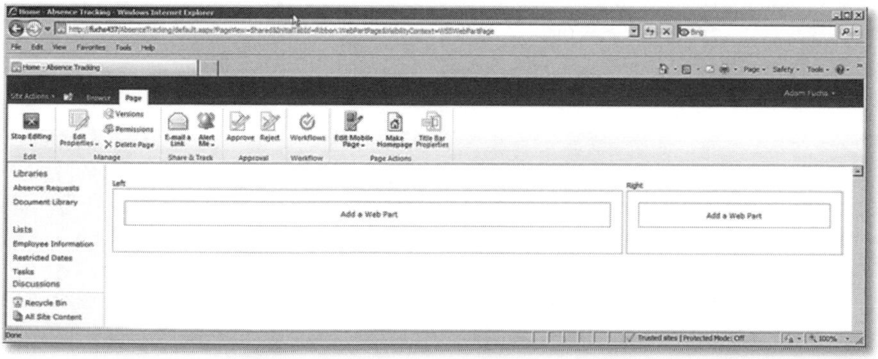

Illustration 563 - The Absence Tracking site home page in edit mode

We are going to simply insert Web Parts on this page and configure them to display the relevant information. We are not going to modify the underlying theme or branding of the page. As such we will work directly in the *SharePoint* user interface.

Inserting and Configuring a Content Editor Web Part

Click on the left **Insert a Web Part** rectangle. The *Ribbon* context will change to *Page Tools>Insert* and the *Insert Web Part* panes will display as shown in **Illustration 564** below. The *Categories* pane displays folders of the Web Parts in each functional category, and the *Web Parts* pane shows the available Web Parts in the selected category. The *About the Web Part* pane provides information about the selected Web Part.

From here you can also select the left or right zone for insertion. Select the different category folders to view the variety of Web Parts that are available out-of-the box. In addition you can upload commercially available Web Parts or create your own.

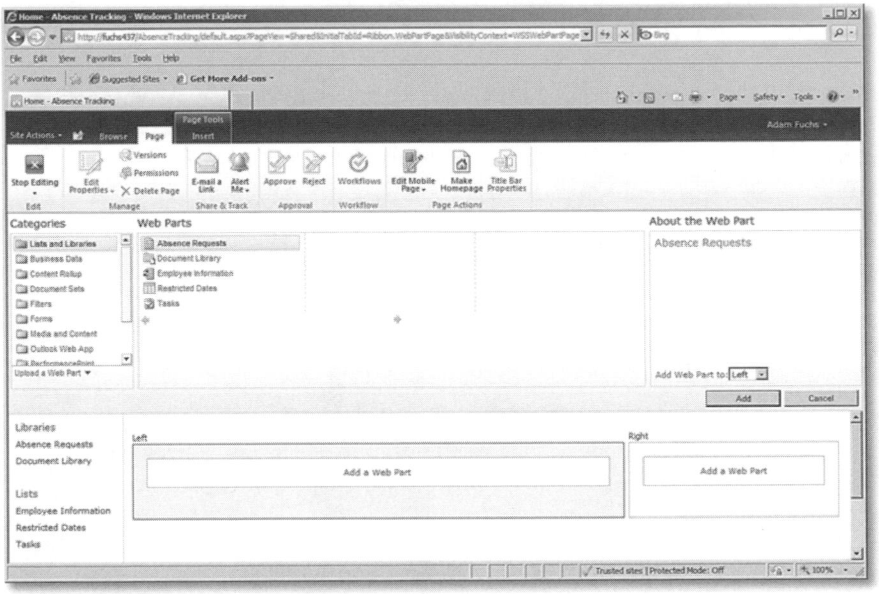

Illustration 564 - The *Insert Web Part* panes will display when Add a Web Part is clicked

Select the **Media and Content** Web Part category and choose the **Content Editor** Web Part. Click the **Add** button and the Web Part will be inserted in the left column. Click on the **Content Editor** link to begin entering text as shown in **Illustration 565** below.

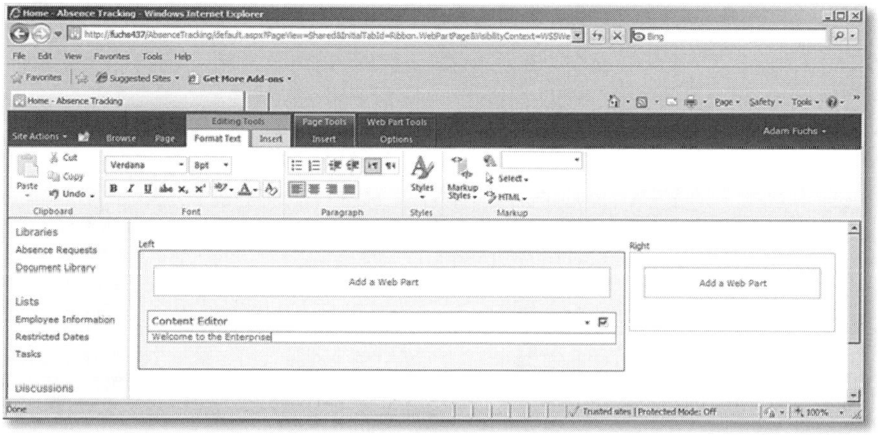

Illustration 565 - Adding a Content Editor Web Part to the page

The *Ribbon* context changes automatically and activates the *Editing Tools>Format Text Ribbon* options. Enter the text "Welcome to the Enterprise Employee Absence Tracking Application" into the Content Editor Web Part. Center the text and make it 18 point Verdana.

Right click on the **web part configuration icon** and select **Edit Web Part** from the drop-down menu as shown in **Illustration 566** below.

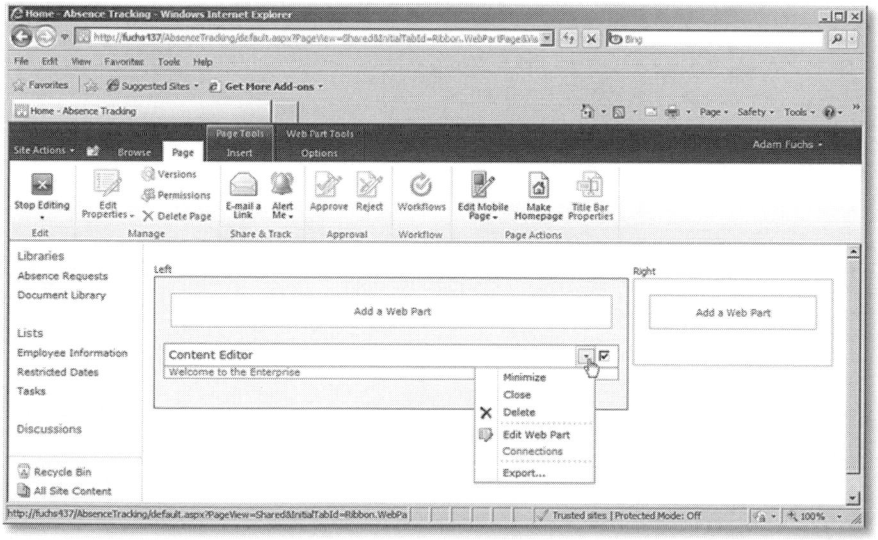

Illustration 566 - Selecting the Edit Web Part option from the web part configuration drop-down menu

Note that one of the drop-down options is *Export*. After editing any Web Part you can save it for reuse on any other SharePoint site page.

Development Note - Component composition, extensibility, reuse and interchangeability has been the holy grail of software development for as long as there has been software. What has prevented truly modular development frameworks from being actualized is the abstraction level of the components. They have existed on too low a level, usually in the form of procedural code that is typically not well documented. What makes *SharePoint* a viable platform for functional reuse and application composition is that the components created in it exist at a higher abstraction level; while functionally complex and sophisticated, they are transparently understandable and usable.

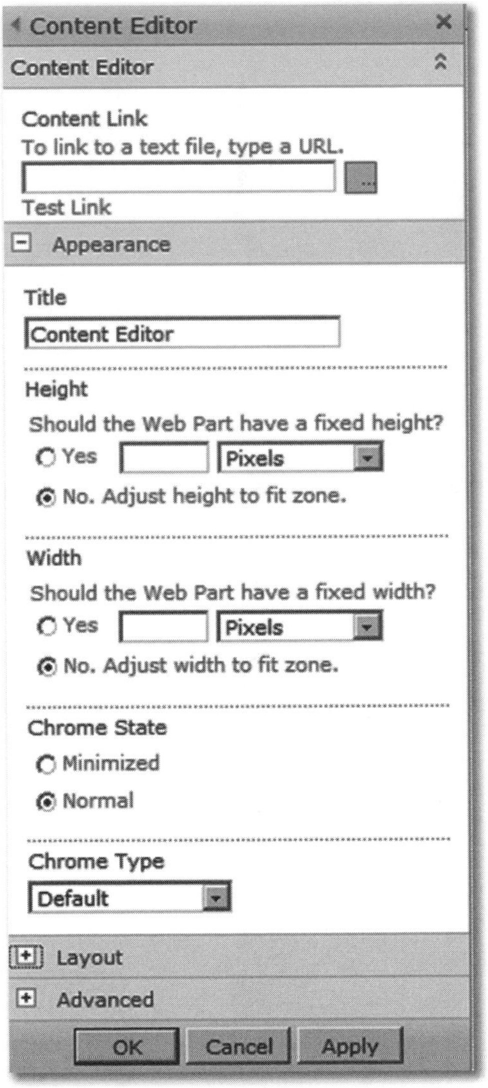

The configuration pane for *the Content Editor* Web Part will display as shown in **Illustration 567** at left. Expand the *Appearance* tab to display the *Appearance* configuration options.

Delete "Content Editor" from the *Title* box and click **OK**.

Create a generic *Announcements* list and name it "Employee Leave Information and Announcements".

Click on **Add a Web Part** on the Right column. Select the **Employee Leave Information and Announcements** Web Part. Right click on the **web part configuration icon** and select **Edit Web Part**. The configuration pane will display. Leave the <*Current view*> for the *Selected View* and choose **No Toolbar** for the Toolbar Type.

Illustration 567 - The configuration pane for the Content Editor Web Part

We are applying this setting because we do not want anyone to be able to change the text in the *Content Editor* Web Part. Click **OK**. The home page should look like **Illustration 568** below.

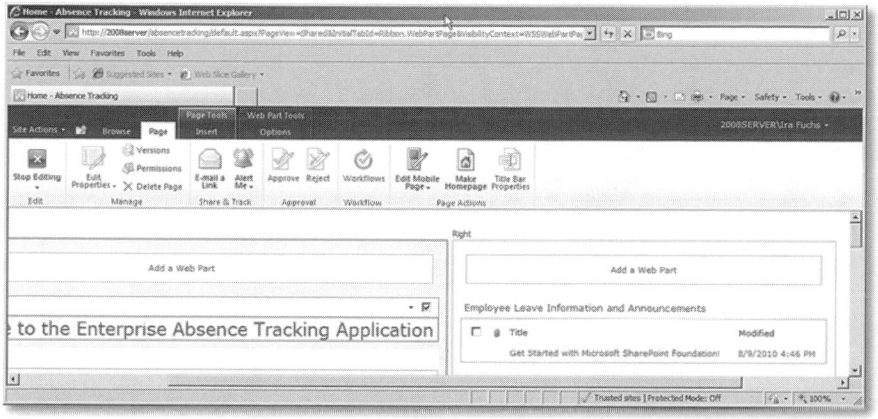

Illustration 568 - The application home page with the Content Editor and the Announcements Web Parts

Inserting and Configuring the New Absence Requests Form Library Web Part

The next Web Part we will add to the application home page is the *New Absence Requests form library* Web Part. Click **Add a Web Part** from the left column. The *Web Part p*anes will display again at the top of the page. Select **List and Libraries** from the *Categories* list and **New Absence Requests** from the *Web Parts* list. Click the **Add** button. The *New Absence Requests* form library Web Part will be inserted above the *Content Editor* Web Part as shown in **Illustration 569** below.

Illustration 569 – Adding the New Absence Requests form library Web Part to the application home page

Place your cursor next to the *New Absence Requests* title and with the right mouse button pressed down drag the Web Part below the *Content Editor* Web Part. The *New Absence Requests form library* Web Part will now be positioned below the *Content Editor* Web Part as shown in **Illustration 570** below.

Note that the Web Part displays the fields from the default *All Documents* view, not the *My Documents* view. That is because we have not yet configured the Web Part to display this view.

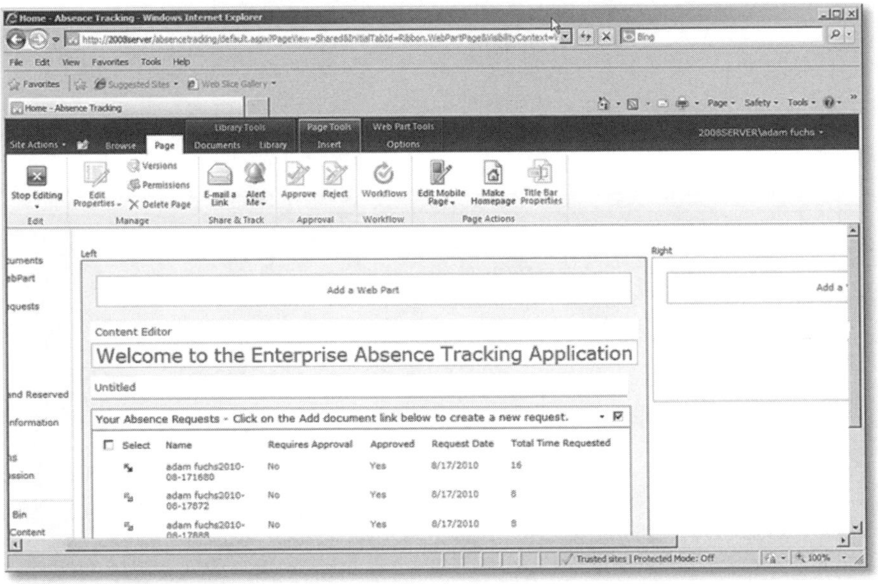

Illustration 570 - Moving the New Absence Requests form library Web Part below the Content Editor Web Part

On the top right of the *New Absence Requests* Web Part click on the **web part configuration icon** and choose **Edit Web Part**. The *List Views Configuration Pane* will display. From the *Selected View* drop-down list choose the **My Documents View**.

For the *Toolbar Type* choose **Full Toolbar**. Expand the *Appearances* tab. In the *Title box* enter "Your Absence Requests - Click on the Add document link below to create a new request."

Change the width of the Web Part to "6.9 Inches". The Web Part configuration pane should look like **Illustration 571** below.

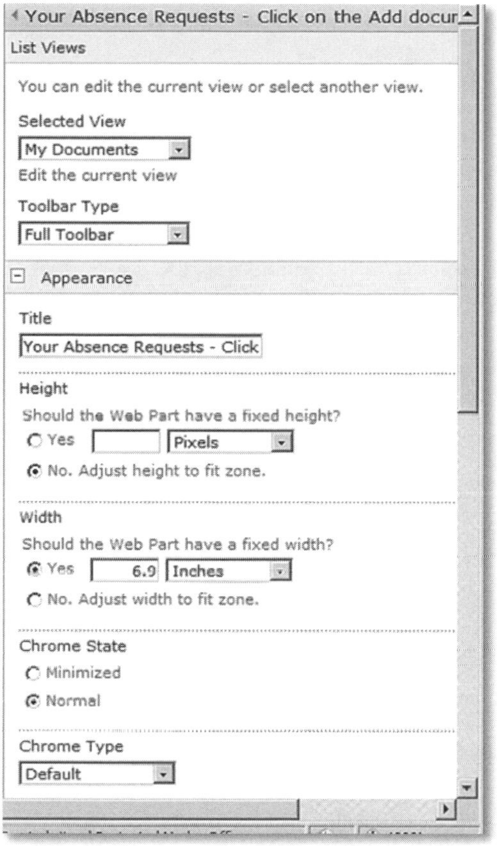

Illustration 571 - The configuration pane for the Absence Requests form library Web Part

Click **OK**. Note that all the columns in the *My Documents View* are displayed in the Web Part. However, we only want the following columns to display in this Web Part:

> *Name*
> *Requires Approval*
> *Approved*
> *Request Date*
> *Total Time Requested*

Open the *New Absence Requests Web Part configuration pane* again. Note that the *Selected View* now displays "*<Current view>*" as shown in **Illustration 572** below. This is because the view specified initially provides the starting point for the *Selected View* information displayed in the Web Part for the list. The default *Selected View* **will always be** the *<Current view>*.

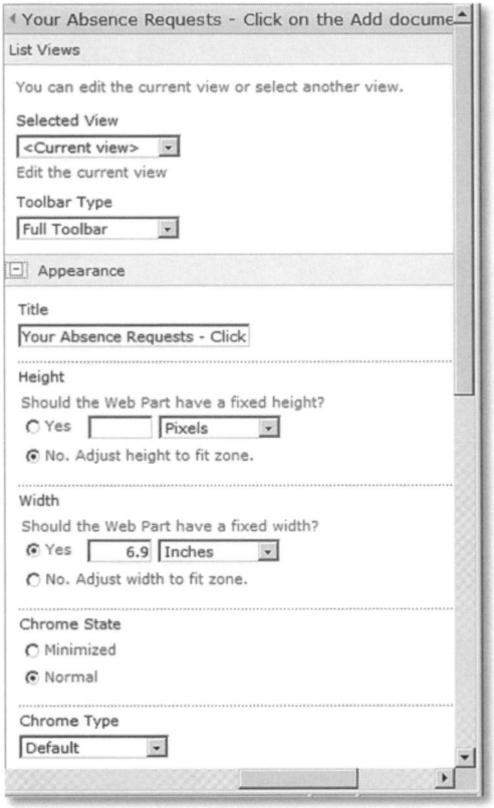

Illustration 572 - The configuration pane for the Absence Requests form library Web Part showing the default <Current view> Web Part view

Click on **Edit the current view** to display the *Edit View*. From here you can modify the view settings *just for* the Web Part view. De-select all the columns except the ones itemized above. Note that the *[Me]* filter is still applied to the *Created By* column. Click **OK**. Now only these columns will display in the *Current view*. Go to the *Absence Requests* library and note that all the original columns in the *My Documents* view are still displaying.

Important Note – an intermittent bug occurs when the default *Summary Toolbar* setting is used with a form library Web Part. Instead of the form opening when you click on *Add documents* from the Web Part the *Upload Document* dialogue will display as shown in **Illustration 573** below. The *Add document* form open action behaves properly when the *Full Toolbar* setting is used.

Illustration 573 – Incorrect New Document dialogue screen that displays when the default Summary Toolbar setting is used with a form library Web Part

Click **OK** to close the Edit Web Part pane and click the **Stop Editing** button on the Ribbon. The application home page will now look like **Illustration 574** below.

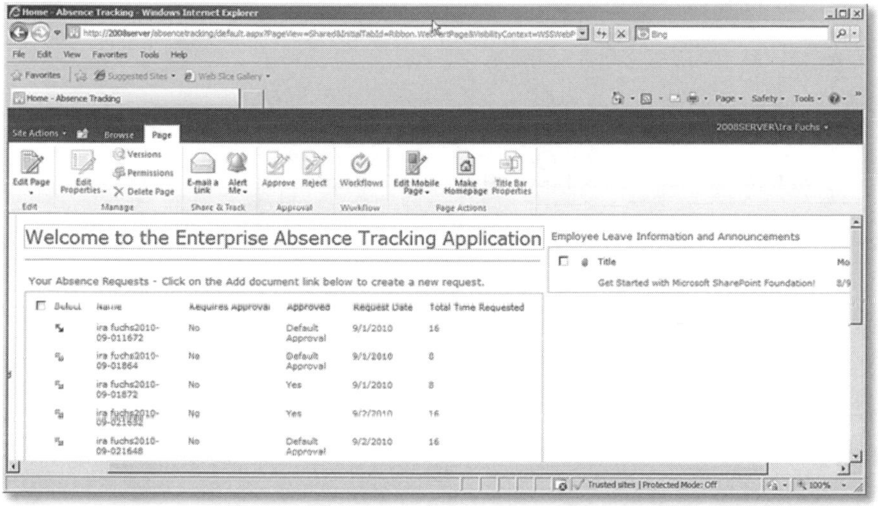

Illustration 574 - The application home page with the Absence Requests form library Web Part added

Inserting and Configuring the InfoPath Form Web Part

Click **Edit Page** again and then click **Add a Web Part**. From the *Categories* pane select **Forms**. In the *Web Parts* pane choose **InfoPath Form Web Part.** With the *Add Web Part to Left* setting selected click the **Add** button. The *InfoPath Form Web Part* will appear on the page as shown in **Illustration 575** below.

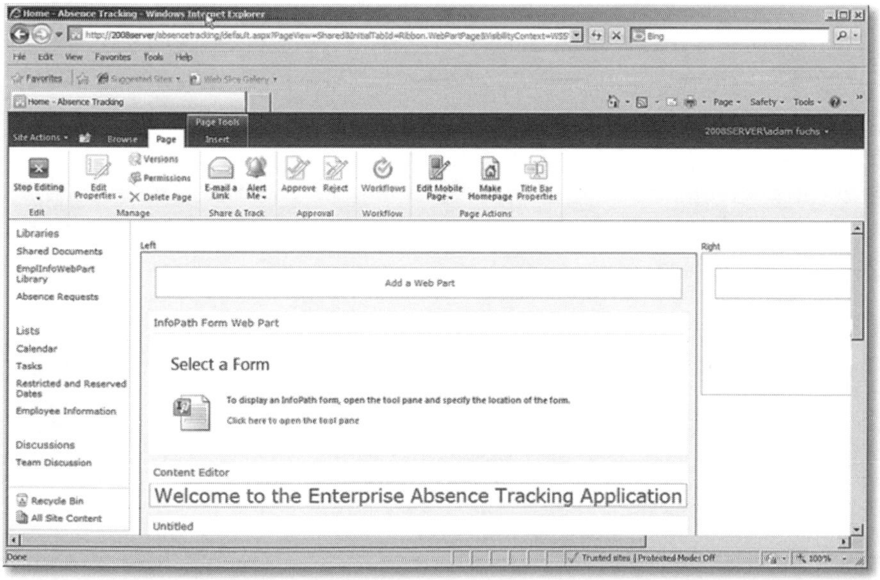

Illustration 575 - The application home page with the InfoPath Form Web Part added

The Web Part needs to be bound to the *InfoPath* form that we just created but before we do that drag the *InfoPath Form Web Part* below the *Content Editor Web Part* and above the *Absence Requests* form library Web Part as shown in **Illustration 576** below.

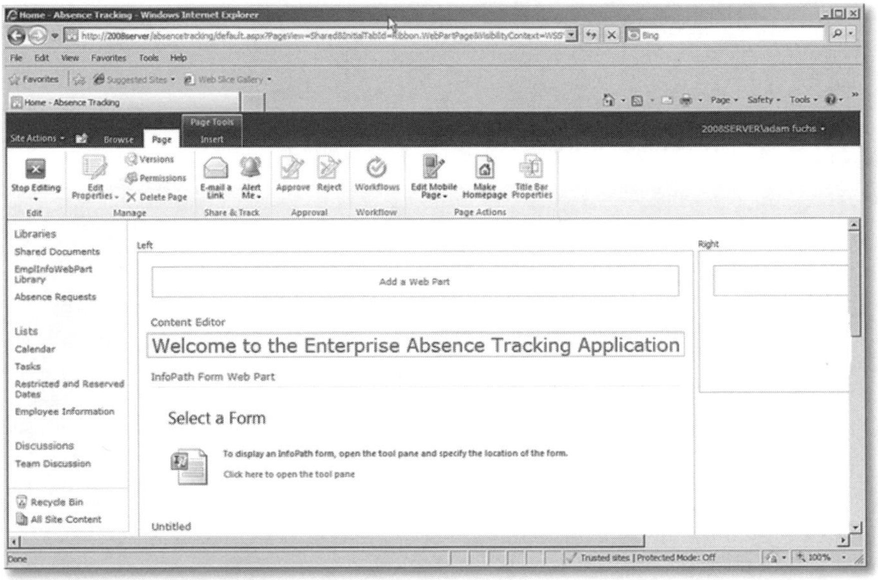

Illustration 576 - The InfoPath Form Web Part moved below the Content Editor Web Part and above the Absence Requests form library Web Part

Click on the **web part configuration icon** [▼] and choose **Edit Web Part** to display the
Web Part configuration pane for the *InfoPath Form Web Part* as shown in **Illustration 577** below.

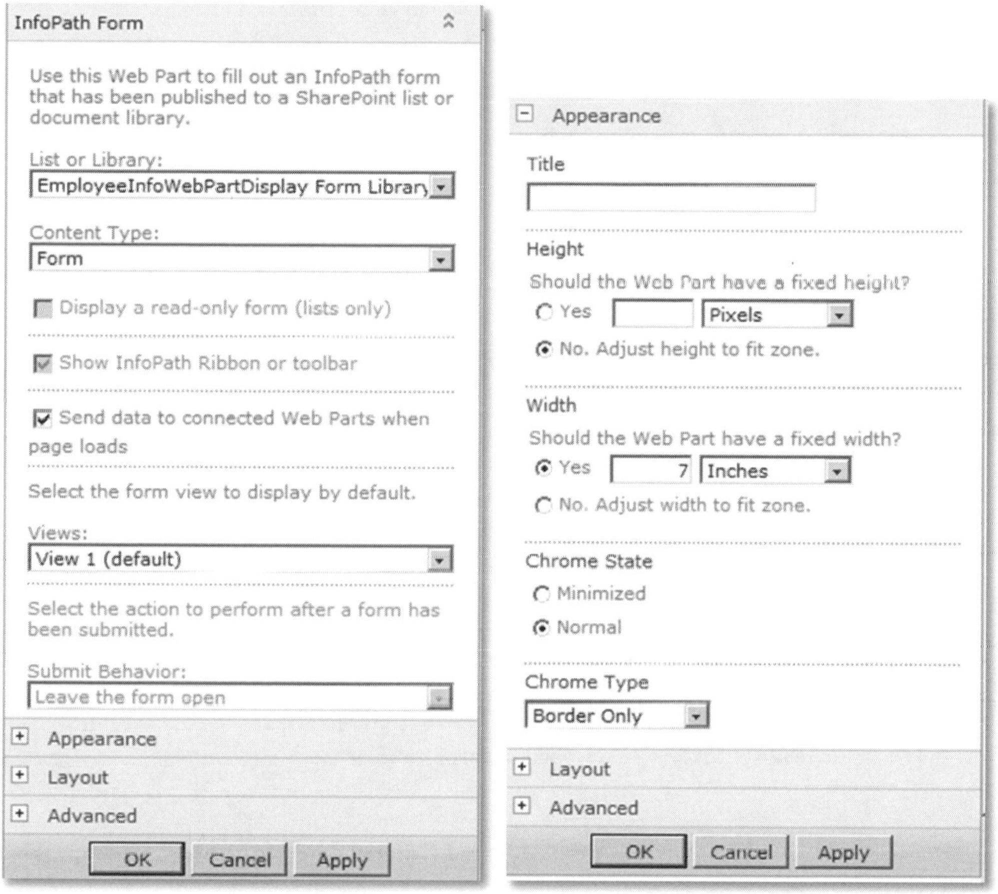

Illustration 577 - The Web Part configuration pane for the InfoPath Form Web Part

In the *List or Library* drop-down list select the **EmployeeInfoWebPartDisplay Form Library**. Expand the
Appearance tab. Delete the default Title text and leave it blank. Change the width of the Web Part to 8 inches
and in the *Chrome Type* drop-down list select **None** as shown in **Illustration 577** above. Click **OK**.

The *InfoPath Form Web Part* displaying the *Employee Information* database record for the current logged in user will now display in the Web Part as shown in **Illustration 578** below.

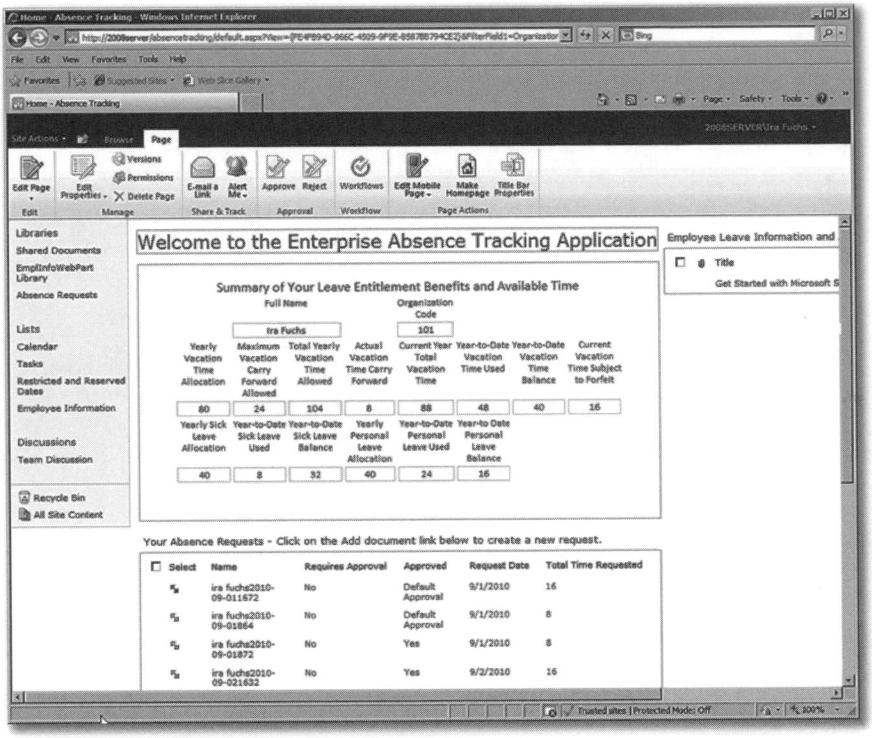

Illustration 578 - The EmployeeInfoWebPartDisplay form rendering in the Web Part

Inserting and Configuring the Web Part for the Restricted and Reserved Dates List

We will add one last Web Part for the *Restricted and Reserved Dates* list and filter it so that it only displays those dates that are applicable to the organization that the current logged-in user is a member of.

Click **Add a Web Part** to be added to the right column. Select the *Restricted and Reserved Dates* list Web Part. After it is inserted on the page drag it below the *Employee Leave Information and Announcements* Web Part.

Click on the **web part configuration icon** and choose **Edit Web Part**. For *Selected View* leave the **<Current view>** and for *Toolbar Type* select **No Toolbar** from the drop-down list. In the *Title box* enter "Restricted and Reserved Dates". Leave all other default settings as shown in **Illustration 579** below. Click **OK**.

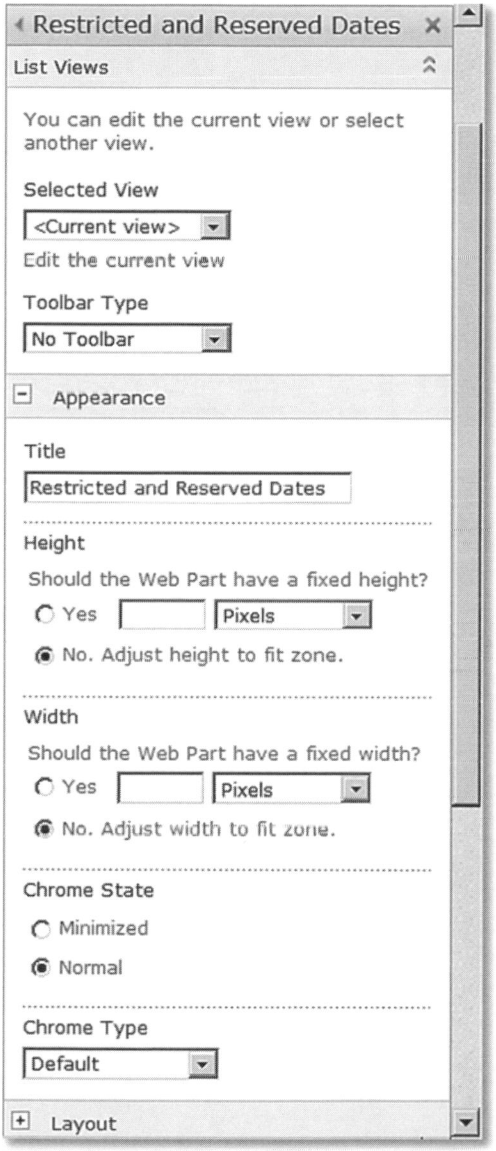

◀ Restricted and Reserved Dates   ✕

List Views   ≽

You can edit the current view or select another view.

Selected View

| <Current view> ▾ |

Edit the current view

Toolbar Type

| No Toolbar   ▾ |

⊟ Appearance

Title

| Restricted and Reserved Dates |

Height

Should the Web Part have a fixed height?

○ Yes [   ] | Pixels   ▾ |

◉ No. Adjust height to fit zone.

Width

Should the Web Part have a fixed width?

○ Yes [   ] | Pixels   ▾ |

◉ No. Adjust width to fit zone.

Chrome State

○ Minimized

◉ Normal

Chrome Type

| Default   ▾ |

⊞ Layout

Illustration 579 - The configuration pane for the Reserved and Restricted Dates list Web Part

Note that all the dates for all organizational units display as shown in **Illustration 580** below. We want to change this so that only the dates for the organizational unit that the current logged-in user is a member of display.

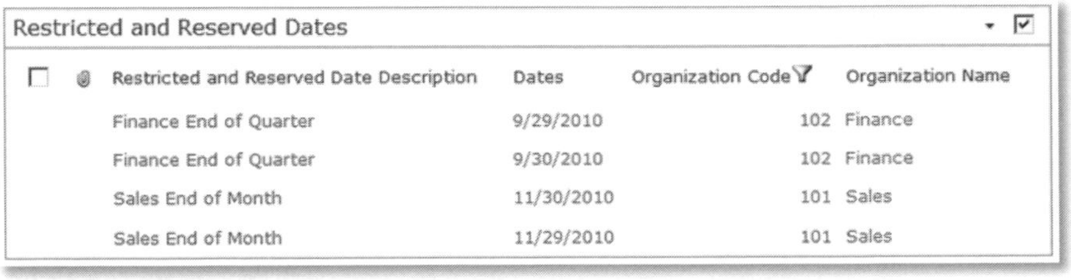

Illustration 580 - Reserved and Restricted Dates Web Part showing dates for all organizations

Click on the web part configuration icon ⌄ and select **Connections**. From the choices that display select **Get Filter Values From**. From the Web Part choices that display select **Your Absence Requests** as shown in **Illustration 581** below.

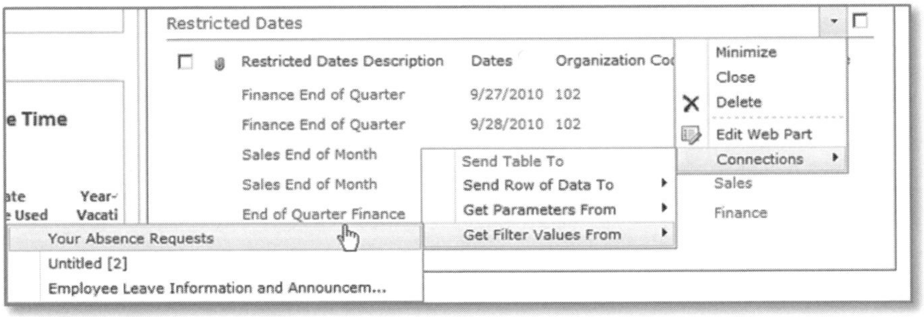

Illustration 581 - Getting the Filter Values from the Your Absence Requests Web Part

The *Configure Connection* dialogue screen will display as shown in **Illustration 582** below.

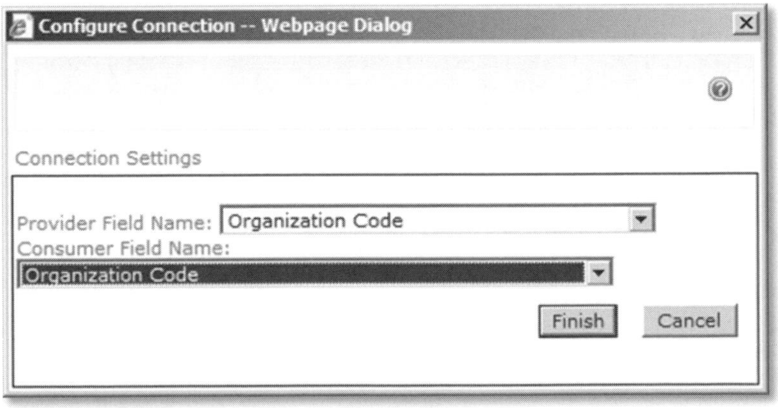

Illustration 582 - The Configure Connection dialogue screen

From the *Provider Field Name* drop-down list select **Organization Code**. From the *Consumer Field Name* drop-down list also select **Organization Code**. Since the Web Part view of the *Absence Requests* form library is filtered by the *[Me]* function, the organization code for the current user will be the value provided by the *Your Absence Requests* Web Part to filter the display of those restricted and reserved dates for that organization.

Click **Finish**. Click **Stop Editing** from the Ribbon. The filtered *Restricted and Reserved Dates* Web Part will now look like **Illustration 583** below with only the dates displaying for Organization Code 101 and a filter icon is shown next to the column title

		Restricted Dates Description	Dates	Organization Code ▼	Organization Name
☐	📎				
		Sales End of Month	7/29/2010	101	Sales
		Sales End of Month	7/30/2010	101	Sales

Restricted and Reserved Dates

Illustration 583 – The Restricted and Reserved Dates Web Part filtered by the Organization Code value obtained from the Your Absence Requests Web Part

> **Note** – The organization code provided by the *Your Absence Requests* Web Part to filter the *Restricted and Reserved Dates* Web Part is not set to display in the *Your Absence Requests* Web Part. It is not necessary for a field column in a list or library to be displayed in a Web Part in order to use it as a filter value.

The placement and configuration of this Web Part completes the composition of the home page for the Employee Absence Tracking application.

Summary of the Features and Functions Covered in this Section

In this section we created the home page for the application and designed it to be a functional portal providing one place where all the relevant information regarding an employee's leave time entitlements is displayed and the employee can create new absence requests and review previously submitted ones. We accomplished this by using the following features and functions:

- We created a *View* of the *Absence Requests* form library filtered on the current logged-in user's credentials in order to display only those requests submitted by the logged-in user and just five of the available column-fields. We then used that *View* for the home page Web Part.

- We created an *InfoPath* form to display the leave time information from the *Employee Information ECT* list on the home page. We used *Form Load* rules to auto-populate the form fields upon opening of the form and configured it to be displayed in read-only mode in the Web Part.

- We placed a Web Part for the *Restricted and Reserved Dates* list and filtered the display of items based on the *Organization Code* from the *Absence Requests* form library Web Part.

Eliminating the View All Site Content Link and Site Actions Menu Option from the Application

Before saving the Site as a Solution for deployment to a testing or production environment you will probably want to remove the *Quick Launch* links for the *Employee Information ECT* list and the *EmplInfoWebPart* form library as these should not be accessible to users of the application.

Illustration 584 – The Site Actions drop-down menu and the All Site Content link on the Quick Launch menu

However, removing the links to these items on the *Quick Launch* menu does not prevent users from finding them easily. By default every *SharePoint* page displays a *View All Site Content* option under *Site Actions* and an *All Site Content* link on the *Quick Launch* navigation pane as shown in **Illustration 584** at left. These links are displayed even to users with Read or View only permissions. Clicking on them will present a page showing all the lists and libraries in the site.

This exposure may be acceptable for *SharePoint* collaboration use cases where the artifacts and information within a site collection or site are not sensitive or restricted. However it is not desirable for users to be able to see all of the underlying artifacts and information in the context of an application such as this one.

When creating applications on any platform it is a fundamental best practice to explicitly expose only what is absolutely necessary to users. There is no reason why a user should see the *Employee Information ECT* list or the *EmplInfoWebPart* library; but with the *View All Site Content* option they can.

There are two methods that we can use to obscure these lists from users. The first is to use the *Hide from Browser* setting for the list in *SharePoint Designer*; the second is to modify the permission settings embedded in the *v4.master* page file that control the display of artifacts on pages based on a user's permissions; any artifact on any page rendered with the *v4.master* page will only be displayed to a user if their access permission level is equal to or greater than the permission level specified in the modified *v4. master* page file.

The first method will hide the list from all users irrespective of their permission settings and the *View all Site Content* option will still be available. The hidden lists will not be displayed on the *Quick Launch* menu nor will they show on the *All Site Content* page. The second method will display the lists and the *View All Site Content* options to users with the appropriate permission levels.

Setting the Hide from Browser Setting in SharePoint Designer

In *SharePoint Designer* go to the summary page for any list or library where you will see the *Settings* section as shown in **Illustration 585** below. The settings options are the same as those available on the *Settings* page of the *SharePoint* user interface with the exception of the *Hide from browser* option; **this setting is only available** in *SharePoint Designer*.

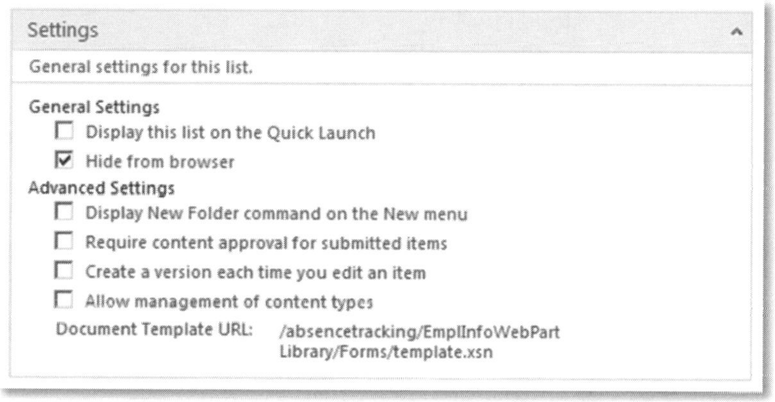

Illustration 585 - The Settings section on the list summary page in SharePoint Designer

De-select the Display this list on the **Quick Launch** check-box and select the **Hide from browser check-box**. If both settings are selected the *Hide from browser* setting will not be activated.

Important Note – The *Hide from browser* setting will not be activated unless you explicitly save the change by clicking on the *Save icon* on the top left corner of the *SharePoint Designer Ribbon*. If you move away from the summary page or exit *SharePoint Designer* before doing this the save the change confirmation dialogue screen as shown in **Illustration 586** below will display. Make sure that you select the Yes button.

Illustration 586 - Save the change dialogue screen

Note – This setting will now hide the list or library in *SharePoint* from everyone. It will also hide the list in *SharePoint Designer*; you will see that the hidden list or library no longer displays in the *SharePoint Designer Lists and Libraries* summary page. To access the summary page for the hidden list or library click

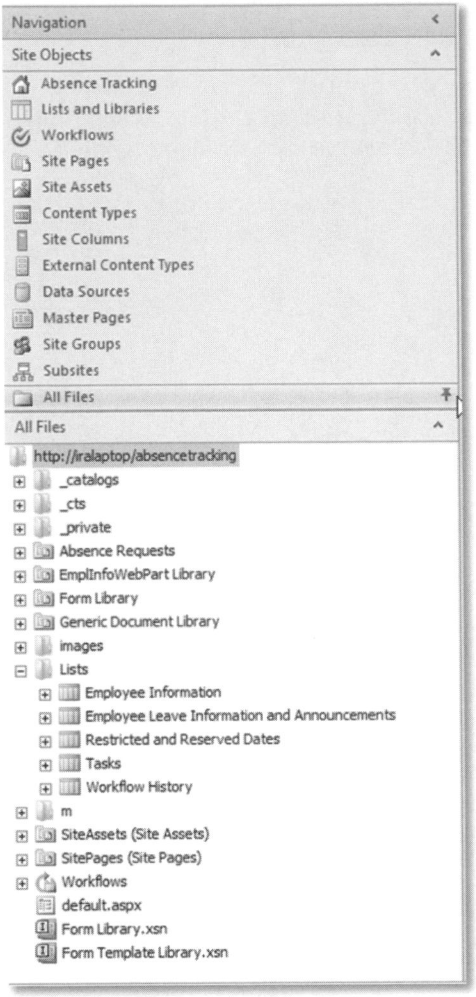

Illustration 587 - All Files folder expanded in SharePoint Designer Navigation pane

on the Pushpin icon to the right of the *All Files* folder on the *SharePoint Navigation* pane as shown in **Illustration 587** at left. This will display all of the artifacts in the site. Libraries are child nodes under the site node and lists are found under the *Lists* folder node. Right click on any list or library node and select *Properties*. The summary page the respective list or library will display and you can access and modify any of its attributes.

Editing the v4.master Page

Open the *Absence Tracking* site in *SharePoint Designer* and select **Master Pages** on the *Navigation* pane. You will see the *v4.master* page in the list of pages as shown in **Illustration 588** below. The *v4.master* page is the underlying *SharePoint* master page that generates the new 2010 user interface.

Double click the **v4.master** page to open it in the *SharePoint Designer* page editor. Select the **Split screen** or **Code** display option to display the HTML and XML code. Select the **Edit** button on the *Ribbon* and then choose the **Find** option to open the *Find and Replace* dialogue box.

With the **Find** tab selected enter "Menuitem_ ViewAllSiteContents" in the *Find what* box. This string will be found in the following code line:

<SharePoint:MenuItemTemplate runat="server" id="MenuItem_ ViewAllSiteContents"

Eight lines below this line you should find the following line of code:

PermissionsString="ViewFormPages"

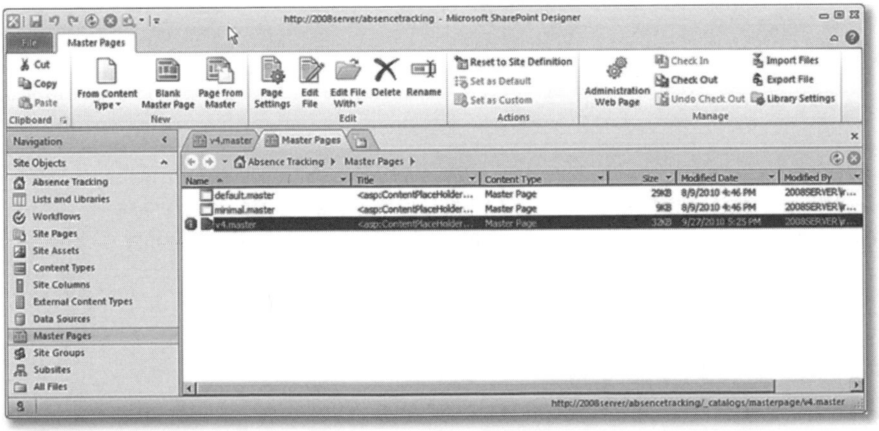

Illustration 588 - v4.master page found on the SharePoint Designer Master Pages page

Change *"ViewFormPages"* in this line to *"ManageWeb"* as shown in **Illustration 589** below.

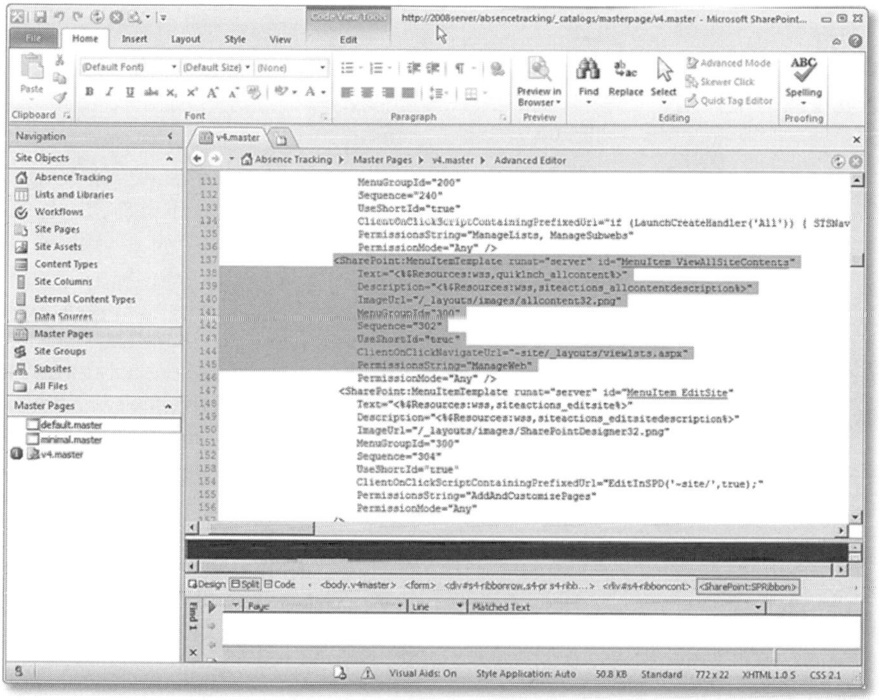

Illustration 589 – Changing the *PermissionsString value* "ViewFormPages" to "ManageWeb" in the v4.master code

Now find the following line of code in the *v4.master* code:

id="idNavLinkViewAllV4"

This should be found directly after the line with the following string:

<SharePoint:ClusteredSPLinkButton

Approximately 4 lines later you will find the following code:

PermissionsString="ViewFormPages"

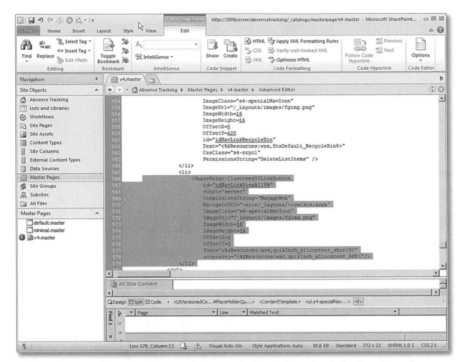

Illustration 590 – The second change of the PermissionsString value "ViewFormPages" to "ManageWeb" in the v4.master code

Again, change the value *"ViewFormPages"* in this line to *"ManageWeb"* as shown in **Illustration 590** at left.

What we are doing by changing these permission values is restricting the presentation of the *View All Site Content* links to only those users or groups who have *Full Control* permission, as the specific *ManageWeb* permission requires *Full Control* as a prerequisite. The list of permissions that can be used in this way can be found at: http://msdn.microsoft. com/en-us/library/ microsoft.sharepoint. spbasepermissions. aspx.

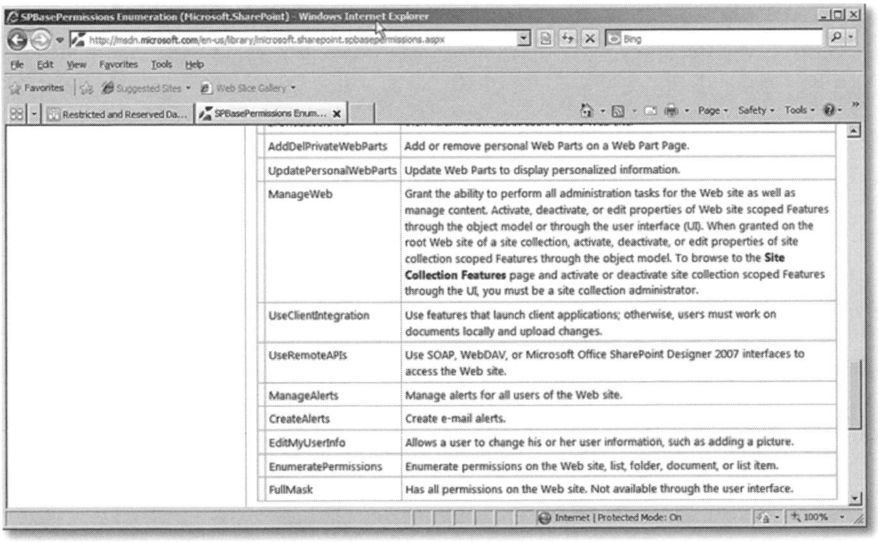

Illustration 591 at left shows some of the specific permissions available. By using specific function permissions that inherit from a general permission class (i.e. Full Control, Contribute, Design, etc.) you can restrict the default objects displayed on master pages to users or groups with those general permissions.

Illustration 591 - Specific function permission values that inherit from general permission classes

Packaging up the Application as a SharePoint Solution Package (WSP)

Congratulations! We have completed building the *Employee Absence Tracking* application. Now you will want to deploy it to another testing or staging environment.

Packaging up the application as a *SharePoint Solution Package* (WSP) allows you to deploy the *Employee Absence Tracking* application to any site collection or site. You can do this from the *SharePoint User Interface* or within *SharePoint Designer.*

In *SharePoint* select **Site Actions** from the *Absence Tracking* home page and choose **Site Settings**. Click on **Save site as template** under *Site Actions* as shown in **Illustration 592** below.

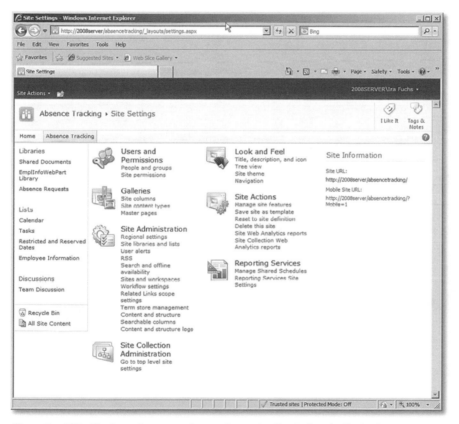

Illustration 592 - The Save site as template option under Site Actions in Site Settings

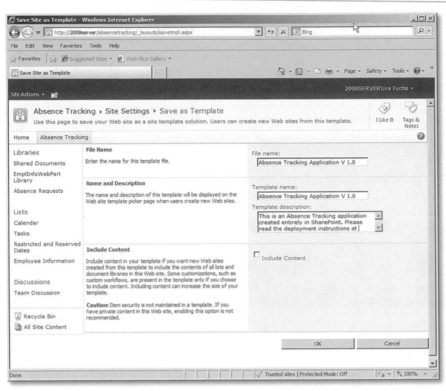

Illustration 593 - The Save as Template page

The *Save as Template* page will display as shown in **Illustration 593** at left.

Enter a *File Name* for the template and a *Template Name and Description*. If you check the *Include Content* check box *SharePoint* will include the list and library item content created as well.

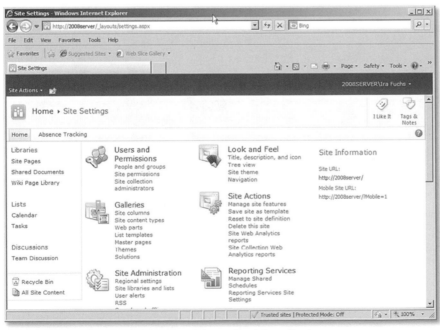

Illustration 594 - The Site Settings page of the top level site collection

Click **OK** and *SharePoint* will generate the *Solution package*. The *Solution package* is stored in the *Solutions Gallery* of the host site collection. Click on **Go to top level site settings** under *Site Collection Administration* to open the *Site Settings* page of the top level site collection as shown in **Illustration 594** at left.

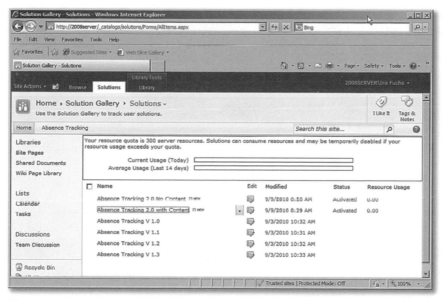

Illustration 595 – Solutions in the Solutions Gallery found at the site collection

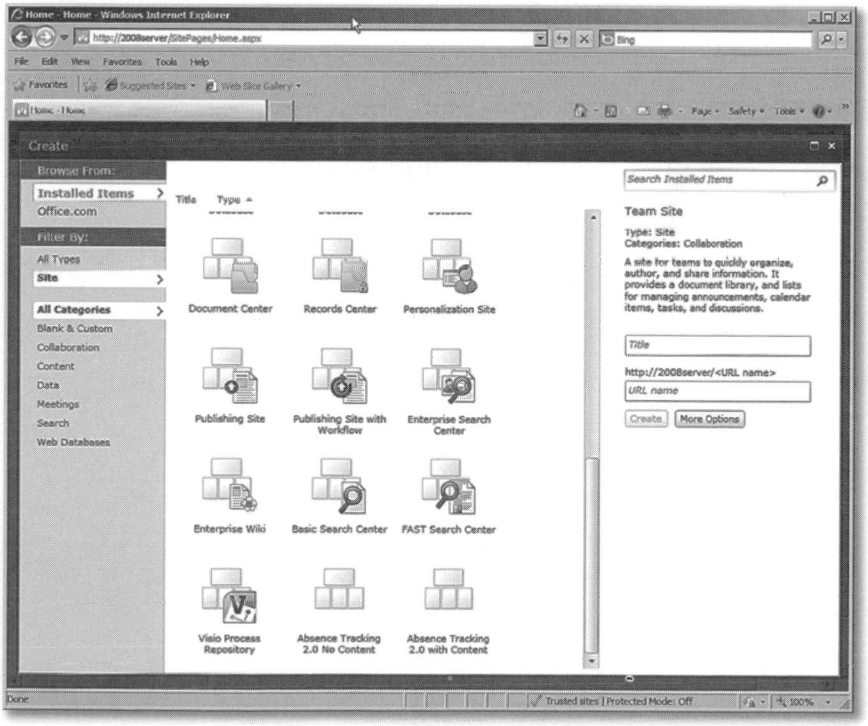

Click on Solutions under *Galleries* to display the *Solutions* page as shown in **Illustration 595** at left.

The *Solution Gallery* page is where you can upload WSP files into the current site collection or copy a *Solution* generated in the current site collection (as we just did) elsewhere. A *Solution* must be activated before it becomes available as a *Site Template*. To *Activate* a *Solution* highlight it and then click on the **Activate** button on the *Ribbon*, or right click on the *Solution* name.

Once a *Solution* is activated it will display in the list of site templates that can be created as shown in **Illustration 596** at left. Since we activated two versions of the application they are both available.

Illustration 596 - Once a Solution is activated it will display in the list of site templates that can be created

Illustration 597 and **Illustration 598** below show the newly created instances of the two saved *Solutions*; the first *Solution* was saved ***without*** content while the second *Solution* was saved ***with*** content.

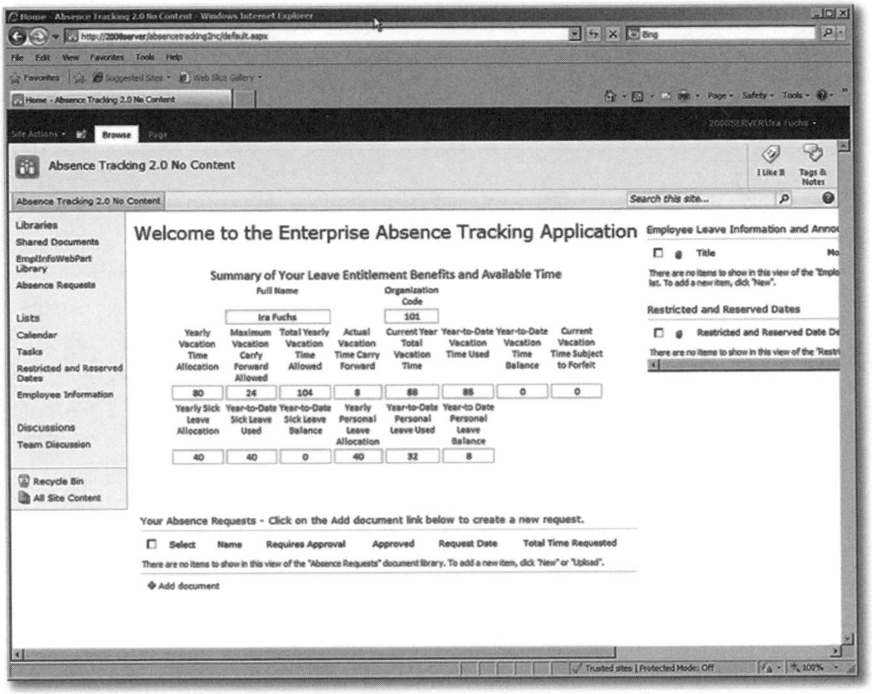

Illustration 597 - Solution saved without content

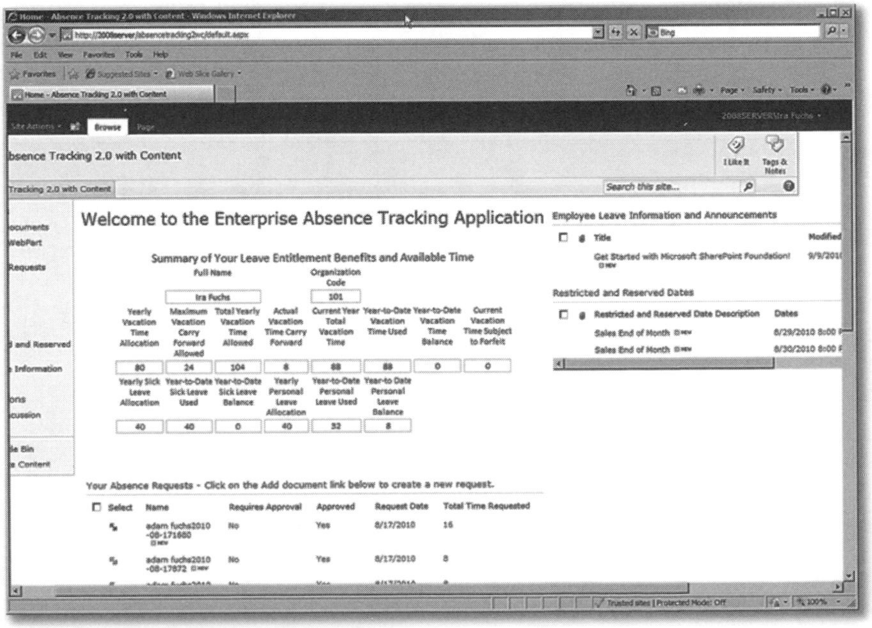

Illustration 598 - Solution saved with content

SharePoint Solution Packages and External Content Types

The *InfoPath* forms used in the application (*Absence Request* and *EmplInfoWebPart*) will work immediately and display information from an instance of the *Employee Information ECT* when the application *Solution* is instantiated on the same farm that the *External Content Type* was created in. This is because *External Content Types* are scoped at the farm level, even though they can be created at a site level. Consequently, an *External Content Type* will be automatically available to any site collection created in the farm, and if the *Solution* generates the list for the *External Content Type*, the information in the external data source will be readily available.

To test this, create a new site collection and open it with *SharePoint Designer*. Click on *External Content Types* in the *Navigation Pane* and the *Employee Information ECT* will be present. Open its *Summary Page* to see its details as shown in **Illustration 599** below. From here you can create a new instance of an ECT list.

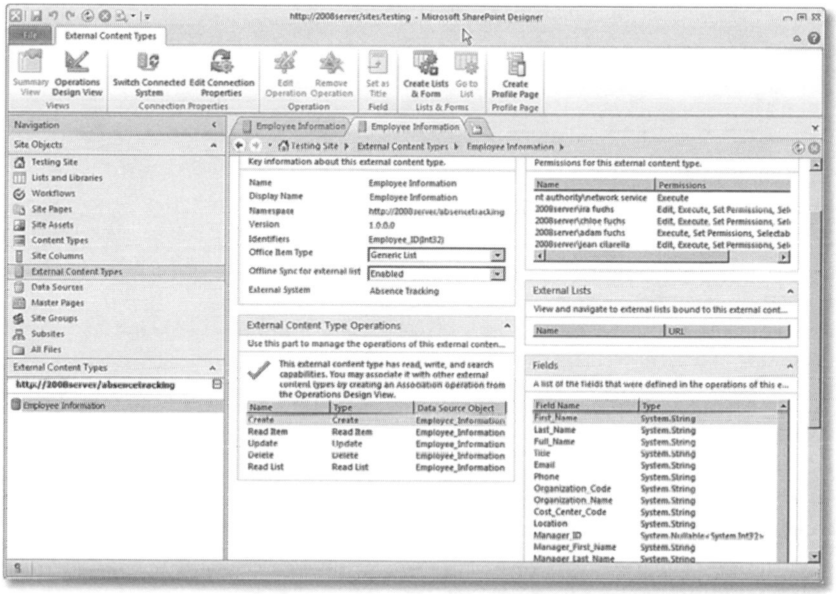

Illustration 599 - The presence of the Employee Information ECT in a new site collection

If you install the *Solution* on a different farm you will have to take the following prerequisite steps prior to creating a site from the *Solution* in order for the application to work properly:

1. Re-create the *Employee Information ECT* using *SharePoint Designer* as described on pages 45 to 55.
2. Create a new instance of the *Absence Tracking* application from the *Solution Package*.
3. Open the new application site in *SharePoint Designer* and create the list for the *Employee Information ECT*.
4. Open the *Absence Request InfoPath* form in *Design* mode and modify the data connections to point to the new addresses of the lists and libraries it will access in the new site.
5. Publish the *Absence Request form template* as a *Content Type*, updating the existing version; and then publish it to the *Absence Requests form library*, again updating the existing form template.
6. Open the *EmployeeInfoWebPartDisplay InfoPath* form in *Design* mode and modify the data connection to the *Employee Information ECT list* and then publish it to the new address of the *Form Template library*.
7. Set the permissions as described in the next section

Setting Site, List and Library Permissions for the New Instances of the Application

In any production deployment of the application you will want to hide the underlying lists and libraries of the site as the application home page provides all of the information and functions applicable to the creation of new absence requests as well as allowing users to access and review existing ones.

Only a small number of managers will need to update the *Restricted and Reserved Dates* list and the *Employee Leave Information and Announcements* list. Managers will have access to the *Absence Requests* library, however the *My Documents View* will be the default view allowing them to see their own submitted requests, and the *Managers View* will only allow them to see requests submitted by the people who directly report to them. No one should have direct access to the *Employee Information ECT* list.

At the site level create the following *SharePoint* Groups with the specified permissions:

- *Application Owners* – This group will contain only those individuals responsible for the maintenance of the application and will have the permission of Full Control
- *Application Users* – This group will contain all the users of the application and have Read permission only.
- *Application Contributors* – This will contain those individuals who will be responsible for creating items in the *Restricted and Reserved Dates* list and posting announcements and documents to the *Employee Leave Information and Announcements* list and will have Contribute permission.

Break permission inheritance for the *Absence Requests* form library and assign the *Application Users* group Contribute permission. This is necessary in order to allow all users to create new absence requests.

> **Note –** setting the most restrictive permissions for all site artifacts at the site level and relaxing permissions only where necessary is a SharePoint best practice.

In addition to these *SharePoint* group settings, you will have to implement the following steps in *Active Directory* and *SharePoint Central Administration*:

1. Create an *Active Directory* security group that corresponds to the *SharePoint Application Users* group specified above. This *Active Directory* security group must be assigned *Object Permissions* for the *Employee Information ECT* in the *Business Data Connectivity Service* as described in the section **Setting the External Content Type Permissions** on pages 56 to 57.

2. Create a *Target Application* and *Impersonation Credential* for the *Employee Information ECT* in the *Secure Store Service* and add the *Active Directory* security group as an impersonator of the *Impersonation Credentials* as described on pages 290 to 294.

Accessing SharePoint User Profile Service Information

We deliberately designed this application so that the user context information used by the application was available in an SQL database representing a Human Resource system. However, many Enterprise *SharePoint* deployments will take advantage of *SharePoint's User Profile Services* to store employee information that can be used by an *InfoPath* application. As such we will describe the technique for accessing this information through its Web Services interface.

Recall that at the beginning of the book we created user profile records for the test accounts that we have been working with. When we later created the *Managers View* of the *Absence Requests* form library we placed a *Current User Web Part Filter* on the page as shown in **Illustration 600** below.

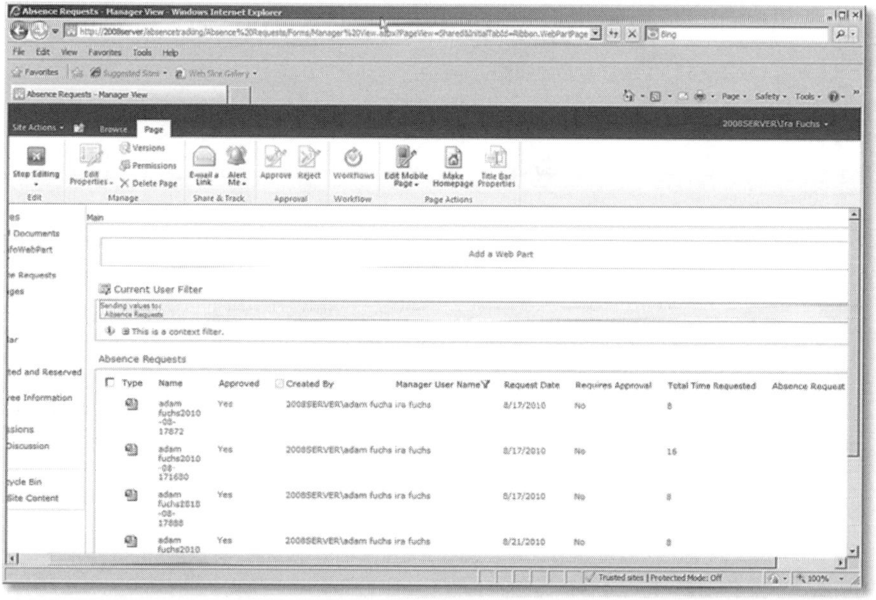

Illustration 600 - The Current User Filter Web Part on the Managers View of the New Absence Requests library

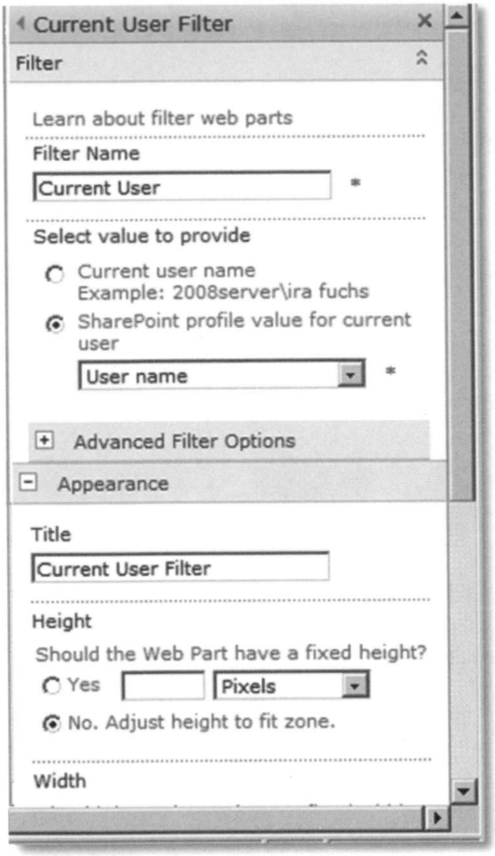

We configured this Web Part to use the *User name* value to filter against the *Manager User Name* column values in the library in order to display only those records where the *Current User* was the manager. This can be seen in **Illustration 601** below.

The *User name* value was obtained from the *SharePoint User Profile Service*. Using the *Current User Filter* on a page is the technique for accessing context information about the current logged-in user within *SharePoint* from the *User Profile Service*. The property information in the *User Profile Service* can also be accessed by *InfoPath* or a custom application through the *User Profile Web Service* interface.

About the SharePoint User Profile Service

The *SharePoint User Profile Service* provides the internal database for User and Group information that *SharePoint* uses for authenticating and granting permissions to *SharePoint* artifacts, as well as the informational attributes exposed in *SharePoint My Sites*. *User Profile Services* is a Farm Level service and its features and functions are managed through the *SharePoint Central Administration* console as shown in **Illustration 602** below.

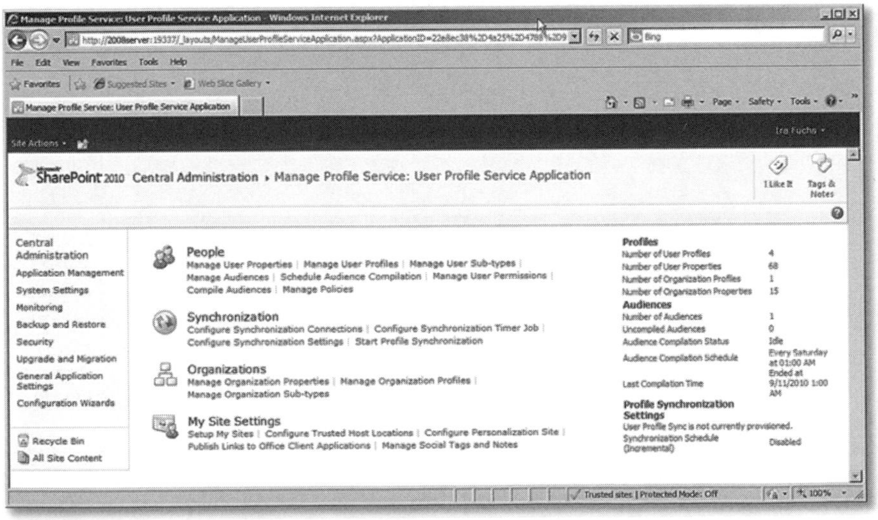

Illustration 601 - Current User Filter configured to use the User name value from the SharePoint User Profile Service

Illustration 602 - User Profile Service Application in SharePoint Central Administration

The information that populates the *User Profile* database typically comes from *Active Directory* and *User Profile Services* can directly communicate with *Active Directory* to auto-populate the *User Profile* database and synchronize changes. *SharePoint User Profile* property fields are mapped to *Active Directory* attributes but additional property fields can be added to the *User Profile* schema. The information in these fields can be filled by the user from their *My Site* and they can also control who can see this information. **Illustration 603** below shows the *Edit User Profile* page in *Central Administration*. The *My Site Edit Profile* page accessible to a user is nearly identical.

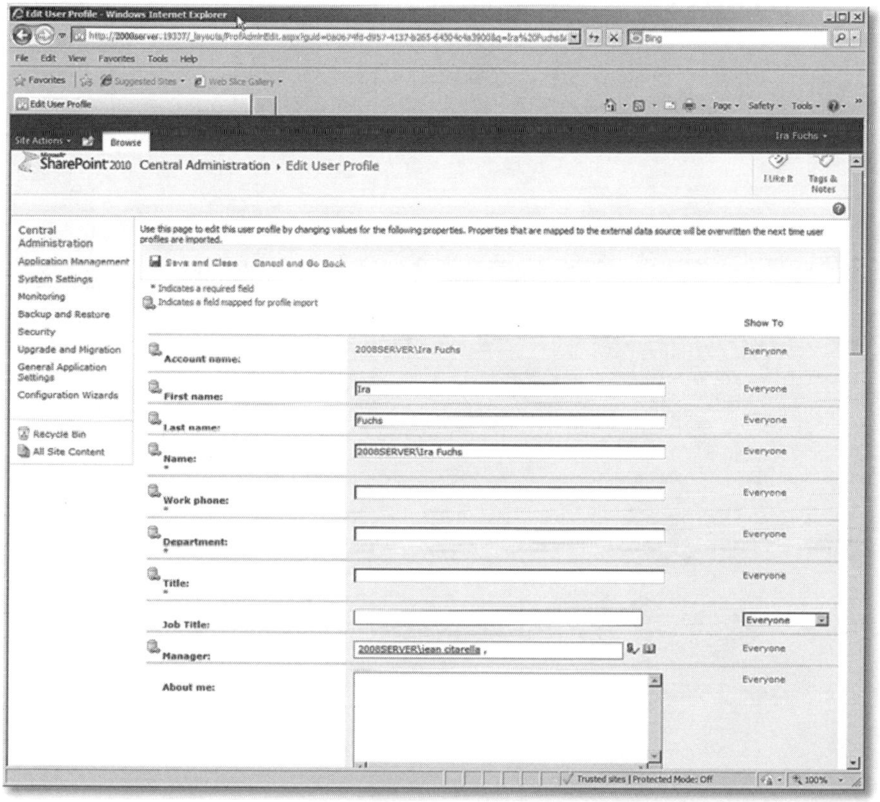

Illustration 603 - The Edit User Profile page in Central Administration

The *Central Administration Manage User Properties* page shown in **Illustration 604** below is where the *User Profile* property fields are managed.

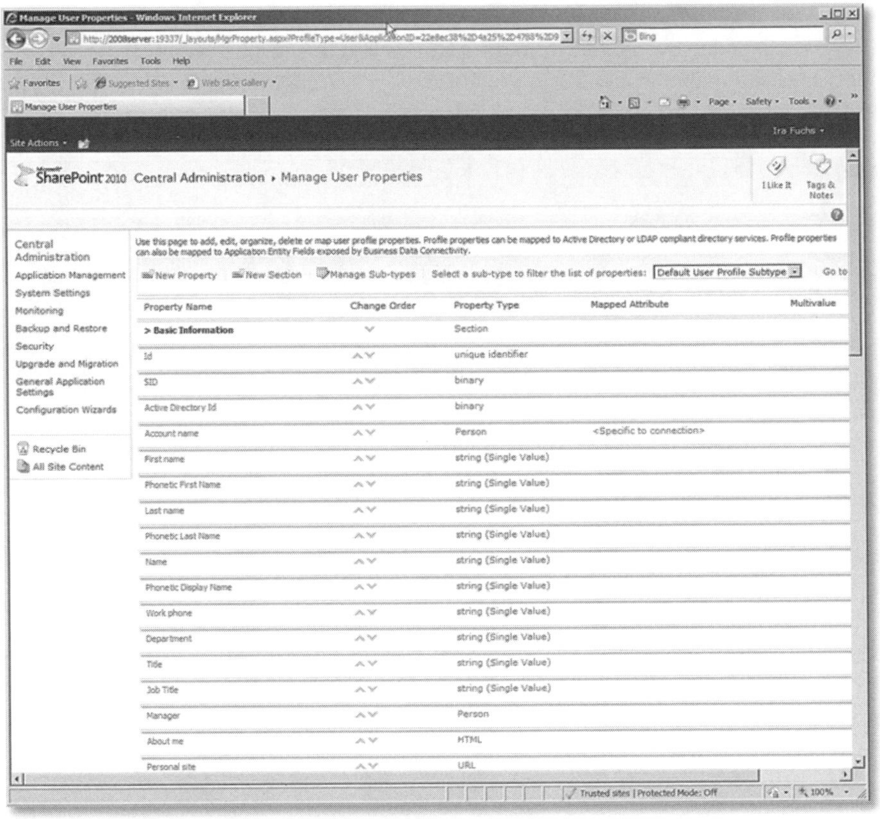

Illustration 604 - The Manage User Properties page in SharePoint Central Administration

Accessing the SharePoint User Profile Web Service from InfoPath

Open *InfoPath* and create a new blank form. Select the **Data Tab** and click the **Data Connections** button and then click **Add** to create a new *Data Connection* to receive information using the *Data Connection Wizard*. In the source screen select **SOAP Web service** as shown in **Illustration 605** below.

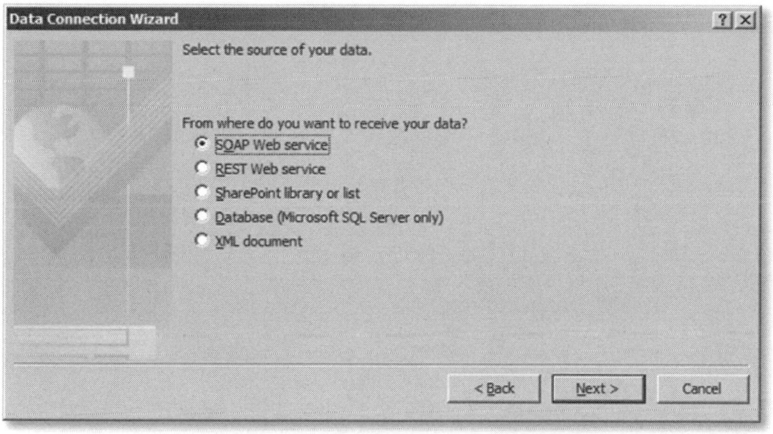

Illustration 605 – The first page of the InfoPath Data Connection Wizard

In the *Web service details* page enter the URL location of the *User Profile Web Service* as shown in **Illustration 606** below. This location will be *_vti_bin/UserProfileService.asmx* entered directly after the name of your server running *SharePoint*.

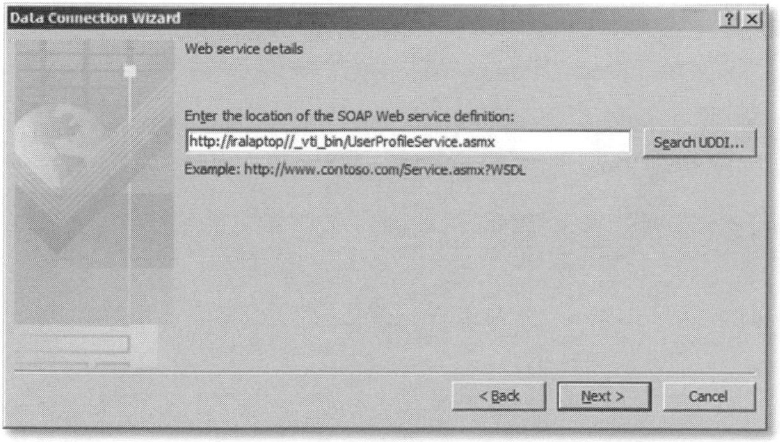

Illustration 606 - The second page of the InfoPath Data Connection Wizard where the URL location of the User Profile Service is specified

Once *InfoPath* has connected to the *User Profile Web Service* it will display the available operations as shown in **Illustration 607** below. Select GetUserProfileByName in the list.

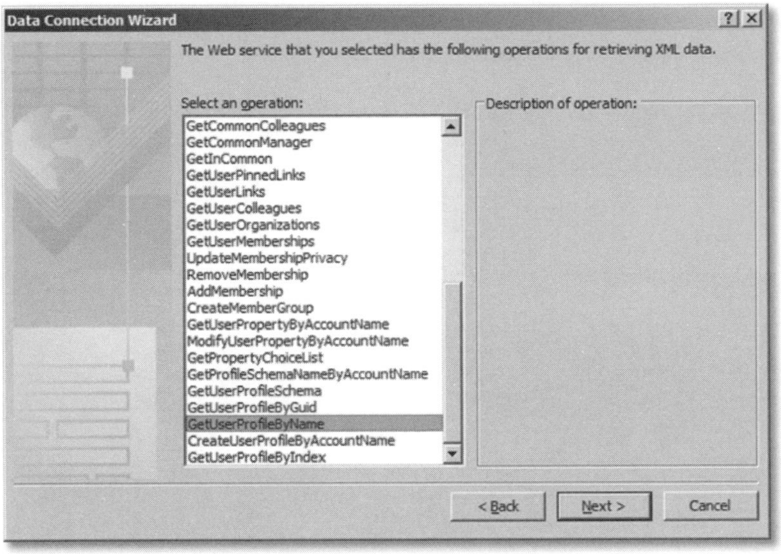

Illustration 607 - The third page of the Data Connection Wizard showing the available operations in the User Profile Service

The screen that follows as shown in **Illustration 608** below will display. This screen allows you to specify the parameter value for the *AccountName* used to query the *User Profile Service*. You *do not* have to enter a value here. *InfoPath* will supply the logged in user's *userName* for the value of this parameter, which is the key to making this an automatic function.

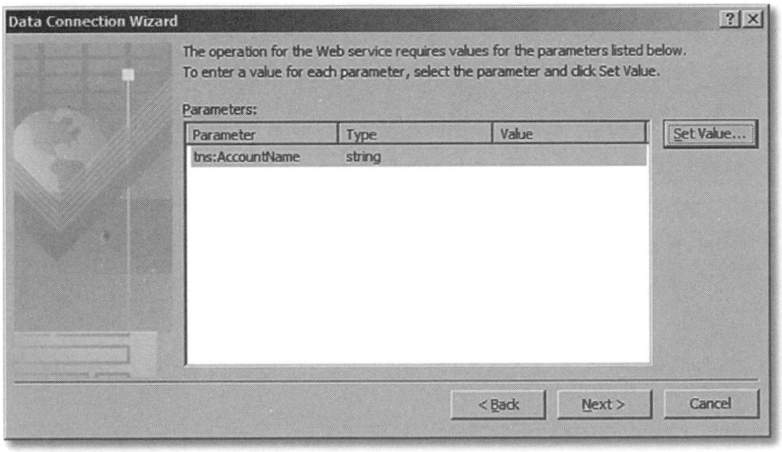

Illustration 608 - The fourth page of the Data Connection Wizard where the AccountName parameter value used to query the service is specified

Finally, enter a name for the data connection. Make sure to check the Automatically retrieve data when form is opened check box as shown in **Illustration 609** below.

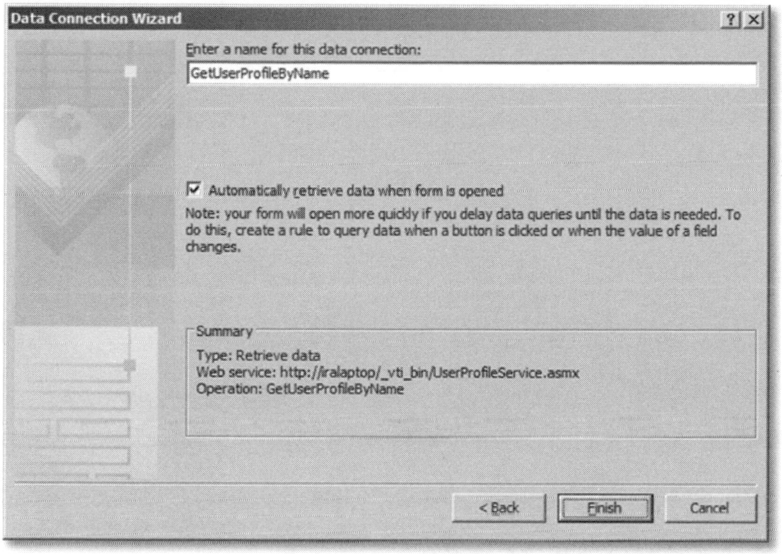

Illustration 609 - The last page of the Data Connection Wizard

Now that we have created the data connection to the *User Profile Web Service* let's try it out. Create a simple form with the fields *First_Name, Last_Name, Account_Name, User_Name* and *Manager* as shown in **Illustration 610** below.

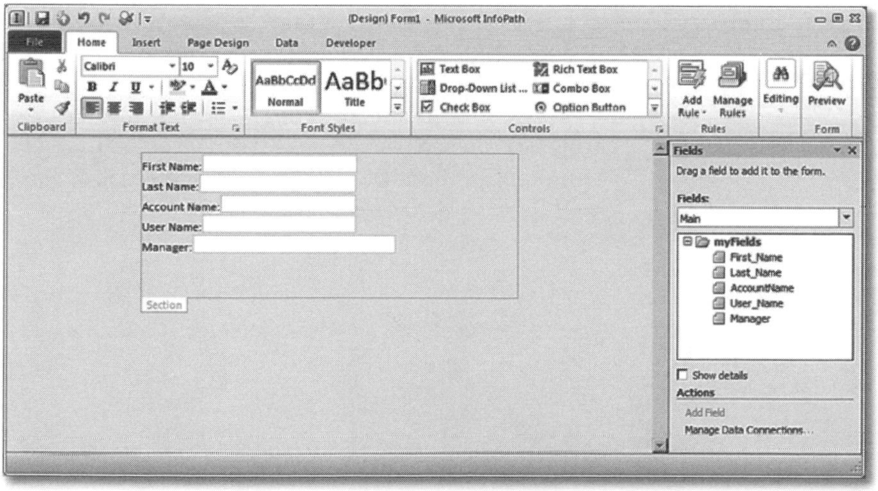

Illustration 610 - A simple form to test the User Profile Service

Right click on the **First_Name** field or **Text Box** control and select **Properties**. Click the **Formula** button and from the *Insert Formula* dialogue screen click the **Insert Field** or **Group** button.

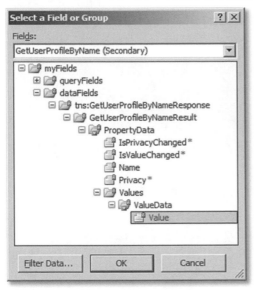

Select the **GetUserProfileByName** *Secondary Data Source* and fully expand the *dataFields* folder as shown in **Illustration 611** at left. Choose the **Value** field inside the *Values\ValuData* folder

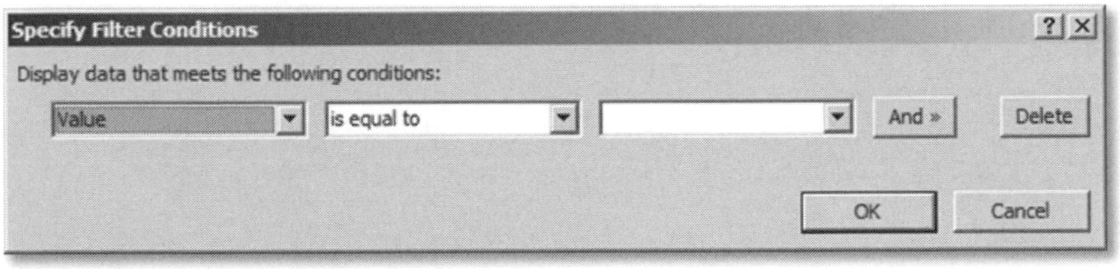

Illustration 611 - The GetUserProfileByName secondary data source information set

Now click the **Filter Data** button. The *Filter Data* dialogue screen will display. Click the **Add** button to open the *Specify Filter Conditions* dialogue screen as shown in **Illustration 612** at left.

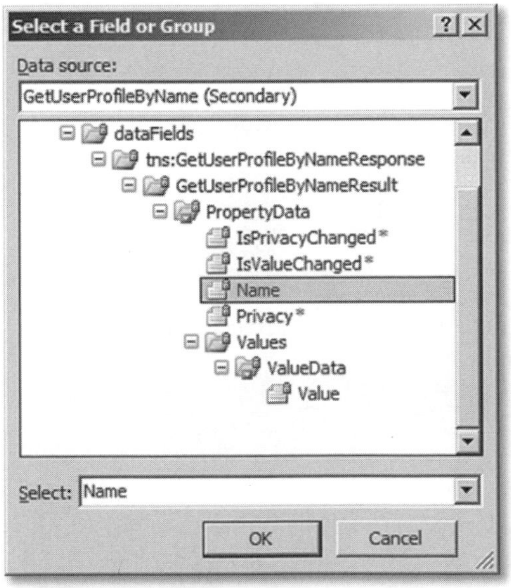

Illustration 612 - The Filter Data dialogue screen

In the first condition drop-down list choose **Select a Field or Group** option. The *Select a Field or Group* selection screen will display the *GetUserProfileByName Secondary Data Source* as shown in **Illustration 613** at left.

Illustration 613 - GetUserProfileByName secondary data source used for the filter

Select the **Name** field node in the *PropertyData* folder as shown above and click **OK**. Leave **is equal to** as the operator in the second condition box. In the third condition box select **Type text** and enter "FirstName" (without the quotation marks). Make sure that you enter this value with a *Capital F and N* as the web service query operation is case sensitive. The completed condition will look like **Illustration 614** below. Click **OK**.

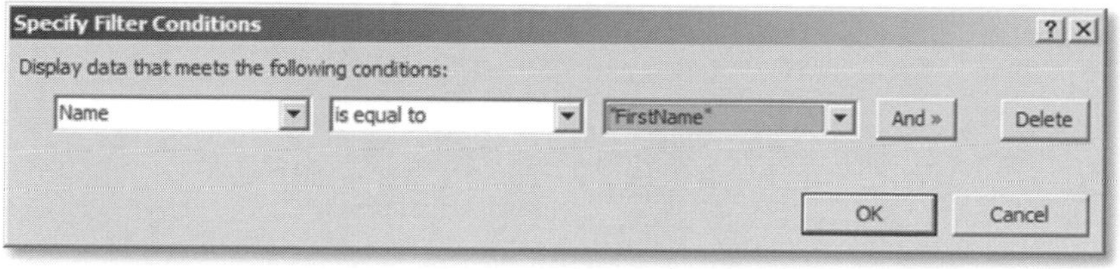

Illustration 614 - The completed filter condition for the formula

The *Filter Data* dialogue screen will look like **Illustration 615** below.

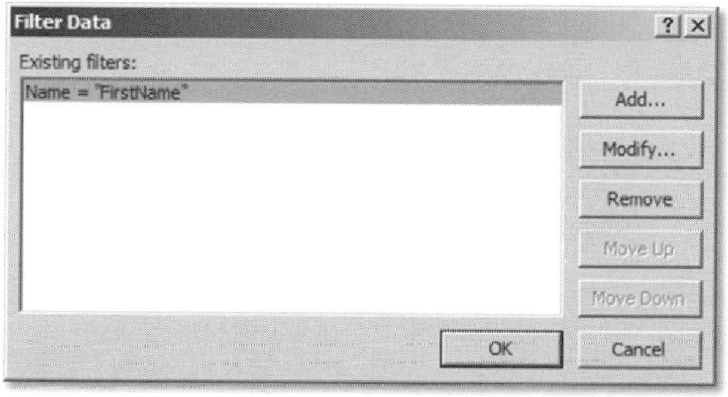

Illustration 615 - The Filter Data dialogue screen

Click **OK**. The *Field or Group Properties* dialogue box for the *First_Name* field will look like **Illustration 616** below. Click **OK** to complete.

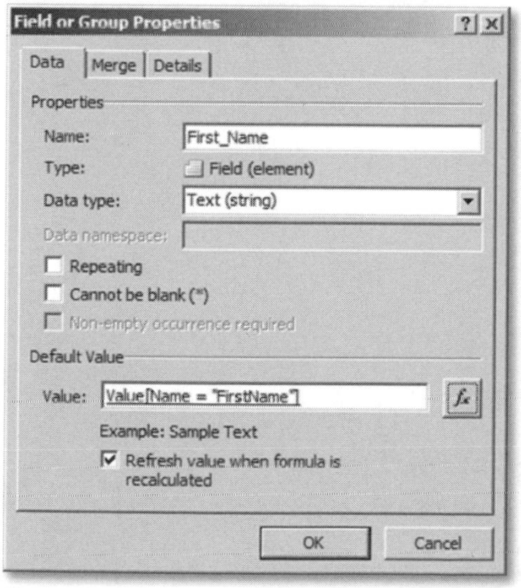

Illustration 616 - The completed formula for the Full_Name Default Value

Now let's test the data connection. Drag the **myFields** folder node to the design surface to automatically generate the form controls as shown in **Illustration 617** below.

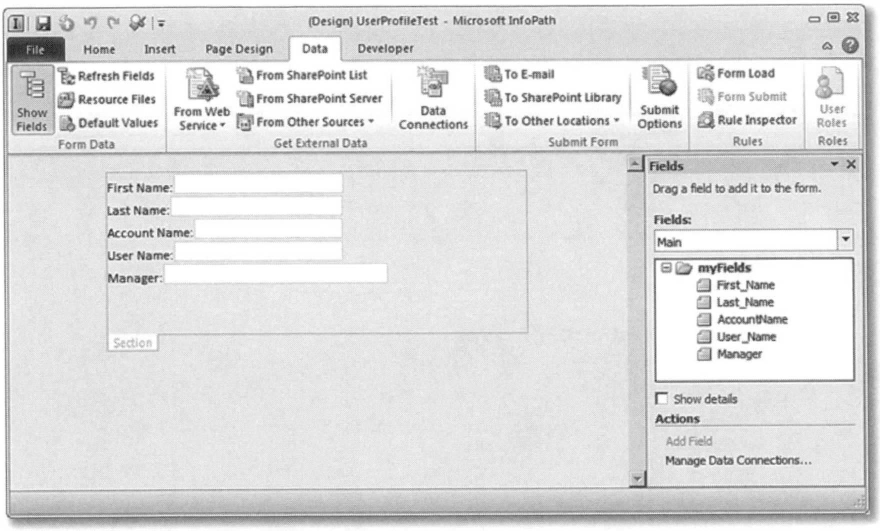

Illustration 617 - Dragging the myFields folder to the design surface to generate the section and form controls

Now click the **Preview** button on the *Ribbon*. The preview will look like **Illustration 618** below displaying the current user's first name obtained from the *User Profile Service* database. Once we set the value for the additional fields using the same procedure above the respective *User Profile Service* information for these fields will display as well.

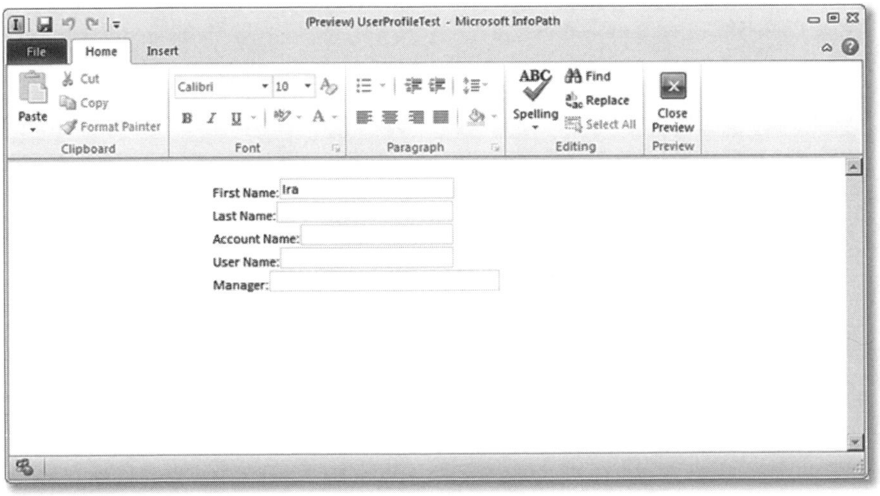

Illustration 618 - Preview of the form showing the First Name field being auto-populated from the User Profile Service

The look-up filtering mechanism used to return the unique value for the *First Name* field is different from the way in which we have accomplished a similar procedure when accessing the *Employee Information* SQL database. Instead of pointing to a corresponding target field for *First Name* in a secondary source and filtering on a *userName* value in the secondary data source, the *User Profile Service* query requires us to point to a generic *Value* field.

Furthermore, the filter used here also requires us to point to a generic *Name* field in the first condition column and supply a literal string for the matching value in the third column of the condition. To understand the logic of this operation an explanation of the schema structure of the *GetUserProfileByName* data source is required.

Open the *Select a Field or Group* dialogue screen as shown in **Illustration 619** below.

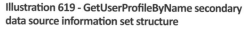

Illustration 619 - GetUserProfileByName secondary data source information set structure

Note that in the *queryFields* group there is a single *AccountName* field. *AccountName* is a property of the *User Profile* and this *queryField* is where the *userName* value is passed to the web service by *InfoPath*. Note that the *PropertyData* group for the query Response\Result set is a repeating group that contains a single *Name* field. This *Name* field is the generic placeholder for the multiple properties in a *User Profile* such as AccountName, FirstName, LastName, Department, Title, Manager, UserName, and so on.

This schema structure allows for the abstract representation of an unlimited and non-deterministic set of property values in the *User Profile* data store. In this manner it is not necessary to literally represent every unique property within the schema. If the schema did so, then the schema would have to be augmented for every new property that was added to the *User Profile*, which is not workable.

The placeholder *Value* field, which itself is embedded in a repeating group within the repeating *PropertyData* group represents the entire set of values for a respective property *Name*. A unique *Value* for the *property Name* is returned when a unique query value, e.g. the *AccountName* is supplied. The web service query logic is thus:

Find the unique *Value* (e.g. "Ira") for the property whose *Name* is *"FirstName"* where the value of the *AccountName* property is the logged in user's *userName*.

To see how this works repeat the filtered look-up steps itemized above for each of the additional form fields. When you are finished doing so preview the form, which will look like **Illustration 620** below.

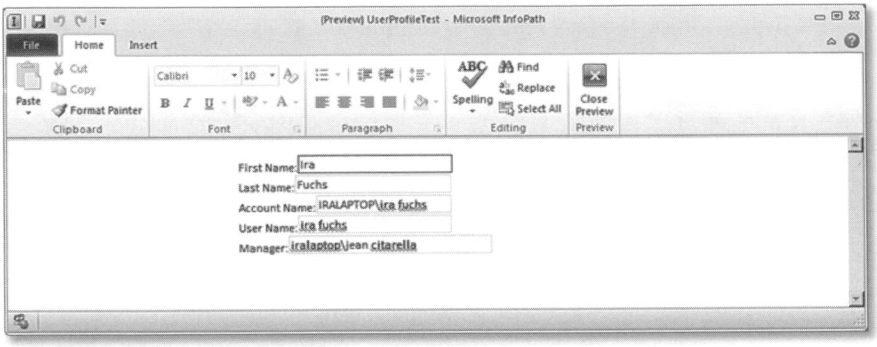

Illustration 620 - The preview of the form after all the values Of the fields have been set using the default value formula

Note that some of the property values (*Account Name* and *Manager*) are returned using the fully qualified *domain\user name* value. This can be stripped out if required using an *InfoPath* string function.

Re-Using a SharePoint Designer Workflow

A Reusable SharePoint Designer workflow, whether or not it is bound to a specific Content Type, can be saved as a *SharePoint Solution Package* (WSP) and re-deployed anywhere. The deployment steps are slightly different than those for deploying a site WSP.

Select a workflow from the *Workflows* page in *SharePoint Designer* and click on the **Save as Template** button on the *Ribbon* as shown in **Illustration 621** below.

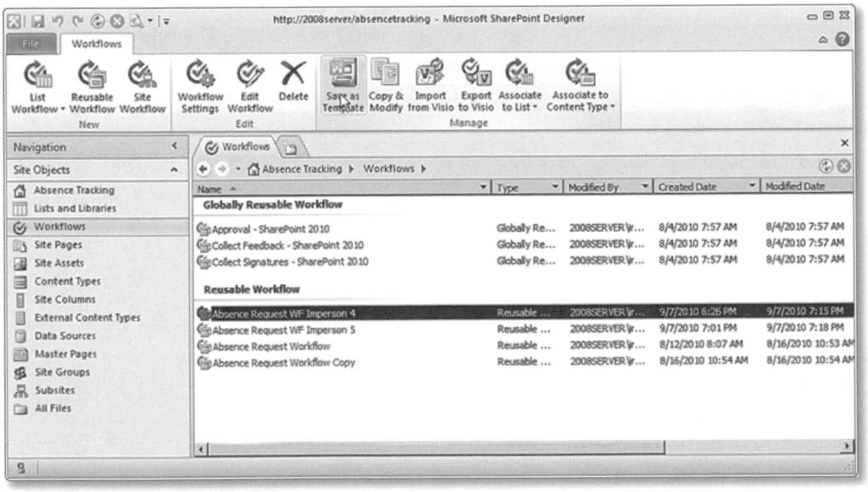

Illustration 621 – Clicking on the Save as Template button to generate a WSP file of a workflow in SharePoint Designer

SharePoint Designer will generate the WSP file for the workflow and save it to the *Site Assets* library. Click on the **Site Assets Library** folder on the *Navigation* pane.

Select the WSP file and click on **Export File** button on the *Ribbon* as shown in **Illustration 622** below.

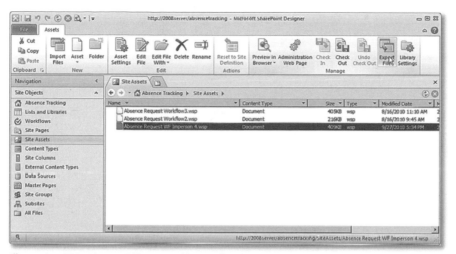

Illustration 622 - The workflow WSP file saved to the Site Assets Library

A dialogue screen will display prompting you for a destination location to save the file.
Place it anywhere of your choice.

From the *SharePoint Site Collection* click **Site Actions**, then **Settings Settings** and then click on **Solutions**.
The *Solutions Gallery* page will open. Click the **Solutions Tab** on the *Ribbon*. The page will look like
Illustration 623 below.

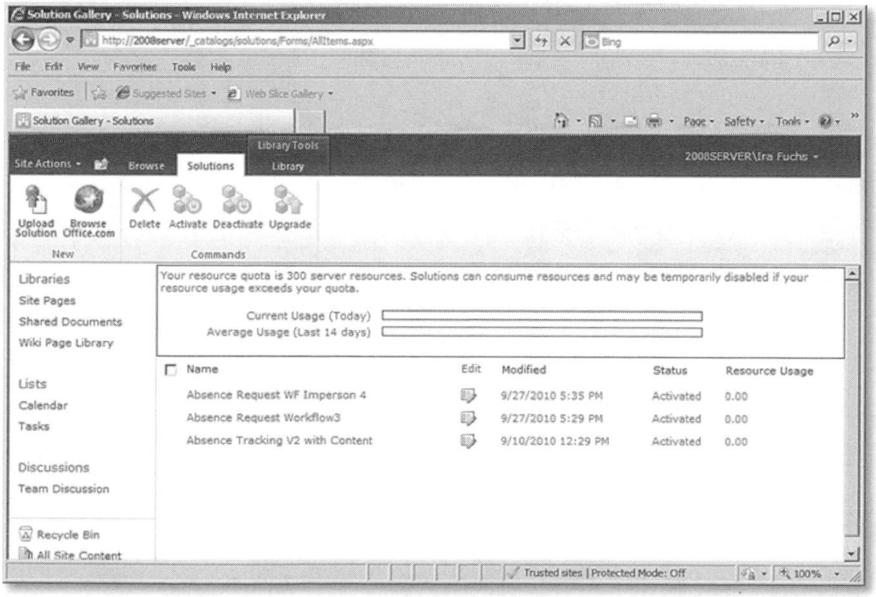

Illustration 623 - The Solutions Gallery page of a site collection

Click on the **Upload Solution** button and navigate to the location where you saved the workflow WSP file where you can select it. Click **OK** and the WSP file will be uploaded to the *Solution Gallery*. Now select the workflow WSP file in the *Solution Gallery* and click **Activate** from the *Ribbon* or by right-clicking on the workflow WSP file name. The *Activate Solution* dialogue screen will display as shown in **Illustration 624** below.

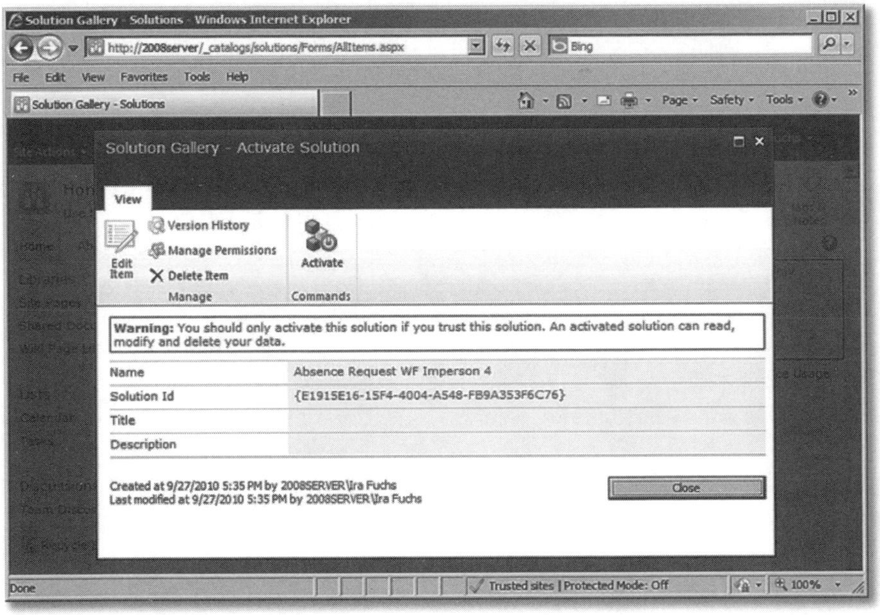

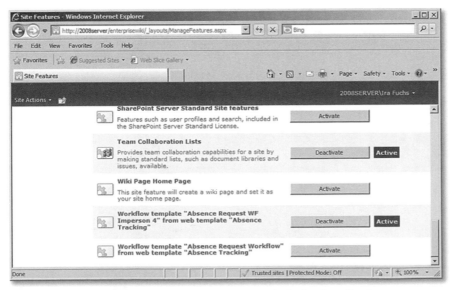

Illustration 624 - Activating the Solution

Click **Activate** and **Close**. Now go to the *Site Settings* page for any site in the site collection and click on the **Manage Site features** link in the *Site Actions* group. Scroll down the page until you see "Workflow template 'your workflow name' from web template "Absence Tracking" as shown in **Illustration 625** below.

Illustration 625 - The Manage Site Features page on any site in the site collection

Click the **Activate** button. Now open the site where you activated the workflow in *SharePoint Designer* and go to the *Workflows* page. The new workflow will be displayed as shown in **Illustration 626** below.

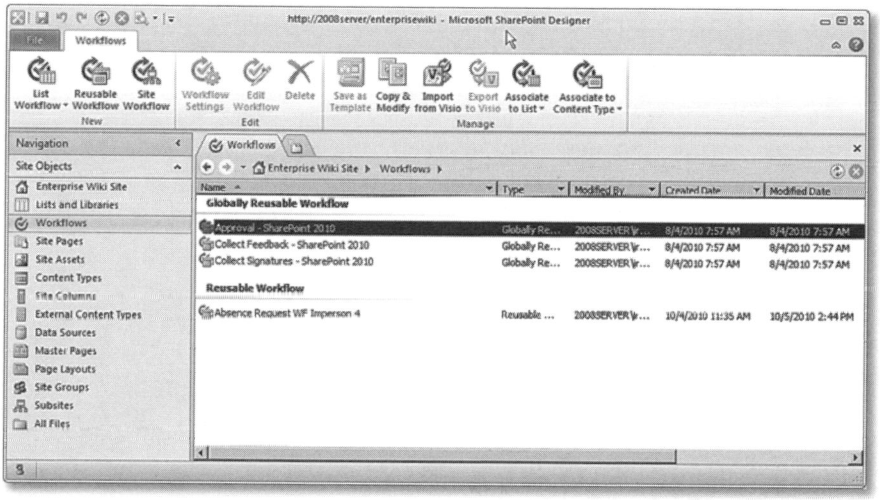

Illustration 626 - The imported and activated workflow template now displaying on the Workflows page of SharePoint Designer

The workflow will need to be re-associated to the *Absence Request form content type* in order to re-bind the *Current Item* list and library field references in the workflow template. In this case you must first publish the *Absence Request* form as a content type to this target site. If we had published the form as a content type at the site collection level the *Absence Request form content type* would be already available to all the sites in the collection. Once this is done you can select the workflow and click on the **Associate to Content Type button** on the Ribbon. The *Absence Request form content type* will appear as a drop down selection.

AfterWord

With the completion of this reference application you now have a good appreciation of SharePoint's capabilities as an enterprise development platform. We could have implemented additional or alternate functions at various places in the application. Some examples of these extensibility points and functional alternatives are:

- The use of additional criteria such as employee level, title, or geography for leave time or carry-forward entitlements
- Using delegation as the mechanism for making sure that an absence request is approved or rejected in a reasonable time frame
- Updating a shared calendar to record and display aggregate employee leave time within an organizational unit
- A workflow that generates alerts of forfeited leave time
- Creating a calendar view of the Reserved and Restricted dates

You can readily implement any or all of these functions right now; you have the knowledge of the methods to do so using rule sets, configuration settings, and workflow capabilities.

Whether you are a professional programmer or an avid SharePoint user you now have a comprehensive understanding of the SharePoint development tools, methodology, and best practices to efficiently create sophisticated enterprise class applications that are extensible, self-documenting, reusable and transportable.

Good luck in your SharePoint application development endeavors!

Index